Adoption Law Manual

CALLOW PUBLISHING

Adoption
Law
Manual

by
Nazreen Pearce

London
Callow Publishing
2006

ISBN 1 898899 82 7

Published by Callow Publishing Limited,
4 Shillingford Street, London N1 2DP
www.callowpublishing.com
Printed and bound in Great Britain by MPG Books Ltd, Bodmin, Cornwall.

Foreword

The Adoption and Children Act 2002 represents the most significant reform in children law since the Children Act 1989, and its full implementation in December 2005 marks a major milestone in the development of adoption practice for those working in agencies and support services, and for practitioners and the courts.

The Act makes fundamental changes in the approach to planning and effecting arrangements for the adoption of children. Underpinning the whole process is the paramountcy of the child's welfare throughout his or her life; this emphasises the permanency which adoption brings, but also involves wider consideration of the child's family relationships and the effect of adoption for the child. Alongside this is a set of procedures for securing the effective and fair determination of proceedings, with provision for a parent to give advance consent to placement and adoption or, where there is no consent, for agencies to seek an order authorising placement and enabling it to implement a decision about the adoption of the child.

The rules made in relation to the conduct of proceedings under the Act also break new ground. The Family Procedure (Adoption) Rules 2005 are the first to be made under powers contained in the Courts Act 2003, and apply to all levels of court. The rules provide a free-standing code for the practice and procedure in adoption cases and will stand as the model for future work on new rules for family proceedings generally.

It is perhaps understandable that the introduction of such significant change should have taken some time. The Act comes into effect a few days after the fifth anniversary of the publication of the White Paper, *Adoption: A New Approach*; the years since then have seen much activity, firstly in the drafting and passage of the Bill and latterly in producing the secondary legislation required to put the Act into practice and in preparing practitioners for the forthcoming changes.

Some of the detail of the operation of the Act has been finalised only in recent weeks and the task facing any author in drawing all these threads together is a daunting one. Nazreen Pearce has more than met the challenge; this work provides a comprehensive guide to the new law and procedures, which is clear and accessible and which will be an invaluable aid to anyone working in or studying adoption practice. The Manual includes detailed coverage of the legal process for both domestic and inter-country adoptions and of the role and responsibilities of adoption agencies and adoption support services; with the text of the Act and the Family Procedure (Adoption) Rules also included, it provides a complete and practical guide which deserves a prominent place on every practitioner's desk.

Philip Waller
Senior District Judge of the Family Division
December 2005

Preface

It has been a time-consuming – sometimes daunting – task, both for me and for my publisher, to ensure that this book would be published in time to complement the coming into force of the Adoption and Children Act 2002 on 30 December 2005. The aim, nevertheless, has been to provide all who may be concerned in the adoption process with an overview of the law and procedure as they affect the child, the birth parents or guardian of the child and the child's extended birth family; prospective adopter(s); local authorities; adoption agencies; legal advisers and many others.

Although the text covers every stage of the adoption process, it is not a comprehensive analysis of the law. Indeed, the speed at which the voluminous subsidiary legislation was issued and continues to be issued has made it difficult – at times almost impossible – to keep up with the changes being made. Some of the statutory instruments, rules and forms which are referred to were issued just days before the book went to press. It has thus not been possible to deal with all the issues or all the statutory and subsidiary provisions. Readers are therefore advised, in all instances, to refer to and follow the relevant statutory provisions, regulations, rules and practice directions. It is hoped that the most important material has, nonetheless, been covered.

All too often, those directly involved in an adoption case are not fully informed and have little or no knowledge of the process, the legal implications and their rights, although the regulations clearly provide for this to take place. It has thus been my hope, and that of the publisher, that the book should be accessible not only to the lawyers, but to all the professional people concerned, perhaps also to non-professionals. In any event, the text has, as far as possible, been written in plain English, and the layout of the book has been designed to be user-friendly.

The opening chapter deals briefly with the background to the new legislation. This is followed by chapters on the substantive law, with individual chapters devoted to the new special guardianship order and placement orders. The new adoption welfare principle/checklist is also specifically considered. The chapters that follow deal with the regulations as they apply to England and Wales. Where the English and Welsh regulations differ, the provisions of both are, usually, set out. Adoptions with a foreign element are covered in later chapters.

Where possible, cross-references are given to avoid duplication, and to assist the reader to find the way around the work.

At the time of writing, the practice directions pursuant to the Family Procedure (Adoption) Rules have not been issued, so the text on procedure (Chapter 25) must be read subject to any new provisions and practice directions which may be published. Nor were all the forms available as the book went to press. It is therefore necessary for readers to trace the appropriate forms, and follow any guidance given by way of notes or otherwise when any application is being contemplated.

Throughout the progress of this book, Pauline Callow, my publisher, has encouraged and spurred me on and worked closely with me. I would like to express my gratitude to her for that, and for her patience and commitment throughout.

I have also had the good fortune to have the invaluable comments and advice of John Williams, Head of the Department of Law at the University of Wales, Aberystwyth.

Finally, I wish to express my gratitude to Philip Waller, the Senior District Judge of the Family Division for providing a foreword at short notice. I am grateful to him, too, for his comments on the text.

Nazreen Pearce
December 2005

Contents

Table of Cases

Table of Statutes

Table of Statutory Instruments

Chapter 1

Introduction

1. The Background

Adoption provides a child with a permanent new family when his natural parents and birth family are not able to care for him. On the making of an adoption order all legal ties between the child and his birth family are severed, with the result that the parents and the birth family no longer have any rights in respect of the child. The natural parents' parental rights and responsibilities are passed to the adoptive parent(s). The child becomes the child of the adoptive parent(s). The child is entitled to the surname of the adoptive parent(s) and to all rights and privileges, including proprietary rights and rights of inheritance, as a natural child of the adoptive parent(s).

This concept was not known to common law. Children were placed with families by agreement but without giving the carer any rights or responsibilities. The absence of any legal recognition was open to abuse, sometimes by all the adults involved, with little, if any, protection for the child or for the often well-meaning carers of the child. The Poor Law Act 1899 attempted to address some issues by enabling guardians to assume parental rights. It did not, however, give the child any status in the new family. (See Cretney, Stephen, *Law, Law Reform and the Family*, 1999, Oxford University Press; and Nigel Lowe in Katz, Eekelaar and MacLean, *Cross Currents – Family Law and Policy in the United States and England*, 2000, Oxford University Press). It was recognised that there was a need to protect the child and his carers, but at the time there was not sufficient will to introduce any legislation.

In 1921, a Parliamentary Committee under the chairmanship of Sir Alfred Hopkinson recommended that the placement of children outside their families should be legally recognised and given legal effect. Between 1924 and 1925, attempts were made to introduce Bills in Parliament, without success. The Report of the Child Adoption Committee, *Adoption of Children* (1926, Cmd 2711, the "Tomlin Report"), under the chairmanship of Tomlin J, raised concerns about the lack of any legal recognition of the relationship between the child and those who cared for the child as their own, and the

1

resulting insecurity which this created for both the child and the carers.

The concerns raised in both these reports, together with the social changes brought about by the First World War, heightened the need for legislation which would set out the basis upon which a child should be placed with prospective adopters and for a court order to be made confirming that placement and identifying the legal effect of such an order.

2. The Early Legislation

Adoption formally became part of English law and received some legal recognition with the passing of the Adoption and Children Act 1926. The Act provided for the transfer of the custody rights and duties of the birth parents to the adopters. It set out the conditions which had to be satisfied before an application could be considered. Safeguards were put in place to ensure that the consent of the parents, particularly that of the mother, was both informed and without compulsion. It confirmed that, on the making of an adoption order, the adopted child would be treated as if he had been born to the adopters in "lawful wedlock". It did not, though, confer any proprietary or inheritance rights on the adopted child.

The 1926 Act was amended by the Adoption and Children Act 1949, which made it possible for a child to be placed without the identity of the adoptive parents being disclosed to the natural parents of the child. These Acts were consolidated by the Adoption Act 1950. The Adoption Act 1958 expanded on the provisions of the Adoption Act 1950.

Between 1958 and 1975 there was a series of Acts, dealing with particular situations which arose as a result of changes in the law applicable to children. The Adoption Act 1960 provided for the revocation of adoption orders made before 1960 in respect of adopted persons who had become legitimated by the subsequent marriage of their parents. The Adoption Act 1964 extended the effects of adoption orders to the Isle of Man and the Channel Islands.

The Adoption Act 1968 gave effect to the Hague Convention on Jurisdiction, Applicable Law and Recognition of Decrees relating to Adoptions which was concluded in 1964 and signed by the United Kingdom on 15 November 1965. The Convention came into force on 23 October 1978 between the United Kingdom, Austria and Switzerland. These were the only countries to ratify the Convention. The Convention provided for adoption orders made in any of the three countries that had ratified the Convention to be given the same status as an order made under the domestic law. These were referred to as Convention adoptions. However, due to the limited number of countries which ratified the Convention, the objective of the Convention – to bring about uniformity in the process of intercountry adoptions – did not materialise, with the result that this procedure was infrequently used.

3. The Adoption Act 1976

In 1972, the Houghton Committee, which had been set up to review the law on adoption, published its report, which led to the law being further amended and consolidated in the Children Act 1975. Not all the provisions of the 1975 Act were put into effect and these were subsequently consolidated in the Adoption Act 1976. The 1976 Act did not, however, come into force until 1 January 1988. Thereafter, it provided the statutory basis of the law on adoption, although it was subject to several amendments, most notably those made by schedule 10 to the Children Act 1989; the Adoption (Intercountry Aspects) Act 1999; the Mental Health Act 1983, schedule 4, paragraph 4; the Human Fertilisation and Embryology Act 1990; the Care Standards Act 2000; and the Adoption and Children Act 2002.

By reason of the delay in implementing the provisions of the Adoption Act 1976, there was a need to review the law on adoption almost immediately it came into force. Adoption law had not kept pace with social changes and the law relating to children generally. In 1989, a working group was established to undertake a further review. A number of discussion papers were published, culminating, in 1992, in the *Review of Adoption Law: Report to Ministers of an Inter-Departmental Working Group: A Consultative Document* (Department of Health and Welsh Office, October 1992, the "Review of Adoption Law 1992"). In 1993 a White Paper was published, and in 1996 a draft Adoption Bill was published, but that Bill was shelved for political reasons. (See *Cretney's Family Law,* 2003, Sweet and Maxwell.)

Although there was a general acceptance that reform of adoption law was necessary, the government of the day did not have the will to address the issue. In the meantime, intercountry adoptions were increasing, with some prospective adopters flagrantly contravening the statutory provisions. This meant that courts were being forced, on occasions, to make orders in favour of applicants who had been assessed as unsuitable to adopt a child, and thus the courts were applying a lower standard in cases where the child, who was the subject of the application, was not habitually resident in the United Kingdom. These cases highlighted what in real terms was a serious abuse, and the trafficking of children for the purposes of adoption.

The United Nations Declaration on Social and Legal Principles relating to the Protection and Welfare of Children, with Special Reference to Foster Placements and Adoptions Nationally and Internationally, General Assembly Resolution 41/85 (3 December 1986), and the United Nations Convention on the Rights of the Child, 1989, set out the basis for reforming the law relating to children, and emphasised the basic rights to which a child was entitled in any decision involving him, including in the process of adoption.

4. The Hague Convention

On 29 May 1993, the Hague Convention on the Protection of Children and

Co-operation in Respect of Intercountry Adoption was concluded. The United Kingdom ratified the Convention in 1994, but no active steps were taken to address the issues raised by the Convention until 1999, when that part of the 1996 Adoption Bill which related to intercountry adoptions was extracted from the Bill, and redrafted as a Bill dealing exclusively with intercountry adoption. The articles of the Hague Convention were incorporated into this Bill and it was introduced as a private member's bill. Parliamentary time was made available. On 27 July 1999 the Adoption (Intercountry Aspects) Act 1999 was passed. The major provisions of the Act did not, however, come into force until 2003, when regulations giving effect to the provisions were put in place.

5.   The Background to the 2002 Act

In 2000, the *Report of the Tribunal of Inquiry into the abuse of children in care in the former county council areas of Gwynedd and Clwyd since 1974: Lost in Care* (HC 201, the "Waterhouse Report") was published. In February 2000 the Prime Minister commissioned a review of adoption by the Performance and Innovation Unit of the Cabinet Office. The review report was published on 7 July 2000 as a consultative document with a commitment by the Prime Minister to modernise the law on adoption, and provide adoption as a realistic option for looked-after children. The report referred to the delay caused in placing children for adoption by efforts directed towards rehabilitation of children with their birth families rather than planning for permanence with an alternative permanent family. The focus of its recommendation was to avoid delay and accelerate the adoption process. There was a brief period of consultation.

On 21 December 2000 the Government published a White Paper, *Adoption: A New Approach,* Cm 5017. In the foreword to the White Paper, the Prime Minister stated that the Government's new approach to adoption was to make "adoption work more clearly, more consistently and more fairly"; that the new approach would make the interests of the children paramount and that the Government wanted "to see more adopters, councils working better, courts performing more transparently. But above all, we want to see vulnerable children safe, in permanent families". The Secretary of State, Mr Milburn, said:

> "Every child should have the best possible start in life. Children do best when they grow into a stable loving family. If children cannot live with their birth parents we have a shared responsibility to make sure they can enjoy the kind of life most of us take for granted."

The key elements of the White Paper included:

(a)   an overhaul and modernisation of adoption law;

(b)   setting targets to increase the number of adoptions of looked after children to 40 per cent by 2004/5, with a view to achieving, if possible, a 50 per cent increase;

(c) the establishment of new national adoption standards;

(d) setting prescribed timescales within which children should be found permanent homes;

(e) the establishment of an adoption register to match children with prospective adoptive parents;

(f) a new right to an independent review for prospective adopters if their applications to be considered for adoption are refused;

(g) the establishment of pre- and post-adoption support services, including financial help and paid adoption leave for prospective adopters;

(h) the provision of an alternative to adoption in the form of "special guardianship" orders.

6. The Adoption and Children Act 2002

On 15 March 2001, the Adoption and Children Bill was presented to Parliament. On 7 November 2002 the Adoption and Children Act received Royal Assent. Some of the provisions were implemented in 2003. These included the provisions which authorised the making of regulations, particularly relating to adoption agencies; the registration of adoption societies and voluntary adoption agencies; adoption support services; and provisions relating to intercountry adoptions. The Adoption (Intercountry Aspects) Act 1999 was brought fully into force on 1 June 2003.

In addition, on 7 August 2001, the National Adoption Standards (LAC(2001) 22) were published to improve adoption services and to ensure that those involved in the process of adoption, and the general public, understood what they could expect from the adoption service. The aim of the standards was to provide a consistent adoption service, to minimise delay in placing children, and to improve permanence planning by prescribing timescales for achieving plans. On the same day, the Adoption Register for England and Wales was launched to accelerate and assist the process of matching approved prospective parents and children waiting to be adopted. Both these services were implemented under the former law.

All the provisions of the Adoption and Children Act 2002 came into force on 30 December 2005. The Adoption (Intercountry Aspects) Act 1999, save for sections 1, 2 and 7 and schedule 1, has been replaced by Chapter 6 of the Adoption and Children Act 2002. The Adoption (Bringing Children into the United Kingdom) Regulations 2003 (SI 2003 No. 1173) have been replaced by the Adoptions with a Foreign Element Regulations 2005 (SI 2005 No. 392). New guidance on such cases from the Department for Education and Skills and the Home Office is, at the time of writing, expected to be provided.

The Adoption and Children Act 2002 also amended the provisions of the

Adoption Act 1976 which prohibited the bringing into the United Kingdom of children who are habitually resident outside the British Islands for the purposes of adoption. It reinforces the former law on illegal placements and advertising, and provides that any arrangements to adopt a child from outside the British Islands must be made through adoption agencies. The penalties for contravention of the provisions have been increased. Again, these provisions were brought into force in 2003.

The welfare principle and the welfare checklist
The most important change brought about by the Act, however, is to bring adoption law into line with the provisions of the Children Act 1989, in stipulating that, whenever a court or adoption agency is coming to a decision relating to the adoption of a child, the paramount consideration must be the child's welfare throughout his life (section 1(1) and (2)). The paramountcy principle is to be applied in relation to all decisions regarding the child, and in any application within the adoption proceedings, for example, when dispensing with a parent's consent.

The Children Act 1989 provides that in any proceedings in which any question with respect to the upbringing of the child arises, the court shall have regard to the general principle that any delay in determining the question is likely to prejudice the welfare of the child. The Adoption and Children Act 2002, section 1(3), provides that the court or the adoption agency must at all times bear in mind that, in general, any delay in coming to the decision is likely to prejudice the child's welfare.

Section 1(3) of the Children Act 1989 (which has come to be known as the "welfare checklist") sets out the factors which a court is obliged to take into account when considering any application under the 1989 Act. Section 1(4) of the Adoption and Children Act 2002 also provides a "welfare checklist" to which a court or an adoption agency is required to have regard. The factors in section 1(4) of the 2002 Act differ slightly from those under the Children Act 1989, but the differences can be said to reflect the differences in outcome between an order under the Children Act 1989 and an adoption order, where the outcome is final and irreversible and results in total severance of the child's links with his birth family. These factors include the child's ascertainable wishes and feelings regarding the decision, considered in the light of the child's age and understanding; the child's particular needs; the likely effect on the child throughout his life of having ceased to be a member of the original family and become an adopted person; the child's age, sex, background and any of the child's characteristics; any harm within the meaning of the Children Act 1989 which the child has suffered or is at risk of suffering; and the child's relationship with members of the extended family and any other person. In this latter regard, consideration must be given to the ability and willingness of any of the child's extended family to provide the child with a secure environment in which the child can develop and otherwise to meet the child's needs; their wishes and feelings; the likelihood of the relationship continuing; and the value of that relationship to the child.

Section 1(5) of the Adoption and Children Act 2002 specifically requires an adoption agency, when placing a child for adoption, to give due consideration to the child's religious persuasion, racial origin and cultural and linguistic background. The new Adoption Agencies Regulations also require the adoption agency to consider these characteristics. Although the Children Act 1989 does not specifically refer to these characteristics, it is implicit that they are important considerations within the provisions of section 1(3)(d).

The "no order" principle
Section 1(6) of the Adoption and Children Act 2002 places a duty on the court not to make any order under the Act unless it considers that making the order would be better for the child than not doing so. This has come to be known as the "no order principle" under the Children Act 1989, which makes similar provisions in section 1(5).

Range of powers
Section 1(6) of the Adoption and Children Act 2002 requires the court or the adoption agency to consider the whole range of powers available to it in the child's case (whether under this Act or the Children Act 1989), as does the Children Act 1989, in section 1(3)(g), where it provides that the court shall have regard to the range of powers available to the court under the Act. The Adoption and Children Act 2002, however, has extended the range of options available for the placement of children to secure permanence and security for the child and legal status to the carer without total severance of the child's ties with his birth family.

Revision of the Children Act 1989
Section 115 of the 2002 Act extends the provisions of the Children Act 1989 by inserting sections 14A to 14G, to provide for a new alternative to adoption, namely that of a "special guardianship order", the effect of which is to give the special guardian some parental responsibility for the child, and restrict the exercise of those rights by the birth parents.

The Adoption and Children Act 2002, schedule 3, amends section 10 of the Children Act to enable a local authority foster carer to apply for a section 8 order (a contact order, prohibited steps order, residence order or specific issue order) in respect of a child who has lived with the foster carer for twelve months. Section 114 of the Adoption and Children Act 2002 further amends section 10 of the Children Act to provide that a residence order may be made to continue until the child has attained eighteen years of age.

Section 112 of the Adoption and Children Act 2002 amends the Children Act 1989 to provide that a step-parent may acquire parental responsibility for a step-child by agreement with the parent (or both parents if both have parental responsibility), or by order of the court.

Persons who may adopt
The Adoption and Children Act 2002 has also extended the categories of person who may now apply to adopt a child, to include unmarried cohabiting couples and same sex-couples. The period for which a child must have lived with the prospective adopter(s) before an adoption order can be made has also been amended (see section 42, pages 33 to 34).

Parental responsibility and consent
Section 111 of the Adoption and Children Act 2002 amends the Children Act 1989 to enable an unmarried father to acquire parental responsibility, not only by agreement or by order of the court, but now also by being registered as the father of the child. If the unmarried father has parental responsibility, by virtue of section 52(6) his consent to an adoption order is necessary; and, if not forthcoming, an application will have to be made for his consent to be dispensed with. Parental consent is now required before placing a child, or when a placement order is sought. Where a parent does not consent to the child's being placed, an application may be made for such consent to be dispensed with. Provision is made for those with parental responsibility to give advance consent for the future adoption of a child, and to withdraw such consent (see sections 20, 47(7) and 52) provided the withdrawal of consent is made before the application for an adoption order is issued. The parent(s) also have the right to apply for permission to oppose the application provided they can satisfy the court that there has been a change of circumstances since the consent was given or the placement order was made.

Under the Adoption and Children Act 2002 there are now effectively three grounds for dispensing with consent, namely: that the parent(s) with parental responsibility cannot be found; that the parent(s) is incapable of giving consent; and that the welfare of the child requires that consent be dispensed with (section 52(1)(a) and (b)).

Contact
Unlike the position under the former law, the Adoption and Children Act 2002 makes specific provisions concerning contact. Section 26(2)(b) provides that an order for contact may be made when a child is placed for adoption. Section 46(6) requires that, before making an adoption order, the court must consider whether there should be arrangements for allowing any person contact with the child. For this purpose, the court is required to consider any existing or proposed arrangements, and to obtain any views of the parties to the proceedings.

Placement orders
Placement orders replace freeing orders. A child may be placed by the local

authority with prospective adopters with the consent of the parent(s) with parental responsibility, or if consent is not forthcoming, by applying for a placement order. If a placement order is made, any care order in existence is suspended while the placement order is in place. The parental responsibility of the parent(s) for the child may then be restricted. Any contact arrangements in existence, whether by agreement or under a court order, come to an end unless an order is made under section 26.

The registers and information

The adopted children register and the adoption contact register will continue to be maintained. Section 79 of the Adoption and Children Act 2002 governs the disclosure of what is referred to as "connecting information" (see page 155). Sections 54 and 56 to 65 make provisions for the nature of the information that the agencies are obliged to keep and the information which they must disclose to adopted adults on request; information which they should disclose to adopted adults and adoptive parents; and information which may be disclosed to the relevant parties at the discretion of the agency. Information referred to as "identifying information" can be accessed only through an adoption agency.

Adoption support services

A duty is placed on each local authority to maintain adoption support services to meet the needs of adopted children and their parents and guardians, prospective adopters and adopted persons, adoptive parents, natural parents and former guardians. The services to be provided include financial support.

Regulations provide for assessments to be carried out when a request is made for adoption support services, and for decisions made by the agencies to be the subject of review by an independent review panel.

7. The Prospects

The Adoption Act 1976 was out of date when it came into force in 1988. Reform of adoption law had been overdue since the 1990s, but for political reasons it did not materialise until, a decade later, the Waterhouse Inquiry was published. That report exposed the need for immediate measures to be taken to protect vulnerable children, and led to the personal involvement of the Prime Minister, who commissioned a review of adoption. Thereafter, the passage of reform took place with alacrity. The Act puts the paramountcy test and the welfare checklist at the heart of any decision relating to the adoption of a child, and thus aligns it with the provisions of the Children Act 1989. Its aim is to encourage more people to adopt children who are in the care system and to speed up the process from the time a child becomes a looked after child to a full adoption order.

The motives no doubt are sincere but there is a risk that, in attempting to meet targets, the child's and the parents' basic human rights may be compromised, overlooked or denied. This is particularly so in cases where a parent has learning difficulties, but, with training and support, could provide good enough parenting; and in cases where reliance is placed on old records to justify the removal of a child and an application for an interim care order, and then a placement order is applied for before appropriate assessments of the mother and the child are completed, thus denying the mother the right to oppose any subsequent adoption application unless the court grants her permission to do so. The Convention on the Rights of the Child recognises the child's right, as far as possible, to know and be cared for by his or her parents. Under article 8 of the European Convention on Human Rights, both the child and his family have a right to respect for private and family life. The European Court of Human Rights has handed down a number of robust decisions on the need to ensure that proper steps are taken towards rehabilitation of children with their birth families. It remains to be seen how far these rights will be respected or eroded as a result of the pressures under which local authorities and the courts will be expected to work and to produce results within targets set by the government.

Chapter 2

Applicants

1. Introduction

Under the Adoption Act 1976, an application for an adoption order could be made only by a married couple or by a single person (Adoption Act 1976, section 14(1)). Joint applications by heterosexual couples who were cohabiting together, or by same-sex couples, could not be entertained. The basis for this view was that a child could be provided with security and permanence only within a traditional family based on marriage. The 1992 *Review of Adoption Law* (Department of Health and Welsh Office, October 1992), while recognising that cohabiting couples had successfully reared adopted children, nevertheless recommended that the restriction should remain. During other reviews carried out in the 1990s, the increase in the divorce rate and in unmarried unions was recognised as a feature of a changing society, but concerns for the need for stability and permanence in a child's life, which it was felt these relationships could not provide, remained. There were also concerns about the lack of legal status of unmarried couples, and therefore of the parties' obligations and responsibilities in the event of a break-up of the relationship. So adoption by married couples only remained the norm.

Despite the restriction, unmarried couples nevertheless wished to adopt children. The courts, having a duty to consider the welfare of the child and promote the child's welfare throughout his life, took steps to address the problem. In appropriate and exceptional cases, the difficulty was overcome by one party to such a relationship making the application to adopt the child, and the couple jointly making an application for a residence order. In *Re AB (Adoption: Joint Residence Order)* [1996] 1 FLR 27, the child had lived with foster parents who were not married. It was recognised that their relationship was stable and that there was a strong bond and attachment between them and the child. The male applicant applied for an adoption order and the couple jointly applied for a residence order. The court found that, although the legal status of each of them towards the child would be different, there was nothing inconsistent in making both an adoption order and a joint residence order, so that both carers of the child would have parental responsibility for the child. The court acknowledged that such orders would be made only in unusual circumstances.

In *Re W (Adoption: Homosexual Adopter)* [1997] 2 FLR 406, a little girl was placed with a woman who was childless and had lived with another woman in a lesbian relationship for ten years. The child had thrived in her care and there was a good relationship between her and the child's mother. The mother nevertheless objected to the child's being adopted by the proposed adopter. Singer J held that the Adoption Act 1976 should not be construed narrowly; the provisions of the Act were drawn widely and did not exclude a person from applying to adopt a child because of the person's homosexual tendencies or relationship. He said:

"the Adoption Act 1976 permits an adoption application to be made by a single applicant, whether he or she at that time lives alone, or cohabits in a heterosexual, homosexual or even an asexual relationship with another person who it is proposed should fulfil a quasi-parental role towards the child. Any other conclusion would be both illogical, arbitrary and inappropriately discriminatory in a context where the court's duty is to give first consideration to the need to safeguard and promote the welfare of the child throughout his childhood."

In *Re E (Adoption: Freeing Order)* [1995] 1 FLR 382, a child with behavioural problems, who was the subject of a care order, was placed with a lesbian single woman, who was an experienced social worker. She was committed to caring for the child and wished to adopt the child. The local authority applied for a freeing order. The mother objected. An order was granted and the order was upheld on appeal.

In *Re T, Petitioner* [1997] SLT 724, the adoption of a child with severe special needs, by a homosexual man and his partner, was allowed. It was held that "any negative factors which may be associated with the applicant's homosexuality must be balanced against the positive factors of the application in the whole context of the child's welfare".

The European Convention on Human Rights and the Human Rights Act 1998 further raised awareness of inequality and discrimination on the basis of sex, sexual orientation, religion, race and culture. This promoted changes in attitudes, particularly as a result of the decisions of the European Court of Human Rights relating to differences in treatment of persons because of their sexual orientation and its effect on the right to family life. In the English courts the decision in *Fitzpatrick v Sterling Housing Association* [2001] 1 AC 27, [1999] 3 WLR 1113, [1999] 4 All ER 705, [2000] 1 FLR 271 (HL) laid the foundation for change, and gradually attitudes towards same-sex couples began to soften. In the context of adoption, the need, and the subsequent drive in government policy, for children to be removed from care and into family homes led to the removal of the restrictions relating to adoption applications by cohabiting heterosexual couples. There were several reasons for this. The most significant was the inequality between the status of the two carers of the adopted child where there was a residence order in favour of both, but an adoption order in favour of one of them alone, one member of the couple's household thus having full legal status and the other not. The law as it stood was also regarded as violating human rights. Other reasons for the change were more practical, in that the restrictions limited the pool of prospective adopters.

At the same time there was a drive to deal with the inequalities in the legal status of persons in same-sex relationships in all fields of law. During 2001 and 2002 there were two Bills – the Relationships (Civil Registration) Bill (Bill 36 2001–02) and the Civil Partnerships Bill (HL Bill 41, 2001-02), both of which were eventually dropped. In the Queen's Speech in November 2003 the Government indicated its commitment to providing same-sex couples equal rights with married couples. It then published the Civil Partnership Bill (HL 53, 2004), which resulted in the Civil Partnership Act 2004. Although it appears that there was no further consultation or discussion on this issue in so far as it affected adoption, there was a stronger move to lift the prohibition on adoption by cohabiting couples, on the basis that the welfare principle, and an appropriate and careful assessment, rather than the domestic status of the applicants, should be the test. The argument gained ground, and during its passage through Parliament the Adoption and Children Bill was amended to extend the meaning of cohabiting couples to same-sex couples.

Assessing the suitability of a cohabiting heterosexual or same-sex couple includes evaluating the nature and length of the relationship, the couple's way of life, the supportive network they have with their families, friends and community, and their social, economic and emotional stability and health.

In removing the bar to adoption by couples other than married couples, the Adoption and Children Act 2002 brought about a significant but contentious change in the law. Section 49(1) of the Adoption and Children Act 2002 provides that an application for adoption can now, subject to the conditions set out in the Act, be made by a couple or by one person.

2. Couples

An application to adopt a child may be made by a couple. Section 144(4) of the 2002 Act, as amended by the Civil Partnership Act 2004, defines a couple to mean:

    (a) a married couple; or

    (b) two people who are civil partners of each other; or

    (b) two people (whether of different sexes or the same sex) living as partners in any enduring family relationship.

"Couple" does not include two people, one of whom is the other's parent, grandparent, sister, brother, aunt or uncle (section 144(5)). The relationships referred to here are relationships of the full blood or half blood, or, in the case of an adopted person, such of those relationships as would exist but for adoption. They include the relationship of a child with his adoptive or former adoptive parents, but not any other adoptive relationship (section 144(6)).

Married couples

As under the former law, there is no specific provision that states whether a marriage which is polygamous, or potentially polygamous, qualifies as a "marriage" for the purposes of adoption. Section 47 of the Matrimonial Causes Act 1973 enables a court to make a declaration concerning the validity of a marriage which was entered into under a law which permits polygamy. It would appear that applicants whose marriage is polygamous or potentially polygamous are likely to be regarded as a married couple (see *Din (Imam) v National Assistance Board* [1967] 2 QB 213, [1967] 2 WLR 257, [1967] 1 All ER 750 (DC) and *Alhaji Mohamed v Knott* [1969] 1 QB 1, [1968] 2 WLR 1446, [1968] 2 All ER 563 (DC).

Enduring family relationships

The Adoption and Children Act 2002 does not provide a definition of an "enduring family relationship". Nor does it set a minimum period for which the couple should have cohabited before they can apply to adopt, as is the case in a number of other European countries. Since the purpose of the legislation is to give children in care a chance to live in a stable family home, the issue may be whether the relationship of the applicants is sufficiently stable to provide for the child in the long term. In contested cases, the contentious matter may be the stability of the relationship. In the case of same-sex couples, where the rate of relationship breakdown appears to be high, it may be that the commitment of the couple will be gauged according to whether or not they have registered their partnership under the Civil Partnership Act 2004.

Age

As under the former law, the Adoption and Children Act 2002 imposes age restrictions on those who wish to adopt. Section 50(1) of the Act provides that, in the case of an application by a couple, both must have attained the age of twenty-one years.

There is no maximum age laid down by the Act. In the past, prospective adopters have found that adoption agencies have imposed an upper age limit of forty for a man and thirty-five for a woman. However, these upper age limits have not always been adhered to, particularly in the case of a child with special needs or a difficult child, or where adoption by an older person is in the interest of the child. In *Re W (Adoption by Grandparents)* [1980] 2 FLR 161, the grandparents of the child, who were in their mid-sixties, applied to adopt their grandson who was then aged seven. A residence order (then, a custody order) had been made in their favour, following the divorce of the child's parents. The mother had virtually disappeared from the child's life and had consented to the adoption. The father opposed the application. At first instance the court refused the application, only by reason of the ages of the applicants. On appeal, the decision was reversed on the ground that the grandparents should be placed in a position to make arrangements for the child's future, including appointing a testamentary guardian. It was held that it was in the best interest of the child to make an adoption order so that the future of the child could be settled as far as possible and not left to chance.

In *Re O (A Minor) (Adoption by Grandparents)* [1985] FLR 546, the child was five years of age when her paternal grandparents applied to adopt her. She had lived with them since she was ten months old. The parents had consented to the adoption and this was supported by the child's guardian. The application was granted on appeal.

In both these two cases the prospective adopters were grandparents of the child, and there were special circumstances. The alternative of a special guardianship order (see Chapter 4) was then not available.

With the trend towards women having children later in life, and the advances in medical science, age may be becoming a less significant barrier. Issues relating to the welfare of the child throughout his life, the ability of the applicant to meet his long-term needs and to provide stability, and the other factors in section 1(4) of the Act may well tend be of greater importance than an applicant's age.

Although no upper age limit is imposed, it is of note that in the context of the interpretation of instruments concerning property, section 69(5) of the Act provides that where it is necessary to determine, for the purposes of a disposition of property effected by instrument, whether a woman can have a child, it must be presumed that once a woman has attained the age of fifty-five years, she will not adopt a person after execution of the instrument. If she does (in spite of section 67) that person is not to be treated as her child or (if she does so as one of a couple) as the child of the other one of the couple for the purposes of the instrument.

Domicile

In the case of an application for adoption by a couple, at least one of the couple must be domiciled in a part of the British Islands (section 49(2)).

Domicile is a concept of law which is relevant in many legal situations which concern personal status. No person can be without a domicile, and a person cannot have more than one domicile at the same time. Under the common law, a person's domicile is determined in English courts under English law (*Dicey and Morris on the Conflict of Laws*, Sweet and Maxwell). For the purposes of an adoption application, the domicile of a person is likewise determined according to English law. Establishing domicile is the first prerequisite to any application to adopt a child; for an applicant who was born and has lived in the British Islands, it should not be difficult.

There are three types of domicile: domicile of origin, domicile of choice and domicile of dependency.

Domicile of origin: A person acquires a domicile of origin at birth from his or her parents. A domicile of origin is capable of persisting during the lifetime of the person. The domicile of a legitimate child born during the lifetime of his father is that of the child's father. If the father dies before the child's birth, the child acquires the domicile of his/her mother at birth. A child's domicile will therefore change if and when the parent(s) change theirs, but his domicile of origin – that which is acquired at birth – will never be lost.

A foundling's domicile of origin is that of the country where he is found.

Domicile of choice: A domicile of choice is acquired when a person leaves his domicile of origin and lives in a country of his choice with the intention of permanently or indefinitely living there. The test is whether the person, having left the domicile of origin, intended to make his home in the new country until the end of his days and until something happens to change his mind; see *IRC v Bullock* [1976] 1 WLR 1178, [1976] 3 All ER 353 and *Re Furse* [1980] 3 All ER 838. In *Udny v Udny* (1869) 1 LR Sc & Div 441, Lord Westbury stated:

"Domicile of choice is a conclusion or inference which the law derives from the act of a man fixing voluntarily his sole or chief residence in a particular place with the intention of continuing to reside there for an unlimited time. This is a description of the circumstances which create or constitute a domicile and not a definition of the term. There must be residence freely chosen, and not prescribed or dictated by any external necessity, such as the duties of office, the demands of creditors, or relief from illness; and it must be residence fixed not for a limited period or particular purpose, but general and indefinite in its future contemplation. It is true that residence originally temporary, or intended for a limited period, may afterwards become general and unlimited, and in such a case so soon as the change of purpose, or *animus manendi*, can be inferred the fact of domicile is established."

If a person, having acquired a domicile of choice, subsequently abandons that domicile and does not acquire another domicile of choice, he reverts to his domicile of origin.

Domicile of dependency: A child under sixteen or a person who is mentally disabled has a domicile of dependency, which is that of his parents. Where the parents are married and living together, the domicile is that of the father. The domicile of an illegitimate child is that of his mother. If the mother changes her domicile, that of the illegitimate child also changes, unless she makes a decision, in the interest of the child, to exercise the power vested in her not to change his domicile when she changes her own. When the parents are separated, the child's domicile is that of the parent with whom he has his home to the exclusion of the other. If the mother dies, the child retains the domicile held by his mother before she died, provided he has not had his home with his father since her death (Domicile and Matrimonial Proceedings Act 1973, section 4). Once a child attains the age of sixteen, he is able to acquire a domicile of choice independently from his parents (Domicile and Matrimonial Proceedings Act 1973, section 3).

An adopted child is treated in law as the child of the adopters, so the domicile of an adopted child is that of his adoptive parents until he attains the age of sixteen, when, again, he may acquire his own domicile of choice.

Habitual residence
In the case of an application by a couple, both applicants must have been habitually resident in a part of the British Islands for a period of not less than one year ending with the date of the application (Adoption and Children Act 2002, section 49(3)).

The term "habitual residence" is not synonymous with "ordinary residence" (*Nessa v Chief Adjudication Officer* [1999] 1 WLR 1937, [1999] 4 All ER 677, [1999] 2 FLR 1116. In *Re J (A Minor) (Abduction: Custody Rights)* [1990] 2 AC 562, [1990] 3 WLR 492, [1990] 2 All ER 961, [1990] 2 FLR 442, Lord Brandon said:

> "The expression is not to be treated as a term of art with some special meaning, but is rather to be understood according to the ordinary and natural meaning of the two words which it contains. The second point is that the question whether a person is or is not habitually resident in a specific country is a question of fact to be decided by reference to all the circumstances of any particular case. The third point is that there is a significant difference between a person ceasing to be habitually resident in country A and his subsequently becoming habitually resident in country B. A person may cease to be habitually resident in country A in a single day if he or she leaves it with a settled intention not to return to it but to take up long-term residence in country B instead. Such a person cannot, however, become habitually resident in country B is a single day. An appreciable period of time and a settled intention will be necessary to enable him or her to become so. During that appreciable period of time the person will have ceased to be habitually resident in country A but not yet have become habitually resident in country B".

Following the decision in *Re J*, the courts placed emphasis on the need to establish residence for "an appreciable period". In *A v A (Child Abduction) (Habitual Residence)* [1993] 2 FLR 225, it was held that a person could not become habitually resident in a country in one day. In *Re F (a Minor) (Child Abduction)* [1992] 1 FLR 548, one month was regarded as sufficient. A stay in a country for a holiday does not amount to the acquisition of habitual residence: *Re O (A Minor) (Abduction: Habitual Residence)* [1993] 2 FLR 594; *Re A (Abduction: Habitual Residence)* [1998] 1 FLR 497. In *Nessa v*

Chief Adjudication Officer [1998] 1 FLR 879, the Court of Appeal considered whether, in order to establish habitual residence, it was necessary to prove that the residence had been for an appreciable period. The court approved the judgment of Lord Brandon in *Re J*, but Thorpe LJ, in his dissenting judgment, took the view that it was not a necessary ingredient; what was important was the quality of the connection of the individual to the relevant society and whether that connection was transitory or enduring. Thorpe LJ was firmly of the view that the meaning of "habitual residence" should not be "confined defined or refined with judge-made rules".

On the other hand, in *Ikimi v Ikimi (Divorce: Habitual Residence)* [2001] EWCA Civ 873, [2001] 3 WLR 672, [2001] 2 FLR 1288, when considering the term "habitually resident" in section 5(2) of the Domicile and Matrimonial Proceedings Act 1973, the Court of Appeal held that the term "ordinarily" and "habitually" had the same meaning in the context of divorce proceedings, but Thorpe LJ seemed to distinguish between the meaning to be given to the term in family cases and the meaning to be given in cases concerning the abduction of children. It can also be argued that the requirement for an "appreciable period" of residence to establish "habitual residence" has crept in by default. In *Swaddling v Adjudication Officer* (C90/97) [1999] All ER (EC) 217, [1999] 2 FLR 184 (ECJ), it was held that a number of factors had to be considered when deciding whether a person has established habitual residence. These include the reasons for coming to the UK, the person's intentions and his family situation.

Whether a person has established habitual residence in a country is therefore a question of fact which must be determined by reference to the particular circumstances of each individual case. There must be an element of voluntariness of residence for settled purposes. The intention must be to take up long-term residence. In deciding the issue the court need not conduct a searching, microscopic inquiry. It is sufficient for the court to stand back and take a general panoramic view of the evidence (*Re B (Minors) (Abduction)* [1993] 1 FLR 998). All that is required is that the purpose to live in the country in question has a sufficient degree of continuity.

Once a person is habitually resident in a country, he does not lose his habitual residence there by reason of temporary absences (*Oundjian v Oundjian* [1980] 1 FLR 198; *Re BM (A Minor) (Wardship: Jurisdiction)* [1993] 1 FLR 495).

Child to have had his home with the applicant(s)
Finally, the child must have had his home with the applicant(s) for the relevant period set out in section 42 (see Chapter 3). Thus, where the child was placed for adoption with the applicant(s) by an adoption agency or in pursuance of an order of the High Court, or where a natural parent seeks to adopt his or her own child, the child must have had his home with the applicant(s) at all times for ten weeks before the application for adoption is

made. In the case of a non-agency application by local authority foster parents, the child should have had his home with them throughout the year preceding the application. In the case of an adoption application by a step-parent or a partner of the child's parent, the child should have had his home with the applicant for a continuous period of six months preceding the application. In any other case, the child must have had his home with the applicant(s) for not less than three out of five years preceding the application.

3. Step-parents

One of the major difficulties in adoption by a step-parent is that the very concept of such an adoption does not sit comfortably with the child's right to know his own identity, because an adoption order has the effect of severing all ties between the child and one side of his family, thus depriving him of forming relationships with one of his birth parents and his/her extended family. The Houghton Report (*Report of the Departmental Committee on the Adoption of Children*, Cmnd 5107, 1972) highlighted this issue, as did the 1992 *Review of Adoption Law* (Department of Health and Welsh Office, October 1992). Under the former law, the court was obliged, in an application by a step-parent, to consider the alternatives to adoption, since it had powers to make any of the orders under section 8 of the Children Act 1989 (a contact order, prohibited steps order, residence order or specific issue order). Under the Adoption and Children Act 2002, the court continues to be under a duty to consider, in applying the welfare principle, whether there are options other than an adoption order which would be in the best interest of the child. To this end, new alternative measures have been introduced which are discussed later (see pages 23 to 26). Although case law under the old law was mainly concerned with whether the natural father was unreasonably withholding consent, these cases may be still be relevant as a guide to, and illustration of, the approach of the court. A summary of some of these cases is therefore given below, to illustrate the difficulties, and to demonstrate the need to assess the advantages and disadvantages of an adoption order, an order under section 8 of the Children Act 1989, or preserving the *status quo* while conferring some legal status on the step-parent.

In conducting this balancing exercise, the words of Ormrod LJ in *Re S (Infants) (Adoption by Parent)* [1977] Fam 173, [1977] 2 WLR 919, [1977] 3 All ER 671 is relevant under the new law. He said that the court:

> "will require considerably more investigation and information than in normal adoption cases, in which a satisfactory report from the guardian *ad litem* is usually sufficient. In many cases it may be desirable that the judge should hear evidence from the natural parent, even if his consent has been obtained, or at least have a detailed statement of his present attitude and of his past relationship with the child from the guardian *ad litem*. It will also be necessary to examine carefully the motives of each

of the adopters, and in this respect the court may require the assistance from the guardian *ad litem*, as the child's advocate, in the form of cross-examination. In fact it will be the duty of the guardian *ad litem*, in this class of case, to draw the attention of the court to the advantages as well as the disadvantages of adoption. It should, perhaps, be borne in mind that one aspect of this type of adoption is its effect on the step-parent. Sometimes it is the step-parent who feels the need to be integrated into the family and who may be helped by an adoption order. He or she, after all is always the last-comer. This may be an advantage to the child or it may not, depending on the personalities involved. There is no doubt that this class of case will now require more investigation than has been the practice in the past."

In *Re S (Adoption Order: Access)* [1976] Fam 1, [1975] 2 WLR 250, [1975] 1 All ER 109, the father of an illegitimate child had had contact with his child. The mother married. She and her husband wished to adopt the child (at the time, a step-parent had to apply jointly with the parent; for the position now, see page 23). The father objected. The application was refused at first instance. On appeal, the parties came to an agreement whereby the father consented to the adoption order subject to an agreement by the mother and the step-father to permit contact between the child and his father to be resumed and to continue, using the court welfare officer as an intermediary. It was held that the court had jurisdiction to impose conditions relating to contact in special circumstances where such an arrangement was necessary in the interest of the child.

In *Re S (Infants) (Adoption by Parent)* (above), the children had grown up with their natural parents and knew their father and had contact with him. A custody (now a residence) order was preferred to an adoption order.

In *Re LA (A Minor)* [1978] 122 SJ 417, [1978] The Times 27 April, the mother and step-father applied for an adoption order after the death of the natural father. The paternal grandparents, who had set up a trust for their grandchild, resisted the application. On appeal it was held that the welfare of the child would not be promoted by the adoption order and that the adoption would sever the child's ties with the paternal family. The application was refused.

In *Re D (Minors) (Adoption by Step-Parents)* [1981] 2 FLR 102, the parents of two girls aged ten and thirteen were divorced. The girls resided with their mother and for about five years the natural father had contact with the children. The mother remarried. Her husband had two children from his former marriage, who lived with him, but had no contact with their mother. The two families integrated and the couple planned to emigrate to Australia. They applied to adopt the two girls. The girls had indicated to the guardian *ad litem* that they wished to be adopted. The father had consented to the adoption and had agreed to the children's names being changed. On appeal, the court made an adoption order but expressed the view that it was difficult to know what criteria should be used in reaching the decision. In the vast majority of cases it would be impossible to show any material advantage to the children in making an adoption order. The court had to consider very difficult psychological issues in coming to the conclusion that the matter could be better dealt with in one way or the other. An important factor was that under section 6 of the Adoption Act 1976 the court was required to ascertain the wishes and feelings of the child regarding the decision. In arriving at his decision, Ormrod LJ said:

"That, to my mind must be an important consideration when dealing with children of the age of these children. They are fully old enough to understand . . . the broad implications of adoption and, if they actively wished to be adopted, even if they cannot give a very coherent reason for that wish, to refuse an adoption in the face of that wish does require . . . some fairly clear reason."

Under the new law the paramount consideration must be the child's welfare and in applying the welfare principle the court is obliged to have regard to all the circumstances, including the factors set out in section 1(4) of the Adoption and Children Act 2002 (see Chapter 9).

In *Re PJ (Adoption: Practice on Appeal)* [1998] 2 FLR 252, the parents of children aged eleven and five had separated in 1991. The children had witnessed domestic violence between their parents. The mother had obtained an injunction and the father, having breached the order, had been committed to prison. Initially the children had indicated that they did not wish to have contact with their natural father and as a result he had not pursued his application for contact with them. The mother and the father both remarried. When the eldest child was almost seventeen, the mother and the step-father applied to adopt the children. The father objected. The guardian *ad litem* supported the application and took the view that the father should accept the children's wishes. Relying on the guardian's report, the father's consent was dispensed with and an adoption order was made. On appeal it was held that the judge at first instance should have questioned the guardian *ad litem*'s reasoning. The evidence, far from showing the children to have been in fear of their father, suggested the reverse; the children's understanding of the effects of an adoption order had been superficial; the guardian *ad litem*'s experience of and expertise on some of the matters she dealt with in her report were questionable and therefore the court should have questioned the guardian *ad litem*'s reasons for her conclusion. The Court of Appeal held that there had been a misdirection and error in the judge's decision. However, since the final order had been made, the older child had attained the age of eighteen and so the case could not be remitted. In the circumstances it would be wrong to remit the case of the younger child and thereby give her a legal status different from that of her brother. Furthermore, the adoption order having been made, setting it aside was more likely to damage the father's relationship with the children than leaving it in place.

In *Re B (Adoption: Father's Objections)* [1999] 2 FLR 215, the child was twelve years of age. His father had not seen him during the first two years of his life. The parents then married, but the marriage was annulled. There was a history of the father's abducting the child from the mother's care, for which he was sentenced to imprisonment. The mother remarried and the child lived with her and the step-father. The natural father's numerous applications for contact were refused. The mother and the step-father applied to adopt the child. The application was supported by the author of the Schedule 2 report and the guardian *ad litem,* but objected to by the father. His objections were based on the loss of the child's links with the paternal family. However, the judge's conclusion was that the welfare of the child demanded an adoption order. On appeal by the father, the Court of Appeal held that the judge had properly applied the twofold test when arriving at his decision. He had taken into consideration the adverse effect on the child of the numerous applications that had been made by the father; the abduction of the child, which had made the child fearful; the child's particular need for stability and security free from such fears; and the child's wish to be adopted and not to be reminded of his father or his links with him. These were all relevant factors, which had been properly taken into account, given the child's maturity and his ability to understand the effect of adoption.

In *Soderback v Sweden* [1999] 1 FLR 250, (2000) 29 EHRR 95, a decision of a Swedish court was challenged on the ground of breach of article 8 of the European Convention on Human Rights (the right to respect for private and family life). The parents of the child had never cohabited. Contact between the natural father and the child had not been regular, due partly to the mother's opposition and partly to the father's problems with alcohol abuse. The mother married and the child lived with her and the step-father. The natural father formed a stable relationship with a woman and sought contact with his daughter. The mother and the step-father applied to adopt the child. The father opposed the application on the basis that an adoption order would deprive him of his family life with his daughter and violate his article 8 rights. The Swedish court made an adoption order on the ground that adoption would be in the best interest of the child. The father appealed to the European Court of Human Rights, which proceeded on the basis that the adoption order amounted to an interference with respect for the father's family life. The issue before the court therefore was one of proportionality. In dismissing the appeal, the European Court of Human Rights took into account:

(a) that the child had been living with her mother since birth and her step-father since she was eight months old. Their relationship had existed for about six and a half years and she regarded him as her father;

(b) that the natural father had had infrequent and limited contact with his daughter; and

(c) the best interests of the child,
and assessed the competing claims. The court concluded that the decision fell
within the margin of appreciation and that the adverse effect of the adoption
order on the natural father's relationship with the child had not been
disproportionate.

It will be observed that when, in past cases, an adoption order has been
made in favour of a step-parent, it has been either subject to conditions, or the
circumstances have been exceptional; in a number of cases the court has
expressed the view that such orders should be made sparingly and only in
exceptional cases. It is submitted that, when applying the welfare test and
balancing all the relevant factors, regard should be had to the irreversible
change in the status of the child and that of his natural parents which occurs
on adoption, namely that all ties with the natural parent whose consent is
dispensed with are severed; and, where the application is made by a parent
and step-parent jointly, the natural parent becomes an adoptive parent.

The Adoption and Children Act 2002 now enables a step-parent to apply
to adopt as a single applicant. Even in such cases, however, it has to be borne
in mind that if the marriage breaks down the adoption order cannot be
revoked. Security, for both the carers of the child and the child, is often
referred to as the reason for making an adoption order, but that security can
be provided from the wide range of alternatives now available which confer
legal rights. In any event, security depends upon the emotional attachment
which a child develops with the adoptive parent, rather than on a legal
document. Finally, on this issue, the need to maintain and preserve the child's
identity is also an important factor.

The Adoption and Children Act 2002 introduces a number of options
which were not previously available to provide legal status to the step-parent
while still maintaining the child's link with the family of the parent with
whom he does not live. These include the acquisition of parental
responsibility, an order under section 8 of the Children Act 1989 and a
special guardianship order. These are considered below.

Acquisition of parental responsibility
Section 112 of the 2002 Act inserts a new section 4A into the Children Act
1989. It provides that where a step-parent is married to the parent with
parental responsibility, the step-parent may acquire parental responsibility for
the child of his or her spouse by agreement between the step-parent and the
natural parent, or with both the natural parents if both have parental
responsibility; this will be a "parental responsibility agreement" within the
definition in section 4(2) of the Children Act 1989. Alternatively, the court
may, on the application of the step-parent, order that the step-parent shall
have parental responsibility for the child.

The procedure to be followed is the same as for the acquisition of
parental responsibility by an unmarried father, as provided by section 4(2) of

the Children Act. The Parental Responsibility Agreement (Amendment) Regulations 2005 (SI 2005 No. 2808) prescribe a form of step-parent parental responsibility agreement (form C(PRA2)). The agreement must be signed by the parent(s) and the step-parent and recorded as prescribed by the Parental Responsibility Agreement Regulations 1991 (SI 1991 No. 1478 as amended).

Where agreement cannot be reached, the step-parent can apply to the court for a parental responsibility order by issuing an application in Form C1. The procedure set out in rule 4.4. of the Family Proceedings Rules 1991 (SI 1991 No. 1247) should be followed. Normally, no written statement is filed with the application. At the directions hearing, the court will give directions for filing written statements and reports, and timetable the case for a final hearing.

Unlike an adoption order, a parental responsibility agreement order is reversible and may be brought to an end by an order of the court on the application of any person who has parental responsibility for the child; or, with the permission of the court, by the child himself (Children Act 1989, section 4A(3), as inserted by the Adoption and Children Act 2002, section 112). In the case of an application by the child, the court may grant permission to make the application only if it is satisfied that the child has sufficient understanding to make the proposed application (section 4A(4)).

Finally, a parental responsibility agreement or order is not available to a partner who is cohabiting with a parent of the child.

Orders under section 8, Children Act 1989
Two further amendments to the Children Act 1989 have been made by virtue of the Adoption and Children Act 2002, schedule 3, paragraphs 54 to 56. These provide that:

(a) a step-parent may now apply for an order under section 8 of the Children Act 1989 if he/she has parental responsibility for the child under the provisions of the amended section 4A of the 1989 Act (see above); and

(b) a step-parent is included in the categories of person who are entitled to apply for a residence order (Children Act 1989, section 10(5) as now amended).

Thus, a step-parent may now apply for a residence order. In addition, the court may make a specific issue order to enable the child to be removed from the jurisdiction for an extended period, or to restrict contact. Where necessary, it may make an order under section 91(14) preventing applications being made for variation or revocation of orders without the permission of the court. See *Re G (A Minor) (Adoption Order)* [1999] 1 FLR 400 where, on appeal, a section 8 order was substituted for an adoption order. By contrast, in *Re B (Adoption) (Father's Objections)* [1999] 2 FLR 215, the adoption order was upheld because of the need for finality, the wishes of the child and the exceptional circumstances of the case.

Duration of a residence order or parental responsibility order

The court may direct that a residence order or parental responsibility order made in favour of a person who is not the parent or guardian of the child (i.e., a step-parent or partner of a child's parent) is to continue in force until the child reaches the age of eighteen years (Children Act 1989, section 12(5), inserted by the Adoption and Children Act 2002, section 114(1)).

A section 8 order can be varied or discharged, but where a residence order has been extended to the child's eighteenth birthday, an application to vary or discharge the order may be made only with the prior permission of the court (Children Act 1989, section 12(6), inserted by the Adoption and Children Act 2002, section 114(1)).

Special guardianship order

Although sections 14A to 14G of the Children Act 1989, inserted by section 115 of the Adoption and Children Act 2002, do not automatically entitle a step-parent to apply for a special guardianship order (see Chapter 4), a step-parent may acquire the right to apply, for example:

(a) under the Children Act 1989, section 10(5)(b), where the child has lived with the step-parent for a period of at least three years; or

(b) the step-parent has the consent of each of the parents who have parental responsibility for the child (Children Act 1989, section 10(5)(c)(iii)); and

(c) without such an application having been made, where the court in any family proceedings considers that a special guardianship order should be made (Children Act 1989, section 14A(6) (b), as inserted by the Adoption and Children Act 2002, section 115).

Contact order

In appropriate cases the court may make an open adoption order, that is, an adoption order combined with a contact order in favour of the natural parent. Indeed, section 46(6) of the Adoption and Children Act 2002 specifically provides that, before making an adoption order, the court must consider whether there should be arrangements for allowing any person contact with the child. For that purpose the court must consider any existing or proposed arrangements and obtain the views of the parties to the proceedings. This provision imposes a duty on the court to address the issue of contact in every case. It is reinforced by section 1(4) of the Act which requires the court to have regard to the child's family links. To ensure that the matter of contact is addressed, the natural parent should be advised, in appropriate cases, to apply for contact within the adoption proceedings.

The availability of the alternative options described above does not prevent the court from making an adoption order in appropriate cases. The decision of the court will turn on the facts of each individual case after applying the welfare principle, the factors set out in section 1(4) of the 2002 Act, and its assessment of the advantages and disadvantages of the various options. The court must also take into account whether making the order would violate article 8 of the European Convention on Human Rights, and, if so, whether interference with such rights is in accordance with the law and necessary in a democratic society for the protection of the rights and freedoms of others including those of the child. It is thus essential that the reports prepared by the local authority and the guardian deal with these issues in detail, and not merely superficially.

4. Single Applicants

An application to adopt a child may be made on the application of one person:

(a) if he/she has attained the age of twenty-one and is not married or a civil partner (Adoption and Children Act 2002, section 51(1) as amended by section 79, Civil Partnership Act 2004). On upper age limits, see pages 14 to 15;

(b) if he/she is a partner of a parent of the child to be adopted and has attained the age of twenty-one years (section 51(2));

(c) who is married and has attained the age of twenty-one years provided:

(i) the person's spouse cannot be found;

(ii) the spouses have separated and are living apart and the separation is likely to be permanent;

(iii) the person's spouse is by reason of ill-health, whether physical or mental, incapable of making an application for an adoption order (section 51(3));

(d) who has attained the age of twenty-one and is a civil partner and:

(i) the person's civil partner cannot be found;

(ii) the civil partners have separated and are living apart and the separation is likely to be permanent; or

(iii) the person's civil partner is by reason of ill-health, whether physical or mental, incapable of making an application for an adoption order (section 51(3A), inserted by the Civil Partnership Act 2004, section 79);

(e) by a mother or father of the child to be adopted where the court is satisfied that:

(i) the other natural parent is dead or cannot be found;

(ii) by virtue of section 28 of the Human Fertilisation and Embryology Act 1990, there is no other parent;

(iii) there is some other reason justifying the child's being adopted by the applicant alone (section 51(4)).

Where the court makes an adoption order under (d) above the court must record that it is satisfied as to the facts in (i) and (ii), or record the reasons for its decision under (iii).

This provision is not dissimilar from the provisions of the Adoption Act 1976, section 15(1) and (2), which were considered by the Court of Appeal and the House of Lords in *Re B (A Minor)* [2001] UKHL 70, [2002] 1 WLR 258, [2002] 1 All ER 641, [2002] 1 FLR 196 (HL), reversing [2001] 1 FLR 589 (CA). This case is a good illustration of the issues to be dealt with by those who prepare reports on applications for adoption orders, and by the courts which make the decisions. In *Re B,* the mother of the child did not inform the genetic father of the pregnancy and wished the child to be placed for adoption without informing the father. She told the local authority that the father was living and working abroad, when he was in fact living in England. By chance, a member of the staff of the local authority saw and recognised the father and the local authority then got in touch with him. He expressed a wish to care for the child and the child was placed with the father when she was two months old. The father then wished to adopt the child to the exclusion of the mother, who did not oppose the application. She did not wish to have contact with the child or to interfere with the father's care of the child. The Official Solicitor, representing the child, opposed the making of an adoption order. The judge at first instance made an adoption order. On appeal, the Court of Appeal set aside the order and replaced it with a residence order until the child was eighteen years of age, with the right to take the child outside England and Wales without the mother's permission. The Court of Appeal also restricted the mother's right to make an application for an order under section 8 of the Children Act 1989 without leave of the court. This order was made on the basis of article 8(2) of the European Convention on Human Rights, and that motherhood in itself was sufficient to establish the right to "family life".

The House of Lords reversed this decision and reinstated the adoption order on the basis that there were no grounds for interfering with the discretion exercised by the judge at first instance; the judge had not misdirected herself, nor had her decision been plainly wrong. It made the decision on the further ground that, in the light of the welfare principle, the child's need for stability and security could be provided only if the father's anxieties that the mother might have a change of heart could be allayed by securing his status. The court also ruled that any interference with the mother's rights under article 8 was both proportionate and necessary in the best interest of the child. Lord Nicholls of Birkenhead, in his judgment, also gave examples of the exceptions listed in section 15(3)(b) of the Adoption Act 1976, which required the court to be satisfied that there was some other reason justifying the exclusion of the other parent; those examples included persistent neglect, ill-treatment and abandonment. His Lordship said:

> ". . . the exception stated in paragraph (b) is altogether open-ended. No doubt this is a deliberate choice of language. I can see no ground for

importing into this exception an unexpressed limitation whereby 'some other reason' must be comparable with the death or disappearance of the other natural parent. What is required by subpara (b) and all that is required, is that the reason whatever it be, must be sufficient to justify the exclusion of the other parent. Whether any particular reason satisfied this test depends on the circumstances."

Section 51(3) and (4) of the 2002 Act (above) now set out the circumstances justifying an adoption order in favour of one parent alone. Although the 2002 Act may have removed the difference in interpretation of the provisions which arose under the 1976 Act, the issue may still be debatable on the broader bases of the welfare test, and proportionality and human rights.

All single applicants must also satisfy the following further require-ments:

    (a) that the applicant is domiciled in a part of the British Islands (see page 15); and

    (b) that the applicant has been habitually resident in a part of the British Islands for a period of not less that one year ending with the date of the application (see page 17); and

    (c) that the child has had his home with the applicant for the relevant period (see page 18).

5. Relatives

Relatives may adopt, provided they satisfy the conditions otherwise applicable, described in this chapter. There is one further requirement, namely that the child must have had his home with the applicant relative(s) for a period of not less than three years, whether continuous or not, during the five years ending with the application, unless the court gives permission to make the application sooner (section 42(5) and (6) of the 2002 Act). The clear indication, therefore, is that in such cases the preferred option would be to apply for one or more of the other options available (see pages 23 to 26).

Section 144 defines "relative", in relation to a child, as a grandparent, brother, sister, uncle or aunt, whether of the full blood or half-blood or by marriage or civil partnership.

6. Procedure

Part 5 of the Family Procedure (Adoption) Rules 2005 (SI 2005 No. 2795) governs the procedure for applying for an adoption order. For the procedure, and for the court in which an application should be made, see Chapter 25, pages 390 and 380.

7. Summary

1. The Adoption and Children Act 2002 imposes certain restrictions on the eligibility of those who may apply to adopt a child. These relate to age, domicile and residence.
2. Couples, irrespective of their marital status, and irrespective of whether they are in a heterosexual relationship or a same-sex relationship, may apply.
3. A step-parent may apply, as a single applicant, to adopt his or her step-child, but the alternatives should be considered and ruled out if appropriate before an application for adoption is made.
4. An application may be made by the mother or father of a child as a sole applicant on satisfying the conditions in section 51(4).
5. An application may be made by one person who is married or is a civil partner, on satisfying the conditions in section 51(3) or 51(3A).

Chapter 3

The Child

1. Statutory Requirements

On an application for an adoption order, the following requirements must be satisfied in respect of a child who is the subject of the application:

(a) the child must be under the age of eighteen years (Adoption and Children Act 2002, section 49(4));

(b) the child must not be or have been married (section 47(8));

(c) the child must not be or have been a civil partner (section 47(8A) of the 2002 Act, inserted by the Civil Partnership Act 2004, section 79(3));

(d) the child must be in England and Wales when the application is made;

(e) the child must have had his home with the prospective adopters for the relevant period, and sufficient opportunities to see the child with the applicant (or in the case of an application by a couple, both of them together) in the home environment must have been given to the adoption agency or the local authority within whose area the home is (section 42).

These requirements are discussed in turn in this chapter.

2. Age

A child who has not attained the age of eighteen years at the date of the application may be the subject of a placement order or an adoption order. The Adoption and Children Act 2002, section 49(4), provides that an application for an adoption order may be made only if the person to be adopted has not attained the age of eighteen years on the date of the application.

Subsection (5) provides that references in the Act to a child, in connection with any proceedings (whether or not concluded) for adoption, (such as a "child to be adopted" or "adopted child") include a person who has attained the age of eighteen years before the proceedings are concluded.

Section 21(4) provides that a placement order comes to an end when the

30

child marries or attains the age of eighteen years.

Section 144 defines a child, except where used to express a relationship, as a person who has not attained the age of eighteen years. A similar definition is given in the Children Act 1989, section 105.

The time at which a person attains a particular age expressed in years is the commencement of the relevant anniversary of the date of birth (Family Law Reform Act 1969, section 9). An adoption order can therefore be made after the child's eighteenth birthday provided the proceedings were commenced before he attained that age. Section 47(9) of the Adoption and Children Act 2002, however, provides that an adoption order may not be made in relation to a person who has attained the age of nineteen years. This may be significant in cases where, although the adoption proceedings were commenced before the child's eighteenth birthday, exceptional circumstances have meant that the final hearing for the adoption order has not taken place by the child's nineteenth birthday.

Child eighteen or over at the final hearing
Where the child has attained the age of eighteen years by the time the application for an adoption order is heard, the court's decision is, as in other cases, based on the application of the welfare principle; the particular circumstances of the case; the assessment of all the circumstances; and the factors set out in section 1(4) of the Adoption and Children Act 2002 (see Chapter 9). The court also takes account of issues arising under article 8 of the European Convention on Human Rights. The following reported cases, decided under the Adoption Act 1976, illustrate the approach of the court to children over eighteen.

In *Re S and J (Adoption: Non-Patrials)* [2004] 2 FLR 111, the applicants were a married couple from Bangladesh but resident in the United Kingdom. They had six children. In 1998 they travelled to Bangladesh and returned to the United Kingdom with two boys aged twelve and ten years. The boys did not have permission from the United Kingdom authorities to enter the United Kingdom, but the applicants succeeded in getting them through immigration control on the basis of a travelling certificate which was not authentic. The boys lived with the couple. On 21 June 1999, the police and immigration authorities discovered the boys and they were removed from the couple but subsequently returned. The couple were charged with immigration offences. They pleaded guilty and were sentenced to 80 hours' community service. They applied for a residence order in respect of both boys and were granted an interim residence order. Subsequently they applied to adopt them. The Home Office was notified of the application, but did not oppose it until late in the proceedings. The children's guardian opposed the application, but the local authority (the "schedule 2 reporter") supported it. At the date of the hearing the older of the two boys was almost eighteen and the younger boy was almost sixteen. Their mother consented to the adoption. Their father could not be traced.

The court found on the evidence that the couple had misled the authorities to achieve an immigration advantage and had also sought to mislead the court regarding the boys' parentage. It was also acknowledged that the older of the two boys was only seven weeks short of his eighteenth birthday and therefore the benefit of adoption to him would come after adulthood, when he would be able to argue all his article 8 rights if the Home Office sought to deport him. The court found, however, that this was not an ordinary case. The couple had genuinely exercised parental responsibility over the boys for five years and proposed to continue to do so indefinitely. Their application was genuine, and in making the application for a residence order and an adoption order they had sought the psychological advantage for the boys that they would have a family life. The court applied the test in section 6 of the Adoption Act 1976, having regard to all the circumstances of the case, first consideration being given to the need to safeguard and promote the welfare of the child throughout his childhood; and the child's ascertainable wishes and feelings having regard to his age and understanding. In so doing the welfare element weighed in favour of granting the application and the adoption order was made. Had the case been decided under the Adoption and Children Act 2002, having regard to the principles set out in section 1(2) and 1(4), the case for making an adoption order would have been even stronger.

Section 1(2) of the 2002 Act imposes a mandatory consideration that in adoption applications the paramount consideration must be the child's welfare throughout his life, whereas under the Adoption Act 1976 the welfare principle was not paramount, but a first consideration among many others. Secondly, the welfare principle was to be considered in so far as it related to the child's childhood, whereas under the new law the child's welfare *throughout his life* is relevant.

In *Re B (A Minor) (Adoption Order: Nationality)* [1999] 2 AC 136, [1999] 2 WLR 714, [1999] 2 All ER 576, [1999] 1 FLR 907, the child, a Jamaican national, entered the United Kingdom with her mother on a visitor's visa to visit her maternal grandparents. The mother returned on the expiry of her visa but the child remained living with her grandparents, who applied for an extension of her stay. The Home Office refused the application. In the meantime, the child's father had died and her mother was living in impoverished circumstances with another daughter and her children. The grandparents applied to adopt the child. On the date of the application the child was sixteen years of age. The court at first instance made an adoption order. The appeal court overturned that decision on the basis that an adoption order would not confer any benefits on the child other than allow her to remain in the United Kingdom. On further appeal, the House of Lords applied the section 6 test. Lord Hoffman in his judgment said:

"Section 6 requires the judge to have regard to all the circumstances and treat the welfare of the child throughout his childhood as the first consideration. I do not see how, consistently with this language, the court could simply have ignored the considerable benefits which would have accrued to J during the remainder of her childhood. . .

It is wrong to exclude from consideration any circumstances which would follow from the adoption whether they are matters which will occur during childhood or afterwards."

Thus the principles set out in the Adoption and Children Act 2002 echo those in *Re B* and *Re S and J*.

In *Re D (A Minor) (Adoption Order: Validity)* [1991] Fam 137, [1991] 2 WLR 1215, [1991] 3 All ER 461, [1991] 2 FLR 66, the child suffered from severe mental handicap and had lived with foster carers, who applied to adopt him. An adoption order was made six days before his eighteenth birthday. The mother of the child appealed on the ground that the order was not necessary to safeguard "his welfare throughout his childhood". The Court of Appeal dismissed the appeal, holding that there was no requirement that benefit during minority was a precondition before an adoption order could be made. The child's age, together with all other relevant factors which would benefit the child not only during childhood but also into adulthood had to be considered.

3. Home with the Prospective Adopters

If the child was placed for adoption with the applicant(s) by an adoption agency or in pursuance of an order of the High Court (for example, in wardship proceedings), or the applicant is a parent of the child, the child must have had his home with the applicant (or in the case of a couple, with one or both of them) at all times during a period of ten weeks before the proceedings are commenced (Adoption and Children Act 2002, section 42(2)).

Where the applicant or one of them is the partner of a parent of the child, the child must have had his home with the applicant(s) at all times during the period of six months before proceedings are commenced (section 42(3)). In transitional cases, however, the period is twelve months (see Chapter 24, page 368).

Where the prospective adopters are local authority foster parents, the child must have had his home with them at all times during the period of one year before the proceedings are commenced (section 42(4)).

In all other cases, for example where the prospective adopters are relatives of the child, the child must have had his home with the applicant (or where the application is by a couple, with one or both of them) for not less than three years (whether continuous or not) during the period of five years preceding the application (section 42(5)). The period for applicants under this category has been extended to three years, in place of the thirteen weeks under the Adoption Act 1976, section 13. This extension may be to stress the inappropriateness of relatives applying for an adoption order save in very exceptional circumstances, and is indicative of the preferred option, which is to consider other alternatives, such as a residence order under section 8 of the Children Act 1989 or a special guardianship order (see Chapter 4).

In the latter two cases (local authority foster parents, and relatives of the child), however, the court may give permission to make an application for adoption even though the time requirements are not met (section 42(6)).

The requirement that the child must have had his home with the applicant(s) for the relevant period is mandatory, section 42(1) providing that an adoption order may not be made unless this requirement is complied with.

4. Opportunities to see the Child and Prospective Adopter(s) at Home
Section 42(7) of the 2002 Act goes on to provide that an adoption order may not be made unless the court is satisfied that there have been sufficient opportunities to see the child with the applicant, or in the case of an application by a couple, both of them, together in the home environment. Such opportunities must be given:

(a) where the child was placed for adoption with the applicant(s) by an adoption agency, to that agency;

(b) in any other case, to the local authority within whose area the home is.

The Adoption Act 1976, section 13, contained a similar requirement. In addition, section 87 of the Children Act 1975 provided that, when considering references to the person with whom a child has his home, absences of the child at a hospital or boarding school, and any other absences, should be disregarded. There was no reference to any absences of the applicant(s), as where, for example, one party may be temporarily absent due to work commitments. The Adoption and Children Act 2002 makes no reference to any absence of the child or the prospective adopters. Where such absences occur, they will have to be considered by the court and it will be for the court to determine whether any such absence should be disregarded. Where the absence of one of the parties is for a lengthy period, the issue will have to be considered against the background of all the circumstances of the case and its impact on the issue.

In *Re Y (Minors) (Adoption: Jurisdiction)* [1985] Fam 136, [1985] 3 WLR 601, [1985] 3 All ER 33, [1986] 1 FLR 152, the court considered the terms "home" and "home environment". In his judgment, Sheldon J stated:

"It is a question to which little or no assistance in finding an answer is provided by ss 107(1) and 87(3) of the 1975 Act. Nor in my view, unless it is to be given for any particular purpose some arbitrary statutory meaning, is the concept capable of precise definition. Nor, too, in my opinion, should a definition be attempted beyond indicating the principal features that a 'home' may be expected to embody. Subject to that, in my judgement it is a question of fact in any particular case whether or not the applicant has a 'home' within the meaning of the 1975 Act.

'Home' is defined in the *Shorter Oxford Dictionary* as: "a dwelling house, house, abode: the fixed residence of a family or household; one's own house; the dwelling in which one habitually lives or which one regards as one's proper abode".

It is a definition which in my judgment, contains the essential elements of a 'home' as it is to be understood for present purposes. I have no doubt that an individual may have two homes; but each in my judgment, to be properly so called, must comprise some element of regular occupation (whether past, present or intended for the future, even if intermittent) with some degree of permanency, based upon some right of occupation whenever it is required, where in the words of Kekewich K in *Re Estlin, Prichard v Thomas* (1903) 72 LJ Ch 687 at 689, 'you find the comforts of what is known as a home' the fixed residence of a family or household."

In a recent case, *Re SL (Adoption: Home in Jurisdiction)* [2004] EWHC 1283 (Fam), [2005] 1 FLR 118, Mumby J agreed entirely with Sheldon J's analysis.

When a child is temporarily absent, for example, at a boarding school, or in hospital, the question whether the child has his home with the prospective adopters is determined by reference to whether or not they continue to exercise parental control over the child: *Re B (An Infant) (No 2)* [1964] Ch 1, [1963] WLR 471, [1963] 3 All ER 125.

5. Reports

Where a child is placed by an adoption agency for adoption, the agency must submit a report on the suitability of the applicants and any other relevant matters, and assist the court in any manner the court directs (Adoption and Children Act 2002, section 43).

Where the child has not been placed with the applicants by an adoption agency the proposed adopters must give notice to the appropriate local authority of their intention to apply for an adoption order.

For details of the requirements concerning reports, see page 217; for the meaning of "appropriate local authority", see page 87.

6. Refusal of Earlier Application

An application to adopt a child may not be made where a previous application to adopt the child was refused by any court, including a court in Scotland, Northern Ireland, the Isle of Man or any of the Channel Islands. The only exception is where there has been a change in circumstances, or for any other reason the court finds that it would be proper to hear the application (Adoption and Children Act 2002, section 48).

Chapter 4

Special Guardianship Orders

1. Introduction

A special guardianship order is an order appointing one or more individuals to be a child's "special guardian". The special guardianship order has been introduced by section 115 of the Adoption and Children Act 2002, which inserts new sections 14A to 14G into the Children Act 1989. It is intended to provide an alternative to an adoption order as a halfway house, the parents of the child retaining parental responsibility when a special guardianship order is made, rather than losing it as under an adoption order. The new order is intended to ensure that stability and permanence for the child are maintained, while security is provided to the child's carers who acquire parental responsibility for the child when the order is made. In appropriate cases, the parents' rights are either restricted or excluded, but their link with the child is maintained because they retain parental responsibility, and, in appropriate cases, their rights of contact with the child.

The order may prove useful, in particular, in cases where the local authority's care plan is for long-term fostering with contact with the birth parents, or placement with a member of the child's extended family. It would also be an alternative to adoption in cases of older children who do not wish to be separated from their birth families, and in cases where, for religious and cultural reasons, adoption is regarded as either inappropriate or unacceptable.

2. The Applicant

Section 14A(5) of the Children Act 1989, as inserted by the Adoption and Children Act 2002, lists the categories of person who are eligible to apply for a special guardianship order. They are:

    (a) any guardian of the child;

    (b) any individual in whose favour a residence order has been made and remains in force with respect to the child;

    (c) any person with whom the child has lived for a period of at least three years. This period need not be continuous, but must not have begun more than five years before, or ended more than three months before, the application is made (section 14A(5)(c), referring to section 10(5)(b), Children Act 1989);

(d) anyone who has the consent of the person or persons in whose favour a residence order has been made (section 14A(5)(c), referring to section 10(5)(c), Children Act 1989);

(e) if the child is in the care of the local authority, any person who has the consent of that authority (section 14A(5)(c), referring to section 10(5)(c), Children Act 1989);

(f) any person who has the consent of those who have parental responsibility for the child (section 14A(5)(c), referring to section 10(5)(c), Children Act 1989);

(g) a local authority foster parent with whom the child has lived for a period of at least one year before the application is made (section 14A(5)(d));

(h) any other person, including the child, who has the permission of the court to make the application (section 14A(3)(b)).

It should be noted that those who are specifically identified as entitled to make an application for a special guardianship order do not include a step-parent.

3. Application for Leave

In cases where a person is required to seek permission to make an application for a special guardianship order, the court is required to have regard to the following matters:

(a) the nature of the proposed application for a special guardianship order;

(b) the applicant's connection with the child;

(c) any risk there might be that the proposed application might disrupt the child's life to such an extent that he would be harmed by it; and

(d) where the child is being looked after by a local authority, the authority's plan for the child's future and the wishes and feelings of the child's parents

(sections 10(9) and 14A(12), Children Act 1989).

Application by the child

Where a child is seeking permission to make the application, the only factor on which the court is specifically directed to be satisfied is that the child has sufficient understanding to make the proposed application (Children Act 1989, sections 10(8) and 14A(12)). Where the court is so satisfied, it has a discretion whether or not to grant permission, but it is not clear what criteria the court should apply. Reported decisions relating to applications under section 10 of the Children Act 1989 (on the powers of the court to make orders under section 8) have differed on whether or not the welfare principle applies to an application made by a child. In *Re S (Contact: Application by Sibling)* [1999] Fam 283, [1999] 3 WLR 504, [1999] 1 All ER 648, [1998] 2 FLR 897 (Fam Div), it was held that the welfare of the child was not paramount, but in *Re C (A Minor) (Leave to Seek Section 8 Orders)* [1994] 1 FLR 26, it was held to be paramount. In any event, the child's interest is a relevant consideration. The court is also likely to have regard to the reasons the child proposes to make the application, and the merit of the proposed application. Although the matters set out in section 1(3) of the Children Act 1989 (the welfare checklist) are not directly relevant, they are factors in determining the application.

Where an application for leave is made by a child, it should be dealt with by the High Court (Practice Direction of 22 February 1993, [1993] 1 FLR 668). If the proceedings are being dealt with in the county court, the application for leave should be transferred to the High Court for determination. The procedure is set out in rule 4.3 of the Family Proceedings Rules 1991 (SI 1991 No. 1247) and rule 3 of the Family Proceedings Courts (Children Act 1989) Rules 1991 (SI 1991 No. 1395).

Application by person other than the child
Section 14A sets out the matters that the court should take into account when determining an application for leave by a person other than the child. These factors are those in section 10(9) of the Children Act, set out in (a) to (d) on page 37 above. Since these factors also govern applications for permission to apply for an order under section 8 of the 1989 Act (contact, prohibited steps, residence and specific issue orders), decisions concerning that provision are therefore relevant to applications for permission to apply for a special guardianship order.

Thus, the matters set out in section 1(1) and 1(3) of the Children Act 1989 (the welfare principle and the welfare checklist) do not apply to applications for leave: *G v F (Contact and Shared Residence: Application for Leave)* [1998] 2 FLR 799, and *Re S (Contact: Application by Sibling)* (above).

The court should have regard to the merits of the proposed application and weigh this with all other factors set out in the subsection. In relation to the risk of disruption, any disruption that would be caused to the child's life if the application were to succeed is also a relevant consideration: *In Re A (A Minor) (Residence Order: Leave to Apply)* [1993] 1 FLR 425.

The section refers to risk of disruption to the child's life to such an extent that he would be harmed by it. "Harm" is defined in section 31(9) of the Children Act as "ill-treatment or the impairment of health or development including, for example, impairment suffered from seeing or hearing the ill-treatment of another".

The court must also have regard to the local authority's future care plan: *In Re M (Prohibited Steps Order: Application for Leave)* [1993] 1 FLR 275.

4. Conditions to be satisfied by the applicant

An applicant for a special guardianship order:

    (a) must be aged eighteen or over (section 14A(2)(a), Children Act 1989, inserted by section 115, Adoption and Children Act 2002);

    (b) must not be a parent of the child who is the subject of the application (section 14A(2)(b)); and

    (c) must give three months' notice to the local authority of his/her intention to make the application. If the child in question is being looked after by a local authority the notice must be served on that local authority. In any other case, the notice must be given to the local authority in whose area the applicant is residing (section 14A(7)). The requirement to give three months' notice does not, however, apply where the court has given permission to apply for a special guardianship order at a final adoption hearing (Adoption and Children Act 2002 section 29(6)).

There is no requirement that joint applicants must be married to one another, and therefore couples living together and same-sex couples may apply for a special guardianship order.

5. Order Made on Court's Own Motion

The court has the power to make a special guardianship order with respect to a child in any family proceedings in which a question arises concerning the welfare of the child, even if an application has not been made, if the court considers that such an order should be made (Children Act 1989, section 14A(6), inserted by section 115 of the Adoption and Children Act 2002).

6. Role of the Local Authority

When a proposed applicant gives notice of his or her intention to apply for a special guardianship order to the local authority, the local authority must investigate the matter, and prepare a report dealing with:

    (a) the suitability of the applicant to be a special guardian;

    (b) all matters set out in the schedule to the Special Guardianship Regulations 2005 (SI 2005 No. 1109) (see below) or the Special Guardianship (Wales) Regulations 2005 (SI 2005 No. 1513, W. 117), as the case may be;

    (c) any matter which the local authority considers to be relevant

(section 14A(8), Children Act 1989, inserted by section 115 of the Adoption and Children Act 2002).

The court may also direct the local authority to conduct such an investigation and prepare a report. The local authority is under a duty to comply with such a direction (section 14A(9)). The local authority may make such arrangements as it sees fit for any person to act on its behalf to conduct the investigation and prepare a report (section 14A(10)), but the court will not make a special guardianship order in the absence of such a report (section 14A(11)).

The schedule to the Special Guardianship Regulations sets out the details to be included in the report for the court under the following headings:

(a) details in respect of the child;

(b) details in respect of the child's family;

(c) details in respect of the wishes and feelings of the child and others;

(d) details in respect of the prospective special guardian or, where two or more persons are jointly prospective special guardians, each of them;

(e) details in respect of the local authority which completed the report;

(f) a summary prepared by the medical professional who provided certain information included in the report;

(g) the implications of the making of a special guardianship order for the child, the child's parent, the prospective special guardian and his family, and any other person the local authority considers relevant;

(h) the relative merits of special guardianship and other orders which may be made under the Act or the Adoption and Children Act 2002 with an assessment of whether the child's long term interests would be best met by a special guardianship order;

(i) a recommendation as to whether or not the special guardianship order sought should be made in respect of the child and, if not, any alternative proposal in respect of the child;

(j) a recommendation as to what arrangements there should be for contact between the child and his relatives or any person the local authority considers relevant.

7. Placement Order in Force

A special guardianship order cannot be made when a placement order is in force unless:

(a) an application has been made for an adoption order; and

(b) the person applying for the special guardianship order has obtained the court's permission under section 29(5) of the Adoption and Children Act 2002, or, if he is a guardian of the child, under section 47(5) of the 2002 Act

(Adoption and Children Act 2002, section 29(5)).

8. Making of Special Guardianship Order

Section 14B(1) of the Children Act 1989 (inserted by section 115 of the Adoption and Children Act 2002) imposes a duty on the court, before it makes a special guardianship order, to consider whether, if the order were

made:
  (a) any contact order should also be made with respect to the child;
  (b) any order under section 8 of the Children Act 1989 which is in force
       in respect to the child should be varied or discharged.
On making a special guardianship order, the court has power to give
permission for the child to be known by a new surname. It may also give
permission, either generally or for a specified period, to the special guardian
to remove the child from the United Kingdom without the written consent of
every person who has parental responsibility for the child or leave of the
court (section 14B(2)).

A special guardianship order, or an order varying one, may contain
provisions which are to have effect for a specified period (section 14E(4)).

A special guardianship order may:
  (a) contain directions about how it is to be carried into effect;
  (b) impose conditions which must be complied with by any person:
       (i)   in whose favour the order is made,
       (ii) who is a parent of the child concerned,
       (iii) who is not a parent of the child but who has parental
             responsibility for him, or
       (iv) with whom the child is living;
  (c) make such incidental, supplemental or consequential provision as
       the court thinks fit
  (sections 14E(5) and 11(7), Children Act 1989).

9. Criteria for Determining the Application

When the court determines an application for a special guardianship order,
the child's welfare is the paramount consideration, as in all applications
under the Children Act 1989 (Children Act 1989, section 1(1)). The court
must also have regard to the principle that delay is likely to prejudice the
welfare of the child (Children Act 1989, section 1(2)), and to the factors set
out in section 1(3) of the Children Act 1989 (the welfare checklist), i.e.:
  (a) the ascertainable wishes and feelings of the child concerned
       (considered in the light of his age and understanding);
  (b) his physical, emotional and educational needs;
  (c) the likely effect on him of any change in his circumstances;
  (d) his age, sex, background and any characteristics of his which the
       court considers relevant;
  (e) any harm which he has suffered or is at risk of suffering;
  (f) how capable each of his parents, and any other person in relation to
       whom the court considers the question to be relevant, is of meeting
       his needs;
  (h) the range of powers available to the court under the Children Act
       1989 in the proceedings in question.

These matters are discussed in more detail in Chapter 9.

10. Effect of a Special Guardianship Order

On the making of a special guardianship order, the special guardian has parental responsibility for the child and, subject to any other order in force under the 2002 Act, is entitled to exercise parental responsibility for the child to the exclusion of any other person with parental responsibility (Children Act 1989, section 14C(1) and (2), inserted by section 115 of the Adoption and Children Act 2002). There are, however, two exceptions to this general rule, in that a special guardianship order does not affect:

(a) the operation of any enactment or rule of law which requires the consent of more than one person with parental responsibility in a matter affecting the child; or

(b) any rights which a parent of the child has in relation to the child's adoption or placement for adoption.

By reason of the fact that a parent of a child who is made the subject of a special guardianship order does not lose parental responsibility, even though his or her rights may be restricted or excluded, the special guardian must obtain the consent of the parent(s) with parental responsibility when important decisions are made in respect of the child. In particular, their consent to the adoption of the child would be required. Further examples of instances when the participation of those who retain parental responsibility is necessary were referred to in the judgment of the former President of the Family Division, Dame Elizabeth Butler-Sloss, in *Re J (Specific Issue Order: Child's Religious Upbringing and Circumcision)* [2000] 1 FLR 571. In this case, the father had applied for a specific issue order that his son, then aged five, should be circumcised. The mother of the child, with whom the child lived, and who was a non-practising Christian, opposed the application. The father's application was dismissed at first instance. On appeal, in her judgment, Dame Elizabeth Butler-Sloss said that:

"there were a small group of decisions made on behalf of a child which, in the absence of agreement of those with parental responsibility, ought not to be carried out or arranged by a one-parent carer although she has parental responsibility under s 2(7) of the Children Act 1989. Such a decision ought not to be made without the specific approval of the court."

She went on to refer to sterilisation, changing a child's surname and circumcision as coming within that group of decisions, and specifically stated that "this requirement for a determination by the court should also apply to a local authority with parental responsibility under a care order".

Furthermore, the new section 14C(3) of the Children Act 1989 specifically provides that while a special guardianship order is in force, no person may cause the child to known by a new surname or remove him from the United Kingdom without the written permission of every person who has parental responsibility for the child, or the permission of the court. This is subject to the right of the special guardian to remove the child from the United Kingdom for a period of less than three months (section 14C(4)).

If the child dies during the currency of the special guardianship order, the special guardian is under a duty to take reasonable steps to notify that fact to each parent of the child who has parental responsibility, and each guardian of the child (section 14C(5)).

A special guardianship order discharges any existing care order or related contact order (section 91(5A), Children Act 1989, inserted by schedule 3, paragraph 68, Adoption and Children Act 2002).

Where a special guardianship order is in force with respect to a child, an application for a residence order may only be made with respect to him, if apart from section 10(7A) of the 1989 Act the leave of the court is not required, with such leave (Children Act 1989, section 10(7A), inserted by schedule 3, paragraph 56 Adoption and Children Act 2002).

11. Variation and Discharge

The Children Act 1989, section 14D(2), as inserted by section 115 of the Adoption and Children Act 2002, provides that a special guardianship order may be varied or discharged by the court of its own motion during any family proceedings in which the welfare of the child arises.

In addition, an application for the variation or discharge of the order may be made by:

(a) the special guardian (or any of them if there are more than one);
(b) any parent or guardian of the child concerned;
(c) any person in whose favour a residence order is in force with respect to the child;
(d) any person who has, or immediately before the making of the special guardianship order had, parental responsibility for the child;
(e) the child himself; or
(f) a local authority designated in a care order with respect to the child (section 14D(1)).

Section 14D(3), however, requires that the following persons must obtain the permission of the court before making the application:

(a) the child;
(b) any parent or guardian of the child;
(c) any step-parent of the child who has acquired, and has not lost, parental responsibility for the child;
(d) any person who, immediately before the making of the special guardianship order, had but no longer has parental responsibility for the child.

The court will not grant permission unless it is satisfied that there has been a significant change in circumstances since the making of the special guardianship order (section 14D(5)). Where the application for permission is made by the child, the court will grant permission only if it is satisfied that he has sufficient understanding to make the proposed application (section 14D(4)).

Where leave is granted, the court is obliged to draw up a timetable with a view to determining the application without delay, and to give such directions as it considers appropriate for the purpose of ensuring so far as is practicable that the timetable is adhered to (section 14E(1)).

It may be appropriate to vary or discharge a special guardianship order where, for example, a child was placed with a relative because the mother was unable to care for the child, but there is then a change of circumstances, as where the mother was a drug addict but has been rehabilitated, and now leads a stable life and can provide good care for the child.

12. Procedure

Application for permission

A request for permission to make an application should be made in accordance with rule 4.3 of the Family Proceedings Rules 1991 (SI 1991 No. 1247), where the application is made in the High Court or county court; and in accordance with rule 3 of the Family Proceedings Courts (Children Act 1989) Rules 1991 (SI 1991 No 1395) if made in the family proceedings court.

In the High Court and the county court, the applicant should file:
(a) the written request for permission, in Form C2. The reasons for the application should be clearly set out; and
(b) a draft of the proposed application, for the making of which leave is sought, together with copies to be served on each respondent.

The applicant must also provide:
(a) the full names and date of birth of the child concerned;
(b) detailed information identifying himself and his relationship with the child;
(c) a brief outline of the reasons for making the application;
(d) the applicant's care plan for the child;
(e) in the case of an application by a child, details of the child's understanding.

The court will either consider the application for permission without a hearing, or direct that the application be listed for an oral hearing, on notice to such other person(s) as the court requires. The court should not refuse the application without an oral hearing.

At a hearing, the issue could be decided on submissions without calling any oral evidence. There may, however, be cases where the court needs to have a fuller inquiry, particularly where the issue relates to the level of understanding of the child, and oral evidence may have to be called. It does not appear that an application for a special guardianship order comes within section 41(6) of the Children Act 1989 (representation of child and of his interests in certain proceedings), and therefore the application for permission does not fall within the meaning of "specified proceedings". It is therefore unlikely that a guardian for the child will be appointed, but the court will invariably appoint a CAFCASS officer to report. Nor is it clear whether public funding will be available in such cases. But where the application is made within care proceedings, there should be no difficulty, as a guardian for the child will have been appointed and public funding will be available to the child and the parents.

Application for the order

Since the special guardianship order has been introduced by way of an amendment to the Children Act 1989, an application for a special guardianship order is an application under the Children Act 1989. The procedure to be followed in making the application is that set out in rule 4.4. of the Family Proceedings Rules 1991, save for paragraph (1)(a) of that rule (rule 4.3.3), when the application is made in the High Court or the county court. For applications made in the family proceedings court, the Family Proceedings Courts (Children Act 1989) Rules 1991, rule 3, sets out the procedure. Form C13A (Supplement for an application for a special guardianship order) is to be used.

13. Special Guardianship Support Services

Section 14F(1) of the Children Act 1989, inserted by section 115 of the Adoption and Children Act 2002, places on every local authority a duty to make arrangements in their areas to provide special guardianship support services, comprising counselling, advice and information, and such other services as are prescribed in relation to special guardianship. The Special Guardianship Regulations 2005 (SI 2005 No. 1109), regulation 3(1), identifies the prescribed services as follows:

    (a) financial support (see below);

    (b) services to enable groups of relevant children, special guardians, prospective special guardians and parents of relevant children to discuss matters relating to special guardianship;

    (c) assistance, including mediation services, in relation to arrangements for contact between a relevant child and his parent or a relative of his, or any other person with whom such a child has a relationship which appears to the local authority to be beneficial to the welfare of the child having regard to the factors specified in section 1(3) of the Children Act 1989;

    (d) services in relation to the therapeutic needs of a relevant child;

    (e) assistance for the purpose of ensuring the continuance of the relationship between a relevant child and a special guardian or prospective special guardian, including:

(i) training for that person to meet any special needs of the child;

(ii) respite care, but where the respite care consists of the provision of accommodation, the accommodation must be provided by or on behalf of a local authority under section 23 of the Children Act (accommodation of looked after children) or by a voluntary organisation under section 59 of the 1989 Act;

(iii) mediation in relation to matters relating to special guardianship orders.

The provision of any of the above services may include giving assistance in cash (regulation 3(2)).

The Special Guardianship (Wales) Regulations 2005 (SI 2005 No. 1513, W. 117) vary slightly. Regulation 3 prescribes the following services in relation to special guardianship:

(a) financial support;

(b) services to enable groups of relevant children, special guardians, prospective guardians and parents of relevant children (or groups consisting of any combination of those individuals) to discuss matters relating to special guardianship;

(c) assistance for relevant children, their parents and related persons in relation to arrangements made for contact between such children and their parents, their former guardians or special guardians or related persons;

(d) services provided in relation to the therapeutic needs of a relevant child;

(e) assistance for the purpose of ensuring the continuance of the relationship between a relevant child and a special guardian or prospective special guardian, including training for that person to meet any special needs of the child and respite care;

(f) where the relationship between a child and his or her special guardian is in danger of breaking down, assistance whose aim is to prevent that occurring, including mediation and organising and holding meetings between such persons as appear to the authority to be appropriate in order to address the difficulties.

"Relevant child"

For the purposes of these regulations a "relevant child" means:

(a) a child subject to a special guardianship order i.e., a child in respect of whom a special guardianship order is in force;

(b) a child in respect of whom a special guardianship order is sought, i.e., a person has given notice to a local authority under section 14A(7) of the Children Act 1989 of his intention to make an application for a special guardianship order in accordance with section 14A(3) of the 1989 Act; or

(c) a child in respect of whom the court has required a report, i.e., a court is considering whether a special guardianship order should be made and has asked a local authority to conduct an investigation and prepare a report pursuant to section 14A(9) of the 1989 Act

(regulation 2(1) of the Special Guardianship Regulations and regulation 1(3) of the Special Guardianship (Wales) Regulations).

In any case where a person who is eighteen years of age or over is in full-time education or training and, immediately before he reached the age of eighteen, financial support was payable in relation to him under the Special Guardianship Regulations then, for the purposes of the continued provision of financial support and any review of financial support, that person is regarded as if he were a child (Special Guardianship Regulations, regulation 2(1)). On financial support, see below.

Prospective special guardian
A "prospective special guardian" is a person who has given notice to a local authority under section 14A(7) of the 1989 Act of his intention to make an application for a special guardianship order in accordance with section 14A(3) of the 1989 Act, or in respect of whom a court has requested that a local authority conduct an investigation and prepare a report pursuant to section 14A(9) of the 1989 Act (Special Guardianship Regulations, regulation 2(1); Special Guardianship (Wales) Regulations, regulation 1(3)).

Securing provision of services
Persons who may provide special guardianship services include a registered adoption society; a registered adoption support agency; a registered fostering agency; a local health board or primary care trust; and a local education authority (Special Guardianship Regulations, regulation 4(1); and see regulation 3(3) of the Special Guardianship (Wales) Regulations which is in slightly different terms).

Services for persons outside the area
A local authority is under a duty to provide special guardianship support services to the following persons who are outside its area:

(a) a relevant child who is looked after by the local authority or was looked after by the local authority immediately before the making of a special guardianship order;

(b) a special guardian or prospective guardian of such a child;

(c) a child of a special guardian or prospective guardian of a relevant child

(Special Guardianship Regulations, regulation 5(1)).

A local authority may however, in its discretion, provide special guardianship support services to persons outside its area where it considers it appropriate to do so (Special Guardianship Regulations, regulation 5(3); Special Guardianship (Wales) Regulations, regulation 3(2)).

The requirement to provide services to persons outside the local authority's area ceases to apply at the end of the period of three years from the date when the special guardianship order is made, except where the local authority is providing financial support under the regulations and the decision to provide that support was made before the making of the order (Special Guardianship Regulations, regulation 5(2)).

Financial support

Financial support may be paid to a special guardian or prospective special guardian to facilitate arrangements for a person to become a special guardian of a child where the local authority considers such arrangements to be beneficial to the child's welfare; or to support the continuation of such arrangements after a special guardianship order is made. Financial support may, however, be paid only where the local authority considers:

    (a) that it is necessary to ensure that the special guardian or prospective special guardian can look after the child;

    (b) that the child needs special care which requires a greater expenditure of resources than would otherwise be the case because of his illness, disability, emotional or behavioural difficulties or the consequences of his past abuse or neglect;

    (c) that it is appropriate to contribute to any legal costs, including court fees, of a special guardian or prospective special guardian, as the case may be, associated with the making of a special guardianship order or any application to vary or discharge such an order; an application for an order under section 8 of the Children Act 1989; or an order for financial provision to be made to or for the benefit of the child; or

    (d) that it is appropriate to contribute to the expenditure necessary for the purposes of accommodating and maintaining the child, including the provision of furniture and domestic equipment, alterations to and adaptations of the home, provision of means of transport and provision of clothing, toys and other items necessary for the purpose of looking after the child

(Special Guardianship Regulations, regulation 6; see also Special Guardianship (Wales) Regulations, regulation 4, which is in slightly different terms).

Financial support may include an element of remuneration, but only where the decision to include it is taken before the special guardianship order is made and the local authority considers such remuneration to be necessary to facilitate arrangements for a person to become a special guardian; this applies only to cases where the special guardian or prospective special guardian has been a local authority foster parent in respect of the child, and an element of remuneration was included in the payments made by the local authority to that person in relation to the fostering. Any such remuneration ceases to be payable after two years from the making of the special guardianship order, unless the local authority considers its continuation to be necessary, having regard to the exceptional needs of the child or any other exceptional circumstances. (Special Guardianship Regulations, regulation 7.)

Financial support may be paid periodically if it is provided to meet a need which is likely to give rise to recurring expenditure; or by a single payment; or, if the local authority and the special guardian or prospective guardian agree, by instalments (Special Guardianship Regulations, regulation 8).

Financial support ceases to be payable to the special guardian or prospective special guardian if the child:

(a) ceases to have a home with him;

(b) ceases full-time education or training and commences employment;

(c) qualifies for income support or job seeker's allowance in his own right; or

(d) attains the age of eighteen years, unless he continues in full-time education or training, when it may continue until the end of the course or training he is then undertaking

(Special Guardianship Regulations, regulation 9).

Where payment is to be made periodically it is not to be paid until the special guardian or prospective guardian agrees that he will:

(a) inform the local authority immediately if the guardian changes his/her address, the child dies, or there is a change in the financial circumstances of the guardian or the needs or resources of the child, or if any of the events which would lead to the cessation of the support occurs (see above);

(b) complete and supply the local authority with an annual statement of his financial circumstances, the financial needs and resources of the child, and his address and whether the child still has a home with him

(Special Guardianship Regulations, regulation 10(1); see also the Special Guardianship (Wales) Regulations, regulation 4(2), which is in slightly different terms).

The local authority has a discretion to impose any other condition it considers appropriate, including the timescale within which, and purposes for which, any payment of financial support should be utilised (Special Guardianship Regulations, regulation 10(2)).

The local authority may suspend or terminate the payment of financial support, and seek to recover all or part of the financial support paid, if any of the above conditions is not complied with, but where the non-compliance is the failure to provide an annual statement, the local authority is under a duty to send to the guardian a written reminder of the need to provide the annual statement and to give the person twenty-eight days within which to comply (Special Guardianship Regulations, regulation 10(3) and (4)).

Notice of any change in the circumstances of the guardian or the child may initially be given orally, but must be confirmed in writing within seven days (Special Guardianship Regulations, regulation 10(1); Special Guardianship (Wales) Regulations, regulation 4(2)).

Assessment

Section 14F(3) of the Children Act 1989 provides that at the request of certain persons, the local authority may carry out an assessment of that person's needs for special guardianship support services, and must to do so if the person, and/or his case, falls within the regulations. The persons who may request assessment are:

(a) a child with respect to whom a special guardianship order is in force;
(b) the special guardian;
(c) a parent;
(d) any other person who is authorised by regulations to make the request.

The local authority has a discretion whether to carry out an assessment at the request of any other person (Children Act 1989, section 14F(4)).

The Special Guardianship Regulations 2005 specify the following persons as persons at whose request the local authority has a duty to carry out an assessment:

(a) a relevant child who is looked after by the local authority or was looked after by the local authority immediately before the making of a special guardianship order;
(b) a special guardian or prospective special guardian of such a child;
(c) a parent of such a child;
(d) a person mentioned in section 14F(3)(a) to (c) of the 1989 Act;
(e) a child of a special guardian;
(f) any person whom the local authority considers to have a significant and ongoing relationship with a relevant child.

In addition to specifying the persons mentioned in section 14F(3)(a) to (c) of the 1989 Act, a prospective special guardian and a child of a special guardian, as eligible to request assessment, the Special Guardianship (Wales) Regulations 2005, regulation 5(1), also specify the following persons as entitled to make a request:

(a) a child in respect of whom a special guardianship order is sought or a child in respect of whom the court has required a report;
(b) a child (other than one referred to above) who is named in a report produced under section 14A(8) of the 1989 Act;
(c) a related person, provided that before the request for an assessment was made arrangements were in place for contact between the person and the relevant child.

The Welsh Regulations also provide that a local authority is not obliged to carry out an assessment unless:

(a) the person who has requested the assessment falls within the categories set out above and either lives in the area of the local authority or intends to live in that area, or is a child looked after by that authority, or is a person in respect of whom the court asked the local authority to prepare a report, or a child to whom such a report relates or would relate; or

(b) in the case of a related person, the relevant child lives or intends to live in the area of the local authority to whom the request is made or is looked after by that authority

(Special Guardianship (Wales) Regulations, regulation 5(2)).

An assessment of a person's needs for special guardianship support services may be carried out by reference only to a particular special guardianship support service where the person whose needs are being assessed has requested a particular special guardianship support service, or it appears to the local authority that the person's needs for special guardianship support services may be adequately assessed by reference only to a particular special guardianship support service (Special Guardianship Regulations, regulation 11(4); Special Guardianship (Wales) Regulations, regulation 5(3)).

If the local authority decides not to carry out an assessment, it must give the person requesting an assessment notice of the proposed decision and the reasons for it. The local authority must also give the person reasonable opportunity to make representations in relation to that decision. (Special Guardianship Regulations, regulation 11(3)).

The assessment procedure: In carrying out an assessment of a person's needs for special guardianship support services, the local authority is under a duty to have regard to the following factors:

(a) the development needs of the child;

(b) the parenting capacity of the special guardian or prospective special guardian;

(c) the family and environmental factors that have shaped the life of the child;

(d) what the life of the child might be like with the particular special guardian or prospective special guardian;

(e) any previous assessments undertaken in relation to the child or the special guardian or prospective special guardian;

(f) the needs of the guardian or of the guardian's family;

(g) where it appears that there is a pre-existing relationship between the guardian and the parent of the child, the likely impact of the special guardianship order on the relationships between that person, that child and that parent

(Special Guardianship Regulations, regulation 12(1).

The corresponding Welsh Regulations provide that the local authority must have regard to:

(i)   the needs of the person being assessed and how these might be met;

(ii) the needs of the relevant child and the family members of any special guardian or prospective special guardian, in so far as they have not been addressed under head (i) above, and how these might be met;

(iii) the circumstances that led up to the making of a special guardianship order in respect of a child subject to a special guardianship order;

(iv) any special needs of a child subject to a special guardianship order arising from the fact that the child has been looked after by a local authority or has been habitually resident outside the British Islands; or that the special guardian is a relative of the child; and

(v)   where the assessment relates to financial support, the relevant requirements in the regulations

(Special Guardianship (Wales) Regulations, regulation 6(1)).

The local authority must, if it considers it appropriate to do so, interview the person whose needs for special guardianship support services are being assessed. Where the needs of a child are being assessed, the local authority must, if it considers it appropriate to do so, interview any special guardian or prospective special guardian of the child, or any adult the local authority considers it appropriate to interview. Where it appears to the local authority that the person may have a need for services from a local health board, primary care trust or local education authority, it must, as part of the assessment, consult that board, trust or authority. (Special Guardianship Regulations, regulation 12(2) and (3); and see Special Guardianship (Wales) Regulations, regulation 6(1)(b) and (c)).

The Welsh regulations contain a provision that the local authority must ensure that the assessment is carried out by, or under the supervision of, an individual who has suitable qualifications, experience and skills for that purpose (Special Guardianship (Wales) Regulations, regulation 6(2)(a)). The local authority must prepare a written report of the assessment (Special Guardianship Regulations, regulation 12(4); Special Guardianship (Wales) Regulations, regulation 6(2)(b)).

Assessment of need for financial support: In determining the amount of any financial support, the local authority must take account of any other grant, benefit, allowance or resource which is available to the person in respect of his needs as a result of becoming a special guardian of the child (Special Guardianship Regulations 2005, regulation 13(2); Special Guardianship (Wales) Regulations, regulation 7(2), which is in slightly different terms). It must also take into consideration:

(a) the financial resources available to the special guardian or prospective special guardian if the child lived with him;

(b) the amount required by the person in respect of his reasonable outgoings and commitments (excluding outgoings in respect of the child);

    (c) the financial needs and resources of the relevant child.

(Special Guardianship Regulations, regulation 13(3)).

The local authority is required to disregard the above considerations where it is considering providing financial support in respect of legal costs, including court fees, in a case where a special guardianship order is applied for in respect of a child who is looked after by the local authority, and the authority supports the making of the order, or an application is made to vary or discharge a special guardianship order in respect of such a child (Special Guardianship Regulations, regulation 13(4)).

The local authority is given a discretion to disregard any of the matters set out under (a) to (c) above where it is considering providing financial support in respect of the initial cost of accommodating a child who has been looked after by the local authority; recurring costs in respect of travel for the purpose of visits between the child and a related person; or any special care required in relation to a child who has been looked after by the local authority. It also has a discretion to disregard those matters where they are considering including an element of remuneration under regulation 7 (see page 48).

Whereas the Welsh Regulations refer to some of the matters set out above, regulation 7(1) requires the local authority, in determining the amount of any financial support, to take account of the following additional factors:

    (d) necessary expenditure on legal costs (to include court fees) in respect of proceedings relating to a special guardianship order or an application for financial provision to be made in relation to, or for the benefit of, the relevant child;

    (e) necessary expenditure in order to facilitate the relevant child having his or her home with a special guardian or prospective special guardian, including any initial expenditure necessary for the purposes of accommodating the child, to include any necessary provision of furniture and domestic equipment, alteration to and adaptations of the home, provision of means of transport and of clothing, toys and other items necessary for the purposes of looking after the child;

    (f) necessary expenditure of the person associated with any special educational needs or special behavioural difficulties of the relevant child including:

        (i) the cost of equipment required for the purposed of meeting any special educational needs of the child,

        (ii) the costs of rectifying any damage in the home in which the child lives, where such costs arise out of the special behavioural difficulties of the child,

        (iii) the costs of placing the child in a boarding school, where that placement is necessary to meet the special educational needs of the child; and

(g) expenditure on travel for the purposes of visits between a relevant child and his or her parent or related persons.

Notification of assessment: After carrying out the assessment and before making any decision, the local authority must give the person requesting the assessment notice of the authority's provisional view. The notice must contain the following information:

(a) a statement of the person's needs for special guardianship support services;

(b) where the assessment relates to his need for financial support, the basis upon which financial support is determined;

(c) whether the local authority proposes to provide him with special guardianship support services;

(d) the services (if any) that are proposed to be provided to him;

(e) if financial support is to be paid to him, the proposed amount that would be payable; and

(f) any proposed conditions under regulation 10(2)

(Special Guardianship Regulations, regulation 15(3) and see Special Guardianship (Wales) Regulations, regulation 8(1) and (2))).

Where the local authority proposes to provide special guardianship support services and is required to prepare a plan (see below), the notice must be accompanied by a draft of that plan (Special Guardianship Regulations, regulation 15(4)).

The local authority must allow the person an opportunity and time to make representations (Special Guardianship Regulations, regulation 15(1); Special Guardianship (Wales) Regulations, regulation 8(3)). The local authority should not make any decision until the person has either made representations to the local authority, or notified it that he is satisfied with the proposed decision and, where applicable, the draft plan; or the period of time for representation has expired (Special Guardianship Regulations, regulation 15(5); Special Guardianship (Wales) Regulations, regulation 8(4)).

Notice of decision: Where, as a result of the assessment and the representations made, the local authority decides that a person has needs for special guardianship support services, it must decide whether to provide such services to that person. After making the decision, the local authority must give notice to the person of that decision and the reasons for it. Where the authority is required to prepare a plan (see below) details of the plan must also be provided. If the decision is to provide financial support the notice must include:

(a) the method of determination of the amount of financial support;

(b) where financial support is to be paid in instalments or periodically, the amount of financial support, the frequency with which payments will be made, the period for which financial support is to be paid, and when payment will commence;

(c) where financial support is to be paid as a single payment, when the payment will be made;

(d) where financial support is to be paid subject to any conditions, those conditions, the date by which they are to be met, and the consequences of failing to meet them;

(e) the arrangements and procedure for review, variation and termination of financial support;

(f) the responsibilities of the local authority under the review procedure and the responsibilities of the special guardian or prospective special guardian pursuant to any agreement relating to any conditions imposed (see page 49)

(Special Guardianship Regulations, regulation 16; and see Special Guardianship (Wales) Regulations, regulation 9(5), which is in slightly different terms.)

Notices: Any notice required to be given must be given in writing. Where the notice is to be given to a child and it appears that the child is not of sufficient age and understanding for it to be appropriate to give him notice, or in all the circumstances it is not appropriate to give him such notice, the notice must be given to his special guardian or prospective special guardian (where applicable), or otherwise to the adult the local authority considers appropriate (Special Guardianship Regulations, regulation 20 and Special Guardianship (Wales) Regulations, regulation 10).

Plan

Under section 14F(6) of the Children Act 1989, if the local authority decides to provide special guardianship support services to a person and the circumstances fall within those provided for in the regulations, the local authority is under a duty to prepare a plan and to keep the plan under review. Under the Special Guardianship Regulations, regulation 14, the local authority is required to prepare a plan if it proposes to provide special guardianship support services to a person on more than one occasion, and the services are not limited to the provision of advice or information.

Where it appears that the person may have a need for services from a local health board, primary care trust or a local education authority, the local authority must consult that board, trust or authority before preparing the plan. Where the person to whom the plan relates lives in the area of another local authority, it must consult that local authority. A copy of the plan must also be provided to those bodies (regulation 14(3)).

See also the (Special Guardianship (Wales) Regulations, regulation 11, which is in broadly similar terms.

Review

Where special guardianship support services are provided, the local authority must review the provision of such services:

    (a) if any change in the person's circumstances, including any change of address, comes to its notice which may affect the provision of special guardianship support service;

    (b) at such stage in the implementation of the plan as it considers appropriate;

    (c) in any event annually (under the Welsh regulations, from time to time)

(Special Guardianship Regulations, regulation 17(2)).

On reviewing the plan, the local authority may decide to vary or terminate the provision of special guardianship support services, or may decide to revise the plan. If it is proposed to vary, terminate or revise the plan, the local authority must, before making the decision, give notice to the person affected by the decision, with reasons. Sufficient opportunity and time must be allowed for the person to make representations (regulation 17(4)). The notice must also contain the information set out in regulation 15(3) (see page 54). Where it is proposed to revise the plan, a draft of the revised plan should also be included with the notice (regulation 17(5)). See also the Special Guardianship (Wales) Regulations, regulation 12, which is in broadly similar terms.

    A decision should be made only after representations have been received, or the time for making representations has elapsed. When a decision is reached, having regard to the review and the representations received, notice of the decision must be given to the person affected by it, together with reasons for the decision and, if applicable, the revised plan (Special Guardianship Regulations, regulation 17(7)).

Review of financial support

The local authority is under a duty to review the financial support:

    (a) annually on receipt of the annual statement (see page 49);

    (b) if any change of circumstances or any breach of a condition comes to its notice; and

    (c) at any stage in the implementation of the plan that it considers appropriate

(Special Guardianship Regulations, regulation 18).

Before making the decision to reduce, terminate or suspend payment of financial support, the local authority has a duty to give the person notice of the proposed decision and an opportunity and the time to make representations. The notice must contain all the relevant information (see page 54). A decision should be taken only after considering any representations received. Once a decision is made, notice of it, with reasons, and if applicable the revised plan, should be given to the person affected by the decision (Special Guardianship Regulations, regulation 18(5) to (8)).

14. Summary

Before making an application for a special guardianship order the following matters should be checked:

1. that the applicant is eligible to make the application, and that the conditions relating to such an applicant have been satisfied;
2. whether the leave of the court is required to make the application;
3. that notice has been given to the relevant local authority of the applicant's intention to make the application;
4. whether the local authority has provided a report, or whether it will be necessary to obtain an order from the court directing the local authority to prepare a report;
5. whether the applicant will be able to satisfy the criteria which the court is required to take into consideration;
6. whether any contact arrangements are in place or proposed;
7. whether the applicant needs special guardianship support services, and if so, whether a request for such services to be provided has been made.

Chapter 5

Placement Orders

1. Introduction

In this chapter, the provisions of the Adoption and Children Act 2002 on placement orders are discussed. These provisions are supplemented by those in the Adoption Agencies Regulations 2005 (SI 2005 No. 389) and the Adoption Agencies (Wales) Regulations 2005 (SI 2005 No. 1313, W. 95). The regulations set out the procedures to be followed for considering and deciding whether a child should be placed for adoption; for assessing prospective adopters; for matching a child with prospective adopters and placing a child with them; the duties of the local authority after placement and the requirements concerning reviews of placements. These matters are considered in Chapter 16. The obligation on adoption agencies to provide appropriate support services is also relevant to the placing of a child for adoption, and is examined in Chapter 17. These chapters should therefore be read together.

A placement order is an order made by a court authorising a local authority to place a child for adoption with any prospective adopters chosen by the authority (Adoption and Children Act 2002, section 21(1)). Placement orders replace freeing orders and provide a new process for placing children for adoption through an adoption agency.

"Placing a child for adoption" refers to the situation where an adoption agency places a child for adoption with prospective adopters, and includes where the agency has placed a child with persons (whether under the 2002 Act or not), leaving the child with them as prospective adopters (section 18(5)).

Under the Adoption Act 1976, the local authority was not obliged to free a child for adoption before placing the child for adoption. Even in situations where the care plan was for adoption, the parents' only opportunity to oppose the adoption of the child was to challenge the care plan within the care proceedings. The first opportunity to challenge the adoption often did not arise until the application to adopt was made.

The objective of the new process is to ensure that the issues leading up to an adoption order are dealt with at an early stage, providing greater certainty, a smoother route to placement with the prospective adopters, and a non-adversarial adoption hearing. The new process should mean that the parent(s) can challenge the proposals at an early stage, instead of at the final hearing of the adoption application. It is also intended to alleviate the anxiety caused to the prospective adopters of a contested hearing.

The new process provides two ways of achieving this. Firstly, the parent(s) will be informed of the adoption plans and may consent to the placement. If the parents' consent is not forthcoming, the local authority can apply for a placement order, the effect of which is to authorise the local authority to place a child for adoption with adopters whom they select.

2. Difference between Placement Orders and Freeing Orders

Under the former law, on the making of a freeing order, the parent(s) lost parental responsibility for the child unless, within twelve months after the making of the freeing order, the child had not been placed for adoption. In such a case the parent(s) could apply for the freeing order to be revoked (Adoption Act 1976, section 20(1)). If the application was granted, the effect was to transfer parental responsibility back to the parent(s). When a placement order is made, by contrast, the parent(s) retain parental responsibility, but must share it with the prospective adopters and the adoption agency.

Thus, once a freeing order was made, the parents' rights were not entirely extinguished, but reserved in limbo to be reactivated in very limited circumstances. They could of course appeal against the making of the freeing order if they had grounds for so doing.

The decision whether to apply for a freeing order where the local authority's care plan was for adoption was discretionary. The practice and policy varied from one local authority to another. Some were more proactive and favoured seeking a freeing order at the same time as the final hearing of the application for the care order, or shortly thereafter. Others were reluctant to consider parallel or twin-track planning during the care proceedings. It was also not unusual, following the making of a care order, for the local authority to place the child with prospective adopters and then encourage them to apply for an adoption order. There was thus no consistency and it led to delay. In addition, where the delay was substantial, parents who had initially conceded that adoption was in the best interests of the child were led to reconsider. They might then withdraw consent; contest the adoption application; seek to reopen the case by, for example, applying for the discharge of the care order and applying for a residence order on the basis of change of circumstances. There were also instances where delay in placing the child resulted in the continuation of contact between the parents and the child, and in such cases that contact could become a live issue on the application for adoption.

Furthermore, in *PC & S v UK* [2002] 2 FLR 631, the European Court of Human Rights criticised the process of issuing proceedings for a care order and a freeing order in respect of a baby, and found that the draconian and irreversible effect of the freeing order breached articles 6 and 8 of the European Convention on Human Rights.

Under the Adoption and Children Act 2002, where the parents' consent to the child's being placed for adoption is not forthcoming, the local authority is obliged to apply for a placement order under section 22 of the Act, so that the issues of consent, dispensation with consent and the appropriateness of the placement can be considered at an early stage.

Where the parents have consented to the placement, or a placement order is made, the parents have a limited right to withdraw consent or apply for the revocation of the placement order.

On the making of a freeing order, save for annual "letter box" contact, contact between the parents and the child came to an end. Although on the making of a placement order, any order under section 8 of the Children Act 1989 (see page 24) also comes to an end, under the provisions of section 26 of the Adoption and Children Act 2002, the court has the power to make a contact order.

3.   Transitional Provisions

For the provisions on applications for freeing orders pending on the coming into force of the Adoption and Children Act 2002, and on children in respect of whom freeing orders have been made but who have not been placed for adoption, see Chapter 24, pages 364 to 367.

4.   How and When a Child may be Placed for Adoption

There are two ways in which a child may be placed for adoption:

   (a) by consent, under section 19 of the 2002 Act; or
   (b) by virtue of a placement order under section 22 of the Act.

Section 18(1) of the Adoption and Children Act 2002 provides that an adoption agency may place a child for adoption with prospective adopters, or where it has placed a child with any persons, leave the child with them as prospective adopters, only as provided in section 19 of the Act, or by a placement order. The only exception is in cases where the child is less than six weeks old.

Section 19 provides that where an adoption agency is satisfied that each parent or guardian of the child has consented to the child's being placed for adoption with the prospective adopters identified in the consent, or with any prospective adopters who may be chosen by the agency, and has not withdrawn the consent, the adoption agency is authorised to place the child for adoption. When consent is not forthcoming or has been withdrawn, the local authority should secure a placement order from the court, authorising it to place the child with adopters whom they select.

Pursuant to section 18(3) of the Act, a child who is placed with the voluntary agreement of the parents or guardian of the child is "looked after" by the local authority.

Child under six weeks old

An adoption agency may place a child who is under six weeks old for adoption, with the voluntary agreement of the parents. Such a placement is not a placement under section 19 or 22 of the Act and the requirements of those sections do not therefore apply. It follows that the parents continue to retain parental responsibility for the child. The adoption agency does not have the authority to restrict the parents' rights of parental responsibility, or contact.

Before placement of such a child, however, the process under Part 5 of the Adoption Agencies Regulations and the Adoption Agencies (Wales) Regulations (duties of adoption agency in respect of proposed placement of child with prospective adopter; see Chapter 16) must be complied with. Regulation 35(3) and (4) (regulation 36(7) in the Welsh regulations) in Part 6 (placement and reviews) goes on specifically to deal with the placement of a child less than six weeks old.

Once the child reaches the age of six weeks, the provisions of section 19 apply and the adoption agency must either obtain the consent of the parents to continue the placement, or the local authority must secure a placement order.

5. Consent

Meaning of consent

Section 52(5) of the Adoption and Children Act 2002 provides that "consent" means "consent given unconditionally and with full understanding of what is involved, but a person may consent to adoption without knowing the identity of the person in whose favour the order will be made".

Consent may be:

(a) specific to identified adopters or to the adoption agency; or

(b) general, that is to adoption by any prospective adopters who may be chosen by the adoption agency; or

(c) combined, that is, consent to placement with particular prospective adopters, or with any other prospective adopters who may be chosen by the adoption agency if the child is removed from, or returned by, the identified prospective adopters (section 19(2)).

Advance consent

In addition, a parent or guardian of the child may give "advance consent" to the child's being adopted in the future. Under the provisions of section 20(1) and (2) of the Adoption and Children Act 2002 the parents' consent to a future adoption order being obtained may be given:

    (a) at the same time as consent for placement for adoption;

    (b) at any subsequent time;

    (c) in relation to prospective adopters who are identified;

    (d) to adoption by any prospective adopters who may be chosen by the adoption agency or the local authority;

    (e) where one parent has given consent for placement for adoption, and at a later date the other parent acquires parental responsibility, the other parent is treated as having given consent at the same time and on the same terms as that given by the first parent (section 52(9) and (10).

Meaning of "parent"

Section 52(6) of the Act provides that "parent" here means a parent with parental responsibility. Thus a step-parent and an unmarried father without parental responsibility are not included. (See also pages 67 to 68.)

Counselling

The adoption agency is required, under regulation 14 of both the Adoption Agencies Regulations and the Adoption Agencies (Wales) Regulations, to provide a counselling service for the parent(s) or guardian of the child, and to explain the procedure for placement and the legal implications of giving consent and "advance consent", and of the placement and adoption orders. In addition, the parent(s) or guardian must be provided with written information. The agency also has a duty to ascertain the parent(s)' or guardian's wishes and feelings about the child and in relation to contact, and their religious and cultural views. These matters are dealt with in detail in Chapter 16.

Procedure

Section 52(7) of the Act requires that the written agreement of the parent(s) or guardian, to placing the child for adoption, must be given on the prescribed form. The form must be witnessed. Regulation 20 of the Adoption Agencies Regulations 2005 (SI 2005 No. 389) and the Adoption Agencies (Wales) Regulations 2005 (SI 2005 No. 1313) provide for a CAFCASS officer (or, in Wales, a Welsh family proceedings officer) to witness documents which signify consent to a placement or adoption order. Where consent for the placement of the child for adoption is given by the parent(s) or guardian in pending proceedings relating to the child, the officer appointed, or the child's guardian if there are care proceedings pending, is the appropriate person to witness the consent of the parents.

On the procedure for documenting, witnessing and filing consent, see Chapter 16, page 209 and Chapter 25, page 413 and the relevant practice direction.

Child less than six weeks old

Consent to the making of an adoption order, given by the mother, is ineffective if given less than six weeks after the child's birth (Adoption and Children Act 2002, section 52(3)).

Effect of consent

Where the parent or guardian of the child has consented to the placement of the child for adoption and the consent has not been withdrawn, or a placement order has been made, the parent or guardian may nevertheless apply to oppose the application for the making of an adoption order, but only if the court gives permission to do so. Permission will not be given unless the court is satisfied that there has been a change of circumstances since the consent was given or, as the case may be, the placement order was made. See section 47(5) and (7) of the 2002 Act.

Withdrawal of consent

A parent or guardian of the child may withdraw consent at any time (section 19(1)). "Advance consent" may also be withdrawn at any time (section 20(3)).

Consent given under section 19 or 20 must be withdrawn on the prescribed form, or by notice to the agency (section 52(8)). The notice may be given by post (section 110)).

Withdrawal of consent to the placement of a child for adoption or of "advance consent" is, however, ineffective if it is given after the application for an adoption order is made (section 52(4)).

Where consent has been given for the placement of a child, and the child has not been placed for adoption but is accommodated by an adoption agency, and the parent or guardian of the child withdraws consent and informs the agency that he or she wishes the child to be returned, the child must be returned to the parent or guardian. The child must be returned within seven days "beginning with the request" (see below), unless an application is, or has been, made for a placement order and the application has not been disposed of (section 31(2)) (see below).

Where the child is placed for adoption by an adoption agency pursuant to section 19 of the Act and the parent or guardian withdraws consent and informs the agency that he or she wishes the child to be returned, the agency must notify the prospective adopters of the withdrawal of consent and request the return of the child. The prospective adopters must return the child to the agency within fourteen days beginning with the day on which notice is given (section 32(1) and (2)). As soon as the child is returned to the adoption agency by the prospective adopters, the agency must return the child to the parent or guardian (section 32(4)). If, before the notice is given, an application for an adoption order, special guardianship order or residence order, or for leave to apply for a special guardianship order or residence order, was made in respect of the child and the application is still pending, the prospective adopters are not required to return the child to the agency unless the court so orders (section 32(5)).

The term "beginning with the request", read literally, means from the date of the request. If the request is sent by second class post, the local authority will barely have time to make an application for a placement order or prepare the child for removal. It could be argued that the provision is not one which sufficiently takes into account the welfare of the child. Where the child has been placed, the obligation on the adoption agency is to return the child to the parent as soon as the child is returned by the prospective adopters to the adoption agency. The prospective adopters are obliged to return the child "within 14 days beginning with the day on which notice is given". Again the issue could arise whether time begins to run from the date the notice is sent, or the date the notice is received. Section 32(2) of the Act imposes a duty on the adoption agency to give notice of the withdrawal to the prospective adopters, but does not specify the form of such notice or the period within which it must be given. It follows that the return of the child cannot take place within fourteen days of the withdrawal of consent by the parent.

Where a child placed for adoption is less that six weeks old or the agency has at no time been authorised to place the child for adoption, and the parent informs the agency that he or she wishes the child returned to him or her, the agency must give notice of the parent's wish to the prospective adopters and they must return the child to the agency within a period of seven days beginning with the day on which notice is given, unless an application is or has been made for a placement order and the application is pending (section 31(3) and (4)).

Again, the meaning of "seven days beginning with the day on which notice is given" may need to be determined. Presumably the notice referred to is the notice given by the local authority to the prospective adopters, but it is not clear whether the seven days run from the date inserted in the notice sent, or the date when the notice is received. Section 110 provides that any notice or information may be sent by post. If time begins to run from the date the notice is sent, and the notice is sent by second class post, it may be two or three days before it is received. In many cases this will not give sufficient time to prepare the child for the move and could be both emotionally and psychologically damaging. In view of the fact that non-compliance with these provisions is made a criminal offence (see Chapter 19, pages 301 to 302), any issues arising under the provisions will have to be considered with sensitivity, applying the welfare principle and the overriding objective.

Dispensing with consent

The consent of the parent or guardian of the child, to the child's being placed for adoption or the making of an adoption order, may be dispensed with if:

(a) the parent or guardian cannot be found;

(b) the parent or guardian is incapable of giving consent (this is to be replaced by "lacks capacity within the meaning of the Mental Capacity Act 2005 to give consent); or

(c) the welfare of the child requires the consent to be dispensed with.

(Section 52(1) of the 2002 Act, and Mental Capacity Act 2005, schedule 6, paragraph 45).

Dispensing with consent is dealt with in detail in Chapter 8.

6. The Application

Conditions which must be satisfied

A placement order cannot be made unless:

(a) the child is the subject of a care order; or

(b) the court is satisfied that the conditions in section 31(2) of the Children Act 1989 are met; or

(c) the child has no parent or guardian (section 21(2) of the 2002 Act); and

(d) each parent or guardian of the child has consented to the child's being placed for adoption with any prospective adopters, or with those chosen by the local authority, and the consent has not been withdrawn; or

(e) the consent of the parent(s) or guardian should be dispensed with (on dispensing with consent, see above and Chapter 8)

(section 21(2) and (3)).

The conditions under section 31(2) of the Children Act 1989 are:

(a) that the child concerned is suffering from, or is likely to suffer, significant harm; and

(b) that the harm, or the likelihood of harm, is attributable to:

(i) the care given to the child, or likely to be given to him if the order were not made and not being what it would be reasonable to expect a parent to give to him; or

(ii) the child is beyond parental control.

"Harm" means ill-treatment or the impairment of health or development including, for example, impairment suffered from seeing or hearing the ill-treatment of another. "Development" means physical, intellectual, emotional, social or behavioural development. "Health" means physical or mental health and "ill-treatment" includes sexual abuse and forms of ill-treatment which are not physical (Children Act 1989, section 31(9)). Where the question of whether harm suffered by a child is significant turns on the child's health or development, his health or development is to be compared with that which could reasonably be expected of a similar child (Children Act 1989, section 31(10)).

The criteria under section 31(2) must be satisfied at the date when proceedings are commenced; or if the child has been accommodated and the arrangements have been remained in place continuously, the date on which those arrangements were first made: *Re M (A Minor) (Care Order: Threshold Criteria)* [1994] 2 AC 424, [1994] 3 WLR 558, [1994] 3 All ER 298, [1994] 2 FLR 577.

7. Parties to the Application

The applicant

Only a local authority may apply for a placement order authorising it to place a child for adoption, with any prospective adopters, who may be chosen by the local authority (section 22 of the 2002 Act and rule 23 of the Family Procedure (Adoption) Rules 2005 (SI 2005 No. 2795)).

Circumstances in which an application is to be made

Section 22 of the Adoption and Children Act 2002 provides four situations in which the appropriate local authority may make an application for a placement order. In three of these situations, the local authority has a mandatory duty to make such an application; in the fourth situation, the local authority has a discretion to apply.

The local authority *must* apply for a placement order if:

(1) (a) the child is placed for adoption by the authority or is being provided with accommodation by it;

(b) no adoption agency is authorised to place the child for adoption;

(c) the child has no parent or guardian or the authority considers that the conditions in section 31(2) of the Children Act 1989 are met; and

(d) the local authority is satisfied that the child ought to be placed for adoption

(section 22(1), 2002 Act);

(2) there is a pending application on which a care order might be made in respect of the child and the local authority is satisfied that the child ought to be placed for adoption; or

(3) the child is the subject of a care order and the appropriate local authority is not authorised to place the child for adoption and the authority is satisfied that the child ought to be placed for adoption (section 22(2), 2002 Act).

The local authority has a discretion to apply for a placement order if the child is subject to a care order and it is the appropriate local authority authorised to place the child for adoption under section 19 of the Act (section 22(3)).

There are two circumstances when the above provisions do not apply, namely:

(a) where any persons have given notice of intention to adopt, unless a period of four months beginning with the giving of notice has expired without their making the application for an adoption order or their application has been withdrawn or refused; or

(b) an application for an adoption order has been made but has not been disposed of

(section 22(5)).

Respondents

The Adoption and Children Act 2002, section 141(3) and (4), requires that every person whose consent to the making of the order is required should be notified of the date and place of the application. The same person(s) must also be notified that, unless he wishes or the court requires, the person need not attend the hearing. If a person whose consent is required cannot be found, any relative, prescribed by rules, who can be found should be notified. Section 144 of the Act defines "relative" in relation to a child as a grandparent, brother, sister, uncle or aunt, whether of the full blood or half blood, or by marriage or civil partnership.

The Family Procedure (Adoption) Rules 2005, rule 23, identifies the following persons as those who should be made respondents to an application for a placement order:

(a) each parent who has parental responsibility for the child or the guardian of the child;

(b) any person in whose favour an order under the Children Act 1989 is in force in relation to the child;

(c) any adoption agency or voluntary organisation which has parental responsibility for, is looking after, or is caring for, the child;

(d) the child; and

(e) the parties or any persons who are or have been parties to proceedings for a care order in respect of the child where those proceedings have led to the application for the placement order.

Step-parent

A step-parent may be a party to an application for a placement order where he or she has acquired parental responsibility by:

(a) obtaining a residence order under section 8, Children Act 1989;

(b) entering into a parental responsibility agreement under the provisions of section 4A, Children Act 1989; or

(c) obtaining a court order granting him/her parental responsibility for the child; or

(d) obtaining a special guardianship order (see Chapter 4).

Unmarried father

The father of a child who is not married to the child's mother does not have parental responsibility for the child, but can acquire parental responsibility if:

(a) he becomes registered as the child's father under the Births and Deaths Registration Act 1953, or the equivalent legislation applicable to Scotland and Northern Ireland; or

(b) he and the mother enter into a parental responsibility agreement providing for him to have parental responsibility; or

(c) he successfully applies to the court to be granted parental responsibility.

Relatives

A number of provisions in the Adoption and Children Act 2002 recognise the importance of members of the extended family. The court and those who are responsible for making decisions about a child have a duty, under section 1(4)(c) of the Act, to consider the likely effect on the child (throughout his life) of ceasing to be a member of the original family and becoming an adopted person. Under section 1(4)(f) the relationship which the child has with relatives, and with any other person in relation to whom the court or agency considers the relationship to be relevant, must be considered. The matters to be taken into account in this context include:

(a) the likelihood of any such relationship continuing and the value to the child of its doing so;

(b) the ability and willingness of any of the child's relatives, or of any such persons, to provide the child with a secure environment in which the child can develop, and otherwise to meet the child's needs; and

(c) the wishes and feelings of any of the child's relatives, or any such person, regarding the child.

Section 1(6) also imposes a duty on the court and the adoption agency to consider the whole range of powers available to it under both the Children Act 1989 and the Adoption and Children Act 2002. A court must observe the "no order" principle, declining to make any order unless it considers that the making of the order would be better for the child than not doing so. To assess these issues, it is necessary for the court and the adoption agency to give those who come within the above categories of person the opportunity to be heard. The local authority is obliged to provide information to the court regarding the steps which have been taken to locate members of the extended family. See section 1(2) and (4) of the Adoption and Children Act 2002 and regulation 16 of the Adoption Agencies Regulations and the Adoption Agencies (Wales) Regulations.

The child

Section 122 of the Adoption and Children Act 2002 amends section 41 of the Children Act 1989 to designate applications for the making or revocation of a placement order as "specified proceedings"; and, in relation to the provisions of section 93 of the 1989 Act, for rules to provide for children to be separately represented in relevant proceedings. Section 41 imposes a duty on the court to appoint a CAFCASS officer (or, in Wales, a Welsh family proceedings officer) for the child, to represent the child's interests in the proceedings. There is also provision for the child to be separately represented where the child has sufficient understanding to instruct a solicitor and wishes to do so, or where it appears to the court that it would be in the child's best interests to be represented by a solicitor.

The Family Procedure (Adoption) Rules 2004, rule 59(1), requires the court to appoint a children's guardian where the child is a party to the proceedings, unless it is satisfied that it is not necessary to do so to safeguard the interests of the child. Rule 59(2) also provides that at any stage of the proceedings where the child is a party, a party may apply for the appointment of a children's guardian, or the court may of its own initiative appoint a children's guardian.

8. Procedure

For the court in which an application for a placement order should be made, see Chapter 25, page 380. The procedure is governed by Part 5 of the Family Procedure (Adoption) Rules 2005 (SI 2005 No. 2795); see Chapter 25, page 392.

9. Duration

A placement order continues in force until:
  (a) it is revoked under section 24 of the 2002 Act; or
  (b) an adoption order is made in respect of the child; or
  (c) the child marries or forms a civil partnership; or
  (d) the child attains the age of eighteen years
  (section 21(4)).

10. Revocation

The Adoption and Children Act 2002, section 24(1), provides that the court may revoke a placement order on the application of any person. This is, however, qualified in section 24(2) to differentiate between those who have an automatic right to apply for the revocation of an order and those who need to obtain the permission of the court to make the application.

The child who is the subject of the placement order, and the local authority in whose favour the placement order was made, may apply for revocation as of right. All other persons, including the child's parent(s) or guardian, must seek the court's permission to do so. An application for permission may be made only if the child has not been placed for adoption by the authority. The court will not grant permission unless it is satisfied that there has been a change in circumstances since the placement order was made. (See section 24(2) and (3).)

The court also has the power to revoke a placement order at the final adoption hearing, if it determines not to make the adoption order and considers that the child should not be placed for adoption (section 24(4)).

For the procedure to apply for revocation, see Chapter 25, page 392.

Declaration by parent(s)

Under section 18(6) of the Adoption Act 1976, before making a freeing order, the court was required to satisfy itself that the parent of the child had been given an opportunity to make, if he or she so wished, a declaration that he preferred not to be involved in future questions concerning the adoption of the child. There was also a duty on the adoption agency to notify the parent if an adoption order was subsequently made. Where the parent did not make a declaration, the adoption agency in whose favour a freeing order had been made had a duty, within fourteen days after the anniversary of the making of the freeing order, to notify the child's parent(s) whether an adoption order in respect of the child had been made, and, if not, whether the child continued to have his home with the person with whom the child had been placed for adoption. Thereafter the adoption agency continued to be under a duty to give notice to the parent of the making of an adoption order if and when made, and in the meantime to keep the parent informed of any change in the child's placement. (Adoption Act 1976, sections 18 and 19.) Where a parent had not made a declaration under section 18(6), the parent had the right to apply, at any time after twelve months of the making of the freeing order, for the revocation of the order if the child had not been adopted and did not have his home with the person with whom he had been placed for adoption.

The Adoption and Children Act 2002, section 20(4), has similar provisions for a parent who has consented to a placement order to notify the adoption agency that he or she does not wish to be informed of any application for an adoption order. However, the parent now also has a right to withdraw such a statement. These provisions thus enable a parent whose circumstances have changed to apply for the revocation of the placement order and for the order to be substituted by any one of the alternative orders which are available; or, in exceptional circumstances, to have the child returned to his or her care.

Application by the child

The child who is the subject of the placement order is directly involved in the proceedings and affected by the order. The Adoption and Children Act 2002 specifically deals with the right of the child to be properly represented and to have separate legal representation where appropriate (see above). The Children Act 1989, section 26A, has also been amended to include provision for advocacy services to be provided to a child who wishes to make or intends to make representations. The assistance provided must include assistance by way of representation to ensure that the child has someone to speak on his or her behalf. The Act also provides for the cases of the children to be kept under review. Furthermore, the Act makes provision for the establishment of a procedure for review by an independent body or organisation to consider, among other matters, the welfare of the child, and to make recommendations. See further pages 277 to 278.

Section 117 of the Adoption and Children Act 2002 also extends the complaints procedure under the Children Act 1989 to provide consistency of approach to all complaints relating to or made by children. The child's right to make representation is therefore protected and assisted.

11. Variation

The court may vary a placement order so as to substitute another local authority for the local authority in whose favour the placement order was made. The application for variation must be made jointly by both local authorities (section 23).

12. Duties of Local Authority to "Looked after" Children

Section 18(3) of the Adoption and Children Act 2002 provides that a child who is placed, or authorised to be placed, for adoption with prospective adopters by a local authority is "looked after" by the authority. Section 22(4) sets out further circumstances in which a child is considered to be looked after. These are where the local authority:

  (a) is under a duty to apply for a placement order; or

  (b) has applied for a placement order in respect of a child and the application has not been disposed of.

This provision thus extends the general duties of the local authority towards looked after children to children who are to be placed for adoption. These duties include the duty to safeguard and promote the welfare of the child, and to make use of the services available for children cared for by their parents as appears to the authority to be reasonable. The local authority continues to have responsibility for managing the child's progress until an adoption order is made, and the child is subject to regular reviews.

Under section 22 of the Children Act 1989, before making any decision with respect to the child, the local authority is obliged to ascertain the wishes of the child, his parents, those who have parental responsibility for him and any other person who is connected to the child. In making decisions relating to the child, the local authority is required to give due consideration to the wishes and feelings of all those persons, and to the child's religious persuasion, racial origin and cultural and linguistic background. The local authority is obliged also to consider the welfare principle and the matters set out in section 1(4) of the Adoption and Children Act 2002 (see page 111).

Section 53 of the Adoption and Children Act 2002, however, stipulates that regulations may provide that, where a local authority is authorised to place a child for adoption, or a child who has been placed for adoption by a local authority is less than six weeks old, the above requirements of the Children Act 1989 may apply with modifications, or not apply. Such regulations may also, in relation to the same children, dispense with the requirements of the Children Act relating to promoting contact with parents and the parents' obligations to contribute towards the child's maintenance (section 53(2)).

Regulation 45(2) of the Adoption Agencies Regulations and regulation 46(2) of the Adoption Agencies (Wales) Regulations provide that in the cases within section 53 of the Adoption and Children Act 2002, the requirement to ascertain the wishes of the parents and of those with parental responsibility, does not apply, but the wishes and feelings of the prospective adopters with whom the local authority has placed the child for adoption must be ascertained and taken into account. The child's religious persuasion, racial origin and cultural and linguistic backgrounds are relevant. Again, in these circumstances, the requirements to promote contact with parents, and the parents' obligation to contribute towards maintenance (under Schedule 2, paragraphs 15 and 21 of the Children Act 1989) do not apply.

The Adoption Agencies Regulations, regulation 45(3) and (4) (regulations 46(3) and (4) of the Adoption Agencies (Wales) Regulations) makes similar modifications to section 61 of the Children Act 1989 (duties of voluntary organisations) as it applies to adoption agencies.

Since there is a general duty, when making any decisions relating to a child placed for adoption, to apply the welfare principle and the factors set out in section 1(4) of the Adoption and Children Act 2002, in appropriate cases the local authority may choose nevertheless to have regard to the wishes and feelings of the parents and others connected with the child, but is under no duty to do so. This approach is to ensure stability for the child, and to give effect to the provisions of the Act which give parental responsibility to the prospective adopters with whom the child is placed, the parents' rights being restricted. Similar provisions apply to the right to contact, although the parents are entitled to apply for an order for contact under section 26 of the Adoption and Children Act 2002 (see page 74). It is advisable to make a cross-application under section 26 for contact in appropriate cases when a placement order is applied for (see further below).

13. Effect of Placement Order

Parental responsibility
When a child is placed for adoption under section 19 of the Adoption and Children Act 2002 (placement with parental consent), or where a placement

order is in force, parental responsibility for the child is given to the agency, and they share this with the parents.

When the child is placed with prospective adopters, parental responsibility is given to them and they share it with the agency and the parents. This means that the parents retain parental responsibility. Under the provisions of section 25(4), however, the agency may make a determination to restrict the parental responsibility of the parent(s). This right could be abused, although its use is discretionary and is subject to the principle that it must be exercised judiciously. In addition, as in all other decisions relating to a child, the agency is under a duty to have regard to the welfare principle and to the factors set out in section 1(4) of the Act (see pages 111 to 112). The child's relationship with his birth family is therefore a relevant consideration in any decision made by the agency, and a decision by an agency to restrict a parent's parental responsibility would be open to challenge. The parent could raise the matter through the complaints procedure (see page 277). Another alternative would be for the parent to withdraw consent and request that the child be returned (see page 63). Finally, an aggrieved parent could raise the issue through legal process.

When a placement order has been made, the parent's parental responsibility is not extinguished, but, pursuant to section 25(4), the agency continues to have power to restrict the exercise of the right. This is not dissimilar from the provisions of section 33 of the Children Act when the child is made the subject of a care order.

Contact

Where an adoption agency is authorised to place a child for adoption, or is placing for adoption a child who is less than six weeks old, any contact order under section 8 or 34 of the Children Act 1989 ceases to have effect (section 26(1) of the 2002 Act); and an application for contact cannot be made under the provisions of the Children Act 1989 while the adoption agency remains authorised to place the child for adoption, or where a child is placed for adoption. By reason of the provisions of section 53 of the Adoption and Children Act and the Adoption Agencies Regulations, regulation 45 (regulation 46 of the Adoption Agencies (Wales) Regulations) (see above), the agency is not under a duty to promote contact with the child; this is in contrast with its obligations in respect of a child in care under a care order.

The adoption agency should nevertheless bear in mind that it has a duty, in making any decision relating to the child, to apply the principles set out in section 1(2) and (4) of the Act, and that in any event the parent has a right to apply to the court for a contact order.

Furthermore, under the Adoption Agencies Regulations, regulation 46, the agency has a duty to consider the contact arrangements, and in so doing it must:

    (a) take into account the wishes and feelings of the parent or guardian of the child, including where appropriate those of a father who does not have parental responsibility for the child;

(b) take into account any advice given by an adoption panel (see page 235); and

(c) have regard to the considerations set out in section 1(2) and (4) of the Act.

It is also under a duty to notify its decision relating to contact to the child; the parent or guardian; where appropriate, an unmarried father without parental responsibility; and any other relevant person. The adoption agency is also obliged to review the contact arrangements in the light of the views of the prospective adopters and any advice given by the adoption panel. Where the adoption agency proposes to make changes to the contact arrangements which affect any of the persons listed above, it must seek the views of those person(s) and take those views into account in deciding what arrangements it should make for contact while the child is placed with prospective adopters.

An application for an order for contact may be made under section 26(2)(b) of the Adoption and Children Act 2002 using Form A53 (see page 393 for the procedure). The court may make an order requiring the person with whom the child lives or is to live, to allow the child to visit or to stay with the person named in the order, or for the child and that person to have some other form of contact.

An application for contact under section 26 may be made by:

(a) the child or the adoption agency;

(b) any parent, guardian or relative;

(c) any person in whose favour there was was provision for contact under the Children Act 1989 before it ceased by virtue of section 26(1);

(d) any person in whose favour a residence order was in force before the adoption agency was authorised to place the child, or placed the child who was less than six weeks old;

(e) the person who had the care of the child under an order made by the High Court under its inherent jurisdiction relating to children, immediately before the agency was authorised to place the child for adoption;

(f) any person who has obtained permission of the court to make the application

(section 26(3)).

In addition, on making a placement order, the court may on its own initiative make an order for contact under section 26 of the Act. Indeed, before making a placement order the court is under a duty to consider the arrangements which the adoption agency has made, or proposes to make, for contact, and invite the parties to the proceedings to comment on the arrangements (section 27(4)). The court may also attach to the order any conditions it considers appropriate (section 27(5)). In determining any issues relating to contact, the court is obliged to apply the welfare principle and the factors set out in section 1(4)) of the Act. In any application for, or connected with, the placement of a child for adoption, the court's attention should be drawn not only to the mandatory duty imposed upon it under section 27(4), but also to the significance of the issue of contact in the light of the absence of any duty on the agency or local authority (in contrast to its position in care proceedings) to promote contact.

After an order for contact under section 26 has been made, the adoption agency may nevertheless refuse to allow contact if it is satisfied that it is necessary to do so in order to safeguard or promote the child's welfare; such a decision may be made only as a matter of urgency and the refusal must not last for more than seven days. The agency must notify those who are affected by the refusal, namely:

(a) the child if he is of sufficient age and understanding;
(b) the person in whose favour the section 26 contact order was made; and
(c) the prospective adopters.

Notification must be given as soon as the decision is made, and must include the date it was made, the reasons for it and the duration of the refusal (regulation 47(1) of both the Adoption Agencies Regulations and the Adoption Agencies (Wales) Regulations). The agency must apply to the court for any variation of a contact order (section 27(1)).

Pursuant to section 27(3) of the Act, provision is also made in the regulations for the parties to vary the terms of a section 26 contact order by agreement. This is subject to the conditions that:

(a) where the child is of sufficient age and understanding, the child's agreement must be obtained;
(b) where the child is placed for adoption, there must be consultation with the prospective adopters with whom the child is placed before the agreement is reached; and
(c) written confirmation of the terms of the agreement must be given to the child if he of sufficient age and understanding, the person in whose favour the section 26 contact order was made and the prospective adopters

(regulation 47(2) of both the Adoption Agencies Regulations and the Adoption Agencies (Wales) Regulations).

A section 26 order remains in force while the adoption agency is authorised to place the child for adoption (or the child is under six weeks old). It may be varied or revoked by the court, on the application of the adoption agency, the child or the person in whose favour the order was made (section 27(1) of the 2002 Act).

The child's surname
Restrictions on changing a child's surname apply where a child is placed for

adoption under section 19, or an adoption agency is authorised to place a child for adoption under that section, or a placement order has been made and remains in force. In these circumstances, a person may not cause the child to be known by a new surname unless the court has given permission to do so, or each parent or guardian of the child gives written consent (section 28(2) and (3) of the 2002 Act). On applying for permission, see page 394.

Removal from the United Kingdom
Where a child is placed for adoption under section 19, or an adoption agency is authorised to place a child for adoption under that section, or a placement order has been made and remains in force, a person may not cause the child to be removed from the United Kingdom unless the court has given permission to do so (for the procedure, see page 394), or each parent or guardian of the child gives written consent (section 28(2) and (3)).

The child may, however, be removed from the United Kingdom for a period of less than one month by a person who provides the child with a home (section 28(4)).

Orders under section 8 of the Children Act 1989 and supervision orders
Where a placement order is in force in respect of a child, any contact order, prohibited steps order, residence order or specific issue order made under section 8 of the Children Act 1989, or any supervision order in respect of the child, ceases to have effect (section 29(2), Adoption and Children Act 2002).

While a placement order remains in force a court may not make a prohibited steps order, residence order, specific issue order, supervision order or child assessment order in respect of the child (section 29(3)). A residence order may, however, be applied for in limited circumstances. These are where an application for an adoption order has been made, and the parent or guardian of the child, or any other person, has applied for permission to oppose the making of an adoption order under section 47(3) or (5) (where consent to the placement for adoption was given) and such permission has been granted (section 29(4)).

Special guardianship orders
Where a placement order is in force, no special guardianship order (see Chapter 4) may be made in respect of the child until an application for an adoption order is made. At that stage, the guardian of the child may apply for a special guardianship order if he has obtained the permission of the court under section 47(5); and any other person who is entitled to apply for a special guardianship order may do so with the leave of the court under section 29(5).

If the court grants a special guardianship order, application should be made for the placement order to be discharged. The criteria to be applied on such an application are the welfare principle, and the factors set out in section

1(4) of the Act (see page 111). By contrast, in the case of an application for a guardianship order the Children Act 1989, the welfare checklist applies.

Care orders
Where the child is the subject of a care order or the court makes a placement order at the same time as making a care order, the care order does not have any effect while the placement order remains in force. The care order does not cease, however; it is merely suspended. On the revocation of the placement order the care order revives without any further order of the court (section 29(1)).

14. Prohibition on Removal from Placement

The Adoption and Children Act 2002, section 30, sets out detailed provisions restricting the removal of a child from its placement; the intention is to avoid harm to the child and disruption of any proceedings concerning the child. The provisions relating to removal depend on whether the removal is from an agency placement or a non-agency placement.

Placement by an agency under section 19
No person may remove from the prospective adopters a child who has been placed for adoption by an adoption agency under section 19 of the Act (consensual placement), or a child so placed who is either less than six weeks old or whom the agency has not been authorised to place for adoption (section 30(1)). Only the adoption agency may remove the child. The parent or guardian must inform the agency if he or she wishes the child returned.

Where a child has not yet been placed for adoption but is being accommodated by a local authority and the local authority has applied for a placement order which is pending, only the local authority may remove the child from his/her accommodation. Any other person will need to apply to the court for permission to do so, and can remove the child only if the court grants leave (section 30(2)).

Where a child is not being placed for adoption but is accommodated by an adoption agency and that agency is authorised to place the child for adoption under section 19 of the Act, or would be so authorised if any consent to placement had not been withdrawn, no person other than the agency may remove the child from the accommodation (section 30(3)). Thus, even where the parent, having initially given consent, later withdraws that consent, the parent cannot remove the child. Only the agency is permitted to do so. If the parent or guardian of the child wants the child returned, he or she must request the return of the child, and the agency must return the child within seven days, unless an application is or has been made for a placement order and the application is pending (section 31(2)).

Where the child is placed for adoption by an adoption agency and either the child is less than six weeks old or the agency has at no time been authorised to place the child for adoption, and a parent or guardian of the child informs the agency that he wishes the child returned to him, the agency is under a duty, on receipt of such a notice, to notify the prospective adopters. They, in turn, have a duty to return the child to the agency within seven days. On the child's return to the agency the agency must return the child to the parent as soon thereafter as possible. (See section 31 and page 301.) This provision does not apply where an application for a placement order is made or has been made and the application is pending (section 31(3)and (4)).

Where the child is placed for adoption by an adoption agency under section 19 and consent to the placement has been withdrawn, then unless an application for a placement order is or has been made and is pending, if the parent or guardian of the child withdraws consent and requests that the child be returned to him, the agency has a duty to notify the prospective adopters of the parent's or guardian's wish. The prospective adopters must return the child to the agency within fourteen days from the date on which notice is given (section 32(1) and (2)). If the child has not been placed, the agency is under a duty to return the child within seven days (section 32). In such a case, the local authority has a duty to apply for a placement order if it considers that a return to the parents would cause the child to suffer significant harm as defined in section 31 of the Children Act 1989. The local authority is under a duty to apply whenever the conditions set out in section 22 of the Act are met (see page 66). Once the application has been issued the child need not be returned, and no person other than the local authority can remove the child, unless the court so orders.

The above restrictions do not, however, apply where, before the request for the return of the child is made, an application for an adoption order, special guardianship order or residence order, or leave to apply for a special guardianship order or residence order was made in respect of the child and has not been disposed of. In such a case the prospective adopters are not obliged to return the child to the agency unless the court orders the child's return (section 32(5)).

The above restrictions on removal do not:

(a) prevent the removal of a child who is arrested (section 30(7)); or
(b) affect the exercise by any local authority or other person of any power conferred by an enactments, other than section 20(8) of the Children Act 1989 (removal of a child from local authority accommodation) (section 30(6)).

Section 20(8) of the Children Act 1989 provides that any person who has parental responsibility for a child may at any time remove the child from accommodation provided by or on behalf of the local authority under section 20. This applies only where the child is placed with the local authority under a voluntary arrangement under the provisions of the Children Act 1989. A parent or guardian who has placed a child for adoption under the provisions of the Adoption and Children Act 2002 does not have the right to remove the child, although he or she may request that the child be returned. It is for the agency or local authority to arrange the removal and return, or apply for a placement order.

Removal of the child by the parent, or the failure of the prospective adopters to return the child when asked to do so, is a criminal offence punishable on summary conviction by three months' imprisonment or a fine, or both (section 30(8)).

Removal after placement order

Where a placement order:

    (a) is in force; or

    (b) has been revoked but the child has not been returned by the prospective adopters, or remains in any accommodation provided by the local authority,

a person other than the local authority may not remove the child from the prospective adopters or from the accommodation provided by the local authority.

If a placement order is revoked, the court determines with whom the child should be placed, and sets a period within which the child should be returned if it determines that the child should not remain with the prospective adopters. There is then an obligation on the prospective adopters to return the child to the local authority (section 31(3) of the 2002 Act). The court may determine that the child be returned to his parent or guardian, in which case the local authority is obliged to do so as soon as the child is returned to the local authority. The court may set a period within which the child should be returned. If the child is accommodated by the local authority, it must return the child immediately (section 34(4)).

Where a child is placed for adoption and the prospective adopters give notice to the agency of their wish to return the child, the agency must receive the child within seven days of the notice being given, and the local authority must notify the parent or guardian of the child of the prospective adopters' decision to return the child (section 35(1)).

Similarly, where the adoption agency takes the decision that the child should not remain with the prospective adopters, the child must be returned by the prospective adopters to the agency within seven days of notice being given to them (section 35(2)). The agency must also give notice to any parent or guardian of the child of the obligation to return the child to the agency (section 35(3))). If, however, before such notice is given to the prospective adopters, an application for an adoption order, special guardianship order or residence order, or for leave to apply for a special guardianship order or residence order, was made in respect of the child and the application has not been disposed of, the prospective adopters are not required to return the child to the agency unless the court so orders (section 35(5)).

Non-compliance by the prospective adopters or the local authority, or removal by any person of a child from its placement without the authority of the court, is an offence. On summary conviction an offender is liable to imprisonment for a term not exceeding three months or a fine, or both (section 34(5)).

Non-agency cases

Sections 36 to 40 of the 2002 Act apply to non-agency cases. In such cases a child may be removed from his placement only in accordance with sections 37 to 40. The people with whom the child has his home are referred to as "the people concerned", and the provisions apply where the people concerned:

    (a) have applied for an adoption order in respect of the child and the application has not been disposed of;

    (b) have given notice of intention to adopt;

    (c) have applied for leave to apply for an adoption order under section 42(6) of the Act and the application has not been disposed of (section 36(1)).

The removal of a child in contravention of section 36 is an offence.

If the people concerned apply for leave to adopt under section 42(6) and their application is granted, the application for leave is not regarded as being disposed of until three days after permission has been granted (section 36(3)). This is to enable the people concerned to make the application for an adoption order.

Where the people concerned have given notice of their intention to adopt, that notice is to be disregarded:

    (a) if four months have elapsed since notice of intention was given and the people concerned have not applied for an adoption order; or

    (b) the notice is a second or subsequent notice of intention to adopt and was given during the period of five months from the preceding notice (section 36(2)).

The above restrictions are, however, subject to the following exceptions:

    (a) they do not apply where the child is arrested (section 36(4));

    (b) where the application for an adoption order is pending, a person who has permission from the court may remove the child;

    (c) a local authority or other person may remove the child in the exercise of a power conferred by any enactment, other than section 20(8) of the Children Act 1989 (section 37).

Local authority foster parents

Where a local authority foster parent has given notice of intention to adopt and the child has had his home with the foster parent at all times for a year, the child may be removed only by:

    (a) a person with parental responsibility for the child who is exercising the power in section 20(8) of the Children Act 1989, except where the child has had his home with the foster parents for five years or more, and they have given notice of intention to adopt, or their application for leave to make an application is pending; or

    (b) a person who has been given permission by the court; or

    (c) a local authority or other person exercising a power conferred by an enactment other than section 20(8) of the Children Act 1989

(section 38).

Partners of parents

Section 39 of the Adoption and Children Act sets out by whom, and the circumstances in which, a child may be removed from the home which the child has had with the partner of his parent where the partner has given notice of an intention to adopt the child.

Provided the child has had his home with the partner for not less than three years during the last five years, the child may be removed by either:

    (a) a person who has been given permission by the court to do so; or

    (b) a local authority or other person in the exercise of a power conferred by any enactment other than section 20(8) of the Children Act 1989

(section 39(2)).

Where the child has not had his home with the partner for at least three of the last five years, that is, for less than three years, the following persons may remove the child:

    (a) a parent or guardian;

    (b) a person who has obtained the permission of the court;

    (c) a local authority or other person in the exercise of a power conferred by any enactment other than section 20(8) of the Children Act 1989

(section 39(3)).

Other non-agency cases

In all other non-agency cases where the person concerned has given notice of intention to adopt, or the people concerned have applied for leave under section 42(6) of the Act for permission to make an application for an adoption order and the application is pending, the following persons may remove the child:

    (a) a person who has obtained the permission of the court;

    (b) a local authority or other person in the exercise of a power conferred by any enactment other than section 20(8) of the Children Act 1989

(section 40).

Offences

On offences in connection with the removal and return of children, see Chapter 19, page 301.

15. Recovery Orders

The applicant

Section 41(2) of the Adoption and Children Act 2002 provides that an application for a recovery order may be made by any person. The section does not refer to any specific categories of person, nor to any conditions which must be satisfied before a person can apply. Section 41, however, provides that a recovery order may be obtained if:

(a) the child has been removed in contravention of the provisions in sections 30 to 35; or

(b) there are reasonable grounds for believing that a person intends to remove a child in contravention of those provisions; or

(c) there has been non-compliance with the provisions under sections 31 to 35.

The order

On the application of any person who satisfies the court of one of the three matters in (a) to (c) above, the court may make any one or more of the following orders:

(a) direct any person who is in a position to do so to produce the child on request to any person mentioned in subsection (4) (see below);

(b) authorise the removal of the child by any authorised person;

(c) require any person who has information as to the child's whereabouts to disclose that information on request to any constable or officer of the court;

(d) authorise a constable to enter premises specified in the order and search for the child, using reasonable force if necessary

(section 41(2)).

Authorised persons

The persons who are authorised to enforce the recovery order are:

(a) any person named by the court;

(b) any constable;

(c) any person who, after the order is made, is authorised to exercise any power under the order by an adoption agency which is authorised to place the child for adoption

(section 41(4)).

These orders are akin to recovery orders under the Children Act 1989 and the Family Law Act 1986. In the case of a recovery order obtained under the 2002 Act, however, it is an offence to obstruct any person in the exercise of a power of removal. A person guilty of this offence is liable, on summary conviction, to a fine. (Section 41(5).)

In relation to an order for the disclosure of the child's whereabouts, the person is under a mandatory duty to provide the information requested even if the information sought might constitute evidence that he had committed an offence (section 41(6)).

Procedure
The procedure on an application for a recovery order is governed by Part 5 of the Family Procedure (Adoption) Rules 2005 (SI 2005 No. 2795); see Chapter 25, pages 389 and 418.

Chapter 6

Preconditions for Applying for an Adoption Order

There are in effect some seven conditions which must be satisfied before an application for adoption is made. Some of these have been dealt with in earlier chapters and others are considered later. The information provided in this chapter is therefore a summary and by way of a checklist towards preparing to make an application to adopt. By this stage, the prospective adopters will have undergone an assessment of their suitability to adopt and been matched with a child. Reference should be made to Chapter 16 for the process of assessment of suitability to adopt, and the extent and nature of the inquiries and investigations which will be made about the prospective adopters, their lifestyle, family and friends.

1. Restrictions on Arranging an Adoption

There are restrictions on who can place a child for adoption. The Houghton Committee (Houghton, Sir W, *Adoption of Children* (Select Committee Report), Cmnd 5107, 1972) had expressed concern regarding the placement of children for adoption by persons other than an authorised adoption agency. It had observed that:

"Adoption is a matter of such vital importance to a child (who is usually too young to have any say in the matter) that society has a duty to ensure that the most satisfactory placements are made. Society manifestly does not do so while it is open to anybody to place a child for adoption. While the court hearing is intended to be a final safeguard, safeguards are needed much earlier. Moreover courts are in a difficulty about refusing to make an adoption order because there is no agency to which the child can be returned. Adoption agencies are increasingly staffed by social workers whose professional skills and knowledge are increasing. Agency practice has built-in safeguards through the Adoption Agencies Regulations and through general accountability to the public."

The Committee's recommendation was that it was essential that the placement of children for adoption should be arranged through the exercise of professional skills and knowledge and that independent placements should not be allowed.

In consequence, section 11 of the Adoption Act 1976 made it unlawful for a person other than an adoption agency to make arrangements for the adoption of a child, or to place a child for adoption, unless the proposed adopter was a relative of the child, or the person was acting in pursuance of an order of the High Court. Any application which suggested that there had been a contravention of the provision had to be referred to the High Court. (see further page 288).

The Adoption and Children Act 2002 confirms the safeguards which existed under the Adoption Act 1976 in the provisions set out in sections 92 to 97. Section 92(1) and (2) prohibit any person who is neither an adoption agency nor acting in pursuance of an order of the High Court from taking any of the following steps:

(a) asking a person other than an adoption agency to provide a child for adoption;

(b) asking a person other than an adoption agency to provide prospective adopters for a child;

(c) offering to find a child for adoption;

(d) offering a child for adoption to a person other than an adoption agency;

(e) handing over a child for adoption to any person other than an adoption agency with a view to the child's adoption by that or another person;

(f) receiving a child handed over to him in contravention of paragraph (e) above;

(g) entering into an agreement with any person for the adoption of a child, or for the purpose of facilitating the adoption of a child, where no adoption agency is acting on behalf of the child in the adoption;

(h) initiating or taking part in negotiations of which the purpose is the conclusion of an agreement within (g) above; and

(i) causing another person to take any steps mentioned above.

As under the previous law, parents, relatives or guardians of the child or a prospective adopter who is a partner of a parent of the child are excluded (section 92(4)).

It is thus essential to ensure that the placement of a child for adoption with the prospective adopters has not contravened this provision.

2. The Applicant(s)

The applicant(s) must meet the requirements relating to competency, eligibility, age, domicile and residence, as set out in Chapter 2.

3.   The Child

Whether or not a child is eligible to be adopted has been dealt with in Chapter 3, but in summary the following requirements have to be met:

(a)   the child must be under eighteen years of age when the application is made. An application may be made only if the child to be adopted has not attained the age of eighteen years on the date when the application is made. An adoption order may be made before the child has attained the age of nineteen years;

(b)   the child must not be married;

(c)   the child must not be or have been a civil partner;

(d)   the child must be resident in the United Kingdom;

(e)   the child must have had his home with the prospective adopters for the relevant period (see below).

4.   The Child to Live with the Adopters before the Application

By reason of the provisions of section 42 of the Adoption and Children Act 2002, it is necessary, before an application for adoption is issued, for the child to have lived with the prospective adopters for the "relevant period". The relevant period differs according to whether the application is by a couple, a partner or spouse of a parent of the child, or a foster carer. The relevant period in respect of the different categories of applicant has been dealt with in Chapter 3, but for ease of reference the provisions are restated here.

Where the child was placed for adoption with the applicant(s) by an adoption agency or in pursuance of an order of the High Court, or the applicant is a parent of the child, the child must have had his home with the applicant, or, in the case of a couple, with one or both of them, at all times for ten weeks before the application for adoption is made (section 42(2)).

Where a child is to be adopted by a step-parent or by a partner of a parent of the child, the child must had had his home with the applicant(s) at all times for six months before the application is made, irrespective of whether or not the application is a joint application (section 42(3)). But the period is extended to twelve months in transitional cases; see Chapter 24, page 368.

In the case of an application by local authority foster parents, the child should have had his home with them throughout the year preceding the application (section 42(4)).

In any other case, the child must have had his home with the applicant, or in the case of an application by a couple, with one or both of them, for not less than three out of five years preceding the application (section 42(5)).

These requirements can be summarised as follows:

Type of placement	Child to live with	ACA 2002
If the child was placed for adoption with the applicant(s): (a) by an adoption agency or (b) in pursuance of a High Court order or (c) the applicant is a parent of the child	The child must have had his home with the applicant(s) or with one or both of a couple at all times during the period of **ten weeks** preceding the making of the application.	s. 42(2)
If the above is not applicable: • if the applicant, or one of the applicants, is the partner or spouse of a parent	The child must have had his home with the applicant(s) at all times during the period of **six months** before the application is made.	s. 42(3)
• if the applicant(s) is/ are a local authority foster parent	The child must have had his home with the applicant(s) at all times during the period of **one year** before the application is made, unless the court gives permission to make the application earlier.	s. 42(4) s. 42(6)
In any other case	The child must have had his home with the applicant or one or both of a couple, for not less than a total of **three years** out of the five years before the application is made, unless the court gives permission to make the application earlier.	s. 42(5)

5.   Opportunity to See the Child

Before an application for adoption is made, the adoption agency or local authority must have had sufficient opportunity to see the child with the applicant, or both applicants together if is a joint application. Such opportunity must have been afforded to the adoption agency in an agency case, or to the local authority in a non-agency placement (for example, where the application is to be by a step-parent, partner of a parent or relative) (section 42(7)).

6.   Notice of Intention to Adopt

Where the child was not placed with the applicant(s) by an adoption agency (that is, in a non-agency placement), the applicant(s) must give notice to the appropriate authority of their intention to adopt. They must give this notice no more than two years, nor less than three months, before the date on which the application to adopt is made. Thus, at least three months' notice of the intention to adopt must be given. (Section 44(2) and (3).)

The appropriate local authority is the local authority for the area in which, at the time of giving the notice of intention to adopt, the applicant(s) have their home, or such other authority as may be prescribed by regulations made under the Adoption and Children Act 2002 (section 44(9)). The Local Authority (Non-Agency Adoptions) (Wales) Regulations 2005 (SI 2005 No.

3113, W. 233), regulation 3, prescribes that, for the purposes of section 44, where the proposed adopters are living overseas when they wish to apply for an adoption order (as, for example, where the proposed adopters are members of the armed forces or in the diplomatic services and posted abroad), the appropriate local authority to which notice should be given is:

(a) where the application is by one person who no longer has a home in Wales, the local authority for the area in which that person's last home in Wales was situated;

(b) where the proposed adopters no longer have a home in Wales, but shared the last home they had in Wales, the local authority for the area in which that home was situated;

(c) where the proposed adopters no longer have a home in Wales, the local authority which the proposed adopters nominate, being the local authority for the area in which the last home in Wales of one of the adopters was situated;

(d) where there are two proposed adopters and neither of them has a home in Wales, but one of them has had a home or homes in Wales, the local authority for the area in which the last of that person's home in Wales was situated.

The requirement therefore is that notice of intention should be given to the appropriate local authority by:

(a) a parent, step-parent or relative;

(b) foster parents with whom the child has been placed by a local authority; or

(c) applicant(s) in relation to a child from overseas.

The notice must be in writing and may be given by post (section 110). This provision is similar to that in section 72(1) of the Adoption Act 1976.

Where the prospective adopter(s), being a foster parent or any other person, seeks to apply for an adoption order but cannot satisfy the conditions relating to the relevant period for which the child has had his home with him, and therefore needs leave from the court to make an application for an adoption order, the notice of intention to adopt may not be given until the application is finally determined by the court and permission is granted to apply for an adoption order (section 44(4) of the 2002 Act).

7. Reports

Where an application for adoption relates to a child placed for adoption by an adoption agency, the agency must submit to the court a report on the suitability of the proposed adopter(s) and on any other matters relevant to the operation of section 1 of the Act, and assist the court in any manner the court directs (section 43).

In non-agency cases, where notice of intention to adopt is given to the local authority, the authority is obliged to check whether the child in respect of whom the notice is served was, immediately before the notice was given, a child who was looked after by another authority. If he was, the authority must, not more than seven days after receiving the notice, inform the other local authority in writing that it has received the notice (section 44(7)).

The local authority must also, upon receiving the notice of intention, arrange for an investigation to be carried out and submit a report on their investigation to the court (section 44(5)). This should include police checks (see page 214). The Local Authority (Non-Agency Adoptions) (Wales) Regulations 2005, regulation 4, specifically requires the local authority, for the purposes of this investigation, to take steps to obtain an enhanced criminal record certificate within the meaning of section 115 of the Police Act 1997, including the matters specified in subsection (6A) of that section, in respect of both the proposed adopter(s) and other members of his household who are over eighteen years of age or over.

If, having given notice of intention, the prospective adopters have not received any communication from the local authority seeking an appointment to see the prospective adopters and the child within a reasonable time, they should pursue the matter with the local authority to ensure that the investigations are set in motion without delay.

The report must include information on the suitability of the prospective adopters and all matters specified in the relevant practice direction (Family Procedure (Adoption) Rules 2005, SI 2005 No. 2795), rule 29(1) and (3)). The relevant matters are likely to be similar to those contained in the schedule 2 report under the former law (Adoption Rules 1984, SI 1984 No. 265, schedule 2). It is suggested that, in addition, all issues relating to the welfare of the child and the matters set out in section 1(3) to (5) of the Adoption and Children Act 2002 should be covered in the report, namely:

(a) the general principle that delay in making a decision is likely to be prejudicial to the child;

(b) the child's ascertainable wishes and feelings regarding the decision considered in the light of the child's age and understanding;

(c) the child's particular needs;

(d) the likely effect on the child (throughout his life) of having ceased to be a member of the original family and become an adopted person;

(e) the child's age, sex, background and any of the child's characteristics which the court or agency considers relevant;

(f) any harm, within the meaning of the Children Act 1989 (see page 38) which the child has suffered or is at risk or suffering;

(g) the relationship which the child has with relatives, and with any other person in relation to whom the court or agency considers the relationship to be relevant, including:

    (i) the likelihood of any such relationship continuing and the value to the child of its doing so;

    (ii) the ability and willingness of any of the child's relatives, or of any such person, to provide the child with a secure environment in which the child can develop, and otherwise to meet the child's needs;

     (iii) the wishes and feelings of any of the child's relatives, or of any such person, regarding the child;

  (h) the child's religious persuasion, racial origin, and cultural and linguistic background.

In carrying out its investigation the local authority is not restricted to the above matters. The report must also include information on all other relevant issues concerning the particular child, such as contact with the birth family, sibling contact and alternatives to adoption.

Qualification of the author of the report

Section 94(1) of the Adoption and Children Act 2002 provides that a person who is not authorised to do so may not prepare a report on the suitability of a child for adoption, a person's suitability to adopt a child, or the adoption or placement for adoption of a child. The Restriction on the Preparation of Adoption Reports Regulations 2005 (SI 2005 No. 1711) set out the categories of person, and the qualifications which they must have, who are authorised to prepare such reports. The matter is fully dealt with in Chapter 16.

Suitability of prospective adopters

Section 45 of the Adoption and Children Act 2002 provides for regulations to be made relating to matters to be taken into account by an adoption agency in determining, or making any report in respect of, the suitability of any person to adopt a child. This includes issues relating to the stability and permanence of the adopters' relationship.

    The Suitability of Adopters Regulations 2005 (SI 2005 No. 1712) set out the matters which the adoption agency should take into account when determining or reporting on the suitability of a person to adopt a child. It too emphasises the need to have regard to the stability and permanence of the relationship of the prospective adopters. The agency must also report on and take into account any information received which indicates that the prospective adopters may be unsuitable to adopt.

    The Adoption Agencies Regulations 2005 (SI 2005 No. 389) and the Adoption Agencies (Wales) Regulations (SI 2005 No. 1313, W.95) govern the exercise by adoption agencies of their functions. This is considered in detail elsewhere (see Chapter 16), but prospective adopters should be aware that the duties include carrying out police checks, inquiring into the prospective adopter's family, and inquiring into the health of the prospective adopters. The adoption agency is under a duty to provide counselling, advice and other information to prospective adopters, but when making any report in respect of the suitability of the prospective adopters the agency is obliged to take into account, amongst other factors:

(a) any information obtained as a consequence of providing counselling services to the prospective adopters;

(b) information obtained in preparation for the placement;

(c) information received as a consequence of carrying out the police checks and on the health of the applicants.

8. Summary

To summarise, therefore, before an application to adopt is made, the following questions should be asked:

1. do the prospective adopters meet the qualifications relating to their status, age, domicile and residence?

2. does the child meet the qualification criteria?

3. has the placement requirement for the relevant period been satisfied; if not, is it appropriate to apply for permission to make the application without meeting the condition?

4. has the required notice been given to the appropriate local authority?

5. has the local authority been afforded sufficient opportunity to see the child with the prospective adopters in their home environment?

6. is the local authority's report ready? If not, has the local authority been asked to give an indication when the report will be ready?

Chapter 7

Conditions for Making an Adoption Order

1. Introduction

Under the Adoption Act 1976, an adoption order could not be made unless the child was free for adoption, or the court was satisfied that:

(a) each parent or guardian of the child, freely and with full understanding of what was involved, had agreed unconditionally to the making of an adoption order; or

(b) the parent's or guardian's agreement to the making of the adoption order should be dispensed with.

The grounds on which consent could be dispensed with were that the parent or guardian:

(a) could not be found or was incapable of giving agreement;

(b) was withholding consent unreasonably;

(c) had persistently failed without reasonable excuse to discharge the parental duties in relation to the child;

(d) had abandoned or neglected the child;

(e) had persistently ill-treated the child;

(f) had seriously ill-treated the child and rehabilitation of the child with the household of the parent or guardian was unlikely.

Section 47 of the Adoption and Children Act 2002 provides that an adoption order may not be made, if the child has a parent or guardian, unless one of three conditions is met. The first condition relates to consent of the parent or guardian; the second relates to the placement of a child for adoption with the prospective adopters in whose favour an order is proposed to be made; and the third condition applies only to Scotland and Northern Ireland. Thus only the first two conditions are relevant to applications made in England and Wales and it is those that are considered in this chapter. The two conditions are in the alternative, i.e., only one of the two conditions has to be satisfied.

As has been observed in Chapter 5, the issue of consent arises at the time a child is being placed for adoption in circumstances where the child is being placed by an agency. In non-agency cases, for example, in an adoption by a step-parent or by a partner or spouse of a parent of the child, or a relative, the issue of consent does not arise until the adoption stage.

In some respects, therefore, the new legislation is not dissimilar from the previous law in so far as the consent of the parent, or dispensing with that consent, remains a crucial issue in any application for an adoption order. The freeing order route under the old law, where it was not necessary to establish placement with prospective adopters, has now given way to the placement route, which can occur only with the agreement of the parent or guardian, or by virtue of a placement order.

The most significant changes relating to consent brought about by the Adoption and Children Act 2002 are the provisions that make it possible for a parent or guardian to give "advance consent" to the adoption of a child; and those permitting the parent to withdraw consent and to oppose the application, notwithstanding consent was given, subject to the court's granting the parent permission to do so.

Where consent is not forthcoming it can be dispensed with. The grounds on which the court may do so, however, are in effect limited to three situations. They are:

   (a) that the parent or guardian of the child cannot be found;

   (b) that the parent or guardian is incapable of giving consent. This provision will be amended when the Mental Capacity Act 2005 comes into force. The second ground on which consent may then be dispensed with will be that the parent or guardian lacks capacity, within the meaning of the Mental Capacity Act 2005, to give consent; and

   (c) that the welfare if the child requires the consent to be dispensed with.

2. Parents

"Parent" is not defined in the Adoption and Children Act 2002 or in the Children Act 1989. However, the persons who have the right to consent to adoption are the parents who have parental responsibility for the child (section 52(6)). A step-parent does not come within this category, although a step-parent's views may be taken into account if he has acquired parental responsibility for the child by a parental responsibility agreement or order, or by a residence order.

Those included in the category of parent are the birth mother, and the birth father if he is married to the mother at the date of birth of the child, or the mother later marries him. A father who is not married to the mother does not have parental responsibility unless he has entered into a parental responsibility agreement or has obtained a parental responsibility order under the Children Act 1989. But such a father has parental responsibility pursuant to the Adoption and Children Act 2002 if be becomes registered as the child's father under the Births and Deaths Registration Act 1953.

3. Guardians

Section 144 of the Adoption and Children Act 2002 gives the term "guardian" the same meaning as in the Children Act 1989, and includes a special guardian within the meaning of the 1989 Act (see Chapter 4 for special guardians). Under the Children Act 1989, section 105, a guardian of a child means a guardian (other than a guardian of the estate of a child) appointed in accordance with the provisions of section 5. The court may, by order, appoint a guardian for a child on the application of any person, or of its own motion in family proceedings if:

    (a) the child has no parent with parental responsibility for him; or

    (b) a residence order has been made with respect to the child in favour of a parent or guardian of his who has died while the order was in force

    (section 5(1) and (2), Children Act 1989).

A parent with parental responsibility may appoint a person to be the child's guardian in the event of the parent's death, and in turn the guardian may appoint another person to take his place in the event of his death (section 5(3) and (4)). The appointment of the guardian by the parent must be in writing, dated and signed; or, if the appointment is made by a will, the will must be attested in accordance with the requirement of the Wills Act 1837.

A person appointed as a child's guardian under section 5 of the Children Act 1989 has parental responsibility for the child. A special guardian also has parental responsibility for the child and is included within the meaning of a guardian.

There may be situations where the application of the above conditions is not straightforward, for example where the case involves a foreign child or a foreign adoption order. Two cases under the former law may be relevant, particularly as the Adoption Act 1976 defined "guardian" in the same terms as under the Adoption and Children Act 2002.

In *Re AMR (Adoption: Procedure)* [1999] 2 FLR 807, a Polish child was cared for by her great grandmother, who was appointed the child's guardian. The child's parents were stripped of parental responsibility for the child. The child was brought to England by her great grandmother and placed with a relative, who wished to adopt her under English law. The question arose whose consent was required – the parents' or the great grandmother's. The court recognised the Polish court order and held that the great grandmother was the guardian for the purposes of the Adoption Act 1976.

In *Re D (Adoption: Foreign Guardianship)* [1999] 2 FLR 865, a Romanian child had been placed in an institution at birth. When she was about thirteen years of age the Romanian court conferred certain parental rights on the hospital in which she was living. The prospective adopters brought the child to England and wished to adopt her. The local authority did not oppose the application, nor did the Official Solicitor. The mother of the child consented to the adoption. The question arose whether it was necessary to apply for the consent of the hospital to be dispensed with. The court gave the words of the Act a strict interpretation and held that since the Adoption Act 1976 provided that "unless the context otherwise requires 'guardian' has the same meaning as in the Children Act 1989", and in section 105 of the Children Act 1989 it meant a "guardian appointed under the Children Act 1989, section 5", it followed that the hospital was not a guardian within the meaning of the Children Act 1989.

Where difficult points such as those above arise in the adoption process, and particularly where they relate to a foreign order or a foreign child, the case should be transferred to, or commenced in, the High Court for determination. Copies of the relevant order should be obtained and translated, and expert evidence on the foreign law and the effect of the order under the domestic law should be obtained (see *Re AMR*, above).

4. Consent (the First Condition)

The court cannot make an adoption order unless it is satisfied that:

(a) each parent or guardian consents to the making of the adoption order; (section 47(2)(a)); or

(b) each parent or guardian has consented under section 20 of the Act and has not withdrawn the consent and does not oppose the making of the adoption order (section 47(2)(b)); or

(c) the consent of each parent or guardian should be dispensed with (section 47(2)(c)).

The three elements described above are referred to in section 47(2) as "the first condition". The nature of consent has been considered in Chapter 5. As under the previous law, consent to an adoption given by the mother, if given less than six weeks after the birth of her child, is ineffective (section 52(3)). Furthermore, although section 52(5) defines consent as "consent given unconditionally and with full understanding of what is involved", as under the previous law, there is no specific requirement that consent must be given freely. This is not to imply that this ingredient is not essential because consent obtained under pressure or by reason of undue influence will not constitute consent. But consent given reluctantly, as is often the case because parents do not wish to give up their child but recognise that adoption is in the child's best interests, is nevertheless effective consent.

A person may consent to adoption without knowing the identity of the persons in whose favour the order will be made (section 52(5)). Where consent is given to the placement of a child for adoption under section 19 of the Act, or advance consent is given under section 20, it must be given on the prescribed form and must be witnessed (section 104(1) and (2)). Details of the procedure for giving consent are set out in rule 28 of the Family Procedure (Adoption) Rules 2005 and the relevant practice direction; see page 413.

Where advance consent is given, whether at the time of placement or at any subsequent time, the consent may be withdrawn, by giving the agency notice on the appropriate form (sections 20(3) and 52(8)), provided such withdrawal occurs before the application for adoption is made (section 52(4)).

A parent or guardian who has given consent and has not withdrawn the consent before the application for an adoption order is made, may not oppose the making of an adoption order unless the court gives permission to oppose. Permission will not be granted unless the court is satisfied that there has been a change of circumstances since the consent was given. The Act does not identify the nature of the change in the circumstances which would justify the granting of permission. The issue may therefore arise whether there has to be an "exceptional" change of circumstances for the court to grant leave. It could be argued that the absence of the word "exceptional" from the section signifies that the legislators did not intend that the change would have to be of an exceptional nature. On the other hand, when considering any application, the court is required to have regard to the child's welfare throughout his life, and it could be said that the change in circumstances must therefore be at least significant and not minimal. The court will also have to balance this with the overriding objective set out in the Family Procedure (Adoption) Rules 2005 (SI 2005 No. 2795; see page 377), and the parents' rights under the European Convention on Human Rights and the Human Rights Act 1998. The rights which will be relevant to consider are those under articles 6 (the right to a fair trial) and 8 (the right to respect for private and family life).

Where consent is not forthcoming, the court may dispense with consent on the grounds set out in section 52(1) of the Act; see Chapter 8.

5. Placements and Placement Orders (the Second Condition)

The second condition to be satisfied before an adoption order may be made, as an alternative to consent as described above, and referred to as "the second condition", is that:

    (a) the child has been placed for adoption by an adoption agency with the prospective adopters in whose favour the order is proposed to be made;

    (b) either:

        (i) the child was placed for adoption with the consent of each parent or guardian and the consent of the mother was given when the child was at least six weeks old; or

        (ii) the child was placed for adoption under a placement order; and

    (c) no parent or guardian opposes the making of the adoption order (section 47(4)).

Where the parent or guardian has given advance consent for the child to be placed for adoption under section 20 of the Adoption and Children Act 2002, then the parent may not oppose the application for an adoption order unless the court grants permission to do so. The same applies where, in proceedings for a placement order, the parent's consent has been dispensed with (see Chapter 8). Leave cannot be granted unless the court is satisfied that there has been a change of circumstances since the consent was given or the placement order was made (section 47(7)). Where permission to oppose is given, the court may still dispense with consent on the ground that the child's welfare so requires (sections 47(2) and 52(1)(b)).

6. Dispensing with Consent

For an adoption order to be made, therefore, the case must fall within the first condition or the second condition. If consent remains in issue, or leave is given to oppose the application, it is open to the applicants to seek an order that consent be dispensed with (see Chapter 8). The child's welfare is now the principal ground for dispensing with the parent's consent. Where there is a conflict between the child's welfare, and therefore the child's rights, and the parent's rights, the court will carry out a balancing exercise, and in so doing must also have regard to the European Convention on Human Rights. This may lead to friction between the domestic law and Convention rights.

7. Summary

1. Where the child has been placed by an agency, the case may fall under either of the two conditions above.

2. Where the parents have consented and that consent has not been withdrawn before the application for adoption is made, the parents cannot oppose the application unless they apply for permission to do so and the court grants permission. Permission will not be granted unless there has been a change of circumstances.

3. Advance consent, unless withdrawn before the application is made, prevents the parents from opposing the application unless the court grants permission to do so.

4. It is not clear what the nature and extent of the change in circumstances must be to justify the court's giving permission. Nor is it clear whether, if a placement order is made and permission to oppose an adoption order is then sought, the court will consider the matter as a whole, or limit its consideration to events since the making of the placement order. The latter seems likely.

5. If permission is granted to the parents to oppose the application for an adoption order, the elements of the second condition (section 47(7)) will not be met and the application will proceed as an application to dispense with consent.

Chapter 8

Dispensing with Consent

1. Introduction

As noted in Chapter 5, section 52 of the Adoption and Children Act 2002 provides for only two grounds for dispensing with consent to the making of an adoption order, namely that the parent cannot be found or lacks capacity within the meaning of the Mental Capacity Act 2005 (when in force); or that the welfare of the child requires consent to be dispensed with. This is in contrast with the eight grounds under the Adoption Act 1976. The ground for dispensation on the basis that the parent is unreasonably withholding consent no longer exists. All the other grounds have been subsumed within the all-embracing requirement that the welfare of the child is the paramount consideration. The two-stage process which the court had to carry out when dispensing with consent under the old law has been removed. This process involved considering, firstly, whether adoption was in the best interest of the child; and, if the answer was in the affirmative, considering, secondly, whether the parent(s) were withholding consent unreasonably. Only if the answer at each stage was in the affirmative could consent be dispensed with. This process has been replaced by a single consideration, that of the welfare of the child. The weight to be attached to parents' wishes and feelings and their interest in maintaining links and ties with the child is debatable, but the court is obliged to have regard to the specific issues raised in section 1(4) and (5) of the 2002 Act (see pages 111 to 112), and to consider the European Convention on Human Rights, and to ensure that the decision it takes does not infringe Convention rights. It would seem that the court will still have to consider the matter of family ties and the child's origin, and that, therefore, the parents' views will feature in the court's consideration. In addition it could be suggested that, having regard to the human rights issues, the court will need to carry out a two-stage process, first considering whether the child's welfare requires consent to be dispensed with; and, secondly, considering whether an adoption order infringes the competing rights under the Convention and, if it does, whether such interference is proportionate to safeguard the child's interest.

2. The Parent or Guardian Cannot be Found

This ground – that the parent or guardian cannot be found – remains the same as under the former law. Case law on the steps which should be taken before it can be said that the parent cannot be found is therefore relevant.

In *Re R (Adoption)* [1967] 1 WLR 34, [1966] 3 All ER 613, the subject of the adoption proceedings had fled a totalitarian state. He had told his parents of his intention before he fled but they did not evince any curiosity about his destination. After he left his homeland there was no communication between him and his parents. He escaped to England and lived with the applicant who assumed full responsibility for him and wished to adopt him. The court was satisfied that any attempt to communicate with the natural parents would not only be embarrassing for them but would expose them to danger, and held that as there were no practical means of communicating with them they could not be found. It could also be said that they were incapable of giving consent.

In *Re F (R) (An Infant)* [1970] 1 QB 385, [1969] 3 WLR 853, [1969] 3 All ER 1101, however, the child had been placed with the applicants by the child's father who was unable to look after him. The applicants applied to adopt the child. The father consented to the adoption. The applicants were not aware of the mother's whereabouts and wrote to her at her last known address, advertised in the press and caused inquiries to be made through the post office, but they failed to approach the natural mother's father, although they had his address and knew he was in touch with the mother. The mother was not served with the application, or the notice of the final hearing when the adoption order was made. Two months later, the mother discovered that an adoption order had been made and took immediate steps to appeal. The mother relied on an affidavit from her father, confirming that she could have been contacted via him. On the evidence, the Court of Appeal stated:

> "We are in no position to express any view whether or not the facts in that affidavit are correct, but, if they are, this is not a case where the mother could not be found, because the words in the section 'cannot be found' must mean cannot be found by taking all reasonable steps. The respondents indubitably took many steps and very thorough steps to find the mother. If, however, it is true that they knew that the mother's father was in touch with the mother and that they knew his address, there is one reasonable step which they omitted to take, and that was to get in touch with the father and ask him to tell the mother what they proposed to do."

Thus the decision of the court was that this was not a case where the mother could not be found. The mother was granted leave to appeal out of time; the adoption order was set aside and the case remitted for a rehearing.

In *Re S (Adoption)* [1999] 2 FLR 374, where the facts were not dissimilar to those in *Re F (R)*, the decision in *Re F (R)* was applied. The applicant sought to adopt the child of her brother on the ground that the mother could not be found and that the mother had failed without reasonable cause to fulfil her responsibility to the child. The report prepared by the local authority included information about the attempts which had been made to locate the mother. At the hearing, the applicant and the natural father had stated that they did not know where the mother was and that she had not been in touch with them. The local authority social worker gave information about the mother's father and sister, but stated that she did not know their address(es). An adoption order was made. The mother appealed, stating that the applicant and her brother, the father of the child, were aware that she could be contacted through her father whose address they knew; and that solicitors acting on her behalf had sent letters to the father at the applicant's address to arrange contact with the child. The court applied the test in *Re F (R)* and held that the proper approach to construing the words "cannot be found" is: "all reasonable steps must be taken, and if even only one reasonable step is omitted, one cannot say that the person cannot be found."

In *Re A (Adoption of a Russian Child)* [2000] 1 FLR 539, the child had been born in Russia in 1996 and placed in a home for children with disabilities. The mother had agreed to the child's being adopted within two days of the child's birth. The applicants followed the correct intercountry adoption procedures to adopt the child. In 1997 an adoption order was made in their favour in Russia. The applicants applied to the English court for an English adoption order. Two issues arose in the proceedings:

(a) in English law, consent of the mother obtained within six weeks of the birth of her child is ineffective; and

(b) the consent for a Russian adoption was not sufficient, as, following the decision in *Re G (Foreign Adoption: Consent)* [1995] 2 FLR 534, the mother's consent to an English adoption was necessary.

The court overcame these issues by making an adoption order not on the basis of consent, but on the basis that consent should be dispensed with on the ground that the mother could not be found. The court considered the interpretation of the phrase "cannot be found" given by Buckley J in *Re R* (above), namely that if there are "no practical means" of communicating with a person whose agreement is required, the person cannot be found, and the interpretation in *Re F (R)* and *Re S* above where the test was that all reasonable steps must be taken. Charles J reconciled these two tests as follows:

"In my judgment, the interpretation of the phrase 'cannot be found' in these two cases are not in conflict. The first refers to 'no practical means' and the second to 'all reasonable steps'. It is important to note that in my judgment correctly neither case refers to possible means or steps. They are therefore authority that all practical means must be employed and all reasonable steps must be taken to find and communicate with the relevant person. What is 'reasonable' and what is 'practical' are not necessarily the same but will often overlay. In my judgment any potential difference does not give rise to difficulty.

> ... The question I should ask myself is whether there are any reasonable steps that can now be taken to inform A's mother of the proposed adoption in England and to seek her properly informed views as to it. In asking myself that question I should consider whether any proposed or possible step is practical and if it would not be then in my judgment it would not be a reasonable step."

On the facts, the court found that it would not be reasonable for steps to be taken to try and find the mother because of the risk that this would give rise to investigation for the purposes of civil litigation against the applicants and possibly third parties; the commercial and personal problems it would cause to the applicants; and the fact that the mother had agreed to an adoption and was informed about the proceedings in Russia but took no part.

The cases of *Re A* and *Re R* can also be distinguished from *Re F (R)* and *Re S* on the facts. *Re A* and *Re R* both involved the adoption of a foreign child, and in both there was evidence of risk: in *Re R* the risk was of endangering life or causing embarrassment; in *Re A* the risk was to the applicants and third parties. In *Re A* the mother had given up her child for adoption, had consented to the adoption and had taken no part in the Russian proceedings, whereas in *Re F (R)* and *Re S* the mother had not given up her child for adoption and had had no inkling that the child might be adopted, nor was there any evidence of any risk to the applicants or the natural parent in making inquiries.

It is thus essential to take all practical and reasonable steps to locate the person whose consent is required. It is the duty of legal advisers to ensure that the applicants are made aware of the serious consequences which may follow, as illustrated by the above cases, should the parent later appear and seek to have the order set aside.

The usual avenues of inquiry are to contact members of the person's extended family and friends, and to consult the electoral register, the council tax register and relevant government or local government departments. Where the enquiry relates to a person who is resident in England, an application may be made to the court for an order addressed to the Inland Revenue, directing the disclosure of the person's whereabouts and last known address to the court. Communication can then be made with the person through the court.

3. Incapable of Giving Consent

The Adoption and Children Act 2002 retains the ground for dispensing with a parent's consent on the basis that the parent or guardian is incapable of giving consent. The provision does not limit the incapacity to mental illness. It is thus wide enough to include mental or physical incapacity whereby a parent or guardian is incapable of giving his or her consent. This ground for dispensing with consent was not often relied upon under the former law.

The words "incapable of giving consent" will be replaced by the words "lacks capacity (within the meaning of the Mental Capacity Act 2005) to give consent" when the Mental Capacity Act 2005 comes into force, thus bringing section 52(1)(a) of the Adoption and Children Act within the wider interpretation given to incapacity. Until the 2005 Act is implemented, cases decided under the former law may serve as good illustrations of how the courts have interpreted this provision.

In *Re R (Adoption)* (above), it was held that where there was no practical means of communicating with the parents, they could be regarded as incapable of giving their consent in that they could not be found.

In *Re L (A Minor) (Adoption: Parental Agreement)* [1987] 1 FLR 400, the court was asked to dispense with the mother's agreement on two alternative grounds, namely that she was incapable of withholding her consent and was therefore incapable of giving her consent; or that she was withholding her consent unreasonably. The mother suffered from mental disorder within the meaning of the Mental Health Act 1983. She was incapable of managing and administering her property and affairs and she was incapable of understanding the meaning and implication of an adoption order and of giving a valid and rational agreement to an adoption order being made. The court nevertheless dispensed with consent on the ground that she was withholding her consent unreasonably. See also *Re A (Adoption of a Russian Child)* (above).

Under the former law, a parent with learning difficulties was invariably psychologically and/or psychiatrically assessed, to ascertain his or her ability to comprehend the wider implications of an adoption order and the ability to make a reasoned decision on the information provided to him or her. In many cases those who lacked the ability to understand the wider implications of an adoption order were considered to be incapable of giving consent or incapable of withholding consent, depending on the degree of their intellectual impairment, in which case consent was dispensed with on that ground. Where the evidence could be equivocal, consent was dispensed with on the ground that it was unreasonably being withheld.

The Law Commission, in Law Comm No. 231 on Mental Capacity, in 1995, recommended that a person is without mental capacity at the material time if he is unable, by reason of mental disability, to make a decision for himself on the matter in question either because:

(a) he is unable to understand or retain the information relevant to the decision, including information about the reasonably foreseeable consequences of deciding one way or another or failing to make the decision; or

(b) he is unable to make a decision based on that information.

Mental disability is disability or disorder of the mind or brain, whether permanent or temporary, which results in an impairment or disturbance of mental reasoning.

It is submitted that an inability to make a decision occurs when the person is unable to comprehend and retain the information which is material to the decision, and especially as to the likely consequences of that decision, or the person is unable to use the information and weigh it in the balance as part of the process at arriving at the decision.

4. Incapacity within the Meaning of the Mental Capacity Act 2005

As noted above, section 52(1)(a) of the Adoption and Children Act 2002 is to be amended by the Mental Capacity Act 2005, which is expected to come into force in the Spring of 2007. The phrase "incapable of giving consent" is to be replaced by "lacks capacity (within the meaning of the Mental Capacity Act 2005) to give consent" (Mental Capacity Act 2005, schedule 6, paragraph 45).

Section 2(1) of the Mental Capacity Act 2005 provides that:

"a person lacks capacity in relation to a matter if at the material time he is unable to make a decision for himself in relation to the matter because of impairment of, or a disturbance in the functioning of, the mind or brain".

It does not matter whether the impairment or disturbance is permanent or temporary (section 2(2)). A lack of capacity cannot be established merely by reference to:

(a) a person's age or appearance; or

(b) a condition of his, or an aspect of his behaviour, which might lead others to make unjustified assumptions about his capacity

(section 2(3)).

The first issue to be considered is whether the person is unable to make a decision. This involves eliciting information from the person and then assessing his ability to retain information and to weigh up the information given to the person. The Mental Capacity Act 2005, in section 3, sets out what constitutes inability to make decisions. It provides that a person is unable to make a decision for himself if he is unable:

(a) to understand the information relevant to his decision. This includes information about the reasonably foreseeable consequences of:

(i) deciding one way or another, or

(ii) failing to make the decision

(section 3(4)). However, a person is not to be regarded as unable to understand the information relevant to a decision if he is able to understand an explanation of it given to him in a way that is appropriate to his circumstances using simple language, visual aids or any other means (section 3(2));

(b) to retain the information. The fact that a person is able to retain information relevant to a decision for a short period does not prevent him from being regarded as able to make the decision (section 3(3));

    (c) to use or weigh that information as part of the process of making the decision; or

    (d) to communicate his decision (whether by talking, sign language or any other means).

Incapacity, therefore, is not limited to mental illness in the traditionally accepted way. It is a broader concept based on impairment of the thought process. Thus people with learning difficulties may come within this broad definition. It will be essential, at a very early stage in the proceedings, for the parent whose consent it is sought to dispense with to be assessed by a qualified psychiatrist or psychologist or both, with experience and expertise in dealing not only with persons with mental illness but also with persons with learning difficulties. The purpose would be to ascertain the extent of the disability and whether, having regard to the provisions of the section, there are any practical steps that can be taken to assist the person's understanding, particularly, as suggested in the section, by visual aids or other means.

The assessment should deal with the extent of the ability of the person to retain relevant information and to make an informed decision. It is the duty of the adoption agency, as far as is reasonably practicable, to ascertain the wishes and feeling of the parent of the child and:

    (a) to provide counselling services for the parent;

    (b) to explain to the parent the procedure in relation to placement for adoption and adoption, including the legal implications of giving consent and of the adoption order, and to provide written information about these matters.

The assessment should deal with whether the ability to retain information, even briefly, leads in the particular case to an affirmative conclusion about the person's understanding of the relevance of the information; the importance and effect of the consequences, both to the person and in relation to the welfare of the child; and the person's ability to make an informed decision on the whole process of adoption. In some cases it may be necessary to show that all attempts have been made to relay the information by assisted means.

The incapacity must be referable to an impairment of, or a disturbance in, the functioning of the mind or brain. It is therefore doubtful whether cases such as *Re R (Adoption)* (above), and *Re A (Adoption of a Russian Child)* (above) would fall within the new provisions.

The Mental Capacity Act 2005, section 1, requires that, in arriving at any decision, certain principles should be applied when considering whether a person lacks capacity. These are:

    (a) a person must be assumed to have capacity unless it is established that he lacks capacity;

    (b) a person is not to be treated as unable to make a decision unless all practicable steps to help him to do so have been taken without success;

(c) a person is not to be treated as unable to make a decision merely because he makes an unwise decision;

(d) an act done, or decision made, under the Act, for on behalf of a person who lacks capacity must be done or made in his interests; and

(e) before the act is done, or decision is made, regard must be had to whether the purpose for which it is needed can be as effectively achieved in a way that is less restrictive of the person's rights and freedom of action.

The question of capacity is therefore issue-specific and subject-specific, particularly in relation to understanding the legal process and the legal proceedings. It is also important to consider whether, in the light of the expert evidence, the person in question has the personal autonomy to make a decision without being influenced by any third party.

Section 16 of the Mental Capacity Act 2005 specifically deals with the power of the court to appoint a deputy to make decisions on behalf of a person who is found to lack capacity in relation to matters concerning his personal welfare and personal property and affairs. "Personal welfare" includes decisions relating to contact with others (section 17(1)(b)); and "property and affairs" includes the conduct of legal proceedings in the person's name or on his behalf (section 18(1)(k)). It will thus be necessary for the court to invite the Official Solicitor to act on behalf of a parent with disability.

In addition, consideration should be given for arrangements to be made for the person to have an independent mental capacity advocate, even where the Official Solicitor has agreed to act and the person has legal representation, in order to offer support to the person throughout the proceedings. Some local authorities provide this service. Section 35 of the Mental Capacity Act 2005 introduces provision for the appointment of "independent mental capacity advocates"; it imposes on the Secretary of State and the National Assembly for Wales a duty to make such arrangements as they consider reasonable to enable independent mental capacity advocates to be available to represent and support persons in acts or decisions relating to medical treatment and the provision of accommodation. The ambit of this section does not extend to adoption proceedings, but section 41 also authorises the Secretary of State to expand the role of the independent mental capacity advocate and to adjust the obligation imposed by section 35. There is therefore scope for extension of this service, but in any event it should be recognised that persons who suffer from learning disabilities are vulnerable persons and should be provided, where appropriate, with support and assistance throughout the legal process.

5. The Child's Welfare

Section 52(1)(b) of the Adoption and Children Act 2002 provides that the court cannot dispense with the consent of any parent or guardian of a child, to the placing of the child for adoption, or to the making of an adoption order in respect of the child, unless it is satisfied that the welfare of the child requires the consent to be dispensed with.

This ground will become the main ground for seeking to dispense with consent, replacing the ground of unreasonably withholding consent under the former law. Although under the old law the parent's rights and interests were balanced with the welfare and interests of the child, the reality was that the welfare test became the more significant issue which turned the scales. In such cases, invariably, passages from the judgments in *Re W (An Infant)* [1971] AC 682, [1971] 2 WLR 1011 were referred to impress the criteria to be used. The most frequently quoted passage was from the judgment of Lord Hailsham:

"The test is reasonableness and not anything else. It is not culpability. It is not indifference. It is not failure to discharge parental duties. It is reasonableness, and reasonableness in the context of the totality of the circumstances. But although the welfare *per se* is not the test, the fact that a reasonable parent does pay regard to the welfare of his child must enter into the question of reasonableness as a relevant factor. It is relevant in all cases if and to the extent that a reasonable parent would take it into account . . . unreasonableness can include where carried to excess, sentimentality, romanticism, bigotry, wild prejudice, caprice, fatuousness or excessive lack of common sense."

And Lord MacDermott's summary of the test:

"the test for deciding whether the consent has been withheld unreasonably is to ask what a reasonable parent, placed in the position of the parent in question would do . . . where the test of unreasonableness falls to be applied in relation to the welfare of the child, the degree of unreasonableness to be proved must be marked in the sense that the parent whose consent is withheld has ignored or disregarded some appreciable ill or risk to be avoided or some substantial benefit likely to accrue if the child is adopted."

Clearly, the welfare of the child, although not the only and paramount test, was a significant criterion on which decisions came to be made.

The changes brought about by the Adoption and Children Act 2002, sections 1(3) and 52(1)(b), make the welfare test not merely significant, but the only and dominant test. This, together with the principles under section 1, to which the court must have regard, means that the child's interests alone dictate the result. So what of the parents' views and interest? Section 1(4) of the Adoption and Children Act 2002 sets out the factors which the court must take into account in making its decision. These include:

    (a) the likely effect on the child (throughout his life) of having ceased to be a member of the original family and become an adopted person;

(b) the child's age, sex, background and any of the child's characteristics which the court or agency considers relevant;

(c) the relationship which the child has with relatives and with any other person in relation to whom the court or agency considers the relationship to be relevant including:

  (i) the likelihood of any such relationship continuing and the value to the child of its doing so,

  (ii) the ability and willingness of any of the child's relatives or of any such person to provide the child with a secure environment in which the child can develop, and otherwise to meet the child's needs;

  (iii) the wishes and feelings of any of the child's relatives, or of any such person, regarding the child.

Section 1(5) of the Act also requires consideration to be given to the child's religious persuasion, his cultural and linguistic background and his ethnicity, and the wide range of powers available. The court should not make any order unless it considers that making the order would be better for the child than not doing so.

It could therefore be argued that the parents' rights are still protected and are to be considered in weighing up issues relating to the relationship between the child and his parents, and to family, cultural, racial and religious ties. These considerations become more pertinent where the child in question is an older child. Where these considerations are significant, although it may be beneficial to the child to remain in his placement, the court nevertheless has a duty to consider alternatives to adoption. The adoption order is, as it were, the last resort, to be made only if the court considers that the making of the order would be better for the child than not to do so. There is also, in appropriate circumstances, the possibility of making a contact order.

Furthermore, in all applications, the court has a duty to consider the human rights implications and it may be that this issue will take more prominence in contested cases. Article 8 of the Convention provides:

"1. Everyone has the right to respect for his private and family life, his home and his correspondence.

2. There shall be no interference by a public authority with the exercise of this right except such as is in accordance with the law and is necessary in a democratic society in the interests of national security, public safety or the economic well-being of the country, for the prevention of disorder or crime, or the protection of health or morals, for the protection of the rights and freedoms of others."

In *Re B (Adoption by One Natural Parent to Exclusion of Others)* [2001] 1 FLR 589, Hale LJ (as she then was) in her judgment acknowledged that:

"An adoption order is undoubtedly an interference by a public authority in the shape of the court which makes it, with the exercise of the right to respect for family life, whether by the child herself or anyone else with whom she enjoys 'family life'. Indeed it is the most drastic interference with that right which is permitted by law. In the right circumstances it is a most valuable way of supplying a child with the 'family life' to which everyone ought to be entitled and of which some children are so tragically deprived . . .

In my view, the relationship of mother and child is in itself sufficient to establish 'family life' even if they are separated at birth. The carrying and giving birth to a child brings with it a relationship between them both which is entitled to respect. Were it otherwise, the state could always interfere without contravening Art 8 by removing children the moment they were born. This only needs stating for it to be recognised how wrong that would be. The state must always justify its actions under Art 8(2).

There are three components to that justification. The first is that the action is 'in accordance with the law': adoption is permitted in these circumstances, but only if there is some reason to justify the mother's exclusion. The second component is that the interference is in pursuit of one of the legitimate aims defined in Art 8(2): the protection of rights and freedoms of others undoubtedly encompasses the protection of the interests of the child. However, the third component is that the intervention must be 'necessary in a democratic society' that is it must be a pressing social need and be proportionate to that need. The more drastic the interference, the greater must be the need to do it."

Although not directly related to adoption, the following cases illustrate the need for evaluating whether the interference is proportionate and necessary and to apply the "fair balance test" in all cases. In *Johansen v Norway* [1997] 33 EHRR 33 a baby was removed from her mother and contact was terminated with a view to the child's being placed for adoption. The European Court of Human Rights held that the denial of contact and parental rights was, in the circumstances, disproportionate and deprived the mother of being reunited with her child, and that such interference should take place only in exceptional circumstances.

In *Olsson v Sweden* [1988] 10 EHRR 259, the court held that there must be sound and weighty considerations before a child is split from his family, and the measures, if taken, must be shown to be proportionate to the legitimate aim pursued. See also *Eriksson v Sweden* [1989] 12 EHRR 183.

These decisions of the European Court of Human Rights were made in care proceedings and refer to the need for proportionality. They are not cases in which the adoption process was challenged. They are mentioned here only as an illustration of the balance which needs to be maintained. By the time a case is dealt with under the adoption procedure, there would necessarily have been an assessment of the family both before and within the care proceedings. In such cases there is usually a history of social services intervention and support before proceedings are commenced. The possibility of rehabilitation would have been considered, attempted and ruled out. The principles enunciated in the cases cannot be relied on, in the context of an application for adoption, with as much force as in the context of care proceedings. It is also important to note that under the new adoption procedure, it is mainly non-agency cases which will come directly as applications for adoption orders. In such cases there will be more scope for alternative options to be considered. In agency cases the procedure for placement of a child for adoption is the first step towards a final adoption application and therefore the opportunity for assessment and rehabilitation would have been offered during these proceedings. The process for planning for the long term future of the child is not a novel idea, as twin-tracking and concurrent planning were recommended by Bracewell J in *Re D and K (Children) (Care Plan: Concurrent Planning)* [2000] 1 WLR 642, [1999] 4 All ER 893, [1999] 2 FLR 872 and adopted by local authorities in planning for the child to avoid delay. In relation to twin-track planning the learned judge said;

> "local authorities traditionally have exhausted the possibility of rehabilitation to parents or extended family before beginning to address the possibility of permanency outside the family. For too long there has been a culture in which adoption has been regarded as the equivalent of failure and therefore a procedure to be considered only as a last resort when all else has been tried and not succeeded. Such sequential planning often promotes delay with serious consequences for the welfare of the child ...
>
> It is now well founded that children deprived of permanent parenting grow up with unmet psychological needs and far too many children have to wait too long before permanent families are found for them when they cannot return to their natural families. The longer the delay the more difficult it is to place children who often become progressively more disturbed in limbo, thereby rendering the task of identifying suitable adoptive families a lengthy and uncertain process. The older the child the greater the risk of breakdown in an adoption placement. It is therefore incumbent on local authorities and guardians to seek to prevent these delays by identifying the options available for the court by twin track planning as opposed to sequential planning."

Twin-track planning means that at an early stage in the proceedings the local authority is obliged to consider two options – rehabilitation with the birth family within a strict and limited time scale, or adoption outside the family. The birth family is informed of the plan at the outset, but given every opportunity to work towards rehabilitation.

Concurrent planning involves the process of working towards a family reunification while at the same time establishing an alternative placement plan. It is usually suitable for young children and babies.

The universality of the welfare principle as set out in section 1(3) to (5) of the Adoption and Children Act 2002, coupled with the observations on the cases made above, and particularly the case of *Re B (Adoption by One Natural Parent to Exclusion of Others)*, should provide some confidence that the courts will not permit the adoption process to be used as a rubber stamp for local authority decisions, but will continue to scrutinise each case on its merits, consider alternative options and safeguard the interests of all those involved in the process.

6. Procedure
An application to dispense with consent should be included in the application for adoption. Part 5 of the Family Procedure (Adoption) Rules (SI 2005 No. 2795) applies to a request, in an application for adoption, to dispense with consent. See Chapter 25, page 389. Rule 27 deals specifically with seeking to dispense with consent and includes provisions on filing a statement of the facts of the case; see page 395.

Chapter 9

The Principles to be Applied

1. Introduction

As in proceedings under the Children Act 1989, the Adoption and Children Act 2002 makes the welfare of the child the central principle to be applied when any decision concerning a child is made. Section 1(1) and (2) of the Act provides that whenever a court or adoption agency is coming to a decision relating to the adoption of a child, the paramount consideration of the court or the adoption agency must be the child's welfare throughout his life.

Section 1(7) of the Act specifically provides that the welfare principle applies in any proceedings for an adoption order, a placement order or a contact order, or for the revocation of any of these orders. It also applies to an application for permission to make an application. Thus, it is not only in relation to the substantive application that the principle is applicable, but in all decisions which have to be taken. The welfare of the child has also been made a deciding factor for dispensing with consent (see Chapter 8).

When considering the welfare of the child, the court or adoption agency must have regard to the following factors (among others):

(a) the child's ascertainable wishes and feelings regarding the decision (considered in the light of the child's age and understanding);

(b) the child's particular needs;

(c) the likely effect on the child (throughout his life) of having ceased to be a member of the original family and become an adopted child;

(d) the child's age, sex, background, and any of the child's characteristics which the court or agency considers relevant;

(e) any harm (within the meaning of the Children Act 1989) which the child has suffered or is at risk of suffering;

(f) the relationship which the child has with relatives, and with any other person in relation to whom the court or agency considers the relationship to be relevant, including:

   (i) the likelihood of any such relationship continuing and the value to the child of its doing so;

   (ii) the ability and willingness of any of the child's relatives, or of any such person, to provide the child with a secure environment in which the child can develop, and otherwise to meet the child's needs;

(iii) the wishes and feelings of any of the child's relatives, or of any such person, regarding the child

(section 1(4)).

An adoption agency, when placing a child for adoption, must give due consideration to the child's religious persuasion, racial origin and cultural and linguistic background (section 1(5)).

Section 1(3) also requires the court and adoption agency at all times to bear in mind that, in general, any delay in coming to a decision is likely to prejudice the child's welfare.

It will be observed that, with appropriate modifications, the "adoption welfare checklist" mirrors the welfare checklist under the Children Act 1989. However, that is not to say that it is only the matters set out in section 1(3) to (5) which are relevant for consideration, because the section clearly states that they are factors '"among others" which should be considered.

2. The Child's Wishes and Feelings

The reference to the child's ascertainable wishes and feelings considered in the light of his age and understanding is in terms similar to those in the Children Act 1989, section 1(3)(a). In addition, under section 22(5)(a) of the Children Act 1989, a local authority is obliged, before making any decision with respect to a child whom they are looking after, or proposing to look after, to give due consideration "having regard to his age and understanding, to such wishes and feelings of the child as they have been able to ascertain". While there is no requirement to *comply* with the child's wishes and feelings, these are nevertheless matters which the local authority is specifically required to consider from the moment the child comes into its care. The Adoption and Children Act 2002, while not giving this factor greater weight than any of the others referred to, nevertheless reinforces the importance of giving it proper consideration. It is one among many other elements which must be considered, and usually has greater importance the older the child. Much depends on the circumstances of the particular case, and on the age, maturity and intellectual understanding of the child. Also relevant may be whether the child's views have been influenced by any other person, and if so, by whom.

The requirement to consider the child's wishes and feelings is not qualified by reference to the age of the child. Decisions made in cases of child abduction, although different in context, may still be of assistance by way of illustration. These cases concern children who object to being returned whence they came, and have attained an age and degree of maturity at which it is appropriate to take their views into account. When considering the child's wishes and feelings it has been held that it is relevant to ascertain whether any views expressed by the child are expressed out of free will and choice and are genuinely held, or whether they have been influenced by some party or person: *Re J (Children) (Abduction: child's objections to return)* [2004] EWCA Civ 428, [2004] 2 FLR 64; *Re R (A Minor: Abduction)* [1992] 1 FLR 105. In *Re G (A Minor) (Abduction)* [1989] 1 FLR 475, the worldly understanding of a nine-year-old was held not sufficiently broad to comprehend all the factors of the case. In *The Ontario Court v M and M (Abduction: Children's objections)* [1997] 1 FLR 475 the children were ten and two years of age. The older child expressed very strong views and the CAFCASS officer's opinion was that it would be profoundly damaging and cause immense distress to the child to be returned. The court found that it would put the child in an intolerable position if returned. In *Re T (Abduction: Child's Objections to Return)* [2000] 2 FLR 192 the child was nine years of age but her views were consistent, clear and reasoned. It was held that the spirit and purpose of the Hague Convention on the Civil Aspects of International Child Abduction, 1980, did not override the respect to be paid to the wishes of the child.

The child's wishes and feelings have to be assessed in the light of his understanding. On what basis should that assessment be made? In most cases, assessments are carried out during care proceedings and/or proceedings for a placement order, so there will have been opportunities to ascertain the child's views. Such views are especially relevant where the agency and the court are dealing with an older child. Case law, where the child has sought separate representation to enable him to express his views, may provide further illustration. In *Re S (Independent Representation)* [1993] Fam 263, [1993] 2 WLR 801, [1993] 3 All ER 36, [1993] 2 FLR 437, on the issue of "understanding", Sir Thomas Bingham MR stated that:

> "in the ordinary way it is no doubt true (at least of children) that understanding increases with the passage of time. But the rule eschews any arbitrary line of demarcation based on age, and wisely so. Different children have differing levels of understanding at the same age. And understanding is not an absolute. It has to be assessed relatively to the issues in the proceedings. Where any sound judgment on these issues calls for insight and imagination which only maturity and experience can bring, both the court and the solicitor will be slow to conclude that the child's understanding is sufficient. . . .

The 1989 Act enables and requires a judicious balance to be struck between two considerations. First is the principle, to be honoured and respected, that children are human beings in their own right with individual minds and wills, views and emotions, which should command serious attention. A child's wishes are not to be discounted or dismissed simply because he is a child. He should be free to express them and decision-makers should listen. Second is the fact that a child is, after all, a child. The reason why the law is particularly solicitous in protecting the interests of children is because they are liable to be vulnerable and impressionable, lacking maturity to weigh the longer term against the shorter, lacking the insight to know how they will react and the imagination to know how others will react in certain situations, lacking the experience to measure the probable against the possible. Everything of course depends on the individual child in his actual situation. For the purposes of the Act, a babe in arms and a sturdy teenager on the verge of adulthood are both children, but their positions are quite different; for one the consideration will be dominant, for the other the first principle will come into its own. The process of growing up is, as Lord Scarman pointed out in *Gillick* [1986] AC 112 at p 186B, [1986] 1 FLR 224 at p 250H a continuous one. The judge has to do his best, on the evidence before him, to assess the understanding of the individual child in the context of the proceedings in which he seeks to participate."

In addition, the United Nations Convention on the Rights of the Child, article 12(1), requires States to:

"assure to the child who is capable of forming his or her own views the right to express those views freely in all matters affecting the child, the views of the child being given due weight in accordance with the age and maturity of the child."

Article 12(2) of the Convention provides that:

"the child shall in particular be provided with the opportunity to be heard in any judicial and administrative proceedings affecting the child, either directly, or through a representative or an appropriate body, in a manner consistent with the procedural rules of national law."

(See also the European Convention on the Exercise of Children's Rights, 25 January 1996, not ratified by the United Kingdom).

3. The Child's Particular Needs

Unlike the Children Act 1989, the Adoption and Children Act 2002 does not specify the particular needs of a child which must be taken into account. The Children Act 1989, in section 1(3)(b), specifically refers to physical, emotional and educational needs. These must be as relevant in adoption proceedings as they are in other proceedings relating to a child and therefore the needs referred to in the 2002 Act must encompass these three aspects. Of particular relevance will be any needs relating to the child's health, whether physical or mental, and any learning or intellectual difficulties which the child may have.

4. The Likely Effect of Being Adopted

The likely effect (throughout the child's life) of ceasing to be a member of the original family and becoming an adopted person is more relevant in respect of older children who are more likely to be sensitive to the reactions of others. See pages 68 and 118.

5. Age, Sex, Background and any Relevant Characteristics

The requirement in section 1(4)(d) to consider the child's age, sex, background and any characteristics which are considered relevant mirrors the provision of section 1(3)(d) of the Children Act 1989. These matters become particularly important when dealing with children who have strong family and cultural links. The word "characteristic" is wide enough to include racial issues. In *Re M (Section 94 Appeals)* [1995] 1 FLR 546, the child was of mixed race. The parents were not married. The father applied for contact and a consent order was made. The mother married a white man. She applied for and was granted a discharge of the contact order by the family proceedings court. On a second appeal to the Court of Appeal, the court considered that the question of race and the child's racial background was an important issue to which careful consideration should have been given by the court in deciding whether or not to allow contact. The appeal was allowed.

6. Harm

The requirement to take into account any harm (within the meaning of section 31(2) of the Children Act 1989) which the child has suffered or is at risk of suffering is similar to that in section 1(3)(e) of the Children Act 1989. "Harm" is defined in section 31(9) of the 1989 Act, as amended by the Adoption and Children Act 2002, as: "ill-treatment or the impairment of health or development including, for example, impairment suffered from seeing or hearing the ill-treatment of another". "Development" means physical, intellectual, emotional, social or behavioural development. "Health" means physical or mental health and "ill-treatment" includes sexual abuse and forms of ill-treatment which are not physical (Children Act 1989, section 31(9)). Where the question of whether harm suffered by a child is significant turns on the child's health or development, his health or development is compared with that which could reasonably be expected of a similar child (Children Act 1989, section 31(10)).

The criteria under section 31(2) of the 1989 Act must be satisfied at the date when proceedings are commenced, or if the child has been accommodated and the arrangements have remained in place continuously, the date on which those arrangements were first made (*Re M (A Minor) Care Order: Threshold Criteria* [1994] 2 AC 424, [1994] 3 WLR 558, [1994] 3 All ER 298, [1994] 2 FLR 577).

It will be noted that "harm" now includes exposure to domestic violence, and violence and ill-treatment generally. This change was a result of the report of the Children Sub-Committee of the Advisory Board of Family Law, published as *A Report to the Lord Chancellor on the Question of Parental Contact in Cases where there is Domestic Violence* (Lord Chancellor's Department, 12 April 2000). The leading authority on the effect on a child of witnessing domestic violence, ill-treatment, harassment and intimidation of others is *Re L; Re V; Re M and Re H (Children) (Contact: Domestic Violence)* [2001] Fam 260, [2001] 2 WLR 339, [2000] 4 All ER 609, [2000] 2 FLR 334, in which the Court of Appeal considered the report mentioned above. In the report, the question of domestic violence in the context of parental contact was highlighted, but it also raised awareness of the impact of violence on children. In her judgment, Dame Elizabeth Butler-Sloss commented on the report:

"Domestic violence takes many forms and should be broadly defined. The perpetrator may be female as well as male. Involvement may be indirect as well as direct. There needs to be greater awareness of the effect of domestic violence on children, both short-term and long-term, as witnesses as well as victims and also the impact on the residential parent. An outstanding concern of the court should be the nature and extent of the risk to the child and to the residential parent and that proper arrangements should be put in place to safeguard the child and the residential parent from risk of further physical and emotional harm ..."

Court rules and application forms have been amended to include information about domestic violence, abuse or other conduct or behaviour or harm which the child who is the subject of the proceedings is said to have suffered or to be at risk of suffering.

Where the harm or the risk of harm is disputed, the allegations should be investigated by the court at a hearing and findings of fact made to establish the truth and to assess the risk of harm to the child. Recently, in *Re K and S (Children)* (Court of Appeal, Civil Division), 16 November 2005 (Lawtel) the judge's failure to take account of matters relating to harassment and violence when making a contact order was considered a "serious deficiency".

Standard of proof

In such cases, the standard of proof required is that of proof on the balance of probability. In *Re H (Minors) (Sexual Abuse: Standard of Proof)* [1996] AC 563, [1996] 2 WLR 8, [1996] 1 All ER 1, [1996] 1 FLR 80, the House of Lords set out the standard of proof required in cases involving children. Lord Nicholls in his judgment ([1996] 1 FLR at page 96) said:

"The balance of probability standard means that a court is satisfied an event occurred if the court considers that, on the evidence, the occurrence of the event was more likely than not. When assessing the probabilities the court will have in mind as a factor, to whatever extent is appropriate in the particular case, that the more serious the allegation the less likely it is that the event occurred and, hence, the stronger should be the evidence before the court concludes that the allegation is established on the balance of probability. Fraud is usually less likely than negligence. Deliberate physical injury is usually less likely than accidental physical injury. A step-father is usually less likely to have repeatedly raped and had non-consensual oral sex with his under-age step-daughter than on some occasions to have lost his temper and slapped her. Built into the preponderance of probability standard is a serious degree of flexibility in respect of the seriousness of the allegation.

Although the result is the same, this does not mean that where a serious allegation is in issue the standard of proof required is higher. It means only that the inherent probability or improbability of an event is itself a matter to be taken into account when weighing the probabilities and deciding whether, on balance, the event occurred. The more improbable the event the stronger must be the evidence that it did occur before, on the balance of probability, its occurrence will be established. Ungoed-Thomas J expressed this neatly in *Re Dellow's Trusts, Lloyd's Bank v Institute of Cancer Research* [1964] 1 WLR 451 at p 455: 'The more serious the allegation the more cogent is the evidence required to overcome the unlikelihood of what is alleged and thus to prove it'."

And (at page 101C) Lord Nicholls said:

"I must emphasise a further point. I have indicated that unproved allegations of maltreatment cannot form the basis for finding by the court that either limb of s 31(2)(a) is established. It is, of course, open to a court to conclude there is a real possibility that the child will suffer harm in the future although harm in the past has not been established. There will be cases where, although the alleged maltreatment itself is not proved, the evidence does establish a combination of profoundly worrying features affecting the care of the child within the family. In such cases it would be open to a court in appropriate circumstances to find that, although not satisfied the child is yet suffering significant harm, on the basis of such facts as are proved there is a likelihood that he will do so in the future."

This standard of proof has recently been affirmed in *Re U (A Child) (Serious Injury: Standard of Proof) Re B* [2004] EWCA Civ 567, [2004] 3 WLR 753, [2004] 2 FLR 263 and *Re T (Abuse: Standard of Proof)* [2004] EWCA Civ 558, [2004] 2 FLR 838, and is referred to as the "cogency test" or in summary: the more serious the allegation the less likely it is that the event occurred and therefore the stronger must be the evidence before a conclusion can be reached that the allegation is established on the balance of probability; and in relation to the risk of harm it means the real possibility of future harm.

7. The Child's Relationships with Relatives and Others

Section 1(4)(f) of the Adoption and Children Act 2002 requires courts and adoption agencies to have regard to the child's relationships with relatives and other relevant persons. The comparable provision in the Children Act 1989 is section 1(3)(f) which refers to "how capable each of the child's parents and any other person in relation to whom the court considers the question to be relevant, is of meeting his needs", which is narrower than the provision in the 2002 Act. Section 1(8) of the 2002 Act provides that "relationships" extend beyond legal relationships and that the term "relative" includes the child's mother and father. Section 144, as amended by the Civil Partnership Act 2004, defines "relative" in relation to a child to mean "grandparent, brother, sister, uncle or aunt, whether of the full blood or half blood or by marriage or civil partnership". Where appropriate, the child's relationships with the identified members of the extended family will need to be considered. Of particular significance is the child's relationship with his or her sibling(s) where the plan is to split them. This is particularly important having regard to the decision of the European Court of Human Rights in *Olsson v Sweden* [1988] 10 EHRR 259, that splitting up a family was a serious interference in family life and must be supported by weighty and sound evidence to justify it. Secondly, section 1(4)(f) requires the court to have regard not only to the value of the relationship of the child with the extended family, but also to the willingness of such person(s) to provide security and stability so as to meet the child's needs and facilitate his development.

It is not unusual for local authorities, and sometimes even a child's guardian, in their eagerness to place a child, to overlook sibling contact after adoption, even though this was provided for in the care plan during care proceedings.

8. Religious, Racial, Cultural and Linguistic Issues

The Adoption and Children Act 2002, section 1(5), provides that, in placing a child for adoption, the adoption agency must give due consideration to the child's religious persuasion, racial origin and cultural and linguistic background. Although this may at first sight appear to be a new criterion introduced into the adoption process, and may appear mandatory, it would seem that this is not the case.

Section 22(5) of the Children Act 1989 appeared to place a duty on the local authority to give due consideration to similar factors; it provided "in making any such decision a local authority shall give due consideration:

    ....

(b) to such wishes and feelings of any person mentioned in subsection (4)(b) and 4(d) (namely the child's parents, any person who is not a parent of the child but who has parental responsibility for the child and any other person whose wishes and feelings the authority considers to be relevant) as they have been able to ascertain; and

(c) to the child's religious persuasion, racial origin and cultural and linguistic background."

However, in *Re P (Children Act 1989 ss 22 and 26 Local Authority Compliance)* [2000] 2 FLR 910, the local authority was proposing not to consult the child's father, who was serving a term of imprisonment for rape and buggery of the child's mother and indecent assault on the child. Nor did it intend to inform him of the arrangements for the children, other than providing him with an annual report. The Court of Appeal held that the provisions of section 22 and the regulations made thereunder were not mandatory but directory in the sense that non-compliance on the part of the local authority would be treated as an irregularity rather then rendering the decision void.

Both section 22 of the Children Act 1989 and section 1(5) of the Adoption and Children Act 2002 require "due consideration" to be given, which means that each factor should be weighed and considered with others, but, in appropriate cases, disregarded.

Thus, issues of race, religion and culture have always been considered when placing children for adoption, and courts have also been mindful of these matters when making adoption orders and applied the welfare test. This is illustrated in the cases summarised below. The difference now is that the process has been incorporated into adoption legislation as one of the principal considerations.

In *Re E* [1964] 1 WLR 51, [1963] 3 All ER 874, the child's mother was Roman Catholic but the child was placed with a Jewish couple who wished to adopt him. The mother objected as she wanted the child to be brought up in her faith. The prospective adopters were willing to undertake to bring the child up as a Catholic. In wardship proceedings, Wilberforce J in his judgment said:

"These authorities establish the basis on which I deal with this case, namely that in wardship proceedings the paramount consideration is the welfare of the infant. Welfare is not limited to material welfare. The religious upbringing is an element of great importance. An illegitimate child's mother's wishes are of great significance and must not merely not be disregarded; they must be very seriously regarded by the court. The court will certainly not substitute its views for hers, but they must be considered with all other matters bearing on the welfare of the child (both long term and immediate). The court is not bound to give effect to them when satisfied that the child's welfare requires otherwise, and in giving effect to them the court has power to do so in such a manner as it may consider to be best in the child's interest."

In *Re J (A Minor) (Adoption Application)* [1987] 1 FLR 455, a child of mixed race was placed with white foster parents who were Jehovah's Witnesses.

The mother objected to the adoption. Her objections were upheld on the basis that the child had West Indian characteristics and that this would lead to the child's drifting from the adoptive parents and seeking out his own ethnic origins. It would therefore not be in the child's best interests to lose his links with his mother.

In *Re N (A Minor) (Adoption)* [1990] 1 FLR 58, the child's parents were Nigerian and not married. The mother placed the child with a white couple pursuant to a private fostering arrangement. The father was in the USA. He remained committed to his daughter and maintained her. The child was unable to visit the father in the USA because of visa regulations. Having cared for the child for over two years, the foster carer indicated her wish to adopt her. The father then received notification from the US authorities that the restriction on his child's visiting him in USA had been lifted, but as soon as the authorities became aware of the foster carer's intention to adopt, the child's visa was suspended. The father applied in wardship proceedings for care and control. The local authority and the guardian were opposed to the adoption because the father had a useful part to play in the child's life in the future; contact with the father would be placed at risk because of the social consequences to the father and the family because of their culture, in which adoption was viewed as a restoration of slavery; the child's security could be assured by granting the foster carer care and control of the child and the child's immigration status was no longer in issue. The court was faced with the question whether the security which an adoption order would give to the carer and the child was offset by the fact that it clearly would not be in the child's interests for her father to feel the shame and distress that, in his culture, an adoption order would cause. The court was satisfied on the evidence that the child could not be moved without immense harm to her psychological development and her psychiatric health both at the time and in the future. However, the father had an important part to play in her life; the court recognised that the concept of adoption was unknown in Nigerian society where children were frequently reared by third parties, so the distress and shame which adoption would bring to the paternal family and the consequences for the child had to be weighed against the security of an adoption order to the foster carer. Applying the welfare test, it was held that adoption was not in the best interests of the child.

In *Re P (A Minor) (Adoption)* [1990] 1 FLR 96, the child was of mixed race. Her father was white European and her mother was Afro-Caribbean. The child was made the subject of a wardship order at birth and placed with a foster parent who wished to adopt her. The child thrived and formed an attachment to the carer. The local authority's objections to adoption were based on a policy that every child should be brought up by a family of the same race and ethnic background as those of the child, and it had a suitable adoptive couple for the child. At first instance the court decided that it was in the child's best interests to be placed with the prospective adopters identified by the local authority. The foster carer appealed. Dismissing the appeal, the Court of Appeal held that although the case was dealt with within wardship proceedings the court had applied the test that the welfare of the child was the first and paramount consideration; based on that test and the evidence before it the conclusion reached that the advantages of bringing up a child of mixed race in a family which matched the child's racial and cultural origins outweighed the circumstances of the child remaining with her current foster carer.

In *Re JK (Adoption: Transracial Placement)* [1991] 2 FLR 340, the child's mother was of the Sikh religion. The child was born out of wedlock and was placed for adoption. The local authority placed the child with short-term foster parents, but the child remained with them longer than had been intended and formed attachments to them and their children. The local authority planned for the child to be placed for adoption with suitably matched prospective adopters, but were unsuccessful because adoption in the Sikh culture was rare and more particularly so where the child was illegitimate. The foster parents wished to adopt the child. The local authority was opposed to the adoption because of its policy of placing children with racially suited adoptive parents. Even though it had not been able to identify such a suitably matched couple the local authority decided to move the child to a bridging placement, as a result of which the foster parents commenced wardship proceedings. The issue for decision was whether the child should remain with the foster parents with a view to adoption, or be moved, in the knowledge that suitable adopters were not available. The court applied the welfare test. It considered the advantages to the child in remaining with the family where she had integrated and settled, where she was attending school with her adoptive siblings, and where she had foster parents who were sensitive to her culture and religion. Against that were the uncertainty and the practical difficulties in trying to place her with a Sikh family, and the stigma of having been born illegitimate with consequent lasting psychological harm to the child. The child was made a ward of court and the foster parents were given permission to apply for an adoption order.

In *Re C (Adoption: Religious Observance)* [2002] 1 FLR 1119, the child was of Jewish, Irish Roman Catholic and Turkish-Cypriot Muslim heritage. The mother described herself as Church of England. In care proceedings the care plan was to place the child for adoption with a Jewish couple with no direct contact with the parents. The parents did not object to the placement. The guardian, however, challenged the local authority's decision to place the child with the Jewish couple on the basis that they were *too* Jewish. The guardian's application for judicial review of the local authority's decision was dismissed. The court held that where the child's heritage was mixed it would be difficult for it to be reflected in the placement and it might well be in the interest of the child to concentrate on one element so long as all the others were sensitively addressed by her carers. The child's religious background had to be weighed against all the other benefits that the placement offered.

Any decision relating to a child must also be considered in the light of United Nations Convention on the Rights of the Child, articles 7 and 8. Article 7(1) provides that a child shall be registered immediately after birth and shall, from birth, have the right to a name, the right to acquire nationality, and, as far as possible, the right to know and be cared for by his parents. Article 8 requires signatory states to undertake "to respect the right of the child to preserve his identity including his nationality, name and family relations as recognised by law without lawful interference".

These rights specifically deal with the preservation of the child's identity and require decision-makers to consider alternatives to adoption, and contact with the birth family following adoption. It could be argued that the effect of adoption in severing the child's links with his birth family threatens the child's rights of identity. It is submitted that, if it is decided that adoption is the only course, the court should ensure that appropriate and complete life story work, with therapy and counselling for the child, where necessary, is undertaken before the order is made. The issue of contact between the child and his parents should be seriously considered and investigated.

These provisions are reinforced by article 9(1) of the Convention which requires states to ensure that a child:

"shall not be separated from his or her parents against their will except when competent authorities subject to judicial review determine, in accordance with applicable law and procedures, that such separation is necessary for the best interests of the child."

Article 9(3) goes on to provide that where a child is separated, the state must respect the right of the child to "maintain personal relations and direct contact with both parents on a regular basis, except if it is contrary to the child's best interests".

These rights and duties must be considered along with the decisions of the European Court of Human Rights in which it has been ruled that the state has an obligation to reunite a parent and child where possible, and the provisions of Article 8 of the European Convention on Human Rights (see pages 134 to 136).

The cases decided under the Adoption Act 1976 demonstrate how the balance is struck between the need to preserve the child's identity, racial and cultural issues, and the overall needs of the child.

9. Delay

The Adoption and Children Act 2002, in section 1(3), provides that the court or adoption agency must at all times bear in mind that, in general, any delay in coming to a decision is likely to prejudice the child's welfare. This provision is not dissimilar from that in section 1(2) of the Children Act 1989, which provides that "in proceedings in which any question with respect to the upbringing of a child arises, the court shall have regard to the general principle that any delay in determining the question is likely to prejudice the welfare of the child".

Taken together, the provisions emphasise the need to avoid delay. A number of steps have been taken to ensure that the care and adoption processes are considered together and not in isolation. Thus the avoidance of delay applies not only within the adoption proceedings but across all aspects of any decision relating to a child.

The National Adoption Standards for England (Department of Health, Local Authority Circular (2001) 22, 7 August 2001) have for some time set timescales within which decisions concerning children should be reached. Section 125 of the Adoption and Children Act 2002 establishes an Adoption and Children Act Register, which contains details of children suitable for adoption and of persons who wish to adopt. Targets have been imposed for the local authorities and the courts, setting timescales within which decisions should be reached; and courts are required to be proactive in managing cases so that directions given by it are adhered to. The former Adoption Agencies Regulations 1983 (SI 1983 No. 1964), which came into force in 1984, required all adoption agencies to establish adoption panels whose function it was to consider each aspect of the agency's adoption work – making plans for children, considering the suitability of prospective adopters and matching individual children with adoptive parents. Recommendations made by the panel had to be taken into account by the agency when making decisions. The Adoption Agencies Regulations 2005 (SI 2005 No. 389) and the Adoption Agencies (Wales) Regulations 2005 (SI 2005 No. 1313, W. 95) make similar provisions, and are dealt with in Chapter 16.

The issue of delay was also highlighted by Bracewell J in *Re D and K (Children) (Care Plan: Concurrent Planning)* [2000] 1 WLR 642, [1999] 4 All ER 893, [1999] 2 FLR 872, and she made recommendations for twin-tracking and concurrent planning to avoid delay in placing children for adoption. The welfare of the child now being paramount in both care proceedings and applications for placement orders and adoption orders, the court should be able to deal with applications for a care and placement order at the same time, or within a relatively short period after a care order has been made where the care plan is for adoption.

However, while adoption agencies and the courts are required to have regard to delay, they are not obliged to do so at the expense of the child's welfare. In appropriate cases delay, if it is planned and purposeful – for example, with a view to rehabilitation with the birth family, or to provide the court with detailed information on which an informed and considered decision can be made – may be justified (see *Re W (Welfare Reports)* [1995] 2 FLR 142; *Hounslow LBC v A* [1993] 1 WLR 291, [1993] 1 FLR 702).

10. The "No Order" Principle

Section 1(6) of the Adoption and Children Act 2002 provides that the court must not make any order under the Act unless it considers that making the order would be better for the child than not making it. This is akin to the fundamental principle which is applied in all applications under the Children Act 1989, and set out in section 1(5), namely, that where a court is considering whether or not to make one or more orders under the Act with respect to a child, it shall not make the order or any of the orders unless it considers that doing so would be better for the child than making no order at all. The effect of the provisions is to encourage those who make decisions about children to consider the least interventionist approach in preference to a draconian measure. To this extent it is in line with the decisions of the European Court of Human Rights; see, for example, *Johansen v Norway* [1997] 23 EHRR 33, page 108. It is also in line with the principle of proportionality embedded in the European Convention on Human Rights and article 8 of the Convention – the right to family life – which has been actively advocated and supported in cases such as *Re K (Minors) (Supervision Orders)* [1999] 2 FLR 303. In that case it was considered that a supervision order under section 31 of the Children Act 1989 should be made only if the children were in need of greater protection than could be given by agreement with the parents working in partnership with the local authority. In *Re O (Care or Supervision Order)* [1996] 1 FLR 755, in considering what the appropriate order was in the circumstances, and applying the no order principle with the requirement that the court should consider the alternatives, Hale J (as she then was) said:

"It must be right to approach the question of the children's interest from the point of view which is exemplified by s 1(5) of the Act, that when considering whether to make any order under this Act the court is not to make an order unless it considers that doing so would be better for the child than making no order at all, and by s 1(3)(g) where it is required to consider the range of powers available under the Act in the proceedings in question. It is accepted by all the parties before this court that the court should begin with a preference for the less interventionist rather than the more interventionist approach. This should be considered to be in the better interests of the children, again unless there are cogent reasons to the contrary".

In *Re O (Supervision Order)* [2001] EWCA Civ 16, [2001] 1 FLR 923, the judge rejected the parent's submission for no order to be made and the local authority's application for a care order. Instead, he made a supervision order because he did not consider that the circumstances would deteriorate so drastically that the local authority would need to remove the children without going to court. The local authority's appeal was dismissed, on the basis (among others) that in the context of the Human Rights Act 1998 proportionality was the key and that:

"where a supervision order is proportionate as a response to the risk presented, a supervision order can be made to work, as indeed the framers of the Children Act 1989 always hoped that it would be made to work".

This "no order" principle complements the requirement that the court and the adoption agency should consider the wide range of options available as an alternative to adoption, and further complements the welfare test.

11. Range of Powers

Section 1(6) of the Adoption and Children Act 2002 requires the court and the adoption agency to consider the whole range of powers available in the child's case, whether under the 2002 Act or the Children Act 1989. The powers or orders which the court should consider on an application for an adoption order, starting from the least interventionist, include:

    (a) applying the "no order principle" and making no order;

    (b) in an application for adoption by a step-parent, granting parental responsibility;

    (c) granting a residence order;

    (d) granting a residence order with a contact or specific issue order, such as a change of name;

    (e) granting a residence order with a restriction under section 91(14) of the 1989 Act to prevent repeated applications;

    (f) granting a special guardianship order, with or without contact;

    (g) granting an adoption order.

Going through each of these options, the court and the adoption agency must weigh up and balance all the factors, and arrive at a decision which is in the interests of the child.

Chapter 10

Effects of an Adoption Order

1. Introduction

The effects of an adoption order are dealt with in Part I, Chapter 4 (sections 66 to 76) of the Adoption and Children Act 2002. Section 66(1) provides that "adoption" means:

    (a) adoption by an adoption order, or a Scottish or Northern Irish adoption order;

    (b) adoption by an order made in the Isle of Man or any of the Channel Islands;

    (c) a Convention adoption (see Chapter 23);

    (d) an overseas adoption (see Chapter 21);

    (e) an adoption recognised by the law of England and Wales and effected under the law of another country.

References to an adopted person include a person adopted within the meaning of Part 4 of the Adoption Act 1976, i.e., section 38 of that Act.

The difference between the definition above and that contained in section 38 of the Adoption Act 1976 is that section 66 extends the meaning to include a "Convention adoption", that is, an adoption effected under the law of a Hague Convention country and certified in pursuance of article 23(1) of the Convention. References to "adoption" in sections 66 to 76 do not, however, include an adoption effected before those sections came into force (section 66(3)).

2. Parental Rights and Duties

An adoption order is an order giving parental responsibility for a child to the adopter(s) (section 46(1) of the 2002 Act). Section 3(1) of the Children Act 1989 defines "parental responsibility" as "all the rights and duties, powers, responsibilities and authority which by law a parent of a child has in relation to the child and his property". It includes the rights, powers and duties which a guardian of the child's estate (appointed before the commencement of section 5, to act generally) would have had in relation to the child and his property. It includes, in particular, the rights of the guardian to receive or recover, in his own name, for the benefit of the child, property of whatever description and wherever situated which the child is entitled to receive and recover (Children Act 1989, section 3(2) and (3)).

Until an adoption order is made, the natural parents, and any other person who has parental responsibility for the child, retain that parental responsibility and their rights are unaffected, save as restricted by any determination made on a placement order (section 46(3)(a) and (b)).

An adoption order has the effect of extinguishing:

(a) the parental responsibility which any person other than the adopter(s) has for the adopted child immediately before the making of the adoption order;

(b) any order made under the Children Act 1989 or the Children (Northern Ireland) Order 1995 (SI 1995 No. 755, NI 2). This includes a residence order, contact order, specific issue order, prohibited steps order, parental responsibility order, guardianship order and a care or supervision order;

(c) any order under the Children (Scotland) Act 1995 other than an excepted order;

(d) any duty arising by virtue of an agreement or an order of a court to make payments, so far as the payments are in respect of the adopted child's maintenance or upbringing for any period after the making of the adoption order

(section 46(2)).

The duty to make payments for the child's maintenance is unaffected where the duty arises by virtue of an agreement:

(a) which constitutes a trust; or

(b) which expressly provides that the duty is not to be extinguished by the making of an adoption order

(section 46(4)).

The above provisions are identical to those in section 12 of the Adoption Act 1976. An adoption order thus extinguishes all previous orders made in respect of the child, and there is no need to apply for the discharge of any such order.

3. Status Conferred by Adoption

As from the date of the adoption (section 67(5)), the child's status alters as follows:

(a) an adopted person is treated in law as if born as the child of the adopter(s) (section 67(1));

(b) an adopted child is the legitimate child of the adopter(s) if adopted by a couple, or by one of a couple under section 51(2) (i.e., adopted by a person who is the partner of a parent of the child) and is to be treated as the child of the relationship of the couple in question (section 67(2));

(c) a child adopted by one of a couple is treated in law as not being the child of any person other than the adopter and the other member of the couple. In any other case he is treated in law as not being the child of any person other than the adopter(s), except where legislation refers to a person's natural parent or any other natural relationship (section 67(3));

(d) where the child is adopted by one of his or her natural parents as a sole adoptive parent, it does not affect any entitlement the child may have to property which depends on relationship to that parent, or as respects anything else depending on that relationship (section 67(4)).

These provisions apply for the interpretation of all enactments or instruments passed or made before or after the adoption, and have effect as respects things done or events occurring on or after the adoption (section 67(6)), except that these provisions do not apply to:

(a) a pre-1976 instrument or enactment insofar as it contains a disposition of property; and

(b) any public general Act in its application to any disposition of property in a pre-1976 instrument or enactment.

An instrument or enactment is a pre-1976 instrument if it was passed or made at any time before 1 January 1976. Insofar as section 69 of the 2002 Act sets out rules of interpretation for instruments concerning dispositions of property (see below), they do not apply to a pre-1976 instrument (2002 Act, schedule 4, paragraphs 17 to 19).

The adopted child thus ceases to be the child of any previous marriage, and an adoption order prevents the adopted child from being illegitimate.

4.   Adoptive Relatives

Relationships which are created by an adoption order may be referred to as "adoptive relationships"; thus an adopter may be referred to as an "adoptive father" or "adoptive mother" etc. (section 68(1)).

Where however, the adoption order has been made on the joint application of a same-sex couple or by a partner of the child's parent where the couple are of the same sex, they will be referred to as "adoptive parents" and not as adoptive mother or adoptive father (section 68(3)).

5.   Testamentary and Proprietary Rights

Rules of interpretation

Section 69 of the Adoption and Children Act 2002 sets out the rules of interpretation which are to apply to any instrument concerning the disposition of property, subject to any contrary indication (see below), and to schedule 4 to the Act.

Where a disposition depends on the date of birth of a child or children of the adoptive parent or parents, the disposition should be interpreted as if the adopted person had been born on the date of adoption; and, as regards two or more persons adopted on the same date, as if they had been born on the same date in the order of their actual births (section 69(2)). This does not affect any reference to a person's age.

The status of the adopted child pursuant to section 67(3) of the Act does not affect or prejudice any vested interest in possession in the adopted person before the adoption, nor any interest expectant (whether immediately or not) on an interest vested in possession (section 69(4)).

Where it is necessary to determine, for the purposes of a disposition of property effected by instrument, whether a woman can have a child:

    (a) it must be presumed that once a woman has attained the age of 55 years she will not adopt a person after execution of the instrument; and

    (b) if she does so, then (in spite of section 67) that person is not to be treated as her child or (if she does so as one of a couple) as the child of the other one of the couple for the purposes of the instrument (section 69(5)).

Contrary indications

An indication contrary to any of the above need not appear on the face of the instrument; it is sufficient if it appears from any surrounding circumstances which are cogent and convincing. The case of *Re Jones's Will Trusts, Jones v Squire* [1965] Ch 1124, [1965] 3 WLR 506, [1965] 2 All ER 828, perhaps best illustrates this point. In 1949 the testator made a will leaving the residue of his estate to be divided equally among his nephews and nieces, including Mrs H. On 1 September 1953 he made a codicil in which he provided that if any of his nephews and nieces predeceased him, their children, if any living at his death, were to take by substitution. Mrs H had two children who were born in 1948 and 1950. She died on 17 September 1953. On 11 November 1953 her first child was adopted. On 1 July 1959, the testator made a new will in the terms of his first will and codicil, and on 22 June 1963 he made a third will containing similar terms. He died on 3 September 1963. The issue was whether the nephew who had been adopted took under the residuary provisions of the will. Buckley J held that the words "unless the contrary indication appears" meant unless the contrary intention appears from any surrounding circumstances which carry conviction in the mind of the court. The effect of the surrounding circumstances on the mind must be cogent and convincing and the evidence must be strong. The fact that the testator's intention in the various wills remained unchanged, and that after his will in 1959 he had made reference to the adopted child as benefiting from the gift, provided strong evidence.

Property devolving with peerages etc

An adoption order does not affect the descent of any peerage or dignity or title of honour (section 71(1)). Nor does it affect the devolution of any property limited (expressly or not) to devolve (as nearly as the law permits) along with any peerage or dignity or title or honour, provided a contrary intention is not expressed in the instrument and has effect subject to the terms of the instrument. This provision is similar to that in section 44 of the Adoption Act 1976.

Trustees and personal representatives

Before conveying or distributing any property, a trustee or personal representative is not under a duty, by virtue of the law relating to trusts or the administration of estates, to enquire whether any adoption has been effected or revoked if that fact could affect entitlement (Adoption and Children Act 2002, section 72(1)). A trustee or personal representative is not liable to any person by reason of a conveyance or distribution of the property, made without regard to any such fact, if he has not received any notice of the fact before the conveyance or distribution. These provisions do not prejudice any right of a person affected to follow the property, or any property representing it, into the hands of a person other than a purchaser who has received it (section 72(2) and (3)).

The provisions of section 72 are in identical terms to those in section 45 of the Adoption Act 1976. The effect is to protect trustees and personal representatives who have made a conveyance or distribution in ignorance of the making or revocation of an adoption order, while leaving the rights of the aggrieved person unaffected.

Testamentary rights

Since an adopted person is to be treated as the legitimate child of his adoptive parent(s), he is in the same legal position as a biological child of his adoptive parents in all respects. A testamentary disposition made before the child was adopted by the adopters will be interpreted so as to give the adopted child inheritance rights under the disposition. Therefore, if a testator has an adopted daughter (whether adopted at the time of the will or later), a gift to his children will include her, and a gift to his grandchildren will include any children of his adopted daughter.

Any interpretation of a disposition which discriminates against an adopted child would be contrary to article 14 of the European Convention (the prohibition of discrimination): *Pla and Puncernau v Andorra* (69498/01) [2004] 2 FCR 630, [2004] ECHR 334. The adopted person has the same rights of inheritance under the will or on the intestacy of his adoptive parent(s) as a natural child of the adoptive parent(s). If an adopted child is disinherited by his adoptive parent(s), he has the same right to apply for reasonable financial provision to be made for him out of the estate of the deceased, under the Inheritance (Provision for Family and Dependants) Act 1975, as if he were the natural child of the deceased adoptive parent.

6. Insurance
Where the natural parent of an adopted child effected insurance with a friendly society, a collecting society or industrial insurance company for the payment, on the death of the child, of money for funeral expenses, the rights and liabilities under the policy are transferred to the adoptive parents as if the adoptive parents had taken out the policy (Adoption and Children Act 2002, section 76). This provision is similar to that contained in section 49 of the Adoption Act 1976.

7. Entitlement to Pension
An adopted child's entitlement to a pension which is payable to or for his benefit, where the child is in receipt of the pension at the time of the adoption order, is not affected by an adoption order (Adoption and Children Act 2002 section 75). This provision is similar to that contained in section 48 of the Adoption Act 1976.

8. Prohibited Degrees of Relationship
An adopted child remains within his natural family for the purposes of the prohibited degrees of marriage and certain sexual offences within the family (Adoption and Children Act 2002, section 74). Section 74 (as amended by the Civil Partnership Act 2004, section 79(7) and the Sexual Offences Act 2003, schedule 6, paragraph 47) provides that section 67 of the Act does not apply for the purposes of a number of enactments, including the table of kindred and affinity in schedule 1 to the Marriage Act 1949 and schedule 1 to the Civil Partnership Act 2004, and section 27 of the Sexual Offences Act 2003 (familial child sex offences). Therefore, any sexual relationship between the adopted child and his natural parents, and marriage between the adopted child and the adoptive parents, are prohibited. But relationships with any member of the adoptive family who are not within the prohibited degrees of consanguinity are not prohibited. Section 67 also does not apply for the purposes of sections 64 and 65 of the Sexual Offences Act 2003 (sex with an adult relative).

The provisions of section 74 are similar to those in section 47 of the Adoption Act 1976.

9. Domicile
An adopted child acquires and retains the domicile of his adoptive parent(s)

until he attains the age of sixteen or marries under that age (Domicile and Matrimonial Proceedings Act 1973; see pages 15 to 17). This is because, under section 67(1) of the 2002 Act, he is treated as the child of the adopter(s).

10. Nationality and Immigration

A child who is not a British citizen acquires British citizenship, from the date of the adoption, if he is adopted in the UK and one of his adoptive parents is a British citizen (British Nationality Act 1981, section 1(5)). Citizenship can be acquired in this way from either the father or the mother. An adopted child who is a British citizen retains his citizenship even if adopted by a person who is of foreign nationality (British Nationality Act 1981, section 1(1)).

Adoption also confers on the adopted person the right of abode in the United Kingdom for the purposes of the Immigration Act 1971 (section 2(1)(a)).

11. State Benefits

Under section 67 of the Adoption and Children Act 2002 an adopted child is to be treated as the legitimate child of his adoptive parents; they are therefore entitled to receive any state benefits in respect of the adopted child for which they are eligible. In calculating entitlement, the adopted child's resources, if any, are taken into account and set off against the amount receivable.

12. Change of Name

Where the prospective adoptive parent(s) wish to give the adopted person a new forename, application for a change of name should be included in the adoption application (Family Procedure (Adoption) Rules 2005 (SI 2005 No. 2795), Part 5; see Chapter 25). On making the adoption order, the child assumes the surname of his adoptive parent(s), and if a change of forename has been applied for, an order to that effect will be made.

Chapter 11

Contact

1. Introduction

When parents separate, one of the issues which causes significant disagreement and difficulty is the question of contact with children, notwithstanding the fact that it is recognised that contact between a child and the non-residential parent is beneficial to the child. It is therefore not surprising that the subject of contact between an adopted child and his birth parents and extended family causes controversy. The benefit or otherwise of contact after adoption has been the subject of considerable research stretching over at least two decades. It demonstrates that "open" adoption (where the child retains contact with the birth family) can in some cases be beneficial to the child, and can strengthen the stability of the placement. Despite this, the reality is that local authority social work policy has tended not to encourage or support contact after adoption, and the legislature has been slow in formulating clear provisions to ensure that contact after adoption is promoted.

This may be because it is simpler and more cost-effective to find and prepare adopters on the assumption that there will be no contact. It may also be the result of the evolution of the law on adoption, not as a product of English common law, but as a creature of statute, devised to deal with the stigma which attached to illegitimacy, and encouraged by those who were conscious of a duty to provide a home for these children, recognise their status, protect them, and avoid their being exploited. The result was the 1926 Adoption and Children Act, which provided that the rights and duties of the natural parent would vest in and be exercisable by the adopter, as if the adopted child was the adopter's legitimate child – a total transfer of parental responsibility and a severance of all ties with the natural parent, with no room for contact between the birth parent and the child. When the Adoption Act 1976 was passed, most adopted children were adopted as babies and the idea that adoption was to give the child a completely new start in life remained.

Since then, the structure of society and its attitudes have changed radically. The majority of children who are taken into the care system are older children. Some of them, whatever their backgrounds, have formed emotional attachments and loyalties to their birth families. As the *Prime Minister's Review of Adoption,* published in July 2000, put it:

"Adoption from care is not about providing couples with trouble-free babies. It is about finding families for children of a range of ages, with challenging backgrounds and complex needs."

The recommendation of the 1992 *Review of Adoption Law* (Department of Health and Welsh Office, October 1992) was for more openness; the need to protect and preserve the child's identity, and for the court to be empowered to make a contact order on an application for an adoption order, were recognised. In the last decade, the development of human rights law has led to greater awareness of the rights of children and of the duty of the state and society to protect those rights. Despite that, the Adoption Act 1976 did not contain any specific or clear provision for contact to be considered or ordered, and therefore the courts have been prevented from taking a more robust approach to contact, even in deserving cases. This has been compounded by the fear of destabilising the placement, and perhaps putting the prospective adopters in a position to specify the terms on which they are prepared to have the child, which might well include determining whether, and if so when and where, contact might take place.

Some of the more significant provisions relating to contact, including the principles under the European Convention on Human Rights, which apply from the time a child is received or taken into care by a local authority until the child is placed for adoption, are summarised below, alongside the approach to contact after adoption under the former law, to illustrate how the Adoption and Children Act 2002 introduces more positive provisions on contact after adoption, and to preserve the child's rights. See also Chapter 16, pages 233 to 234 on the duty of adoption agencies to consider contact.

2.   The Right to Family Life

The most important provision in relation to the protection of family life is article 8 of the European Convention on Human Rights. It provides:

"1. Everyone has a right to respect for his private and family life, his home and his correspondence.

2. There shall be no interference by a public authority with the exercise of this right except such as is in accordance with the law and is necessary in a democratic society in the interests of national security, public safety or the economic well-being of the country, for the prevention of disorder or crime, for the protection of health or morals, or for the protection of the rights and freedoms of others."

Both adults and children enjoy this right, and any interference with it must fall within the specific justifications set out in article 8(2). The right to contact falls within the all-encompassing right to family life.

In numerous cases, the European Court of Human Rights has emphasised the duty of the state to take reasonable steps to enforce contact, but two recent decisions perhaps best illustrate the approach which has been taken. In *Hansen v Turkey* (36141/97) [2004] 1 FLR 142, (2004) 39 EHRR 18, the children were taken on holiday to Turkey by their father, who was Turkish. He failed to return them to their mother with whom they lived in Iceland. The mother obtained a custody order in the Icelandic courts, but the Turkish courts, after proceedings lasting six years, during which the mother was allowed to see the children only twice, granted custody to the father with contact to the mother. Despite the order, contact was denied to her and the courts failed to enforce the order effectively. The mother complained to the European Court of Human Rights for infringement of her right to family life under article 8. The court found that Turkey had violated the mother's rights in failing to take effective enforcement measures; and, in the light of the father's consistent refusal to comply with the contact order, the authorities should have taken measures, including coercive measures, against the father of a type which were likely to lead to compliance. Further, the court found that, even though the children had been exposed to immense pressure as a consequence of the media attention which the case attracted, the authorities had failed to take any steps to facilitate contact; in particular, they failed to seek advice from social services, a psychologist or child psychiatrist to facilitate the reunion of the mother with her children and to create a more co-operative atmosphere between the mother and the children.

In *Kosmopoulou v Greece* (60457/00) [2004] 1 FLR 800, the mother separated from the father, leaving the child with the father in Athens. In proceedings relating to the child, custody of the child was granted to the father and contact to the mother. On the father's application, the contact order was set aside. There followed numerous proceedings relating to whether the mother should have contact in circumstances where the court found that the mother should have contact, and that the child's reluctance to see her mother was due to the father's behaviour. When the child refused to see her mother, however, the court dismissed the mother's application, despite a psychiatrist's report recommending that contact should take place. The mother complained to the European Court of Human Rights that her article 8 rights had been violated. The court ruled:

> "It follows from the concept of family law on which Art 8 is based, that a child born of a marital union is *ipso jure* part of that relationship; hence, from the moment of the child's birth and by the very fact of it, there exists, between him or her and his or her parents a bond amounting to 'family life' which subsequent events cannot break save in exceptional circumstances."

On the issue of the state's obligation, the European Court of Human Rights reaffirmed its repeated rulings that article 8 rights include a right for parents to have measures taken with a view to the reunification of children with their parents, and an obligation upon national authorities to take such measures:

"This applies not only to cases dealing with the compulsory taking of children into public care and the implementation of care measures, but also where contact and residence disputes concerning children arise between parents and/or other members of the children's family."

While recognising that the state's obligation to take measures to facilitate reunion is not absolute, the court confirmed the obligation to take effective preparatory steps to enable reunification to take place:

"The nature and extent of such preparation will depend on the circumstances of each case, but the understanding and co-operation of all concerned is always an important ingredient. Whilst national authorities must do their utmost to facilitate such co-operation, any obligation to apply coercion in this area must be limited since the interests as well as the rights and freedoms of all concerned must be taken into account and more particularly the best interests of the child and his or her rights under Art 8 of the Convention. Where contact with a parent might appear to threaten those interests or interfere with those rights, it is for the national authorities to strike a fair balance between them."

In dealing with the child's interest, on the facts of the case, the court found that, in failing to take appropriate action despite the psychiatrist's report, the state had failed in its obligation.

By reason of article 8, therefore, there is an obligation on the public authorities and the courts to promote and take all necessary measures to facilitate contact, even where circumstances are difficult, and to take active and effective steps to enforce contact. It is only in exceptional circumstances that contact should be denied; where there is a conflict between the rights of the parents and others, and the child, a fair balance has to be struck. When making any decision, the welfare of the child throughout his life must be considered.

3. Public Law Cases

Schedule 2, paragraph 15, to the Children Act 1989 provides that where a child is being looked after by a local authority, the authority shall, unless it is not reasonably practicable or consistent with his welfare, endeavour to promote contact between the child and:

(a) his parents;

(b) any person who is not a parent of his but who has parental responsibility for him; and

(c) any relative, friend or other person connected with him.

Section 34(1) of the 1989 Act provides that where a child is in the care of a local authority, the authority shall (subject to the other provisions of the section) allow the child reasonable contact with:

(a) his parents;

(b) any guardian of his;

(c) where there was a residence order in force with respect to the child immediately before the care order was made, the person in whose favour the order was made; and

(d) where, immediately before the care order was made, a person had care of the child by virtue of an order made in the exercise of the High Court's inherent jurisdiction with respect to children, that person.

Thus there is a duty on the local authority to take all steps necessary to promote contact. It can refuse contact only under the section 34(6), namely, if it:

(a) is satisfied that it is necessary to do so in order to safeguard or promote the child's welfare; and

(b) the refusal is decided upon as a matter of urgency and does not last for more than seven days.

Both the child's position, and that of the parents or any other person who is connected to the child, are protected by the requirement that if the local authority wishes to continue to deny contact it must make an application to the court for authority to do so; the court may make such order as it considers appropriate, including an order authorising the local authority to refuse contact. Section 34(3) and (4) allow the child and any person referred to in (a) to (d) above to make an application for contact. The court is thus given a specific and clear power to regulate contact.

If the local authority applies for authorisation to deny contact and is unsuccessful, the child may apply for contact to be considered and regulated by the court. It is also open to the parent(s) and any other person affected to challenge the local authority's decision. Where there is a dispute about the nature and extent of contact, the local authority, the child, the parent(s) or other(s) affected should apply for the matter to be considered by the court.

On determining any such application, the court has the power to attach, to any order it makes, such conditions as it considers appropriate (Children Act 1989 section 34(7)). An application under section 34 may be made at the same time as the application for the care order itself, or later. Thus, if the arrangements in the care plan for contact are not adhered to by the local authority, or if, by reason of a change in circumstances, the original care plan for contact needs to be reconsidered, the matter may be revisited and the court may vary or discharge an order made under section 34 (section 34(9)). When making a full care order, the court cannot, by virtue of these provisions, retain control by providing for a general review of contact or by retaining the child's guardian to oversee contact. See *Re B (A Minor) (Care Order Review)* [1993] 1 FLR 421 and *Kent County Council v C* [1993] Fam 57, [1992] 3 WLR 808, [1993] 1 All ER 719, [1993] 1 FLR 308.

It is during the care proceedings that the public authority must undertake the groundwork to determine whether contact with the birth parents or the extended family should continue in the future. The initial decision may be made by the permanency panel which determines whether or not it is in the best interest of the child to be placed for adoption. The local authority's care plan inevitably follows any proposal by the panel for contact after adoption. It is the local authority's fostering and adoption team, and adoption agencies, who are responsible for finding prospective adopters. There is enormous pressure on them to find placements, and this will continue under the new regime. The controversy attaching to contact after adoption introduces added pressure, but the issue of contact should be dealt with in a positive way at an early stage, all concerned starting with the principle that contact should be promoted at all times, even at the adoption stage, unless the circumstances suggest otherwise.

It is not uncommon, when the care plan is for adoption, for the care plan to propose that contact should come to an end, even if a placement has not been identified. In such cases the local authority may seek an order permitting them to refuse contact under section 34(4) of the Children Act 1989 (see above). Sometimes, contact arrangements are included in the care plan but the details are left to the discretion of the local authority and no order for contact is made. The local authority may then vary, or even reduce, the level of contact. Often, when contact is reduced, the parents do not reapply for contact to be considered by the court, with the result that by the time the adoption application is made, contact has become insignificant in the process and the damage has been done.

In determining any issue of contact, the court must apply the welfare principle in section 1 of the Children Act 1989. It must also have regard to the human rights of both the child and the parents under article 8 of the European Convention on Human Rights, and the rulings of the European Court of Human Rights on reunification and refusal of contact with a child in care (see above). The cases cited above are as relevant in cases where the child is in care as they are in private disputes between warring parents. In addition, the cases mentioned below set out the obligations of the local authority in this regard.

In *K and T v Finland* (25702/94) (No 1) [2000] 2 FLR 79, [2000] 3 FCR 248, (2001) 31 EHRR 18, a mother who suffered from schizophrenia had been hospitalised several times. During her second pregnancy, her older child was voluntarily placed in care. As soon as the baby was born, the baby was removed from the care of the mother under an emergency protection order. Contact was permitted only on a supervised basis. Despite improvement in the care given to the children by their father, the children were placed with foster carers and contact was restricted. The parents complained to the European Court of Human Rights that the authorities, by not having given them any chance to care for their children and restricting contact, had interfered with their article 8 rights. The complaint was upheld. The court ruled that extraordinary and compelling reasons were needed to justify physical removal of a baby from its mother and the restriction or termination of contact between a child and its parents. The failure to take appropriate steps towards reunification of the child with its parents was also criticised.

In *KA v Finland* (27751/95) [2003] 1 FLR 696, it was held:

"As the court has reiterated time and again, the taking of a child into public care should normally be regarded as a temporary measure, to be discontinued as soon as circumstances permit, and any measures implementing such care should be consistent with the ultimate aim of reuniting the natural parent and child. The positive duty to take measures to facilitate family reunification as soon as reasonably feasible will begin to weigh on the responsible authorities with progressively increasing force as from the commencement of the period of care, subject always to it being balanced against the duty to consider the best interests of the child . . .

A greater scrutiny is called for in respect of any further limitations, such as restrictions placed by those authorities on parental rights of access. Such further limitations entail the danger that the family relations between the parents and a young child are effectively curtailed. The minimum to be expected of the authorities is to examine the situation anew from time to time to see whether there has been any improvement in the family's situation. The possibilities of reunification will be progressively diminished and eventually destroyed if the biological parents and child are not allowed to meet each other at all or only so rarely that no natural bonding between them is likely to occur."

In *Haase v Germany* (11057/02) [2004] 2 FLR 39, seven children, including a new-born baby, were removed from their parents without hearing the parents, and their parental rights were withdrawn. At a second hearing, directed by the appeal court, the district court withdrew the parents' rights and refused the parents access to the children. The European Court of Human Rights was not satisfied that there were extraordinary compelling circumstances for the authorities to take such intrusive action.

The Children Act 1989 thus protects the right of contact between a child and his parent(s) and others, and imposes a duty on the local authority to promote and facilitate contact while the child is looked after by the local authority. This is reinforced by the provisions of article 8 of the Convention and the decisions of the European Court of Human Rights. Refusal of contact can be justified only when there are exceptional and compelling reasons for such a draconian step. The issue of contact is therefore an essential element in any care proceedings, and particularly where the care plan is for adoption. Thus, where appropriate, contact should be considered in great detail by those who represent the parents and the child, and by the court. The aspects to be considered include the likely effect on the child if contact should cease, the relationship which the child has with his parents and the extended family, and the benefit to the child of any such relationship, even though these matters are not specifically referred to in the Children Act 1989. It should be remembered that the welfare checklist is not exhaustive, and the court is entitled to consider any matter which affects the child. The extent and nature of the child's relationships with others is also an important issue which the local authority is required to take into consideration when preparing the care plan.

If questions of contact are raised during the care proceedings, the local authority is put on notice of them, and must take them into account in any care plan it proposes, particularly where it is considering twin-track or concurrent planning. It must also take them into account in family-finding and assessing the suitability of prospective adopters. If a care order is made without contact having been raised and considered, it will become difficult to pursue the issue in a meaningful way in later proceedings for a placement order or an adoption order. Any agreement for contact should therefore be in clear terms, and, if necessary, incorporated into any order the court makes.

4.   Contact under the Adoption Act 1976

There was no specific provision in the 1976 Act for the court to consider or order contact. When contact was sought in adoption proceedings, the provision in section 12(6) of the Act was relied on to support the court's power to consider the application and to make an order. Section 12(6) provided that: "An adoption order may contain such terms and conditions as the court thinks fit". In making any decision relating to the adoption of the child, the court and the adoption agency were required to have regard to the "need to safeguard and promote the welfare of the child throughout his childhood". This was the first consideration among other unspecified factors, and there was a proviso that so far as practicable the wishes and feelings of the child, having regard to his age and understanding, should be given due consideration.

When the Children Act 1989 came into force, the parent(s) or other interested parties were given the right to apply for contact within the adoption proceedings. They could also seek permission to apply for an order under section 8 of the Act, which included an order for contact after the adoption order was made. These applications, however, were considered in the context of the provisions of the Adoption Act 1976. It is not surprising, therefore, that the courts, particularly when faced with the possibility that the placement might be destabilised or even break down if such an order was made, were reluctant to make contact orders, or to make an adoption order subject to any conditions, unless the prospective adopters were in agreement. The effect was to empower prospective adopters to determine issues of contact, regardless of the merits of the case. A good example is the case of *Re S (Contact: Application of Sibling)* [1999] Fam 283, [1999] 3 WLR 504, [1999] 1 All ER 648, [1998] 2 FLR 897, in which two siblings were adopted by different adopters. The girl was aged nine when she discovered that her brother, then seven, was suffering from cystic fibrosis. On finding out about her brother's condition, she became very distressed and wished to see him. The social worker approached the boy's adoptive parent to discuss the issue, but the boy's adoptive parent refused to consider any contact, and stated that the efforts made to persuade her to do so were undermining her care of the child. The girl applied for leave to have contact with her brother. The evidence in support of the application included evidence of two child psychologists that contact between the siblings would be in the interests of the children. The expert's evidence and the application were rejected, the court holding:

> "This approach is not one where the court asks what the court making the adoption order would have considered to be in the best interest of the relevant child, or children, at the time the adoption order was made if the present circumstances had then existed, but is one that recognises that the relevant adopters could not have had an adoption order on terms forced upon them and thus that the discretion and freedom of action given to them by the adoption order to safeguard and promote the welfare of the child should be respected."

In rejecting an application for contact after adoption, reliance was placed on Lord Ackner's observations in *Re C (A Minor) (Adoption Order: Conditions)* [1989] AC 1, [1988] 2 WLR 474, [1988] 1 All ER 705, [1988] 2 FLR 159:

> "No doubt the court will not, except in the most exceptional circumstances, impose terms and conditions as to access to members of the child's natural family to which the adopting parents do not agree. To do so would be to create a potentially frictional situation which would be hardly likely to safeguard or promote the welfare of the child. Where no agreement is forthcoming the court will, with very rare exceptions, have to choose between making an adoption order without terms or conditions as to access, or to refuse to make such a order and seek to safeguard access through some other machinery, such as wardship, To do otherwise would be merely inviting future and almost immediate litigation."

A similar reason for refusing the application, which was for contact limited to indirect contact by way of cards, was given in *Re D (A Minor) (Adoption Order: Conditions)* [1992] 1 FCR 461.

On the other hand, in *Re T (Adopted Children: Contact)* [1995] 2 FLR 792, an adult sibling of the adopted children had made an application for contact at the time of the adoption application. That application had then been withdrawn on the basis of an agreement that the adopters would provide annual reports on the children, and an adoption order was made. The adopters subsequently resiled from the agreement. The Court of Appeal found that the adopters' failure to comply with the terms of the agreement was a change of circumstances, as it had induced the withdrawal of the application for contact, and had formed the basis on which the adoption was granted; it could therefore be challenged. See also *Re T (Adoption: Contact Order)* [1995] 2 FLR 251, where the adopters had agreed to allow the mother some contact but no contact order was made.

Over time, the possibility of an application for contact, coupled with the statutory duties imposed on the local authority and the human rights issues, led local authorities to give some consideration to the issue of contact when seeking adoptive families. It became the norm to ensure that at least annual indirect "letter box" contact was encouraged and maintained. In other cases it was possible, with the right professional approach and through mediation, to come to an agreement, which was formally recorded by being incorporated into the adoption order by way of a preamble.

5. Contact under the Adoption and Children Act 2002

There are two separate provisions in the Adoption and Children Act 2002 on the issue of contact, one of which applies when a placement order is made, the other when an application for adoption is being considered.

When a placement order is sought

Sections 26 and 27 of the Adoption and Children Act 2002 specifically deal with the issue of contact when a placement order is being sought. Section 26 provides that when an adoption agency is authorised to place the child for adoption, or where it places for adoption a child who is less than six weeks old, any contact order made under the Children Act 1989 (i.e., an order under section 8 or 34) ceases to have effect. Subsection 26(2)(a) prohibits the making of any application for contact under the Children Act 1989 within the placement proceedings.

There are rights, however:

(1) to make an application for contact and for the court to determine such an application under section 26(2)(b) of the Act, which provides that:

"the court may make an order under this section requiring the person with whom the child lives, or is to live, to allow the child to visit or stay with the person named in the order, or for the person named in the order and the child otherwise to have contact with each other."

Section 26(3) identifies the persons who may apply for such an order.

Provisions, similar to those in section 34(4) of the Children Act, are made for the adoption agency to refuse contact, but only in the limited circumstances set out in section 27(2) of the 2002 Act. Such refusal is restricted to a period of seven days, which means that the adoption agency must bring the matter before the court for determination if it wishes the termination or restriction of contact to continue. The persons affected by the refusal are also entitled to make an application.

The provisions under the 2002 Act appear not as wide as those under section 34(1) of the Children Act 1989, which places on the local authority a duty to allow reasonable contact. However, it must be implicit that there is a duty to promote contact, as the child remains a "looked after" child and therefore the provisions of schedule 2, paragraph 15 (see page 136) apply in respect of a child who is placed for adoption. If not, it is submitted that in appropriate circumstances the provisions of article 8 of the Human Rights Convention and the decisions of the European Court of Human Rights can be relied on (see above, pages 134 to 135);

(2) under section 26(4) of the 2002 Act, for the court, on its own initiative, to make such an order when it makes a placement order, that is, even where a formal application for contact has not been made;

(3) for the court to consider the arrangements which the adoption agency has made, or proposes to make, for contact, and to invite the parties to the proceedings to comment on those arrangements. The court has a mandatory duty under section 27(4) of the Adoption and Children Act 2002 to do this;

(4) for the court to attach any conditions to the contact order under section 26 of the Adoption and Children Act 2002 as it considers appropriate (section 27(5)).

In contrast with the provisions of the Adoption Act 1976, the Adoption and Children Act 2002 thus clearly makes the issue of contact a specific factor which must be considered before a placement occurs. The court's hands are not tied by a *fait accompli,* as previously. In addition, the "no order" principle, the duty under section 1(6) to consider the range of options, the welfare principle (which specifically includes consideration of the child's relationship with the birth family, section 1(4)) at all levels and stages of the decision-making process, and the duty to consider the human rights issues, all send a clear message to local authorities, adoption agencies and the courts that the links between the child and his family, and the preservation of his identity, are to be seriously considered; only exceptionally compelling reasons can justify the drastic and draconian measure of breaking those links or abandoning the child's identity.

On making an adoption order
Section 46(6) of the Adoption and Children Act 2002 provides that, before making an adoption order, the court must consider whether there should be arrangements for allowing any person contact with the child. For that purpose the court must consider any existing or proposed arrangements and obtain any views of the parties to the proceedings. This is a mandatory provision and thus the court must not only consider the issue of contact between the child and those who are connected with the child, but must also be proactive

in inviting interested parties to make representations. This is reinforced by section 26(5) which expressly allows an interested party to make an application for a contact order under section 8 of the Children Act 1989 within the adoption proceedings, and for that application to be heard together with the application for the adoption order. The other matters discussed at page 142 above also apply here.

It is submitted that in both applications (for the adoption order and for contact):

(a) the child's welfare is paramount;

(b) both the adoption agency and the court are under a duty to apply the welfare principle;

(c) the "no order" principle applies;

(d) the duty to consider alternative options applies; and

(e) most significantly, article 8 of the European Convention is relevant, and the decisions of the European Court of Human Rights apply.

This lends force to the argument that the issue of contact should be seriously considered, and is not a matter which the prospective adopters should be permitted to dictate or control, as was the case in the past. It is up to the local authorities and adoption agencies to acknowledge this change in the concept of adoption, and to convey this information to prospective adopters in a positive light. It can best be put across in the words of Simon Brown LJ in *Re E (A Minor) (Care Order: Contact)* [1994] 1 FLR 146:

> "even when the s 31 criteria are satisfied, contact may well be of singular importance to the long-term welfare of the child: first, in giving the child the security of knowing that his parents love him and are interested in his welfare; secondly, by avoiding any damage or loss to the child in seeing himself abandoned by his parents; thirdly, by enabling the child to commit himself to the substitute family with the seal of approval of the natural parents; and fourthly, by giving the child the necessary sense of family and identity. Contact, if maintained, is capable of reinforcing and increasing the chances of success of a permanent placement, whether on a long-term fostering basis or by adoption."

Procedure

For the court in which an application for a contact order should be made, see Chapter 25, page 380. The procedure is governed by Part 5 of the Family Procedure (Adoption) Rules 2005 (SI 2005 No. 2795); see Chapter 25, page 393. Part 5 applies also to an application to vary or revoke a contact order under section 27; see page 394.

6. Summary

Sections 26, 27 and 46(6) of the Adoption and Children Act 2002 make important changes on the question of contact between the child and his birth family, which is of particular significance in relation to older children. The intention is to ensure that the issue is actively addressed and not sidelined.

Protective measures under domestic statute law, and the decisions of the European Court of Human Rights on contact and article 8 of the European Convention, are sufficient to make all those concerned in making decisions relating to children aware that contact needs to be considered positively and seriously; the principle must be in favour of contact. If that is not understood and put into effect, then it may require a dramatic change in the thinking of the courts, and robust decisions and clear directions by the judiciary, to ensure that public bodies and prospective adopters do not hold the court and other interested parties to ransom and defeat the purpose of the legislation.

It is also important that those who represent parents, other interested parties and the children themselves, should not be complacent. They should tackle the issue of contact at every stage of the decision-making process from the first step taken by the local authority, which can be interpreted as interference with parental rights and infringement of article 8 rights, through the proceedings for a care order, placement order and adoption order. Each case must be considered on its own facts. There may still be cases where contact, other than indirect "letter box" contact, despite everything that has been said in this chapter, may not be in the child's best interest.

Chapter 12

Amendment, Revocation, Cancellation and Setting Aside of an Adoption Order

1. Amendment

Schedule 1, paragraph 4(1) and (2), to the Adoption and Children Act 2002 provides for the amendment of an adoption order. There are two specific situations in which an order may be amended. The court which made an adoption order may, on the application of the adopter or the adopted person, amend the order:

(a) by the correction of any error in the particulars contained in the order; or

(b) if satisfied that, within the period of one year beginning with the date of the order, any new name:

  (i) has been given to the adopted person (whether in baptism or otherwise), or

  (ii) has been taken by the adopted person,

  either in place of or in addition to a name specified in the particulars required to be entered in the adopted children register in pursuance of the order, by substituting or, as the case may be, adding that name in those particulars.

The adopter(s) or the adopted person are the only persons who can apply.

An application for the amendment of an adoption order may be made using the procedure in Part 9 of the Family Procedure (Adoption) Rules 2005 (SI 2005 No. 1795), unless any practice direction requires that this procedure is not be used (rule 86(3)(b)). The relevant practice direction should be consulted for any further requirements relating to the procedure; the text below is subject to any such requirements. The application may be made without notice in the first instance, although the court may require notice of the application to be served on such person(s) as it thinks fit. The respondents to the proceedings will be those who were parties to the adoption proceedings (rule 86(4)(a)). The applicant must file an application notice unless:

(a) a practice direction permits the application to be made without filing an application notice; or

(b) the court dispenses with the requirement for an application notice (rule 87).

The application notice must state what order the applicant is seeking and briefly why the order is being sought.

The application notice must be accompanied by any written evidence in support of the application. If the application notice contains sufficient information in support of the application, provided it is verified by a statement of truth, the applicant may rely on the matters set out in the application notice (rules 90(2) and 91(2)). It is always good practice to provide a draft of the order which is sought.

The court will undertake service of all relevant documents with a notice of the date, time and place where the application will be heard (rule 91(1)). The court has powers to dispose of the application without notice being served but if it does, the order must contain a statement that the parties have a right to make an application to set aside or vary the order within seven days of service of the order on the person making the application (rules 93 and 94). In such a case the notice of the application, the supporting evidence and the order made should be served on the respondents, unless the court directs otherwise (rule 93(2)). The court may also abridge time for service or direct, in the circumstance of the case, that sufficient notice has been given and hear the application. The court may also deal with the application without a hearing where the terms of the order sought are agreed, or the parties agree that the court should dispose of the application without a hearing, or the court does not consider that a hearing would be appropriate (rule 92).

The notice must be served on each of the respondents to the application, unless a practice direction or the court permits otherwise.

Where the court amends the adoption order, the court must send the Registrar General a notice specifying the amendments, and must give sufficient particulars of the order to enable the Registrar General to identify the case (schedule 1, paragraph 4(3), Adoption and Children Act 2002). The Registrar General must amend the entry in the adopted children register accordingly. See Chapter 13 for the adopted children register.

Where an adoption order has been amended, any certified copy of the relevant entry in the adopted children register must be a copy of the entry as amended, without the reproduction of any note or marking relating to the amendment. A copy or extract of an entry in any register or record is deemed to be an accurate copy if, and only if, the marking and the cancellation have been omitted from it (schedule 1, paragraph 4(7) and (8)).

2. Revocation

The Adoption and Children Act 2002, section 55 and schedule 1, paragraph 4(3) and (4), provide for the revocation of a direction in an adoption order, or of an adoption order.

The court which made an adoption order may revoke a direction for the marking of an entry in the registers of live-births, the adopted children register or other records included in the order. It may do so on the application of any person concerned, but only if it is satisfied that the direction was wrongly included in the order (schedule 1, paragraph 4(3)).

Where a person adopted by his father or mother alone has subsequently become a legitimated person by the marriage of his parents, the court which made the adoption order may, on the application of any of the parties concerned, revoke the order (section 55(1)). This is the only case when revocation of an adoption order is permitted. If a child is adopted by one of his natural parents and his or her partner, and they then separate, the adoption order may not be revoked. Likewise, in the case of an adoption by a step-parent, the adoption order may not be revoked if the parties divorce.

An application for the revocation of an adoption order under the above provisions may be made by any person who is affected by it.

An application for the revocation of a direction to the Registrar General, or for the revocation of an adoption order, may be made without notice in the first instance, although the court may require notice of the application to be served on such person(s) as it thinks fit (rule 93; see above). The procedure under part 9 of the Family Procedure (Adoption) Rules (above) applies, unless a practice direction provides otherwise.

For the procedure for an application under section 55, see Chapter 25, page 419.

Where the application is granted, the court must send the Registrar General a notice informing him of the revocation and giving sufficient particulars of the order to enable the Registrar General to identify the case (schedule 1, paragraph 4(4) and rule 112(1)(b)(iii) of the Family Procedure (Adoption) Rules 2005). The Registrar General must cause the marking of the entry in the registers of live-births, the adopted children register or other records to be cancelled (paragraph 4(5)).

3. Cancellation

Where an adoption order is quashed, or an appeal against an adoption order is allowed, the court must give directions to the Registrar General to secure that any entry in the adopted children register and any marking of an entry in that Register, the registers of live-births or other records as the case may be, in pursuance of the order is cancelled (schedule 1, paragraph 4(6)). In the case of cancellation on legitimation, the court must communicate the revocation to the Registrar General (rule 112(1)(b)(iii), Family Procedure (Adoption) Rules 2005), who must then cancel or secure the cancellation of the entry in the adopted children register relating to the adopted person, and the marking with the word 'Adopted' of any entry relating to the adopted person in the registers of live-births or other records.

A copy or extract of an entry in any register or other record, being an entry the marking of which has been cancelled, will not be treated as an accurate copy unless both the marking and the cancellation are omitted from it (schedule 1, paragraphs 4(8) and 6(3)).

4. Setting Aside

Except where a child is legitimated by the subsequent marriage of his parents (section 55(1)) an adoption order is irrevocable. An adoption order which is good on the face of it, but which was made in favour of two persons to a void marriage, remains a valid order until it is set aside. In *Re Skinner (An Infant) Skinner v Carter* [1948] Ch 387, [1948] 1 All ER 917, the mother of a child married in 1941 and a step-parent adoption order was made in the couple's favour in 1942. In 1947 the step-father was convicted of bigamy and served a term of imprisonment. On his release, the mother applied for maintenance for the child. Her application was granted. The father appealed on the ground that the marriage which formed the basis of the adoption order was void. The court held that the adoption order remained valid.

It is not clear whether an adoption order which the court was induced to make without jurisdiction can be set aside by judicial review or an appeal (see the judgment of Simon Brown LJ in *Re B (Adoption: Jurisdiction to Set Aside)* [1995] Fam 239, [1995] 3 WLR 40, [1995] 3 All ER 333, [1995] 2 FLR 1). In *Re Skinner,* Lord Green MR said:

> "This adoption order is not like a judgment for damages or anything of that kind. Status is a serious and important thing and it might very well be thought to be more consistent with public policy that once status is purported to be changed, changed it should remain."

This decision was confirmed in *Re F (Infants) (Adoption Order: Validity)* [1977] Fam 165, [1977] 2 WLR 488, [1977] 2 All ER 777, where the facts were not dissimilar, except that the step-father obtained a divorce from his former wife, and the parties had their marriage annulled and then remarried. They applied for a declaration as to the status and effect of the adoption orders. The county court judge concluded that he did not have jurisdiction to hear the matter. The couple appealed to the Court of Appeal and asked for the adoption orders to be set aside. It was held that the court was not obliged as a matter of law to set aside the orders. The orders remained valid. The court considered that the application was misconceived and, in the interests of justice, declined to exercise its discretion and set aside the orders.

Adoption orders have, however, been set aside in exceptional circumstances, for example where there has been a mistake, fraud or an irregularity. In *Re F (R) (An Infant)* [1970] 1 QB 385, [1969] 3 WLR 853, [1969] 3 All ER 1101, the mother was not notified of the adoption proceedings. When she discovered that her child had been adopted, she appealed and applied for the order to be set aside. Salmon LJ said "I think that this court has an inherent jurisdiction to set aside the adoption order and remit the case for reconsideration". Karminski LJ said:

"It would be, in my view, wholly wrong to say that in a case of this kind where we are dealing with an infant, this court has no jurisdiction to correct a mishap – I do not say error – of the kind that has happened here."

In *Re M (Minors) (Adoption)* [1991] 1 FLR 458, two children were adopted by their mother and step-father with the consent of the natural father, who was not aware that his former wife was terminally ill. The mother died within three months of the adoption order. The children expressed a wish to live with their natural father. Two years later, the natural father's application for permission to appeal out of time, and to appeal against the order, was granted. The order was set aside on the ground of mistake.

In *Re B (Adoption: Jurisdiction To Set Aside)* [1995] Fam 239, [1995] 3 WLR 40, [1995] 3 All ER 333, [1995] 2 FLR 1, it was held that the facts of *Re M* were exceptional and the court had specifically stated that the decision was not to be taken as being a precedent.

In *Re K (Adoption and Wardship)* [1997] 2 FLR 221, a Bosnian child was found and taken to an orphanage. Journalists wished to bring her to England for treatment. The Bosnian government granted permission for the child to leave the country and appointed a guardian. An English couple agreed to foster her. The child was treated and returned to the couple, who applied to adopt her. By then, adoption of Bosnian children had been stopped. In addition, the child's grandfather and an aunt had been located and wanted the child returned to them. A guardian *ad litem* was not appointed in the adoption proceedings, but directions were given to notify the Bosnian guardian of the proceedings. The guardian failed to respond. An adoption order was made. The Bosnian guardian and the grandfather of the child appealed, and applied for the order to be set aside. The appeal was allowed because of a number of serious irregularities in the proceedings which led to the denial of justice. The Bosnian guardian had not been joined as a party; a guardian *ad litem* for the child had not been appointed; the Home Office had not been served with the proceedings; there was no firm evidence that the child's parents were dead; and the case had not been transferred to the High Court. These irregularities were sufficiently serious to amount to a denial of justice to the child's family and her guardian. Further inquires revealed that the foster parents had not acted in good faith. However, while accepting the couple's appalling behaviour towards the child, because the child had formed attachments to the English couple, the child was made a ward of court, and care and control was granted to the couple with conditions attached.

In *Re B (Adoption: Jurisdiction To Set Aside)* (above), the applicant was the adopted person. His father was a Muslim; his mother a Catholic. The parents never married. The mother placed the child for adoption and he was adopted by an orthodox Jewish couple who believed that the child was of

Jewish parentage; they brought him up as a Jew. The applicant was not permitted to settle in Israel. He traced his father but could not live in Kuwait. He applied to have the adoption order set aside. His application was dismissed. He appealed. His appeal was dismissed. The court held that there was no statutory provision which allowed for the revocation of an adoption order save where there were exceptional circumstances. Swinton Thomas LJ said:

> "An adoption order has a quite different standing to almost every other order made by a court. It provides the status of the adopted child and the adoptive parents. The effect of an adoption order is to extinguish any parental responsibility of the natural parents. Once an adoption order has been made, the adoptive parents stand to one another and the child in precisely the same relationship as if they were his legitimate parents, and the child stands in the same relationship to them as to legitimate parents. Once an adoption order has been made the adopted child ceases to be the child of his previous parent and becomes the child for all purposes of the adopters as though he were their legitimate child."

And:

> "There is no case which has been brought to our attention in which it has been held that the court has an inherent power to set aside an adoption order by reason of a misapprehension or mistake. To allow considerations such as those put forward in this case to invalidate an otherwise properly made adoption order would, in my view, undermine the whole basis on which adoption orders are made, namely that they are final and for life as regards the adopters, the natural parents, and the child . . . It would gravely damage the life-long commitment of adopters to their adoptive children if there is a possibility of the child, or indeed the parents subsequently challenging the validity of the order. I am satisfied that there is no inherent power in the courts in circumstances such as arise in this case to set aside an adoption order."

The cases where the orders had been set aside were distinguished on the ground of a denial of justice. In relation to them (see above) Swinton Thomas said:

> ". . . It is fundamental to the making of an adoption order that the natural parent should be informed of the application so that she can give or withhold her consent. If she has no knowledge at all of the application then, obviously, a fundamental injustice is perpetrated. I would prefer myself to regard those cases not as cases where the order has been set aside by reason of procedural irregularity, although that has certainly occurred, but as cases where natural justice has been denied because the natural parent, who may wish to challenge the adoption, has never been told that it is going to happen."

5. Summary

1. An adoption order may be amended or cancelled if the circumstances come within the provisions of schedule 1, paragraph 4.
2. An adoption order may be revoked only if it comes within the specific provisions of section 55(1) of the Adoption and Children Act 2002 (i.e., on legitimation).
3. An adoption order may be set aside only if there are exceptional circumstances which amount to a serious and significant irregularity and/or a denial of justice.

Chapter 13

The Registers

1. Introduction

The obligation of the Registrar General to maintain a register of adopted children was first introduced in the Adoption and Children Act 1926 and has been re-enacted in subsequent legislation. Under section 50 of the Adoption Act 1976, the Registrar General was required to maintain, at the General Register Office, an adopted children register, and an index to that register. The register could be searched, and certified copies of any entry in the register could be obtained. The Registrar General was not permitted to furnish any person with any information contained in, or with any copy or extract from, any such register, except in accordance with section 51 of the Act or under an order of court. Section 51 provided the machinery whereby an adopted person might apply to the Registrar General for particulars to enable him to obtain a copy of his birth certificate, provided he was eighteen years of age.

The question whether the adopted person's right to such information was absolute or subject to public policy considerations was addressed by the Divisional Court in *R v Registrar General ex parte Smith* [1991] 2 QB 393, [1991] 2 WLR 782, [1991] 2 All ER 88, [1991] 1 FLR 255. The applicant was an adult who had been adopted but had expressed extreme hatred for his adoptive parents. He was convicted of murder and was sentenced to life imprisonment. While in prison he strangled an inmate, believing him to be his adoptive mother. He was diagnosed as suffering from a mental disorder. He applied under section 51(1) for disclosure of his birth records. The registrar was concerned about the safety of the natural mother if the information was disclosed to the applicant. The applicant applied for judicial review. It was held that the applicant was entitled to the information, subject to the right to refuse to supply it on the ground of public policy where, on the evidence, there was a real risk of a serious crime being committed or serious danger to a member of the public. The application was refused.

In *Re H (Adoption: Disclosure of Information)* [1995] 1 FLR 236, the court was concerned with three issues:

(a) the practice to be established on an application by an individual or organisation for disclosure of information;

(b) how the court's discretion was to be exercised;

(c) the procedure to be followed.

The court held that the burden on the applicant was no more than the ordinary burden to show cause, by establishing a case of sufficient weight and justification to persuade the judge of the reasonableness of the order and that it was inappropriate for the application to be made without notice to the Registrar General. In *Re D v Registrar General* [1997] 2 WLR 739, [1997] 1 FLR 715, Sir Stephen Brown P said that the court, in the exercise of its discretion, should order disclosure only in exceptional circumstances, and that an exceptional need to know the information must be established. Curiosity on the part of the parent was not sufficient justification for the disclosure.

President's Direction of 17 December 1998, *Adopted Children Register: Restriction on Disclosure,* [1999] 1 FLR 35, provided that in adoption proceedings, where it is feared that the security of a placement may be put at risk if information relating to the child in the adopted children register is open to inspection, the High Court may restrict disclosure. In an appropriate case, an order may be made under the court's inherent jurisdiction directing that, during the minority of the child, the Registrar General shall not disclose the details of the adoption entered in the adopted children register to any person without leave of the court.

An application for such an order should be made to the High Court. If the application is issued in the county court, it should be transferred to the High Court for determination; if the application is made before the adoption order has been made, the adoption proceedings should also be transferred. Pursuant to section 100(3) of the Children Act 1989, a local authority is required to obtain leave to make such an application.

2. The Adopted Children Register

Sections 77 to 82 of the Adoption and Children Act 2002 (as amended by section 79(8) and (9) of the Civil Partnership Act 2004), schedules 1 and 2 to the Act, and the Adopted Children and Adoption Contact Registers Regulations 2005 (SI 2005 No. 924) ("the Registers Regulations", which have been corrected and reprinted) set out the provisions relating to the registration of adoptions under the 2002 Act. The Forms of Adoption Entry Regulations 1975 (SI 1975 No. 1959) continue to apply in relation to an adoption order made before 30 December 2005. The Registration of Foreign Adoption Regulations 2003 (SI 2003 No. 1255) continue to apply in relation to an adoption order made or adoption effected before 30 December 2005 where an application has been made pursuant to schedule 1, paragraph 3(1) to the Adoption Act 1976 (registration of foreign adoptions).

Role of the Registrar General

Under the Adoption and Children Act 2002, the Registrar General must continue to maintain in the General Register Office a register, called the adopted children register (section 77(1)) and an index of it (section 78(1)). Schedule 1, paragraph 1, requires every adoption order to contain a direction to the Registrar General to make an entry in the adopted children register in the form set out in schedule 1 (England) or 2 (Wales) to the Registers Regulations. This gives details of the date, place and country of birth (or registration district) of the child. It also sets out the name, surname and sex of the child, and details of the adoptive parents and the date the adoption order was made or the adoption effected.

The adopted children register is not open to public inspection or search (section 77(2)). However, any person may search the *index* and obtain a certified copy of any entry in the adopted children register (section 78(2)). This right is subject to the terms, conditions and regulations as to payment of fees and otherwise, applicable under the Births and Deaths Registration Act 1953 and the Registration Service Act 1953, in respect of searches in the index, certified copies of entries in the registers of live-births and the supply of certified copies of entries (section 78(4)). Further, a person is not entitled to have a certified copy of an entry in the adopted children register relating to an adopted person who has not attained the age of eighteen years unless the applicant provides the Registrar General with the particulars set out in regulation 10 of the Registers Regulations. Those particulars are:

(a) the full name of the adopted person;

(b) the date of birth of the adopted person; and

(c) the full names of the adoptive parent or parents.

The Registrar General is also required to make traceable the connection between any entry in the registers of live-births or other records which has been marked "Adopted", and any corresponding entry in the adopted children register (section 79(1)). This ensures that the adopted person is able to trace and obtain access to his birth certificate. For the marking of records with the word "Adopted", see below, pages 158 and 161.

The Act provides three separate procedures for the disclosure of information by the Registrar General:

(a) Under section 79(4), where a person was adopted before sections 56 to 65 of the 2002 Act (the provisions on disclosure of information relating to a person's adoption) came into force, the court may, in exceptional circumstances, order the Registrar General to give information to a person (the adopted person). The information which may be ordered to be disclosed is that kept pursuant to section 79(1) (above), and any other information which would enable an adopted person to obtain a certified copy of the record of his birth (section 79(3)). The provisions of schedule 2 to the Adoption and Children Act 2002 (see below) apply to this category of applicant.

(b) Under section 79(5), on an application for the like information made in writing (Registers Regulations, regulation 11) by the appropriate adoption agency. The Registrar General is under a duty to provide the information relating to an adopted person whose record is kept by the Registrar General to the adoption agency. This differs from the position under the former law where an adopted person could himself apply directly to the registrar. The appropriate agency is:

(i) if the person was placed for adoption by an adoption agency, that agency, or (if different) the agency which keeps the information in relation to the person's adoption,

(ii) in any other case, the local authority to which notice of intention to adopt was given (section 65).

For the procedure to assist an adopted person in tracing the appropriate adoption agency, see below.

(c) Under section 79(7) (as amended by section 79 of the Civil Partnership Act 2004), an adopted person who is under eighteen years of age and intends to marry or form a civil partnership, and whose record of birth is kept by the Registrar General, may apply for information. The application by the adopted person must be made in writing and signed by the adopted person (Registers Regulations 2005, regulation 13). The Registrar General is under a duty to inform the applicant whether or not it appears from the information contained in the register of live-births or other records that the applicant and the intended spouse or civil partner may be within the prohibited degrees of relationship for the purposes of the Marriage Act 1949.

A fee may be payable before the information is disclosed (section 79(8)).

In addition, pursuant to the Disclosure of Adoption Information (Post-Commencement Adoptions) Regulations 2005 (SI 2005 No. 888) regulation 20, the Registrar General is required to:

(a) disclose to any person (including an adopted person), at his request, any information which the person requires to assist him to make contact with the appropriate adoption agency; and

(b) disclose to the appropriate agency any information which the agency requires about an entry relating to the adopted person on the adoption contact register.

The appropriate adoption agency must pay any fee that the Registrar General determines is reasonable for the disclosure of the information (regulation 20(2)).

Disclosure to a person adopted before the 2002 Act

A person adopted before the commencement of sections 56 to 65 of the 2002 Act may apply for a certified copy of the record of his birth provided he has attained the age of eighteen years. The application must be made to the

Registrar General, in writing, by the adopted person and signed by him. The Registrar General is under a duty to give the applicant any information necessary to enable the applicant to obtain a certified copy of the record of his birth, subject to the following.

(a) Before giving any information to the applicant the Registrar General must inform the applicant that counselling services are available, and identify where such services may be obtained. Counselling services are available from a registered adoption society; or an organisation within section 144(3)(b) of the Adoption and Children Act 2002; or an adoption society registered under article 4 of the Adoption (Northern Ireland) Order 1987 (SI 1987 No. 2203 NI 22). If the applicant is in England and Wales, the services are available at the General Register Office or from any local authority or registered adoption support agency. If the applicant is in Scotland, counselling services are available from any council constituted under section 2 of the Local Government etc (Scotland) Act 1994; and, in the case of Northern Ireland, from any Board (2002 Act, schedule 2, paragraph 2(1)).

(b) If the applicant chooses to receive counselling from a person or body whose details are provided to the applicant by the Registrar General, the Registrar General must send to the person or body chosen by the applicant the information to which the applicant is entitled (schedule 2, paragraph 2(4)).

(c) Where the adopted person seeking the information was adopted before 12 November 1975, the Registrar General must not give information to the applicant unless the applicant has attended an interview with a counsellor arranged by a person or body from whom counselling services are available as set out above.

(d) Where the Registrar General is prevented by reason of (c) above from giving information to a person who is not living in the United Kingdom, the Registrar General may give the information to any body which the Registrar General is satisfied is suitable to provide counselling to the adopted person, and which has notified the Registrar General that it is prepared to provide such counselling (schedule 2 paragraph 4(2)).

To obtain information relating to the connection between any entry in the registers of live-births with any other record which has been marked "Adopted" and any corresponding entry in the adopted children register, the adopted person must apply to the court. The court will permit disclosure only in exceptional circumstances. It should be noted that the adopted person does not need to go through an adoption agency, but can make the application directly to the court. If the application is granted, the Registrar General is obliged to pass on the information to the adopted person directly.

Further, section 98 of the Adoption and Children Act 2002 now provides the framework for a service for persons who were adopted before 30 December 2005, and the birth families of such persons, to obtain information about each other and to facilitate contact between them. These provisions are in addition to those described above, and are considered in Chapter 15.

Disclosure to a person adopted after the 2002 Act
A person adopted after the coming into force of the 2002 Act who wishes to trace the connection between any entry in the register of live-births or other records which has been marked "Adopted", and any corresponding entry in the adopted children register, must apply through the appropriate adoption agency.

Section 60(2) provides that an adopted person has the right, at his request, to receive information which would enable him to obtain a certified copy of the record of his birth, only via an adoption agency and not directly from the Registrar General. The Disclosure of Adoption Information (Post-Commencement Adoptions) Regulations 2005 (above), regulation 19, imposes a duty on the adoption agency, if it does not have the information, to seek it from the Registrar General. When applying for the information the adoption agency must make the application in writing and provide the Registrar General with:

(a) the name, date of birth and country of birth of the adopted person;

(b) the name of the adoptive father and mother; and

(c) the date of the adoption order.

There is, however, an exception to this right, in that the High Court may order that the information is not disclosed. The High Court may make such an order on an application by the appropriate agency if it is satisfied that the circumstances are exceptional (section 60(2)(a) and (3); and see *R v Registrar General ex parte Smith*, above.

On the disclosure of information relating to adoptions, see also Chapter 14.

3. The Registration of Adoption Orders
Paragraph 1(1) of schedule 1 to the Adoption and Children Act 2002 provides that every adoption order must contain a direction to the Registrar General to make an entry in the adopted children register. The entry must take the form prescribed by the Registers Regulations 2002, regulation 2(1), and set out in schedule 1 if the order is made in England, and in schedule 2 if the order is made by a court in Wales. The adoption order must also contain a direction to secure that the entry in the register of live-births or record in question is marked with the word "Adopted". Where the adoption order relates to a child who has been previously adopted, the order must contain a direction to the Registrar to mark the previous entry in the adopted children register with word "Re-adopted" (schedule 1, paragraph 1(2) and (3)).

A copy of the adoption order, any Convention order and any order authorising a proposed foreign adoption must be sent by the court to the Registrar General within seven days of the making of the order. The Registrar General has a duty to comply with the direction contained in the order (schedule 1, paragraph 1(4) and rule 112 of the Family Procedure (Adoption) Rules 2005).

The following must likewise be sent to the Registrar General: an order directing the correction of any errors in the particulars contained in an adoption order; an order rectifying any entry or markings in the adopted children register and the register of live-births or other records; and the cancellation of the entry on legitimation. The Registrar General must then amend any marking of an entry in the adopted children register, the register of live-births or other records. Where such an entry has been so marked, and the Registrar General is notified that the order has been quashed, or that an appeal against the order has been allowed, or that the order has been revoked, the Registrar General is under a duty to secure that the marking is cancelled (schedule 1, paragraph 2(4)).

"Records" includes certified copies kept by the Registrar General of entries in any register of births, and "register of live-births" means the registers of live-births made under the Births and Deaths Registration Act 1953 (section 82(1)).

A certified copy of an entry in the adopted children register which is sealed or stamped with the seal of the General Register Office is evidence of the adoption to which it relates (section 77(4)). Where an entry in the adopted children register contains a record of the date of birth of the adopted person, or of the country or district of his birth, a certified copy of the entry in the register is evidence of that information.

Similar provisions apply in relation to the registration of adoptions made in Scotland, Northern Ireland, The Isle of Man and the Channel Islands (schedule 1, paragraph 2).

Where the adoption order is made by a court sitting in Wales, in respect of a child born in Wales or a child who is treated as having been born in the registration district and sub-district in which that court sits, and the adopter so requests before the order is drawn up, the court must obtain a translation into Welsh of the particulars set out in the order. Within seven days of the making of the order, a copy of the order and of any translation into Welsh must be sent to the applicant (rules 111(2) and 112(5) of the Family Procedure (Adoption) Rules 2005).

4. The Registration of Convention and Overseas Adoptions

Schedule 1, paragraph 3, to the Adoption and Children Act 2002 makes provision for the registration of Convention and overseas adoptions, on application, provided the "prescribed requirement" is met. The "prescribed requirement" is that, at the time the Convention adoption or overseas adoption is effected, the adoptive parent or, in the case of a couple, both adoptive parents, are habitually resident in England or Wales (Registers Regulations, regulation 3). For Convention adoptions in general, see Chapter 23, and for overseas adoptions, Chapter 21.

The applicant(s)

The persons who are qualified to make the application for registration are:

(a) the adoptive parent or, in the case of a couple, one of the adoptive parents of the adopted child;

(b) any other person who has parental responsibility, within the meaning of section 3 of the Children Act 1989, for the adopted child;

(c) the adopted person if he has attained the age of eighteen years (Registers Regulations, regulation 4).

Form of application

The application must be in writing and signed by the person making it. It must be in the form prescribed by the Registers Regulations 2005, regulation 2(2), and set out in schedule 1 in the case of an adopted child habitually resident in England, and in schedule 2 in the case of an adopted child habitually resident in Wales. It must be accompanied by the following documents and information:

(a) in the case of a Convention adoption, a copy of the certificate sent to the adoptive parents by the relevant Central Authority in accordance with regulation 32 of the Adoptions with a Foreign Element Regulations 2005 (SI 2005 No. 392) and the date on which the adoption was effected;

(b) in the case of an overseas adoption, the evidence in accordance with article 4 of the Adoption (Designation of Overseas Adoptions) Order 1973 (SI 1973 No. 19), or an order made under section 87(1) of the Adoption and Children Act 2002 that the adoption has been effected, and the date on which the adoption was effected.

(c) particulars of the child namely:

  (i)   the child's full name on adoption and any previous names,

  (ii) the child's sex,

  (iii) the child's date of birth,

  (iv) the place and country of the child's birth,

  (v)   the full names and any previous names of the child's natural mother and father,

  (vi) the full name, any previous names, address and occupation of the adoptive parent or parents, and

  (vii) the capacity in which the person is making the application.

(d) where the documents or information are not in English or Welsh, a

translation into English of the application, signed and endorsed by
the translator with:

(i)   the name and address and occupation of the translator; and

(ii)   a statement to the effect that the translation is true and accurate

(Registers Regulations, regulation 5).

If the Registrar General is satisfied that he has sufficient particulars relating
to a child adopted under a Convention or overseas adoption to enable an entry
to be made in the adopted children register, he is under a duty to make an
entry. Further, if he is satisfied that an entry in the registers of live-births or
other records relates to the child, he must secure that the entry is marked
"Adopted", followed by the name, in brackets, of the country in which the
adoption order was made; or, in the case of an overseas adoption, secure that
the overseas registers of birth is so marked (schedule 1, paragraph 2(1) and
(2) of the 2002 Act).

5.   The Adoption Contact Register

An adoption order severs all links between the child and his birth family. The
Adoption and Children Act 1949 made it possible for a child to be placed
without the identity of the adoptive parents being disclosed to the natural
parents. This secretive process was continued in the 1976 legislation which
provided for the prospective adopters to apply for a serial number in respect
of their application so that their identity would not be disclosed. The evidence
filed in the proceedings is treated as confidential and can be disclosed only if
the court grants permission. The United Nations Convention on the Rights of
the Child recognised the right of the child to his identity, including his
nationality, name and family relations as recognised by law without unlawful
interference (article 8). The *Review of Adoption* published in 1992 referred to
the child's right to know his background and his identity, and encouraged the
idea that adopters should be open with the child about his adoptive status. It
also recognised the need to have information about the family in relation to
medical issues. The Adoption Act 1976, section 51(1), made provision for an
adopted person who had attained the age of eighteen years to obtain a
certified copy of his birth certificate. Section 51A required the Registrar
General to maintain, at the General Register Office, a two-part register called
the adoption contact register. Part 1 of the register contained information
about adopted children, and Part 2 concerned relatives of adopted persons.
The Adoption and Children Act 2002 section 80(1) requires the Registrar
General to continue to maintain the adoption contact register.

Part 1

In order to make an entry in Part 1 of the register, the adopted person must
give notice expressing his wish to make contact with his relatives.
"Relatives" includes any person who would have been related to the adopted

person, but for the adoption, by blood (including half blood), marriage or civil partnership. The notice must be in the form set out in schedule 3 to the Registers Regulations. The adopted person has a right to withdraw the notice at any time.

The Registrar General may make an entry in Part 1 only if:

(a) a record of the adopted person's birth is kept by the Registrar General;

(b) the adopted person has attained the age of eighteen years;

(c) the Registrar General is satisfied that the adopted person has such information as is necessary to enable him to obtain a certified copy of the record of his birth

(section 80(3), 2002 Act).

An entry in Part 1 must contain the full name, address and date of birth of the adopted person together with the following information:

(a) any relative with whom the adopted person wishes to have contact together with the name of that relative if known;

(b) any relative with whom the adopted person does not wish to have contact, together with the name or that relative if known

(Registers Regulations, regulation 6(1)).

The fee payable to make the entry in Part 1 of the register is £15 (Registers Regulations, regulation 9(1)).

Part 2

An entry in Part 2 of the register contains information about person(s) who have given notice expressing their wishes, as relatives of an adopted person, to make contact with the adopted person. Such a person must have attained the age of eighteen, and the Registrar General must be satisfied that the person is a relative of the adopted person and has such information as is necessary to enable him to obtain a certified copy of the record of the adopted person's birth (section 80(4) and (5)).

"Relative", for these purposes, means any person who (but for his adoption) would be related to him by blood (including half blood) or marriage or civil partnership (section 81(2) as amended by the Civil Partnership Act 2004).

The notice expressing the wish to make contact must be in the form set out in schedule 4 to the Registers Regulations (regulation 7(2)). The information required to be given is the full name, address, and date of birth of the relative of an adopted person, together with the following additional information:

(a) the name of the adopted person with whom it is sought to have contact; or

(b) the fact that the person does not wish to have contact with the named adopted person.

The fee payable on making an entry in Part 2 is £30 (Registers Regulations,

regulations 9(2)).

Under the Adoption Act 1976 the Registrar was under a duty to disclose to an adopted person the details of any relative in respect of whom there was an entry in Part 2. Section 80(6) of the Adoption and Children Act 2002 makes provision for regulations to be made for the disclosure of information to persons included in both sections of the register. Regulation 8 of the Registers Regulations requires the Registrar General to give an adopted person whose name is in Part 1 of the register, in writing, the name of any relative of the adopted person whose name appears in Part 2, and who has asked for contact with the adopted person. The Registrar General must also provide an address, at or through which the adopted person can contact the relative.

The adoption contact register is not open to the public for inspection or search (section 81(1)).

Reference should be made to the corrected and reprinted version of the Adopted Children and Adoption Contact Registers Regulations 2005 (SI 2005 No. 924).

Pre-Commencement Adoptions
For the role of the Registrar General in supplying information from the adoption contact register to an intermediary agency in respect of an adoption before 30 December 2005, see Chapter 15.

6. The Adoption and Children Act Register
On the Adoption and Children Act Register, see Chapter 16, page 229.

Chapter 14

The Disclosure of Information

1. Introduction

The adoption process is by its very nature sensitive, from the points of view of the child, the natural parent(s) and the adoptive parent(s). Since 1926 when adoption first became the subject of statute law, information relating to adoption proceedings has been treated with confidentiality. In particular, the guardian's report was treated with utmost confidentiality, and the parties in the adoption proceedings had no right to see it except in so far as the court, in its discretion, permitted disclosure. When disclosure was allowed, it was restricted to matters which were considered to weigh against the party to whom disclosure was granted, and to such parts of the report as were considered to affect the party's case. See *Re G (TJ) (An Infant)* [1963] 2 QB 73, [1963] 2 WLR 69, [1963] 1 All ER 20; *Re PA (An Infant)* [1971] 1 WLR 1530, [1971] 3 All ER 522; and *Re M (An Infant) (Adoption: Parental Consent)* [1973] 1 QB 108, [1972] 3 WLR 531, [1972] 3 All ER 321.

The Adoption Rules 1984 (SI 1984 No. 265), in rule 53(2), made inroads into this rule by providing for controlled disclosure, by way of inspection, to a party referred to in a confidential report supplied to the court by an adoption agency, a local authority, a reporting officer or a guardian *ad litem* for the purposes of the hearing. Disclosure was restricted to that part of such a report which referred to the party in question, subject to any direction given by the court. Rule 53(3) provided that the information obtained by any person in the course of or relating to any adoption proceedings should be treated as confidential, and could be disclosed only if disclosure was necessary for the exercise of that person's duties; or the information was requested by a court, public authority, the Registrar General or other person authorised in writing by the Secretary of State to obtain the information for the purposes of research.

The Adoption Agencies Regulations 1983 (SI 1983 No. 1964), regulation 15(2), permitted an adoption agency to provide access to its case records and indexes, and to disclose information in its possession, in specific instances. It also permitted disclosure for the purposes of carrying out its functions as an adoption agency, and for the purposes of authorised research on condition that the adoption agency kept a record of any access to information given, or disclosure made. These provisions were the subject of a number of cases, for example where disclosure was sought in a criminal trial or appeal. This led to the Practice Note (*Adoption: Disclosure: Attorney General*) of 14 January 1990.

The issue was raised more recently in *Gunn-Russo v Nugent Care Society* [2001] EWHC Admin 566, [2002] 1 FLR 1, where the adopted person discovered the identity of her birth mother and remained in direct contact with her until her mother died. She had also traced her half-sibling, but her father died before she could locate him. Her adoptive parents had died. She requested information from the adoption agency's files but the agency was not prepared to disclose the information, arguing that it remained confidential regardless of the passage of time or the death of the persons concerned. The Secretary of State had also been reluctant to direct the agency to disclose the information. The adopted person sought judicial review of the decision. Granting the application, the court held that the wide discretion given by the regulations had to be exercised against the background of the legislation and in the context of the circumstances of the case. The ambit of the duty of confidence depended on the nature of the obligation and the interest which it was intended to protect. Great care had to be exercised before confidential records are disclosed. A balance needed to be struck between disclosure and maintaining confidence, and in appropriate cases it was necessary to look at each document in relation to which disclosure was sought, and to consider, having regard to the passage of time, whether there was any compelling reason why the document should not be disclosed, having regard to the fact that a great many public documents are now disclosed after a lapse of thirty years.

Section 26 of the Children Act 1975 made it possible for an adopted person, on attaining the age of eighteen, to have access to his birth records. This section was replaced, as from 1 January 1988, by section 51 of the Adoption Act 1976, which provided for the adopted person to obtain such information as was necessary to enable him to obtain a certified copy of the record of his birth from the Registrar General. This section was extended by the Children Act 1989 which added section 51A to the Adoption Act 1976. Under this section the Registrar General was required to maintain a two-part register called the adoption contact register (see Chapter 13).

There were thus three avenues through which information about the adopted person could be obtained, namely the adoption agency, the court and the Registrar General.

Having regard to the sort of difficulties which resulted in cases like *D v Registrar General* [1997] 2 WLR 739, [1997] 1 FLR 715 and *R v Registrar General ex parte Smith* [1991] 2 QB 393, [1991] 2 WLR 782, [1991] 2 All ER 88, [1991] 1 FLR 255 (see Chapter 13), there was clearly a need for reform. In addition, with increasing use of the European Court of Human Rights to challenge domestic law, the rights enshrined in the European Convention and decisions of the European Court of Human Rights began to raise awareness of the need to strike a better balance between concerns about privacy and the right to disclosure in relation to adoption.

The new provisions

The Adoption and Children Act 2002, sections 54 and 56 to 65, now regulate the disclosure of information relating to an adopted person, using the adoption agency as a filter. All applications for disclosure must now be made through the appropriate adoption agency. This is the only gateway.

The provisions in sections, 54 and 56 to 65 deal with:

(a) disclosure to prospective adopters during the adoption process;

(b) information which the adoption agency is obliged to keep;

(c) restrictions on the disclosure of "protected" information;

(d) disclosure of other information;

(e) disclosure of information to adopted adults;

(f) disclosure of protected information about adults and children; and

(g) counselling.

Also under these provisions, the Register General continues to have a duty to maintain the adopted children register and the adoption contact register (see Chapter 13).

The overall legal framework is designed to provide consistency in the information kept by adoption agencies about adopted persons, birth relatives, prospective adopters and others involved in the adoption process, and in the way in which information is disclosed.

2. Disclosure to Prospective Adopters

Regulations require adoption agencies, in prescribed circumstances, to disclose, in accordance with regulations, prescribed information to prospective adopters (Adoption and Children Act 2002, section 54). These are discussed in Chapters 15 and 16.

3. Information to be Kept by Adoption Agencies

The information which an adoption agency must keep in relation to an adopted person, and the form and manner in which such information should be kept (referred to as "section 56 information") is regulated by the Disclosure of Adoption Information (Post-Commencement Adoptions) Regulations 2005 (SI 2005 No. 888) (the "Disclosure Regulations"), regulations 3 to 8.

The "section 56" information

The obligation to keep the information rests with the adoption agency which placed the adopted person for adoption, or the adoption agency to which the case records of the adopted person (or any information mentioned in regulation 4(3)) have been transferred (regulation 3) (see below).

The information required to be kept by the adoption agency is set out in Part 3 of the Adoption Agencies Regulations 2005 (SI 2005 No. 389) and the Adoption Agencies (Wales) Regulations 2005 (SI 2005 No. 1313, W. 95), and regulation 4(2) of the Adoption Agencies Regulations 1983 (SI 1983 No. 1964). Under the 2005 Regulations, regulation 12, the adoption agency must set up a case record in respect of the child and place on it:

(a) the information and reports obtained by the agency while complying with its duties under the regulations;

(b) the child's permanence report (see page 206);

(c) the written record of the proceedings of the adoption panel under regulation 18, its recommendation and the reasons for its recommendation, and any advice given by the panel to the agency (see page 208);

(d) the record of the agency's decision and any notification of that decision under regulation 19 (see page 209);

(e) any consent to placement for adoption under section 19 of the Adoption and Children Act 2002 (placing a child with parental consent, see page 61);

(f) any consent to the making of a future adoption order under section 20 of the 2002 Act (advance consent, see pages 61 to 62);

(g) any form or notice withdrawing consent under section 19 or 20 (see page 63) or 20(4)(a) or (b) of the 2002 Act (notice not to be kept informed of adoption or withdrawal of such notice);

(h) a copy of any placement order in respect of the child; and

(i) any other documents or information obtained by the agency which it considers should be included in that case record.

The equivalent regulation for Wales refers only to any information obtained and any report, recommendation or decision made by virtue of the regulations.

In addition, the adoption agency must place on the child's record documents and information which the agency obtains while carrying out its statutory duties:

(a) An adoption agency has a duty to provide counselling services for the child and to explain to the child the legal implications of adoption; where appropriate it must provide written information about these matters. It must also investigate the child's wishes and feelings regarding the adoption, the child's religious and cultural upbringing, and contact with his parent(a), guardian, relative(s) or other person(s). Any information gathered during this process must be placed on the child's records.

(b) An adoption agency must provide a similar service for the parent or guardian of the child, and information obtained from those persons must be placed in the case records.

(c) Under regulations 15 to 17 of the Adoption Agencies Regulations and the Adoption Agencies (Wales) Regulations, the adoption agency is required to obtain information about the child's physical and mental health and that of his birth parents and siblings, and the information set out in schedule 1 to the regulations, and to prepare the child's permanence report. The medical reports, the permanence report and the schedule 1 information must be placed on the child's case records.

(d) The recommendations of the adoption panel, its decision and reasons for the decision, are also relevant documents (Adoption Agencies Regulations, regulation 12).

(e) The request to CAFCASS to appoint a CAFCASS officer to witness any consent of the parent or guardian must also be placed on record.

Section 56 of the 2002 Act and the Disclosure Regulations, regulation 4(3), require the adoption agency to keep:

(a) any information that has been supplied by a natural parent or relative or other significant person in the adopted person's life with the intention that the adopted person may, should he wish, be given that information;

(b) any information supplied by the adoptive parents or other persons which is relevant to matters arising after the making of the adoption order;

(c) any information that the adopted person has requested should be kept;

(d) any information given to the adoption agency in respect of an adopted person by the Registrar General that would enable an adopted person to obtain a certified copy of the record of his birth;

(e) any information disclosed to the adoption agency about an entry relating to the adopted person on the adoption contact register;

(f) any information required to be recorded in relation to disclosure given (see regulations 10, 14 and 18, below);

(g) the record of any agreement obtained for the purposes of disclosure of protected information (see regulation 11, below); and

(h) any other identifying information (2002 Act, section 57(1)). "Identifying information" means information which, whether taken on its own or together with other information disclosed by an adoption agency, identifies the person, or enables the person to be identified (section 57(4)).

Regulation 4(4) provides, however, that the agency is not required to keep information in (a) to (c) above if it considers that:

(a) it would be prejudicial to the adopted person's welfare to do so; or

(b) it would not be reasonably practicable to keep it.

In summary, the information that the adoption agency must keep is:

(a) the matters set out in regulation 4(3), which include information obtained by the agency from the child's birth family and other significant people in the child's life, and information obtained by the agency from the Registrar General under section 79(5) (information which would enable an adopted child to obtain a certified copy of his birth certificate and information about an entry on the adoption contact register);

(b) information which, whether taken on its own or with other information, would enable a person to be identified, and which is referred to as "protected information";

(c) background information.

Storage of records

There are two sets of regulations which provide for the storage of the records concerning adopted children. The Disclosure Regulations, regulation 5, provides that the adoption agency must ensure that the section 56 information in relation to a person's adoption is at all times kept in secure conditions, and in particular that all appropriate measures are taken to prevent theft, unauthorised disclosure, damage, loss or destruction. The Adoption Agencies Regulations 2005, regulation 39 (regulation 40 of the Adoption Agencies (Wales) Regulations) makes similar provisions relating to the child's case records and the prospective adopter's case records. These requirements extend to information stored electronically. Since the information is sensitive and confidential, the implication is that it should not be transmitted by FAX or e-mail. See also pages 374 and 405 on the keeping of information.

Preservation of section 56 information

The Disclosure Regulations, regulation 6, provides that the adoption agency must keep the section 56 information in relation to a person's adoption, no matter what its format, for at least one hundred years from the date of the adoption. However, under the Adoption Agencies Regulations 2005, the adoption agency is required to keep the child's case record and the case records of the prospective adopter(s) for such period as it considers appropriate. The Disclosure Regulations were made and laid before Parliament after the Adoption Agencies Regulations, and it is submitted that it is the provisions of these regulations which must therefore apply, although it could be argued that the former provisions give the agency a discretion. See also the Adoption Support Agencies (England) and Adoption Agencies (Miscellaneous Amendments) Regulations 2005 (SI 2005 No. 2720), regulation 14(2) and the Adoption Support Agencies (Wales) Regulations 2005 (SI 2005 No. 1514, W. 118), regulation 18(2) on the keeping of records relating to adoption support services; see page 277.

Transfer of information

The provisions for the transfer of section 56 information to another adoption agency, local authority or other body are dealt with in the Disclosure Regulations and the Adoption Agencies Regulations.

Under the Disclosure Regulations, regulation 7, where a registered adoption agency intends to cease to act or exist as such, it must transfer any section 56 information it holds in relation to a person's adoption:

   (a) to another adoption agency, having first obtained the approval of the registration authority (the Commission for Social Care Inspection or, in Wales, the National Assembly) for such transfer;

   (b) to the local authority in whose area the society's principal office is situated;

   (c) in the case of a society which amalgamates with another registered adoption society to form a new registered adoption society, to the new body.

Where the activities of a registered adoption society that transfers its records to another adoption society were based principally in the area of a single local authority, it must give notice of the transfer to that authority.

When an adoption agency transfers information, it must give written notification of the transfer to the registration authority.

Under the Adoption Agencies Regulations 2005, regulation 43 (regulation 44 of the Adoption Agencies (Wales) Regulations), an adoption agency is permitted to transfer a copy of the child's case records or the case records of the prospective adopter or part of that record to another adoption agency when it considers this to be in the interests of the child or the prospective adopter. Such a situation would arise, for example, if the adoptive family moves home from one area to another. The agency must keep a written record of any such transfer.

Where an adoption agency intends to cease to act or exist, it must first obtain the registration authority's approval for the transfer of section 56 information. It must then transfer the case records to another adoption agency; or to a local authority in whose area the society's principal office was situated; or, where it amalgamates with another society, to the new body. Any adoption agency receiving the section 56 information is subject to the duties outlined above in respect of securing, storing, safeguarding and disclosing such information.

Regulation 7(2) of the Disclosure Regulations requires a registered adoption society that transfers its records to another adoption agency to give written notice of the transfer to the local authority in whose area its activities were principally based. This is to ensure that those seeking information are able to trace the source from which it may be obtained. The registration authority must in any event be informed of the transfer in writing.

4. Restrictions on Disclosure

Section 57 of the Adoption and Children Act 2002 restricts the disclosure of the following documents, referred to as "protected information", save in accordance with sections 60 to 64 and regulations made thereunder:

(a) any section 56 information kept by an adoption agency which is about an adopted person or any other person, and is or includes identifying information about the person in question. For the meaning of "identifying information" see page 168;

(b) any information received and kept by the agency following a disclosure by the Registrar General under section 79(5) (see page 156) which would enable the adopted person to obtain a certified copy of the record of his birth or an entry in the adoption contact register.

5. Permitted General Disclosure

The disclosure of information by an adoption agency, in so far as disclosure is permitted, is either discretionary or mandatory.

An "adoption agency", in relation to an adopted person or to the information relating to his adoption, and for the purposes of the provisions of section 56 to 65, is:

(a) if the person was placed for adoption by an adoption agency, that agency, or (if different) the agency which keeps the information in relation to his adoption;

(b) in any other case, the local authority to which notice of intention to adopt was given

(Adoption and Children Act 2002, section 65).

Discretionary disclosure

The adoption agency has a discretion to disclose section 56 information that is not "protected information" as it thinks fit for the purposes of carrying out its functions as an adoption agency (Disclosure Regulations, regulation 8(1)). This discretion enables the agency to share information provided by the birth family and others who may have played a significant role in the child's life with the adoptive parents and *vice versa*, subject of course to the consent of the interested parties. The information given to the birth family will include information about how the child is getting on at school and with the adoptive family, and any achievements of the child. Information passed on to the adoptive parents may include medical information relating to the birth family and other information which may assist the adoptive parents with the care of the child. Where information is shared, a written record must be kept.

The adoption agency may also disclose section 56 information, including protected information, to:

(a) a registered adoption support agency or another adoption agency which provides services to the adoption agency in connection with any of its functions under section 61 or 62 (see below) of the Adoption and Children Act 2002; or

(b) a person who is authorised in writing by the Secretary of State to obtain information for the purposes of research

(Disclosure Regulations, regulation 8(2)).

Before such information is disclosed, the agency should seek the views, on the disclosure sought, of the person to whom the information relates. It must also ensure that the agency requesting the information has the skills to conduct the work for which the information is required. It would be prudent, when providing the information, to obtain an undertaking from the agency that the information will be used for the specified purpose only.

Where the information is required for research, a similar undertaking should be obtained, with an added provision that any published report or finding should not disclose any material which could identify any person involved in an adoption.

Mandatory disclosure for purposes of inquiries etc

An adoption agency must disclose section 56 information, including protected information, to assist various authorities and departments to make decisions relating to the establishment of inquiries and investigations dealing with complaints, and in connection with an independent review of a qualifying determination (see page 220). The disclosure of section 56 information must be made to:

(a) those holding an inquiry under section 17 of the Adoption and Children Act 2002 (inquiry ordered by a Minister into any matter connected with the functions of an adoption agency), or section 81 of the Children Act 1989 (inspection of children's homes etc), for the purposes of such inquiry;

(b) the Secretary of State, for example to consider whether to hold an inquiry under section 81 of the 1989 Act;

(c) the registration authority, for example in connection with inspection of the agency's services;

(d) subject to the provisions of sections 29(7) and 32(3) of the Local Government Act 1974 (investigations and disclosure), the Commission for Local Administration in England, for the purposes of any investigation conducted in accordance with Part 3 of that Act. This relates to cases where a complaint is being investigated by a local government ombudsman, but disclosure should be limited and restricted;

(e) any person appointed by the adoption agency for the purposes of the consideration by the agency of any representations (including the investigation of complaints under the Voluntary Adoption Agencies and Adoption Agencies (Miscellaneous Amendments) Regulations

2003, SI 2003 No. 367);

(f)   a panel constituted under section 12 of the Adoption and Children Act 2002 to consider a qualifying determination in relation to the disclosure of section 56 information;

(g)   a court having power to make an order under the Adoption and Children Act 2002 or under the Children Act 1989, for example, in connection with proceedings for judicial review

(Disclosure Regulations, regulation 9).

When such disclosure is made, the adoption agency is required to make a written record, which must include:

(a)   a description of the information disclosed;

(b)   the date on which the information was disclosed;

(c)   the person to whom the disclosure was made;

(d)   the reason for the disclosure

(Disclosure Regulations, regulation 10).

The record made should be detailed and comprehensive.

Disclosure in pursuance of agreement

An adoption agency is permitted to disclose protected information in pursuance of a prescribed agreement to which the adoption agency is a party (Adoption and Children Act 2002, section 57(5)). The agreements to which this section relates are:

(a)   an agreement made between the adoption agency, and a person aged eighteen or over at the time the agreement was made, as to the disclosure of protected information about him; or

(b)   an agreement made between the adoption agency and each of the following persons as to the disclosure of protected information about them or about the adopted person:

(i)   the adoptive parent(s) of the adopted person;

(ii)   each person who, before the adoption was made, was a parent with parental responsibility for the adopted person

(Disclosure Regulations, regulation 11(1)).

Where an agreement is reached, the adoption agency is under a duty to keep a written record of the agreement. The record must also include:

(a)   the full names and signatures of the persons who are parties to the agreement;

(b)   the date on which the agreement was made;

(c)   the reasons for making the agreement;

(d)   the details of the information which it was agreed should be disclosed; and

(e)   details of any agreed restrictions on the circumstances in which the information may be disclosed

(Disclosure Regulations, regulation 11(2)).

Before entering into such an agreement, the agency should ensure that the person concerned is aware of and understands the legal implications. Where necessary, counselling should be offered to the person before the agreement is signed. Any agreement reached must be for the benefit of the child's welfare. It would be prudent to renew the terms of the agreement periodically to ensure that it remains valid.

6. Disclosure to an Adopted Adult

Under section 60 of the Adoption and Children Act 2002, an adult adopted person has a right, save in exceptional circumstances, to request and receive, from the appropriate adoption agency (for the meaning of "appropriate" adoption agency, see page 156), any information which would enable him to obtain a certified copy of any record of his birth, and certain information disclosed to the adopters by the agency.

Withholding of information

The High Court has the power, on an application made to it by an appropriate adoption agency, to prevent disclosure of such information if it is satisfied that the circumstances are exceptional (see Chapter 13, pages 154 and 158). The application by an adoption agency to withhold information must be made in accordance with the procedure in Part 10 of the Family Procedure (Adoption) Rules 2005 (SI 2005 No. 2795), rules 86(3), 97(2) and 105). The application must:

(a) state that Part 10 applies to the application;

(b) set out the question which the applicant wants the court to decide or the order which the applicant is seeking, and the legal basis for the application, including details of the exceptional circumstances to justify non-disclosure;

(c) if the application is being made under an enactment, state what that enactment is (here, section 60(3) of the 2002 Act);

(d) if the applicant is applying in a representative capacity, state that capacity; and

(e) if the respondent is to appear in a representative capacity, state that capacity

(rule 98(1)).

The respondent to the application will be the person seeking the information. The respondent should return the acknowledgment of service within fourteen days of service of the application on him (rule 100). The time limit where service is to be effected outside the jurisdiction is to be set by practice direction. A respondent who fails to return the acknowledgment of service will be permitted to attend the hearing but will not be able to take part in the hearing unless the court gives permission to do so (rule 101).

Written evidence must be filed by the parties in support of their respective cases, as provided for in rule 102 or as directed by the court. If the time limit is not adhered to, the written evidence cannot be relied upon in court unless the court gives permission. The court may require or permit a party to give oral evidence.

Agency not in possession of information sought

Where the agency does not have the relevant information sought, it must apply to the Registrar General for it on behalf of the adopted person (Disclosure Regulations, regulation 19(1)). When making the application to the Registrar General the agency must provide the name, date of birth and country of birth of the adopted person, the names of the adopted person's adoptive parents and the date of the adoption order (regulation 19(2)). On receiving the application, the Registrar General is under a duty to provide the information (regulation 20).

Information from the court

Pursuant to section 60(4), an adopted person also has a right, at his request, to receive from the court which made the adoption order a copy of the following:

    (a) the application form for the adoption order, but not the documents attached to that form;

    (b) the adoption order and any other orders relating to the adoption proceedings;

    (c) orders allowing any person contact with the child after the adoption order was made; and

    (d) any other document or order referred to in the relevant practice direction.

(Family Procedure (Adoption) Rules, rule 84).

The relevant practice direction issued pursuant to the Family Procedure (Adoption) Rules should also be consulted for further procedural requirements.

To obtain the information, the adopted person must file in the court a request for the document or order, in Form A64. When providing the information requested, the court is obliged to remove any protected information from any copy document or order disclosed (rule 84(2); see below).

This right to information is not given to a person under eighteen years of age.

The adopted person is not entitled to any reports made to the court by a CAFCASS officer, the local authority or an adoption agency, without the permission of the court. The Family Procedure (Adoption) Rules 2005 are silent on the procedure for seeking such permission, but it is expected that a practice direction may deal with the matter. The relevant practice direction pursuant to the 2005 Rules should therefore be consulted.

Pre-Commencement adoptions

Section 98 of the Adoption and Children Act 2002 now provides the framework for a service for persons who were adopted before 30 December 2005, and the birth families of such persons, to obtain information about each other and to facilitate contact between them. These provisions are in addition to those set out above, and are considered in Chapter 15.

7. Disclosure of Protected Information about Adults

Section 61 of the Adoption and Children Act 2002 deals with the disclosure of protected information about adults. "Protected information" means information which would be protected information under section 57(3) of the 2002 Act, if the agency, rather than the court, gave the information (Family Procedure (Adoption) Rules, rule 84(4)). Where a person applies to the appropriate agency for protected information and none of the information sought relates to a person who is a child at the time of the application, the adoption agency has a discretion whether or not to disclose the information. The adoption agency is required to consider the application in three stages. Firstly, the adoption agency is not required to disclose unless it considers it appropriate to do so. It must therefore consider whether or not it would be appropriate to provide the information sought. Secondly, if the agency decides that it is appropriate to disclose the information, it must, before doing so, obtain the views of the person to whom the information relates. Any objection by such a person to disclosure is a relevant consideration. Thirdly, in deciding whether or not it is appropriate to disclose the information requested, the agency must consider:

(a) the welfare of the adopted person;
(b) any views obtained from interested parties;
(c) any prescribed matters; and
(d) all the other circumstances of the case.

Thus, even if a person who is affected by the disclosure consents to its disclosure, the adoption agency may still decide to refuse the application if, having considered the factors in (a) to (d) above, it comes to the conclusion that it would not be appropriate to do so.

The section does not apply to a request for information made by an adopted person for information to enable him to obtain his birth records or information which the adoption agency is authorised to give (see *Discretionary disclosure,* above).

The application

An application to an adoption agency for disclosure of protected information must be in writing and must state the reason for the application. On receipt of the application, the adoption agency must take all reasonable steps to confirm the identity of the applicant or any person acting on his behalf, for example by the production of a passport, driving licence or birth certificate, and that any person acting on his behalf is authorised to do so. (Disclosure Regulations, regulation 13.) A person may be authorised to act for a person seeking information where that person is under a disability. Identification should be sought of both the person requesting the information, and the person who purports to act on his behalf.

8.   Disclosure of Protected Information about Children

Section 62 of the Adoption and Children Act 2002 concerns the disclosure of protected information about children. Where a person applies for disclosure of protected information which includes information about a child, the agency is not required to give that information unless it considers it appropriate to do so (section 62(2)). The procedure the agency must then follow depends on whether the person in respect of whom information is sought has or has not attained the age of eighteen.

Child under eighteen

If the request relates to a child under eighteen, then, before it decides whether or not to disclose the information, the adoption agency must take all reasonable steps to obtain:

    (a) the views of any parent or guardian of the child; and

    (b) the views of the child, if the agency considers it appropriate to do so having regard to his age and understanding and to all the other circumstances of the case

(section 62(3)).

It would also be desirable to obtain the views of the child's adoptive parent(s).

The adoption agency is required to ensure that any views obtained are recorded in writing.

In deciding whether it is appropriate to proceed with the application and disclose information relating to a child:

    (a) if the child is an adopted child, the child's welfare must be the paramount consideration;

    (b) in the case of any other child, the agency must have particular regard to the child's welfare

(section 62(6)).

The adoption agency must also consider:

    (a) the welfare of the adopted person;

    (b) any views obtained under section 62(3) and/or (4) (above – from the parent or guardian of a child, the child, and any person who has attained the age of eighteen); and

    (c) all the circumstances of the case

(section 62(7)).

Again, the adoption agency must ensure that any views obtained are recorded in writing.

Thus, the agency has a discretion whether or not to disclose the information. Even where it considers it might be appropriate to disclose information it should do so only if it is satisfied that it would be in the interest of the child. The applicant does not have a right to request a review of the decision since it concerns a child.

Person eighteen or over

Where the application for disclosure relates to a person who, at the date of the application, has attained the age of eighteen years, the adoption agency:

    (a) must take all reasonable steps to obtain the views of that person as to the disclosure of the information. The adoption agency is required to ensure that any views obtained are recorded in writing.

    (b) must have regard to:

        (i)   the welfare of the adopted person (where the person is not an adopted child),

        (ii) the views of the person to whom the request relates,

        (iii) any prescribed matters, and

        (iv) all the circumstances of the case

    (section 62(4) and (7)).

The adoption agency should disclose the information only if it considers it appropriate to do so (section 62(5)).

Any person who is affected by the determination of the adoption agency may apply for a review of that determination under section 12 of the Adoption and Children Act 2002 (see below).

The application

An application to an adoption agency for the disclosure of protected information must be in writing and must state the reason for the application. On receipt of the application, the adoption agency must take all reasonable steps to confirm the identity of the applicant, for example by the production of a passport, driving licence or birth certificate, or any person acting on his behalf, and that any person acting on his behalf is authorised to do so (Disclosure Regulations, regulation 13). A person may act for another where the person seeking the information is under a disability.

9.   Independent Review

Any person who is affected by the determination of the adoption agency may apply, under the provisions of section 12 of the Adoption and Children Act 2002, for a review of the following qualifying determinations:

    (a) not to proceed with an application from any person for disclosure of protected information;

(b) to disclose information against the express views of the person in respect of whom the information is sought;

(c) not to disclose information about a person to the applicant where that person has expressed the view that the information should be disclosed

(Disclosure Regulations, regulation 15(1)).

The adoption agency must give the applicant, where the decision is made against him, or the person to whom the protected information relates ("the relevant person") as the case may be, written notification of the determination. The notice must state the reasons for the determination and advise the relevant person that he may apply to the Secretary of State within forty working days, beginning with the date on which the notification was sent, for review of the determination by an independent review panel (regulation 15(2)).

Upon receiving such an application, the Secretary of State notifies the adoption agency that the relevant person has applied for review. Within ten days of receipt of the notification, the adoption agency must send to the Secretary of State the following documents and information:

(a) a copy of the application for disclosure of information;

(b) a copy of the notification given to the relevant person of the determination and his right to a review;

(c) the record of any views obtained by the agency under section 61(3) of the 2002 Act; and

(d) any additional information requested by the panel

(Disclosure Regulations, regulation 15(3)).

The adoption agency must not take any action on its determination before the end of the forty day period within which the relevant person has a right to apply for a review. If that person has asked for a review before the independent review panel, the adoption agency may not act on its determination until the review panel has made its recommendation (regulation 15(4)). The review panel's decision takes the form of a recommendation to the agency in respect of its decision. The agency must consider the recommendation and decide whether or not to confirm its original "qualifying decision" (regulation 15(5)).

For the purposes of the above provisions "working day" means any day other than a Saturday or Sunday, Christmas Day, Good Friday or a day which is a bank holiday within the meaning of the Banking and Financial Dealings Act 1971 (Disclosure Regulations, regulation 15(6)(b)).

10. Counselling

An adoption agency is under a duty to provide information about the availability of counselling services to persons:

(a) seeking information (for example, the adopted person or the birth family), who are affected by the issue of disclosure under the above provisions; or

(b) considering objecting or consenting to the disclosure of information by the agency (whose views have been sought under section 61(3) or 62(3) or (4)); or

(c) considering entering into an agreement with the agency to share protected information (see above, page 173).

The information provided must include information about the fees that may be charged by the person providing counselling (Disclosure Regulations, regulation 16).

When counselling is requested, the agency must itself provide counselling, or make arrangements for it to be provided by:

(a) another adoption agency or a registered adoption support agency;

(b) where the person is in Scotland, a Scottish adoption agency;

(c) if the person is in Northern Ireland, an adoption agency registered under article 4 of the Adoption (Northern Ireland) Order 1987 (SI 1987 No. 2203 NI 22) and any Board; or

(d) if the person is outside the United Kingdom, any person or body outside the United Kingdom who appears to the agency to correspond in its function to an adoption agency or an adoption support agency

(Disclosure Regulations, regulation 17).

The agency must ensure that an adoption support agency which provides counselling is registered to provide such services. It must also satisfy itself that the adoption support agency has appropriately qualified and experienced staff to provide the necessary services to meet the needs of the particular person.

Disclosure of information for counselling

An adoption agency is permitted to disclose any information, including protected information, which is required for the purposes of providing counselling to any person with whom it has made arrangements to provide counselling. It must make a written record of any such disclosure made in the person's case records (2002 Act, section 63(3) and the Disclosure Regulations, regulation 18).

11. Offence

A registered adoption society which discloses any information in contravention of section 57 of the Act is guilty of an offence and is liable on summary conviction to a fine (Disclosure Regulations, regulation 21). See also Chapter 19, page 302.

12. Summary

1. The adoption agency is the first point of call for access to information about an adoption.
2. The adoption agency is under a duty to keep a case record of all relevant information relating to the child and the adoptive parents.
3. The adopted person has a right to information which would enable him to obtain a certified copy of his birth record, unless the High Court orders otherwise.
4. The disclosure of certain information is at the discretion of the adoption agency; in respect of other information, the agency has a duty to disclose.
5. Regulations set out the factors that the agency must take into account when making its decision.
6. In some instances, a person who is aggrieved by the agency's decision has a right to request an independent review. The agency must notify the applicant of this right.
7. The agency has a duty to offer counselling and secure such counselling for all relevant persons concerned in the process of disclosure.

Chapter 15

Intermediary Services: Pre-Commencement Adoptions

1. Introduction

Section 98 of the Adoption and Children Act 2002 makes provision for regulations to be made to assist persons adopted before 30 December 2005, who have attained the age of eighteen years, to obtain information about their adoption, and to facilitate contact between them and their relatives. For these purposes, "relative" means any person who (but for his adoption) would have been related to the adopted person by blood (including half blood), marriage or civil partnership (section 98(7) as amended by section 79(10), Civil Partnership Act 2004). It also makes provision for regulations to require registered adoption support agencies, the Registrar General and adoption agencies to disclose information or restrict the disclosure of information. The section thus provides the framework for a very specific service to be provided to persons who were adopted before 30 December 2005, and the birth families of such persons, to obtain information about each other and to facilitate contact between them. The aim is to address the difficulties that would otherwise be faced by persons adopted before the coming into force of the current regime on disclosure of information; without these new provisions, such persons would have little or no information enabling them to trace persons from whom they have been separated by adoption.

The Adoption Information and Intermediary Services (Pre-Commencement Adoptions) Regulations 2005 (SI 2005 No. 890, the "Intermediary Services Regulations") and the Adoption Information and Intermediary Services (Pre-Commencement Adoptions) (Wales) Regulations 2005 (SI 2005 No. 2701, W.190, the "Intermediary Services (Wales) Regulations") identify the agencies which are to provide the services – known as "intermediary services", and to whom such services may be provided. It sets out the procedure to be adopted by both the applicant who seeks such services and the agency which provides them. This new regulatory structure enables an intermediary agency to seek information to assist an adopted adult person and his adult birth relatives to obtain information about each other, subject to obtaining the necessary consents, and to facilitate contact. An intermediary support agency is able to provide support and advice to the persons concerned. The right to request this service is additional to the right which the adopted person has, on reaching eighteen, to apply to the Registrar General for the information needed to obtain a certified copy of his birth record (see pages 156 to 158). It is also additional to the adopted person's right to apply to the appropriate adoption agency for access to his adoption records (see page 158).

2.   The Provision of Intermediary Services

Only a registered adoption support agency or an adoption agency is authorised to provide intermediary services. The adoption support agency must be registered under Part 2 of the Care Standards Act 2000 to provide intermediary services. These services are available only to adopted persons who have attained the age of eighteen and must be provided in accordance with the requirements set out in the regulations. An adoption agency which is the appropriate agency in relation to an adopted person, which provides information solely about that person's adoption, does not provide an intermediary service. If these conditions are met, the agency constitutes an adoption support service for the purposes of section 2(1) of the 2002 Act. See Intermediary Services Regulations, regulations 3 and 5(3) and Intermediary Services (Wales) Regulations, regulation 3.

3.   Services to be Provided

The services to be provided by the intermediary agency comprise:
   (a)   assisting adopted persons over eighteen, who were adopted before 30 December 2005, to obtain information in relation to their adoption; and
   (b)   facilitating contact between such person and their relatives
   (Intermediary Services Regulations and Intermediary Services (Wales) Regulations, regulation 4(1)).
The services also include securing counselling, advice and other information to such persons (Intermediary Services Regulations and Intermediary Services (Wales) Regulations, regulation 10). An intermediary agency may also assist a relative of person adopted before 30 December 2005 to contact an adopted person (Intermediary Services Regulations and Intermediary Services (Wales) Regulations, regulation 5(1)).

   Where the intermediary agency has limited capacity to deal with such applications, it is required to give priority to applications in respect of adoptions before 12 November 1975 (Intermediary Services Regulations and Intermediary Services (Wales) Regulations, regulation 5(2)). The reason for this is that the birth relatives of such a person would now be elderly, making time of the essence.

The intermediary agency should have the expertise to investigate; to gather information and assess it; and to contact, advise, prepare, support and counsel the individuals concerned. Regulation 4(2) (see above) distinguishes between the provision of an intermediary service and the function of the adoption agency to disclose information to the adopted person in relation to his adoption. The adoption agency is the first point of contact for an adopted person seeking information about his adoption and his family. The intermediary agency therefore needs to establish clearly what information is being sought by the applicant and whether the usual steps have already been taken to trace the person he wishes to contact or about whom he seeks more information.

4. Procedure on Receipt of the Application

Where an application is received by an intermediary agency from a person who was adopted before 30 December 2005 for assistance in contacting a relative, or from a relative of a person adopted before that date for assistance in contacting the adopted person, before proceeding with the application, the agency must confirm certain details. These are the identity of the applicant or any person acting on his behalf; the age of the applicant, to ensure that he is eighteen or over; and that any person acting on the applicant's behalf is authorised to do so. Where the applicant is a relative of the adopted person, the agency must confirm that the person is related to the adopted person (Intermediary Services Regulations and the Intermediary Services (Wales) Regulations, regulation 11). The applicant and the subject of the application must both be aged eighteen or over. If, during the course of the inquiry, it is discovered that the subject of the application is or may be under the age of eighteen, the application should not be proceeded with (Intermediary Services Regulations and Intermediary Services (Wales) Regulations, regulation 5).

5. Counselling

Once the identification is confirmed, counselling should be offered to the applicant. There are two specific provisions in the regulations which deal with the need to provide counselling. Regulation 10 of both the Intermediary Services Regulations 2005 and Intermediary Services (Wales) Regulations requires the agency to provide applicants with written information about the availability of counselling, the persons who offer such counselling services, and the fees that may be charged for the service.

If the person concerned asks for counselling services to be provided, the intermediary agency must secure the provision of such services for him, by providing the service itself or arranging the service to be provided by:

(a) another adoption agency or registered adoption support agency (if the person is in England or Wales);

(b) a Scottish adoption agency if the person is in Scotland;

(c) if the person is in Northern Ireland, an adoption society which is registered under article 4 of the Adoption (Northern Ireland) Order 1987 or any Health and Social Services Board established under article 16 of the Health and Personal Social Services (Northern Ireland) Order 1972 or where the functions of the Board are exercisable by a Health and Social Services Trust, that trust; or

(d) if the person is outside the United Kingdom, any person or body outside the United Kingdom who appears to the agency to correspond in its functions to a body mentioned in (a) to (c) above)

(Intermediary Services Regulations 2005 and Intermediary Services (Wales) Regulations, regulation 10(3), (4) and (5)).

The intermediary agency is also under a duty to seek any other information required to trace the subject of the inquiry, to enable that person to make an informed decision whether to consent to the disclosure sought. Regulation 12(3)(c)(iii) of both the English and the Welsh regulations requires the intermediary agency to seek information for counselling the subject and the applicant before the decision is taken by him. It must also seek information for the purposes of counselling the applicant.

These provisions clearly recognise the importance of counselling as a support service to assist the individuals concerned with the difficult feelings they will undoubtedly experience, and to help them to deal with the outcome of the inquiry and any decisions which they make. The further and perhaps more specialised services provided by the adoption support agency should also be considered in difficult cases. Before doing so, the intermediary agency must verify that the adoption support agency is registered to provide the particular service and has the expertise to do so.

6. Sources of Information

The intermediary agency has four main sources from which it may seek information: appropriate adoption agencies, a local authority, the Registrar General and the courts.

Appropriate adoption agency

The intermediary agency must take reasonable steps to contact the appropriate agency which was involved in the adoption, since that agency should have information on the adopted person's case records. Both the adoption agency and the intermediary must ascertain whether a veto exists (see below) which prevents the disclosure of any information. Where there is no veto, the appropriate agency is obliged to take reasonable steps to provide the information sought and to disclose the information, including identifying information as is necessary for the purpose (Intermediary Services Regulations, regulation 12(4); Intermediary Services (Wales) Regulations, regulation 12(5)). Based on the information it holds, the adoption agency may also be able to assist and advise the intermediary agency on whether or not, and if so how, to proceed with the application. The adoption agency may charge an intermediary agency such fee as it determines to be reasonable for providing the information requested or for giving its views under regulation 12 (Intermediary Services Regulations and Intermediary Services (Wales) Regulations, regulation 18(4)).

When the appropriate adoption agency has been identified, it is important to establish whether a veto exists, whether the subject of the application has at any time expressed his views to the agency about future contact with any relative of his, or about his being approached with regard to such contact. Regulation 8 of the Intermediary Services Regulations 2005 and Intermediary Services (Wales) Regulations provides that a veto applies where the subject is the adopted person and that person has notified the appropriate agency in writing that he does not wish to be contacted by an intermediary agency in relation to an application under the regulations; or that he wishes to be contacted only in specified circumstances or by specified persons. It is the duty of the adoption agency, before the veto is registered, to take appropriate steps to advise and counsel the person of the implications, particularly where the veto is in absolute terms. The adopted person should also be informed of his right to amend or withdraw the veto at any time, and how this can be done, if he wishes to do so. Where the veto is a qualified one, the agency should ensure that the specified circumstances are clearly identified, and the person is advised about the need for him to be informed of special circumstances that could affect him, for example, a serious medical condition. Section 80 of the 2002 Act makes specific provision for recording information in Part 2 of the adoption contact register on the wishes of the relatives of an adopted person as to making contact with the adopted person (see Chapter 13). An adopted person also has a right to specify the relatives with whom he does or does not wish to have contact. Both these provisions reflect respect for the person's right to privacy.

The agency must keep a written record of such a veto on the adopted person's case record and ensure that it is made known to any intermediary agency which requests information (Intermediary Services Regulations and Intermediary Services (Wales) Regulations, regulation 8(2)).

If no veto is in place, the intermediary agency must ascertain from the adoption agency whether the subject has at any time expressed a view to the agency about future contact with any relative, or about being approached with regard to such contact; ascertain the agency's views as to whether the application is appropriate having regard to the relevant criteria (see below); and seek any other information required to trace the subject, enable him to make an informed decision on whether or not to consent to the disclosure sought and offer him and the applicant counselling. (Intermediary Services Regulations and Intermediary Services (Wales) Regulations, regulation 12.)

The Registrar General
The intermediary agency should, where appropriate, contact the Registrar General for information on the adoption contact register. The request for information to the Registrar General may be made where the intermediary agency has been unable to identify the appropriate adoption agency or ascertains that the adoption in question was a non-agency adoption; or where the appropriate adoption agency, having been identified, confirms that it does not hold the necessary information, for example because its files have been destroyed ((Intermediary Services Regulations and Intermediary Services (Wales) Regulations, regulation 13(2)). The appropriate agency may also make a request to the Registrar General for information, where it does not hold the information (Intermediary Services Regulations and Intermediary Services (Wales) Regulations, regulation 13(3)).

Information on the adoption contact register may assist in pursuing the application and provide information on which the intermediary agency can make an informed decision whether or not to proceed with the application. In order to obtain the information, the agency should request the information in writing from the Registrar General.

The Registrar General is under a duty to take all reasonable steps to comply with the written request for information from the intermediary agency (Intermediary Services Regulations and Intermediary Services (Wales) Regulations, regulation 14(1)). If the Registrar General does not have the information sought he must provide the intermediary agency with written confirmation of that fact, together with details of the court that made the adoption order (Intermediary Services Regulations and Intermediary Services (Wales) Regulations, regulation 14(2)). He is entitled to charge a fee of £10 for providing the information (Intermediary Services Regulations and Intermediary Services (Wales) Regulations, regulation 18(3)).

The request for information should include information which would enable an application to be made for a certificate from the adoption contact register and information from that register.

The court
Where the Registrar General certifies that he does not have the information, a request in writing should be made to the court that made the adoption order. The court may charge an intermediary agency a fee not exceeding £20 for providing the information (Intermediary Services Regulations and Intermediary Services (Wales) Regulations, regulation 18(5)).

The court which made the adoption order generally has the information filed in the proceedings. A request to the court may become appropriate, for instance where the local authority or the adoption agency has lost the records, or the records have been destroyed. On receiving the request, the court must disclose any information requested by the intermediary agency that is contained in the court records. If the court does not have the information, it must inform the intermediary agency in writing of the fact. The information must give details of the searches that have been made of the records; if the court considers that the information may be found in the records of another court, it must provide that information to the intermediary agency with details of the court. (Intermediary Services Regulations and Intermediary Services (Wales) Regulations, regulation 15.)

7. Discretion Whether or not to Proceed

The agency it is not obliged to proceed with or continue with the application where it considers that it would not be appropriate to do so. In deciding whether or not it would be appropriate to do so the agency must have regard to all the circumstances and the following matters:

(a) the welfare of the applicant, the person in relation to whom the information is sought, and any other person who may be identified or otherwise affected by the application. Where the subject of the application is under eighteen years of age the agency must not proceed further with the application in relation to that subject;

(b) any views of the appropriate agency that was involved in the adoption, having regard to the information disclosed by them (see below);

(c) any information obtained from the adoption contact register; and

(d) any veto recorded under regulation 8

(Intermediary Services Regulations and Intermediary Services (Wales) Regulations, regulation 6).

8. Disclosure

Before disclosing to the applicant any identifying information about the person in relation to whom the inquiry is being made (the subject), the intermediary agency must obtain that person's consent. For this purpose "identifying information" means information which, whether taken on its own or together with other information in the possession of the applicant, would enable the applicant to identify or trace the subject. Before obtaining such consent, the agency is required to ensure that the subject has had sufficient information to make an informed decision whether or not to give consent. If the subject has died or is incapable of giving his consent, the agency is permitted to disclose such information as it considers appropriate having applied the criteria set out in regulation 6 above (Intermediary Services Regulations and Intermediary Services (Wales) Regulations, regulation 7). The agency may, however, disclose to the applicant information which is not identifying information where it would be appropriate to do so (Intermediary Services Regulations and Intermediary Services (Wales) Regulations, regulation 9).

An agency must not proceed with an application and should not disclose information where the subject is the adopted person and he has notified the appropriate agency (that is, the agency involved in the adoption) that he does not wish to be contacted by an intermediary agency in relation to such an application, or that he wishes to be contacted only in specified circumstances. (Intermediary Services Regulations and Intermediary Services (Wales) Regulations, regulation 8(1)).

The intermediary agency may disclose non-identifying information provided it considers it appropriate to do so having applied the criteria set out in regulation 6 (above).

Any information received by the intermediary must be treated as confidential. Disclosure may be made to the Registrar General, the court or the appropriate adoption agency for the purpose of obtaining information under regulation 12 or 13 (see above). It may also be disclosed to the appropriate adoption agency to ascertain its views. Such information as is necessary to enable the subject to make an informed decision may be disclosed to the subject. Where counselling services are provided in connection with the application, such disclosure as is necessary may be made to the person who is to provide the counselling services (Intermediary Services Regulations and Intermediary Services (Wales) Regulations, regulation 16).

9. Fees

The intermediary agency may charge such fees as it deems reasonable for processing the application, for providing counselling services or making arrangements for such services to be provided outside the United Kingdom (Intermediary Services Regulations and Intermediary Services (Wales) Regulations, regulation 18(1) and (2)).

10. Offence

It is an offence, punishable on summary conviction by a fine not exceeding £5,000, for an intermediary agency to disclose information in contravention of regulation 7 without reasonable excuse (Intermediary Services Regulations and Intermediary Services (Wales) Regulations, regulation 17). See also Chapter 19, page 302.

Chapter 16

Adoption Agencies

1. Introduction

The Report of the Departmental Committee on the Adoption of Children (the *Houghton Report*, Cmnd 5107, 1972) acknowledged that:

> "a voluntary social work agency is not accountable for its work in the same way as a statutory body. In the absence of this public accountability, arrangements must be made to ensure its capability to undertake this kind of work."

The committee accepted that a voluntary adoption agency was required to register with the local authority in whose area its administrative centre was situated, but found that the existing system of registering voluntary adoption societies was "ineffective and the criteria (were) too narrow". The committee's recommendation was that "broader criteria should be laid down and registration by the central government would be the most effective way of ensuring good standards throughout the country".

As a result of the recommendations, section 3(1) of the Adoption Act 1976 was enacted. It provided for a body which was a voluntary society and which desired to act as an adoption society or, if it was already an adoption society and desired to continue to act as such, to apply, subject to regulations under section 9(1) of the Act, to the Secretary of State for approval. The Adoption Agencies Regulations 1983 (SI 1983 No. 1964) regulated adoption agencies. Section 1(4) of the Adoption Act 1976 provided that a local authority or approved adoption society may be referred to as an adoption agency. Schedule 10, paragraph 30, to the Children Act 1989 extended the definition to include an adoption agency within the meaning of section 1 of the Adoption (Scotland) Act 1978 and article 3 of the Adoption (Northern Ireland) Order 1987 (SI 1987 No. 2203 NI 22). A further amendment to section 1(5) of the Adoption Act 1976 defined a voluntary adoption agency as an "appropriate voluntary organisation which is an adoption society in respect of which a person is registered under the Care Standards Act 2000, part 2, and the Voluntary Adoption Agencies and the Adoption Agencies (Miscellaneous Amendments) Regulations 2003 [SI 2003 No. 367]".

In the White Paper *Adoption: a New Approach* (Cm 5017, December 2000), the Government set out its proposals to increase the use of adoption for children in care. It was therefore necessary to provide support for those directly involved in the process – the child, the natural parent(s) and the prospective parent(s) – and to regulate the bodies which would be authorised to provide that support, so that they would be accountable and would meet certain acceptable standards.

The Adoption and Children Act 2002 sets about this by introducing measures referred to as "adoption support services", and by providing for the revision of the existing adoption agencies regulations. This chapter deals with the provisions which regulate the establishment of adoption panels, and the duties of adoption agencies in respect of children and prospective adopters in relation to adoption and placing children for adoption. The provisions relating to adoption support services are considered in Chapter 17.

The following regulations apply to adoption agencies from 30 December 2005 and have been made pursuant to section 9(1) of the Adoption and Children Act 2002:

(a) the Adoption Agencies Regulations 2005, SI 2005 No. 389 (the "Agencies Regulations");

(b) the Suitability of Adopters Regulations 2005, SI 2005 No. 1712;

(c) the Adoption Agencies (Wales) Regulations 2005 (SI 2005 No. 1313 (the "Agencies (Wales) Regulations");

(d) the Restriction on the Preparation of Adoption Reports Regulations 2005 (SI 2005 No. 1711); and

(e) the Independent Review of Determinations (Adoption) Regulations 2004, SI 2004 No. 190 as amended;

(f) the Independent Review of Determinations (Adoption) (Wales) Regulations 2005, SI 2005 No. 1819, W. 147.

The National Adoption Standards
Also relevant are the National Adoption Standards for England (Department of Health, 2001) and the National Minimum Standards for Local Authority Adoption Services in Wales. The National Adoption Standards for England, provide, in respect of adoption services, as follows:

"E. Councils
Corporate and senior management responsibilities
A comprehensive adoption service to meet the needs of children, birth families, adoptive parents and adopted adults will be planned corporately and provided in collaboration with other relevant agencies.

1. Councils will plan and deliver adoption services with local health and education bodies (including schools), voluntary adoption agencies, the local courts and other relevant agencies, including, where applicable, other councils.

2. There will be clear policies for adoption, including post-adoption services, which are set out in Children and Young People's Strategic Plans or

equivalent local plans.

3. Councillors will carry out their responsibilities as corporate parents and receive regular information on the management and outcomes of the service they are responsible for providing.

4. Senior managers, with a clear management link to Director level, will ensure that adoption is an integral part of the council services for children, and will be involved in the strategic planning, delivery and monitoring of the adoption service.

5. A senior manager will have direct operational responsibility for all parts of the adoption service including planning, management and delivery of the adoption service, and performance management through quality assurance systems. This includes making sure that: a) Each child has a named social worker and an agreed care plan; b) Timescales for planning, decision making and adoptive placements are met; c) Staff are subject to the necessary safeguard checks; d) Staff have the necessary skills and knowledge, or access to them, and are supervised; e) Managers, councillors and panel members have access to necessary training and skills development; f) Procedures, guidance and sound professional practice are followed; g) Quality standards are set and consistently maintained; h) Management information systems inform service provision.

6. Councils, with the relevant agencies listed in 1), will provide or commission a comprehensive range of pre- and post-adoption services consistent with any national framework or regulation. These will facilitate and support adoption and meet the needs of children who move between local authority areas. Criteria for access to services will be clear, concise and understandable.

F. Adoption Agencies and Services – Council and Voluntary
Each council and voluntary adoption agency will provide a high quality adoption service.

1. Children's welfare and safety will be put first, and their rights, needs and wishes, elicited, recorded and taken into account at all times.

2. Agencies will agree, and follow, policies and procedures for adoption which are clear, concise and easily understood. They will be made available to those affected by adoption, staff and the general public.

3. Councils and voluntary adoption agencies will work together to plan and deliver a co-ordinated package of services to meet the needs of the child.

4. The second and every subsequent review of a looked after child will consider permanence. Where adoption is the plan, reviews will evaluate the success of the plan in meeting the child's needs and specify any new objectives required to meet those needs.

5. Timescales will be met, taking account of the individual child's needs. The senior manager will monitor performance against timescales.

6. Agencies will plan, implement and evaluate effective strategies to recruit sufficient adopters to meet the needs of children waiting for adoption locally and nationally, especially those from diverse ethnic and cultural backgrounds and disabled children.

7. Agencies will have thorough and timely assessment processes in accordance with Sections A, B and C using the dimensions in the Framework for the Assessment of Children in Need and their Families. Children and adults will

be prepared for adoption in accordance with Sections A and C.

8. Careful and thorough checks will be made on prospective adopters, members of their households and agency staff.

Adoption panels:

9. Agencies will arrange enough adoption panels to avoid any delays in considering children for adoption, approval of adopters and matching, and to meet the following timescales: a) Panels will receive all necessary information from agencies no later than 6 weeks from the completion of the assessment report; b) Where a review has agreed that adoption is the plan, the adoption panel will make its recommendation within 2 months; c) Panel recommendations will be conveyed orally to applicants, children and birth parents within 24 hours.

Agency decision making:

Agencies will ensure that timely decisions are taken on panel recommendations and to meet the following timescales: a) Decisions will be taken within 7 working days of the adoption panel recommendation; b) Decisions will be conveyed orally to the applicants, the child and the birth parents within 24 hours; c) Decisions will be confirmed in writing within 7 working days.

11. Where an adoption is at risk of breaking down, all agencies involved in the placement will cooperate to provide support and information to all parties without delay.

12. When an adoption has broken down all agencies involved will cooperate to provide support to the child and the adoptive parents, and ensure that the birth parents are informed.

13. Agencies will have effective systems for managing and keeping safe information from all the people affected by adoption.

14. Agencies will have representations and complaints procedures that comply with regulations and guidance.

There are separate standards for the inspection of agencies; these can be obtained from the website of the Commission for Social Care Inspection (www.csci.org.uk).

2. Definitions

A local authority or registered adoption society may be referred to as an adoption agency (Adoption and Children Act 2002, section 2(1)).

A "registered adoption society" means a voluntary organisation (i.e., a body other than a public or local authority, the activities of which are not carried on for profit) which is an adoption society registered under part 2 of the Care Standards Act 2000. In relation to the provision of any facility of the adoption service, however, references to a registered adoption society or to an adoption agency do not include an adoption society which is not registered in respect of that facility (section 1(2) and (3)). The "adoption service" is the services maintained by local authorities (section 2(1)). An adoption society is a body whose functions consist of or include making arrangements for the adoption of children (section 2(5)). Only a corporate body may be registered as an adoption society under part 2 of the Care Standards Act 2000 (section 2(4)).

3. The Adoption Panel

All adoption agencies have been required to have adoption panels since the Adoption Agencies Regulations 1983 came into force in 1984. The new regulations confirm this in regulation 3(1) of both the English and Welsh regulations. On 30 December 2005, however, all members of the panels established under the 1983 regulations ceased to hold office. Thereafter, a member of an old panel is disqualified from holding office as a member of a new adoption panel of the same adoption society for a specified period; see *Term of office*, below.

Under the Agencies Regulations and the Agencies (Wales) Regulations, an adoption agency is obliged to establish a new adoption panel in compliance with the new regulations (see below).

Each aspect of the adoption agency's work – from making adoption plans, considering the suitability of prospective adopters and matching individual children with adoptive parents – must be considered by the panel, whose duty it is to advise and make recommendations to the adoption agency on these issues.

Composition

The panel must consist of no more than ten members. The members include the chairperson, who must be appointed by the adoption agency and must be a person who is not disqualified (see below) and who has the skills and experience necessary for chairing an adoption panel (regulation 3(2) of both the Agencies Regulations and the Agencies (Wales) Regulations). A vice chairperson must also be appointed, whose duty is to act as chair if the appointed chairperson is absent or his office is vacant. In addition, the panel must comprise:

    (a) two social workers, each with at least three years' relevant post-qualifying experience;

    (b) in the case of a registered adoption society, one person who is a director, manager or other officer concerned with the management of that society;

    (c) in the case of a local authority, one member of that authority; in the case of Wales one elected member of the authority;

    (d) one or more medical advisers to the adoption agency;

    (e) at least three other persons (referred to as "independent members") of whom at least two must, where reasonably practicable, have personal experience of adoption, for example, an adopted person over eighteen years of age and an adoptive parent

(regulation 3(3) of both the Agencies Regulations and the Agencies

(Wales) Regulations).

The objective is that this group of people will pool their experiences and expertise, offer an informed perspective, and bring knowledge and scrutiny to the adoption agency's work.

Joint panels

Two or more (but in Wales, not more than three) local authorities may together establish a panel, known as a "joint adoption panel". If such a panel is established it must consist of no more than eleven members. The panel must include:

    (a) a chairperson with the appropriate qualifications (see above);

    (b) two social workers with at least three years' relevant post-qualifying experience;

    (c) one member of any of the local authorities;

    (d) a medical adviser to one of the local authorities; and

    (e) at least three independent members including, where reasonably practicable, at least two persons with personal experience of adoption

(Agencies Regulations, regulation 3(5)).

The Agencies (Wales) Regulations, regulation 3(5), varies slightly. It provides that where a joint panel is established:

    (a) each local authority must appoint two persons to the panel, one of whom must be a social worker and the other must be an elected member of that authority;

    (b) by agreement between the local authorities there must be appointed:

        (i) a person to chair the panel who is not an elected member of any of the local authorities whose panel it is, and has the skills and experience necessary for chairing the adoption panel,

        (ii) at least three independent members, including, where reasonably practicable, at least two persons with personal experience of adoption,

        (iii) two members of the panel either of whom will act as chair if the person appointed to chair the panel is absent or their office is vacant, and

        (iv) the medical adviser to one of the authorities.

Disqualified persons

The following persons are classed as disqualified from taking an appointment of chairperson of an adoption panel in England:

    (a) in the case of a registered adoption society, a person who is, or has been within the last year, a trustee or employee, or is related to an employee, of that society; or

    (b) in the case of a local authority, a person who has been, within the last year, a member or employee, or is related to an employee, of that authority. For these purposes, a person (A) is related to another person (B) if A is:

(i) a member of the household of, or married to or the civil partner of, B, or

(ii) a son, daughter, mother, father, sister or brother of B; or

(iii) the son, daughter, mother, father, sister, brother of the person to whom B is married or with whom B has formed a civil partnership

(Agencies Regulations, regulation 3(7)).

Independent members

The following persons cannot be appointed as independent members of an English adoption panel:

(a) in the case of a registered adoption society, a person who is, or has been within the last year, a trustee or employee, or related to an employee, of that society;

(b) in the case of a local authority, a person who is, or has been within the last year, employed by that authority in its children and family social services, or is related to such a person, or is or has been within the last year a member of that authority; or

(c) the adoptive parent of a child who was placed for adoption with him by the adoption agency ("Agency A"), or by another adoption agency where he had been approved as suitable to be an adoptive parent by agency A, unless at least twelve months have elapsed since the adoption order was made in respect of the child

(Agencies Regulations, regulation 3(6)).

In Wales, a person cannot be appointed as an independent member of an adoption panel if that person:

(a) is or has been within the last year employed, in the case of a registered adoption society by that society, or in the case of a local authority, by that authority, to carry out any of the social services functions of that authority;

(b) in the case of a local authority, is or has been an elected member of that authority within the last year;

(c) in the case of a registered adoption society, is or has been within the last year a trustee or concerned in the management of that agency;

(d) is an adoptive parent with whom the agency has placed a child for adoption, or whom the agency has approved as suitable to be an adoptive parent, unless at least two years have elapsed since the adoption order was made in respect of the child;

(e) is related, in the case of a registered adoption society, to a person employed by that agency; or in the case of a local authority, to a person employed by that authority to carry out any of the social services functions of that authority. A person (A) is related to

another person (B) if A is:
(i)   a member of the household of, or married to or the civil partner of, B,
(ii) the son, daughter, mother, father, sister or brother of B, or
(iii) the son, daughter, mother, father, sister or brother of the person to whom B is married or with whom B has formed a civil partnership
(Agencies (Wales) Regulations, regulation 3(6) and (7)).

Term of office
A member of an adoption panel can hold office for a term not exceeding three years (five years in Wales) and may not hold office for the adoption panel of the same adoption agency for more than three years in total. In Wales a person may not hold office for the adoption panel of the same adoption agency for more than two consecutive terms without an intervening period of at least three years. A medical adviser member may hold office only for so long as he is the medical officer of the adoption agency. (Regulation 4(1) and (2) of both the Agencies Regulations and the Agencies (Wales) Regulations).

As noted above, on 30 December 2005, all existing members of adoption panels ceased to hold office. Such a person is disqualified from holding office on the new panel of the same adoption society as follows:
(a) where the term of office of that member was extended by the adoption agency, for more than one term;
(b) where that member was in his first term of office as a member, for more than two terms; and
(c) in any other case, for more than one term
(Agencies Regulations, regulation 10(3) to (5)).
The corresponding provision for Wales (Agencies (Wales) Regulations, regulations 4 and 10(3)) is that a member of the old panel may be appointed to the new panel for a maximum of five years, minus the term already served as a member of the old panel.

Resignation and termination of office
A member of an adoption panel may resign from office at any time by giving one month's notice in writing to the adoption agency. An adoption agency may terminate a member's office at any time if it is of the opinion that the member is unsuitable or unable to remain in office. The notice of termination must be given in writing and must set out the reasons for the termination. (Regulations 4(3) and (4) of both the Agencies Regulations and the Agencies (Wales) Regulations 2005.)

The appointment of a person who is a member of a joint adoption panel may be terminated only with the agreement of all the local authorities concerned (regulation 4(5) of both the Agencies Regulations and the

Agencies (Wales) Regulations 2005).

Quorum

At least five members, and in the case of a joint adoption panel at least six, including the chairperson or vice chairperson and at least one of the social workers or one of the independent members, must be present to form a quorum (regulation 5(1) and (2) of both the Agencies Regulations and the Agencies (Wales) Regulations 2005).

Records

An adoption panel is under a duty to make a written record of its proceedings and recommendations, and the reasons for its recommendations (regulation 5(3) of both the Adoption Agencies Regulations and the Adoption Agencies (Wales) Regulations).

Fees

A local authority may pay any member of its adoption panel a reasonable fee (regulation 6 of both the Agencies Regulations and the Agencies (Wales) Regulations).

Medical adviser

The adoption agency is under a duty to appoint at least one registered medical practitioner to be the agency's medical adviser. The medical adviser(s) must be consulted in relation to the arrangements for access to and disclosure of information concerning the health of children, the prospective adopters and the natural parents (regulation 9 of both the Agencies Regulations and the Agencies (Wales) Regulations).

Agency adviser

An adoption agency must appoint a senior member of staff to be the agency adviser. In the case of a joint adoption panel, the local authorities whose panel it is, by agreement, must appoint a senior member of staff of one of them to be the agency adviser. In either case, the adviser must be a social worker of at least five years' relevant post-qualifying experience and must have, in the opinion of the adoption agency, relevant management experience. The Welsh regulation does not require the social worker to have at least five years' experience.

The duties of the agency adviser are:
    (a) to assist the agency with the appointment, including re-appointment, termination and review of appointment of members of the adoption panel;
    (b) to be responsible for the induction and training of members of the adoption panel;
    (c) to be responsible for liaison between the agency and the adoption

panel, monitoring the performance of members of the panel and the administration of the panel; and

(c)   to give such advice to the adoption panel as the panel may request in relation to any case or generally

(regulation 8 of both the Agencies Regulations and the Agencies (Wales) Regulations).

The National Adoption Standards

By virtue of the National Adoption Standards, adoption agencies are required to arrange enough adoption panels to avoid delays in considering children for adoption, approving prospective adopters and matching children with prospective adoptive adopters. They are also required to meet the following timescales, unless compliance would not be in the child's best interest in the particular case:

(a)   the adoption panel should receive all necessary information from the agency within six weeks of the completion of the child's permanence report;

(b)   where, at a review, it has been agreed that adoption is the plan, the adoption panel's recommendation should be made within two months of the review;

(c)   the agency must decide whether the child should be placed for adoption within seven working days of the adoption panel's recommendation where adoption has been identified as the permanence plan;

(c)   the panel's recommendation should be conveyed orally to the child's parent(s) or guardian, the child and any prospective adopters, within two working days, and written confirmation should be sent to them within five working days

(National Adoption Standards for England; see also the National Minimum Standards for Local Authority Adoption Services for Wales).

4.   Deciding Whether a Child Should be Placed for Adoption

The provisions of the regulations made under the Adoption and Children Act 2002 concerning the duties of adoption agencies must be considered together with the general duty of the local authority, under sections 22 and 23 of the Children Act 1989, in relation to children who are looked after by them. A child is "looked after" if he is being voluntarily accommodated by the local authority, or is the subject of a care order under the Children Act 1989, or if care proceedings in respect of him have been issued. The local authority has a duty to such children to identify a permanence plan by the four-month review. The range of options available must be considered at the review. The options include rehabilitation of the child with his parents or birth family, with appropriate support; placement with foster carers or in a residential institution; and placement for adoption. The views of the child, his parents and others with parental responsibility must be ascertained, and the options explained to them. See the National Adoption Standards for England and the National Minimum Standards for Local Authority Adoption Services for Wales.

Under regulations 11 to 17 of both the Agencies Regulations and the Agencies (Wales) Regulations, an adoption agency's duties towards a child whom the agency is considering for adoption include the following:

    (a) to open the child's case records;

    (b) to provide counselling and information for the child and ascertain the child's wishes and feelings;

    (c) to provide counselling and information for, and ascertain the wishes of, the child's parent(s) or guardian and others;

    (d) to obtain information about the child;

    (e) to obtain information about the child's family;

    (f) to prepare the child's permanence report for the adoption panel.

The child's case record

The adoption agency is under a duty to set up a child's case record and place on it:

    (a) all the information gathered by it in relation to the duties referred to above;

    (b) the child's permanence report;

    (c) a written record of the proceedings of the adoption panel, its recommendations and reasons for them, and any advice given by the panel to the agency;

    (d) a record of the agency's decision and any notification of that decision (see below);

    (e) any parental consent obtained to the placement of the child for adoption;

    (f) any advance consent obtained for the adoption of the child;

    (g) any form or notice of withdrawal of consent under section 19 or 20, or notice under section 20(4)(a) or (b), of the Adoption and Children Act 2002;

    (h) a copy of any placement order in respect of the child;

    (i) any other documents or information obtained by the agency which it considers should be included in the case record

(Agencies Regulations, regulation 12(1)).

Where an adoption agency places on a child's case record any notice under section 20(4) of the Adoption and Children Act 2002 (statement by a parent or guardian who has given advance consent to adoption that he does not wish to be informed of any application for an adoption order, or the withdrawal of such a statement), the adoption agency must notify the court in which the proceedings for an adoption order have been commenced (Agencies

Regulations, regulation 12(2) and see the Family Procedure (Adoption) Rules 2005 (SI 2005 No. 2795), rule 24, in Chapter 25, page 398).

The Agencies (Wales) Regulations, regulation 12, instead simply provides that the adoption agency must place on the case record "any information obtained and any report, recommendation or decision made by virtue of these Regulations". It goes on specifically to require that where the child is looked after, or is provided with accommodation under section 59(1) of the Children Act 1989, the local authority or, as the case may be, the registered adoption society must obtain any information which is required to be obtained by the regulations from the records maintained with respect to the child under the 1989 Act, and place that information on the case record. Presumably, this would be covered under (a) above in an English case.

Counselling etc for the child
Local authorities have long been under a duty to establish and maintain within their areas services designed to meet the needs, in relation to adoption, of children who may be adopted, their parents and guardians, prospective adopters, adopted persons and their natural parents, adoptive parents and former guardians. This duty is continued under the Adoption and Children Act 2002. These services are referred to as the "adoption service", which includes "adoption support services" – counselling, advice and information, and other services (Adoption and Children Act 2002 sections 2(1), (3) and (6)). This duty is further reinforced in regulation 13 of both the Agencies Regulations and the Agencies (Wales) Regulations. Regulation 13 provides that the adoption agency must, so far as is practicable:

   (a) provide a counselling service for the child;

   (b) explain to the child in an appropriate manner the procedure in relation to, and the legal implications of, adoption, and provide him with appropriate written information about these matters; and

   (c) ascertain the wishes and feeling of the child regarding the possibility of placement for adoption with a new family and his adoption; his religious and cultural upbringing and contact with his parents, guardian, other relatives or any other person the agency considers relevant.

The needs of children from minority cultural backgrounds must be addressed. There may be language or cultural issues to be considered, so that effective communication is achieved when information is given to the child.

When giving information to the child, it is important to ensure that the child understands the reasons for the agency's decision that he or she should be placed for adoption, and the effect of the order on him and his parents. The effect it will have on contact should also be clearly explained. When seeking to ascertain the child's wishes and feelings, it is essential that the child understands that his views are only one of the factors which will be taken into account.

Where the adoption agency is satisfied that the duties under regulation 13 have been carried out by another agency, it is not required to repeat the process (regulation 13(2)). Where, however, the child has continuing needs or there has been a change of circumstances, or where, for example, counselling is continuing, the duties referred to above remain. Disclosure of information should be sought from the agency which first provided those services, to assist the present agency to meet the child's needs.

Counselling etc for the parent or guardian and others
Regulation 14 of both the Agencies Regulations and the Agencies (Wales) Regulations concerns the requirement to provide counselling and information for the parent or guardian of the child, and others, and to ascertain the wishes and feelings of these persons. Thus, an adoption agency must so far as is practicable:

(a) provide a counselling service for the parent or guardian of the child;
(b) explain to him the procedure in relation to both placement and adoption; the legal implications of giving consent to placement for adoption and advance consent; and the legal implications of a placement order and an adoption order. In addition, the parent or guardian must be given written information of these matters;
(c) ascertain the wishes and feelings of the parent or guardian of the child and any other relevant person concerning the placement of the child for adoption and his adoption, including any wishes and feelings about the child's religious and cultural upbringing and contact with the child if a placement or adoption order is made.

Where the parent or other relevant person's first language is not English, the adoption agency must establish whether the person needs an interpreter to explain the above matters. It is important to ensure that the information given is understood and that the person is able to make an informed decision. Cultural and religious differences and any disabilities, including learning difficulties or intellectual impairment, must be taken into account to impart meaningful information. Similar factors should be considered when offering counselling (see below). The effect of adoption on contact between the parent or other person and child must be made clear. The right to apply for contact under section 26 of the 2002 Act, and the court's duty under section 46 to consider arrangements for contact, should be explained. Any information gathered during this process should be recorded and placed on the child's case record. Any consent or advance consent of any parent or guardian must be given in the form required by the relevant practice direction under rule 28 of the Family Procedure (Adoption) Rules 2005 (SI 2005 No. 1795).

Where counselling is offered but not accepted, there is a continuing duty to support the parent or guardian throughout the adoption process, and to continue to offer counselling. It is also important that the parent's wishes and feelings are clearly recorded on the child's case records.

Under the Adoption Agencies Regulations 1983, the agency was required to obtain, so far as was practicable, such particulars of the parents or guardian, and, having regard to his age and understanding, the child, as were referred to in Parts 1 and 3 to 5 of the schedule to the regulations, together with any other relevant information which may be requested by the adoption panel. In *Z County Council v R* [2001] 1 FLR 365, the issue was whether the local authority, when applying for a freeing order, was obliged to tell the mother's relatives of the existence of the baby and inquire whether any of them might wish to offer the child a home, and whether the guardian *ad litem* was under a duty to do so. The mother opposed any approach being made to her family and stated that none of them could offer the child a secure and stable home. Holman J considered the issue under domestic law and under the European Convention on Human Rights. In relation to domestic law, he held that none of the statutory provisions, regulations or rules imposed on the local authority or the guardian a duty to inform or consult members of the family in a case where, as here, the mother had concealed her pregnancy from her family. He concluded that on the particular facts of the case it would not be in the child's best interest to reveal the information to the mother's family. In relation to Convention rights, while the court held that a family life within article 8(1) existed between the child and his extended family, interference with that right by not approaching the child's extended family was in accordance with the provision in article 8(2) which permitted adoption orders, and, striking a balance between those rights and the necessity to protect the child, it was necessary in the case to preserve confidentiality. It was, however, stressed that this conclusion was reached on the facts and was not intended to suggest that the extended family could simply be ignored on the wish of the mother.

Both the 2002 Act and the regulations now specifically require consideration to be given to the effect of the loss of relationship between the child and his original family, including his relatives and others who may play a significant role in the child's life, and the wishes of the relatives must be considered. At every stage of the process in coming to a decision relating to the adoption of the child, those concerned in making the decision are required to consider the welfare test and all the matters set out in section 1(4) to (7). It would seem that only in very exceptional circumstances could the information-gathering process not include the extended family. (See further below.)

In the case of the father of a child who does not have parental responsibility, but whose identity is known to the adoption agency, the service available to the parent with parental responsibility must also be made available to the father and the agency's duties to him are as set out above, unless the agency is satisfied that these duties have been carried out by another agency. In addition, it is the duty of the agency to ascertain, so far as is possible, whether the father wishes to acquire parental responsibility for the child, or intends to apply for a residence order, contact order or any other order under the Children Act 1989, for example the discharge of a care order or of an order for contact under section 34 of the 1989 Act if the child is in care.

As in the case of relatives, so in the case of the father without parental responsibility, there may be circumstances which permit the local authority not to contact him. An example arose in *Re M (Adoption: Rights of Natural Father)* [2001] 1 FLR 745, where the evidence disclosed that the father was violent and dangerous and subjected the mother to serious domestic violence in the presence of an older child. The father also had a series of criminal convictions for violent offences. The court excused the local authority from trying to locate and seek to interview the father. However, it was stressed that only in exceptional circumstances would it be appropriate to depart from the general rule that a father should be informed. Where it was felt that it would not be in the interest of the child to do so, authority from the court should be sought. Such an application would have to be justified on grounds that not approaching the father was necessary to protect the child, because there were grounds for believing that doing so would result in real danger or serious violence. It was also held that on the particular facts of the case the interference with the father's rights was justified.

Re H (A Child) (Adoption: Disclosure); Re G (A Child) (Adoption: Disclosure) [2001] 1 FLR 646 concerned two unmarried mothers who had each placed her child for adoption with the local authority on the basis she would not be asked to disclose the identity of the child's father. In *Re H* the mother and father had lived together and had had an older child with whom the father had contact. The mother had concealed the second pregnancy from the father and the extended family. In *Re G* the mother and father had never lived together but the relationship had faded and they were not in contact with each other. In each case the local authority sought the guidance of the court on whether the father should be consulted about the adoption and whether he should be joined as a party. In directing, in *Re H*, that the father should be informed, and in *Re G* that he should not, the facts of the cases were distinguished on the basis of the relationships between the parents. However, generally on the issue of confidentiality and the involvement of a father without parental responsibility in adoption proceedings, Dame Elizabeth Butler-Sloss P said:

"A considerable confidentiality is clearly important but it ought not, in the majority of cases, deprive the father of his right to be informed and consulted about his child. In my view, social workers counselling mothers ought to warn them that at some stage, the court will have to make a decision in adoption proceedings as to whether to add the father as a respondent to the proceedings. The father should therefore be told as soon as possible in order to reduce delay, and certainly before the child is placed with prospective adopters. If the mother refuses to disclose the identity of the father, her reasons must be carefully considered and, unless those reasons are cogent it would be wise for the local authority to seek legal advice at an early stage. If necessary the local authority should follow the prudent course adopted by [one of the authorities in the case] of an application to the court for directions on whether to notify the father."

In *Re J (Adoption: Contacting Father)* [2003] EWHC 199, [2003] 1 FLR 933 the mother had a baby at the age of sixteen years, at which time her relationship with the father had ended and they had no contact with each other. They had not lived together. She gave the local authority details of the father on the basis that the father would not be informed. The child was diagnosed as suffering from severe cystic fibrosis. The local authority sought a declaration from the court that it was in the child's best interest for the father to be informed. The mother objected. The court declared that it was lawful for the local authority to place the child for adoption without informing the father and seeking his views; the exceptional circumstances of the case took it outside the general rule which required the father to be informed about the adoption. There had been no family life within the context of article 8 of the European Convention on Human Rights between the father and the mother; the fact that it was unlikely that the father or his family would wish to care for the child outweighed any potential advantage to the child.

The provisions of the Adoption and Children Act 2002 and the regulations have reinforced the requirement to inform the father where his identity is known. But where there are exceptional circumstances, which warrant an exception to the rule, a direction should be sought from the High Court under the Family Procedure (Adoption) Rules 2005, rule 108 (see page 382), to absolve the local authority from its obligations.

On the issue of the infringement of Convention rights, much depends on the particular facts of the case. To avoid breaching article 8, it would have to be established, for example, that the parents have not lived together as a family unit; or that they did not have any meaningful relationship at the time of conception and leading up to the child's birth; or that there were some other exceptional circumstances, such as the need to protect the mother and the child from serious violence or danger, justifying the interference with the father's right to family life under the Convention. The case law under the former law is relevant to issues which may arise under the Adoption and Children Act 2002 and the Agencies Regulations because, under regulation 7(3) of the 1983 regulations, there was an express duty on the adoption agencies to contact the unmarried father of the child and involve him in the process.

Information about the child

Regulation 15 of the Agencies Regulations requires an adoption agency to obtain two specific types of information:

(a) the information specified in part 1 of schedule 1 to the regulations. This information includes the child's personal details and information about his cultural background, legal status, care history, a physical description and a description of his personality and interests, likes and dislikes, his educational history, his relationships with his family and others, and arrangements for contact; and

(b) to make arrangements for the child to be examined by a registered medical practitioner and for such other medical and psychiatric examination or tests as may be recommended by the agency's medical adviser, and in each case to obtain a written report on the child's health. This is known as the child's health report. It must record any treatment which the child is receiving and the matters set out in part 2 of schedule 1. No medical examination may be carried out, however, if the child is of sufficient understanding to make an informed decision and refuses to submit to the examination or other tests.

The medical examination need not be carried out if the medical adviser advises that it is not necessary (regulation 15(2)). It is for the medical adviser to consider whether he has sufficient information to provide an accurate report on the child's health. The adoption agency, however, must make arrangements for other medical and psychiatric examinations of, and other tests on, the child to be carried out, and to obtain reports recommended by the medical adviser. (regulation 15(3)).

Similar provisions are made in the regulation 15 of the Agencies (Wales) Regulations.

Information about the child's family

The adoption agency must obtain, so far as is practicable, the information about the child's family specified in part 3 of schedule 1 (in the case of Wales the information specified in parts 3 and 4 of schedule 1) and the information about each of the child's natural parents and brothers and sisters of the full blood or half blood, as specified in part 4 of schedule 1 to the Agencies Regulations. See regulation 16 of both the Agencies Regulations and the Agencies (Wales) Regulations.

The permanence report

The adoption agency is under a duty to prepare a written report, referred to as the child's "permanence report" which must include:

(a) the information specified in parts 1 and 3 of schedule 1 to the Agencies Regulations, or, in Wales, in parts 1, 3 and 4 of schedule 1 to the Agencies (Wales) Regulations;

(b) a summary of the child's health report;

(c) the wishes and feelings of the child on placement for adoption and adoption, his religious and cultural upbringing and contact with his parent, guardian or other relative or with any other relevant person;

(d) the wishes and feelings of the child's parent or guardian, or his natural father not having parental responsibility, on placement, adoption, religious and cultural upbringing and contact with the child;

(e) the views and proposals, if any, of the agency with regard to contact between the child and his parents, relatives or other relevant persons;

(f) an assessment of the child's emotional and behavioural development and related matters;

(g) an assessment of the parenting capacity of the child's parent and father without parental responsibility;

(h) a chronology of the decisions and actions taken by the agency with respect to the child;

(i) an analysis of the options for the future of the child which have been considered, and the reason adoption is considered the preferred option;

(j) any other information that the agency considers relevant. The welfare principle, the factors set out in the welfare checklist, issues relating to the child's religious persuasion, racial origin and cultural and linguistic background, and the no order principle, will be relevant considerations

(regulation 17 of both the Agencies Regulations and Agencies (Wales) Regulations).

Copies of the report, edited where appropriate, should be provided to the parent(s). A copy may also be provided to the child, if he is of sufficient age and understanding.

The adoption agency must send the permanence report to the adoption panel, together with the child's health report, any other reports obtained under regulation 15, and information about the health of both the child's parents (regulation 17(2) of both the Agencies Regulations and Agencies (Wales) Regulations).

The author of the permanence report

Only a person who is appropriately qualified may prepare a report about the suitability of a child for adoption, or of a person to adopt a child, or about the adoption or placement for adoption of a child (Adoption and Children Act 2002, section 94(1)). The author of the report must be:

(a) (i) a social worker who is registered in the register for social workers maintained in accordance with section 56 of the Care Standards Act 2000, or the register maintained by the Scottish Social Services Council under section 44 of the Regulation of Care (Scotland) Act 2001, and who is employed by a local authority or registered adoption society; and

(ii) who has at least three years' post-qualifying experience in child care social work, including direct experience of adoption work; or

(b) (i) a person who is participating in a course approved by a council under section 63 of the Care Standards Act 2000 for persons wishing to become social workers, and is employed by, or placed with, a local authority or registered adoption society as part of that course; and

(ii) is supervised by a social worker who is employed by the local authority or registered adoption society in question and who has at least three years' qualifying experience in child care social work, including direct experience of adoption work

(The Restriction on the Preparation of Adoption Reports Regulations 2005, SI 2005 No. 1711, regulations 2 and 3).

The role of the adoption panel

The adoption panel has its own identity, separate from that of the agency. An adoption agency may not delegate decision-making to the panel, but it is required to refer to the panel the question whether adoption is in the best interest of the child; if the panel recommends that it is, it may at the same time give advice to the agency about the arrangements which the agency proposes to make for allowing any person contact with the child. Where the agency is a local authority, the panel may also recommend that the authority apply for a placement order in respect of the child. Regulation 18 of both the Agencies Regulations and the Agencies (Wales) Regulations requires the adoption panel to consider the case of every child referred to it by the adoption agency and to make a recommendation to the agency as to whether the child should be placed for adoption.

In considering what recommendation to make, the adoption panel must have regard to the duties imposed upon the adoption agency by section 1 of the Adoption and Children Act 2002, namely the welfare principle; the factors set out in the welfare checklist; issues relating to the child's religious persuasion, racial origin and cultural and linguistic background; the duty to consider the whole range of powers available; and the no order principle. The panel must also consider and take into account the reports and other information submitted to it by the adoption agency and described above. It may request the agency to obtain any other additional, relevant information which the panel considers necessary, and must obtain legal advice in relation to the case. It must thus be satisfied that the agency's proposal for adoption was arrived at having explored and discounted all the options available.

A person who is not a member of the panel may not attend its meetings. In *R v North Yorkshire County Council ex parte M* (No 2) [1989] 2 FLR 79, the guardian *ad litem* wished to attend the meeting of the adoption panel to make representations to the panel. It was held that although it was incumbent on the local authority to listen to the guardian *ad litem*'s views, that did not imply that the guardian *ad litem* was entitled to decide how the adoption panel, or any other branch of the local authority, should conduct its affairs, nor was she entitled to insist on attending meetings.

The recommendation made by the panel is taken into account by the adoption agency when making its decision

The guidance from the Department of Health, *Adoption: Achieving the Right Balance* (LAC 98 20) states that:

"adoption continues to provide an important service for children offering a positive and beneficial outcome, research shows that generally adopted children make very good progress through childhood and into adulthood compared to children brought up with their own parents and do considerably better than children who have remained in care throughout most of their childhood."

The adoption agency is obliged to take into account the recommendation of the adoption panel in coming to a decision about whether the child should be placed for adoption, but no member of the adoption panel must take part in any decision made by the adoption agency. The adoption panel therefore has a separate entity from the agency, providing an important independent element, and providing impartiality and objectivity.

The adoption agency's decision, with reasons for it, must be recorded in the child's case record. The agency must also notify the child's parent or guardian of its decision, in writing. The father of the child who does not have parental responsibility should also be notified if his identity and whereabouts are known and if the agency considers it appropriate to do so (regulation 19(3)).

The consent of the parent or guardian

Where the parent or guardian of a child is willing to consent to the placement of the child for adoption, or to the future making of an adoption order, the adoption agency may request CAFCASS to appoint an officer of the service, or may request the National Assembly of Wales to appoint a Welsh family proceedings officer, for the purposes of obtaining and witnessing the consent. In Wales, the request is made directly to the National Assembly. The request must be accompanied by the following information and documents:

(a) a certified copy of the child's birth certificate;

(b) the name and address of the child's parent or guardian;

(c) a chronology of the actions and decisions taken by the adoption agency with respect to the child;

(d) confirmation by the adoption agency that it has counselled and explained to the parent or guardian the legal implications of both consent to placement under section 19 of the Adoption and Children Act 2002 or, as the case may be, to the making of a future adoption order under section 20 of the Act, and provided the parent or guardian with written information about this, together with a copy of the written information provided to him; and

(e) such information about the parent or guardian or other information as the adoption agency considers the officer may need to know

(Agencies Regulations and Agencies (Wales) Regulations, regulation 20 and schedule 2).

The consent form, duly signed by the parent or guardian and witnessed by the CAFCASS or Welsh family proceedings officer, should be placed on the child's case record, as should any notice given by the parent under section 20(4)(a) of the Adoption and Children Act 2002 (that he does not wish to be informed of any application for an adoption order), or any withdrawal of consent.

The Family Procedure (Adoption) Rules 2005 (SI 2005 No. 2795), rule 28, requires that the consent of any parent or guardian of a child, to the child's being placed for adoption or to the making of an adoption order in the future, must be in the form specified by the relevant practice direction, or a form to the like effect. Consent to the making of an adoption order or to the making of an order by the High Court giving parental responsibility for the child to foreign prospective adopters with a view to the child's being adopted outside the United Kingdom, may be given in the form required by the relevant practice direction or a form to the like effect. Any form of consent executed in Scotland must be witnessed by a justice of the peace or a sheriff (rule 28(4)). Any form of consent executed in Northern Ireland must be witnessed by a justice of the peace. A form of consent executed outside the United Kingdom must be witnessed by:

(a) any person for the time being authorised by law in the place where the document is executed to administer an oath for any judicial or other legal purpose;

(b) a British Consular officer;

(c) a notary public; or

(d) if the person executing the document is serving in any of the regular armed forces of the Crown, an officer holding a commission in any of those forces.

Where the child is less than six weeks old, the consent of the mother to placement for adoption, or adoption, of her baby should not be sought (section 52(3) of the 2002 Act). Any consent given by the mother while the child is less than six weeks old would be invalid. Where the mother is willing to have her child placed for adoption, an agreement to that effect should be entered into and signed by the mother. The agreement should be placed on the child's case records. Before the agreement is made, the parent(s) or guardian of the child should be offered counselling. They should also be informed that they continue to have parental responsibility for the child until either they can give their formal consent when the baby is over six weeks old, or a placement order or adoption order is made. Their rights to contact with the child should also be explained.

The National Adoption Standards

The National Adoption Standards set out the principles which apply to domestic adoptions through adoption agencies. Adoption agencies are required to apply these principles when discharging their duties towards looked after children. The standards also provide a guide for children, birth families and prospective adopters to what they should expect from the adoption services. In respect of children, the standards provide that the needs and wishes, welfare and safety of the looked after child are the centre of the adoption process. They state:

"The needs and wishes, welfare and safety of the looked after child are at the centre of the adoption process.

1. Children whose birth family cannot provide them with a secure, stable and permanent home are entitled to have adoption considered for them.

2. Whenever plans for permanence are being considered, they will be made on the basis of the needs of each looked after child, and within the following timescales: a) The child's need for a permanent home will be addressed at the four month review and a plan for permanence made; b) Clear timescales will be set for achieving the plan, which will be appropriately monitored and considered at every subsequent review; c) Where adoption has been identified as the plan for the child at a review, the adoption panel will make its recommendation within 2 months.

Where adoption is the plan:

3. The timescales below will be followed, taking account of the individual child's needs: a) A match with suitable adoptive parents will be identified and approved by panel within 6 months of the agency agreeing that adoption is in the child's best interest; b) In care proceedings, where the plan is adoption, a match with suitable adoptive parents will be identified and approved by panel within 6 months of the court's decision; c) Where a parent has requested that a child aged under 6 months be placed for adoption, a match with suitable adoptive parents will be identified and approved by panel within 3 months of the agency agreeing that adoption is in the child's best interest.

4. Every child will have his or her wishes and feelings listened to, recorded and taken into account. Where they are not acted upon, the reasons for not doing so will be explained to the child and properly recorded.

5. All children will have a named social worker who will be responsible for them throughout the adoption process.

6. Children will be given clear explanations and information about adoption, covering what happens at each stage (including at court), and how long each stage is likely to take in their individual case.

7. Children will be well prepared before joining a new family. This will include clear appropriate information on their birth family and life before adoption, and information about the adopters and their family. Children are entitled to information provided by their birth families, which will be kept safe both by agencies and adopters. It will be provided to adopted children, or adults, at a time and in a manner that reflects their age and understanding, as well as the

nature of the information concerned.

8. Children will be matched with families who can best meet their needs. They will not be left waiting indefinitely for a 'perfect family'.

9. Every effort will be made to recruit sufficient adopters from diverse backgrounds, so that each child can be found an adoptive family within the timescales in 3) above, which best meets their needs, and in particular: a) which reflects their ethnic origin, cultural background, religion and language; b) which allows them to live with brothers and sisters unless this will not meet their individually assessed needs. Where this is the case, a clear explanation will be given to them and recorded.

10. The child's needs, wishes and feelings, and their welfare and safety are the most important concerns when considering links or contact with birth parents, wider birth family members and other people who are significant to them.

11. Adoption plans will include details of the arrangements for maintaining links (including contact) with birth parents, wider birth family members and other people who are significant to the child and how and when these arrangements will be reviewed.

12. Children are entitled to support services that meet their assessed needs. These include advice and counselling, health, education, leisure, and cultural services, and practical and financial help when needed. Information from agency records will be made available to the child when they are of an age and level of understanding to comprehend it.

13. Where there are difficulties arising from an adoption or a proposed adoption, or where an adoption or proposed adoption breaks down, a child will receive support and information without delay.

14. Children placed for adoption and adopted children will be informed of their right to make representations and complaints and will be helped to do so if this is required. . . .

Birth parents and birth families

Birth parents and birth families are entitled to services that recognise the lifelong implications of adoption. They will be treated fairly, openly and with respect throughout the adoption process.

1. Agencies will work with birth parents and significant birth family members to enable effective plans to be made and implemented for their child(ren).

2. Every effort will be made to ensure that birth parents and significant birth family members have a full understanding of the adoption process, the legal implications, and their rights.

3. Birth parents will have access to a support worker independent of the child's social worker from the time adoption is identified as the plan for the child.

4. Birth parents and birth families (including siblings) will have access to a range of support services both before and after adoption, including information about local and national support groups and services.

5. Birth parents will have the opportunity to give their account of events, and to see and comment on what is written about them in reports for the adoption panel, and in information passed to the adopters.

6. Birth parents and families will be supported to provide information that the adopted child needs. This will include information about the adopted child's birth and early life, the birth family's views about adoption and contact and

up-to-date information about themselves and their situation.

7. Where it is in the child's best interest for there to be ongoing links, including contact, with birth parents and families (including siblings separated by adoption), birth families will be involved in discussions about how best to achieve this and helped to fulfil agreed plans, e.g. through practical or financial support.

8. Where adoptive parents have agreed to inform the agency of the death of the adopted child or the breakdown of the adoption, birth parents or the 'next of kin' at adoption will, if they wish, be informed by the adoption agency.

9. Birth parents and birth families will be informed of their right to make representations and complaints."

Summary of process for deciding whether a child is to be placed for adoption
When considering whether a child should be placed for adoption:

1. The agency sets up the child's case record.
2. The agency provides counselling and information to the child and the parent(s) or guardian of the child, and ascertains their wishes and feelings.
3. The agency obtains information about the child.
4. The agency obtains information about the family.
5. The agency prepares the child's permanence report.
6. The agency sends the matter to the adoption panel for its recommendation and advice.
7. On receiving the panel's recommendation, the agency decides whether or not the child should be placed for adoption, and sends written notification of the decision to the child's parent(s) or guardian.
8. Where the child's parent is prepared to consent to placement under section 19 or 20, the agency should ask CAFCASS to appoint an officer of the service.

5.   Assessing and Approving Prospective Adopters

Once it has been decided that a child is to be placed for adoption, the next stage in the process is to assess and approve the prospective adopters. Thus, first, before placing a child with prospective adopters, the adoption agency is under a duty to:

(a) provide a counselling service for the prospective adopter(s);

(b) in the case of a child from outside the United Kingdom, explain to the prospective adopter(s) the procedure for adopting a child from the country in question and the legal implications of so doing;

(c) in any other case, explain the legal implications of, and procedure in relation to, placement for adoption and adoption; and

(d) provide written information about the above matters,

unless these duties have already been carried out by another adoption agency. (Regulation 21 of both the Agencies Regulations and the Agencies (Wales)

Regulations.) This duty requires the adoption agency to ensure that the prospective adopter(s) are given details of children who have been placed and are awaiting placement. The prospective adopter(s) should also be informed of the legal requirements which they will have to meet before they can be considered as prospective adopter(s) (see Chapter 2). In this respect, it is always advisable for prospective adopter(s) to seek legal advice. The procedure for making the application to the agency to be considered as prospective adopter(s) should be explained. This includes giving information about the enquiries, police check and health checks that will be made. It also includes ensuring that the prospective adopter(s) know and understand the various stages of the assessment, approval, matching and placement process before the adoption application can be made; and explaining the review and complaints procedures.

The prospective adopter's case record
When an adoption agency receives a written application, in the form provided by the agency, from a prospective adopter, the agency must set up a case record in respect of the prospective adopter and consider his suitability to adopt a child. The agency may ask the prospective adopter for any further information it may reasonably require. See regulation 22 of both the Agencies Regulations and the Agencies (Wales) Regulations. Regulation 22(3) of the Agencies Regulations goes on to specify that the adoption agency is required to place on the case record the following documents and information:

(a) the application by the prospective adopter for an assessment of his suitability to adopt a child;
(b) the information and reports obtained by the agency under the regulations;
(c) the prospective adopter's report and his observations on that report (see below);
(d) the written record of the proceedings of the adoption panel under regulation 26, its recommendation and the reasons for it, and any advice given by the panel to the agency;
(e) the record of the agency's decision;
(f) where there has been a request for a review of the decision (see page 220), the recommendation of the review panel;
(g) where applicable, the prospective adopter's review report and his observations on that report; and
(h) any other document or information obtained by the adoption agency which it considers should be included in that case record.

Police checks
In assessing suitability to adopt, the agency must first take steps to obtain, in respect of the prospective adopter(s) and any member of his household who

214

is over the age of eighteen, an enhanced criminal record certificate within the meaning of section 115 of the Police Act 1997, including the matters specified in subsection (6A) of that section.

If a prospective adopter or a member of his household aged eighteen or over has been convicted of a specified offence committed at the age of eighteen or over, or has been cautioned by a constable in respect of any such offence which he admitted when the caution was administered, he is not to be considered suitable to adopt a child. The specified offences are:

(a) an offence against a child;

(b) an offence specified in part 1 of schedule 3 to the Agencies Regulations (rape and sex offences);

(c) a breach of any of the prohibitions and restrictions relating to pornography in relation to prohibited goods which include indecent photographs of children under the age of sixteen years (see section 170 of the Customs and Excise Management Act 1979 and section 42 of the Customs Consolidation Act 1876);

(d) any other offence involving bodily injury to a child, other than an offence of common assault or battery.

In addition, an adoption agency may not consider a person suitable to adopt a child if he, or any member of his household aged eighteen or over, has been convicted of, or cautioned for (and, when cautioned, admitted the offence) any of the following offences, even though these offences have been repealed:

(a) an offence specified in paragraph 1 of part 2 of schedule 3 committed at the age of eighteen or over (rape and sex offences); or

(b) offences which fall within paragraph 2 or 3 of part 2 of schedule 3 (other sex offences and offences of indecency).

Where an adoption agency becomes aware that a prospective adopter or a member of his household has been convicted of or cautioned for any of these offences, the agency must notify the prospective adopter as soon as possible that he cannot be considered suitable to adopt a child. See regulation 23 of both the Agencies Regulations and the Agencies (Wales) Regulations.

Where the police check discloses an offence which does not fall within regulation 23(3) or (4), the adoption agency has a discretion whether or not to proceed with the application. Its decision and reasons for it must be placed on the prospective adopter's case record. The information received by the agency is confidential and, if the application is a joint one, must not be disclosed to the person's partner or spouse (Police Act 1997, section 124).

Preparation for adoption
The adoption agency is obliged to make arrangements for the prospective adopters to receive preparation for adoption, unless it is satisfied that the requirements have been carried out by another agency. Preparation for adoption includes providing the prospective adopter with information about

the following matters:

(a) the age range, sex, likely needs and background of children who may be placed for adoption by the adoption agency;

(b) the significance of adoption for a child and his family;

(c) contact between a child and his parent or guardian or other relatives where a child is authorised to be placed for adoption or is adopted;

(d) the skills which are necessary for an adoptive parent;

(e) the adoption agency's procedures in relation to the assessment of a prospective adopter and the placement of a child for adoption; and

(f) the procedure in relation to placement for adoption and adoption

(regulation 24, Agencies Regulations and regulation 25, Agencies (Wales) Regulations).

Further information

If the adoption agency forms a view, after carrying out the police checks and the preparation work described above, that the prospective adopter may be suitable to adopt a child, the agency must go on to the next stage, which consists of obtaining further information about the adopter(s). The information to be obtained is specified in part 1 of schedule 4 to the Agencies Regulations and the Agencies (Wales) Regulations. It includes information about the prospective adopter's extended family, home, neighbourhood, community, employment, income and expenditure, reasons for wishing to adopt, his feelings about adoption and its significance, and his parenting capacity. (Agencies Regulations, regulation 25(1) and (2) and Agencies (Wales) Regulations, regulation 26(1) and (2).)

Medical report

The adoption agency must obtain a written report from a registered medical practitioner about the health of the prospective adopter following a full examination, covering the matters set out in part 2 of schedule 4, unless the agency has received advice from its medical adviser that such a report is unnecessary (Agencies Regulations, regulation 25(3)(a) and Agencies (Wales) Regulations, regulation 26(3)(a)).

References

A prospective adopter is required to provided personal references and the adoption agency must obtain a written report of the interviews with the referees nominated (Agencies Regulations, regulation 25(3)(b) and Agencies (Wales) Regulations, regulation 26(3)(b)).

Information from the prospective adopter's local authority

The adoption agency must ascertain from the local authority in whose area the prospective adopter(s) has his home whether it has any information on the adopter which may be of relevance to the assessment, and, if so, obtain a written report from that authority. (Agencies Regulations, regulation 25(4) and Agencies (Wales) Regulations, regulation 26(3)(c).) The purpose of this is to ascertain whether there is any record of child protection issues in respect of the prospective adopter(s).

Matters to be taken into account
In making any report in respect of the suitability of any person to adopt, the adoption agency must take into account:
  (a) any information obtained as a consequence of providing counselling services to the prospective adopter;
  (b) any information obtained in consequence of the preparation for adoption (see above);
  (c) any information received as a consequence of obtaining an enhanced criminal record certificate (see above);
  (d) in the case of a Convention adoption, any additional information obtained about the prospective adopter as a consequence of regulation 15(4) of the Adoptions with a Foreign Element Regulations (SI 2005 No. 392, see page 349);
  (e) the written reports of the medical practitioner, the referees and the local authority (see above).
(The Suitability of Adopters Regulations 2005 (SI 2005 No. 1712), regulation 3).
Where the agency is assessing the suitability of a couple to adopt, it should also have regard to the need for stability and permanence in their relationship (Suitability of Adopters Regulations, regulation 4(2)). Where a person is putting himself or herself forward as a single prospective adopter, and that person is in a relationship, the stability and permanence of the relationship may nevertheless be a relevant factor to be considered and assessed.

The prospective adopter's report
The adoption agency has to prepare a written report (the "prospective adopter's report") which must include:
  (a) the information about the prospective adopter(s) as specified in part 1 of schedule 4;
  (b) a summary, written by the agency's medical adviser, of the state of health of the prospective adopter;
  (c) any relevant information from the local authority in whose area the prospective adopter(s) lives;
  (d) the observations of the agency on the police checks, the preparation for adoption and the provision of information about adoption;
  (e) the agency's assessment of the prospective adopter's suitability to adopt a child; and
  (f) any other information which the agency considers relevant
(Agencies Regulations, regulation 25(5); Agencies (Wales) Regulations,

regulation 26(4)).

Where the prospective adopter(s) has applied to adopt a child from outside the United Kingdom, the report should also include the name of the country from which the prospective adopter(s) wishes to adopt a child, confirmation that the prospective adopter(s) meets the eligibility requirements of that country, and the agency's assessment of the prospective adopter's suitability to adopt a child from outside the British Islands. (Agencies Regulations, regulation 25(6)). Further, the Agencies (Wales) Regulations, regulation 26(5)(c), requires the report to include any additional information obtained as a consequence of the requirements of the country of origin.

Where the adoption agency is of the opinion that the prospective adopter(s) is unlikely to be considered suitable to adopt a child, it may proceed to make the prospective adopter's report even though it has not obtained all the information required by the regulations (Agencies Regulations, regulation 25(7)). In coming to its decision, the matters taken into account by the adoption agency may be limited to any information received which is specified in part 1 of schedule 4 to the Agencies Regulations; the medical report; the referee's report; and the report from the local authority in whose area the prospective adopter(s) lives (Suitability of Adopters Regulations 2005, regulation 5).

Otherwise, the adoption agency should notify the prospective adopter(s) that his application will be presented to the adoption panel, give him a copy of the prospective adopter's report, and invite him to send any observations in writing to the agency within ten working days beginning with the date on which the notice is sent. At the end of the ten days, or earlier if a response is received from the prospective adopter(s), the adoption agency must send to the adoption panel the prospective adopter's report, the report of the registered medical practitioner, the reports on the interviews with the referees and the local authority's report. The adoption agency should also obtain, so far as is reasonably practicable, any other relevant information and send that information to the panel. See Agencies Regulations, regulation 25(8) to (10); Agencies (Wales) Regulations, regulation 26(6) to (8). The agency should also obtain any other relevant information requested by the panel, and send it to the panel (Agencies Regulations, regulation 25(10); Agencies (Wales) Regulations, regulation 26(10)).

Function of the adoption panel

The function of the panel is to consider the case and make a recommendation to the agency as to whether the prospective adopter(s) is suitable to adopt a child. Before making a recommendation the adoption panel must invite the prospective adopter(s) to attend a meeting of the panel. In considering what recommendation to make, the adoption panel may consider and take into account all the information and reports submitted to it; it may request the agency to obtain other relevant information; and it may obtain legal advice.

Where the adoption panel makes a positive recommendation to the adoption agency, the panel may advise the agency about the number of children the prospective adopter(s) may be suitable to adopt, their age(s), sex(es), likely needs and background(s).

See the Agencies Regulations, regulation 26; and the Agencies (Wales) Regulations, regulation 27.

Determining suitability to adopt

It is for the adoption agency to decide whether a prospective adopter is suitable to adopt; no member of the panel may take any part in the agency's decision. In determining the suitability of a prospective adopter, the adoption agency must take into account:

(a) the prospective adopter's report;

(b) the medical report and the report of the referees;

(c) the recommendation of the adoption panel;

(d) any other relevant information obtained by the agency at the request of the panel;

(e) where regulation 12 of the Foreign Element Regulations 2005 applies, any additional information obtained as a consequence of chapter 1 of part 3 of those regulations (see page 349);

(f) the need for stability and permanence

(Suitability of Adopters Regulations 2005, regulation 4).

Where the agency is considering the suitability of a couple to adopt, it should have regard to the need for stability and permanence in their relationship (Suitability of Adopters Regulations 2005, regulation 4(2)).

Notification to prospective adopters

Where the adoption agency decides that the prospective adopter(s) is suitable to adopt a child, it must notify him in writing of the decision (Agencies Regulations, regulation 27(3); Agencies (Wales) Regulations, regulation 28(3)).

If the decision is negative, the adoption agency must notify the prospective adopter(s) in writing that it proposes not to approve him as suitable to adopt a child (a "qualifying determination") with its reasons. The notification must include the recommendation of the adoption panel if that recommendation is different from the decision reached. Finally, it must advise him that he may, within forty working days (in Wales, twenty), beginning with the date on which the notification is sent, either submit any representations he wishes to the agency, or apply to the Secretary of State (in Wales, the National Assembly) for a review of the qualifying determination by an independent review panel. (Agencies Regulations, regulation 27(4); Agencies (Wales) Regulations, regulation 28(4); Independent Review of Determinations (Adoption) (Wales) Regulations 2005, regulation 4.)

If the prospective adopter(s) does not make any representations or apply for a review, the adoption agency should proceed to make its decision and notify the prospective adopters of it in writing, together with its reasons. If, on the other hand, representations are made, these, together with all the relevant information, must be resubmitted to the adoption panel for further consideration. The adoption panel must reconsider the case and make a fresh recommendation. (Agencies Regulations, regulation 27(5) to (7); Agencies (Wales) Regulations, regulation 28(5) to (7).)

The agency must then make a decision on the case on the basis of matters set out in (a) to (e) above. Where the referral to the adoption panel was made on receipt of representations, the agency must also take into account both the original recommendation of the panel and the fresh recommendation. Where the prospective adopter(s) applied for an independent review, the adoption agency must make a decision only after taking into account any recommendation of the independent review panel (see below) and the original recommendation of the adoption panel. It must then send a written notification of its decision to the prospective adopters. If the decision is negative, it must also state its reason for the decision and send a copy of the adoption panel's recommendation if this is different from the agency's decision. (Agencies Regulations, regulation 27(7) and (8); Agencies (Wales) Regulations, regulation 28(8) and (9).)

Independent review of qualifying determination
If a prospective adopter seeks an independent review of a qualifying determination as described above, the review is undertaken by a panel constituted for the purpose by the Secretary of State or the National Assembly. The review panel is independent of adoption agencies. It should be noted, however, that referral to the independent review panel is not an appeal process; nor does it deal with complaints against an adoption agency. A separate procedure for making complaints is available. The review panel cannot overturn the decision of the adoption agency. It may only review the information before it and request further information. It can then make a recommendation to the adoption agency as to the suitability or otherwise of the prospective adopter(s) to adopt a child, but not a *specific* child. The adoption agency is required to take into account any recommendation of the independent review panel when making its final decision on the prospective adopter's suitability to adopt a child.

The independent review of qualifying determination was set up by the Independent Review of Determinations (Adoption) Regulations 2004 (SI 2004 No. 190), made under the provisions of the Adoption Act 1976. These regulations applied to England only. The regulations made provision for the review by an independent review panel of a determination by an adoption agency that it did not propose to approve a prospective adopter as suitable to adopt a child. The Independent Review of Determinations (Adoption) (Wales) Regulations 2005 (SI 2005 No. 1819, W.147), made under sections

9(1), (2) and (4) and 12(1) to (3) of the 2002 Act, provide for such reviews. Presumably, similar regulations will be made for the continuation of this process in England. At the time of going to press, new regulations for England had not been issued. Reference is therefore made in the text to the 2005 Welsh regulations and the 2004 English regulations, on the basis that any new English regulations will be similar to the Welsh provisions and/or the 2004 regulations. The prospective adopter(s) should be reassured that there is no material difference between the two sets of regulations so far as the review process is concerned.

Processing an application for review: The prospective adopter(s) must, within forty days (in Wales, twenty) from the date of the qualifying determination, apply for a review. The application must be made in writing and set out the reasons/grounds for the request for review (regulation 9 of the Independent Review of Determinations (Adoption) Regulations 2004 and regulation 11 of the Independent Review of Determinations (Adoption) (Wales) Regulations 2005). The application should be acknowledged by the Secretary of State. The 2004 regulations set no time limit within which the acknowledgement should be given, but the Welsh regulations (regulation 12) provide that the National Assembly must acknowledge in writing, within five working days, receipt of any request made. The Secretary of State or the National Assembly should also, within the same period, notify the adoption agency of the request, and send a copy of the application for review (regulation 10(a) of the Independent Review of Determinations (Adoption) Regulations 2004 and regulation 13 of the Welsh regulations).

A panel is then constituted by the Secretary of State or the National Assembly. Regulation 13(2) of the Welsh regulations requires the National Assembly to appoint the panel within twenty-five days of receipt of the request, and to set a date for the panel to meet and review the qualifying determination. Regulation 13(3) requires the date for the review to be no later than three months after the date on which the determination is referred. Regulation 10(c) and (d) of the 2004 English regulations specify no time limit within which the panel should be appointed by the Secretary of State, nor any time limit within which the review should take place.

The prospective adopter(s) and the adoption agency must be notified of the date, time and venue of the panel meeting. Under the Welsh provisions notice must be given not less than five working days before the date fixed for the review. It is, however, likely that this information will be provided much earlier, having regard to the fact that the prospective adopter may wish to amend or provide further grounds, and/or to provide details for consideration by the panel; regulation 10(f) of the Independent Review of Determinations (Adoption) Regulation 2004 imposed a duty on the Secretary of State to inform the prospective adopter(s) in writing that he/she could provide to the panel further details of the grounds of the application, in writing, in the period up to two weeks before the review meeting, and orally at the review meeting.

The constitution and functions of the review panel: The panel is drawn from a list of persons appointed and serving as members of adoption agency panels (the "central list") kept by the Secretary of State or the National Assembly (as the case may be) who are considered, by reason of their skills, to have the qualifications or experience to be members of a panel. Regulation 4 of the Independent Review of Determinations (Adoption) Regulations 2004 provides that the review panel should consist of no more than ten members. The Independent Review of Determinations (Adoption) (Wales) Regulations 2005, regulation 5, provides for no more than five persons to be appointed as members of the panel. The panel should, where reasonably practicable, include an adoptive parent and an adopted person who has attained the age of eighteen. Under the Independent Review of Determinations (Adoption) Regulations 2004, the members of the panel included a chair, two social workers with at least three years' relevant post-qualifying experience, a registered medical practitioner and at least four other people. Although not specifically referred to in the regulations, it is implicit that all personnel on the panel would have some experience of working in the field of adoption or have knowledge or experience relevant to the adoption process. Regulation 5 of the 2005 Welsh regulations provides that the five members of the panel should include an adoptive parent and an adopted person. It also provides that the panel must be advised by a social worker within the meaning of Part IV of the Care Standards Act 2000, who should have at least five years' post-qualifying experience in adoption and family placement work; a registered medical practitioner with expertise in adoption work; and, where the panel considers it appropriate, a legal adviser with knowledge and expertise in adoption legislation.

A review panel is not permitted to deal with the determination unless at least four of its members, including the chair or vice chair, meet as a panel.

The panel is obliged to keep written records of its reviews of qualifying determinations, and the reasons for its recommendations, and ensure that the records are kept secure (regulation 8 of the Independent Review of Determinations (Adoption) Regulations 2004 and regulation 10 of the Independent Review of Determinations (Adoption) (Wales) Regulations 2005). The 2004 regulation also provides that the record must be retained for a period of twelve months from the date on which the recommendation is made.

A member or an adviser who is or was employed, whether paid under a contract of service or for services, or as a volunteer, at any time in the preceding two years, by the adoption agency against whose qualifying determination a review is being sought, is disqualified from playing any role in the review procedure (Independent Review of Determinations (Adoption)

(Wales) Regulations 2005, regulation 5(3)). The Independent Review of Determinations (Adoption) Regulations 2004, regulation 4(3), provides for a person to be disqualified from being appointed to the panel if:

   (a) he or a member of his family was involved in the making of the qualifying determination in question;

   (b) he is employed by the adoption agency which made the qualifying determination in question, or was employed by that agency within the period of two years prior to the date on which the qualifying determination was made;

   (c) where the adoption agency which made the qualifying determination is a local authority, he is an elected member of that local authority or was such a member within the period of two years prior to the date on which the qualifying determination was made;

   (d) where the adoption agency which made the qualifying determination is an appropriate voluntary organisation, he is concerned with the management of that agency or was so concerned within the period of two years prior to the date on which the qualifying determination was made;

   (e) he was approved as a prospective adopter by the adoption agency which made the qualifying determination in question;

   (f) in the case of an adopted person, the adoption agency which made the qualifying determination was the adoption agency which arranged his adoption; or

   (g) he knows, in a personal or professional capacity, the person making the application.

The term "employed" under both sets of regulations means employed under a contract of service or a contract for services, or as a volunteer.

A "member of his family" is defined in the Independent Review of Determinations (Adoption) Regulations 2004, regulation 4(4)(b), as "his spouse, a member of his household or a son, daughter, mother, father, sister or brother of his or of his spouse".

A chairperson, with expertise in adoption work, and having the skills and experience necessary for chairing a panel, is appointed to chair the panel. One of the members of the panel is appointed as a vice-chair to act as chair if the chairperson is absent or the office is vacant. Payment may be made to any member of the panel, of such expenses by the Secretary of State, or such fees by the National Assembly, at their discretion, as is considered reasonable (regulation 6 of the Independent Review of Determinations (Adoption) Regulations 2004 and regulation 8 of the Independent Review of Determinations (Adoption) (Wales) Regulations 2005).

Procedure to be followed by the adoption agency: Where an adoption agency receives notification of a prospective adopter's request for a review, the agency is obliged, within ten working days of receipt of that notification, to send to the Secretary of State the following information:

(a) all the information which was placed before the adoption panel in accordance with regulation 25 of the Agencies Regulations;

(b) any relevant information in relation to the prospective adopter(s) which was obtained by the agency after the documents and information were passed to the adoption panel;

(c) the qualifying determination and the reasons for it

(Agencies Regulations, regulation 28).

For Wales, the Agencies (Wales) Regulations, regulation 29(2), is more specific. It requires the adoption agency to send to the independent review panel the following information:

(a) all the reports and information which were sent to the adoption panel in accordance with regulation 26;

(b) any written representations made by the prospective adopter(s);

(c) any other reports or information sent by the adoption agency to the adoption panel;

(d) the record of the proceedings of the adoption panel, its recommendations and the reasons for its recommendations; and

(e) the notification, together with the reasons sent by the adoption agency to the prospective adopter(s) in accordance with regulation 28(4)(a) and (b).

Who may attend before the review panel: The prospective adopter(s) may attend the meeting of the panel with a McKenzie friend. A prospective adopter(s) who has any disability may bring a helper. Where English is not the prospective adopter's first language, an interpreter may also be brought. The expenses of the helper or interpreter will not, though, be paid by the panel. It will be for the prospective adopter(s) to make the necessary arrangements and meet the expenses.

At the review meeting the panel may ask the prospective adopter(s) questions.

The adoption agency is also entitled to be represented at the panel meeting. It is desirable that the agency is represented by the person who carried out the original assessment, so that any questions asked by the panel can be dealt with.

Procedure of the review panel: All relevant papers submitted by the prospective adopter(s) and the adoption agency must be placed before the panel not less that five working days before the date fixed for the review (Independent Review of Determinations (Adoption) (Wales) Regulations) 2005, regulation 13(2) to (5)). It is the duty of the review panel to review the qualifying determination and make a recommendation to the adoption agency which made it, as to whether or not a prospective adopter is suitable to be an adoptive parent. The panel will consider and take into account the agency's determination and reasons and the adoption panel's recommendations. It will also have regard to all the information which was presented to the adoption panel and any other information that has come to light since its decision, together with the grounds for review and information provided by the prospective adopter(s).

Recommendation of the review panel: The panel's recommendation will be that of the majority. The panel may either give its decision on the date fixed for the review or reserve its decision. The recommendation of the panel, with its reasons for it, and whether the recommendation was a unanimous one or by a majority, has to be recorded immediately in a document which must be signed and dated by the chairman. It is the duty of the Secretary of State or the National Assembly (as the case may be) without delay, and, in Wales, in any event within ten working days of the recommendation being made, to send a copy of it to the adoption agency which made the qualifying determination and to the prospective adopter(s) (Independent Review of Determinations (Adoption) (Wales) Regulations 2005, regulation 14).

Procedure following the recommendation of the review panel: Where the prospective adopter(s) have applied for a review, the adoption agency should make its decision on his suitability to adopt only after taking into account the recommendation of the independent review panel and the original recommendation of the adoption panel. The adoption agency's decision must be notified to the prospective adopter(s), and a copy of the decision must be sent to the Secretary of State. (Agencies Regulations, regulation 27(8) and (9); Agencies (Wales) Regulations, regulation 28(8) and (9).)

Review of approval
Where an adoption agency has approved a person as suitable to adopt a child, the agency is under a duty to review the approval whenever it considers it necessary to do so, and in any event must do so not more than one year (in Wales, two years) after approval, and thereafter at intervals of not more than one year (in Wales, two years). This is to ensure that there has not been any change in the circumstances of the prospective adopter(s), such as the separation of a couple, the birth of a child, or a criminal conviction. The review should encompass all the relevant factors set out at page 219. The requirement for review does not, however, apply where the child has been placed for adoption with the prospective adopter(s) or, in the case of a foreign child, the prospective adopter(s) has visited the child in the country where the child is habitually resident and has confirmed in writing that he wishes to proceed with the adoption. (Agencies Regulations, regulation 29(1) and (2) and Agencies (Wales) Regulations, regulation 30(1) and (2).)

In carrying out the review, the adoption agency must make such inquiries and obtain such further information as it considers necessary in order to review whether the prospective adopter(s) continues to be suitable to adopt a child, and seek and take into account the views of the prospective adopter(s) (Agencies Regulations, regulation 29(3); Agencies (Wales) Regulations, regulation 30(3)).

The Agencies (Wales) Regulations contain additional requirements. Thus, the adoption agency must consider, as part of each review:

(a) why no child has been placed with the prospective adopter;

(b) any arrangements for the provision of adoption support services and whether they should continue or be modified;

(c) where the child has been returned to the agency, the reasons for the child's return; and

(d) whether the prospective adopter is still suitable to adopt a child

(Agencies (Wales) Regulations, regulation 30(4)).

The adoption agency is also required to set out in writing the arrangements for the review, and draw those arrangements to the attention of the prospective adopter(s) and any other relevant person. It is also under a duty to record in writing and place on the prospective adopter(s)' case record:

(a) the information obtained in respect of the prospective adopter(s);

(b) details of the proceedings at any meeting arranged by the agency to consider the review; and

(c) details of any decision made

(Agencies (Wales) Regulations, regulation 30(5)).

Termination of approval

If the adoption agency considers that the prospective adopter(s) is no longer suitable to adopt a child, it must:

(a) prepare a prospective adopter's review report which must include the agency's reasons and any other information which the agency considers relevant;

(b) notify the prospective adopter(s) that his case has been referred to the adoption panel; and

(c) give him a copy of the report, inviting him to send any observations to the agency within ten working days beginning with the date on which the report is sent.

If the prospective adopter(s) makes representations, these, together with the prospective adopter's review report, are resubmitted to the adoption panel. If the adoption panel requires further information, the adoption agency must provide it.

The panel considers the review report, together with the prospective adopter'(s) observations and any other information passed to it, following which the panel makes a recommendation to the agency as to whether the prospective adopter(s) continues to be suitable. Following the panel's recommendation the adoption agency make its decision. If the decision is negative the procedure outlined above in respect of qualifying determinations must be followed. See Agencies Regulations, regulation 29(4) to (8) and Agencies (Wales) Regulations, regulation 30(6) to (11).

Duties in relation to a child resident outside the British Islands
Where an adoption agency decides to approve a prospective adopter(s) as suitable to adopt, in relation to a child who is habitually resident outside the British Islands, the agency is required to send to the Secretary of State or, in Wales, the National Assembly:

(a) written confirmation of the decision and its recommendation in relation to the number of children the prospective adopter(s) may be suitable to adopt, their age(s), sex(es), likely needs and background;

(b) the medical report, referees' report, any local authority's report, the prospective adopter's report and other information placed before the adoption panel;

(c) all records of the proceedings of the adoption panel, its recommendation and the reasons for the recommendation;

(d) if the prospective adopter(s) applied for the review of a qualifying determination, the record of the proceedings of the independent review panel, its recommendation and the reasons for it; and

(e) any other information relating to the case which the Secretary of State or the National Assembly or the foreign authority may require

(Agencies Regulations, regulation 30 and Agencies (Wales) Regulations, regulation 31).

The National Adoption Standards
The National Adoption Standards, in respect of prospective adopters provide as follows:

"People who are interested in becoming adoptive parents will be welcomed without prejudice, responded to promptly and given clear information about recruitment, assessment and approval. They will be treated fairly, openly and with respect throughout the adoption process.

1. Information on becoming an adoptive parent will be provided, including what is expected of adopters. Applicants will be given the opportunity to hear about preparation and support services available to adopters, and to talk to others who have adopted children.

2. Clear information will be given about children locally and across the country who need families to help prospective adopters decide whether to proceed further.

3. Written eligibility criteria and details of the assessment and approval process will be provided. a) Applicants will be considered in terms of their capacity to look after children in a safe and responsible way that meets their developmental needs. Where agencies have specific eligibility criteria e.g. because the agency has particular religious beliefs, applicants will be told what these are and, if necessary, be referred to another agency. People will not be automatically excluded on the grounds of age, health or other factors, except in the case of certain criminal convictions. b) The assessment and

approval process will be comprehensive, thorough and fair. An explanation will be given of the need for status checks and enquiries to be made about prospective adopters and members of their household.

4. There will be clear written timescales for each stage. Applicants can expect: a) Written information sent in response to their enquiry within 5 working days. b) Follow up interviews/invitation to an information meeting within 2 months c) Agencies will prioritise applications that are more likely to meet the needs of children waiting for adoption. Where agencies and applicants decide to proceed, a decision on the outcome will be made by the agency following the Adoption Panel within six months of the receipt of the formal application. Where the agency decides not to proceed applicants will be informed in writing and advised of the options open to them. d) If b) and c) follow each other without a gap, the whole process from enquiry to decision should not take more than 8 months. Panels will record reasons for delays.

5. Foster carers who make a formal application to adopt children in their care will be entitled to the same information and preparation as other adopters and be assessed within four months.

6. Applicants will be kept informed of progress throughout. They will receive a copy of the assessment report at least 28 days before an adoption panel and have the opportunity to comment on the report, and, if they wish, to attend the adoption panel and be heard.

7. Prospective adopters will be informed of their right to make representations and complaints."

Prospective adopters should be informed orally of the agency's decision within two working days, and written confirmation should be sent to them within five working days.

Summary of the procedure for assessing and approving prospective adopters
1. The agency offers information and counselling to the prospective adopter(s).
2. The agency considers the application.
3. The agency carries out police checks and obtains medical reports and references.
4. The agency prepares the prospective adopter's report and other reports.
5. The agency provides a copy of the prospective adopter's report to the applicant and invites comments, and sends the report to the adoption panel.
6. The adoption panel considers the case, makes recommendations and gives advice.
7. The agency decides whether or not the prospective adopter(s) are suitable to adopt a child.
8. If the agency decides to approve the prospective adopter(s), it notifies them of the decision and arranges for matching and placement. The agency also informs the parent(s) or guardian of the child.
9. If the agency decides not to approve the prospective adopter(s), it must inform them and notify them of their right to make representations for

review by the adoption panel or the independent review panel.

10. The agency makes a decision on receiving the recommendation of the adoption panel or the independent review panel. If it decides to approve the application, it notifies the prospective adopters. If it decides to refuse the application, it must inform the prospective adopters.

11. If the prospective adopters are approved but a child is not placed with them, the agency must carry out reviews. The outcome of each review must be notified to the prospective adopters.

Summary of timescale in respect of prospective adopters

1. The prospective adopter(s) should be sent written information within five working days of enquiring about the adoption process.

2. The adoption panel should be sent information about the prospective adopter(s) within six weeks of the completion of the prospective adopters' report.

3. The adoption panel's recommendation on the suitability of the prospective adopters should be made within eight months of receipt of their formal application.

4. The agency should make its decision whether or not to approve the prospective adopter(s) within seven working days of the panel's recommendation, and the prospective adopter(s) should be informed of the decision orally and in writing of the decision.

6.   The Adoption and Children Act Register

The background

In the White Paper, *Adoption – A New Approach* (2000, Cm 5017), the Government accepted a recommendation to establish a new adoption register, initially to cover England and Wales, to tackle delays in finding suitable adoptive placements for children. The proposals were set out in paragraphs 6.8 to 6.12 as follows:

"8. The Register will provide a national infrastructure for adoption services. It will hold information on approved adoptive families and children for whom adoption is the plan. This information will be used to suggest families for children where a local family is either not desirable or cannot be found within a reasonable period of time.

9.   Councils will be required to place details of all children waiting to be adopted and approved adoptive families on the Register. They will need to obtain the consent of the children, subject to their age and understanding, and families before doing so. The Government will also encourage voluntary adoption agencies to make full use of the Register.

10.   Adoptive families will be placed on the Register as soon as they are approved for adoption, and children when the plan for adoption is

made. This will enable the Register to produce non-identifying data on the characteristics of the two groups, and the success of the matching process.

11. Following the initial placement of a child or family on the Register for information purposes, social workers will be given an agreed period of time to find a family or child locally. This period may be extended for adoption agencies involved in local and regional consortia arrangements.

12. At the end of this agreed period, or immediately where finding a family locally is not in the best interests of the child, the Register will be used to suggest matches between children and adoptive families. A team of staff with social work expertise will offer advice on these matches, which will then be considered locally by the children and families' social workers."

The intention was to have the register set up by July 2001 under powers then in place. A register was established by the Department of Health in August 2001 and a number of adoption agencies have been "piloting" it; see Department of Health Circular LAC 2002(5). The register permits adoption agencies to carry out their own research for local matches, or regional matches if the agency is part of a consortium, within specified times.

Under the scheme which has operated, before submitting details for entry on the register, an adoption agency is required to obtain the consent of the child in question if he is able to understand what is proposed and its implications. It is for the social worker to decide whether the child has such understanding and is competent to make an informed decision. Consent should be obtained in writing, and placed on the child's case records. The consent given must be unequivocal. Consent from the prospective adopters is also required. The person giving the consent must have a clear understanding of how the information will be used. He must also have a full understanding of how the register operates, namely who will have access to the register; the consequences of being included on the register; and the type of information which he will be required to provide. The social worker should go through the required details carefully with the prospective adopter. If the consent of the child or the prospective adopter is not forthcoming, the details may not be entered on the register. The issue of consent must be reviewed periodically to ensure that it is still valid. Any change in the information appearing on the register must be notified.

The child's details are not submitted for entry on the register until the adoption agency has confirmed that adoption is in the child's best interest. Where care proceedings are pending, registration cannot take place until a final order is made. Information about a prospective adopter should be submitted as soon as he is approved. Adoption agencies are encouraged to consider any links between children and adopters suggested by the register and report back. If a link is not to be pursued, the agency is expected to give its reasons.

Once forms have been submitted to the register, adoption agencies are given timescales to search for local matches. For children, the maximum time for a local match is three months, with a further three months if the agency belongs to a consortium. In the case of a prospective adopter, it is six months for a local match, with a further three months if the agency belongs to a consortium.

The statutory provisions

Sections 125 to 131 of the Adoption and Children Act 2002 concern the Adoption and Children Act Register. Section 125 confirms the proposals in the White Paper by providing that an Order in Council may be made, providing for the Secretary of State to establish and maintain a register to be called the Adoption and Children Act Register. The register would contain prescribed information about children who are suitable for adoption; about prospective adopters who are suitable to adopt; and about persons included in the register in respect of things occurring after their inclusion. The Order may also provide for the register to contain information for the purpose of giving assistance in finding persons with whom children may be placed for purposes other than adoption. By virtue of section 125(2)(b), the Order may apply any of the provisions of sections 126 to 131 with or without modification for the purpose of finding persons with whom children may be placed for purposes other than adoption. The register is not to be open to public inspection (section 125(3)).

A child is suitable for adoption if an adoption agency is satisfied that the child ought to be placed for adoption. Prospective adopters are suitable to adopt a child if an adoption agency is satisfied that they are suitable to have a child placed with them for adoption (section 131(2)).

An adoption agency means a local authority in England or a registered adoption society whose principal office is in England (section 130(1)), but an Order may provide for any requirements imposed on adoption agencies in respect of the register to apply to Scottish local authorities and voluntary organisations providing adoption services; and to local authorities in Wales and registered adoption societies whose principal offices are in Wales (section 130(1) and (2)).

Section 126 authorises the Secretary of State to make arrangements to delegate to an organisation any of the functions assigned to him by Order under section 125, of establishing and maintaining the register, and disclosing information entered in, or compiled from information entered in, the register. The Secretary of State may make arrangements for payments to be made to the organisation for this service (section 126(2)). If the Secretary of State makes any such arrangements, the organisation would be required to carry out the functions in accordance with any directions given by the Secretary of State (section 126(3)). Any arrangements made by the Secretary of State must be made in consultation with and with the agreement of the Scottish Ministers (if the register applies to Scotland) and of the Assembly if the register applies to Wales (section 126(4)).

An organisation to whom such functions are delegated may be authorised to act as agent for the payment of or receipt of sums payable by adoption agencies to other adoption agencies, and may require adoption agencies to pay or receive such sums through the organisation. The organisation must perform such functions in accordance with any directions given by the Secretary of State; such directions may be of general or special application. Directions given by the Secretary of State require the agreement of the Scottish Ministers if any payment agency provision applies to Scotland, and of the Assembly if any payment agency provision applies to Wales (section 127).

The Order under section 125 may specify the information which must be provided by adoption agencies to the Secretary of State or the registration organisation for entry in the register, and the form and manner in which that information must be given (section 128(1) and (2)). A fee may be payable to the Secretary of State or the registration organisation for registering the information in the register. The consent of the prospective adopters and the children (or prescribed person) must first have been obtained before any information is included in the register, no doubt to protect their right to respect for family life and privacy (section 128(3) and (4)).

Prescribed information entered in the register may be disclosed by the Secretary of State or the registration organisation only in accordance with the provisions of section 129. These are:

(a) where an adoption agency is acting on behalf of a child who is suitable for adoption, to the agency to assist in finding prospective adopters with whom it would be appropriate for the child to be placed;

(b) where an adoption agency is acting on behalf of prospective adopters who are suitable to adopt a child, to the agency to assist in finding a child appropriate for adoption by them

(section 129(2)).

Information may also be disclosed by the Secretary of State or the registration organisation to any prescribed person for use for statistical or research purposes, or other prescribed purposes (section 129(3)). Disclosure may be subject to terms and conditions (section 129(6)).

The Order made under section 125 may prescribe the steps to be taken by adoption agencies in respect of information received by them (section 129(4)). A fee may be payable to the Secretary of State or the registration organisation by adoption agencies in respect of information given to them (section 129(7)). A person who discloses information otherwise than in accordance with the provision of section 129 is guilty of an offence. On summary conviction, an offender is liable to imprisonment for a term up to three months or a fine of £5,000 or both (section 129(8) and (9)).

At the time of writing (November 2005), no Order in Council pursuant to the above provisions has been made.

7. Matching and Approval of Placements

An adoption agency is under a duty to take certain steps relating to the proposed placement of a child for adoption. These again include an information-gathering and giving process; an assessment of the adoptive family's needs; the preparation of an adoption placement report; and the submission of the information to the adoption panel for its recommendation and decision. At this stage the agency needs to consider and compare alternative prospective adopters for a particular child, and assess their respective abilities to meet the child's needs.

The proposed placement

When the adoption agency has identified prospective adopter(s) for a child, and is considering placing the child with him, the adoption agency is under a duty to:

(a) provide the prospective adopter(s) with the child's permanence report and any other relevant information;

(b) meet the prospective adopter(s) to discuss the placement;

(c) ascertain the views of the prospective adopter(s) about the placement and the agency's proposals for contact with the child;

(d) provide a counselling service for, and any further information to, the prospective adopter(s)

(Agencies Regulations, regulation 31; Agencies (Wales) Regulations, regulation 32).

The Agencies (Wales) Regulations contain additional requirements. Regulation 32(1)(c) requires the agency to ascertain the prospective adopter's views on the child's assessed needs for adoption support services and on any restrictions on the exercise of parental responsibility by the prospective adopter(s). Under regulation 32(2), once the above procedure has been completed but before the next step is taken by the adoption agency, the prospective adopter(s) must confirm in writing his agreement to the proposed placement. The agency is also required, again under regulation 32(2), where the child is of sufficient age and understanding, to counsel the child and tell the child about the prospective adopters, their family circumstances and home environment; and ascertain the child's views about the proposed placement, contact arrangements and any restrictions of the prospective adopter's parental responsibility.

Assessment of needs and preparation of the adoption placement report

If the adoption agency is the local authority, it must, before placing a child for adoption, assess whether the child, the prospective adopter(s), or the prospective adoptive family needs adoption support services. Where the agency is a registered adoption society, it must notify the prospective adopter(s) that he may request that such an assessment be carried out by the local authority in whose area he lives. If he does so request, the agency passes to the relevant authority, at its request, a copy of the child's permanence report and the prospective adopter's report (Agencies Regulations, regulation 31(2); Agencies (Wales) Regulations, regulation 32(2)).

The agency must also consider the arrangements for allowing any person contact with the child, and whether the parental responsibility of any parent or guardian or of the prospective adopter is to be restricted to any extent. It must prepare a written report, referred to as "the adoption placement report", which should include:

(a) the reason for proposing the placement;

(b) the information gathered by the agency when it informed the prospective adopter(s) of the placement (see above);

(c) where the agency is a local authority, its proposal for the provision of adoption support services for the adoptive family;

(d) the proposal for contact between the child and any person;

(e) any other relevant information;

(f) (in England only) the agency's proposals for restricting parental responsibility where appropriate

(Agencies Regulations, regulation 31(2)(d); Agencies (Wales) Regulations, regulation 32(3)(d)).

Referral to the adoption panel
Once an adoption agency decides to place the case before the adoption panel for its consideration, the agency must notify the prospective adopter(s) of its intention to do so and give him a copy of the placement report. The notification must include an invitation to the prospective adopter(s) to make any observations in writing to the agency within ten days beginning with the date on which the notification is sent.

At the end of the ten-day period, or earlier if the observations have been received, the agency must send to the adoption panel the adoption placement report; the child's permanence report; the prospective adopter(s) report; and its observations. If the adoption panel requests further information in connection with the placement, the agency must provide that information to the panel. (Agencies Regulations, regulation 31(3) to (5); Agencies (Wales) Regulations, regulation 32(4), (5) and (8)).

The regulations provide for situations where more than one adoption agency is concerned in a particular case. Thus, where one agency (agency A) intends to refer the proposed placement to the adoption panel, and another agency (agency B) made the decision that the child should be placed for adoption or that the prospective adopter(s) is a suitable person to adopt the child, agency A can refer the proposed placement to the adoption panel only if it has consulted agency B about the proposed placement. In either case agency A must open a child case record and a prospective adopter's case record, and place on the appropriate record the information and documents it receives from agency B. (Agencies Regulations, regulation 31(6) and (7) and see Agencies (Wales) Regulations, regulation 32(6)).

Functions of the adoption panel in relation to a proposed placement
The adoption panel must consider the proposed placement and make a recommendation to the adoption panel whether the child should be placed with the prospective adopter(s). The adoption panel may make the recommendation only if:
 (a) all three decisions – to recommend that the child be placed for adoption, that the prospective adopter(s) is suitable to adopt a child, and that the child be placed with the prospective adopter(s) – are made at the same meeting; or
 (b) the adoption agency, or another adoption agency, has already made a decision that the child should be placed for adoption and that the prospective adopter(s) is suitable to adopt a child.
In other words, the recommendation on the placement may not be made before the recommendations that the child be placed for adoption, and that the prospective adopter(s) are suitable to adopt. (Agencies Regulations, regulation 32(1) and (5); Agencies (Wales) Regulations, regulation 33(4)).

In considering a proposed placement, the adoption panel must have regard to:
 (a) the fact that it is under a duty, when making any decision in relation to the child, to apply the welfare principle and the welfare test set out in section 1(2), (4) and (5) of the Adoption and Children Act 2002 (see page 111 *et seq*);
 (b) all the information contained in the various reports placed before it. The adoption panel may ask for more information and seek legal advice if it considers it necessary;
 (c) where the agency is the local authority, the arrangements it proposes for the provision of adoption support services for the adoptive family;
 (d) the arrangements for contact between the child and any other person;
 (e) (under the Welsh regulations) whether an application for a placement order should be made; and
 (f) whether the parental responsibility of any parent or guardian or the prospective adopter(s) should be restricted and if so, to what extent.
(Agencies Regulations, regulation 32(2); Agencies (Wales) Regulations, regulation 33(3)).

The adoption agency's decision
On receiving the adoption panel's recommendation, the adoption agency must decide whether or not the child should be placed for adoption with the prospective adopter(s). In making that decision, it must take into account the recommendation of the adoption panel, and apply the welfare principle and the adoption welfare test. No member of the adoption panel may take part in this decision. The agency must then:

(a) notify the prospective adopter(s) of the decision in writing;

(b) notify in writing the parent or guardian, if his whereabouts are known, and the father of the child if his identity is known, that the child has been placed for adoption;

(c) if the decision is to place the child with the prospective adopter(s), explain to the child, in an appropriate manner having regard to the age and understanding of the child, its decision; and

(d) place on the child's case records:

    (i) the prospective adopter's report,

    (ii) the adoption placement report and the prospective adopter's observations,

    (iii) the written record of the proceedings of the adoption panel and its recommendation and reasons for the recommendation, and

    (iv) any advice given by the panel to the agency and the record of the notification of the agency's decision

(Agencies Regulations regulation 33; Agencies (Wales) Regulations, regulation 34).

The adoption agency must place on the child's record and in the prospective adopter's record the decision and the reasons for it (regulations 12 and 22 of both the Agencies Regulations and the Agencies (Wales) Regulations).

Functions of the adoption agency where the child is from overseas
Certain additional duties arise in the case of a proposed adoption of a child who is habitually resident outside the British Islands. Where an adoption agency receives from a foreign authority information about a child to be adopted by a prospective adopter(s), the agency must send a copy of the information to the prospective adopter(s) unless it is aware that the prospective adopter(s) has already received a copy. It must consider the information and meet the prospective adopter(s) to discuss the information and, if appropriate, provide counselling, and give him any further information as may be required. (Agencies Regulations regulation 34; Agencies (Wales) Regulations, regulation 35.)

Summary of the procedure for matching and approving a proposed placement
1. The agency identifies a match and provides the prospective adopter(s) with the child's permanence report.

2. The agency meets the prospective adopter(s) to discuss the proposed placement and ascertain their views.
3. If the placement is to proceed, the agency assesses the prospective adopter's need for adoption support services and considers the arrangements for contact.
4. The agency notifies the adopters that it has referred the case to the adoption panel and gives them a copy of the adoption placement report.
5. The agency refers the proposed placement to the adoption panel for approval. The panel may seek legal advice and/or ask for more information. It then makes a recommendation and may give advice.
6. On receipt of the panel's recommendation, the agency makes a decision on the placement and notifies the prospective adopter(s), the parent(s) or guardian and the child.

8. Placement and Reviews

Procedure to be followed before placement

Once the decision is taken to place a child with the identified prospective adopter(s), the adoption agency must, as soon as possible (in Wales, seven days before the child is placed), send the prospective adopter(s) an adoption placement plan in respect of the child. The adoption placement plan must include the information set out in schedule 5 to the Agencies Regulations, or schedule 6 to the Agencies (Wales) Regulations.

Where the child already has his home with the prospective adopter(s), the adoption agency must notify the prospective adopter(s) in writing of the date on which the child is placed for adoption with him by that agency.

A child who is less than six weeks old should not be placed for adoption unless the parent or guardian of the child has agreed in writing that the child may be placed for adoption.

The agency is authorised to place the child for adoption with the prospective adopter(s) only after:

(a) it has been notified by the prospective adopter(s) that he wishes to proceed with the placement;

(b) it has sent to the prospective adopter's general practitioner written notification of the proposed placement, together with a written report of the child's health history and current state of health;

(c) it has sent to the local authority (if that authority is not the adoption agency) and Primary Care Trust or Local Health Board (Wales) in whose area the prospective adopter has his home, written notification of the proposed placement; and

(d) where the child is of compulsory school age, it has sent to the local education authority in whose area the prospective adopter(s) has his home, written notification of the proposed placement; and information about the child's educational history, and whether he has been or is likely to be assessed for special educational needs under the Education Act 1996.

The adoption agency must notify the prospective adopter(s) in writing of any change to the adoption placement plan and must place on the child's case records a copy of the adoption placement plan and any amendments made to that plan. Where the child is less than six weeks old and a placement order has not been made, but the parents have agreed to the placement, a copy of the agreement must be placed on the child's record. See Agencies Regulations, regulation 35; Agencies (Wales) Regulations, regulation 36.

Reviews

Where an adoption agency is authorised to place a child for adoption but has not done so, the agency must carry out a review of the child's case not more than three months after the date on which the agency was first authorised to place the child, and thereafter not more than six months after the date of the first review, until the child is placed for adoption.

Where a child has been placed for adoption, the agency must ensure that the child and the prospective adopter(s) are visited within one week of the placement, and thereafter at least once a week for four weeks. Written reports of each such visit must be made. Advice and assistance to the prospective adopter(s) must also be provided as the agency considers necessary. A review of the child's case must be carried out not more than four weeks after the date on which the child was placed for adoption (the first review); and again not more than three months after the first review; and thereafter not more than six months after the date of the previous review, unless the child is returned to the agency by the prospective adopter(s) or an adoption order is made. See Agencies Regulations, regulation 36; Agencies (Wales) Regulations, regulation 37.

Matters to be considered on review: When carrying out a review, an adoption agency is under an obligation to ascertain so far as is reasonably practicable, and to consider, the views of the child having regard to his age and understanding. It must also ascertain and take account of the views of the prospective adopter(s) with whom the child is placed for adoption, and the views of any other person the agency considers relevant. In addition, the agency must have regard to the following matters:

    (a) whether the adoption agency remains satisfied that the child should be placed for adoption;

    (b) the child's needs, welfare and development, and whether any changes need to be made to meet his needs or assist his development;

    (c) the existing arrangements for contact and whether they should continue or be altered;

    (d) where the child is placed for adoption, the arrangements in relation to the exercise of parental responsibility for the child, and whether they should continue or should be altered;

(e) the arrangements for the provision of adoption support services for the adoptive family and whether there should be any reassessment of the need for those services;

(f) in consultation with the appropriate agencies, the arrangements for assessing and meeting the child's health care and educational needs;

(g) the frequency of the reviews.

(Agencies Regulations, regulation 36(5) and (6); Agencies (Wales) Regulations, regulation 37(6) and (7)).

Where the child is subject to a placement order but has not been placed at the time of the six-month review, the local authority must establish why the child has not been placed and consider what further steps should be taken in that respect. It must also consider whether it remains satisfied that the child should be placed for adoption. (Agencies Regulations, regulation 36(7); Agencies (Wales) Regulations, regulation 37(8).)

Notification of review: The outcome of each review must be notified to:

(a) the child if he is of sufficient age and understanding;

(b) the prospective adopter(s); and

(c) any other relevant person.

The adoption agency must record in writing, in the child's case record, all the information it obtains during review visits, including the views expressed by the child; details of any proceedings of any meeting arranged by the agency to consider any aspect of the review of the case; and details of any decision made in the course of the review.

If a child is returned to the adoption agency, a review must be carried out between twenty-eight days and forty-two days of the child's return. In Wales, the review must be carried out no later that twenty-eight days after the date on which the child is returned. When carrying out the review the agency must have regard to all the matters set out in paragraphs (a), (b), (c) and (f) above.

See Agencies Regulations, regulation 36(8) to (10); Agencies (Wales) Regulations, regulation 37(9) to (11).

Independent reviewing officer: Section 118 of the Adoption and Children Act 2002, which came into force in September 2004, amended section 26 of the Children Act 1989 (review of cases of looked after children). In particular, it amended section 26(2)(e) (requirement to consider the discharge of a care order) to encompass a review of the care plan and its amendment if necessary. The amendment was made as a consequence of the fact that, on making a care order, responsibility for the child is transferred to the local authority and the court had no control over any decisions made in respect of the child, nor could it monitor the child's progress in care, and the House of Lords' rejection of the suggestion that the care plan should contain "starred milestones" (*Re S (Children) (Care Order: Implementation of Care Plan); Re W and B (Children) (Care Order: Adequacy of Care Plan)* [2002] UKHL 10, [2002] 2 AC 291, [2002] 2 WLR 720, [2002] 2 All ER 192, [2002] 1 FLR 815). The amendment to the Children Act 1989 requires the local authority to appoint an independent reviewing officer whose function is to participate in the review process, monitor the local authority's functions and refer a case to CAFCASS where appropriate. The Agencies Regulations, regulation 37(1) and the Agencies (Wales) Regulations, regulation 38(1), impose a duty on a local authority, or a registered adoption society which is a voluntary organisation providing accommodation for a child, to appoint an independent reviewing officer in respect of each child authorised to be placed for adoption, to carry out the functions set out in section 26(2A) of the Children Act 1989.

Qualification of the independent reviewing officer: The independent reviewing officer must be a social worker registered in a register maintained by the General Social Care Council or by the Care Council for Wales under section 5 of the Care Standards Act 2000, or in a corresponding register maintained under the laws of Scotland and Northern Ireland. He must have sufficient relevant social work experience to undertake the duties required of the independent reviewing officer under section 26(2A) of the Children Act 1989. The Agencies (Wales) Regulations, regulation 38(1), requires the independent reviewing officer to hold a social work diploma, a social work degree or an equivalent qualification recognised by the Care Council for Wales. (Agencies Regulations, regulation 37(2) and (3); Agencies (Wales) Regulations, regulation 38(2).)

A person who is an employee of the adoption agency may not be appointed as independent reviewing officer if he is:

(a) involved in the management of the case, or under the direct management of a person involved in the management of the case; or

(b) a person with management responsibilities in relation to a person involved in the management of the case; or

(c) a person with control over the resources allocated to the case

(Agencies Regulations, regulation 37(4); Agencies (Wales) Regulations, regulation 38(3)).

Functions of the independent reviewing officer: The independent reviewing officer must:

(a) so far as is reasonably practicable, attend any meetings in connection with the review of the child's case and chair any such meeting that he attends;

(b) so far as is reasonably practicable, take steps to ensure that the review is conducted in accordance with regulation 36 (in Wales, regulation 37);

(c) ensure that the child's views are understood and taken into account;
(d) ensure that the persons responsible for implementing the decision taken in consequence of the review are identified;
(e) ensure that any failure to review the case as provided for in the regulations (see above), or to take steps to make arrangements agreed at the review, is brought to the attention of persons at an appropriate level of seniority within the adoption agency;
(f) assist the child to obtain legal advice, if the child wishes to take proceedings on his own account, or establish whether an appropriate adult is able and willing to provide such assistance to bring proceedings on the child's behalf

(Agencies Regulations, regulation 37(5) to (7); Agencies (Wales) Regulations, regulation 38(5) to (7)).

The adoption agency must inform the independent reviewing officer of any significant failure to make the arrangements agreed at a review, and any significant changes in the child's circumstances after the review (Agencies Regulations, regulation 37(8); Agencies (Wales) Regulations, regulation 38(7)).

Withdrawal of consent
A parent or guardian of a child, having given consent or advance consent to the child's being placed for adoption, may later withdraw that consent in accordance with section 52(8) of the Adoption and Children Act 2002. In such a case, if the adoption agency is a local authority, it must immediately review its decision to place the child for adoption; if it decides to apply for a placement order, it must notify the parent or guardian of the child, the child's father where appropriate, and, if the child is placed for adoption, the prospective adopter(s) with whom the child is placed (see page 63). Where the consent was given to an adoption agency other than a local authority, and is withdrawn, the agency must immediately consider whether it should notify the local authority in whose area the child is living. (Agencies Regulations, regulation 38; Agencies (Wales) Regulations, regulation 39.)

Contact
Where it has been decided to place a child for adoption, the adoption agency is required to consider what arrangements it should make for allowing any person contact with the child (the "contact arrangements"). In doing so, the adoption agency is required to take account of the wishes and feelings of the parent or guardian of the child. Where the father of the child does not have parental responsibility but it is appropriate to take into account his wishes and feelings, the adoption agency must do so. It must also be guided by the welfare principle and the factors set out in the adoption welfare checklist.

Any arrangements the agency makes relating to contact must be notified to:

(a) the child if he is of sufficient age and understanding;

(b) the parent or guardian of the child if his whereabouts are known;

(c) the father of the child if appropriate;

(d) any other person in whose favour there was a contact order; and

(e) any other relevant person.

Before a child is placed for adoption, the adoption agency is required to review the arrangements for contact in the light of the views of the prospective adopter(s) and any advice given by the adoption panel. If it is then proposed to make any changes to the arrangements, the views of the child, his parent or guardian, his father and any other relevant person must be sought; those views must be taken into account when deciding the arrangements for contact while the child remains in the placement. The adoption agency must set out the contact arrangements in the contact plan and keep the arrangements under review. See Agencies Regulations, regulation 46; Agencies (Wales) Regulations, regulation 47.

Pursuant to section 27 of the Adoption and Children Act 2002, an adoption agency may refuse contact that would otherwise be required by virtue of an order, if it is satisfied that it is necessary to do so to safeguard or promote the child's welfare. The refusal must be decided upon as a matter of urgency and may not have effect for more than seven days. Section 27(3) provides that regulations may make provisions as to the steps to be taken by the agency when it seeks to refuse contact; the circumstances in which, and conditions upon which, the terms of an order made under section 26 may be varied by agreement; and the notification which the agency is required to give in respect of any variation or suspension. Regulation 47 of the Agencies Regulations (regulation 47(3) of the Agencies (Wales) Regulations) specifically deal with those matters.

Thus, where it is decided to refuse contact that would otherwise be required by virtue of an order under section 26 of the Adoption and Children Act 2002, the agency must inform the following persons of its decision:

(a) the child if he is of sufficient age and understanding;

(b) his parent or guardian;

(c) his father if appropriate; and

(d) the prospective adopter(s) if the child has been placed.

If an order under section 26 of the Adoption and Children Act 2002 has been made, it may be departed from only if a written agreement had been reached between the agency and the person in whose favour the order was made, and:

(a) the child agrees to the change;

(b) there was consultation before the agreement was reached with the prospective adopter(s) if the child is placed with them; and

(c) the agency has given written confirmation to the child, the parent or guardian and father of the child, and the prospective adopter/s if the child has been placed with them for adoption

(regulation 47(2) of both the Agencies Regulations and the Agencies

(Wales) Regulations).

Case records and disclosure
These matters are fully dealt with in Chapter 14.

National Adoption Standards
The National Adoption Standards for England make the following provisions in respect of adoptive parents:

> *"Children will be matched with approved adopters who can offer them a stable and permanent home and help and support will be provided to achieve a successful and lasting placement.*

1. Approved adopters will be given clear written information about the matching, introduction and placement process, as well as any support to facilitate this that they may need. This will include the role of the Adoption Register for England and Wales.
2. Before a match is agreed, adopters will be given full written information to help them understand the needs and background of the child and an opportunity to discuss this and the implications for them and their family.
3. There will be access to a range of multi-agency support services before, during and after adoption. Support services will include practical help, professional advice, financial assistance where needed and information about local and national support groups and services.
4. Adoptive parents will be involved in discussions as to how they can best maintain any links, including contact, with birth relatives and significant others identified in the adoption plan.
5. Adoptive parents will be encouraged to keep safe any information provided by birth families via agencies and to provide this to the adopted child on request, or as they feel appropriate.
6. Adoptive parents whose adopted child has decided to explore their birth heritage will be supported to deal with the impact of this decision.
7. Where there are difficulties with the placement or the adoption breaks down the agencies involved will cooperate to provide support and information to the adoptive parents and the child without delay.
8. Agencies will ask adoptive parents whether they are prepared to agree to notify the agency if an adopted child dies during childhood or soon afterwards.
9. Adoptive parents will be informed of their right to make representations and complaints."

Summary of the procedure for placement and review
1. The agency notifies the prospective adopter(s) in writing before the child is placed.
2. The agency carries out reviews in respect of children who have been placed and those who have not.
3. The agency visits the child at the required intervals.
4. The agency has regard to prescribed matters when carrying out reviews.
5. The agency notifies the outcome of reviews to the prospective adopters.

Summary of timescales

The following is a summary of the timescales which should be applied unless, having regard to the welfare test, it would not be in the interest of the child to do so:

1. The child's need for a permanent home should be addressed, and a permanence plan prepared at the four month review.
2. The case should be presented to the adoption panel within six weeks of the completion of the permanence report.
3. A placement with prospective adopter(s) should be identified and approved by the adoption panel within six months of the agency's decision to place a child for adoption.
4. A placement for a child who is under six months old should be identified and approved by the panel within three months of the agency's decision to place the child for adoption, if the parent has requested that the child should be placed for adoption.
5. The adoption panel should make its recommendation within two months of a review where a placement has been identified.
6. The decision to place a child with prospective adopters should be made within seven days of the panel's recommendation.
7. The adoption agency must make its final decision within seven days of the adoption panel's recommendation.
8. The parents or guardian and the father with parent responsibility should be informed of the agency's decision orally within two working days and in writing within five working days.

9. Transitional Provisions

Article 3(1) of the Adoption and Children Act 2002 (Commencement No. 10 Transitional and Savings Provisions) Order 2005, SI 2005 No. 2897, provides that, as a general rule, where, on 30 December 2005 (the date the 2002 Act came fully into force), a case is in progress, any action or decision taken before that date under the regulations formerly in force, is treated as if it were an action or decision taken under the corresponding provision of the Adoption Agencies Regulations 2005 or the Adoption Agencies (Wales) Regulations 2005. There are certain exceptions. See Chapter 24.

Chapter 17

Adoption Support Services

1. Introduction

The Adoption and Children Act 2002, section 3(1), provides that each local authority must continue to maintain within its area a service designed to meet the needs of certain persons in relation to adoption, and provide the requisite facilities. Those persons are:

    (a) children who may be adopted and their parents and guardians;

    (b) persons wishing to adopt a child; and

    (c) adopted persons, their parents, natural parents and former guardians.

Section 3(2)(b) provides that those facilities must include making and participating in arrangements for the provision of adoption support services. Section 3(4) permits a local authority to make arrangements for securing the provision of facilities by registered adoption societies, or other persons authorised by regulations to provide services.

Section 2 of the Adoption and Children Act 2002 defines "adoption support services" to mean counselling, advice and information, and any other services, in relation to adoption, prescribed by regulations.

In addition, section 4 creates a new right for certain persons to ask to have their needs for adoption support services assessed. The local authority is obliged to carry out such an assessment. If, during the assessment, it appears that there may be a need for health or education services, the local authority must notify the appropriate health or education authority. It may also seek the assistance of another local authority where appropriate (section 4(8) to (11) of the 2002 Act).

If the local authority decides to provide any adoption support services to a person, and the circumstances fall within a specified description, the local authority is obliged to prepare a plan, in accordance with which the adoption support services are to be provided; it must keep the plan under review. (Section 4(5).)

Section 4(6) authorises the making of regulations concerning the provision of assessments, preparing and reviewing plans and the provision of adoption support services. Subsection (7) sets out in detail the matters which

may, in particular, be the subject of regulations:
  (a) the circumstances in which specified persons are to have a right to request an assessment of their needs;
  (b) the type of assessment to be carried out, or the way in which it is to be carried out;
  (c) the way in which a plan is to be prepared;
  (d) the way in which, and the time at which, a plan or the provision of adoption support services is to be reviewed;
  (e) the considerations to which a local authority is to have regard in carrying out an assessment or review, or preparing a plan;
  (f) the circumstances in which a local authority may provide adoption support services subject to conditions;
  (g) the consequences if such conditions are not met, including the recovery of any financial support provided by the local authority;
  (h) the circumstances in which services may be provided for persons outside the area of the local authority;
  (i) the circumstances in which a local authority may recover from another local authority the expense of providing adoption support services to any person.

Sections 125 to 131 provide for the establishment of the Adoption and Children Act Register. The object is to facilitate matching prospective adopters with children suitable for adoption, by providing information about children who are suitable for adoption and about persons wishing to adopt. The register is discussed in Chapter 16; see page 229.

Further, registered adoption support agencies and adoption agencies now provide intermediary services to assist those adopted before the coming into force of the 2002 Act to obtain information about their relatives and to make contact with them, and *vice versa*. These services are discussed in Chapter 15.

As will be observed, the statutory duties now imposed on local authorities are more extensive than under the former law, and apply to wider categories of person.

The Adoption Support Services Regulations 2005 (SI 2005 No. 691, the "Support Services Regulations") in force from 30 December 2005, make provision for such services. The Adoption Support Services (Local Authorities) (Wales) Regulations 2005 (SI 2005 No. 1512, W.116, the "Support Services (LAs) (Wales) Regulations") apply to Wales. These regulations contain definitions of words and phrases which, in some instances, differ from those provided in the Adoption and Children Act 2002. These are dealt with below and throughout the text. The duties imposed on local authorities in relation to adoption, such as assessing prospective adopters and establishing a procedure for reviewing a "qualifying determination" are dealt with in Chapter 16.

2. Prescribed Services

As noted above, section 2(6) of the Adoption and Children Act 2002 defines "adoption services" to mean counselling, advice and information, and any other services prescribed by regulations. Regulation 3 of both the Support Services Regulations and the Support Services (LAs) (Wales) Regulations specify services which are so prescribed as adoption support services. They are:

(a) financial support (see below);

(b) services to enable groups of adoptive children, adoptive parents and natural parents or former guardians of an adoptive child to discuss matters relating to adoption;

(c) assistance, including mediation services, in relation to arrangements for contact between an adoptive child and a natural parent, natural sibling, former guardian or a related person of the adoptive child. The Support Services (LAs) (Wales) Regulations do not refer to mediation under this head;

(d) services in relation to the therapeutic needs of an adoptive child. The Support Services (LAs) (Wales) Regulations refer to services "that may be provided *to an adoptive parent* in relation to the therapeutic needs of an adoptive child;

(e) assistance for the purpose of ensuring the continuance of the relationship between an adoptive child and his adoptive parent, including training for the adoptive parents to meet any special needs of the child, and respite care. If respite care takes the form of providing accommodation, it must be provided by or on behalf of a local authority under section 23 of the Children Act 1989 or by a voluntary organisation under section 59 of that Act. Although the Welsh regulations do not mention the provision of accommodation, it must be assumed that sections 23 and 59 apply;

(f) assistance where disruption of an adoptive placement or of an adoption arrangement following the making of an adoption order has occurred or is in danger of occurring. This includes making arrangements for the provision of mediation services and organising and running meetings to discuss disruptions in such placements or arrangements.

The above services may include giving cash (Support Services Regulations, regulation 3(3)). There is no equivalent of this in the Support Services (LAs) (Wales) Regulations.

In addition to the above services, regulation 3 of both the Adoption Support Agencies (England) and the Adoption Agencies (Miscellaneous Amendments) Regulations 2005 (SI 2005 No. 2720) identify the following additional services as adoption support services:

(a) any services prescribed in regulation (b) to (f) above that are provided in the case of an adoption of a child by his natural parent,

or the partner of his natural parent;
  (b) assistance to adoption agencies in preparing and training adoptive parents;
  (c) assistance to:
    (i) adopted persons who have attained the age of eighteen,
    (ii) relative of such persons,
to facilitate contact between such adopted persons and their relatives. Relatives include persons who, but for the adoption, would be related to the adopted person by blood, half blood, marriage or civil partnership.

In the case of the adoption of a child by his natural parent or the partner of his natural parent, respite care that consists of the provision of accommodation must be accommodation provided by or on behalf of a local authority for looked after children under section 23 of the Children Act.

3. Definitions

For the purposes of the regulations only, "adoptive child" means:
  (a) a child who has been adopted or in respect of whom a person has given notice of his intention to adopt under section 44 of the Adoption and Children Act 2002; or
  (b) a child whom an adoption agency has matched with a prospective adopter or placed for adoption
  (regulation 2(1) of both the Support Services Regulations and the Support Services (LAs) (Wales) Regulations).

For the purposes of continuing to provide financial support and any review of that support (see below), "child" includes a person who has attained the age of eighteen years and is in full time education or training, and, immediately before he attained the age of eighteen, he was an adoptive child and financial support was payable in relation to him (Support Services Regulations, regulation 2(2)).

  "Agency adoptive child" means a child:
  (a) who has been adopted after having been placed for adoption by an adoption agency; or
  (b) whom an adoption agency has matched with a prospective adopter or placed for adoption; or
  (c) whose adoptive parent has been a local authority foster parent in relation to him (unless the local authority oppose the adoption)
  (Support Services Regulations, regulation 2(1)).

In the Welsh regulations, an "adoptive child" is an agency adoptive child or a non-agency adoptive child. For the purposes of providing financial support, the phrase includes an adopted child who has attained the age of eighteen years and is in full time education and training. An agency adoptive child is a child:
  (a) in respect of whom an adoption agency has decided, in accordance

with regulation 34 of the Adoption Agencies (Wales) Regulations
2005, that a person would be a suitable adoptive parent for the child;
  (b) whom an adoption agency has placed for adoption; or
  (c) who has been adopted after having been placed for adoption by an
       adoption agency
(Support Services (LAs) (Wales) Regulations, regulation 2(1)).
"Adoptive parent" means:
  (a) a person who has adopted a child or has given notice under section
       44 of his intention to adopt a child; or
  (b) a person with whom an adoption agency has matched a child or has
       placed a child for adoption
(Support Services Regulations, regulation 2(1)).
In the Welsh regulations, in addition to (a) and (b) above, a person whom an
adoption agency has decided would be a suitable person to adopt a particular
child is also referred to as an adoptive parent (Support Services (LAs)
(Wales) Regulations, regulation 2(1)).

4. Persons to whom Adoption Support Services are Provided

Section 3(3) of the Adoption and Children Act 2002 requires that adoption
support services *must* be provided to persons falling within certain
descriptions, and *may* be provided to certain other persons. Regulation 4 of
both the Support Services Regulations and the Support Services (LAs)
(Wales) Regulations identify the categories of person to whom specified
services are available.

Counselling, advice and information
Counselling advice and information must be available to:
  (a) children who may be adopted, their parents and guardians;
  (b) persons wishing to adopt a child;
  (c) adopted persons, their adoptive parents, natural parents and former
       guardians;
  (d) children who are natural siblings (whether full or half blood) of an
       adoptive child;
  (e) children of adoptive parents (whether or not adopted);
  (f) related persons in relation to adoptive children. A related person in
       relation to the child is a grandparent, brother, sister, uncle or aunt
       whether of the full blood or half blood or by marriage, and any other
       person with whom an adoptive child has a relationship which
       appears to the local authority to be beneficial to the welfare of the
       child.
(See regulation 4(1), Support Services Regulations.)
Category (f) takes account of the provisions of the welfare checklist in
section 1(4)(f) of the Act, which provides that regard must be had to the

relationship which the child has with relatives, and with any other person if the court or agency considers the relationship to be relevant. The matters to be addressed include the likelihood of any such relationship continuing and the value to the child of its doing so; the ability and willingness of any of the child's relatives, or of any such other person, to provide the child with a secure environment in which the child can develop, and otherwise to meet the child's needs; and the wishes and feelings of any of the child's relatives or such other person(s), regarding the child.

The Welsh regulations (regulation 4(1)) extend counselling, advice and information only to those in (a) to (d) above, not to children of the adoptive parents or persons related to the adoptive child.

Financial support
The nature and extent of financial support provided by a local authority is considered at page 253. This service may be provided to an adoptive parent of an agency adoptive child (regulation 4(3) of both the Support Services Regulations and the Support Services (LAs) (Wales) Regulations).

Services to enable discussion
Services to enable groups of adoptive children, adoptive parents, natural parents and former guardians of adoptive children to discuss matters relating to adoption are to be available to:
    (a) an adoptive parent of an agency adoptive child;
    (b) an agency adoptive child;
    (c) a natural parent, namely a natural parent whose child has been matched or placed for adoption by an agency or has been adopted following such a placement, or (in England) a former guardian of an agency adoptive child
(regulation 4(4) of both Regulations).

Contact
Assistance, including mediation services to resolve issues relating to contact between the adoptive child and his natural parents, siblings, former guardian or a related person of the adoptive child, is provided by the local authority to the following persons:
    (a) an adoptive parent of an agency adoptive child;
    (b) an agency adoptive child;
    (c) a child who is a natural sibling, whether of the full or half blood, of an adoptive child;
    (d) a natural parent, former guardian or related person in relation to an agency adoptive child
(Support Services Regulations, regulation 4(5); and see Support Services Regulations (Wales), regulation 4(5)).

Therapeutic services
Services to meet the therapeutic needs of an adoptive child must be provided
to an agency adoptive child, an adoptive child from overseas and an adoptive
child in the case of a Convention adoption (regulation 4(6) of both sets of
regulations).

Continuance or disruption of relationships
Assistance for the purpose of ensuring the continuance of the relationship
between an adoptive child and his adoptive parents, and assistance where
disruption of the placement has occurred or is in danger of occurring, is
provided to an adoptive child irrespective of whether the placement relates to
a local child, an overseas child or a child from a Convention country. It is
also provided to an adoptive parent of such a child, and a child of the
adoptive parent, irrespective of whether the child is that person's natural
child or an adopted child. See regulation 4(7) of both the Support Services
Regulations and the Support Services (LAs) (Wales) Regulations.

5. The Provision of Services

Section 3(4) of the Adoption and Children Act 2002 allows a local authority
to secure the provision of adoption support services by a registered adoption
society or other persons, rather than providing them itself. The persons
qualified to provide the services or facilities are another local authority; a
registered adoption support agency (see below); a Local Health Board or
Primary Care Trust/NHS trust; and a local education authority (regulation
5(1) of both the Support Services Regulations and the Support Services (LAs)
(Wales) Regulations).

An "adoption support agency" is defined in the Adoption and Children
Act 2002 as an undertaking, the purpose of which, or one of the purposes of
which, is the provision of adoption services. An undertaking is not an
adoption support agency, however, merely because it provides information in
connection with adoption. "Undertaking" has the same meaning as in the
Care Standards Act 2000, section 121 (Adoption and Children Act 2002
section 8(1)). The following are excepted from the definition of "adoption
support agency", as they are regulated under specific provisions which apply
to them: a registered adoption society, a local authority, a local education
authority, a Special Health Authority, a Primary Care Trust or NHS
foundation trust (in Wales, a Health Authority or Local Health Board), NHS
trust or NHS foundation trust (Adoption and Children Act 2002 section 8(2)
as amended by the Social Care (Community Health and Standards) Act 2003,
schedule 4, paragraph 125).

Additionally, the Adoption Support Agencies (England) and Adoption
Agencies (Miscellaneous Amendments) Regulations 2005 (above), regulation
4, excepts from the definition of adoption support agency the following:

(a) a barrister or a solicitor of the Supreme Court, who is providing adoption support services in the course of his practice;

(b) an undertaking which merely provides services to enable groups of adoptive children, adoptive parents and natural parents or former guardians of an adoptive child to discuss matters relating to adoption;

(c) an undertaking which merely provides respite care in relation to adoption and is a care home, children's home or domiciliary care agency, in respect of which a person is registered under Part 2 of the 2000 Act.

Under the Support Services Regulations, an adoption society is a registered adoption support agency if it is registered under Part 2 of the Care Standards Act 2000 as amended. The Welsh regulations emphasise that an adoption support agency which is not registered to provide a particular service is not a registered adoption support agency in respect of that service. See regulation 5(2) of both the Support Services Regulations and the Support Services (LAs) (Wales) Regulations.

Adoption support services adviser

The local authority is obliged to appoint an adoption support services adviser, whose function is:

(a) to give advice and information to those who may be affected by the adoption or proposed adoption of a child, including information about services that may be appropriate and how to obtain those services;

(b) to give advice, information and assistance to the local authority, including advice, information and assistance concerning the assessment of needs for adoption support services (see below), the availability of such services and the preparation of plans required under section 4(5) of the Adoption and Children Act 2002;

(c) consult with and give advice, information and assistance to another local authority where appropriate.

The Welsh regulations also include in (c) giving the advice and information under (b) where a child is to be placed by another local authority, and where a person in respect of whom there is a plan in place moves to the area of another local authority.

The person appointed as adoption support services adviser must have sufficient knowledge and experience of the process of adoption and its effect on persons likely to be affected by an adoption, for the purposes of the work he is to perform.

See regulation 6 of both the Support Services Regulations and the Support Services (LAs) (Wales) Regulations.

Services for persons outside the area

Pursuant to section 4 of the Adoption and Children Act 2002, a local authority is obliged to provide adoption support services to the following persons who are outside its area:

(a) an agency adoptive child whom the authority has placed for adoption, or who has been adopted after being placed for adoption by the authority;

(b) an adoptive parent of such a child;

(c) a child of such an adoptive parent, whether or not adopted.

This duty ceases three years after the adoption order is made, except in relation to any financial support provided by the local authority where the decision to provide support was made before the adoption. The local authority is not prevented from providing adoption support services to persons outside its area where it considers it appropriate to do so, and therefore it is within its discretion to do so even if the case falls outside the regulations (Support Services Regulations, regulation 7 and Support Services (LAs) (Wales) Regulations, regulation 15).

Regulation 7 of the Welsh regulations contains further provisions concerning the situation where a local authority (the "placing authority") is considering the placement of a child who is looked after with a prospective adopter who is resident in the area of another authority (the "recovering authority"). The placing authority must consult the recovering authority, in writing, about the placement, and the results of the assessments undertaken in accordance with section 4(1) and (2) of the Adoption and Children Act 2002, and in particular about the ability of the agencies in the area of the recovering authority to provide any identified adoption support services. A placing authority must allow twenty working days following the consultation before the placement of the child can be considered by the adoption panel. When the recovering authority has responded in writing to the consultation undertaken, that response must be taken into account by the adoption panel when considering the placement of the child under regulations 18 and 19 of the Adoption Agencies (Wales) Regulations, SI 2005 No. 1313, W. 95. See also regulation 15(3) and (4), Support Services (LAs) (Wales) Regulations

For the recovery of expenses between local authorities, see below.

6. Financial Support

Circumstances in which financial support is payable

Financial support is paid to an adoptive parent only for the purpose of supporting the placement of the adoptive child, or the continuation of the adoption arrangements after an adoption order is made. It is payable only where (Support Services Regulations, regulation 8(2)):

(a) it is necessary to ensure that the adoptive parent can look after the child. It is implicit, having regard to the meaning given to the phrase "adoptive parent" in the regulations (see page 249), that this includes offering the service at every stage of the adoption process. The Support Services (LAs) (Wales) Regulations, regulation 11, is more specific in that it provides for financial support where the child has not been placed with the adoptive parent for adoption, and financial support is required to ensure that the adoptive parent can look after the child; and where the child has been placed or has been adopted, and financial support is necessary to ensure that the adoptive parent can continue to look after the child;

(b) the child needs special care which requires greater expenditure or resources by reason of illness, disability, emotional or behavioural difficulties or the continuing consequences of past abuse or neglect. This would cover situations such as those which arose in *A v Essex County Council* [2003] EWCA Civ 1848, [2004] 1 WLR 1881, [2004] 1 FLR 749;

(c) on account of the age or ethnic origin of the child it is necessary for the local authority to make special arrangements to facilitate the placement or the adoption; or where it is desirable that the child be placed with the same adoptive parent as his brother or sister (whether of the full blood or half blood) or with a child with whom he has previously shared a home. The Welsh provisions are set out in regulation 11(2)(e) and (g) and differ slightly in that the provision in relation to the age and ethnicity of the child includes taking account of the sex of the child, and it appears to be limited to special arrangements to facilitate the "placement of the child for adoption", whereas the English provisions refer to making any "special arrangements to facilitate the placement or the adoption";

(d) such support is to meet recurring costs in respect of travel for the purpose of visits between the child and a related person. The Welsh equivalent of this provision is contained in regulation 12(4)(g) of the Support Services (LAs) (Wales) Regulations, under issues relating to the assessment of the amount of financial support to be provided and the considerations which must be taken into account;

(e) the local authority considers it appropriate to make a contribution to meet the legal costs, including fees payable to a court, in relation to an adoption, expenditure for the purpose of introducing an adoptive child to his adoptive parent, and expenditure necessary for accommodating and maintaining the child, including the provision of furniture and domestic equipment, alterations to and adaptations of the home, provision of means of transport and provision of clothing, toys and other items necessary for the purpose of looking after the child. The Welsh equivalent of this provision appears in regulation 12(4)(a) to (c). In addition, the Support Services (LAs) (Wales) Regulations, regulation 12(4)(e) and (g) specify two additional circumstances when financial support may become payable, namely in relation to the cost of placing a child in boarding school where the placement is necessary to meet the special needs of the child, and the cost of meeting the special needs of the child, including needs arising out of serious disability or illness.

Remuneration for former foster parent

Where an adoptive parent has been a local authority foster parent and an element of remuneration was included in the payments made by the local authority to the adoptive parent in relation to his fostering the child, financial support may include an element of remuneration. But this may be done only where the decision to include the element of remuneration was taken before the adoption order was made, and the local authority considers it to be necessary to facilitate the adoption. However, the element of remuneration ceases to be payable at the end of the period of two years from the adoption order, unless the local authority considers its continuation to be necessary having regard to the exceptional needs of the child or any other exceptional circumstances (Support Services Regulations, regulation 9). Remuneration to an adoptive parent for the care of the child is not permitted. The payment to the foster carer is an exception by reason of the particular circumstances in which the placement arises.

The Welsh equivalent of this provision is contained in regulation 12(8) and (9) of the Support Services (LAs) (Wales) Regulations, under the provision which deals with the assessment of the amount to be paid. It is similar to the provisions described above, except that the two-year period is referred to as the "second anniversary" occurring two years after the date of the adoption in respect of the child. In relation to the circumstances which may give rise to payments being made after that date, regulation 12(10) specifically refers to financial support necessary to ensure that the adoptive parent will be able to continue to look after the child; or to meet the child's special needs by reason of illness, disability, emotional or behavioural difficulties or the continuing consequences of past abuse or neglect; or by reason of the child's sex, age or ethnicity; or where it is desired to place the child's sibling with the adoptive parent. "Foster parent", in the context of the Welsh provisions, has the same meaning as in the Fostering Services (Wales) Regulations 2003 (SI 2003 No. 237, W.35) (Support Services (LAs) (Wales) Regulations, regulation 2(1)).

Payment of financial support

Where a local authority decides that financial support should be given, it may be paid in a single payment, except where the local authority and the adoptive parent agree that it should be paid by instalments, or where it is provided to meet a need which is likely to give rise to recurring expenditure, in which case it may be paid periodically. It is for the local authority to specify how and when payments are to be made. See regulation 10 of the Support Services Regulations. The equivalent provision for Wales is regulation 13(4) of the Support Services (LAs) (Wales) Regulations.

Cessation of financial support
Any financial support given by a local authority ceases to be payable to an adoptive parent if the child:
    (a) ceases to have a home with the adoptive parent;
    (b) ceases full-time education or training and commences employment;
    (c) qualifies for income support or jobseeker's allowance in his own right;
    (d) attains the age of eighteen years, unless he continues in full-time education or training, when it may continue until the end of the course or training he is then undertaking
(Support Services Regulations, regulation 11; Support Services (LAs) (Wales) Regulations, regulation 17(7)).

Conditions attached to financial support
Where financial support is payable periodically, it is not payable until the adoptive parent, or, in the case of an adoption by a couple, each adoptive parent, has agreed to the following conditions:
    (a) that he will inform the local authority immediately if he changes his address, or the child dies; or any changes occur which would lead to the payments ceasing (see above); or there is a change in his financial circumstances or the financial needs or resources of the child, which may affect the amount of financial support payable to him. This information must be conveyed to the local authority in writing;
    (b) that he will complete and supply the local authority with an annual statement of his financial circumstances, the financial needs and resources of the child and his address, and whether the child still has a home with him.
The local authority may impose such other conditions as it considers appropriate, including the timescale within which, and purposes for which, any payment of financial support should be utilised. See regulation 12 of the Support Services Regulations.

An equivalent provision in the Support Services (LAs) (Wales) Regulations is contained in regulation 11(3) and 13(3). Regulation 11(3) refers to the local authority's reaching an agreement with the adoptive parents. It provides that before financial support is payable, the local authority must require the adoptive parents to agree to inform it immediately if they change their address; if the child's home is no longer with them (or either of them); if the child dies; or if there is any change in their financial circumstances or the financial needs or resources of the child. Regulation

13(3) refers to the terms of the agreement as a condition of the financial support.

Termination and suspension of payment
Non-compliance with any condition imposed on the provision of financial support entitles the local authority to suspend or terminate payment. It also entitles the local authority to recover all or any part of the financial support it has paid. Where the non-compliance consists of failure to provide an annual statement, a reminder must be sent and the person given twenty-eight days from the date on which the notice was sent within which to comply before any steps are taken to suspend or terminate the financial support (Support Services Regulations, regulation 12(3) and Support Services (LAs) (Wales) Regulations, regulation 17(4)).

Assessment for financial support
In determining the amount of financial support to pay, the local authority is required to take account of any other grant, benefit, allowance or resource available to the person in respect of his needs as a result of the adoption of the child. In addition, the local authority is obliged to take account of:
   (a) the person's financial resources, including any tax credit or benefit which would be available to him if the child lived with him. Tax credit has the same meaning as in the Tax Credits Act 2002;
   (b) the amount required by the person in respect of his reasonable outgoings and commitments (excluding outgoings in respect of the child); and
   (c) the financial needs and resources of the child.
   (Support Services Regulations, regulation 15(3)).
The matters set out under the heading *Circumstances in which financial support is payable*, on pages 253 to 255, are also relevant considerations. The Support Services (LAs) (Wales) Regulations, regulation 12(4), set these out as relevant considerations where the local authority is considering providing financial support in respect of expenditure for purposes of supporting the placement of the child with the adoptive parent for adoption, and the continuation of that placement following the making of an adoption order.
   The three considerations in (a) to (c) above may, however, be disregarded where financial support is being considered in respect of the initial costs of accommodating an agency adoptive child; recurring costs in respect of travel for the purposes of visits between the child and a related person; any special arrangements or special care required by reason of illness, disability, emotional or behavioural difficulties or the continuing consequences of past abuse or neglect of the adoptive child; or where it is necessary to make special arrangements to facilitate the placement by reason of the child's age, sex, ethnicity or the desirability of placing a sibling in the same household. The considerations in (a) to (c) above may also be

disregarded where the local authority is considering including an element of remuneration paid to an adoptive parent who has been the foster parent of the child (see above). (Support Services Regulations, regulation 15(5).)

Further, the local authority *must* disregard the above three matters where it is considering providing financial support in respect of legal costs, including fees payable to a court, where an adoption order is applied for in respect of an agency adoptive child, or expenditure for the purposes of introducing an agency adoptive child to his adoptive parents.

The Support Services (LAs) (Wales) Regulations, regulation 12(3), (5) and (6), make similar provisions, save that they provide that any recommendations in relation to the adoptive parent or the adoptive child, made by the adoption panel to the local authority on a matter referred to in regulations 18 and 27 of the Adoption Agencies (Wales) Regulations, may not be taken into account in such a case.

7. Request for Assessment

As noted in the introduction to this chapter, section 3(1) of the Adoption and Children Act 2002 places a duty on each local authority to continue to maintain within its area a service designed to meet the needs in relation to adoption of:

    (a) children who may be adopted;

    (b) their parents and guardians;

    (c) persons wishing to be adopted; and

    (d) adopted persons, their adoptive parents, natural parents and former guardians,

  and for that purpose to provide the requisite facilities.

Section 4(1) of the Act obliges the local authority, at the request of any of the above-mentioned persons, or any other person specified in regulations, to carry out an assessment of that person's needs for adoption support services. Persons other than those referred to in section 3(1) who may apply for adoption support services are identified in regulations as follows:

    (a) a child of an adoptive parent (whether or not adopted);

    (b) a child who is a natural sibling (whether of full blood or half blood) of an adoptive child;

    (c) a related person in relation to the adoptive child

  (Support Services Regulations, regulation 13(1)).

The Support Services (LAs) (Wales) Regulations, regulation 7(1), makes similar provisions but, under (b), it specifically refers to the child's natural brother or sister (whether of the full blood or half blood) to make clear that the child's adoptive sibling does not come within this provision, but under (a). In addition, in (c) above, it limits the assessment to a related person in connection with arrangements for contact between that person and an adoptive child where arrangements for such contact have been made before the request for assessment.

Where a request for an assessment is made by a person falling within any one or more of the above categories, and the request relates to a particular support service, or it appears to the local authority that the person's needs for adoption support services may be adequately assessed by reference to a particular adoption support service, the local authority may carry out the assessment by reference only to that service (Support Services Regulations, regulation 13(2); Support Services (LAs) (Wales) Regulations, regulation 7(2)). "Particular adoption support service" here means counselling, advice and information in relation to adoption or any of the prescribed services referred to in regulation 3 (see above).

Regulation 13(3) specifically excludes assessment for a service if the person in question does not come within the description of persons (in regulation 4, see above) who are eligible for that particular service.

Matters to be taken into consideration on assessment

In carrying out an assessment of a person's needs for adoption support services the following matters are considered relevant:

(a) the needs of the person being assessed and how these might be met;

(b) the needs of the adoptive family and how these might be met;

(c) the needs, including developmental needs, of the adoptive child and how these might be met;

(d) the parenting capacity of the adoptive parent(s);

(e) wider family and environmental factors;

(f) where the child is or was placed for adoption or matched for adoption, the circumstances that led to the child's being so placed or matched;

(g) any previous assessments of needs for adoption support services undertaken in relation to that person

(Support Services Regulations, regulation 14(1)).

The Support Services (LAs) (Wales) Regulations, regulation 8(1), differs in that it does not include the parenting capacity of the adoptive parents, or the wider family and environmental factors, as relevant considerations. In relation to the needs of the person requesting the assessment, it provides that where the assessment has been requested by a related person, the local authority should have regard to the needs of that person only so far as they relate to his or her need for assistance so as to enable him or her to take part in arrangements for contact with the adoptive child that were made before an assessment was requested. Regulation 8(1)(d) also includes as a relevant factor "any special needs of the adoptive child arising from the fact that the child has been looked after by a local authority, the child has been habitually resident outside the British Islands, and the adoptive parent is a relative of the child".

Interview and report

Both the English and the Welsh regulations require the local authority, where it considers it appropriate to do so, to interview the person requesting assessment. Where the person is an adoptive child, it must also interview the adoptive parent(s). In any event, the local authority must prepare a report of the assessment (Support Services Regulations, regulation 14(3) and Support Services (LAs) (Wales) Regulations, regulation 8(5)).

Referrals to other agencies

Where it appears that there may be a need for the provision of services, by a Primary Care Trust, NHS trust or NHS foundation trust, a Local Health Board, or a local education authority, for the person who is being assessed, the local authority is required, as part of the assessment, to consult the appropriate agency (Support Services Regulations, regulation 14(4); Support Services (LAs) (Wales) Regulations, regulation 8(4)).

Plan

Section 4(5) of the Adoption and Children Act 2002 requires the local authority, if it decides to provide any adoption support services, to prepare a plan for the provision of those services and keep the plan under review. This requirement is relevant if the services are to be provided on more than one occasion, as is specifically recognised in regulation 16(2) of the Support Services Regulations and regulation 10(1) of the Support Services (LAs) (Wales) Regulations.

Where the local authority considers that there may be a need for the provision of services by a Primary Care Trust, NHS Trust or NHS foundation trust, a Local Health Board, or an education authority, it is required to consult the appropriate trust or authority before preparing the plan. It must also nominate a person to monitor the provision of the services. (Support Services Regulations, regulation 16(3) and (4); Support Services (LAs) (Wales) Regulations, regulation 10(3) and (4)).

Notice of assessment

On completing the assessment but before deciding whether to provide adoption support services, the local authority is required to give notice of the proposed decision to the person requesting the services, and allow that person an opportunity to make representations. The notice must contain:
 (a) a statement of the person's needs for adoption support services;
 (b) where the needs relate to financial support, the basis upon which financial support is determined;
 (c) whether it is proposed to provide adoption support services to him;
 (d) the services, if any, which it is proposed to provide;
 (e) if financial support is to be paid, the proposed amount that would be payable and any conditions attached to it;

(f) where appropriate, a copy of the draft plan under section 4(5) of the Act;

(g) details of the right to make representations and the time within which they must be made.

The local authority cannot make a decision until the person has made representations or notified the local authority that he is satisfied with the proposed decision, and, where applicable, with the draft plan; or the time limit has expired. (Support Services Regulations, regulation 17; Support Services (LAs) (Wales) Regulations, regulation 9).

Decision to provide support

In making its decision whether or not to provide support services, the local authority is under a duty to have regard to the assessment and any representations made following the notice given to the person whose case has been assessed. It must decide whether that person has a need for adoption support services, and, if he does, whether the local authority proposes to provide such services and on what conditions.

Notice of decision

Written notice of the decision, together with reasons for it, and where appropriate a copy of the plan, must be given to the person requesting the assessment, together with details of the person who has been nominated to monitor the plan.

Where the local authority has decided to provide financial support, the notice must also include details of:

(a) the method of determination of the amount;

(b) where the payment is to be made in instalments or periodically;
   (i)   the amount of financial support,
   (ii)   the frequency with which payment will be made,
   (iii) the period for which financial support will be paid,
   (iv)   when the first payment is to be made;

(c) where the amount is to be paid in a single payment, the date on which it is to be paid;

(d) any conditions imposed, the date, if any, by which the conditions are to be met and the consequences of failing to meet those conditions;

(e) the arrangements and procedure for review, variation and termination of financial support;

(f) the responsibilities of the local authority when carrying out the review (see below) and that of the adoptive parent as set out in regulation 12 (see above)

(Support Services Regulations, regulation 18; Support Services (LAs) (Wales) Regulations, regulation 13(5)).

Any notice required to be given must be given in writing to:

(a) the person who requested the assessment if he is an adult;

261

(b) the child, unless it appears that the child is not of sufficient age and understanding for him to be given such notice, or in all the circumstances it would be inappropriate to give him such notice. Here the notice should be given to the adoptive parent, or to the adult whom the local authority considers most appropriate

(Support Services Regulations, regulation 22).

Regulation 14 of the Support Services (LAs) (Wales) Regulations makes the same provision, but is more specific in identifying the adult person to be served, referring to "a suitable adoptive parent for the child", the "person with whom the child has been placed", and "the person by whom the child has been adopted" and "the person who proposes to adopt the child".

8. Reviews

Services other than financial support

Where the local authority is providing, or in the preceding twelve months has provided, adoption support services for a person, it must review the provision of such services. The duty to review arises where the local authority becomes aware of any change in the person's circumstances; at any stage in the implementation of the plan as the authority considers appropriate; and in any event, annually. The procedure for assessment, set out in regulations 14 and 15 of the Support Services Regulations and regulation 8(1) to (4) of the Support Services (Wales) Regulations, applies to a review as it does to an initial assessment.

If the local authority proposes to vary or terminate the provision of adoption support services, then before making the decision it must give the person affected an opportunity to make representations. Notice of the proposal must therefore be given to him and he must be allowed sufficient time to make the representations. (Support Services Regulations, regulation 19(1) to (3) and Support Services (LAs) (Wales) Regulations, regulation 16).)

The notice must contain the information set out under the heading, *Notice of assessment,* above, and, if the local authority proposes to revise the plan, a draft of the plan should be enclosed with the notice. (Support Services Regulations, regulation 19(5); Support Services (LAs) (Wales) Regulations, regulation 17(8).)

The local authority should not make a decision until it has received the representations of the person affected, or the time for making representations has expired. When coming to its decision the local authority is required to have regard to the representations made. It may vary or terminate the provision of adoption support services and, where appropriate, revise the plan. Notice of the decision must be given, together with reasons for the decision, and, where appropriate, a copy of the revised plan. (Support Services Regulations, regulation 19(6); Support Services (LAs) (Wales) Regulations, regulation 16(4).)

Financial support paid periodically

The local authority is required to review the provision of financial support:

    (a) annually, on receipt of the adoptive parents' financial statement under regulation 12 (England) or 17 (Wales) (see page 256);

    (b) if any relevant change of circumstances or any breach of a condition comes to its notice; and

    (c) at any stage in the implementation of the plan as it considers appropriate.

In carrying out the review the local authority must apply the same considerations as when carrying out an assessment (see above).

The local authority has a right to review, suspend or cease payment of financial support and seek to recover all or part of the financial support it has paid if any conditions on the provision of such support has not been complied with. Where, though, the breach consists of failure to provide the annual statement, a reminder should be sent, with a notice that compliance should take place within twenty-eight days.

If the local authority proposes to reduce or terminate the financial support or revise the plan, it is under a duty first to notify the person of the proposal, give the person an opportunity to make representations, and allow the person time to do so. The notice must contain a statement of the person's needs and the basis upon which the financial support is assessed, whether the local authority proposes to provide financial support, and, if so, the amount and any conditions attached.

When carrying out the review, the local authority should consider the representations made and give notice of its decision, with reasons, and a revised plan, if appropriate, to the person assessed.

See Support Services Regulations, regulation 20 and Support Services (LAs) (Wales) Regulations, regulation 17.

9. Recovery of Expenses between Local Authorities

Section 4(10) of the Adoption and Children Act 2002 provides that where it appears to a local authority that another local authority could, by taking any specified action, help in the exercise of any of its functions, it (the "paying authority") may request the help of that other local authority, specifying the action in question. Where a local authority (the "recovering authority") provides adoption support services to any person in consequence of such a request from another local authority, the recovering authority may recover the expenses of providing those services from the paying authority. This provision does not, however, apply where the recovering authority has provided counselling, advice and information under section 2(6)(a) of the Adoption and Children Act 2002, or the recovering authority is providing services to the following persons who are outside the authority's area:

    (a) an agency adoptive child whom the authority has placed for adoption or who has been adopted after having been placed for adoption by the authority;

(b) an adoptive parent of such a child;

(c) a child of such an adoptive parent (whether or not adopted)

(Support Services Regulations, regulations 23 and 7(1); Support Services (LAs) (Wales) Regulations, regulation 15(1)).

10. Fees

Pursuant to section 11 of the Adoption and Children Act 2002, adoption agencies are permitted to charge fees to persons to whom facilities are provided as part of the adoption service. They are also permitted to pay fees to persons providing or assisting in providing such facilities. Local authorities may also charge for the facilities of the adoption service in connection with the adoption of a child brought into the United Kingdom for the purpose of adoption, a Convention adoption, an overseas adoption or an adoption effected under the law of a country or territory outside the British Islands.

In relation to Wales, see the Local Authorities (Prescribed Fees) (Adoptions with a Foreign Element) (Wales) Regulations 2005 (SI 2005 No. 3114, W. 234), page 336.

11. Transitional Provisions and Revocations

The following regulations are revoked as of 30 December 2005:

(a) the Adoption Allowance Regulations 1999 (SI 1999 No. 2030);

(b) the Adoption Support Services (Local Authorities) (England) Regulations 2003 (SI 2003 No. 1348);

(c) the Adoption Support Services (Local Authorities) (Wales) Regulations 2004 (SI 2004 No. 1011, W.108).

Any assessment, plan, review or any adoption support service which was in the course of preparation or was in place under the former regulations is treated, with effect from 30 December 2005, as an assessment plan, review or service provided under the new regulations (Support Services Regulations, regulation 24; Support Services (LAs) (Wales) Regulations, regulation 18). See also Chapter 25, page 375.

Chapter 18

Adoption Support Agencies

1. Introduction

In the past, local authorities and voluntary adoption agencies and societies have worked together to meet the needs of children placed for adoption, the natural families of such children, and prospective adopter(s). The Adoption and Children Act 2002 extends the support services that must be provided in connection with adoption. As already noted in Chapter 17, section 3 imposes on each local authority a duty to maintain, in its area, a service designed to meet the needs, in relation to adoption, of children who may be adopted; their parents and guardians; persons wishing to adopt a child; and adopted persons, their parents, natural parents and former guardians. For that purpose, the local authority must provide the requisite facilities. These services are collectively referred to as "the adoption service" (section 2(1) of the 2002 Act). The service includes "adoption support services", comprising counselling, advice and information, and any other support services prescribed by regulations. The Adoption Support Services Regulations 2005 (SI 2005 No. 691) and the Adoption Support Services (Local Authorities) (Wales) Regulations 2005 (SI 2005 No. 1512, W. 116) prescribe such other services, and are considered in Chapter 17. In addition, the Adoption Support Agencies (Wales) Regulations 2005 (SI 2005 No. 1514, W. 118) list the prescribed services (see **2.** below), and it will be observed that these include offering assistance to adopted persons to obtain information about, and facilitate contact with, their parents and relatives and *vice versa*. The Adoption Information and Intermediary Services (Pre-Commencement Adoptions) (Wales) Regulations 2005 (see Chapter 15) set out the procedure to be followed by an adopted person and his birth family who wish information about each other and to make contact with each other, and the agency which is authorised to provide this service. In addition, the Local Authority Adoption Service (Wales) Regulations 2005 (SI 2005 No. 3115, W. 235) make provisions in relation to local authorities in Wales which provide an adoption service within the meaning of section 43(3)(a) of the Care Standards Act 2000.

The English provisions relating to these services are set out in the following regulations:

    (a) the Adoption Support Agencies (England) and Adoption Agencies (Miscellaneous Amendments) Regulations 2005 (SI 2005 No. 2720), which extend the prescribed services (see below);

    (b) the Adoption Information and Intermediary Services (Pre-Commencement Adoptions) Regulations 2005 (SI 2005 No. 890), which deal with services offering assistance to an adopted person who was adopted before 30 December 2005 to obtain information and facilitate contact with his birth family and *vice versa*. This has been discussed in Chapter 15;

    (c) the Disclosure of Adoption Information (Post-Commencement) Adoptions) Regulations 2005 (SI 2005 No. 888) which deal with similar services for persons adopted after 30 December 2005. These are considered in Chapter 13 at page 156.

Section 3(4) of the Adoption and Children Act 2002 permits a local authority to provide any of the requisite facilities by securing the provision of these services by registered adoption agencies, or by other persons who are within a description prescribed by regulations. Section 3(5) confirms that these facilities must be provided in conjunction with the local authority's other social services and with registered adoption societies in its area, so that help may be given in a co-ordinated manner, without duplication, omission or avoidable delay. Section 2(2) of the Act, however, provides that a person cannot carry on or manage an adoption services agency without being registered under Part 2 of the Care Standards Act 2000 to provide that facility.

Section 9(1) of the Adoption and Children Act 2002 makes provision for regulations to be made relating to the exercise by local authorities, voluntary adoption agencies and adoption support agencies of their functions in relation to adoption. Section 10(1) identifies some of the areas which such regulations should cover. These include:

    (a) the persons who are fit to be employed for the purposes of functions relating to adoption;

    (b) the fitness of premises;

    (c) the management and control of operations;

    (d) the number of persons, or persons of any particular type, working for the purposes of those functions;

    (e) the management and training of persons working for the purposes of those functions; and

    (f) keeping information.

In relation to voluntary adoption agencies and adoption support agencies, section 10(3) provides that the regulations may cover, among others, matters relating to the fitness and qualifications of personnel in managerial positions; the financial position of the agency; and the welfare of the children placed by the agency, including the promotion and protection of their health.

Section 10(4) of the Act particularises some of the matters which may be covered by subsidiary legislation on the conduct of such agencies, to include:

(a) the facilities and services to be provided;

(b) the keeping of accounts;

(c) notifying the registration authority of events which occur in the premises used for the purposes of an agency;

(d) notifying the registration authority when the manager of an agency proposes to be absent, arrangements for running the agency in the manager's absence, and notifying any intention to change the identity of the manager;

(e) notifying the registration authority of changes in ownership of an agency or of the identity of any of its officers, and paying the appropriate fee; and

(f) arrangements for dealing with complaints.

The Adoption Support Agencies (England) and Adoption Agencies (Miscellaneous Amendments) Regulations 2005 (SI 2005 No. 2720, the "Support Agencies (England) Regulations") and the Adoption Support Agencies (Wales) Regulations 2005 (SI 2005 No. 1514, W. 118, the "Support Agencies (Wales) Regulations") make provisions which regulate the management of adoption support agencies, and cover the issues specifically referred to in sections 9(1) and 10(1), (3) and (4) of the Act. These matters are described in this chapter.

2. The Prescribed Adoption Support Services

Regulation 3 of the Support Agencies (England) Regulations lists the prescribed adoption support services as follows:

(a) any services prescribed in regulation 3(1)(b) to (f) of the Adoption Support Services Regulations (see Chapter 17) that are provided in the case of an adoption of a child by his natural parent or the partner of his natural parent;

(b) assistance to adoption agencies in preparing and training adoptive parents;

(c) assistance to adopted persons who have attained the age of eighteen, or relatives of such persons,

to facilitate contact between such adopted persons and their relatives. "Relative" here means any person who, but for his adoption, would be related to him by blood, including half-blood, marriage or civil partnership.

Where a child is adopted by his natural parent or the partner of his natural parent, respite care that consists of the provision of accommodation must be accommodation provided by or on behalf of a local authority under section 23 of the Children Act 1989 (accommodation of looked after children) or by a voluntary organisation under section 59 of that Act.

The regulations specifically except from being regarded as an adoption support agency a barrister or solicitor who is providing adoption support services in the course of his practice. Also excepted is any undertaking which merely provides:

(a) services to enable groups of adoptive children, adoptive parents and natural parents or former guardians of an adoptive child to discuss matters relating to adoption;

(b) respite care in relation to adoption, and is a care home, children's home or domiciliary care agency in respect of which a person is registered under Part 2 of the Care Standards Act 2000.

Under the Support Agencies (Wales) Regulations 2005, regulation 2, the prescribed services are:

(a) assistance to adoptive parents, adoptive children and related persons in relation to arrangements for contact between an adoptive child and a natural parent or a related person of the adoptive child;

(b) services that may be provided in relation to the therapeutic needs of the child in relation to that adoption;

(c) assistance for the purpose of ensuring the continuance of the relationship between the child and adoptive parent, including training for adoptive parents for the purpose of meeting any special needs of the child arising from that adoption;

(d) assistance where disruption in an adoption arrangement or placement has occurred or is in danger of occurring, including mediation and organising and running meetings to discuss disruption in adoption or placements;

(e) assistance to adopted persons who have attained the age of eighteen in obtaining information in relation to their adoption, or facilitating contact between such persons and their relatives; and

(f) assistance to relatives of adopted persons who have attained the age of eighteen in obtaining information in relation to that adoption or facilitating contact between such persons and the adopted person.

3. Information about Adoption and Facilitating Contact: Wales

The Support Agencies (Wales) Regulations go on to provide in more detail for the services in (e) and (f) above; this is considered below. In addition, the Adoption Information and Intermediary Services (Pre-Commencement Adoptions) Regulations 2005 (SI 2005 No. 890) and the Adoption Information and Intermediary Services (Pre-Commencement Adoptions) (Wales) Regulations 2005 (SI 2005 No. 2701, W. 190) make specific provisions for adoption support agencies to provide to persons who were adopted before 30 December 2005, and the birth families of such persons, information about each other and to facilitate contact between them. This has been considered in Chapter 15. The position relating to post-commencement adoptions is considered in Chapter 14. The information provided in this chapter should be read in conjunction with what is said in Chapters 14 and 15.

In Wales, an adoption support agency which provides the services in (e) and (f) above is not required to commence providing such services, or having begun to provide those services, to continue doing so, if the agency considers it would not be appropriate to do so. In deciding whether or not it would be appropriate to do so, the agency must have regard to all the circumstances, and:

(a) the welfare of the adopted person requesting the service;

(b) the welfare of the relative requesting the service;

(c) any information held by the Registrar General on the adoption contact register (see Chapter 13); and

(d) any information recorded which suggests that the person does not wish to be contacted, or wishes to be contacted only in specified circumstances (see below)

(Support Agencies (Wales) Regulations, regulation 11(1), (2) and (3)). The agency cannot in any event provide these services to a person who is under eighteen years of age, unless there are exceptional circumstances. Even then, the person with parental responsibility for the child must give consent, as must the child if he is competent; if he is not competent, his wishes or feelings must be taken into account (Support Agencies (Wales) Regulations, regulation 11(4)).

An adoption support agency must not disclose any "identifying information" about "the subject" to a person requesting information under (e) and (f) without the consent of the subject. For these purposes, "identifying information" means information which, whether taken on its own or together with other information possessed by the person requesting it, enables the subject to be identified and traced (see also page 188). The "subject" is the person whom the person requesting information seeks to contact, or about whom he seeks information. When seeking the subject's consent, the agency is under a duty to ensure that that person has been given sufficient information to make an informed decision whether or not to consent to the disclosure sought. If the subject has died or is incapable of giving consent, the agency has a discretion to disclose such identifying information as it considers appropriate, but it must first take into consideration the welfare of those who may be affected by the disclosure, and obtain the views of the persons who might be so affected. (Support Agencies (Wales) Regulations, regulation 12.)

An agency must not proceed with an application, and should not disclose information, where the subject is the adopted person or a relative of the adopted person, and that person has notified the agency in writing that he does not wish to be contacted by the agency, or that he wishes to be contacted only under specified circumstances or by a specified person. The agency is obliged to keep a record of such a veto. (Support Agencies (Wales) Regulations, regulation 13.)

An agency may disclose information which is not regarded as identifying information, provided it considers that it would be appropriate to disclose the information to the adopted person or relative making the request. (Support Agencies (Wales) Regulations, regulation 14.)

An agency which provides services to assist adopted persons to obtain information about, or facilitate contact with, their birth families, must provide written information about the availability of counselling. Such information must be given to anyone who requests adoption support services which include disclosure of any of the information referred to above, and to any person who is the subject of an application for information and is considering whether or not to consent to disclosure. The agency may provide such counselling services itself, or make arrangements for them to be provided by another registered provider of adoption support services, or by a person who provides such services under contract to a registered provider. Information relating to the availability of counselling must include a description of the person offering counselling, and the fees that may be charged. See Support Agencies (Wales) Regulations, regulation 15.

4. Fitness of the Registered Provider

The Support Agencies (England) Regulations, regulation 7, provides that a person shall not carry on an agency unless he is fit to do so. A person is not regarded as fit unless the person:

(a) is an individual who carries on the agency otherwise than in partnership with others and satisfies the requirements set out below, or in partnership with others, and he and each of the partners satisfy the requirements below;

(b) is a partnership and each of the partners satisfies the requirements below; or

(c) is an organisation which has given the registration authority details of the person who has the management of the agency, referred to as the "responsible individual" (see below).

A person must not carry on an agency if:

(a) he has been adjudged bankrupt or sequestration of his estate has been awarded and (in either case) he has not been discharged and the bankruptcy order has not been annulled or rescinded;

(b) he is a person in respect of whom a bankruptcy restrictions order or an interim bankruptcy restrictions order under schedule 4A to the Insolvency Act 1986 has effect;

(c) he has made a composition or arrangement with his creditors and has not been discharged in respect of it

(Support Agencies (England) Regulations, regulation 7(4)).

5.   The Responsible Individual

An organisation is prohibited from carrying on an agency unless it fulfils two conditions concerning a person known as the "responsible individual", namely:

    (a) it has given notice to the registration authority (in England, the National Care Standards Commission; in Wales, the National Assembly) of the name, address and position in the organisation of a person (the "responsible individual") who is a director, manager, secretary or other officer of the organisation and is responsible for the supervision and management of the agency; and

    (b) the responsible individual is a person of suitable integrity and good character to carry on the agency, is physically and mentally fit to do so, and has made available full and satisfactory information or documentation of each of the matters specified in schedule 2 to the regulations

(Support Agencies (England) Regulations, regulations 7(2) and (3); Support Agencies (Wales) Regulations, regulation 5(2) and (3)).

The information required under schedule 2 includes:

    (a) where appropriate, an enhanced criminal record certificate issued under section 115 of the Police Act 1997 (in Wales, in respect of which less than three years have elapsed since it was issued); or, in any other case, a criminal record certificate under section 113 of the Police Act 1997 and in England under section 115(6A) of that Act (in Wales, in respect of which less than three years have elapsed since it was issued). The certificate must cover matters specified under section 113(3A) or (3C) or 115(6A) or (6B) of that Act; such matters include, for example, whether the person's name appears on the list kept under section 1 of the Protection of Children Act 1999 of individuals considered unsuitable to work with children;

    (b) proof of identity;

    (c) two written references, one of which must be from the person's most recent employer, if any;

    (d) if the person has previously worked with children or vulnerable adults, then, so far as is reasonably practicable, verification of the reason the employment came to an end;

    (e) documentary evidence of qualifications; and

    (f) a full employment history, together with a satisfactory written explanation of any gaps.

6.   The Registered Manager

The person who is registered under Part 2 of the Care Standards Act 2000 as the person carrying on the agency ("the registered provider") is under a duty to appoint a manager ("the registered manager") to manage the agency, and to notify the registration authority of the name of the person appointed and the date the appointment takes effect. In Wales, where the local authority provides the adoption service within the meaning of section 43(3)(a) of the Care Standards Act 2000, it must appoint one of its officers to manage the adoption service, and must notify the National Assembly of the name and address of the person appointed, and the date on which the appointment is to take effect. If the manager appointed ceases to be manage the service, the National Assembly must be notified immediately (Local Authority Adoption Service (Wales) Regulations 2005, SI 2005 No. 3115, W. 325, regulation 6).

The person appointed must be of suitable integrity and good character; have the qualifications, skills and experience necessary to manage the agency; and be physically and mentally fit to do so. The information set out in schedule 2 to the both the English and the Welsh regulations (see above) must be obtained in respect of the registered manager. See Support Agencies (England) Regulations, regulations 8 and 9, and Support Agencies (Wales) Regulations, regulations 6 and 7. In Wales, where the local authority provides an adoption service, it must obtain the information set out in schedule 3 to the Local Authority Adoption Service (Wales) Regulations 2005: regulation 7.

7. Training and Standards of Work

The registered provider must ensure that the registered manager undertakes from time to time such training as is appropriate to ensure that he has the experience and skills necessary for managing the agency (Support Agencies (England) Regulations, regulation 10(3); Support Agencies (Wales) Regulations, regulation 8(3)). Regulation 10(2) of the English regulations additionally requires that if the registered provider is an individual, he too must undertake the like training. Regulation 8(2) of the Local Authority Adoption Service (Wales) Regulations 2005 requires a manager appointed by a local authority also to undertake training to ensure that he/she has the skills necessary to manage the adoption service. If the registered provider is an organisation or a partner, such training is to be undertaken by the responsible individual or one of the partners, as the case may be. Regulation 8(2) of the Welsh regulations requires the registered provider to ensure that the responsible individual undergoes this training.

The registered person and any responsible individual (in Wales, the registered provider and the registered manager) are under a duty, having regard to the size of the agency and its statement of purpose, and the need to safeguard and promote the welfare of those receiving adoption support services from the agency, to carry on the agency with sufficient care, competence and skill: Support Agencies (England) Regulations, regulation 10(1); Support Agencies (Wales) Regulations, regulation 8(1). Regulation 10(1) of the English regulations additionally requires the registered provider and any responsible individual, when discharging this duty, to have regard also to the number of needs of those receiving adoption support services from the agency. Regulation 8(1) of the Local Authority Adoption Service (Wales) Regulations 2005 makes similar provisions in respect of a manager appointed by a local authority which provides an adoption service within the meaning of section 43(3)(a) of the Care Standards Act 2000.

It is a criminal offence to contravene regulation 10 or 8, and contravention is punishable on summary conviction with a fine of up to £5,000. (Adoption and Children Act 2002, section 9(3); Support Agencies (England) Regulations, regulation 29(1); Support Agencies (Wales) Regulations, regulation 32(1)).

Regulation 11 of the English Regulations (regulation 9 of the Welsh regulations) further requires that where the registered person or the responsible individual is convicted of any criminal offence, whether in Wales or elsewhere, he must immediately notify the Secretary of State or the National Assembly of the date and place of conviction, the offence of which he was convicted and the penalty imposed.

8. Statement of Purpose and Children's Guide

The regulations contain provisions requiring the compilation of certain documents relating to the objectives and methods of working of adoption support agencies.

Statement of purpose

The person who is the registered provider or registered manager (see above) (the "registered person") must compile, in relation to the agency, a written statement of purpose, which must consist of the following matters:

    (a) the aims and objectives of the agency;

    (b) the name and address of the registered provider and, where applicable, the registered manager and the responsible individual;

    (c) any conditions in force in relation to the registration under Part 2 of the Care Standards Act 2000 of the registered provider and, if applicable, the registered manager;

    (d) the relevant qualifications and experience of the registered provider and, if applicable, the registered manager;

    (e) the number, relevant qualifications and experience of the staff working for the purposes of the agency;

    (f) a description of the organisational structure of the agency;

    (g) a description of the services offered by the agency;

    (h) the procedures for assessing the needs of those requesting adoption support services from the agency;

    (i) the system in place to monitor and evaluate the provision of services to ensure that the services provided by the agency are effective and of an appropriate quality standard;

(j) a summary of the complaints procedure;

(k) the name, address and telephone number of the registration authority (Support Agencies (England) Regulations, regulation 5(1) and schedule 1; see also Support Agencies (Wales) Regulations, regulation 3(1) and schedule 1, which is in broadly the same terms).

In addition, the Local Authority Adoption Service (Wales) Regulations 2005, regulation 3 and schedule 1, which makes similar provisions for Wales, requires a local authority that provides an adoption service to include in its statement of purpose:

(a) the arrangements that the local authority has put in place to assess and make provision for adoption support services; and

(b) the procedures for recruiting, preparing, assessing, approving and supporting prospective adoptive parents.

A copy of the statement of purpose must be provided by the registered person to the registration authority (in England, the Commission for Social Care; in Wales, the National Assembly). A copy must also be made available, upon request, for inspection by:

(a) any person working for the purposes of the agency;

(b) any person receiving adoption support services from the agency or acting on behalf of a child receiving such services from the agency;

(c) any person making enquiries about receiving adoption services from the agency on his behalf or on a child's behalf; and

(d) any local authority

(Support Agencies (England) Regulations, regulation 5(2) and (3); Support Agencies (Wales) Regulations, regulation 3(2) and (3)).

The Local Authority Adoption Service (Wales) Regulations 2005, regulation 3(2), also provides that the local authority must make a copy of the statement of purpose available, upon request, for inspection by:

(a) children who may be adopted, their parents and guardians;

(b) persons wishing to adopt a child;

(c) adopted persons, their parents, natural parents and former guardians;

(d) persons who are seeking an assessment of their needs for the provision of adoption services by the authority.

It also requires the local authority to ensure that the adoption service is at all times conducted in a manner which is consistent with its statement of purpose.

The children's guide

The registered person, in relation to an agency which provides adoption support services, is also under an obligation to provide a written guide to the agency, the "children's guide". It should include a summary of the agency's statement of purpose; a summary of the complaints procedure; and the address and telephone number of the registration authority. The Local Authority Adoption Service (Wales) Regulations 2005, regulation 4, schedule

2, further require, in respect of Wales, that the children's guide must include:
- (a) a summary of the procedures where adoption is identified as the appropriate plan for the child;
- (b) information about the role of the adoption support services advisor and a summary of the procedure for seeking an assessment for the provision of adoption support services;
- (c) details of how a child may have access to the services of an advocate who is independent of the authority to assist him or her in bringing a complaint or making representations under the complaints procedures;
- (d) the name and address and telephone number of the Children's Commissioner for Wales.

The guide should be in a form which is age-appropriate and appropriate to the understanding and communication needs of the children to whom the agency provides adoption support services. The registered person must provide a copy of the children's guide to the registration authority; to any adult acting on behalf of a child to whom the agency provides adoption support services; and, subject to the child's age and understanding, to the child. See Support Agencies (England) Regulations, regulation 5(4) to (6); Support Agencies (Wales) Regulations, regulation 3(4) to (6), and Local Authority Adoption Service (Wales) Regulations 2005, regulation 4(1) and schedule 2. Regulation 4(2)(b) and (c) of the latter regulations also requires a local authority which provides an adoption service to provide a copy of the children's guide to every prospective adopter with whom the authority has placed a child for adoption.

Review
Both the statement of purpose and the children's guide must be kept under review and, where appropriate, revised. Within twenty-eight days of any revision, the registered person must notify the registration authority of the revision. A copy of any revision to the children's guide should also be made available to any adult who is acting on behalf of a child to whom the agency supplies adoption support services, and, subject to his age and understanding, to each such child. See Support Agencies (England) Regulations, regulation 6; Support Agencies (Wales) Regulations, regulation 4.

Non-compliance
Failure to comply with these provisions, or with any condition in relation to the registration of the registered provider under Part 2 of the Care Standards Act 2000, is an offence; on summary conviction a fine not exceeding £5,000 may be imposed (Adoption and Children Act 2002, section 9(3); Support Agencies (England) Regulations, regulation 29; Support Agencies (Wales) Regulations, regulation 32(1).

9. Written Policy

The registered person is required to make arrangements for the protection and safety of children receiving adoption support services from the agency. The Support Agencies (England) Regulations, regulation 12, the Support Agencies (Wales) Regulations, regulation 16 and the Local Authority Adoption Service (Wales) Regulations, regulation 10, require the registered person in relation to an adoption agency (and, in Wales, the local authority) which provides adoption support services to prepare and implement a written policy to safeguard from abuse or neglect children who are or may be receiving adoption services from the agency or the local authority. It must also set out the procedure that would be followed if an allegation of abuse or neglect were made. The regulation requires that this procedure should in particular make arrangements for three specific issues:

(a) for liaison and co-operation with any local authority which is, or may be, making child protection enquiries in respect of the child. This includes any enquires carried out by a local authority in connection with its duty under the Children Act 1989 relating to the protection of children;

(b) for written records to be kept of any allegations of abuse or neglect, and the actions taken in response; and

(c) for accessing information which would enable the agency, and those to whom adoption support services are provided, to contact the following bodies regarding any concern about child welfare or safety: the local authority in whose area the agency is situated, any other local authority on behalf of which the agency is providing adoption support services to a child, and the registration authority.

"Child protection enquiries" means any enquiries carried out by a local authority in the exercise of any of its functions conferred by or under the Children Act 1989, relating to the protection of children; See Support Agencies (England) Regulations, regulation 12(3); Support Agencies (Wales) Regulations, regulation 16(3).

It is a criminal offence to contravene any of the above provisions, punishable on summary conviction by a fine not exceeding £5,000. (Adoption and Children Act 2002, section 9(3); Support Agencies (England) Regulations, regulation 29(1); Support Agencies (Wales) Regulations, regulation 32(1)).

10. Records

The registered person is under a duty to keep and update records, which must include the personal details of each person to whom the agency is providing adoption support services. The records must indicate whether those persons are children who may be adopted, their parents or guardians; or prospective adopters; or adopted persons, adoptive parents, natural parents, former guardians and related persons. The Support Agencies (England) Regulations require the records to indicate whether the person is an adoptive child or an adopted person who has attained the age of eighteen or, if not, his relationship to an adoptive child or adopted person. The records must state the service that has been requested; any assessment of needs provided by a local authority; the services which were in fact provided; and whether the services were provided on behalf of a local authority or another person or organisation. (Support Agencies (England) Regulations, regulation 14; Support Agencies (Wales) Regulations, regulation 18.)

Regulation 14(2) of the English regulations requires the records to be retained for such period as the registered provider considers appropriate. In Wales, the records must be kept for seventy-five years from the date of the last entry. This provision should be considered along with the provisions on the keeping of adoption case records under the regulations discussed on disclosure in Chapter 14 (see pages 169 to 170).

Contravention of these regulations is a criminal offence; on summary conviction a fine not exceeding £5,000 may be imposed. The registration authority may bring proceedings against a person who was once, but no longer is, a registered person, in respect of a failure to comply with regulation 18. (Adoption and Children Act 2002, section 9(3); Support Agencies (England) Regulations, regulation 29(1); Support Agencies (Wales) Regulations, regulation 32.)

Transitional provision
Regulation 15 of the Support Agencies (England) Regulations provides that the Adoption Agencies Regulations 1983 (SI 1983 No. 1964) apply to case records held by an adoption support agency on 30 December 2005 by virtue of regulation 16(2A) of the 1983 regulations (transfer of case records) in relation to the adoption of a person adopted before that date, as they apply to the case records of an adoption agency.

11. Complaints
Pursuant to section 10(4)(i) of the Adoption and Children Act 2002, the registered person in relation to an adoption agency which is registered to provide adoption support services is required to establish a written procedure for considering complaints made by or on behalf of any person who has requested, or to whom the agency has provided, adoption support services. The Support Agencies (England) Regulations require the complaints procedure to be available also to persons who have been refused adoption support services (regulation 16(1)).

The Support Agencies (England) Regulations, regulation 16, and the Support Agencies (Wales) Regulations, regulation 19, require that the procedure formulated must include provision:

(a) for an opportunity for informal resolution of a complaint at an early stage;

(b) to ensure that no person who is the subject of a complaint takes part in its consideration other than, if the registered person considers it appropriate, at the informal resolution stage only;

(c) for dealing with complaints about the registered person or (in England) the responsible individual; and

(d) in the case of an agency providing adoption support services to children, for complaints to be made by a person acting on behalf of a child.

The registered person is required to ensure that a copy of the complaints procedure is provided to every person working for the purposes of the agency. It is also obligatory to provide a copy of the complaints procedure, upon a request made on behalf of any person to whom the agency has provided adoption support services, or any person acting on behalf of a child. In this event, the copy of the complaints procedure must also contain the name, address and telephone number of the registration authority and details of the procedure (if any) which has been notified to the registered person by the registration authority for making complaints about the agency.

The registered person must take the following steps if a complaint is made:

(a) ensure that the complaint is fully investigated;

(b) ensure, so far as is reasonably practicable, that, within twenty-eight working days (in Wales, twenty) of the complaint being received by the agency, the complainant is informed of the outcome of the investigation and of the action (if any) which it is proposed to take in response to the complaint; and

(c) ensure that a written record is made of any complaint, details of the investigation made, the outcome and any action taken in consequence. The English regulations require that the record must be retained for at least three years from the date it is made.

Registered persons are also required to:

(a) take all reasonable steps to ensure that a child is enabled to make a complaint and that a person is not subjected to any reprisals by the agency for making the complaint;

(b) at the request of the registration authority, supply a statement containing a summary of any complaints made during the preceding twelve months and the action taken in response.

See Support Agencies (England) Regulations, regulation 17; Support Agencies (Wales) Regulations, regulation 20.

In respect of Wales, where a local authority is providing an adoption service within the meaning of section 43(3)(a) of the Care Standards Act 2000, the Local Authority Adoption Service (Wales) Regulations 2005, regulation 18, requires the local authority to:

(a) ensure that a written record is made of any complaint, including details of the investigation and the outcome, and any action taken in consequence. The record must be retained for at least three years from the date it is made; and

(b) supply to the National Assembly at its request a statement containing a summary of any complaints made in respect of the adoption service during the preceding twelve months and the action (if any) taken as a result.

A contravention or failure to comply with any of the above provisions is an offence by virtue of section 9(3) of the Adoption and Children Act 2002; on summary conviction, a fine not exceeding £5,000 may be imposed (Support Agencies (England) Regulations, regulation 29(1); Support Agencies (Wales) Regulations, regulation 32(1)).

12. Staff

Pursuant to section 10(1)(a) of the Adoption and Children Act 2002, regulation 18 of the Support Agencies (England) Regulations, and regulation 21 of the Support Agencies (Wales) Regulations, require the registered person to ensure that the agency has a sufficient number of suitably qualified, competent and experienced persons working for the purposes of the agency, having regard to the size of the agency, its statement of purpose and the need to safeguard and promote the health and welfare of children to whom the agency provides adoption support services.

The personnel employed by the agency should be fit to work for the purposes of the agency in that they must:

(a) be of integrity and good character;

(b) have the qualifications, skills and experience necessary for the work to be performed, with documentary evidence of any relevant qualification;

(c) be physically and mentally fit for the work they are required to undertake; and

(d) have provided full and satisfactory information relating to a criminal record certificate under sections 113 and 115 of the Police Act 1997; references; verification of the reason any previous employment ended, particularly if the position held was one which included work with children or vulnerable adults; and their full employment histories

(Support Agencies (England) Regulations, regulation 19 and schedule 2; Support Agencies (Wales) Regulation, regulation 22 and schedule 2).

Similar provisions are made by regulation 11 of the Local Authority Adoption Service (Wales) Regulations 2005 in respect of Wales where a local authority provides an adoption service within the meaning of section 43(3)(a) of the Care Standards Act 2000. Regulation 12 goes on to provide that, in Wales, a local authority must not employ a person to work for the purposes of its adoption service unless that person is fit to work for the purposes of an adoption service. Nor may the local authority allow a person employed other than by the authority, in a position where that person may in the course of his or her duties have regular contact with children who may be or have been placed for adoption or who may receive or are receiving adoption support services from the authority, unless that person is fit to work for the purposes of an adoption service.

Employing staff

The Adoption and Children Act 2002, section 10(1)(e), provides for regulations to be made concerning the management and training of persons working for the purposes of the agency's functions. The Support Agencies (England) Regulations, regulation 20, and the Support Agencies (Wales) Regulations, regulation 23, require the registered person to ensure that all permanent staff employed by the agency to carry out its functions must first satisfactorily complete a period of probation. All persons employed by an agency must receive appropriate training, supervision and appraisal, and must be enabled, from time to time, to gain further qualifications appropriate to the work they perform. Every member of staff must also be provided with a job description outlining his or her responsibilities. For Wales, the Local Authority Adoption Service (Wales) Regulations 2005, regulation 13, makes similar provision where the adoption service is provided by a local authority.

Disciplinary procedure

The registered person (in Wales, the local authority if it is providing the adoption service) is required to operate a disciplinary procedure which, in particular, provides for the suspension of an employee where necessary in the interests of the safety or welfare of the persons to whom the agency provides adoption support services. The disciplinary procedure should also provide that proceedings will be instituted for any failure on the part of an employee to report an incident of abuse or suspected abuse of a child to:

    (a) the registered person;

    (b) an officer of the registration authority;

    (c) a police officer;

    (d) an officer of the NSPCC; or

    (e) an officer of a local authority in whose area the agency is situated, or (in England only) in whose area the child is living or in whose area the child is placed for adoption, if this is a different authority.

See Support Agencies (England) Regulations, regulation 21; Support Agencies (Wales) Regulations, regulation 24; Local Authority Adoption Service (Wales) Regulations, regulation 14.

Records

The registered person is required to maintain and keep up to date records of each person working for the purposes of the agency, for a period of at least fifteen years from the date of the last entry. The record must contain personal details of the person; his address; qualifications relevant to, and experience of, working with persons receiving adoption support services; and (in relation to an agency which provides adoption support services to children) qualifications relevant to, and experience of, work involving children.

The record must also contain details of the date a person's employment commenced and when it is to cease; and whether the person is employed by the registered provider under a contract of service or for services, or by someone other than the registered provider, or is a volunteer. Details of the nature of the job, including the job description, whether the employment is full-time or part-time, and the number of hours for which the person is employed by or contracted to work for the registered provider each week, must also be recorded.

Finally, in respect of each employee, a record must be made of training, supervision and appraisal; and of any disciplinary action taken against him, any complaint made against him or concerning him and the outcome of such complaint; and any other matters in relation to his employment. See Support Agencies (England) Regulations, regulation 22 and schedule 3; Support Agencies (Wales) Regulations, regulation 25 and schedule 3.

Where a local authority in Wales provides an adoption service within the meaning of section 43(3)(a) of the Care Standards Act 2000, it is also under a duty to keep a similar record of persons employed by it (Local Authority Adoption Service (Wales) Regulations 2005, regulation 16 and schedule 4).

Offences

Contravention of, or failure to comply with, any of the provisions of regulations 10 to 22 (England) or 21 to 25 (Wales) is an offence; on summary conviction, a fine not exceeding £5,000 may be imposed. The registration authority may bring proceedings against a person who was once, but no longer is, a registered person, in respect of a failure to comply with regulation 25. See Adoption and Children Act 2002, section 9(3); Support Agencies (England) Regulations, regulation 29(1); Support Agencies (Wales) Regulations, regulation 32. For defences and restrictions see below and Chapter 19.

13. Premises

Section 10(1)(b) of the Adoption and Children Act 2002 provides for regulations to be made concerning the fitness of premises used by local authorities, voluntary adoption agencies and adoption support agencies. Section 10(1)(f) contemplates regulations in relation to the keeping of information. The Support Agencies (England) Regulations, regulation 23 and the Support Agencies (Wales) Regulations, regulation 26, provide that a registered person must not use premises for the purposes of the agency unless the premises are suitable for the purpose of achieving the aims and objectives set out in its statement of purpose. It also imposes a duty on the registered person to ensure that there are adequate security arrangements at the premises, in particular that there are secure facilities for the storage of records and that any records which are, for any reason, not on the premises, are nevertheless kept in conditions of appropriate security.

In Wales, where an adoption service within the meaning of section 43(3)(a) of the Care Standards Act 2000 is provided by a local authority, similar provisions apply to that local authority (Local Authority Adoption Service (Wales) Regulations 2005, regulation 17).

Contravention of, or failure to comply with, any of the above provisions is an offence; on summary conviction, a fine not exceeding £5,000 may be imposed. (Adoption and Children Act 2002, section 9(3); Support Agencies (England) Regulations, regulation 29(1); Support Agencies (Wales) Regulations, regulation 32.)

14. Finances and Accounts

Section 10(4)(b) of the Adoption and Children Act 2002 provides that regulations under section 9 may make provision as to the conduct of voluntary adoption agencies and adoption support agencies, and, in particular, as to the keeping of accounts. The Support Agencies (England) Regulations, regulation 25 and the Support Agencies (Wales) Regulations, regulation 28, require a registered provider to carry on the agency in such manner as is likely to ensure that it will be financially viable for the purposes of achieving the aims and objectives set out in its statement of purpose, and to ensure that adequate accounts are maintained and kept up to date. On the request of the registration authority, the registered provider must provide the registration authority with such information and documents as it may require for the purpose of considering the financial viability of the agency, including:

    (a) the annual accounts of the agency certified by an accountant; and

    (b) a certificate of insurance for the registered provider in respect of liability which may be incurred by him in relation to the agency in respect of death, injury, public liability, damage or other loss.

The Welsh regulations also include under this heading:

    (c) a reference from a bank expressing an opinion as to the registered provider's financial standing;

    (d) information as to the financing and financial resources of the agency; and

    (e) information as to any of the organisation's associated companies.

Contravention of, or failure to comply with, any of the above provisions is an offence; on summary conviction, a fine not exceeding £5,000 may be imposed. (Adoption and Children Act 2002, section 9(3); Support Agencies (England) Regulations, regulation 29(1); Support Agencies (Wales) Regulations, regulation 32).

15. Notices to the Registration Authority

Notice of absence

Section 10(4)(d) and (e) of the Adoption and Children Act 2002 provides for notice to be given to the registration authority of periods of absence of the manager of an adoption support agency. The Support Agencies (England) Regulations, regulation 26, and the Support Agencies (Wales) Regulations, regulation 29, provide that where the registered person, if he has the day-to-day charge of the agency, or the registered manager (in Wales, the manager) proposes to be absent from the agency for a continuous period of twenty-eight days or more, the registered person must (save in exceptional circumstances) give at least one month's written notification of the proposed absence to the registration authority. A shorter period may be accepted by the registration authority by agreement.

In Wales, each local authority that provides an adoption service within the meaning of section 43(3)(a) of the Care Standards Act 2000 must establish a system to ensure that where the manager proposes to be or is absent from the local authority for a continuous period of twenty-eight days or more, an identified person is responsible for the management of the adoption service until such time as the manager returns or (as the case may be) a new manager is appointed by the authority (Local Authority Adoption Service (Wales) Regulations 2005, regulation 15).

The notice must specify:

(a) the length or proposed length of the absence;

(b) the reason for the absence;

(c) the arrangements which have been made for running the agency during the absence;

(d) details and qualifications of the person who will be responsible for the management of the agency during the absence; and

(e) the arrangements that have been made or proposed for appointing another person to manage the agency during the absence, including the proposed date by which the appointment is to start.

Where the absence arises out of an emergency, the registered person is under a duty to give notice within a week of its occurrence, giving the details specified above. If the registered person or manager has been absent for a continuous period of twenty-eight days or more, and notification as required has not been given to the registration authority, the registered person is required without delay to give such notice, with the particulars specified above. Within seven days (in Wales, five days) of the return of the registered person or manager, the registration authority should be notified of the date of his return.

Contravention of, or failure to comply with, any of the above provisions is an offence; on summary conviction, a fine not exceeding £5,000 may be imposed. (Adoption and Children Act 2002, section 9(3); Support Agencies (England) Regulations, regulation 29(1); Support Agencies (Wales) Regulations, regulation 32).

Notice of changes

Pursuant to section 10(4)(f) and (g) of the Adoption and Children Act 2002, regulations provide that the registered person must notify the registration authority, in writing, as soon as is practicable, of the following events:

(a) a person other than the registered person carries on or manages the agency;

(b) a person ceases to carry on or manage the agency;

(c) the name and address of the registered provider, if an individual, is changed;

(d) where the registered provider is a partnership, there is any change in the membership of the partnership;

(e) where the registered provider is an organisation, any change in its name or address, or of a director, manager, secretary or similar officer, or in the identity of the responsible individual;

(f) where the registered provider is an individual, a trustee in bankruptcy is appointed or the registered provider makes any composition or arrangement with his creditors;

(g) where the registered provider is a company, a receiver, manager, liquidator or provisional liquidator is appointed in respect of the registered provider.

If more than one person is registered in respect of an agency and one of them dies, the other must, without delay, notify the registration authority of the death, in writing. Where a single person is registered, and he dies, his personal representative must give the notice. See Support Agencies (England) Regulations, regulation 27, and Support Agencies (Wales) Regulations, regulation 30 which is in slightly different terms.

Contravention of, or failure to comply with, any of the above provisions is an offence; on summary conviction, a fine not exceeding £5,000 may be imposed. (Adoption and Children Act 2002, section 9(3); Support Agencies (England) Regulations, regulation 29(1); Support Agencies (Wales) Regulations, regulation 32.)

Notification of conviction

Where the registered person or the responsible individual or a manager is convicted of any criminal offence, whether in England and Wales or elsewhere, he must immediately notify the registration authority in writing,

specifying:
(a) the date and place of the conviction;
(b) the offence of which he was convicted; and
(c) the penalty imposed.
(Support Agencies (England) Regulations, regulation 11; Support Agencies (Wales) Regulation, regulation 9; Local Authority Adoption Service (Wales) Regulations, regulation 9).
Failure to comply with this provision is a criminal offence; on summary conviction a fine not exceeding £5,000 may be imposed. (Adoption and Children Act 2002, section 9(3); Support Agencies (England) Regulations, regulation 29(1).)

16. Appointment of Liquidator
Where a person is appointed:
(a) receiver or manager of the property of a company or partnership which is a registered provider of an agency;
(b) liquidator or provisional liquidator of a company which is a registered provider of an agency; or
(c) (in England), trustee in bankruptcy of an individual who is a registered provider of an agency,
he must notify the registration authority immediately of his appointment, stating the reasons for it. If the agency has no manager, the person appointed must take steps to appoint a manager to take full-time day-to-day control of the agency. Not more than twenty-eight working days (in Wales, twenty) after his appointment, the person appointed must notify the registration authority of his intentions regarding the future operation of the agency. See Support Agencies (England) Regulations, regulation 28; Support Agencies (Wales) Regulations, regulation 31.

Contravention of, or failure to comply with, any of the above provisions is an offence by virtue of section 25(2) of the Care Standards Act 2000.

17. Notices to the Relevant Authority
Regulation 24 of and schedule 4 to the Support Agencies (England) Regulations. and regulation 27 of and schedule 4 to the Support Agencies (Wales) Regulations, provide that when certain events take place, the registered person must, without delay, notify the specified body or bodies. The events in question are:
(a) a referral to the Secretary of State pursuant to section 2(1)(a), Protection of Children Act 1999 of an individual working for an agency. This must be notified to the registration authority;
(b) the death or serious injury of an adult or child in the course of receiving adoption support services from the agency. This must be

reported to the registration authority; the primary care trust; the local health board; the relevant authority; and, where it was a child who died (or, in Wales, was seriously injured), the Secretary of State. Any oral notice given must be confirmed in writing within fourteen (in Wales, ten) working days. The "relevant authority" means the local authority in whose area the agency is situated. In relation to a child who has died or sustained serious injury in the course of receiving adoption support services, it means any local authority on behalf of which the agency was providing the services to the child under section 3(4)(b) of the Adoption and Children Act 2002. The "local health board" and "primary care trust" means the local health board or primary trust in whose area the child who has died or sustained serious injury was living at the time of the incident.

18. Fees

Regulations under section 9 of the Adoption and Children Act 2002 will provide for the fees which may be charged by adoption agencies for providing facilities as part of the adoption service, and the fees which may be paid by adoption agencies to persons providing or assisting in providing such facilities. Regulations will also prescribe the fees which may be charged by local authorities for providing prescribed facilities of the adoption service where the facilities are provided in connection with:

(a) the adoption of a child brought into the United Kingdom for the purposes of adoption; or

(b) a Convention adoption, an overseas adoption or an adoption effected under the law of a country or territory outside the British Islands.

For regulations which have been made in respect of Wales, see page 336.

Fees may also be charged by adoption agencies for providing counselling in connection with the disclosure of information in relation to a person's adoption. Regulations will also provide for agencies to publish their fees or make them known to the prospective adopter(s) before providing the service. Agencies are also required to provide an applicant with a written statement setting out what is included in the fee.

19. Proceedings in Relation to Offences

In relation to any contravention of, or failure to comply with, any of the provisions of the regulations discussed in this chapter, the registration authority must not institute any proceedings against a person unless:

(a) the person is a registered person. A registration authority may, however, bring proceedings against a person who was once, but no longer is, a registered person, in respect of a failure to comply with regulations 14 to 22 of the Support Agencies (England) Regulations (regulations 18 to 25 in Wales);

(b) the person has been given notice specifying the respects in which it is alleged he has contravened the regulations or failed to comply with them; what actions he is required to take in order to comply; and the time, not exceeding three months, within which the registered person should take action and make representations;

(c) the period specified in the notice has not expired; and

(d) where action was required to be taken following the notice, the action has not been taken

(Support Agencies (England) Regulations, regulation 29; see also Support Agencies (Wales) Regulations, regulation 32, which does not include (b) to (d) above).

Chapter 19

Restrictions and Offences

At various points throughout this text, it is noted that certain matters are made offences pursuant to the Adoption and Children Act 2002 and to regulations made under the Act. In this chapter, the principal restrictions and prohibitions under the 2002 Act, and the offences created in connection with them, are described.

1. Introduction

The Adoption Act 1976, section 11(1), provided that no person other than an adoption agency could make arrangements for the adoption of a child, unless the proposed adopter was a relative of the child, or the person was acting in pursuance of an order of the High Court. Section 11(3) made it a criminal offence for a person to take part in the management or control of a body of persons other than an adoption agency which existed for the purpose of making arrangements for the adoption of children; or in any other way to contravene the provisions of section 11(3); or to receive a child placed with him other than by an adoption agency. Section 72(3) gave a very wide definition of the phrase "making arrangements for the adoption of a child". Thus, a person was deemed to have made arrangements for the adoption of a child if he entered into or made any agreement or arrangement for, or for facilitating, the adoption of a child by any other person, whether the adoption was effected or intended to be effected in Great Britain or elsewhere; or if he initiated or took part in any negotiations, the purpose or effect of which was the conclusion of any agreement or the making of any arrangement therefor; or if he caused another to do so. Section 1(3A) of the 1976 Act defined "adoption" to include the adoption of children, wherever they were habitually resident, effected under the law of any country or territory within or outside the British Islands. In relation to the proposed adoption of a child resident outside the British Islands, section 72(3A) of the 1976 Act, as amended, provided that arrangements for the adoption of a child included references to arrangements for an assessment for the purpose of indicating whether or not a person was suitable to adopt a child. With certain specified exceptions, section 57(1) of the 1976 Act made unlawful the making or giving to any person of any payment or reward for or in consideration of the adoption by that person of a child; or the grant by that person of any agreement or consent required in connection with the adoption of a child; or the handing over of a child by that person with a view to the adoption of the child; or the making by that person of any arrangements for the adoption of a child.

Despite the wide provisions of the Act and the illegality of placements made in breach of those provisions, the reality was that a court faced with an adoption application in breach of these provisions did not refuse the application. The child's welfare, being the first consideration, outweighed any contravention and public policy considerations, so that breach of the statutory restrictions was not an absolute bar. Just two examples serve to demonstrate the approach taken. In *Re C (A Minor) (Adoption: Legality)* [1999] Fam 128, [1999] 2 WLR 202, [1999] 1 FLR 370, a childless woman aged thirty-nine had approached two social services departments and an adoption agency, but had been rejected as a suitable prospective adopter. She sought information from a Guatemalan support group which put her in touch with a contact in Guatemala. She paid a lawyer in Guatemala to deal with the legal process. She paid £300 for a home study which was wholly inadequate, and described by Johnson J as "striking for its superficiality". She had neither gone to Guatemala nor seen the child, but she successfully adopted a child in Guatemala. The child was handed over to her in Amsterdam and she then brought the child to England. She gave notice of her intention to adopt the child to her local social services department. Both the guardian and the local authority were concerned about the ability of the applicant to meet the child's needs and about the child's future, but were faced with the problem that, in the circumstances, leaving the child with the applicant was the least damaging of the options available. The court held that, in arranging to have the home study report prepared and paying for it, the applicant was in breach of section 11 or 57 or both, and guilty of a criminal offence. It also held that the arrangements the applicant made with the Guatemalan lawyers and the agreement to pay them were in breach of section 57(2) of the Act. Despite the applicant's unlawful acts, however, the court held that these did not represent an absolute bar. Further, although concerned by the deliberate evasion of the statutory procedures, which meant that the court had to apply to the child a lower standard of protection than would apply to a British child in domestic adoption proceedings, and thus operating a two-tier system, the court was bound by section 6, under which the child's welfare was the first consideration; the disadvantage to the child if the order was not made outweighed the other considerations.

The case of *Flintshire County Council v K* [2001] 2 FLR 476 highlighted the flagrant abuse of the system. An American couple made a decision to give up their unborn twins for adoption. They used a private adoption agency.

Within four months of their birth the twins were placed with prospective adopters by the agency, but the mother removed them after about a month. In the meantime the agency contacted a couple in England, who had signed a co-ordination contract with the agency about the availability of the twins for adoption, and paid the agency $12,500. The couple had also commissioned a private home study report. The couple flew to California, and paid a further $1,200. As a result of police involvement instigated by the original couple, the English couple flew to Arkansas with the twins, where the mother consented to the adoption of the twins by the English couple. The father of the twins also consented to the adoption. An adoption order was made by the court in Arkansas, although the mother had not been resident there. The English couple returned to England with the twins, without immigration clearance. The couple subsequently gave their story to the newspapers. The local authority in the meantime issued care proceedings. An emergency protection order was obtained and the twins were placed in the care of foster parents. The mother of the children sought their return to the USA. The English couple applied for residence orders. The application for residence orders was rejected, the court having found that the couple's plans had been misguided and that the twins had suffered and were continuing to suffer significant harm; the couple's conduct raised concerns that the twins would suffer harm if they were returned to the couple. The court made a care order on the basis that the local authority would arrange for the twins to be returned to Missouri where the appropriate court has made an order granting protective custody to the Division of the Family Services pending the resolution of the matters before the count.

See also *Re Adoption Application (Non-Patrial: Breach of Procedures)* [1993] Fam 125, [1993] 2 WLR 110, [1993] 1 FLR 947, *Re An Adoption Application* [1992] 1 WLR 596, [1992] 1 FLR 341, and *Re AW (Adoption Application)* [1993] 1 FLR 62; pages 298 to 299. These and other cases raised concerns regarding trafficking in children, and an awareness that the statutory provisions in place were insufficient to prevent children from sometimes being placed in unsuitable placements, in effect supporting the two-tier system referred to by Johnson J in *Re C*, above.

The Adoption and Children Act 2002 addresses this problem by extending the provisions on bringing into the United Kingdom a child resident outside the United Kingdom. Those provisions now apply to bringing or causing to bring into the United Kingdom a child under an external adoption effected within the preceding six months. Heavier penalties for breaches of the provisions are also introduced, with a view to deterring prospective adopters from contravening the restriction.

2. Restrictions on Arranging Adoptions
Section 92 of the Adoption and Children Act 2002 extends the former

provisions of sections 11 and 72(3) of the Adoption Act 1976. Section 92(1) prohibits any person, who is neither an adoption agency nor acting in pursuance of an order of the High Court, from taking any of the steps listed in section 92(2). Those steps are:

(a) asking a person other than an adoption agency to provide a child for adoption;

(b) asking a person other than an adoption agency to provide prospective adopters for a child;

(c) offering to find a child for adoption;

(d) offering a child for adoption to a person other than an adoption agency;

(e) handing over a child to any person other than an adoption agency with a view to the child's adoption by that or another person;

(f) receiving a child handed over to him in contravention of (e) above;

(g) entering into an agreement with any person for the adoption of a child;

(h) initiating or taking part in negotiations of which the purpose is the conclusion of an agreement within (g) above; and

(i) causing another person to take any of the steps mentioned in (a) to (h).

The term "agreement" includes an arrangement, whether or not it is enforceable (section 92(7)(a)).

Paragraphs (d), (e), (g), (h) and (i) above do not apply if the prospective adopters are (or if one of them is) parents, relatives or guardians of the child, or if the prospective adopter is the partner of a parent of the child (section 92(3)).

Offences

Section 93(1) of the 2002 Act makes it a criminal offence for a person to contravene section 92(1). It also provides that if that person is an adoption society, the person who manages the society is also guilty of the offence.

Section 93(2) and (3) provide two defences to a prosecution under section 93(1), namely:

(a) if a person is charged with receiving a child handed to him by a person other than an adoption agency with a view to the child's adoption by him or another person, he is not guilty unless it is proved that he knew or had reason to suspect that the child was handed over to him in contravention of (e) above;

(b) a person is not guilty of an offence of causing a person to take any of the steps mentioned in (a) to (h) above unless it is proved that he knew or had reason to suspect that the step taken would contravene the paragraph in question.

The defences are available only if sufficient evidence is adduced to raise an issue as to whether the person knew, or had reason to suspect, that the child was handed over to him in contravention of section 92, or that the step(s) taken would contravene the relevant provisions (section 93(4)). See also the Electronic Commerce Directive (Adoption and Children Act 2002) Regulations 2005, SI 2005 No. 3222.

A person found guilty of an offence under section 93 is liable, on summary conviction, to imprisonment for a term not exceeding six months or a fine not exceeding £10,000, or both (section 93(5)).

A prosecution under section 93 may be brought within six months from the date on which evidence, sufficient in the opinion of the prosecutor to warrant the proceedings, came to his knowledge, but may not be brought more than six years after the commission of the offence (section 138).

Likely effect of the new provisions
As has already been noted, when the welfare of the child was the first among many other considerations which the court had to take into account, courts were reluctant to refuse an application for adoption even where there had been blatant breaches. Under section 1(2) of the Adoption and Children Act 2002, the welfare of the child throughout his life is the paramount consideration. It therefore seems unlikely that the court's approach will be any different. Indeed, the argument that a child should remain in his placement, particularly where the child has been in the care of the applicant for some time and has settled with the applicant, is likely to be even stronger. It remains to be seen whether a court will, in those circumstances, condone an act which Parliament has clearly indicated remains a criminal offence, and whether prosecutors will consider a breach sufficiently serious to commence proceedings.

3. Restrictions on Reports

Section 94 of the Adoption and Children Act 2002 introduces a new provision which places restrictions on the preparation of reports in connection with adoption. It provides that a person who is not within a prescribed description may not, in any prescribed circumstances, prepare a report for any person about the suitability of a child for adoption, or of a person to adopt, or about the adoption or placement for adoption of a child.

The Restriction on the Preparation of Adoption Reports Regulations 2005 (SI 2005 No. 1711) make supplementary provisions. Regulation 3 provides that a person is within a "prescribed description" for the purposes of section 94(1) if he is a social worker employed by or acting on behalf of an adoption agency and satisfies at least one of the conditions set out in regulation 3(2) (on length of post-qualifying experience, and supervision); or he is participating in a social work course and is employed by or placed with an adoption agency as part of that course, and satisfies the condition in regulation 3(2)(b) (concerning supervision). The prescribed circumstances are the preparation of reports on specified subjects pursuant to the Adoption Agencies Regulations 2005 (SI 2005 No. 389), the Adoption Agencies (Wales) Regulations 2005 (SI 2005 No. 1313, W.95), and the Adoptions with a Foreign Element Regulations 2005 (SI 2005 No. 392); pre-adoption and post-adoption reports; and reports pursuant to sections 43, 44(5) and 84(1) of the Adoption and Children Act 2002 (see Chapters 16, 22 and 23).

The purpose of the statutory provision, combined with the regulations, is to ensure that assessments and reports required in connection with the adoption of a child are carried out and prepared by those with the appropriate qualifications. To add weight to these provisions, section 94(2) makes contravention a criminal offence.

Offences

Section 94(2) and (3) provide that if a person contravenes the provisions of section 94(1) or causes a person to prepare a report, or submit to any person a report which has been prepared, in contravention of that subsection, he is guilty of an offence. If a person who works for an adoption society contravenes section 94(1), or causes a person to prepare a report, or submits to any person a report, which has been prepared in contravention of that subsection, the person who manages the society is also guilty of the offence (section 94(3)).

A person is not, however, guilty of the offence of causing a person to prepare a report, or submit to any person a report which has been prepared, in contravention of section 94(1) unless it is proved that he knew or had reason to suspect that the report would be or had been prepared in contravention of section 94(1). But this defence is available only if sufficient evidence is adduced to raise an issue as to whether the person knew or had reason to suspect that the report was so prepared (section 94(4)).

A person found guilty of this offence is liable, on summary conviction, to imprisonment for a term not exceeding six months or a fine not exceeding £5,000, or both (section 94(5)).

A prosecution under section 94 may be brought within six months from the date on which evidence, sufficient in the opinion of the prosecutor to warrant the proceedings, came to his knowledge, but may not be brought more than six years after the commission of the offence (section 138).

4. Prohibition of Certain Payments

Section 95 of the Adoption and Children Act 2002 prohibits any payment (save for the exceptions provided) which is made for or in consideration of:

(a) the adoption of a child;
(b) giving any consent required in connection with the adoption of a child;
(c) the removal from the United Kingdom of a child who is a

Commonwealth citizen, or is habitually resident in the United Kingdom, to a place outside the British Islands for the purpose of adoption;

(d) a person (who is neither an adoption agency nor acting in pursuance of an order of the High Court) taking any step mentioned in section 92(2) (see **2.** above);

(e) preparing, causing to be prepared or submitting a report, the preparation of which contravenes section 94(1) (see **3.** above).

A payment is excepted from the provisions of section 95 of the Adoption and Children Act 2002 if:

(a) it is made by virtue of, or in accordance with provision made by or under, the Adoption and Children Act 2002, the Adoption (Scotland) Act 1978 or the Adoption (Northern Ireland) Order 1987;

(b) it is made to a registered adoption society by a parent or guardian of a child, or a person who adopts or proposes to adopt a child, in respect of expenses reasonably incurred by the society in connection with the adoption or proposed adoption of the child;

(c) it is made in respect of any legal or medical expenses incurred or to be incurred by any person in connection with an application to a court which he has made or proposes to make for an adoption order, a placement order, or an order for contact under section 26 or for parental responsibility, in order to adopt a child outside the British Islands under section 84 of the Adoption and Children Act 2002;

(d) it is made in respect of the removal of a child from the United Kingdom for the purposes of adoption where the prospective adopters are the parents, guardians or relatives (or one of them) of the child, or a step-parent or person with parental responsibility for the child, or the child is removed under the authority of an order under section 49 of the Adoption (Scotland) Act 1978 or article 57 of the Adoption (Northern Ireland) Order 1987, and the payment is made in respect of the travel and accommodation expenses reasonably incurred in removing the child from the United Kingdom for the purposes of adoption

(section 96).

Offences

It is a criminal offence for a person:

(a) to make any payment other than as permitted;

(b) to agree or offer to make any such payment; or

(c) to receive or agree to receive or attempt to obtain any such payment

(Adoption and Children Act 2002, section 95(3)).

A person convicted of such an offence is liable, on summary conviction, to imprisonment for a term not exceeding six months or a fine not exceeding £10,000, or both (section 95(4)).

A prosecution under section 95 may be brought within six months from the date on which evidence, sufficient in the opinion of the prosecutor to warrant the proceedings, came to his knowledge, but may not be brought more than six years after the commission of the offence (section 138).

5. Restrictions on Advertisements

Section 123 of the Adoption and Children Act 2002 prohibits the publication or distribution of an advertisement or information, or causing such an advertisement or information to be published or distributed, which indicates that:

(a) a parent or guardian of a child wants the child adopted; or

(b) a person wants to adopt a child;

(c) a person other than an adoption agency is willing to take any of the steps in paragraphs (a) to (e) or (g) to (i) of section 92(2) (see **2.** above);

(d) a person other than an adoption agency is willing to receive a child handed over to him with a view to the child's adoption by him or another; or

(e) a person is willing to remove a child from the United Kingdom for the purposes of adoption.

The above provisions do not apply to publication or distribution by or on behalf of an adoption agency, which includes a Scottish or Northern Irish adoption agency. "Adoption agency" here includes a prescribed person outside the United Kingdom exercising functions corresponding to those of an adoption agency, if the functions are being exercised in prescribed circumstances. The Secretary of State is empowered, in consultation with the Scottish Ministers, the Department of Health, Social Services and Public Safety, and the Assembly, to prescribe regulations to authorise organisations outside the United Kingdom to carry out the functions of an adoption agency. This should facilitate and regulate the adoption of children from outside the United Kingdom, and, it is to be hoped, encourage those who wish to adopt not to take desperate and illegal measures, but to use legal channels to achieve their aims.

The phrase "publishing or distributing" an advertisement means publishing or distributing it to the public, and includes doing so by electronic means, for example, by means of the internet. In this connection, see the Electronic Commerce Directive (Adoption and Children Act 2002) Regulations 2005, SI 2005 No. 3222.

"Public" includes selected members of the public as well as the public generally or any section of the public. "Information" includes information about how to do anything which, if done, would constitute an offence under section 85 or 93, or of section 11 or 50 of the Adoption (Scotland) Act 1978, or article 58 of the Adoption (Northern Ireland) Order 1987 (whether or not the information includes a warning that doing the thing in question may constitute an offence), and information about a particular child as a child available for adoption (Adoption and Children Act 2002, section 123(3) and (4)).

Offence

Section 124 of the Adoption and Children Act 2002 makes it an offence to breach the restrictions imposed by section 123(1) of the Act. As in relation to other offences, section 124(2) provides that a person is not guilty of the offence unless it is proved that he knew or had reason to suspect that section 123 applied to the advertisement or information, but this defence is available only if sufficient evidence is adduced to raise an issue as to whether the person had the knowledge or reason to suspect that the section applied to the advertisement or information.

A person found guilty of this offence is liable, on summary conviction, to imprisonment for a term not exceeding three months or a fine not exceeding £5,000, or both (section 124(3)).

6. Restrictions on Bringing Children from Overseas

Section 83 of the Adoption and Children Act 2002 prohibits a person who is habitually resident in the British Islands (the "British resident") from bringing, or causing another to bring, a child who is habitually resident outside the British Islands into the United Kingdom for the purposes of adoption by the British resident. It also prohibits the British resident at any time from bringing, or causing another to bring, into the United Kingdom a child adopted by the British resident under an external adoption effected within the preceding six months. References to adoption, or to a child adopted by the British resident, here include references to adoption, or to a child adopted, by the British resident and another person. Section 83 does not apply if the intention is that the child will be adopted under a Convention adoption order. "External adoption" means an adoption, other than a Convention adoption, effected under the law of any country or territory outside the British Islands, whether or not the adoption is an adoption within the meaning of Chapter 4 of the Act (see section 66, page 126) or a full adoption within the meaning of section 88(3) – namely an adoption by virtue of which the child is to be treated in law as not being the child of any person other than the adopter(s).

Section 83(4), (5) and (6) of the Act provides for regulations to be made dealing with the requirements to be met by a person intending to bring, or cause another to bring, a child into the United Kingdom. The Adoptions with a Foreign Element Regulations 2005 (SI 2005 No. 392) have been made and came into force on 30 December 2005. They are dealt with in Chapter 22.

Offences

Section 83(7) of the Adoption and Children Act 2002 makes it an offence for a person to bring, or cause another to bring, a child into the United Kingdom at any time in circumstances where the restrictions in section 83 apply, unless he has complied with any requirement or condition imposed by regulations made under section 83(5).

Regulation 59 of the Adoptions with a Foreign Element Regulations 2005 makes it an offence for a person to fail to comply with regulation 26, 27 or 33. Regulation 26 requires the prospective adopter to give notice to the relevant authority if he does not wish to proceed with the adoption. Regulation 27 provides that where the relevant local authority is of the opinion that it is not in the interest of the child who has been placed with the prospective adopter to remain in the placement, it must notify the prospective adopter and he must return the child within seven days of the notice being given to him. Under Regulation 33, where a court refuses to make a Convention adoption order, or the application for such an order is withdrawn, the prospective adopter must return the child to the relevant local authority within the time determined by the court.

A person found guilty of an offence under section 83 is liable, on summary conviction, to imprisonment for a term not exceeding six months or a fine not exceeding £5,000, or both; and, on conviction on indictment, to imprisonment for a term not exceeding twelve months or a fine, or both (Adoption and Children Act 2002, section 83(8)).

A person found guilty of any of the offences under the Adoptions with a Foreign Element Regulations is liable on summary conviction to imprisonment for a term not exceeding three months or a fine not exceeding £5,000 or both (regulation 59).

7. Restrictions on Taking Children out of the United Kingdom

A child who is a Commonwealth citizen or is habitually resident in the United Kingdom must not be removed from the United Kingdom to a place outside the British Islands for the purpose of adoption, unless the conditions set out in section 85(2) of the Adoption and Children Act 2002 are met (section 85(1)).

"Removing" a child from the United Kingdom includes arranging to do so, and the circumstances in which a person arranges to remove a child from the United Kingdom include those where he:

(a) enters into an arrangement for the purpose of facilitating such a removal of the child;

(b) initiates or takes part in negotiations, of which the purpose is the conclusion of an arrangement within (a) above; or

(c) causes another person to take any steps as mentioned in (a) or (b) above.

An arrangement includes an agreement (whether or not enforceable).

A person may, however, remove a child from the United Kingdom in two circumstances:

    (a) a person who intends to adopt a child under the law of another country or territory outside the British Islands may remove the child from the United Kingdom where he has been granted parental responsibility for the child by an order of the High Court. The removal of the child must comply with the Adoptions with a Foreign Element Regulations 2005, regulation 10 (see page 325);

    (b) a child may be removed from the United Kingdom under the authority of an order under section 49 of the Adoption (Scotland) Act 1978 or article 57 of the Adoption (Northern Ireland) Order 1987

(Adoption and Children Act 2002, section 85(2)).

Offences

It is a criminal offence for a person to remove a child from the United Kingdom in breach of the above restrictions; or arrange to do so by entering into an arrangement for facilitating such a removal; or initiate or take part in any negotiations for the purpose of concluding an arrangement for the removal of the child from the United Kingdom; or cause another person to take any such steps (Adoption and Children Act 2002, section 85(4)).

A person is not guilty of causing another to enter into an arrangement, or initiate or take part in negotiations, unless it is proved that he knew or had reason to suspect that the step taken would contravene section 85(1) of the Act, but this defence applies only if sufficient evidence is adduced to raise an issue as to whether the person knew or had reason to suspect that the step was in breach of section 85(3)(a) or (b) (section 85(5)).

A person guilty of this offence is liable, on summary conviction, to imprisonment for a term not exceeding six months or a fine not exceeding £5,000, or both; and, on conviction on indictment, to imprisonment for a term not exceeding twelve months or a fine, or both (section 85(6)).

Extra-territorial effect

There are conflicting decisions on whether the provisions of the Adoption Act 1976 corresponding to those discussed above had extra-territorial effect. Some of the decisions in which the subject arose are described below.

In *Re an Adoption Application* [1992] 1 WLR 596, [1992] 1 FLR 341, a couple who wished to adopt were over the eligible age to adopt through English agencies. The male applicant was a solicitor who was under criminal investigation for deception. The couple commissioned and paid for a private home study with a view to adopting a child from overseas. They contacted lawyers in Ecuador and travelled to Ecuador, but abandoned their intention to adopt a child from Ecuador. They then contacted a lawyer in El Salvador, to whom the man paid $7,000. In due course the couple was notified that a newborn baby was available for adoption. Within four weeks of the child's birth, consent to the adoption was obtained; the male applicant travelled to El Salvador and returned to England with the child; he was met by his wife at the airport. An entry clearance certificate for the child had not been obtained; the entry clearance officer at the British Embassy in El Salvador had not had the opportunity to make inquiries as required under the Home Office circular on intercountry adoptions. The couple notified the local authority of their intention to adopt the child, but did not disclose the pending criminal trial of the male applicant. A formal adoption order was made in El Salvador about five months after the child's removal to England. The male applicant was convicted on fourteen counts of obtaining property by deception and fourteen counts of procuring the execution of a valuable security by deception; he was sentenced to four years' imprisonment. The local authority, with some misgivings, supported the application. The guardian opposed the making of an adoption order on the basis of the circumstances, the serious breaches of sections 11 and 57 of the Adoption Act 1976, and for public policy reasons.

On the issue of the breach under section 11(1), the court found that the placement of the child with the female applicant at the airport constituted an arrangement for the adoption of a child by a person other than an adoption agency, but that the High Court could excuse it and that authorisation could be given retrospectively. On the breach of section 57, the court considered the provisions of section 57 with those of section 72(3), and held that the payments made by the couple for the home study report and the lawyers in El Salvador were in breach of the provisions, but nevertheless concluded that considerations of public policy did not outweigh considerations of the child's welfare and that an adoption order should be made. The court thus found that the provisions had extra-territorial effect.

In *Re AW (Adoption Application)* [1993] 1 FLR 62, a couple aged sixty-two and sixty had an adopted child and wished to adopt another child. They were aware that they would not be eligible to adopt a child in England because of their age, the instability of their marital relationship and the male applicant's alcoholism. They deliberately set out to evade the legal provisions, in that they agreed with a pregnant woman who did not want her baby that she should give birth in Germany and that they would have her baby. They paid her £1,000 in England, and other costs and expenses while she remained in Germany. The male applicant and another lady then travelled to Germany and returned with the baby to England. Thereafter they set about misleading the authorities and concealing the circumstances. In construing the provisions of section 29(1) of the Adoption Act 1958, which was replaced on 1 January 1988 by section 11 of the Adoption Act 1976, Bracewell J held that the placement of the child with the applicants was in breach of the section, and that, although it did not have extra-territorial effect, it applied in the case as the arrangements had been made in England. With regard to section 50(1) of the 1958 Act – the forerunner of section 57 of the Adoption Act 1976 – the court found the section did not have extra-territorial effect. Bracewell J said:

> "I have reached the conclusion that there is no extraterritorial jurisdiction . . . With the greatest respect to Hollings J in *Re An Adoption Application*, to which I have already referred and to *Re F*, I find that there is not any extraterritorial jurisdiction and I do not agree with the comments therein."

In *Re Adoption Application (Non-Patrial: Breach of Procedure)* 1993] Fam 125, [1993] 2 WLR 110, [1993] 1 FLR 947, a couple who wished to adopt a child contacted a lawyer in El Salvador with a view to adopting a baby. They obtained a home study report and medical reports. These were sent to the lawyer, who was paid £4,750. The wife travelled to El Salvador and returned with the baby. The court in El Salvador made an adoption order in the couple's favour. The couple also gave notice to the local authority of their intention to adopt the child in accordance with English law. The court found that the handing over of the child by the wife to her husband, with the intention that they should jointly apply to adopt the child, was caught by the provisions of section 11 of the 1976 Act. The payment made to the lawyer could constitute a breach of section 57 of the 1976 Act, subject to the issue of extra-territoriality. Douglas Brown J held that neither section 11 nor section 57 had extra-territorial effect. He said:

> ". . . neither s 11 nor s 57 has extraterritorial effect. In the first place there is an established presumption that, in the absence of clear and specific words to the contrary, a statute does not make conduct outside the jurisdiction a criminal offence . . . Secondly, in the Adoption Act 1976 there are positive provisions excluding extraterritorial effect. The extent of the statute is dealt with in s 74(3) which provides that the Act extends to England and Wales only. Section 74(3), which I have already referred to, expressly refers to adoption in "Great Britain or elsewhere" but does not apply those words to "agreement or arrangement". The preponderance of judicial opinion is to the same effect: see *Re A (Adoption: Placement)* [1988] 2 FLR 133 where Anthony Lincoln J held that s 29 of the Adoption Act 1958 had no extraterritorial effect . . ."

In *Re WM (Adoption: Non Patrial)* [1997] 1 FLR 132, the child was born in El Salvador. The mother wished to give up her child and contacted a lawyer. An English couple wished to adopt a child from overseas. They contacted the lawyer and paid him £5,000 to arrange for them to adopt the child. An adoption order was made and the couple brought the child to England. The couple then applied to adopt him in England, but before the application was heard the couple separated. The child lived with the adoptive mother. The court found that the payment had been in breach of section 57 of the 1976 Act, although it had been made outside the jurisdiction; and that the placement had been in contravention of section 11. The court held that the section 11 breach did not prevent the court from making the adoption order. and that, in so far as the breach of section 57 was concerned, the court would exercise its discretion and authorise the payment retrospectively.

In *Re C (A Minor) (Adoption: Legality)* [1999] Fam 128, [1999] 2 WLR 202, [1999] 1 FLR 370 (see page 289 for the facts), where the payment was transmitted from the United Kingdom to Guatemala, Johnson J rejected the argument that the payment was not made until it had been received, and held that the payment was made when it was transmitted and therefore there had been a breach of section 57.

8. The Removal and Return of Children

It is a criminal offence for any person, other than the adoption agency, to remove a child from his prospective adopters where the child is placed for adoption by an adoption agency under section 19; or a child is placed for adoption by an adoption agency and either the child is less than six weeks old or the agency has at no time been authorised to place the child for adoption. A person guilty of this offence is liable, on summary conviction, to imprisonment for a term not exceeding three months or a fine not exceeding £5,000, or both (Adoption and Children Act 2002, section 30(8)).

A prospective adopter with whom a child less than six weeks old has been placed, or who is providing accommodation for a child, must return the child if notified to do so by the adoption agency that placed the child with him. This must be done within seven days of the notice being given. Failure to comply is a criminal offence, and if found guilty the person is liable, on summary conviction, to imprisonment for a term not exceeding three months or a fine not exceeding £5,000, or both (Adoption and Children Act 2002, section 31(5)).

Where a child is placed for adoption with a prospective adopter with the consent of his parent, and the consent is then withdrawn, then, unless an application is or has been made for a placement order, the agency must give notice to the prospective adopter of the withdrawal of consent and request the return of the child within fourteen days of notice being given. Failure by the prospective adopter to return the child is a criminal offence. If found guilty, the prospective adopter is liable, on summary conviction, to imprisonment for a term not exceeding three months or a fine not exceeding £5,000, or both (Adoption and Children Act 2002, section 32(3)).

Where a child has been placed for adoption by a local authority and an application for a placement order has been refused, the prospective adopter must return the child to the local authority on a date determined by the court. Failure to comply with the order is a criminal offence. The prospective adopter is liable, on summary conviction, to imprisonment for a term not exceeding three months or a fine not exceeding £5,000, or both (Adoption and Children Act 2002, section 33(3)).

Where a placement order in respect of a child is in force or has been revoked, but the child has not been returned by the prospective adopter or remains accommodated by the local authority, it is a criminal offence for any person to remove the child from the prospective adopter or from the accommodation provided by the local authority. A person found guilty is liable, on summary conviction, to imprisonment for a term not exceeding three months or a fine not exceeding £5,000, or both (Adoption and Children Act 2002, section 34(2) and (5)).

Section 36(6) of the Adoption and Children Act 2002 makes it an offence to remove a child from the person with whom the child was placed in a non-agency case, where that person has applied for an adoption order and the application has not been disposed of; or has given notice of intention to adopt the child or has applied for leave to apply for an adoption order under section 42(6) and the application is pending. A person who removes the child in these circumstances commits an offence and is liable, on summary conviction, to imprisonment for a term not exceeding three months or a fine not exceeding £5,000, or both. Similarly, where a parent is able to remove his child, the person with whom the child is living must return the child to the parent immediately the request for the child's return is made. Failure to do so is an offence and an offender is liable, on summary conviction, to imprisonment for a term not exceeding three months or a fine not exceeding £5,000, or both (Adoption and Children Act 2002, section 36(6)).

Where a court makes a recovery order under section 41 of the Adoption and Children Act 2002, any person who intentionally obstructs a person exercising a power of removal is guilty of an offence and is is liable on summary conviction to a fine not exceeding £1,000 (Adoption and Children Act 2002, section 41(5)).

It is an offence for a parent or guardian to remove a child from the custody of a person with whom the child has his home, without leave of the court, where an application for an adoption order under the Adoption Act 1976 remains pending after the coming into force of the 2002 Act (Adoption Act 1976, section 27); see Chapter 25, page 364.

A prospective adopter who fails to comply with a requirement to return the child within seven days of notice being given under section 35(2) (see page 79) commits a criminal offence, and is liable, on summary conviction, to imprisonment for a term of not more than three months or a fine, or both (Adoption and Children Act 2002, section 35(4)).

9. Disclosure of Information

Disclosure of any protected information in contravention of section 57 of the Adoption and Children Act 2002 by a registered adoption society (see Chapter 14) is a criminal offence. The society would be liable, on summary conviction, to a fine not exceeding £5,000 (Adoption and Children Act 2002, section 59 and the Disclosure of Adoption Information (Post-Commencement Adoptions) Regulations 2005, SI 2005 No. 888, regulation 21).

Disclosure of information on the Adoption and Children Act Register otherwise than in accordance with section 129 of the 2002 Act is an offence. On summary conviction, an offender is liable to a term of imprisonment not exceeding three months, a fine of £5,000, or both (see Chapter 16, page 232).

10. Offences by Bodies Corporate and Unincorporated Bodies

Where any offence under the Adoption and Children Act 2002 committed by a body corporate is proved to have been committed with the consent or connivance of, or to be attributable to any neglect on the part of, any director, manager, secretary or other similar officer of the body, or a person purporting to act in any such capacity, that person, as well as the body, is guilty of the offence and liable to be proceeded against and punished accordingly (Adoption and Children Act 2002, section 143(1)).

Where the affairs of a body corporate are managed by its members, section 143(1) of the Act applies in relation to the acts and defaults of a member in connection with his functions of management as it applies to a director or a body corporate (section 143(2)).

Where an offence under the Act committed by an unincorporated body is proved to have been committed with the consent or connivance of, or attributable to any neglect on the part of, any officer of the body or any member of its governing body, he as well as the body is guilty of the offence and liable to be proceeded against and punished accordingly. Proceedings for an offence alleged to have been committed under the Act by an unincorporated body should be brought in the name of that body (and not in the name of any of its members). For the purposes of any such proceedings in England and Wales or Northern Ireland, any rules of court relating to the service of documents have effect as if that body were a corporation. A fine imposed on an unincorporated body on its conviction for an offence under the Act should be paid out of the funds of the body. See section 143(3) to (6) of the 2002 Act.

Where an offence under the 2002 Act committed by a partnership is proved to have been committed with the consent or connivance of, or to be attributable to any neglect on the part of, a partner, he, as well as the partnership, is guilty of the offence and liable to be proceeded against and punished accordingly (section 143(7)).

11. Offences in Relation to Intermediary Services

Save in certain specified circumstances referred to in regulation 7(2) of the Adoption Information and Intermediary Services (Pre-Commencement Adoptions) Regulations 2005 (SI 2005 No. 890) and the Adoption

Information and Intermediary Services (Pre-Commencement Adoptions) (Wales) Regulations 2005 (SI 2005 No. 2701, W. 190) (see Chapter 15), an intermediary must not disclose any identifying documents to a person who requests assistance to obtain information about his adoption or to facilitate contact. Contravention of regulation 7, without reasonable cause, is an offence. The intermediary agency would be liable, on summary conviction, to a fine not exceeding £5,000 (regulation 17).

12. Offences in Relation to Adoption Support Agencies

Section 9(3) of the Adoption and Children Act 2002 contemplates regulations providing that a person who contravenes or fails to comply with any provision of regulations under the section is to be guilty of an offence. The Adoption Support Agencies (England) and Adoption Agencies (Miscellaneous Amendments) Regulations 2005 (SI 2005 No. 2720), regulation 29, makes it an offence to contravene or fail to comply with the provisions of regulations 5(1) to (7), 6, 7(1) and (4), 8(2), 9(1), 10, 11, 12(1) and (2), 13, 14, 16 to 18, 19(1), 20, 21(1), 22, 23, 24(1) and (2), 25, 26 and 27(1). These regulations are discussed in Chapter 18. On summary conviction, an offender is liable to a fine not exceeding £5,000. The registration authority may not, however, bring proceedings against a person in respect of such a contravention or failure to comply unless:

    (a) he is a registered person;

    (b) the requisite notice has been given;

    (c) the period specified in the notice, within which the registered person may make representations to the registration authority, has expired;

    (d) where the notice specifies any action that is to be taken within a specified period (see below), the period has expired and the action has not been taken within that period.

A notice under (b) must specify:

    (a) in what respect the registered person has contravened or is contravening any of the regulations, or has failed or is failing to comply with the requirements of any of the regulations;

    (b) what action, in the opinion of the registration authority, the registered person should take so as to comply with any of those regulations; and

    (c) the period, not exceeding three months, within which the registered person should take action.

The registration authority may bring proceedings against a person who was once, but no longer is, a registered person, in respect of a failure to comply with regulation 14 (records with respect to services) or 22 (records with respect to staff).

    The Adoption Support Agencies (Wales) Regulations 2005 (SI 2005 No. 1514, W. 118) make similar provisions; see Chapter 18.

Chapter 20

Adoptions with a Foreign Element

1. Introduction

The principles by reference to which the law on intercountry adoptions and the recognition of foreign adoptions has been formulated are enshrined in a number of international declarations and conventions to which the United Kingdom is a party. These instruments provide the legal framework for the relevant domestic law. An appreciation of some of the background elucidates the reasons for, and the purpose of, the domestic process which has been laid down in respect of adoptions with a foreign element, and in particular those now known as "Convention adoptions". The relevant statutory provisions include, in particular, the Adoptions with a Foreign Element Regulations 2005 (SI 2005 No. 392) and the Convention on the Protection of Children and Co-operation in respect of intercountry Adoptions 1993 (the "Hague Convention").

The most important international instruments, which form the backbone of the legislative framework on the rights of the child, include:

- the United Nations Declaration on Social Legal Principles relating to the Protection and Welfare of Children with special reference to Foster Placements and Adoptions Nationally and Internationally, adopted by General Assembly Resolution 41/85 of 3 December 1986;
- the United Nations Convention on the Rights of the Child, 1989 (see below);
- the Convention on the Protection of Children and Co-operation in respect of Intercountry Adoption, 1993 (the "Hague Convention", see below);
- Recommendation 1443/2000, *International adoption: respecting children's rights*, adopted by the Parliamentary Assembly of the Council of Europe on 26 January 2000;
- the European Parliament's Resolution on Improving the Law and Co-operation between Member States on the Adoption of Minors, of 12 December 1996.

The central theme which runs through the international instruments is the principle that the best interest of the child must be the determining factor in any decision that is made relating to a child.

2. The United Nations Convention on the Rights of the Child

The United Nations Convention on the Rights of the Child of 20 November 1989 was ratified by the United Kingdom on 15 January 1992. The preamble, *inter alia*, restates that in the Universal Declaration of Human Rights, the United Nations proclaimed that "childhood is entitled to special care and assistance". The preamble to the Convention further confirms that the family:

"as the fundamental group of society and the natural environment for the growth and well-being of all its members and particularly children, should be afforded the necessary protection and assistance so that it can fully assume its responsibilities within the community."

It recognises that the child, "for the full and harmonious development of his or her personality, should grow up in a family environment, in an atmosphere of happiness, love and understanding". The child "should be fully prepared to live an individual life in society, and brought up in the spirit of the ideals proclaimed in the Charter of the United Nations, and in particular in the spirit of peace, dignity, tolerance, freedom, equality and solidarity". It emphasises that "in all countries in the world, there are children living in exceptionally difficult conditions, and that such children need special consideration", with due account taken of "the importance of the traditions and cultural values of each people for the protection and harmonious development of the child"; and recognises "the importance of international co-operation for improving the living conditions of children in every country, in particular in the developing countries".

Article 2 of the UN Convention provides that states who are parties to the Convention should respect and ensure the rights set out in the Convention to each child within their jurisdiction without discrimination of any kind, irrespective of the child's or his "parent's or legal guardian's race, colour, sex, language, religion, political or other opinion, national, ethnic or social origin, property, disability, birth or other status".

Under article 2(2), states are required to take all appropriate measures to ensure that the child is protected against all forms of discrimination or punishment on the basis of the status, activities, opinions or beliefs of the child's parents, guardians or family members.

Article 3 provides that:

"1. In all actions concerning children, whether undertaken by public or private social welfare institutions, courts of law, administrative authorities or legislative bodies, the best interest of the child shall be a primary consideration.

2. States Parties undertake to ensure the child such protection and care

as is necessary for his or her well-being, taking into account the rights and duties of his or her parents, legal guardians or other individuals legally responsible for him or her and, to his end, shall take all appropriate legislative and administrative measures.

3.   States Parties shall ensure that the institutions, services and facilities responsible for the care or protection of children shall conform with the standards established by competent authorities, particularly in the areas of safety, health, in the number and suitability of their staff as well as competent supervision."

Article 7 confirms the child's right to an identity, requiring that a child shall be registered immediately after birth and shall have a right to a name, the right to acquire a nationality and, as far as possible, the right to know and be cared for by his or her parents. Article 8 goes on to provide that states are obliged to ensure the implementation of these rights. In addition, states undertake to respect "the right of the child to preserve his or her identity" and to this end are required, if a child is illegally deprived of some or all the elements of his or her identity, to provide appropriate assistance and protection with a view to re-establishing his or her identity speedily.

Article 9 requires states to ensure that a child is not separated from his parents against their will, except where such separation is necessary for the best interests of the child, for example where there has been abuse or neglect of the child, but in any such case the parents should be given an opportunity to take part in any proceedings and to express their views. Where the separation of a child from his parents is inevitable, the state is obliged to respect the right of the child to maintain his relationship and for direct contact with his parents unless it is found to be contrary to the interests of the child.

The Convention also protects the right of a child who is capable of forming his or her own views, to express those views freely in all matters affecting the child, and where appropriate to be provided with the opportunity to be heard and represented in any proceedings which affect the child (article 12).

Where, having taken account of the child's right to the preservation of family life, it is nevertheless considered that it is in the child's best interest that he should not live with his parents, the state is required to provide protection and assistance and to ensure alternative care for the child. Article 20(3) specifically states that such care:

"could include, *inter alia*, foster placement, kafalah of Islamic law, adoption or if necessary placement in suitable institutions for the care of children. When considering solutions, due regard shall be paid to the desirability of continuity in a child's upbringing and to the child's ethnic, religious, cultural and linguistic background."

In states which recognise and permit adoption, the state is required to ensure that "the best interests of the child shall be the paramount consideration". In particular, states must:

"(a) ensure that the adoption of a child is authorized only by competent authorities who determine, in accordance with applicable law and procedures and on the basis of all pertinent and reliable information, that the adoption is permissible in view of the child's status concerning parents, relatives, and legal guardians; and that, if required, the persons concerned have given their informed consent to the adoption on the basis of such counselling as may be necessary;

(b) recognise that intercountry adoption may be considered as an alternative means of [caring for the child], if the child cannot be placed in a foster care or an adoptive family or cannot in any suitable manner be cared for in the child's country of origin;

(c) ensure that a child concerned in an intercountry adoption enjoys safeguards and standards equivalent to those existing in the case of national adoption;

(d) take all appropriate measures to ensure that, in intercountry adoptions, the placement does not result in improper financial gain for those involved in it;

(e) promote, where appropriate, the objectives of the present article by concluding bilateral or multilateral arrangements or agreements and endeavour, within this framework, to ensure that the placement of the child in another country is carried out by competent authorities or organs."

(Article 21.)

3. The Hague Convention

As noted in Chapter 19, the Adoption Act 1976 contained provisions which appeared to safeguard at least some of the rights described above, but in reality it fell short of so doing, even where children were brought into the United Kingdom in blatant breach of adoption procedures. Taking into account the welfare of the child, courts were prepared to acquiesce in such breaches and make orders in favour of applicants who had been found to be unsuitable to adopt a child in the United Kingdom; the effect was to apply a lower standard in respect of children from overseas.

This abuse, and trafficking in children, led to the Convention on Protection of Children and Co-operation in respect of Intercountry Adoption of 29 May 1993 (the "Hague Convention"). The Convention was ratified by the United Kingdom on 27 February 2003 and entered into force in the United Kingdom on 1 June 2003.

The United Nations Convention on the Rights of the Child (above) forms the basis of the Hague Convention. The preamble to the Hague Convention recognises that the child, for the full and harmonious development of his personality, should "grow up in a family environment, in an atmosphere of happiness, love and understanding"; and repeats that each state should take appropriate measures to enable a child to remain in the care of his family of origin. It recognises that, if this is not possible, intercountry adoption may offer the advantage of a permanent family to a child for whom a suitable family cannot be found in his or her state of origin. The preamble also emphasises the need to take measures to ensure that intercountry adoptions are made in the best interests of the child and with respect to the child's fundamental rights; and the need to prevent the abduction or sale of, or traffic in, children. It confirms the desirability of establishing common provisions which take account of these principles, and those set out in the United Nations Convention, and the United Nations Declaration on Social and Legal Principles relating to the Protection and Welfare of Children etc, 1986.

Objectives

The objectives of the Hague Convention are set out in article 1 as follows:

"(a) to establish safeguards to ensure that intercountry adoptions take place in the best interests of the child and with respect for his or her fundamental rights as recognised in international law;

(b) to establish a system of co-operation amongst Contracting States to ensure that those safeguards are respected and thereby prevent the abduction, the sale of, or traffic in children;

(c) to secure the recognition in Contracting States of adoptions made in accordance with the Convention."

The Convention applies:

"where a child habitually resident in one Contracting State (the 'State of origin') has been, is being, or is to be moved to another Contracting State ('the receiving State') either after his or her adoption in the State of origin by spouses or a person habitually resident in the receiving State, or for the purposes of such an adoption in the receiving State or in the State of origin." (Article 2(1).)

Preconditions for adoption within the Convention

The key requirements in respect of the natural parents or guardian of the child are that an adoption within the scope of the Convention may take place only if the competent authorities of the state of origin:

(a) have established that the child is adoptable;

(b) have determined, after possibilities for placement of the child within the state of origin have been given due consideration, that an intercountry adoption is in the child's best interests;

(c) have ensured that:

(i) those whose consent is necessary for adoption have been appropriately counselled and have been informed of the effects of their consent, in particular whether or not an adoption will result in the termination of the legal relationship between the child and his or her family of origin,

    (ii) such persons have given their consent freely, in the required legal form and expressed or evidenced in writing,

    (iii) the consents have not been induced by payment or compensation of any kind and have not been withdrawn, and

    (iv) the consent of the mother, where required, has been given only after the birth of the child;

(d) have ensured, having regard to the age and degree of maturity of the child, that:

    (i) he or she has been counselled and duly informed of the effects of the adoption and of his or her consent to the adoption, where such consent is required,

    (ii) consideration has been given to the child's wishes and opinions;

    (iii) the child's consent to the adoption, where such consent is required, has been freely given, in the required legal form, and expressed or evidenced in writing, and

    (iv) such consent has not been induced by payment or compensation of any kind.

(Article 4.)

In relation to prospective adopters, the competent authorities of the receiving state must have determined that the prospective adopters are eligible and suitable to adopt a child. They must have ensured that the prospective adopters have been counselled, and that the child is or will be authorised to enter and reside permanently in that state (article 5).

In relation to articles 4 and 5, the Convention provides that there shall be no contact between the prospective adopters and the child's parents or any other person who has the care of the child until the requirements of article 4(c) and (d) (above) and article 5(a) (determination that prospective adopters are eligible and suitable to adopt) have been met, unless the adoption takes place within a family or unless the contact is in compliance with the conditions established by the competent authority of the state of origin (article 29)

Obligations of contracting states

The Convention imposes certain obligations on the contracting states. These are:

(a) contracting states must designate a "Central Authority" to discharge the duties imposed by the Convention (article 6); and Central Authorities must co-operate with each other and promote co-operation to protect children and to achieve the other objects of the Convention (article 7);

(b) states must accredit bodies to work as adoption agencies. These bodies must be non-profit making (article 11);

(c) states must take all appropriate measures to prevent financial or other gain in connection with adoption, and deter all practices contrary to the object of the Convention (article 8).

It is also the duty of each contracting state to:

(a) collect, preserve and exchange information about the situation of the child and the prospective adopters so far as is necessary to complete an adoption;

(b) facilitate, follow and expedite proceedings with a view to obtaining the adoption;

(c) promote the development of adoption counselling and post-adoption services in their state;

(d) provide evaluation reports about experience with intercountry adoption; and

(e) reply to justified requests from other Central Authorities or public authorities for information about a particular adoption situation (article 9).

Accredited and non-accredited bodies

As regards accredited bodies, the Central Authority in each state is obliged to take all appropriate measures to ensure that accreditation is granted only to, and maintained only by, bodies who have demonstrated the competence to carry out the tasks entrusted to them. Accredited bodies are required to be non-profit making and must be manned by qualified staff who have been appropriately trained and have experience to work in the field of intercountry adoption. The composition, operation and financial situation of accredited bodies must be subject to supervision by the competent authorities of the state. An accredited body should be permitted to act in another contracting state only if authorisation to do so has been given by the competent authorities in both states. The designation of the Central Authorities, and, where appropriate, the extent of their functions, with details of the accredited bodies, must be exchanged between the contracting states. See articles 10 to 13.

Article 22 of the Hague Convention permits the contracting states to allow non-accredited persons to make arrangements for intercountry adoptions, provided that such persons or bodies are subject to the supervision of the competent authorities of that state. Article 22 requires that, where such an arrangement is permitted by a contracting state, the state must ensure that the persons or bodies meet the requirements of integrity, professional competence, experience and accountability of that state, and that the persons or bodies are qualified by their ethical standards and by training or experience to work in the field of intercountry adoption.

Where a contracting state allows non-accredited persons or bodies to make arrangements for intercountry adoptions, it is obliged to provide, to the Permanent Bureau of the Hague Conference on Private International Law, the names and addresses of those persons and bodies; but in any event where such an arrangement is permitted, all reports on the prospective adopters or the child must be prepared under the responsibility of the Central Authority or other public body accredited to do so.

Procedural requirements
The receiving state: The Hague Convention sets out the procedural requirements which must be followed in intercountry adoptions. Prospective adopters habitually resident in one contracting state, wishing to adopt a child who is habitually resident in another contracting state, must apply to the Central Authority in the state of their habitual residence. If that Central Authority is satisfied that the prospective adopters are eligible and suitable to adopt a child, it must prepare a report, including information about their identity; eligibility and suitability to adopt; background; family and medical histories; social environment; reasons for seeking to adopt; ability to undertake an intercountry adoption; and the characteristics of the children whom they would be qualified to care for. The Central Authority of the receiving state must then transmit the report to the state of origin. See articles 14 and 15.

The state of origin: The duties of the state of origin are:
    (a) to satisfy itself that the child is adoptable; if it so satisfied, to prepare a report including information about the child's identity, adoptability, background, social environment, family history, medical and family histories and any special needs;
    (b) to give due consideration to the child's upbringing and to his ethnic, religious and cultural background;
    (c) ensure that consents have been obtained in accordance with article 4; and
    (d) determine, on the basis of the reports relating to the child and the prospective adopters, whether the envisaged placement is in the best interests of the child.

On completion of the report, the Central Authority of the state of origin must transmit it to the Central Authority of the receiving state, with proof of the necessary consents and the reasons for its determination on the placement, taking care not to reveal the identities of the mother and the father if, in the state of origin, these identities may not be disclosed.

In addition, it is the duty of the Central Authority, before taking any decision to transfer the child into the care of the prospective adopters, to ensure that:
    (a) the Central Authority of the receiving state has the prospective adopters' continued agreement for the child to be placed in its care with a view to adoption;
    (b) the Central Authority of the receiving state has approved such a decision, where such approval is required by the law of that state or by the Central Authority of the state of origin;

(c) it has been determined that the prospective adopters are eligible and suited to adopt the child;

(d) authorisation has been or will be given for the child to enter and reside permanently in the receiving state

(article 17).

Article 28, however, provides that the Convention does not affect any law of a state of origin which requires that the adoption of a child habitually resident within that state take place in that state; or which prohibits the child's placement in, or transfer to, the receiving state prior to adoption.

Reciprocal duties: Furthermore, the Central Authorities of both the state of origin and the receiving state must:

(a) take all necessary steps to obtain permission for the child to leave the state of origin and to enter and reside permanently in the receiving state, i.e., obtain immigration entry clearance;

(b) ensure that the transfer of the child takes place in secure and appropriate circumstances and, if possible, in the company of the prospective adopters;

(c) keep each other informed about the adoption process and the measures taken to complete it, as well as the progress of any probationary period where this is required

(articles 18 and 19.)

Duty to protect the child

The Hague Convention places a duty on a receiving state to protect the child once transfer has taken place. This includes a duty, where it appears to the Central Authority that the continued placement of the child with the prospective adopters in not in the child's best interests, to take all necessary measures to protect the child. In such a case the Central Authority is required to remove the child from the prospective adopters and to make alternative temporary arrangements for the care of the child pending consultation between the Central Authorities of the two states. Where the placement breaks down, the receiving state is under a duty, in consultation with the Central Authority of the state of origin, to arrange alternative long-term care. An alternative placement with a view to adoption by new prospective adopters should be considered only if the Central Authority of the state of origin has been duly informed of the arrangements and, it follows, their approval has been obtained. If all else fails, arrangements should be made for the child to be returned if his or her interests so require. Where the child is of sufficient age and maturity, he should be consulted and his consent should be obtained before any steps are taken. See article 21.

Recognition of adoption by contracting states

In order to ensure reciprocity, each contracting state is required, at the time of signature, ratification, approval or acceptance of the Convention, to notify, to the depositary of the Convention, the identity and the functions of the authority or authorities which are competent to certify the making of an adoption order. It must also give notice of any change which may from time to time occur in the designation of these authorities.

Adoptions made in countries which have ratified the Hague Convention are recognised by other contracting states, provided the adoption is certified by the competent authority of the state of the adoption. The certificate must specify when and by whom the agreements of the central authorities of both states pursuant to article 17(c) – that the adoption may proceed – were given. Recognition may be refused only if the adoption is manifestly contrary to the public policy of the state in question, taking into account the best interests of the child. (Articles 23 and 24.)

Effect of adoption
Articles 26 and 27 of the Hague Convention deal with the effect of an adoption order on both the adopters and the child. The Convention deals with cases where the adoption is a "full" adoption, as in the United Kingdom, resulting in the total severance of legal ties between the child and his parents and the birth family; and an adoption which is not regarded as terminating all existing rights, sometimes referred to as a "simple" adoption.

Article 26(1) provides that the recognition of an adoption includes recognition of:

(a) the legal parent-child relationship between the child and his adoptive parents;
(b) parental responsibility of the adoptive parents for the child; and
(c) the termination of a pre-existing legal relationship between the child and his natural parents if the adoption has this effect in the contracting state where the adoption was made.

Where the adoption order has the effect of terminating the legal relationship between the child and his natural parents, the child must enjoy, in the receiving state and in any other contracting state where the adoption is recognised, rights equivalent to those resulting from adoptions having this effect in each such state. The child also has such other rights as are more favourable for the child and which may apply under the law in the contracting state which recognises the adoption.

Where an adoption granted in the state of origin does not have the effect of terminating a pre-existing legal parent-child relationship (a "simple" adoption), the adoption may be converted to a "full" adoption in a receiving state which recognises the adoption under the Convention, provided:

(a) the law of the receiving state so permits; and
(b) the consents of the relevant persons under article 4(c) and (d) (consents of the relevant persons and of the child) have been or are given for the purposes of such an adoption

(article 27(1)).

Article 27(2) makes provision for such a converted adoption to be recognised in other contracting states on the production of a certified order of such an adoption.

Confidentiality, disclosure and preservation of documents

It is the duty of the competent authorities of a contracting state to ensure that information held by them concerning a child's origin, in particular information concerning the identity of his or her parents, as well as the child's medical history, is preserved. The authorities must also ensure that the child, or his or her legal representative, has access to such information, under appropriate guidance, is so far as is permitted by the law of that state. See article 30.

Personal data gathered or transmitted under the Convention, particularly data relating to reports on adoptive parents and children, should be used only for the purposes for which they were gathered or transmitted (article 31).

Prohibition of payments

Article 32 prohibits the obtaining of improper financial or other gain from an activity related to an intercountry adoption. Reasonable costs and expenses, including professional fees of persons involved in the adoption process, may be charged or paid. (Article 32(1) and (2).) This provision corresponds to that in section 95 of the Adoption and Children Act 2002 (see page 293).

Article 32(3) provides that the directors, administrators and employees of bodies involved in the adoption process should not receive remuneration which is unreasonably high in relation to the services rendered.

The Children and Adoption Bill, before Parliament at the time of writing, contains a clause inserting into the Adoption and Children Act 2002 a section 91A, which would enable the Secretary of State to charge, and determine the level of fee to be paid by, adopters and prospective adopters for services provided or to be provided by him in relation to adoptions with a foreign element. By way of confirmation that this provision is not intended to permit profit-making, there would be a duty on the Secretary of State to secure that the income from fees would not exceed the total cost of providing the services in relation to which the fees would be charged.

Breaches

Where a competent authority finds that any provision of the Convention has not been respected, or that there is a serious risk that it may not be respected, it has the duty immediately to inform the Central Authority of its state. The Central Authority has a duty to ensure that appropriate measures are taken to deal with the non-compliance (article 33).

Where the non-compliance relates to an offence having been committed, it is the responsibility of the Central Authority to ensure that effective steps are taken to pursue the matter. If there has been a breach of any of the relevant regulations, e.g., by the accredited body, the Secretary of State has a duty to ensure that appropriate action is taken against the body or the relevant responsible person.

Delay

Article 35 of the Hague Convention specifically requires the contracting states to act expeditiously in the process of adoption. The Adoption and Children Act 2002 meets with this requirement in providing, in section 1(3), that the court or adoption agency must at all times bear in mind that, in general, any delay in coming to a decision is likely to prejudice the child's welfare. The various regulations and guidelines also set out time limits within which decisions should be made.

Two or more systems of law applicable in a state

Where a state, with regard to adoption, has two or more systems of law applicable to different categories of person, or has different territorial units which have their own rules in respect of adoption, the state should not be bound to apply the Convention where a state with a unified system of law would not be so bound.

Contracting states are given the freedom to enter into agreements with one or more other contracting states with a view to improving the application of the Convention. However, these agreements may derogate only from the provisions of articles 14 to 16 (procedural requirements for adoptions) and 18 to 21 (transfer of the child). See articles 38 and 39.

4. Domestic Law

When the Hague Convention was ratified, the Adoption Act 1976 was the framework for adoptions in England and Wales. As noted in Chapter 19, the provisions of the Act were not always adequate to prevent abuses, and when breaches occurred, action was rarely, if ever, taken against the offenders. Applications for the adoption of children brought to England in contravention of the provisions were usually granted, the court often applying a lower standard of assessment; in some cases applications were granted even where adoption would not have been considered appropriate if the child had been an English or Welsh child.

It was not until the Adoption (Intercountry Aspects) Act 1999 that action was taken to bring the law into line with the provisions of the Convention. The 1999 Act came into force on 1 June 2003, amending the 1976 Act to regulate intercountry adoption in England, Wales and Scotland. The Act enabled the United Kingdom to ratify the Hague Convention. The main provisions of the 1999 Act had the effect of placing a duty on local authorities to provide, or arrange to provide, intercountry adoption services. It enabled those who chose to adopt a child in accordance with the Hague

Convention to apply to register the adoption at the Office of the Registrar General for England and Wales, and for the adopted child to acquire British citizenship, provided certain conditions were met.

The Adoption and Children Act 2002 further amended the 1976 Act. The amendments included provisions extending the restriction on bringing children into the United Kingdom by inserting section 56A; authorising the Secretary of State to make regulations in respect of prospective adopters who are not habitually resident in the United Kingdom; and increasing penalties for breaches of the provisions. The Secretary of State was also authorised to make regulations requiring prospective adopters to apply to be assessed for eligibility and suitability to adopt a child not habitually resident in the United Kingdom, and other requirements of the Hague Conventions.

Corresponding regulations were made, and came into effect on 1 June 2003. These included the Intercountry Adoption (Hague Convention) Regulations 2003 (SI 2003 No. 118); the Adoption (Bringing Children into the United Kingdom) Regulations 2003 (SI 2003 No. 1173); and the Registration of Foreign Adoptions Regulations 2003 (SI 2003 No. 1255).

As from 30 December 2005, with the coming into full force of the Adoption and Children Act 2002, the Adoption (Intercountry Aspects) Act 1999, sections 3, 6, 8, 9 and 11 to 13 cease to have effect. The sections of the Act which will continue to be effective in relation to England and Wales are:

    (a) section 1, which makes provision for regulations to be made for giving effect to the Hague Convention, to comply with article 6(1) of the Convention;

    (b) section 2, which identifies the Central Authority for England as the Secretary of State, and in Wales, the National Assembly. As in cases of child abduction, the Central Authority is the gateway to all applications relating to adoptions under the Hague Convention. Section 2(3) and (4) of the 1999 Act makes provision for adoption societies to be accredited to provide intercountry adoption services in accordance with articles 9 to 11 of the Convention, and places a duty on local authorities to provide or arrange to provide an intercountry adoption service (see below);

    (c) section 7, which makes provision for the acquisition of British citizenship by an adopted child who is not a British citizen but has been adopted under a Convention adoption;

    (d) schedule 1, which incorporates the articles of the Hague Convention and underpins the provisions of the Adoption and Children Act 2002 which apply to adoptions with a foreign element.

5. The Adoption and Children Act 2002

The current statutory framework

The Adoption and Children Act 2002, together with such of the provisions of the Adoption (Intercountry Aspects) Act 1999 as remain in force (see above), is now the primary legislative framework for adoptions with a foreign element which take place in England and Wales. The key secondary legislation includes the Adoption Agencies Regulations 2005 (SI 2005 No. 389); the Adoption Agencies (Wales) Regulations 2005 (SI 2005 No. 1313, W.95); the Adoptions with a Foreign Element Regulations 2005 (SI 2005 No. 392); the Suitability of Adopters Regulations 2005 (SI 2005 No. 1712); and the Restriction on the Preparation of Adoption Reports Regulations 2005 (SI 2005 No. 1711). As will be observed from the provisions of both international conventions, the practice and professional standards applied in relation to intercountry adoptions must be no different from those which apply in domestic adoptions.

Duties of local authorities and adoption agencies
Local authorities with social services responsibilities are required to establish and maintain an adoption service that extends to intercountry adoptions. Their duties, and the duties of adoption agencies, when arranging intercountry adoptions are the same as those relating to domestic adoptions. Those duties include:
  (a) providing information about overseas adoption;
  (b) offering counselling for both the prospective adopter and the child;
  (c) carrying out assessments of the eligibility and suitability of prospective adopters;
  (d) carrying out assessments of the child; and
  (e) matching children to prospective adopter(s).
Now, however, local authorities and accredited voluntary adoption agencies have to consider the requirements set out in the Adoptions with a Foreign Element Regulations 2005. These regulations deal with the process in relation to Convention and non-Convention adoptions, and adoptions of children from overseas. See Chapters 21, 22 and 23.
    Adoptions with a foreign element may feature a number of scenarios, for example:
  (a) adoptions of children from non-Convention countries by prospective adopters who are habitually resident in the British Islands;
  (b) overseas adoptions of children who are habitually resident in the British Islands;
  (c) overseas adoptions, i.e., adoptions in non-Convention countries;
  (d) adoptions of children from Convention countries;
  (e) adoptions of British children; and
  (f) adoptions of British children by adopters in Convention countries.

Domicile and habitual residence
The regulations and procedure which apply to these types of adoption are dealt with in Chapters 21, 22 and 23. However, issues of domicile and

habitual residence arise in such cases. Both these issues have been touched on in Chapter 2, but where the circumstances are unclear, or there is uncertainty, specialist advice should be sought.

Entry to the United Kingdom
Section 83 of the Adoption and Children Act 2002 restricts the freedom of a person who is habitually resident in the British Islands to bring or cause to be brought a child who is habitually resident outside the British Islands into the United Kingdom for the purposes of adoption by the British resident. The Adoptions with a Foreign Element Regulations set out the process which must be followed to enable a foreign child to be brought into the United Kingdom. When bringing a child into the United Kingdom the immigration status of the prospective adopter(s) is relevant. Where a prospective adopter(s) who is a British citizen and habitually resident in the United Kingdom is seeking to adopt a child from a Convention country, there should be no difficulty in obtaining entry clearance; and on adoption the child will automatically receive British citizenship (see pages 132, 317 and 322). Where the child has been adopted by a British citizen in a country which is not a Convention country but is listed in the Adoption (Designation of Overseas Adoption) Order 1973 (SI 1973 No. 19, as amended by SI 1993 No. 690), the adoption is referred to as an "overseas adoption". Although this adoption ranks as an adoption order, entry clearance for the child to enter the United Kingdom is required.

Where the prospective adopter has a temporary right to stay in the United Kingdom, for example pursuant to a work permit, it will be difficult to satisfy the precondition of domicile and habitual residence. It is therefore highly unlikely that such a person would be able to adopt a child in the United Kingdom under the Convention, as it is unlikely that the Central Authority would be able to confirm that the child would be permitted to enter the United Kingdom and to live here permanently. The only option for such a person would be to adopt in a country whose adoptions are recognised as "overseas adoptions".

Nationals of the European Economic Area are permitted to enter the United Kingdom and to live here. However, in order to adopt in the United Kingdom, such a person would have to satisfy the conditions of domicile and habitual residence in section 49 of the 2002 Act. Whether such an applicant would be permitted to adopt a child from a Convention country appears to be a moot point; it would seem that, as the prospective adopter is able to enter and live in the United Kingdom without restrictions, and can apply to remain here indefinitely after four years, it would be unlikely that the Central Authority would not be able to obtain and give assurances that the child would be able to enter and live here permanently. There appears to be no restriction on a national of the European Economic Area adopting a child in a country whose adoptions are recognised as "overseas adoptions".

A prospective adopter who has indefinite leave to remain in the United Kingdom would more than likely satisfy the section 49 conditions. He should therefore be able to adopt a child in the United Kingdom, or a child from a Convention country, or adopt a child from a country whose adoptions are recognised as "overseas adoptions". Entry clearance for the child would be needed.

6. Summary
The United Nations Convention on the Rights of the Child underpins the provisions of the Hague Convention, which has, in turn, been incorporated into domestic law. The basic principles which apply to adoptions from countries which have ratified the Hague Convention may be summarised as follows:
1.   Where a child cannot be cared for by his own family, attempts should always be made to place him with a family in his country.
2.   Intercountry adoption should take place only if it is in the best interest of the child.
3.   Standards equivalent to those which apply in domestic adoptions should be applied to intercountry adoptions. The child's safety, protection and welfare should not be compromised.
4.   The natural parents' consent must be obtained and given freely and without inducement or undue influence.
5.   The prospective adopters must be assessed for eligibility and suitability.
6.   Appropriate assessments of the child must be carried out and the child must be appropriately matched with the prospective adopter(s).
7.   The child's immigration status should be confirmed and assurances given that the child will be able to enter the country of his prospective adopter(s) and live there permanently.
8.   Only those persons or agencies who are appropriately accredited, monitored and supervised should engage in providing intercountry adoption services.
9.   Accredited agencies and those involved in arranging intercountry adoptions should not make a profit from the process.
10. The procedure set out in the secondary legislation made under the Adoption and Children Act 2002 should be followed.
11. The following issues relating to the prospective adopter(s) should be clarified before starting the process:
    (a) domicile;
    (b) habitual residence; and
    (c) immigration status.

Chapter 21

Overseas Adoptions

1. Introduction

An "overseas adoption" is defined in the Adoption and Children Act 2002, section 87(1), as an adoption of a description specified in an order made by the Secretary of State, being a description of adoptions effected under the law of any country or territory outside the British Islands, but does not include a Convention adoption. Section 87(2) provides that regulations may prescribe the requirements to be met in respect of an adoption of any description effected after the commencement of the regulations for it to be an overseas adoption for the purposes of the Act. Section 87(3) provides that the Secretary of State must exercise his powers under the section to secure that subsequently effected adoptions of any description are not overseas adoptions for the purposes of the Act if he considers that they are not likely, within a reasonable time, to meet the prescribed requirements.

As noted in Chapter 20, where a child has been adopted in one of the designated countries, the adoption is recognised in the United Kingdom and it is not necessary to seek an adoption order in the domestic courts.

See Chapter 19, page 296, for the restrictions on bringing children from overseas to the United Kingdom for adoption.

2. The Designated Territories

Under the former law, the Adoption (Designation of Overseas Adoptions) Order 1973 (SI 1973 No. 19, as amended by SI 1993 No. 690), set out in the schedule the list of countries which have been designated. The list appears below. It is likely that the list will be applied to overseas adoptions after the commencement of the Adoption and Children Act 2002.

Commonwealth countries and British overseas territories: Anguilla, Australia, Bahamas, Barbados, Belize, Bermuda, Botswana, British Virgin Islands, Canada, Cayman Islands, The Republic of Cyprus, Dominica, Ghana, Gibraltar, Guyana, Jamaica, Kenya, Lesotho, Malawi, Malaysia, Malta, Mauritius, Montserrat, Namibia, New Zealand, Nigeria, Pitcairn, St Christopher and Nevis, St Vincent, Seychelles, Singapore, South Africa, Sri Lanka, Swaziland, Tanzania, Tonga,

Trinidad and Tobago, Uganda, Zambia, Zimbabwe.

Other countries and territories: Austria, Belgium (including the Antilles), People's Republic of China, Denmark (including Greenland and the Faroes), Fiji, Finland, France (including Reunion, Martinique, Guadeloupe and French Guiana), Germany, Greece, Hong Kong, Iceland, Ireland, Republic of, Israel, Italy, Luxembourg, The Netherlands (including the Antilles), Norway, Portugal (including the Azores and Madeira), Spain (including the Balearics and the Canary Islands), Surinam, Sweden, Switzerland, Turkey, the United States of America, Yugoslavia.

3. Preconditions for Recognition of Overseas Adoptions

To constitute an "overseas adoption", the adoption order must have been made under statutory provisions in the designated country, and may not be an adoption obtained under customary or other law. Article 3 of the Adoption (Designation of Overseas Adoptions) Order provides that the adoption order must relate to a child who is under the age of eighteen and who is not married.

A prospective adopter(s) who wishes to adopt a child from one of the designated countries must still comply with the statutory and procedural requirements set out in the Adoptions with a Foreign Element Regulations. However, once an adoption order has been made in the designated country, the adoption is automatically recognised in the United Kingdom as a valid adoption, and therefore, unlike an adoption order obtained in a non-designated country, the prospective adopter(s) do not have to apply for an adoption order in the United Kingdom.

4. Entry to the United Kingdom

When bringing into the United Kingdom a child who is the subject of an overseas adoption, entry clearance is required. The entry clearance officer must be satisfied of the validity of the adoption order. Alternatively, and perhaps preferably, the adoptive parents could apply for the child to be registered as a British citizen before the child is brought into the United Kingdom. To achieve this, they should obtain a British passport for the child from the British Diplomatic Post. This will enable the child to be brought to the United Kingdom without the need for entry clearance.

But if the child has not acquired British citizenship before coming to the United Kingdom, the entry clearance officer, on being satisfied that the overseas adoption is genuine, allows the child to enter the United Kingdom for a limited period of time so as to enable the adopter, if he is a British citizen, to obtain British citizenship for the child. If the adopter is not a British citizen, the child is permitted to remain in the United Kingdom so long as the adopter has a right to remain here. The adopter would have to apply for the child to remain in the United Kingdom on that basis.

Where a final overseas adoption has not yet been made, the child may nevertheless be permitted to enter the United Kingdom, but again for a limited period to enable the overseas adoption to be finalised. When the final order is made, application should be made for the necessary forms and information on the procedure to be followed to the Home Office, Nationality Group, PO Box 306, Liverpool L2 7XS.

An overseas adoption should be registered in the adopted children register (see Chapter 13).

5. Annulment of an Overseas Adoption

Under the former law, the High Court had jurisdiction to order that an overseas adoption should cease to be valid in Great Britain on the ground that it was contrary to public policy or that the authority which purported to authorise the adoption was not competent to entertain the case. The Adoption and Children Act 2002 makes similar provisions. Section 89 provides that the High Court may, on an application made under section 89(2) of the Act:

(a) by order provide for an overseas adoption or a determination under section 91 (which includes determinations to revoke or annul an adoption order) to cease to be valid on the ground that the adoption or determination is contrary to public policy, or that the authority which purported to authorise the adoption or make the determination was not competent to entertain the case; or

(b) decide the extent, if any, to which a determination under section 91 has been affected by a subsequent determination under that section.

Section 91 of the Adoption and Children Act 2002 applies where an authority of (*inter alia*) any British overseas territory has power under the law of that country or territory to authorise or review the authorisation of an adoption order made in that country or territory, or to give or review a decision revoking or annulling such an order. If such an authority makes such a determination in the exercise of that power, then that determination has effect for the purpose of effecting, confirming or terminating the adoption in question, or as the case may be, confirming its termination.

Save as aforesaid the validity of an overseas adoption or a determination under section 91 cannot be called into question in proceedings in any court in England and Wales (Adoption and Children Act 2002, section 89(4)).

The provisions of section 89 echo those in article 24 of the Hague Convention (see page 314) which provides that the recognition of an adoption may be refused in a contracting state only if the adoption is manifestly contrary to its public policy, taking into account the best interests of the child. Applying the principles of the Hague Convention, and the Convention on the Rights of the Child, it would appear that the court would have to be satisfied that there were exceptional circumstances to justify annulling an order on public policy grounds. Such grounds may exist where there have been serious breaches of the provisions of section 83 of the Act or of the principles set out in the Conventions, or, for example, there is evidence of child trafficking or fraud.

The procedure for applications under sections 89 and 91 falls within Part 5 of the Family Procedure (Adoption) Rules 2005 (SI 2005 No. 2795) and is described in Chapter 25; see page 389. An application for a section 89 order must be made within two years beginning with the date on which the Convention adoption or Convention adoption order, or the overseas adoption or determination under section 91, was made (Family Procedure (Adoption) Rules 2005, rule 109).

6.   Taking Children out of the United Kingdom for Adoption

Restrictions

The Adoption and Children Act 2002, section 85, provides that a child who is a Commonwealth citizen or is habitually resident in the United Kingdom must not be removed from the United Kingdom to a place outside the British Islands for the purposes of adoption unless:

(a)   the prospective adopters have parental responsibility for the child by virtue of an order made under section 84; or

(b)   the child is removed under the authority of an order under section 49 of the Adoption (Scotland) Act 1978 or article 57 of the Adoption (Northern Ireland) order 1987

(section 85(1) and (2)).

Removing a child from the United Kingdom includes arranging to do so, and the circumstances in which a person arranges to remove a child from the United Kingdom include those where he:

(a)   enters into an arrangement for the purposes of facilitating such a removal of the child;

(b)   initiates or takes part in any negotiations of which the purpose is the conclusion of an arrangement within (a) above; or

(c)   causes another person to take any step mentioned in (a) or (b) above.

An "arrangement" includes an agreement (whether or not enforceable) (section 85(3)).

Section 85(4) makes it a criminal offence for any person to remove a child from the United Kingdom in contravention of the above provisions. A person charged with the offence cannot, though, be convicted unless it is proved that he knew or had reason to suspect that the step taken would contravene section 89(1) (section 89(5)).

Preconditions for removing a child from the United Kingdom

The decision to remove a child for adoption outside the United Kingdom is generally made by a local authority, which may decide that the interest of a child in its care would best be served by the child's being adopted by an identified person in another country. The prospective adopter in such cases is usually a relative of the child or someone who is known to the family. Before a child is removed from the United Kingdom, it is necessary for the person seeking to adopt the child under the law of a country or territory outside the British Islands to apply, under section 84 of the Adoption and Children Act 2002, for an order from the High Court giving parental responsibility for the child to the prospective adopter.

An order for parental responsibility for a child under section 84 may not be made unless the following conditions are met:

(a) the requirements prescribed by regulations are satisfied (section 84(3));

(b) at all times during the preceding ten weeks the child's home was with the applicant, or, in the case of an application by two people, both of them (section 83(4)).

The Adoptions with a Foreign Element Regulations, regulation 10, sets out the requirements which must be satisfied before a section 84 order may be made. Where the child is placed for adoption by an adoption agency the court must be satisfied that the agency:

(a) has complied with all the requirements set out in the Adoption Agencies Regulation 2005, regulations 11 to 20 and their equivalents for Wales (see Chapter 16). These include requiring the adoption agency to open the child's case record; provide counselling and information; where the child is of sufficient age and understanding, ascertain his wishes and feelings regarding the placement and contact with his natural family; and consider the child's religious and cultural upbringing. Counselling must also be provided to the natural parents and others with whom the child has had a relationship, and their wishes and feelings must be ascertained and considered. The legal implications of the placement and the adoption must be explained to them. The adoption agency is also required to obtain information about the child's extended family and prepare a permanence report which must be placed before the adoption panel. The adoption panel must have recommended the adoption and the agency must have decided that the placement is in the best interest of the child. In coming to the decision, the adoption agency must apply the welfare test and consider all the factors set out in section 1(4) to (6) of the 2002 Act;

(b) has submitted to the court:

(i) the reports and information referred to in regulation 17(2) and (3) of the Adoption Agencies Regulations 2005 or the corresponding Welsh provisions, i.e., the child's permanence report; the child's health report and the reports of any other examination recommended by the medical adviser; information relating to the health of the child's natural parents; and any other information presented to the adoption panel at its request,

    (ii)   the recommendation made by the adoption panel in accordance with regulations 18 and 33 and their Welsh equivalents (see Chapter 16). The procedure for the placement of the child, set out in regulations 31 to 33 must be complied with,

    (iii) the adoption placement report prepared in accordance with regulation 31(2)(d) of the Adoption Agencies Regulations 2005 or the corresponding Welsh provision. When the decision is taken to place the child with the prospective adopter(s), the adoption agency is required to assess the adoptive family's needs for adoption support services. Issues of contact should be addressed in the assessment, and the agency is required to prepare a written adoption placement report,

    (iv) the reports and information obtained in respect of the visits and reviews referred to in regulation 36 of the Adoption Agencies Regulations 2005 or the corresponding Welsh provision. Following placement, the adoption agency is required to carry out periodic visits and reviews. In doing so, it must consider the welfare principle and all the factors set out in section 1(4) to (6) of the Act and the matters listed in regulation 36(6) (regulation 37(6) of the Welsh regulations). The adoption agency must ensure that the following are recorded in writing: the information obtained in the course of a review or visit, details of meetings arranged to consider any aspect of the review, and any decision taken as a result. The court should be provided with all the reports and other information gathered,

    (v)   the report prepared on the suitability of the prospective adopters, and on any other relevant matter referred to in section 1 of the Act;

  (c) has confirmation in writing from the relevant foreign authority that the prospective adopter has been counselled and has had explained to him the legal implications of adoption; that a suitability report on the prospective adopter has been prepared and that it has been determined that he is eligible and suitable to adopt in the country or territory in which the adoption is to be effected; and that the child is or will be authorised to reside permanently in that foreign country or territory;

  (d) has confirmation in writing from the prospective adopter that he will accompany the child when taking him out of the United Kingdom and entering the country or territory where the adoption is to be effected. In the case of a couple, confirmation is required, if it is the case, that it has been agreed between the agency and the foreign relevant authority that only one of them should accompany the child.

The adoption agency is not required to notify the Department for Education and Skills of the decision to place the child with prospective adopters overseas.

Modification which apply to section 84 cases

Section 84(6) of the Adoption and Children Act 2002 provides that regulations may provide for any provision of the Act which refers to adoption orders to apply, with or without modifications, to orders under section 84. The Adoptions with a Foreign Element Regulations, regulation 11, sets out the provisions of the Act which have been modified, so as to substitute "order under section 84" in place of "adoption order". They are:

(a) section 1(7)(a) (coming to a decision relating to adoption of a child);
(b) section 18(4) (placement for adoption by agencies);
(c) section 21(4)(b) (placement orders);
(d) section 22(5)(a) and (b) (application for placement orders);
(e) section 24(4) (revoking placement orders);
(f) section 28(1) (further consequences of placement);
(g) section 29(4)(a) and (5)(a) (further consequences of placement orders);
(h) section 32(5) (recovery by parent etc. where child placed and consent withdrawn);
(i) section 42(7) (sufficient opportunity for adoption agency to see the child);
(j) section 43 (reports where child placed by agency);
(k) section 44(2) (notice of intention to adopt);
(l) section 47(1) to (5), (8) and (9) (conditions for making orders);
(m) section 48(1) (restrictions on making applications);
(n) section 50(1) and (2) (adoption by a couple);
(o) section 51(1) to (4) (adoption by one person);
(p) section 52(1) to (4) (parental etc. consent);
(q) section 53(5) (contribution towards maintenance); and
(r) section 141(3) and (4)(c) (rules of procedure).

7. Summary of the Procedure

1. The adoption agency identifies the prospective adopters.
2. The adoption agency obtains a report from the relevant foreign authority on suitability, and confirmation that the child will be allowed to enter the country and live there permanently.
3. The suitability report is considered, with other information, to decide whether or not it should be pursued; if it is not to be pursued, the foreign authority and the prospective adopters are notified.
4. The procedure set out in the Adoption Agencies Regulation is followed, and a report placed before the adoption panel.
5. The panel makes its recommendation, which is then considered by the

agency.

6. If the decision is positive, a placement plan report is prepared and sent to the adopters, who are then required to decide whether they wish to go ahead with the application. If the decision is negative, the adopters should be informed of the decision and the right for a review by an independent review panel.

7. If the prospective adopters wish to proceed, a meeting between the child and the prospective adopters is arranged and observed. A report is prepared and a decision taken on whether or not the placement should go ahead. If it is decided to go ahead, a placement plan is prepared and the placement begins.

8. The child remains in the placement for ten weeks before any application for a parental responsibility order can be obtained.

9. The court has to be satisfied that the requirements set out in regulation 11 of the Adoptions with a Foreign Element Regulations 2005 have been complied with.

10. If a section 84 order is made, leave is given to remove the child from the United Kingdom.

11. If leave is refused, or the placement is not considered appropriate or breaks down, a request is made for the return of the child and the prospective adopters must comply.

Chapter 22

Non-Convention Adoptions

1. Introduction

"Non-Convention adoptions" include the adoption of a child in a country whose adoption orders are not recognised in the United Kingdom. Adoptions in many countries in the Far East, and in Central and South America, for example, fall into this category. A child adopted in such a country by a person resident in the United Kingdom may be brought to the United Kingdom, but the procedure is strictly controlled and an adoption order in the United Kingdom must be applied for. The counselling and screening procedures are now as rigorous as for a domestic adoption. This chapter deals with adoptions of this kind.

A non-Convention adoption also includes an "overseas adoption", which means "an adoption of a description specified in an order made by the Secretary of State, being a description of adoptions effected under the law of any country or territory outside the British Islands, but does not include a Convention adoption" (Adoption and Children Act 2002, section 87). The designated countries are listed on pages 321 to 322, and include commonwealth countries, British overseas territories, many European countries and the United States. Where a child has been adopted from a country which is a "designated" country, the adoption is recognised in the United Kingdom as an adoption order and it is not necessary to apply for an adoption order from a court in the United Kingdom. Overseas adoptions are the subject of Chapter 21.

2. Restriction on Bringing Children into the United Kingdom

Section 83(1) of the Adoption and Children Act 2002 makes it a criminal offence for a person who is habitually resident in the British Islands:

(a) to bring, or cause another to bring, a child who is habitually resident outside the British Islands into the United Kingdom for the purposes of adoption by the British resident; or

(b) at any time to bring, or cause another to bring, into the United

Kingdom a child adopted by the British resident under an external adoption (a non-Convention adoption) effected within the period of six months ending with that time.

On summary conviction, an offender may be imprisoned for up to six months, or fined up to £5,000, or both; and, on conviction on indictment, imprisoned for up to twelve months, or fined, or both.

The Children and Adoption Bill

The Children and Adoption Bill (HL Bill 25), before Parliament at the time of writing, makes provision for the Secretary of State to suspend intercountry adoptions from a particular country if he has concerns about the practices in that country in connection with the adoption of children. The provisions in clause 8 of the Bill would authorise the Secretary of State to apply "special restrictions" in respect of children being brought into the United Kingdom for adoption, where he has reason to believe that, because of practices taking place in a country outside the British Islands ("the other country"), and irrespective of the fact that the other country is a Convention country, in connection with the adoption of children, it would be contrary to public policy to further the bringing of children into the United Kingdom. The cases where it is intended the provision should apply are where a British resident:

(a) wishes to bring, or cause another to bring, a child who is not a British resident into the United Kingdom for the purpose of adoption by the British resident, and, in connection with the proposed adoption, there have been, or would have to be, proceedings in the other country or dealings with authorities or agencies there; or

(b) wishes to bring, or cause another to bring, into the United Kingdom a child adopted by the British resident under an adoption effected, within the period of twelve months ending with the date of the bringing in, under the law of the other country.

When exercising this power, the Secretary of State would have to give reasons for applying the restriction. He would publish a list of the restricted countries, which would be kept under review. The restriction order would be cancelled if the Secretary of State, in consultation with the National Assembly for Wales and the Department of Health, Social Services and Public Safety in Northern Ireland, has reason to believe that for public policy reasons the restriction no longer applies. See clause 9.

The special restrictions would require the appropriate authority dealing with the adoption not to take any steps which he or it might otherwise have taken to further the bringing of a child into the United Kingdom unless the prospective adopters satisfy the appropriate authority, or in relation to Northern Ireland, in a non-Convention case, the Secretary of State, that the appropriate authority should take those steps despite the special restrictions. Regulations would provide the criteria to be applied and the procedure to be followed in determining whether or not the appropriate authority should exercise its discretion in such cases. See clause 10.

Adoptions of children from particular countries by UK citizens has in the past been suspended when there have been concerns as a result of investigations carried out by the Department for Education and Skills in collaboration with others about practices in relation to adoption in the other country. These have related to matters such as the obtaining of consents of the birth parents, and financial gain by those concerned in the adoption process. Other specific matters of concern would be where there is evidence of falsification of official documents, of extensive involvement by facilitators, of procurement of children for intercountry adoption by coercion and of paying birth mothers to give up their children, and corruption.

Clause 11 of the Bill provides for the Secretary of State to make regulations providing for him to specify, in relation to the restricted list, a particular step in the adoption process, for example, the forwarding of a matching report or providing the certificate of suitability and eligibility, and one or more additional conditions which would have to be met in respect of a child brought into the United Kingdom in either of the two cases referred to above. The intention is that where a restriction has been declared and a step listed, a person would not be able to bring a child to the United Kingdom in the specified cases unless he could show that the step was taken and the additional conditions met. It would seem that when a suspension has been declared in respect of a country, only in exceptional circumstances would the Secretary of State permit the application by prospective adopters to proceed. In determining such applications the Secretary of State would need to take account of the welfare principle and the best interest of the child, and all the facts of the particular case.

The Bill contains a provision making it an offence for a person to bring a child into the United Kingdom or cause another person to bring the child without having met such condition(s). The penalty, on summary conviction or indictment, would be twelve months' imprisonment, a fine, or both.

It is proposed to insert a new section, 91A, and amend section 83 of the 2002 Act:

    (a)   section 91A would entitle the Secretary of State to charge a fee to adopters or prospective adopters for services provided by the Secretary of State in relation to adoptions to which section 83 applies. (Provision has been made for local authorities to charge for certain services provided by them to prospective adopters; see page 336);

    (b)   the time limit in section 83(1)(b) of the Act would be extended from six months to twelve months;

    (c)   where, after the child has been brought into the United Kingdom for the purposes of adoption, and a notice of intention to adopt has been given to the local authority, the local authority would be required to discharge certain functions in respect of him, to be set out in regulations. The intention is to exclude the child in respect of whom a notice of intention has been served from the definition of a "privately fostered child".

The objective is to tighten control on intercountry adoptions and to dissuade prospective adopters from attempting to circumvent the restrictions on bringing to the United Kingdom children who are not habitually resident in the United Kingdom. It may also be a way to persuade the "other country" to implement the Hague Convention.

3. The Preconditions

Section 83(4) of the Adoption and Children Act 2002 requires a person who is habitually resident in the British Islands to comply with certain conditions before adopting, or bringing into the United Kingdom for adoption, a child who is not habitually resident in the British Islands. The conditions are specified in the Adoptions with a Foreign Element Regulations 2005 (SI 2005 No. 392, the "Foreign Element Regulations"), as follows:

(a) the prospective adopter(s) must apply in writing to an adoption agency for an assessment of his eligibility and suitability to adopt a child, and provide to the agency any information it requires for the purposes of the assessment (regulation 3);

(b) prior to the child's entry into the United Kingdom, the Secretary of State must issue a certificate confirming to the relevant foreign authority that the prospective adopter(s) has been assessed and approved as eligible and suitable to be an adoptive parent in accordance with Part 4 of the Adoption Agencies Regulations 2005 or the corresponding Welsh provisions (see page 213 *et seq*); and that if entry clearance and leave to enter and remain as may be necessary is granted, and not revoked or curtailed, and an adoption order is effected, the child will be authorised to enter and reside permanently in the United Kingdom;

(c) before visiting the child in the state of the child's habitual residence (the state of origin), the prospective adopter(s) must notify the adoption agency of the details of the child to be adopted; provide the adoption agency with any information and reports received from the relevant foreign authority; and meet with the adoption agency to discuss the proposed adoption and information received from the relevant foreign authority. The "relevant foreign authority" means the person or body outside the British Islands performing functions in the country in which the child is, or in which the prospective adopter is, habitually resident, which correspond to the functions of an adoption agency or of the Secretary of State in respect of adoptions with a foreign element;

(d) the prospective adopter(s) must visit the child in the state of origin;

where the prospective adopters are a couple, each of them must do so;

(e) after that visit, the prospective adopter(s) must confirm in writing to the adoption agency that he has done so and that he wishes to proceed with the adoption; provide the adoption agency with any additional reports and information received on or after that visit; and notify the adoption agency of his expected date of entry into the United Kingdom with the child;

(f) the prospective adopter(s) must accompany the child on entering the United Kingdom unless, in the case of a couple, the adoption agency and the relevant foreign authority have agreed that it is necessary for only one of them to do so;

(g) except where an overseas adoption (see page 329) is or is to be effected, the prospective adopter(s) must, within fourteen days of the date on which the child is brought into the United Kingdom, give notice to the relevant local authority of the child's arrival in the United Kingdom, and of his intention either to apply for an adoption order in accordance with section 44(2) of the Adoption and Children Act 2002, or not to give the child a home.

The relevant local authority in relation to the prospective adopter(s) is the local authority within whose area he has his home or, where he no longer has a home in England or Wales, the local authority for the area in which he last had his home. Where the prospective adopter(s) has given notice of his intention to adopt or not to adopt, as the case may be, and subsequently moves his home into the area of another local authority, he must, within fourteen days of that move, confirm in writing to that authority the child's entry into the United Kingdom, and that notice of his intention to apply for an adoption order in accordance with section 44 of the Adoption and Children Act 2002 has been given to another local authority, or not to give the child a home has been given.

See regulation 4.

4. Information, Counselling and Advice

The local authority has certain duties when it receives a request for information about intercountry adoption, and when an application is made to proceed with such an adoption.

Initial inquiries

Before a prospective adopter(s) makes the decision to adopt a child who is not habitually resident in the United Kingdom, he should obtain information about the process, about what is expected of him at each of the stage of that process, and how each of the statutory and procedural requirements set out above will be met. Some of these issues, as they relate to bringing a child into the United Kingdom from a non-Convention country for the purposes of adoption, are covered in this chapter.

When prospective adopters seek information, from a local authority or a voluntary adoption agency, about intercountry adoptions, they should be provided with as much information as possible, both orally and in writing. This should include an explanation of the legal implications of such an adoption, details of the procedure, and, if available, information about the children who may be available for adoption. Prospective adopters should also be made aware of the fact that assessments of suitability and eligibility cannot be circumvented, and that such assessments are carried out by the local authority or by a voluntary adoption agency. Information about the role of the Department for Education and Skills in the adoption process (see page 337) must also be explained. Prospective adopters should also understand the role of the relevant foreign authority in the matching process, and the need to obtain immigration entry clearance, and the potential difficulties. Prospective adopters may not know of the need to travel to the country where the child is habitually resident to visit the child, and to accompany him if it is decided to go ahead with the adoption. This, and the costs, should be clearly explained. Finally, the process of obtaining a full adoption order in the United Kingdom must be explained.

On deciding to make an application for adoption
Where a prospective adopter decides to make an application to adopt a child from a non-Convention country, or a country which is not a designated country, the duties of the adoption agency are as set out in the Adoption Agencies Regulations 2005 (SI 2005 No. 389) or the Adoption Agencies (Wales) Regulations 2005 (SI 2005 No. 1313, W.95). These are described in detail in Chapter 16. Thus, the adoption agency is obliged to provide counselling services for the prospective adopter(s) and explain the procedure in relation to, and the legal implications of, adopting a child from the country in question. Prospective adopters should be encouraged to obtain information on the adoption laws of the country where the child is. The preparation for adoption should take the same form as for a domestic adoption. The prospective adopters should be assisted to understand the legal implications of intercountry adoptions, and the criteria which will be applied in carrying out the assessment of suitability and eligibility. The likely timescale should be explained, to ensure that prospective adopters understand that there are no shortcuts, and that any circumvention of the procedure carries the risk of a criminal prosecution, and the likelihood of never being able to adopt a child.

Prospective adopters should be made aware that they will have to travel to the child's country of origin, and may need to stay there for a period of time while the matching, placement and legal processes are carried out. They will also have to accompany the child to the United Kingdom. Prospective adopters should be advised to ascertain the likely cost of the whole process.

An adoption agency is required to provide prospective adopters with written information about the intercountry adoption process and the legal implications.

5. Assessment of Eligibility and Suitability

When an adoption agency receives an application in writing from prospective adopter(s) for an assessment of suitability to adopt a child, the adoption agency is required to set up a prospective adopter's case record. The prospective adopter's domicile and habitual residence need to be explored, and police checks carried out. References are taken up and medical reports obtained. Checks are made of the home, the family, employment, social and community life, and the status and circumstances of the prospective adopter. Reasons for wishing to adopt a child are also relevant. The assessment covers all the issues required to be covered for a domestic adoption under the Adoption Agencies Regulations 2005 and the Adoption Agencies (Wales) Regulations 2005, as described in Chapter 16.

The prospective adopter's report

The adoption agency is under a duty to prepare a prospective adopter's report as required by regulation 25 of the Adoption Agencies Regulations, regulation 26 of the Adoption Agencies (Wales) Regulations, and the Suitability of Adopters Regulations 2005 (SI 2005 No. 1712). Regulation 25(6) of the Adoption Agencies Regulations (regulation 26(5) of the Welsh regulations) requires the prospective adopter's report to include:

    (a) the name of the country from which the prospective adopter wishes to adopt;

    (b) confirmation that the prospective adopter(s) is eligible to adopt a child under the laws of that country;

    (c) additional information obtained as a consequence of the requirements of that country;

    (d) the agency's assessment of the prospective adopter's suitability to adopt a child who is habitually resident outside the United Kingdom and who is habitually resident in that particular country.

Notification of unsuitability

Where it is considered that the prospective adopter(s) is unlikely to be considered suitable to adopt, the adoption agency must notify the prospective adopter(s), provide him with a copy of the report, and invite him to make observations thereon in writing within ten working days, so that any such observations may be placed with the report before the adoption panel for its consideration. The procedure set out in regulations 26 to 29 of the Adoption Agencies Regulations and regulations 27 to 31 of the Adoption Agencies (Wales) Regulations, including the right to make further submissions to the agency or apply to the Secretary of State for a review by an independent panel, applies to non-Convention cases as it does to domestic cases; see Chapter 16.

Referral to the adoption panel
All assessments must be referred to the adoption panel; they must include a recommendation as to the suitability and eligibility of the prospective adopter(s). The assessment should specify the number of children the prospective adopter(s) should be approved to adopt, the age range of the children likely to be suitable, their sex(es) and any other relevant information. See page 219.

Notice of approval to the prospective adopter(s)
The adoption agency should inform the prospective adopter(s) of the panel's decision. It should also inform the prospective adopter(s) that he should not bring or cause the child to be brought into the United Kingdom until he has received notification from the Department for Education and Skills (see below). The prospective adopter(s) should also be warned that if he goes ahead without the appropriate certificate having been issued and served on him, he is at risk of being prosecuted for an offence under section 83 of the Adoption and Children Act 2002, and of not being able to adopt the child.

Fees for services provided by local authorities
Section 95 of the Adoption and Children Act 2002 prohibits any payment (other than excepted payments) to be made for or in consideration of, *inter alia*, the adoption of a child, or preparing, causing to be prepared or submitting a report about the suitability of a child for adoption, or of a person to adopt a child, or about the adoption or placement for adoption of a child. The Local Authorities (Prescribed Fees) (Adoptions with a Foreign Element) (Wales) Regulations 2005 (SI 2005 No. 3114, W. 234), regulation 3, provide that where facilities are provided by a local authority in Wales in connection with:
  (a) the adoption of a child brought into the United Kingdom for the purposes of adoption; or
  (b) a Convention adoption, an overseas adoption or any other adoption effected under the law of a country or territory outside the British Islands,
it may charge a fee to a prospective adopter and an adopter. The facilities in question are:
  (a) facilities in accordance with the Adoption Agencies (Wales) Regulations 2005 (SI 2005 No. 1313, W.95) and the Adoptions with a Foreign Element Regulations 2005 (SI 2005 No. 392);
  (b) facilities in the discharge of any function imposed on a local authority by or in accordance with the Foreign Element Regulations

or by the Act, as modified or applied by the Foreign Element regulations, except:

(i) for facilities provided under regulation 5,

(ii) for the provision of counselling which is not followed by receipt of a written application for assessment of suitability,

(iii) for the provision of information prior to the receipt of a written application for an assessment of suitability to adopt a child under regulation 14(1) of the Foreign Element Regulations;

(iv) for the provision of information to prospective adopter(s), meeting with prospective adopter(s) or providing counselling to prospective adopter(s) in accordance with regulation 19(2) of the Foreign Element Regulations, and

(v) for the submission of a report in accordance with regulation 29(2) of the Foreign Element Regulations (see page 354);

(c) the submission of a report to a relevant foreign authority when the report is not a requirement for the making of a Convention adoption or overseas adoption under the law of the foreign country in which the child is habitually resident.

The fees charged must be reasonable, and limited to the local authority's costs and expenses properly incurred in providing the facilities. It is to be noted that fees may not be charged for providing counselling which is not followed by receipt by a local authority of a written application for an assessment of suitability to adopt a child who is habitually resident outside the British Islands, or for the provision of information prior to receipt by a local authority of an application for such an assessment.

The fees charged must not include any element in respect of the costs and expenses incurred by the local authority in connection with any complaint made about any aspect of the local authority's adoption service, or representation submitted to the local authority in accordance with regulation 28 of the Adoption Agencies Regulations (see pages 223 to 224) or in respect of a review of a qualifying determination under section 12 of the Act (see page 220).

Presumably, similar provisions will be made in relation to services provided by English local authorities.

If requested to do so, the local authority must provide details of the method by which the fee has been calculated.

6. The Role of the Department for Education and Skills or National Assembly

Referral of case to the Department
When an adoption agency approves a prospective adopter(s) as suitable to adopt a child, it must then send to the Secretary of State, or, in Wales, the National Assembly:

(a) written confirmation of the decision and any recommendation the agency may make in relation to the number of children the prospective adopter(s) may be suitable to adopt, their age(s), sex(es), likely needs and background(s);

(b) all the documents and information which were passed to the adoption panel; this includes the prospective adopter's report and the prospective adopter's observations if any, medical reports, references, any information received from any local authority, and any other information obtained by the adoption agency during the assessment;

(c) the record of the proceedings of the adoption panel, its recommendation and the reasons for its recommendation;

(d) if the prospective adopter(s) applied to the Secretary of State for a review by an independent panel of a qualifying determination, the record of the proceedings of that panel, its recommendation and the reason for the recommendation; and

(e) any other information relating to the case which the Secretary of State or the relevant foreign authority may require.

(Adoption Agencies Regulations, regulation 30; Adoption Agencies (Wales) Regulations, regulation 31; see page 227.)

Application to the Department for Education and Skills or National Assembly
Once the prospective adopter(s) has been approved, the application and the relevant documents must, as described above, be submitted to the Department for Education and Skills, or the National Assembly, where the application is checked to ensure that the relevant statutory requirements and procedures have been followed and that all the relevant information has been provided. If any information is missing or the correct procedure has not been followed, the Department or Assembly contacts the adoption agency. If the Department or Assembly requires any further information from the prospective adopter(s) it notifies him.

If the relevant foreign authority requires the documents to be translated, notarised or legalised, the prospective adopter(s) is notified and provided with information about where and how to obtain the necessary services.

When all the statutory and procedural requirements have been complied with, the Department or Assembly issues a certificate to the relevant authority in the country where the child lives. The certificate confirms that the prospective adopter(s) has been assessed and approved as eligible and suitable to adopt a child and, subject to any entry clearance and immigration requirements, the child will be permitted to enter and live in the United Kingdom.

Forwarding documents to the relevant foreign authority
The Department for Education and Skills, or the National Assembly, then

forwards the application and the documents to the relevant foreign authority in the country where the child is habitually resident (the child's state of origin) and notifies the adoption agency and the prospective adopter(s) that this has been done.

When the prospective adopter(s) has been approved as suitable to adopt a child and the processed application has been sent to the relevant foreign authority in the state of origin, that authority considers the application and carries out a matching process. The prospective adopter(s) are placed on a waiting list until the matching process is completed. The time it takes to match a child with the prospective adopters depends on the country in which the child is living and all the circumstances.

The fact that the assessment of prospective adopters in the United Kingdom has been positive does not necessarily mean that an application will be accepted by the relevant foreign authority. Alternatively, a situation could arise where the prospective adopter(s) is suitable, but a child who is a suitable match is not available.

Review
In the meantime, the adoption agency is required to review the approval of prospective adopter(s) periodically as provided for in regulation 29 of the Adoption Agencies Regulations and regulation 30 of the Adoption Agencies (Wales) Regulations. A review should take place whenever the adoption agency considers it necessary, but in any event not more than one year after approval and thereafter at intervals of not more than a year, until the prospective adopter(s) has visited the child in the country in which the child is habitually resident, and has confirmed in writing that he wishes to proceed with the adoption. If there is any change of circumstances, the adoption agency must follow the procedure set out in the regulations. A change of circumstance may arise, for example, where a single applicant marries or cohabits with a partner, a child is born to the applicant or his partner, a couple separates, or by reason of ill-health.

Positive match
Where the prospective adopter(s) is matched with a child, the relevant authority of the state of origin informs the Department for Education and Skills or National Assembly and provides the Department/Assembly with information about the child. The Department/Assembly then usually forwards the information to the prospective adopter(s) and the adoption agency. In some instances the information about the match may be sent to the prospective adopter(s) directly by the relevant foreign authority. If this happens, it is the duty of the prospective adopter(s) to notify the adoption agency, and, if the agency has not received a copy of the information, to forward a copy to the agency.

Regulation 34 of the Adoption Agencies Regulations 2005 (regulation 35 of the Adoption Agencies (Wales) Regulations) provides that where the adoption agency receives from the relevant foreign authority information about a child to be adopted by a prospective adopter it has a duty:

(a) to send a copy of the information to the prospective adopter(s) unless it is aware that the prospective adopter(s) has received a copy;

(b) to consider that information and meet with the prospective adopter(s) to discuss the information; and

(c) if appropriate, to provide counselling services for, and any further information to, the prospective adopter(s) as may be required.

The Adoption Support Services Regulations 2005 (SI 2005 No. 691) and the Adoption Support Services (Local Authorities) (Wales) Regulations 2005 (SI 2005 No. 1512, W.116) apply to prospective adopters for intercountry adoptions as they do in domestic cases. See Chapter 17. The provisions of regulation 31 of the Adoption Agencies Regulations (regulation 32 of the Adoption Agencies (Wales) Regulations), on placements, also apply.

It is important that the meeting takes place as soon as practicable after the information has been received. The guidance issued by the Department suggests that it should take place within ten working days of receiving the information, where this is reasonably practicable. As in a domestic adoption, the prospective adopter should be given time and reasonable assistance to consider the information. In particular, it is desirable that the adoption agency should go through with the prospective adopter(s) the information about the child and any assessment of the child, and consider any special medical or other needs that the child may have.

Adoption support services

Any prospective adopter is entitled to adoption support services, and so the adoption agency has a duty to provide prospective adopters with written information about requesting an assessment of their needs for adoption support services. Where the adoption agency is a voluntary adoption agency it should notify prospective adopters that they may ask their local authority to carry out a needs assessment. See Chapter 17.

If the information discloses that the child may have special needs, it is important for the adoption agency to consider this with its medical adviser and seek his views. The adoption agency should in such cases provide the prospective adopter(s) with its medical adviser's view of the health needs of the child. Conversely it is important that prospective adopters recognise that, although the information from the relevant foreign authority may suggest that the child is healthy and developing well, neither the agency nor the Department for Education and Skills or National Assembly can give any guarantee of the accuracy of such information. By contrast with domestic adoptions, where considerable information is gathered about the child, his medical history and his natural parents and family, in the case of intercountry adoptions, such information may not be available, or, if available, may be scant or inaccurate. The child could have physical, health and emotional needs which are not disclosed in the information supplied. It is therefore important that prospective adopters take time to consider the information carefully before deciding to go ahead with the adoption.

If the prospective adopter(s) decides not to proceed with the proposed match, he will be expected to give reasons for his decision in writing. It is also open to him to request another match to be considered by the relevant foreign authority.

Visiting the child
If the prospective adopter(s) decides to proceed with the adoption, he will need to make arrangements to visit the child as required by regulation 4(2)(c) of the Foreign Element Regulations. Regulation 4(2)(c) requires that in the case of a joint application by a couple, they are both required to visit the child in the state of origin.

After the visit to the state of origin, the prospective adopter(s) must confirm to the adoption agency, in writing, that he has visited the child, and state whether or not he has decided to proceed with the adoption. This is the second occasion on which the prospective adopter(s) has an opportunity to withdraw from the adoption process. If he decides to proceed, the prospective adopter must then provide the adoption agency with any additional reports, information or other material that he has received during or after the visit, and notify the adoption agency of the expected date of return to the United Kingdom (Foreign Element Regulations, regulation 4(2)(d)).

On receipt of confirmation from the prospective adopter(s) of his decision, the adoption agency must notify the Department for Education and Skills or the National Assembly of that decision, and confirm that the prospective adopter(s) has visited the child. If the adoption process is to proceed, it is for the relevant foreign authority to make the necessary arrangements to place the child with the prospective adopter(s); to complete the adoption process in the state of origin; and for the adopter(s) to return to the United Kingdom with the child, with the necessary documentation with a view to obtaining an adoption order under English law. The prospective adopter(s), however, need to obtain entry clearance for the child to enter the United Kingdom before he leaves the state of origin.

Bringing the child to the United Kingdom
Once the adoption procedures in the state of origin have been completed and entry clearance obtained, the prospective adopter(s) must accompany the child to the United Kingdom (regulation 4(3), Foreign Element Regulations). In the case of a joint application by a couple, the adoption agency and the relevant foreign authority may agree that it is necessary for only one of the couple to accompany the child (regulation 4(3)).

On arrival in the United Kingdom, the entry clearance officer requires confirmation from the Department for Education and Skills or National Assembly that all the statutory and procedural requirements have been complied with. On being so satisfied, the child is permitted entry into the United Kingdom for a limited period to enable the prospective adopter(s) to complete the adoption process in accordance with UK law.

7. Procedure Following Arrival in the United Kingdom

Within fourteen days of arriving in the United Kingdom with the child, the prospective adopter(s) must notify the adoption agency of the child's arrival and of the prospective adopter's intention to proceed with the adoption or not.

Duties of the adoption agency
The adoption agency is then under a duty:

  (a) if it has not already done so, to set up a case record in respect of the child and place on it any information it has received from the relevant foreign authority, any other adoption agency involved, the prospective adopter(s), the entry clearance officer and the Secretary of State or National Assembly for Wales as the case may be (Foreign Element Regulations, regulation 5(1)(a); see also the Adoption Agencies Regulations, regulations 12 and 39 to 44 and their equivalents for Wales; Chapter 16);

  (b) to send to the prospective adopter's general practitioner written notification of the arrival in England or Wales of the child, together with a written report of the child's health history and current state of health, so far as is known;

  (c) to send to the Primary Care Trust or (in Wales) Local Health Board in whose area the prospective adopter(s) has his home, written notification of the arrival in England or Wales of the child (see also regulation 35 of the Adoption Agencies Regulations and its equivalent in Wales, pages 237 to 238);

  (d) where the child is of compulsory school age, to send to the local education authority in whose area the prospective adopter(s) has his home, written notification of the arrival of the child in England or Wales and information, if known, about the child's educational history and whether he is likely to be assessed for special educational needs under the Education Act 1996;

  (e) to ensure that the child and the prospective adopter(s) are visited within one week of receipt of the intention to adopt, and thereafter at intervals of not less than once a week until a review required by regulations (see below) is carried out, and thereafter at such frequency as the authority may decide;

  (f) to carry out a review of the child's case not more than four weeks after receipt of the notice of intention to adopt and:

(i) to visit and, if necessary, review not more than three months after that initial review, and

(ii) thereafter not more than six months after the date of the previous visit,

unless the child no longer has his home with the prospective adopter(s) or an adoption order is made

(Foreign Element Regulations, regulation 5(1)(a) to (f), and see regulation 36 of the Adoption Agencies Regulations and regulation 37 of the Adoption (Wales) Regulations, Chapter 16);

(g) when carrying out the review, to consider the following matters:

(i) the child's needs, welfare and development, and whether any changes need to be made to meet his needs or assist his development,

(ii) the arrangements for the provision of adoption support services and whether there should be any re-assessment of the need for those services, and

(iii) the need for further visits and reviews

(Foreign Element Regulations, regulation 5(1)(g), and see regulation 36(5) of the Adoption Agencies Regulations and its equivalent for Wales, pages 238 to 239);

(h) to ensure that:

(i) advice is given as to the child's needs, welfare and development,

(ii) written reports are made of all visits and reviews of the case and placed on the child's case records, and

(iii) on such visits, where appropriate, advice is given as to the availability of adoption support services.

It is essential that all the relevant information is recorded on the child's case records.

Application for adoption

The prospective adopter(s) should apply for and obtain an adoption order in the United Kingdom. The procedure to be followed is the same as for a domestic application, save that the application must be made within two years of giving notice of intention to adopt, and the minimum period of time the child must have lived with the applicants before an adoption order is made is six months if the statutory conditions referred to above have been complied with. If they have not been complied with, the child must have lived with the applicants for at least twelve months before an adoption order is made (see below and see pages 86 to 87). For the procedure to be followed, see Chapter 25.

Application for adoption not made

If the prospective adopter(s) fails to make an application for an adoption order within two years of the receipt by the local authority of the notice of intention to adopt, the local authority must review the case. The matters it should consider when carrying out the review are:

(a) the child's needs, welfare and development, and whether any changes need to be made to meet his needs or assist his development;

(b) the arrangements, if any, in relation to the exercise of parental responsibility for the child;

(c) the terms upon which leave to enter the United Kingdom was granted and the immigration status of the child;

(d) the arrangements for the provision of adoption support services for the adoptive family and whether there should be any re-assessment of the need for those services;

(e) in conjunction with the appropriate agencies, the arrangements for meeting the child's health care and educational needs

(Foreign Element Regulations, regulation 5(4)).

Where the prospective adopter(s) has moved home to the area of another local authority, he should notify the original local authority of this. The original local authority is obliged to notify the local authority to whose area the prospective adopter(s) has moved within fourteen days of receiving notice of the change of address, and forward the following information:

(a) the name, sex, date and place of birth of the child;

(b) the prospective adopter'(s) name, sex and date of birth;

(c) the date on which the child entered the United Kingdom;

(d) where the original local authority received notification of intention to adopt, the date of receipt of such notification, whether an application for an adoption order has been made, and the stage of those proceedings; and

(e) any other relevant information.

(Foreign Element Regulations, regulation 5(5).)

8. Effect of Placement in the United Kingdom

Section 83(6)(a) of the Adoption and Children Act 2002 provides that where a child is brought into the United Kingdom for adoption in circumstances where section 83 (restrictions on bringing children into the United Kingdom – see page 296) applies, regulations may provide for any provision of Chapter 3 of the Act (placement for adoption and adoption orders) to apply with modification, or not to apply. The Foreign Element Regulations, regulations 6 to 9, make the following modifications to the relevant provisions of the Act.

Change of name and removal from the United Kingdom

Section 28(2) has been modified to provide that where a child enters the United Kingdom in the circumstances where section 83(1)(a) applies, a person may not cause the child to be known by a new surname, or remove the child from the United Kingdom, unless the court gives permission, or each parent or guardian of the child gives written consent. Section 83(1)(a) applies where a British resident brings, or causes another to bring, a child who is habitually resident outside the British Islands into the United Kingdom for the purpose of adoption by the British resident.

The procedure for seeking the court's consent to a change of name or removal from the United Kingdom is governed by Part 5 of the Family Procedure (Adoption) Rules 2005 (SI 2005 No. 2795); see Chapter 25, page 394.

Return of the child

Section 35 of the Adoption and Children Act 2002 is modified to provide that:

(1) where a child enters the United Kingdom in circumstances where section 83(1) applies and the prospective adopter(s) give notice to the local authority of their wish to return the child, the local authority must:

  (a) receive the child from the prospective adopter(s) within seven days of receipt of the notice, and

  (b) give notice to the Secretary of State or, as the case may be, the National Assembly, of the prospective adopter's wish to return the child;

(2) where a child enters the United Kingdom in circumstances where section 83(1) applies and the local authority:

  (a) is of the opinion that the child should not remain with the prospective adopters, and

  (b) gives notice to them of its opinion,

  the prospective adopters must, not later than the end of the period of seven days beginning with the giving of the notice, return the child to the local authority;

(3) if the agency gives notice under (2)(b) above it must also give notice to the Secretary of State or, as the case may be, the Assembly

(Foreign Element Regulations, regulation 8.)

Failure to return the child

A prospective adopter who fails to comply with a requirement to return the child within seven days of notice being given under section 35(2) commits a criminal offence, and is liable, on summary conviction, to imprisonment for a term of not more than three months or a fine, or both (Adoption and Children Act 2002, section 35(4)).

Effect of notice to return the child if proceedings are pending
Where a local authority gives notice to the prospective adopter(s) that it is of the opinion that the child should not remain with them, but before the notice was given an application for an adoption order, special guardianship order or residence order, or for leave to apply for a special guardianship order or residence order, was made in respect of the child, and the application has not been disposed of, the prospective adopter(s) are not required to return the child to the local authority unless the court so orders.

Requirement for child to live with prospective adopter(s)
Where the prospective adopter(s) has complied with the statutory and procedural requirements for applying to adopt a child who is habitually resident outside the United Kingdom, as outlined above, and makes an application for an adoption order, section 42(3) of the Act does not apply to him. Section 42(3) requires that, if the applicant, or one of the applicants, is the partner or a parent of the child, the child must have had his home with the applicant(s) for six months before the application. Furthermore, the provision which requires that the child should have had his home with the applicants for a minimum period where the applicant is not a partner of the child's parent or a local authority foster carer (section 42(4) and (5)) is reduced to six months in the case of an intercountry adoption application. Where the child has been brought into the United Kingdom without having complied with the statutory requirement imposed in section 83(4) and the Foreign Element Regulations, the period for which the child must have had his home with the prospective adopters is twelve months (Foreign Element Regulations 2005, regulation 9).

9. Transitional Provisions
For the transitional provisions relating to non-Convention cases in progress on 30 December 2005 when the Adoption and Children Act 2002 came fully into force, see Chapter 24, page 370.

Chapter 23

Convention Adoptions

1. Introduction

A "Convention adoption" is an adoption effected under the law of a country outside the British Islands, in which the Convention on Protection of Children and Co-operation in respect of Intercountry Adoption (the Hague Convention) is in force, and certified in pursuance of article 23(1) of the Convention (see section 66 of the Adoption and Children Act 2002). The Hague Convention has been incorporated into domestic law by virtue of the Adoption (Intercountry Aspects) Act 1999. The aim of the Convention is to ensure that intercountry adoptions take place in the best interests of the child, and with respect for his or her fundamental rights as recognised in international law; and to establish a common basis and principles on which arrangements for intercountry adoptions should be made between contracting member states. Adoption orders made under the Convention are recognised in all member states. The provisions of the Convention are discussed in Chapter 20, which describes the statutory and procedural requirements which must be met by prospective adopters to ensure that they do not fall foul of the restrictions imposed on the transfer of children to and from the United Kingdom for the purposes of adoption. The statutory provisions which restrict such movements are dealt with in Chapter 21. Anyone who wishes to adopt a child from a Hague Convention country must comply with the provisions of the Convention and of the Adoptions with a Foreign Element Regulations 2005 (SI 2005 No. 392, the "Foreign Element Regulations").

Contravention of these provisions is a criminal offence punishable by imprisonment, a fine, or both. If a child is brought into, or removed from, the United Kingdom in contravention of sections 83 and 85, the offence is punishable, on summary conviction, by imprisonment for not more than six months or a fine or both; and on, conviction on indictment, by imprisonment for not more than twelve months, a fine, or both. Breach of certain requirements of the Foreign Element Regulations is also a criminal offence (see page 297).

See also the Children and Adoption Bill, outlined on page 330.

2.   Where the United Kingdom is the Receiving State

The Foreign Element Regulations, regulations 12 to 34, apply where a person or a couple, habitually resident in the British Islands, wishes to adopt a child who is habitually resident in a Convention country outside the British Islands.

Age and residency

To qualify to adopt a child from a Convention country, a prospective adopter must satisfy the authorities, if the application is to be made by a single person, that he has attained the age of twenty-one years and has been habitually resident in a part of the British Islands for a period of not less than one year immediately preceding the making of the application. Where the application is made by a couple, they must both have attained the age of twenty-one and satisfy the residency requirement (Foreign Element Regulations, regulation 13(2)).

The application

Once the prospective adopter(s) has taken an informed decision that he wishes to adopt a child who is habitually resident in a Convention country outside the British Islands, he must apply in writing, to an adoption agency that is accredited to undertake intercountry adoptions, for a determination of eligibility and an assessment of his suitability to adopt a child. The prospective adopter must co-operate in providing the adoption agency with any information it requires for the purposes of the assessment. See Foreign Element Regulations, regulation 13(1)).

Counselling and provision of information

Before carrying out the assessment, the adoption agency is obliged to provide to the prospective adopter(s) counselling services as required under regulation 21(1)(a) of the Adoption Agencies Regulations 2005 or the corresponding Welsh provision (see page 213).

The adoption agency is also required to explain to the prospective adopter(s) the procedure in relation to, and the legal implications of, adopting a child from the state of origin (the state where the child is habitually resident) in question. The information given usually includes information about the process of assessment and matching; the role of the Department for Education and Skills (in Wales, the National Assembly); the immigration implications and processes; and the actions which the prospective adopter(s) will have to take once he has been approved as a suitable person to adopt a child. The prospective adopter(s) may need to attend meetings arranged by the adoption agency to assist in understanding the process and the issues which arise. In particular, prospective adopter(s) should be fully assisted in understanding the implications not only of UK adoption law but also of the law of adoption in the child's state of origin. The requirement for the prospective adopter to visit the child in the state of origin, and to accompany him to the United Kingdom, and the costs and other consequences, need to be addressed carefully. Written information on these matters must be provided. If the adoption agency to whom the application has been made is satisfied that the prospective adopter(s) has already received counselling and been provided with the relevant information from another authorised agency, this requirement can be dispensed with. (Foreign Element Regulations, regulation 14.)

Assessment of eligibility and suitability

In assessing eligibility and suitability, the adoption agency checks the age and residence of the prospective adopter(s), and their immigration status, under both British law and the law of the state of origin. It is important that this issue is addressed first.

In carrying out the assessment, the adoption agency must apply the requirements relevant to domestic adoptions under regulations 22 to 25 of the Adoption Agencies Regulations 2005 or the corresponding Welsh provisions, described in Chapter 16. This entails carrying out police checks and obtaining enhanced criminal records certificates, and obtaining health reports, written reports of the interviews with referees and reports from the local authority. A prospective adopter's report is prepared for submission to the adoption panel. In a Convention adoption case, the prospective adopter's report includes the following information, in addition to that required in a domestic case:

    (a) the state of origin from which the prospective adopter wishes to adopt a child;

    (b) confirmation that the prospective adopter is eligible to adopt a child under the law of that state;

    (c) any additional information obtained as a consequence of the requirements of that state; and

    (d) the agency's assessment of the prospective adopter's suitability to adopt a child who is habitually resident in that state.

All the information obtained by the adoption agency is placed on the prospective adopter's case record. See regulation 15 of both the Adoption Agencies Regulations and the Adoption Agencies (Wales) Regulations, pages 205 to 206.

The agency's decision and notification

The adoption agency must notify to the prospective adopter(s) its decision on suitability. If the decision is that the prospective adopter(s) is not suitable to adopt a child, the agency must give its reason, and a copy of the recommendation of the adoption panel. The prospective adopter is informed of his right to challenge the decision by seeking a review by an independent review panel. The process would continue as in a domestic case (see page 220).

Review and termination of approval

Once a prospective adopter has been approved, the adoption agency is required to review the approval as set out in regulation 29 of the Adoption Agencies Regulations or regulation 30 of the Adoption Agencies (Wales) Regulations, until the adoption agency has received from the relevant Central Authority written notification that the agreement under article 17(c) of the Convention (see below) has been made (Foreign Element Regulations, regulation 17).

Procedure following decision on suitability

Once the adoption agency decides that a prospective adopter is suitable to adopt a child from the state of origin in question, it must send certain documents and information to the "Central Authority", which, for England, is the Department for Education and Skills, and, for Wales, the National Assembly. The documents and information to be sent are:

  (a) written confirmation of the decision and any recommendation the agency may make in relation to the number of children the prospective adopter(s) may be suitable to adopt, their age(s), sex(es), likely needs and background(s);

  (b) the enhanced criminal record obtained under regulation 23 of the Adoption Agencies Regulations or the corresponding Welsh provision;

  (c) all the documents and information which were passed to the adoption panel in accordance with regulation 25(9) of the Adoption Agencies Regulations or the corresponding Welsh provision;

  (d) the record of the proceedings of the adoption panel, its recommendation and the reasons for its recommendation; and

  (e) any other information relating to the case as the relevant Central Authority or the Central Authority of the state of origin may require. (Foreign Element Regulations, regulation 18(1).)

If, at any stage before an agreement is made under article 17(c), the agency determines that the prospective adopter(s) is no longer suitable, or the prospective adopter(s) decides not to proceed, the agency must inform the Department or Assembly (regulation 20, Foreign Element Regulations).

Fees

On the charging of fees by the local authority, see pages 264, 286 and 336.

The role of the Department for Education and Skills or National Assembly

On receipt of the application, the Department's or Assembly's case worker checks that all the requirements have been complied with, requesting further information if necessary. If the Department or Assembly is satisfied that the adoption agency has complied with the duties and procedures imposed by the regulations, and that all the relevant information has been supplied by the agency, the Department or Assembly, as the Central Authority, is obliged to send to the Central Authority of the state of origin, the following documents and information:

(a) the prospective adopter's report;

(b) the enhanced criminal record certificate;

(c) a copy of the adoption agency's decision and the adoption panel's recommendation;

(d) any other information that the Central Authority of the state of origin may require; and

(e) a certificate confirming that the documentation is in order and the relevant procedures have been complied with. It also confirms that the prospective adopter(s) has been assessed and approved as eligible and suitable to be an adoptive parent in accordance with the relevant statutory provisions; and that, subject to entry clearance and any immigration requirements, the child will be allowed to enter and remain in the United Kingdom

(Foreign Element Regulations, regulation 18(2)).

If any documents need to be translated, notarised or legalised, the prospective adopter(s) are notified of this and given information on how to secure these services; the translated, notarised or legalised documents are then forwarded with the other documents.

The Department or Assembly also notifies the adoption agency and the prospective adopter(s) in writing that the certificate and all the documents and information have been forwarded to the Central Authority of the state of origin (regulation 18(3)).

The matching process

The Central Authority in the state of origin considers the application. If it approves the application, it places the prospective adopter's name on the list of approved adopters. When a suitable child is matched with the prospective adopter(s), the Central Authority of the state of origin prepares a report on the child, including information about the child and his identity, adoptability, background, social environment, family history, medical history (including that of the child's family) and any special needs of the child. It gives due consideration to the child's upbringing and to his ethnic, religious and cultural needs, and ensures that all the necessary consents have been obtained from those who have parental responsibility for the child. It goes on to determine, on the basis of the reports relating to the child and the prospective adopter(s), whether the placement is in the best interests of the child. It then transmits to the Central Authority in the United Kingdom its report on the child, proof that the necessary consents have been obtained and the reason for the decision to place the child with the applicants. This information is known as the "article 16 information".

On receipt of the article 16 information, the Department for Education and Skills, or the National Assembly, as the Central Authority, sends the information on to the adoption agency. See the Foreign Element Regulations, regulation 19(1) and article 16 of the Hague Convention.

The adoption agency's role following approval

The adoption agency considers the article 16 information, and sends a copy to the prospective adopter(s). It arranges a meeting with the prospective adopter(s) to discuss the information, the proposed placement and the availability of adoption support services. Where appropriate, it provides counselling and further information (Foreign Element Regulations, regulation 19(2)). Arrangements are then made for the prospective adopter(s) to visit the child in the state of origin, and to confirm whether or not he wants to proceed with the application. Where the application has been made by a couple jointly, they must both visit the child.

Procedure following the visit to the child

After visiting the child, the prospective adopter(s) must, if it is the case, confirm to the adoption agency his intention to proceed. He is required to confirm in writing to the adoption agency that he has visited the child and has provided the adoption agency with additional reports and information received on or after that visit; and that he wishes to proceed to adopt that child. (Foreign Element Regulations, regulation 19(3).)

On receiving this confirmation, the adoption agency notifies the Department for Education and Skills or National Assembly in writing that the requirements of regulation 19(3) have been satisfied and that the agency is content that the application should proceed.

On receipt of the information, the Department or Assembly notifies the Central Authority of the state of origin of the prospective adopter's intention to go ahead and for the adoption process to proceed. It also provides confirmation relating to entry clearance (see page 322). For this purpose it liaises with the Home Office to obtain written confirmation on the immigration issue. The Central Authorities of both states then reach an agreement that the adoption may proceed as required by article 17(c) of the Hague Convention. See the Foreign Element Regulations, regulation 19(4). Should there be any difficulty over the immigration issue, the adoption agency is notified and must then provide the necessary support services to the prospective adopter(s). If the adoption cannot go ahead, all relevant documents sent to the adoption agency must be returned.

Proposed adoption not proceeding

There are three clear instances in which a proposed placement may not proceed. First, where the prospective adopter(s) withdraws and notifies the adoption agency that he does not wish to adopt. In this event the adoption agency must notify the Department or Assembly and return the relevant documents to it. It is the responsibility of the Department or Assembly to notify the Central Authority of the state of origin and send the documents to it. (Foreign Element Regulations, regulation 20(3).)

The second instance arises where, before agreement under article 17(c) is reached, the state of origin notifies the Department or Assembly that it has decided that the placement should not proceed. In this event the adoption agency is notified of the decision and in turn notifies the prospective adopter(s). The article 16 information must then be returned to the Department or Assembly, which is obliged to return it to the Central Authority in the state of origin. (Foreign Element Regulations, regulation 20(1).)

Thirdly, during the periodic review of the prospective adopter(s) before the article 17(c) agreement is reached, the adoption agency may determine that the prospective adopter(s) is no longer suitable to adopt a child. In this event it is the duty of the adoption agency to notify the Department or Assembly and return the article 16 information. The Central Authority of the state of origin is notified and the documents returned to it. (Foreign Element Regulations, regulation 20(2)).

Procedure following the article 17(c) agreement
Once confirmation has been received that both states have agreed that the adoption can proceed, the prospective adopter(s) must:

(a) notify the adoption agency of his expected date of entry into the United Kingdom with the child;

(b) confirm to the adoption agency when the child is placed with him by the competent authority in the state of origin;

(c) accompany the child on entering the United Kingdom. In the case of a couple they must both accompany the child unless it has been agreed that only one of them need do so.

(Foreign Element Regulations, regulation 21.)

The prospective adopter(s) then have a choice – to apply for an adoption order in the state of origin, or to continue the adoption process in the United Kingdom (see below).

The adoption agency also has obligations. Before the child enters the United Kingdom it must:

(a) send to the prospective adopter's general practitioner written notification of the proposed placement, together with the report on the child's medical history and current state of health as far as is known;

(b) send to the local authority, if that authority is not the adoption agency, and the Primary Care Trust or (in Wales) the Local Health Board in whose area the prospective adopter(s) lives, written notification of the proposed arrival date of the child;

(c) where the child is of compulsory school age, send to the local education authority in whose area the prospective adopter(s) has his home information about the child's education history and, where appropriate, state, if it is the case, that the child is likely to be assessed for special educational needs under the Education Act 1996.

(Foreign Element Regulations, regulation 22.)

If the child is placed with the prospective adopter(s) by the competent authority of the state of origin for a probationary period, and the prospective adopter(s), having applied for a Convention adoption in the child's state of origin, returns to England or Wales with the child before the probationary period is completed, and the Convention adoption is then made in the state of origin, the relevant local authority must, if requested by the competent authority of the state of origin, provide a report about the placement and any other matter raised in the request. It must do so within such period as the competent authority reasonably requires. (Foreign Element Regulations, regulation 29.)

Convention adoption not made before entry

If it is decided to adopt the child under the laws of England and Wales, the prospective adopter(s) must, within fourteen days of entry into the United Kingdom with the child, notify the relevant local authority of the child's arrival in the United Kingdom and of his intention to adopt the child in accordance with section 44(2) of the Adoption and Children Act 2002. If he has changed his mind, then he must give notice that he does not intend to give the child a home. (Foreign Element Regulations, regulation 24.) If the prospective adopter(s) moves to the area of another local authority, he must, within fourteen days of the move, inform that local authority and give a similar notice.

Where the prospective adopter(s) have indicated an intention to proceed, the requirements and procedure in relation to a domestic adoption apply. The adoption agency must follow the procedure set out in regulations 24 to 27 of the Adoption Agencies Regulations or the corresponding Welsh provisions (see Chapter 16). The information concerning the child received from the state of origin and the competent foreign authority is placed on the child's case records (Foreign Element Regulations, regulation 26).

Prospective adopter(s) unable to proceed

Where a prospective adopter(s) gives notice that he does not wish to proceed to adopt a child who has been placed with him for adoption, the relevant local authority requests the return of the child, and the child must be returned to and received by the local authority within seven days of the giving of the notice. The local authority is also under a duty to inform the Department for Education and Skills or (in Wales) the Assembly, as the Central Authority, of the decision of the prospective adopter(s). See Foreign Element Regulations, regulation 26.

If, in the course of the reviews and inquiries which the local authority is obliged to make, it comes to the decision that the continued placement of the child is not in the best interests of the child, it must give notice to the prospective adopter(s) of its opinion and request that the child is returned to it. It must also inform the Department or Assembly of its decision. In this event, the prospective adopter(s) is under a duty to return the child within seven days of the date of the notice, unless adoption proceedings in respect of the child were commenced before the notice was received. In the latter case, if the proceedings are still pending, the prospective adopter(s) is not obliged to return the child unless the court so directs. See Foreign Element Regulations, regulation 27.

Breakdown of placement

If a placement breaks down in any one or more of certain circumstances, the local authority is permitted to place the child for adoption with another prospective adopter(s) who is habitually resident in the United Kingdom, if it considers that such a placement would be in the best interests of the child. The circumstances in which it may do so are where:

(a) the prospective adopter does not wish to proceed with the adoption and gives notice of his intention under regulation 26 of the Foreign Element Regulations;

(b) the child is withdrawn from the placement under regulation 27;

(c) an application for a Convention adoption is refused;

(d) a Convention adoption which is subject to a probationary period cannot be made; or

(e) a Convention adoption order or a Convention adoption is annulled under section 89(1) of the Adoption and Children Act 2002.

Where an alternative placement has been identified and the prospective adopter(s) appropriately assessed under the Foreign Element Regulations as eligible and suitable, the adoption agency must notify the Department or Assembly. If the child is of sufficient age and understanding, his views and feelings must be ascertained, and regard had to those wishes and feelings; his consent to the proposals should also be obtained. The Central Authority of the state of origin is then informed of the proposed placement, and attempts made to reach an agreement with the state of origin for the placement to continue. If this cannot be achieved, and it is decided that it would not, after all, be in the best interests of the child to be placed with another prospective adopter in England and Wales, arrangements are made between the Central Authorities of both States for the child to be returned. See Foreign Element Regulations, regulation 28.

Application for Convention adoption order

Where a prospective adopter(s) serves notice on the local authority of his intention to apply for a Convention adoption, the report under section 44(5) of the Adoption and Children Act 2002 (see page 89) must include:

(a) confirmation that the certificate of eligibility and approval has been sent to the Central Authority of the state of origin in accordance with regulation 18 of the Foreign Element Regulations 2005;

(b) the date on which the Article 17(c) agreement was made and details of the reports of the visits and reviews made

(Foreign Element Regulations, regulation 30).

Before a Convention adoption order is made, the court must be satisfied that:

(a) the applicant, or both applicants in the case of a couple, has/have been habitually resident in any part of the British Islands for a period of not less than one year immediately preceding the date of the application;

(b) the child to be adopted was, on the date of the Article 17(c) agreement, habitually resident in a Convention country outside the British Islands; and

(c) where one member of a couple (in the case of an application by a couple) or the applicant (in the case of an application by one person) is not a British citizen, that person is authorised to enter and remain permanently in the United Kingdom

(Foreign Element Regulations, regulation 31).

Procedure on making a Convention adoption order

Where a court in England and Wales makes a Convention adoption order, a copy of the order should be sent to the Department for Education and Skills, or (in Wales) the National Assembly, as Central Authority. The Department or Assembly must then issue a certificate in the form in schedule 2 to the Foreign Element Regulations, confirming that the adoption has been made in accordance with the Convention. A copy of the certificate is sent to the state of origin, the adoptive parent(s) and the adoption agency or the relevant authority.

Where a Convention adoption is made and a certificate under article 23 of the Convention is received by the Department or Assembly, it must send a copy of the certificate to the adoptive parent(s) and the adoption agency or relevant local authority.

(Foreign Element Regulations, regulation 32).

Refusal, withdrawal or annulment

If an application for a Convention adoption order is refused or withdrawn, the prospective adopter(s) must return the child to the relevant local authority within the period specified by the court. Where a Convention order is annulled under section 89(1) of the Adoption and Children Act 2002, a copy of the order must be served on the Department or Assembly, which in turn must forward a copy to the Central Authority in the state of origin. See

Foreign Element Regulations, regulations 33 and 34.

3. Where the United Kingdom is the State of Origin

Where a prospective adopter(s) who is habitually resident in a Convention country outside the British Islands wishes to adopt a child habitually resident in the British Islands, the requirements and procedure set out in Foreign Element Regulations, regulations 35 to 51, must be followed.

The adoption agency must ensure that the child, if he is of sufficient age and understanding, is given information; and that his wishes and feelings are taken into account. The principles laid down in section 1(2) to (6) of the Adoption and Children Act 2002 (see Chapter 9) must be applied in making any decision relating to the adoption of the child.

Counselling and information for the child

The adoption agency is under a duty to provide a counselling service for the child. It must also provide the child with information about the legal process and implications of a Convention adoption, in an age-appropriate way. It must ascertain the child's wishes and feelings on the placement, having made him aware of the fact that the prospective adopter(s) is habitually resident in the receiving state. Written information must also be provided of all the matters which need to be dealt with as provided by regulation 13 of both the Adoption Agencies Regulations and the Adoption Agencies (Wales) Regulations (see page 201), and the Foreign Element Regulations, regulation 36. If the child has already received counselling and information from another agency, it is not necessary to repeat the process.

Counselling and information for the parent, guardian and others

The process set out in regulation 14 of the Adoption Agencies Regulations and the Adoption Agencies (Wales) Regulations for counselling and providing information to the parent or guardian of the child, and to other significant persons (see page 202), applies to Convention adoptions as it does to domestic adoptions. This duty is owed to the child's father where his identity is known. Written information must also be provided. See the Foreign Element Regulations, regulation 37.

Permanence report and panel's recommendation

A permanence report must be prepared in accordance with regulation 17 of the Adoption Agencies Regulations 2005 and the Adoption Agencies (Wales) Regulations (see pages 206 to 207). In addition to the usual requirements, it must include a summary of the possibilities for placing the child within the United Kingdom, and an assessment of whether an adoption by a person in the particular receiving country is in the child's best interests.

The adoption agency should have received a report prepared by the receiving state, in accordance with article 15 of the Convention, on the eligibility and suitability of the prospective adopter(s), including information about the person's identity, background, family and medical history, social environment, reasons for seeking to adopt and ability to undertake an intercountry adoption. This report, together with the adoption agency's observations on it and the other reports and information required under regulation 17 of the Adoption Agencies Regulations or its Welsh equivalent, must be placed before the adoption panel. In addition to the matters set out in regulation 17 (see page 207), the adoption panel must, when making its recommendation, consider and take into account the report under article 15 and the adoption agency's observations on it. See Foreign Element Regulations, regulation 39.

The decision of the adoption agency
Where the decision of the adoption agency is in the affirmative, it must notify the Department for Education and Skills or, in Wales, the National Assembly, of the name, sex, and age of the child; the reason it considers the child may be suitable for such an adoption; whether a prospective adopter has been identified, and if so any relevant information; and any other information that may be required. The child's name is placed on a list of children maintained by the Department or Assembly as the Central Authority (the "Convention list"), which is available for consultation by other authorities within the British Islands. If the adoption agency decides that a Convention adoption is no longer in the child's best interests, it must inform the Department or Assembly, so that the child's name may be removed from the Convention list. See the Foreign Element Regulations, regulation 41.

The role of the Department for Education and Skills and National Assembly
Where the Department for Education and Skills or, in Wales, the National Assembly, receives an article 15 report, it must first satisfy itself that:
   (a) the prospective adopter is habitually resident in the receiving state, or, in the case of couple, that they are both habitually resident in the receiving state;
   (b) the prospective adopter(s) wishes to adopt a child from the British Islands;
   (c) the prospective adopter(s) satisfies the age criteria set out in section 50 and 51 of the Adoption and Children Act 2002 (see page 14).
On being so satisfied, the Department or Assembly consults the Convention lists maintained within the British Islands to find an appropriate match. Where a match between a particular child and the prospective adopter(s) has already been identified, and the criteria set out above are satisfied, the article 15 report is forwarded to the relevant adoption agency. Where a match is still to be found, the article 15 report may be circulated among the other Central Authorities in the British Islands with a view to finding a possible match

from their lists. If a match is found, that authority sends the article 15 report to the relevant local authority.

Proposed placement and referral to the adoption panel

Where the adoption agency is considering placing a child with a particular prospective adopter(s), it must have regard to the article 15 report and place the report before the adoption panel for its consideration, along with all other matters specified in the relevant regulations (see pages 208 to 209). The panel is obliged to have regard to the article 15 report, along with any other information received, when it makes its recommendation. See the Foreign Element Regulations, regulations 43 and 44.

The adoption agency makes its decision in accordance with regulation 33 of the Adoption Agencies Regulations 2005 (regulation 34 of the Adoption Agencies (Wales) Regulations) (see page 236), save that for the purposes of a Convention adoption, paragraph (3), which requires it to inform the prospective adopter(s) of its decision, does not apply. If the decision is that the placement is not to proceed, however, the article 15 report must be returned, together with any other documents and information provided, to the Department or Assembly, which then forwards it to the receiving State. See Foreign Element Regulations, regulation 45.

Where the decision is to go ahead with the placement, the adoption agency has to prepare a report for the purposes of article 16(1) of the Convention (see pages 351 to 352). The report must include the information set out in schedule 1 to the Adoption Agencies Regulations or the Adoption Agencies (Wales) Regulations, and the reason for the adoption agency's decision. This report, together with any court orders made in respect of the child (such as a placement order or confirmation that the parent has consented to the proposed adoption) must then be sent to the Department or Assembly. The Department or Assembly then forwards it to the Central Authority in the receiving state. See the Foreign Element Regulations, regulation 46.

Preconditions for placement

Before agreement is reached under article 17(c), the Department or the National Assembly must have confirmation from the Central Authority of the receiving state that:

(a) the prospective adopter(s) has agreed to adopt the child and has received necessary counselling;

(b) the prospective adopter(s) has confirmed that he will accompany the child to the receiving state. In the case of a joint application by a couple, it may be agreed that only one of them should do so;

(c) it is content that the adoption should proceed;

(d) where a Convention adoption is to be effected, it has explained to the prospective adopter(s) the need to make an application in

England or Wales for a parental responsibility order under section 84(1) of the Adoption and Children Act 2002; and

(e) the child is or will be authorised to enter and reside permanently in the Convention country if a Convention adoption is effected or a Convention adoption order is made.

Before an article 17(c) agreement is reached, confirmation on all the above matters is required. In addition, the adoption agency needs to confirm that:

(a) the prospective adopter(s) has visited the child;

(b) the agency has met with the prospective adopter(s) and explained the need to make an application for a parental responsibility order under section 84(1) of the Adoption and Children Act 2002 before the child is removed from the United Kingdom; and

(c) the prospective adopter(s) has confirmed that he is content for the adoption to proceed

(Foreign Element Regulations, regulation 47).

Parental responsibility order

Section 84(3) of the Adoption and Children Act 2002 provides that an order giving parental responsibility before adoption abroad may not be made unless any requirements prescribed by regulation are satisfied. Regulation 48 of the Foreign Element Regulations sets out the requirements, which are that:

(a) the competent authority of the receiving state must have:

(i) prepared an article 15 report,

(ii) determined and confirmed in writing that the prospective adopter(s) is eligible and suitable to adopt,

(iii) ensured and confirmed in writing that the prospective adopter(s) has been counselled as may be necessary, and

(iv) determined and confirmed in writing that the child is or will be authorised to enter and reside permanently in that state;

(b) the adoption agency has:

(i) prepared the article 16(1) report,

(ii) confirmed in writing that it has complied with the requirements of part 3 of the Adoption Agencies Regulations (regulations 11 to 20; see Chapter 16) or the corresponding Welsh provisions,

(iii) obtained and made available to the court the recommendation of the adoption panel in relation to whether the child should be placed for adoption and in relation to the proposed placement, the adoption placement report, reports on reviews carried out, and confirmation that the prospective adopter will accompany the child to the receiving state.

The procedure for seeking an order under section 84 is governed by Part 5 of the Family Procedure (Adoption) Rules 2005 (SI 2005 No. 2795); see Chapter 25, page 389.

Convention adoption order

Where an application for a Convention adoption order is applied for, the local authority's report under section 43(a) and 44(5) of the Adoption and Children Act 2002 must include a copy of the article 15 report, the article 16(1) report and written confirmation of the article 17(c) agreement.

A Convention adoption order will not be made unless the residency requirement – that the applicant has been habitually resident in the Convention country for twelve months preceding the application – has been satisfied. The court also needs confirmation that the child was habitually resident in part of the British Islands before the article 17(c) agreement was made, and that the competent authority has confirmed that the child is authorised to enter and remain permanently in the Convention country in which the applicant is a habitual resident. See the Foreign Element Regulations 2005, regulations 49 and 50.

Procedure following a Convention adoption order

Once a Convention adoption order has been made in England or Wales, a copy of it should be sent to the Department for Education and Skills or (in Wales) the National Assembly, which must then issue a certificate in the form in schedule 2 to the Foreign Element Regulations that the adoption has been made in accordance with the Convention. A copy of the certificate is sent to the Central Authority of the receiving state and the relevant local authority. Where a Convention adoption order is made outside England or Wales, the Department or National Assembly receives, from the Central Authority of the receiving state, a certificate under article 23 of the Convention confirming that a Convention adoption has been made. On receipt of the certificate the Department or Assembly should send a copy to the relevant local authority. See the Foreign Element Regulations, regulation 51.

For the procedure for applications in connection with a Convention adoption order after it has been made (for example, for annulment, or a determination that it should cease to be valid on grounds of public policy), see Chapter 25, page 389.

4. Offences

It is an offence for any person to:
- (a) contravene or fail to comply with the requirements in regulation 26 of the Foreign Element Regulations; or
- (b) fail to return a child to the local authority when the placement of the child with that person has been withdrawn under regulation 27; or
- (c) fail to return the child within the period specified by a court when the application for a Convention adoption order is refused.

On summary conviction, an offender is liable to imprisonment for not more than three months or a fine of not more than £5,000, or both. See the Foreign Element Regulations, regulation 59.

5. Transitional Provisions

For the transitional provisions relating to Convention cases in progress on 30 December 2005 when the Adoption and Children Act 2002 came fully into force, see Chapter 24, page 369.

Chapter 24

Transitional Provisions

1. Introduction

The main provisions on the transition to the new regime under the Adoption and Children Act 2002 are set out in schedule 4 to the 2002 Act and the Adoption and Children Act 2002 (Commencement No. 10 Transitional and Savings Provisions) Order 2005, SI 2005 No. 2897, the "Transitional and Savings Provisions Order". The various regulations made under the 2002 Act, in particular those concerning adoption support services, also contain certain transitional provisions.

Paragraph 1(1) of schedule 4 to the Adoption and Children Act 2002 provides that any reference in Part 1 of the 2002 Act, or in any other enactment, instrument or document, to any provision in Part 1, or to things done or required to be done under Part 1, should be construed as including references to any corresponding provision repealed by the 2002 Act, so far as the nature of the reference permits. This means that, for example, if a decision was made before 30 December 2005, under the Adoption Agencies Regulations 1983 (SI 1983 No. 1964), that a person is suitable to adopt a child, the decision is treated a having been made under the 2005 regulations (see Chapter 16, page 213). Again, any notice given by a person to a local authority of intention to adopt a child under section 22(1) of the Adoption Act 1976 is treated as have been given under section 44(1) of the 2002 Act (see Chapter 6, page 87).

Paragraph 1(2) of schedule 4 to the 2002 Act provides that any reference in any enactment, instrument or document to a provision repealed by the 2002 Act, or things done or required to be done under a repealed provision, is to be construed as a reference to the corresponding provision in the 2002 Act or to the things done or required to be done or falling to be done under the corresponding provision, so far as the nature of the reference permits. This means that a decision taken before 30 December 2005 stands as a decision taken under the new regime.

Orders already made are not affected by the implementation of the 2002 Act. A pending application will proceed under the 1976 Act.

2. Freeing Orders

Pending application

An application for a freeing order made before 30 December 2005 which has not been disposed of immediately before the 2002 Act comes into force, is not affected by the 2002 Act if the child in relation to whom the application is made has his home with a person with whom he has been placed for adoption by an adoption agency. The application continues to be dealt with under the 1976 Act (paragraph 6 of schedule 4 to the 2002 Act). "Not disposed of" means that the application is pending. In the context of a freeing order, by virtue of rule 47(2) of the Adoption Rules 1984 (SI 1984 No. 265), this means that the application has been issued. See also schedule 4, paragraph 1, to the 2002 Act. Furthermore, notwithstanding the repeal of the provisions in the Adoption Act 1976 set out in schedule 5 to the 2002 Act, section 18 of the Adoption Act 1976 (freeing for adoption) continues to have effect:

- (a) where the application for a freeing order was made before 30 December 2005 and is still pending on 30 December 2005; and
- (b) the child in relation to whom the application is made is not immediately before the 30 December 2005 placed for adoption by the adoption agency

(article 10, Transitional and Savings Provisions Order).

An application for a freeing order cannot be made after 30 December 2005.

Where, on 30 December 2005, an application for a freeing order is pending and the child is in the care of the adoption agency making the application and the parent does not consent to the freeing order being made, the parent or guardian must not remove the child from the person with whom the child has his home without the permission of the court. Thus, section 27 of the Adoption Act 1976 continues to apply, notwithstanding the repeal of the provisions in the Adoption Act 1976 set out in schedule 5 to the 2002 Act (article 9 of the Transitional and Savings Provisions Order). If such removal occurs, the court may, on the application of a person from whose custody a child has been removed in breach of section 27, pursuant to section 29 of the 1976 Act, order the person who has removed the child to return the child to the applicant. Where there are reasonable grounds for believing that another person is intending to remove the child from the applicant's custody, the court's power under section 29(2) to direct that the other person must not remove the child from the applicant continues. If the child is not returned to the applicant, the court may make a recovery order under section 29 of the 1976 Act (article 9(b), Transitional and Savings Provisions Order).

Freeing order made but adoption order not made

Where a freeing order was made before 30 December 2005 it remains a valid order and is not affected by the provisions of the 2002 Act. The adoption agency in whose favour the order was made continues to retain parental responsibility for the child (schedule 4, paragraph 7, to the 2002 Act). If the child has been freed for adoption under section 18 of the 1976 Act but is not placed for adoption, the adoption agency may place the child for adoption. The adoption agency does not have to comply with the requirements of section 18 of the 2002 Act regarding the placement of the child, nor does it have to comply with the requirement in section 22 of the 2002 Act that the adoption agency must obtain a placement order (article 4(a) of the Transitional and Savings Provisions Order). The application for an adoption order will, however, proceed under the 2002 Act. So where a child is free for adoption but has not yet been placed and a recommendation has not been made, the freeing order enables the local authority to place the child for adoption under the 2002 Act. Regulation 35 of the Adoption Agencies Regulations 2005 and the corresponding Welsh regulation, relating to placement (see page 237) applies to such cases as if the adoption agency was authorised to place the child for adoption,but the child is not for the time being placed but is subject to a placement order. (See article 4(b), Transitional and Savings Provisions Order.)

Article 3(6) of the Transitional and Savings Provisions Order (see below) makes clear that all placements made under the 1983 regulations must be treated as if they were made under the 2005 regulations. Therefore, as from 30 December 2005, all placements must be monitored and reviewed in accordance with regulation 36 of the Adoption Agencies Regulations 2005 and its Welsh equivalent (see page 238).

Except for the right to receive reports on the child, pending his adoption, and to apply for a revocation order in an appropriate case (see below) the parental responsibility of the parent(s) or of any other person who had parental responsibility for the child before the order was made, remains extinguished. Any application for the revocation of a freeing order will be dealt with under the provisions of the Adoption Act 1976 and the 1984 Adoption Rules.

A former parent who was given an opportunity to make a declaration under section 18(6) of the Adoption Act 1976 (that he prefers not be involved in future questions concerning the adoption of the child), but did not do so, retains the right to be notified, within fourteen days of the first anniversary after the making of the freeing order, whether an adoption order has been made in respect of the child; and if not, whether the child has his home with a person with whom he has been placed.

If, at the time the notice is given to the former parent, an adoption order has not been made in respect of the child, the adoption agency must notify the parent when the adoption order is made. Until the adoption order is made, the former parent must also be notified whenever the child is placed for adoption or ceases to have his home with a prospective adopter(s).

Revocation
The former parent of the child retains the right to apply for the revocation of

the freeing order at any time after twelve months from the making of the freeing order, and to seek to resume parental responsibility and to make an application for an order under section 8 of the Children Act 1989, provided that:

(a) an adoption order has not been made in respect of the child; and

(b) the child has not had his home with a person with whom he has been placed.

If the child has his home with the prospective adopter(s) but an adoption order has not been made, the former parent would not have the right to apply for revocation. Should the placement with the prospective adopters break down, the former parent would have the right to apply for the revocation of the freeing order (*R v Derbyshire County Council ex parte T* [1990] Fam 164, [1990] 2 WLR 101, [1990] 1 All ER 792, [1990] 1 FLR 237 and *Re G (A Minor) (Adoption: Freeing Order)* [1997] AC 613, [1997] 2 WLR 747, [1997] 2 All ER 534, [1997] 2 FLR 202). Since, in such a case, an application for revocation would be made under section 20 of the 1976 Act, the test which would apply is that set out in section 6 of the 1976 Act. The court would have to have regard to all the circumstances, first consideration being given to the welfare of the child. Invariably, the application for the revocation of the freeing order is accompanied by an application for an order under the Children Act 1989. The welfare principle enshrined in section 1 of the 1989 Act therefore applies to such an application.

If such an application is made, the adoption agency having parental responsibility for the child must not place the child for adoption without the permission of the court (section 20(1), Adoption Act 1976).

The revocation of a freeing order operates:

(a) to extinguish the parental responsibility given to the adoption agency under the order;

(b) to give parental responsibility for the child to the child's mother; and where the child's father and mother were married to each other at the time of his birth, the father; and

(c) to revive:

(i) any parental responsibility agreement,

(ii) any parental responsibility order made under section 4(1) of the Children Act 1989;

(iii) any care order within the meaning of the Children Act 1989, and

(iv) any appointment of a guardian in respect of the child (whether made by a court or otherwise) extinguished by the making of a freeing order.

The provision for the revival of the care order has been inserted by virtue of schedule 4, paragraph 7(2), to the Adoption and Children Act 2002. Previously, on the making of the freeing order a care order ceased to have effect. Parental responsibility was transferred to the adoption agency alone, and was no longer shared with the parent. If an adoptive placement for the child could not be found, neither the child nor the adoption agency had the right to apply for revocation. The child therefore entered into a legal vacuum, and was described by Wall J in *Re C (Adoption: Freeing Order)*1999] Fam 240, [1999] 1 WLR 1079, [1999] 1 FLR 348 as a "statutory orphan". In *Re C*, the child had been freed for adoption but after some eight years he was not adopted. It was accepted by the mother and the local authority that she should be able to share parental responsibility for the child, but because she had signed a declaration under section 18(6) she could not apply for the revocation of the freeing order, nor could the local authority, the child or the adoption agency. To overcome the problem, the court's inherent jurisdiction had to be invoked to revoke the freeing order.

Where the former parent has made a declaration that he prefers not to be involved in future questions concerning the adoption of the child, the former parent cannot make an application for revocation. In such a case the inherent jurisdiction of the court would have to be invoked (see *Re C (Adoption: Freeing Order)*, above; *Re J (Freeing for Adoption)* [2000] 2 FLR 58).

The Family Procedure (Adoption) Rules 2005 (SI 2005 No. 2795) do not make any reference to the procedure to be followed in such cases. The procedure under the former Adoption Rules should therefore be followed, and where an application includes an application for an order under section 8 of the Children Act, the Family Proceedings Rules 1991 (SI 1991 No. 1247) apply.

Preconditions for adoption order
Schedule 4 paragraph 7(3), to the 2002 Act provides that where a freeing order is in force and an application for an adoption order is made under the 2002 Act, the third condition in section 47(6) of the 2002 is to be treated as satisfied. Section 47 sets out the conditions which must be satisfied before an adoption order can be made. Under subsection (6) the third condition is that the child is free for adoption by virtue of a freeing order made in Scotland or in Northern Ireland. The effect of the provision in Schedule 4 is to add an English freeing order to the third condition.

3. Adoption Orders

Pending application
Schedule 4, paragraph 8, to the 2002 Act provides that nothing in the 2002 Act affects any application for an adoption order under section 12 of the Adoption Act 1976 where:

  (a) the application has been made and has not been disposed of immediately before the repeal of that section; and
  (b) the child in relation to whom the application is made has his home, immediately before that repeal, with a person with whom he has

been placed for adoption by an adoption agency.

Pending applications will be dealt with under the Adoption Act 1976 and the 1984 Rules. Orders will be made under the 1976 Act.

In respect of a pending application for an adoption order in a non-agency case, article 11 of the Transitional and Savings Provisions Order provides that nothing in the 2002 Act affects any such application in respect of which notice has been given to the local authority by virtue of section 22 of the Adoption Act 1976, and the application was made and not disposed of immediately before 30 December 2005.

An application is "made" when it is issued, and is not disposed of until a final order is made or the application is dismissed. Thus any application made for an adoption order before 30 December 2005 will proceed under the former law.

Application by the partner of the child's parent

Schedule 4, paragraph 9, to the 2002 Act makes a specific provision in relation to an application for adoption by the partner of a child's parent. Under section 22(1) of the Adoption Act 1976, an adoption order could not be made in respect of a child who was not placed with the applicant by an adoption agency unless the applicant had, at least three months before the date of the order, given notice to the local authority within whose area he had his home of his intention to apply for the adoption order. Section 42(2) of the 2002 Act, which is the corresponding provision, again provides that an adoption order may not be made unless the prospective adopter(s) has given notice to the appropriate local authority of his intention to apply for the adoption order. However, section 42(3) of the 2002 Act provides that an application for an adoption order may not be made, if the applicant or one of the applicants is the partner of a parent of the child, unless the child has had his home with the applicant(s) at all times during the period of *six* months preceding the application. This provision has been varied by paragraph 9 of schedule 4 to the 2002 Act, which extends the period for which the child must have had his home with the applicants in such a case to *twelve* months. Paragraph 9 provides that where a notice in respect of a child by the prospective adopters under section 22(1) of the 1976 Act is treated, by virtue of paragraph 1(1) of schedule 4 to the 2002 Act, as having been given for the purposes of section 44(2), section 42(3) has effect as if for "six months" there were substituted "twelve months." In such cases, the alternatives to adoption which are now available under the 2002 should be considered before applying for an adoption order.

Restrictions on removing a child

Notwithstanding the repeal of the provisions in the Adoption Act 1976 set out in schedule 5 to the 2002 Act, sections 27 and 29 of the 1976 Act continue to have effect where an application for an adoption order is pending on 30

December 2005 (article 9, Transitional and Savings Provisions Order). A parent or guardian of the child who has agreed to the making of the adoption order is not entitled to remove the child from the custody of the person with whom the child has his home except with the leave of the court; that is, section 27 of the 1976 Act continues to apply. Removal of the child is an offence. If such removal occurs, the court may, on the application of a person from whose custody a child has been removed in breach of section 27, pursuant to section 29 of the 1976 Act, order the person who has removed the child to return the child to the applicant. Where there are reasonable grounds for believing that another person is intending to remove the child from the applicant's custody, the court's power under section 29(2) to direct that the other person must not remove the child from the applicant continues to apply to such an application. If the child is not returned to the applicant, the court may make a recovery order under section 29 of the 1976 Act.

4. Adoptions with a Foreign Element
Where a child who has been habitually resident outside the United Kingdom has been lawfully brought into the United Kingdom for adoption, the applicant(s) must give notice to the local authority of his intention to adopt; no adoption order can be made unless the notice was given at least three months before the date of the proposed adoption order (Adoption (Bringing Children into the United Kingdom) Regulations 2003, SI 2003 No. 1173, regulation 5(b)).

Section 13 of the Adoption Act 1976 was amended by schedule 4, paragraph 10, to the 2002 Act, to insert an additional subsection (1A). It provides that, where an adoption is proposed to be effected by a Convention adoption order, the order should not be made unless at all times during the preceding six months the child had his home with the applicants or one of them. This provision came into force on 1 June 2003.

Further amendments were made to the provision which restricts bringing children into the United Kingdom, by the insertion of section 56A, and the provision for regulations to be made setting out the conditions which prospective adopters have to meet, the procedure to be followed and the penalties to be imposed in relation to any breaches of the statutory provisions. These are already in force and have been considered in Chapter 20 (see page 317, and see further below).

5. Pending Hague Convention Cases
Subject to the exceptions set out below, the general rule is that where a case is in progress on 30 December 2005, any action or decision taken before 30 December 2005 under the provisions of the Intercountry Adoption (Hague Convention) Regulations 2003 (SI 2003 No. 118) is to be treated as if it were

an action or decision taken under the corresponding provision of Part 3 of the Adoptions with a Foreign Element Regulations 2005 (SI 2005 No. 392) (article 6 of the Transitional and Savings Provisions Order 2005).

The exceptions are:

(a) where, before 30 December 2005, an adoption panel has considered:

(i) whether or not adoption by a person habitually resident in a Convention country outside the British Islands is in the best interests of the child; or

(ii) whether a prospective adopter is suitable to adopt a child;

and no decision on that question has been made by the adoption agency before 30 December 2005, the Intercountry Adoption (Hague Convention) Regulations 2003 apply for the purposes of making that decision (article 6(3), Transitional and Savings Provisions Order);

(b) where an adoption agency is minded to make a decision under the Intercountry Adoption (Hague Convention) Regulations 2003 whether before 30 December 2005, or, where regulation 6(3) (see above) applies, on or after that date, as to whether a prospective adopter is suitable to adopt a child, the Intercountry Adoption (Hague Convention) Regulations 2003 and the Independent Review of Determinations (Adoption) Regulations 2004 (SI 2004 No. 190), continue to apply for the purposes of making representations or reviewing any qualifying determination in relation to that decision. The time periods referred to in the regulations are increased from twenty-eight days to forty working days and from seven days to ten working days. (Article 6(4), Transitional and Savings Provisions Order).

6. Non-Convention Adoptions

The Transitional and Savings Provisions Order contains provisions concerning the conditions to be met by prospective adopters under section 83(5) of the 2002 Act. Where, before 30 December 2005, the prospective adopter received notification from the Secretary of State that a certificate referred to in regulation 5(a) of the Adoption (Bringing Children into the United Kingdom) Regulations 2003 has been issued, then:

(a) if the prospective adopter has visited the child but the child has not entered the United Kingdom before 30 December 2005, regulation 4(2)(b) to (d) of the Adoptions with a Foreign Element Regulations 2005 (see page 341) do not apply;

(b) if the child has entered the United Kingdom but the prospective adopter has not given notice of intention to adopt pursuant to regulation 5(b) of the Adoption (Bringing Children into the United Kingdom) Regulations 2003, the provisions of regulation 4(2)(b) to

(d) and (3) of the Adoptions with a Foreign Element Regulations 2005 (see page 341) do not apply

(article 7, Transitional and Savings Provisions Order).

7. The Functions of Local Authorities

Three situations concerning the functions of local authorities require consideration in the context of transitional provisions:

(a) where notice of intention to adopt was given to the local authority before 30 December 2005 by a prospective adopter, as a consequence of regulation 5(b) of the Adoption (Bringing Children into the United Kingdom) Regulations 2003 or regulation 15 of the Intercountry Adoption (Hague Convention) Regulations 2003, then regulation 5 of the Adoptions with a Foreign Element Regulations 2005 (see page 342) applies, subject to (b) and (c) below;

(b) where the local authority has not visited the child and the prospective adopter by 30 December 2005, and more than one week has elapsed since receipt of the notice of intention to adopt, 30 December 2005 is treated as the date on which the notice of intention is received for the purposes of regulation 5(1)(e) and (f) of the Foreign Element Regulations 2005 (see page 342);

(c) where the local authority has visited the child and prospective adopter(s), the reviews and frequency of visits imposed by regulations 5(e) to (h) of the Foreign Element Regulations (see pages 342 to 343) must be complied with if this has not already been done. Where the review to consider the matters referred to in regulation 5(e) to (h) has not taken place by 30 December 2005, that date is to be treated as the date of receipt of the notice of intention to adopt for the purposes of regulation 5(1)(f)

(article 8, Transitional and Savings Provisions Order).

8. Annulment etc of Overseas Adoptions

An application for the annulment of an overseas adoption order, which is pending in the High Court on 30 December 2005, is unaffected by anything in the 2002 Act (article 12, Transitional and Savings Provisions Order).

9. Application for Parental Rights

An application under section 55 of the 1976 Act, for a parental responsibility order for a British child, by a person who is intending to adopt a child outside the United Kingdom, which is pending in the High Court on 30 December 2005 is unaffected by anything in the 2002 Act (article 12, Transitional and Savings Provisions Order). Pending applications are dealt with under the

1976 Act. Applications made on or after 30 December 2005 must meet the requirements of the 2002 Act.

10. Parental Orders under the Human Fertilisation and Embryology Act 1990

Notwithstanding the repeal of the provisions of the Adoption Act 1976 set out in schedule 5 to the 2002 Act, the 1976 Act continues to have effect in respect of applications for orders under the Human Fertilisation and Embryology Act 1990, with such modifications (if any) as may be specified in regulations made under the 1990 Act (article 14, Transitional and Savings Provisions Order). The regulations also make minor amendments to regulation 2 of the Parental Orders (Human Fertilisation and Embryology) Regulations 1994 (SI 1994 No. 2767) and article 2(o) of the Adoption and Children Act 2002 (Commencement No. 9) Order 2005 (SI 2005 No. 2213). Articles 15 and 16 of the Transitional and Savings Provisions Order provide that those repeals do not affect the operation of the Local Authority Adoption Services (England) Regulations 2003 (SI 2003 No. 370).

11. Restrictions on Advertising

Section 58 of the Adoption Act 1976 was amended by the Adoption and Children Act 2002, schedule 4, paragraph 14, to make it unlawful to publish any advertisement that the parent or guardian of a child desires to cause a child to be adopted, or that a person desires to adopt a child, or to make arrangements for the adoption of a child. The prohibition extends to publishing by electronic means for example by means of the internet. This provision applies to applications for adoptions made under the former law.

12. Child Ceasing to be a "Protected Child"

In consequence of the repeal of sections 32 to 36 of the Adoption Act 1976 by schedule 5 to the 2002 Act, a child ceases to be a "protected child" and becomes a privately fostered child within the meaning of section 66 of the Children Act 1989. Article 5 of the Transitional and Savings Provisions Order makes provisions for such a child as follows:

(a) If the person who is fostering the child is disqualified from doing so by the Disqualification from Caring for Children (England) Regulations 2002 (SI 2002 No. 635) or the Disqualification from Caring for Children (Wales) Regulations 2004 (SI 2004 No. 2695, W. 235), made under section 68 of the Children Act 1989, the foster carer is treated as having obtained the consent of the local authority until such time as the local authority notifies him that such consent is refused.

(b) The foster carer in such a case is not regarded as in breach of regulation 5 of the Children (Private Arrangements for Fostering) Regulations 2005 (SI 2005 No. 1533) or the corresponding Welsh regulations, which require a person fostering a child privately to notify the local authority of such an arrangement, provided:

    (i) the foster carer has given the local authority the information required under that regulation whether by way of notice of intention to adopt or otherwise, or

    (ii) if he has not provided that information, the foster carer does so no later than 30 January 2006.

(c) The local authority must carry out its duties under regulation 7 of the relevant Children (Private Arrangements for Fostering) Regulations 2005 no later than 7 February 2006.

(d) In relation to subsequent visits and for the purposes of regulation 8 of the Children (Private Arrangements for Fostering) Regulations and the corresponding Welsh regulations, the private fostering arrangement is treated as beginning on 30 December 2005.

13. Adoption Agencies

The 2002 Act makes extensive provisions, including those contained in regulations, in relation to the facilities to be provided by local authorities as adoption support services. These are discussed in Chapter 17. These were to be provided as part of the service to be maintained under section 1(1) of the Adoption Act 1976. The 2005 regulations, made under the 2002 Act, provide for the revocation of previous regulations and for transitional provisions. Schedule 5 to the Act repeals the whole of the 1976 Act except for part 4 and paragraph 6 of schedule 2. Parts 1 to 4 of the Voluntary Adoption Agencies and Adoption Agencies (Miscellaneous Amendments) Regulations 2003 (SI 2003 No. 367) are unaffected by the repeal of the Adoption Act 1976.

Article 3(1) of the Transitional and Savings Provisions Order provides that, as a general rule, where, on 30 December 2005, a case is in progress, any action or decision taken before that date under the 2003 Regulations must be treated as if it were an action or decision taken under the corresponding provision of the Adoption Agencies Regulations 2005 (SI 2005 No. 389) or the Adoption Agencies (Wales) Regulations 2005 (SI 2005 No. 1514, W.95).

This rule is subject to the following exceptions:

(a) Where, on 30 December 2005, an adoption panel has considered but not decided whether adoption is in the best interest of a child, whether a prospective adopter is suitable to adopt a child or whether a child should be placed for adoption with a particular prospective adopter, the 1983 Regulations continue to apply for the purposes of making that decision (article 3(3)). The process thereafter is governed by the 2003 regulations.

(b) Where the adoption agency is minded to make a decision as to a prospective adopter's suitability to adopt a child, the 2003 regulations and the Independent Review of Determinations (Adoption) Regulations 2004 continue to apply for the purposes of making representations or reviewing any qualifying determination in relation to that decision. In this event the time limits of twenty-eight days and seven days specified in regulation 11A of the 1983 Regulations are increased to forty working days and ten days respectively (article 3(4) and (5)).

(c) Where an adoption agency has made a decision, whether before 30 December 2005 or on or after that date, following a decision made by an adoption panel before 30 December 2005, that a prospective adopter is suitable to adopt a particular child, the 2003 Regulations continue to apply in relation to placing the child with that prospective adopter. Section 18 of the Adoption and Children Act 2002 does not apply to such a placement. Any such placement must be treated as if it were made under the Adoption Agencies Regulations 2005 or the Adoption Agencies (Wales) Regulations 2005 (article 3(6)).

(d) Where a child is placed for adoption by an adoption agency before 30 December 2005, or the situation is as under (c) above, section 22 of the 2002 Act, which requires the adoption agency to apply for a placement order, does not apply (article 3(7)).

Records and disclosure of information
In the case of a person adopted before 30 December 2005, the Adoption Agencies Regulations 1983 continue to have effect in so far as they relate to the retention, storage, transfer and disclosure of information concerning that person's adoption; section 9 of the Adoption Act 1976 continues to have effect for the purposes of amending or revoking those regulations (article 13, Transitional and Savings Provisions Order).

Adoption panels
All members of the existing panels ceased to hold office on 30 December 2005 (regulation 10(1), Adoption Agencies Regulations 2005). Adoption agencies must establish a new panel in accordance with the 2005 regulations. See Chapter 16, page 194.

Medical adviser
A medical adviser nominated under the 1983 regulations is treated as if appointed under the 2005 regulations, by virtue of schedule 4, paragraph 1, to the 2002 Act.

14. Adoption Support Services

In relation to adoption support services the Adoption Support Services Regulations 2005 (SI 2005 No. 691), regulation 24, and the Adoption Support Services (Local Authorities) (Wales) Regulations 2005 (SI 2005 No. 1512, W. 116), regulation 18, make the following provisions:

(a) the Adoption Allowance Regulations 1991, the Adoption Support Services (Local Authorities) (England) Regulations 2003 and the Adoption Support Services (Local Authorities) (Wales) Regulations 2004 are revoked;

(b) the following are treated, with effect from 30 December 2005, as an assessment plan or service under the 2005 regulations: any assessment which was requested or being prepared, and any plan or adoption service or review which was in the course of preparation, or in place or being provided under the 2003 or 2004 regulations as the case may be;

(c) in relation to adoption support agencies, regulation 35 of the Adoption Support Agencies (Wales) Regulations provides that an adoption agency which, immediately before 30 December 2005, was carrying on or managing an agency may continue to carry on or to manage the agency without being registered under the Care Standards Act 2000 during the period of three months beginning with that date and if, within that period, application is made for registration, until the application is finally disposed of or withdrawn. "Finally disposed of" means twenty working days following the grant or refusal of registration, and, if an appeal is made, the date when the appeal is finally determined or abandoned.

15. Independent Review of Determinations

The right to an independent review of determinations made by a local authority in relation to adoption was inserted into section 9 of the Adoption Act 1976 as section 9A and came into force on 1 April 2004. Regulations made under this provision are considered in Chapter 16.

16. Venue

The Children (Allocation of Proceedings) Order 1991 (SI 1991 No. 1677 as amended), and the Children (Allocation of Proceedings) (Amendment No. 2) Order 2005 (SI 2005 No. 2797) contain transitional provisions on the allocation of proceedings. See Chapter 25, page 380.

Chapter 25

Procedure

1. Introduction

The Family Procedure (Adoption) Rules 2005 (SI 2005 No. 2795) introduce a new procedural code. They apply a unified procedure to be followed in the High Court, the county court and the magistrates' courts. Many of the rules are similar, and in some instances identical, to the Civil Procedure Rules 1998 (SI 1998 No. 3132) and therefore a standardised procedure is, where appropriate, in place.

The Family Procedure (Adoption) Rules 2005 provide for proceedings under the Children and Adoption Act 2002 to be subject to an overriding objective, which is to enable courts to deal with cases justly, having regard to the welfare issues involved.

Like the Civil Procedure Rules, the Family Procedure (Adoption) Rules 2005 are to be accompanied by practice directions, which will contain further details and will evolve over time. They will have mandatory effect. At the time of writing (November 2005), it is understood that practice directions on the following subjects are to be issued:

- hearings by a single justice of the peace (Part 2, rule 7(1)(c)(ii)(bb));
- court documents (Part 2, rule 9(4));
- civil restraint orders (Part 3, rule 16);
- forms (Part 4, rule 17 and Part 5, rule 28);
- who receives a copy of the application form for orders in proceedings (Part 5 rule 24(1)(b)(ii));
- the first directions hearing – adoptions with a foreign element (Part 5, rule 26(3));
- reports by the adoption agency or local authority (Part 5, rule 29(3));
- reports by registered medical practitioners ("health reports") (Part 5, rule 30(2));
- service (Part 6, section 1);
- service out of the jurisdiction (Part 6, section 2);
- litigation friends (Part 7, section 1);
- communication of information relating to proceedings (Part 8, rule

78(1)(b));
- disclosing information to adopted adult (Part 8, rule 84(1)(d));
- other applications in proceedings (Part 9);
- alternative procedures for applications (Part 10);
- human rights, joining the Crown (Part 13);
- interim injunctions (Part 14);
- evidence (Part 15);
- depositions and court attendance by witnesses (Part 16);
- experts (Part 17);
- change of solicitor (Part 18);
- appeals (Part 19).

The information given in this chapter is based on the 2002 Act and the 2005 rules, and must be read subject to the provisions of the practice directions. The equivalent provisions in the Civil Procedure Rules may provide guidance.

2. Overriding Objective and Case Management

In dealing with any application before it, when it exercises any power given to it by the rules or interprets any rule, the court must apply the overriding objective to deal with the case justly, having regard to the welfare issues involved (rule 1). This requires the court to have regard to the welfare checklist in the Children Act 1989 Act or the Adoption and Children Act 2002, as appropriate. In many cases there are competing interests, and the rights of all parties must be considered before striking a balance between those interests. The rights under the European Convention on Human Rights need to be considered also. Brooke LJ, in *Goode v Martin* [2001] EWCA Civ 1899, [2002] 1 WLR 1828, [2002] 1 All ER 620, stated:

"We now possess more tools for enabling us to do justice than were available before April 1999. Since then, the Civil Procedure Rules and the provisions of the 1998 Act [the Human Rights Act] have come into force. By the former we must seek to give effect to the overriding objective of dealing with cases justly when we interpret any rule (see CPR 1.2(b)). By the latter we must read and give effect to subordinate legislation, so far as it is possible to do so, in a way which is compatible with the Convention rights set out in schedule 1 to the Act (see section 3(1) of the 1998 Act)."

See also *Re B (Disclosure of Other Parties)* [2001] 2 FLR 1017, where Mumby J struck a balance between the competing rights of the father to a fair trial, and the rights of the mother and the children to family and privacy, and applied the principles set out in the House of Lords decision in *Re D (Minors)* [1996] AC 593, [1995] 3 WLR 483, [1995] 4 All ER 385, [1995] 2 FLR 687 .

Rule 1(2) of the Family Procedure (Adoption) Rules provides that dealing with the case justly includes:

(a) ensuring that it is dealt with expeditiously and fairly;

(b) dealing with the case in ways which are proportionate to the nature, importance and complexity of the issues;

(c) ensuring that the parties are on an equal footing;

(d) saving expense; and

(e) allotting to it an appropriate share of the court's resources, while taking into account the need to allot resources to other cases.

The issue of dealing with the case expeditiously and fairly may arise where a parent makes an application late in the proceedings, perhaps for further assessments to enable him to care for the child, or where an application is made for permission to oppose an application for a placement order or an adoption order.

The parties and their legal representatives must assist the court to further the overriding objective by ensuring that the court's management of the case is complied with. See rule 3. They are required to cooperate with each other and with the court in fixing a timetable and adhering to it, so that a trial date is honoured. Where experts are instructed, their availability will affect case management, and parties and their legal advisers should cooperate with the court to avoid delay, particularly bearing in mind the principle in section 1(3) of the 2002 Act (see pages 122 to 123). The cost to the Legal Services Commission is also a relevant consideration. The court's duty to be proactive is further emphasised in that active management of a case includes (see rule 4(1)):

(a) encouraging the parties to cooperate with each other in the conduct of the proceedings;

(b) identifying at an early stage the issues (for example, considering the range of options within the extended family) and who should be a party to the proceedings;

(c) deciding promptly which issues need full investigation and hearing and which do not; and the procedure to be followed in the case;

(d) deciding the order in which the issues are to be resolved;

(e) encouraging the parties to use an alternative dispute resolution procedure if the court considers it appropriate (on issues of contact, for instance), and facilitating the use of such procedure;

(f) helping the parties to settle the whole or part of the case;

(g) fixing timetables or otherwise controlling the progress of the case (as applies in all public law cases);

(h) considering whether the likely benefits of taking a particular step justify the cost of taking it;

(i) dealing with as many aspects of the case as it can on the same occasion;

(j) dealing with the case without the parties needing to attend at court. This can be done by hearing cases by video link or telephone conferencing. It is submitted, however, that in cases where there are multiple parties, perhaps with learning and other difficulties, sometimes including language barriers, it would be difficult to conduct a case fairly without the attendance of the parties, save in the simplest of cases;

(k) making use of technology; and

(l) giving directions to ensure that the case proceeds quickly and efficiently.

Those who are experienced in dealing with public law cases and the application of the *Protocol for Judicial Case Management in Public Law Children Act Cases* (2003) will not find much that is unfamiliar in any of the matters referred to above.

3. Costs

Unless the context otherwise requires, the Family Procedure (Adoption) Rules 2005 apply to proceedings in the High Court, the county court and the magistrates' courts. In relation to costs in adoption proceedings, the Civil Procedure Rules apply as follows:

(a) Rule 35.15 applies in detailed assessment proceedings in the High Court and the county court, that is, the court appoints one or more persons (an assessor) under section 70 of the Supreme Court Act 1981 or section 63 of the County Courts Act 1984. An assessor is appointed to assist the court, by bringing his skill and experience, in dealing with costs assessments. The assessor takes such part in the proceedings as the court may direct, and in particular the court may:

(i) direct the assessor to prepare a report for the court on any matter in the proceedings; and

(ii) direct him to attend the whole or any part of the proceedings to advise the court on any matter.

If the assessor prepares a report for the court before the proceedings, the court sends a copy to each of the parties, who may use the report in the trial. The assessor's remuneration is determined by the court and forms part of the costs of the proceedings. The court may direct any party to pay into court a specified sum in respect of the assessor's fees, in which case the assessor will not be asked to act until the sum has been deposited into court.

(b) Subject to paragraph (4), Parts 43, 44 (except 44.3(2) and (3) and 44.9 to 44.12A), 47 and 48 and rule 45.6, with the modification that a costs officer in rule 43.2(1)(c)(ii) includes a district judge of the Principal Registry of the Family Division, apply. Appropriate amendments are made to the rule and to rule 48.7(1) of the Supreme Court Act 1981 to include the magistrates' court.

(c) Parts 50 and 70 to 74 of, and schedules 1 and 2 to, the Civil Procedure Rules so far as they are relevant to the enforcement of orders made in proceedings in the High Court and the county court, with the necessary modifications.

(d) Part 47 of the CPR does not apply to proceedings in the magistrates' court (family proceedings court)

(rule 5).

The procedure in relation to special guardianship orders is governed by the Family Proceedings Rules 1991 (SI 1991 No. 1247); see Chapter 4, pages 44 to 45. See also below, on venue.

4. Venue

The Children (Allocation of Proceedings) Order 1991 (SI 1991 No. 1677) as amended, and the Children (Allocation of Proceedings) (Amendment No. 2) Order 2005 (SI 2005 No. 2797), set out the provisions for the allocation of proceedings under the Adoption and Children Act 2002, between the High Court, the county court and the magistrates' courts. They identify the proceedings which must be commenced in the High Court and the magistrates' court. They identify the county courts in which certain proceedings must be commenced. They regulate the transfer of cases between different courts and categories of court. They provide for the Principal Registry of the Family Division of the High Court to be treated as an adoption centre and an intercountry adoption centre.

Transitional provisions

The Children (Allocation of Proceedings) Order 1991 continues to apply to applications under the Adoption Act 1976 for:

(a) an adoption order (section 12);

(b) freeing for adoption (section 18);

(c) the revocation of a freeing order (section 20);

(d) the variation of a freeing order to substitute one adoption agency for another (section 21);

(e) a restriction on removing of child where adoption proceedings are, or an application for a freeing order is, pending (section 27(1) and (2));

(f) the return of a child taken away in breach of section 27 (section 29);

(g) the annulment of an overseas adoption (section 53);

(h) the adoption of children abroad (section 55)

(Children (Allocation of Proceedings) (Amendment No. 2) Order 2005, article 2).

Under the Adoption Act 1976, section 62(3), if the child was in England or Wales, the application was made in the Family Division of the High Court; a divorce county court, or any other prescribed court authorised by rules made under section 75 of the County Courts Act 1984; or in a magistrates' court. The appropriate magistrates' court was the court within whose area the child was, or, where the application was for a freeing order, within whose area a parent (not the guardian) of the child was. A number of county courts on each circuit were and continue to be designated as adoption centres, where applications for adoption orders and related proceedings must be issued (President's Adoption Guidelines Booklet: *Adoption Proceedings: A New Approach* [2001] Fam Law 810). Any of the above applications must therefore be issued at an adoption centre, and any application which affects the original order, for example an application to extend, vary or discharge the order, must be commenced in the court where the original order was made (Children (Allocation of Proceedings) Order 1991, article 4). If the proceedings are issued in another divorce county court, they are transferred to the appropriate adoption centre.

The Children (Allocation of Proceedings) Order 1991, as amended, provides for the transfer of cases between courts horizontally, vertically and downwards. Applications may be transferred to an appropriate court applying the general principle that delay is prejudicial to a child, and the welfare test. A county court may transfer a case to the High Court if, having regard to the welfare principle, it is considered that the proceedings are appropriate for determination in the High Court and that such determination would be in the interest of the child (article 12).

Proceedings under the 2002 Act
The Children (Allocation of Proceedings) (Amendment No. 2) Order 2005 amends the 1991 Order to make provision for proceedings under the 2002 Act, and the amendments made to the Children Act 1989 by section 115, which introduces the special guardianship order (see Chapter 4). It also identifies the county courts which are designated to deal with the more specialised cases with a foreign element. In this regard it creates two distinct classes of county court: adoption centres and intercountry adoption centres. Schedule 3 to the Order lists the following county courts as adoption centres:

> Aberystwyth; Birmingham; Blackburn; Bolton; Bournemouth; Bow; Bradford; Brentford; Brighton; Bristol; Bromley; Cambridge; Canterbury; Cardiff; Carlisle; Chelmsford; Chester; Coventry; Croydon; Derby; Exeter; Guildford; Ipswich; Kingston Upon Hull; Lancaster; Leeds; Leicester; Lincoln; Liverpool; Llangefni; Luton; Macclesfield; Manchester; Medway; Middlesbrough; Milton Keynes; Newcastle upon Tyne; Newport (Gwent); Northampton; Norwich; Nottingham; Oxford; Peterborough; Plymouth; Pontypridd; Portsmouth; Reading; Rhyl; Romford; Sheffield; Southampton; Stockport; Stoke on Trent; Sunderland; Swansea; Swindon; Taunton; Teesside; Telford; Truro; Warrington; Watford; Wolverhampton; Worcester; York.

The following county courts are intercountry adoption centres:

> Birmingham; Bournemouth; Bristol; Cardiff; Chester; Exeter; Leeds; Liverpool; Manchester; Newcastle upon Tyne; Nottingham; Portsmouth.

Proceedings to be commenced in the High Court
Under the provisions of the Adoption and Children Act, the following applications must be commenced in the High Court. If the proceedings are commenced in the county court, they should be transferred to the High Court:

(a) an application for an order under section 84, for parental responsibility before adoption of a child abroad (see pages 324 to 326);

(b) an application for a direction under section 88, that the provisions of section 67(3) (status conferred by adoption) do not apply, or do not apply to any extent specified in the direction;

(c) an application for an order under section 89, for the annulment of a Convention adoption or Convention adoption order; for a declaration that an overseas adoption or determination under section 91 should cease to be valid on the ground of public policy or that the authority which authorised or made the adoption order was not competent to entertain the case; or a declaration or determination of the extent, if any, to which a determination under section 91 has been affected by a subsequent determination under that section (see page 323);

(d) proceedings for a Convention adoption order (see Chapter 23), or an adoption where section 83 of the 2002 Act (restrictions on bringing children into the UK; see page 296) applies (Children (Allocation of Proceedings) Order 1991, article 3A). These applications may also be commenced in a county court;

(e) an application for a direction under rule 108 (see page 205). Such an application may be made, where no proceedings have started, by an adoption agency or local authority, asking the High Court for directions on the need to give a father without parental responsibility notice of the intention to place a child for adoption;

(f) an application where infringement of Convention rights is raised or a claim is made for a declaration of incompatibility in accordance with section 4 of the Human Rights Act 1998 (rule 116). A deputy High Court judge and a district judge, including a district judge of the Principal Registry of the Family Division, is not authorised to deal with such applications (rule 7(2)).

Proceedings to be commenced in the High Court or county court
Proceedings for a Convention adoption order, or an adoption order where section 83 of the Adoption and Children Act 2002 (restrictions on bringing foreign children into the United Kingdom for adoption) applies, must be commenced in the High Court or in an intercountry adoption centre (Children (Allocation of Proceedings) Order, 1991, article 3A as amended by article 7 of the 1995 (Amendment No. 2 Order).

In all other cases the application may be made in the High Court, a designated county court which is classified as an adoption centre or intercountry adoption centre as appropriate, or a magistrates' court (family proceedings court).

The county court
A designated county court is one that is designated:
    (a) as a divorce county court under an order made under the Matrimonial and Family Proceedings Act 1984;
    (b) as a civil partnership proceedings county court by an order made under section 36A, Matrimonial Proceedings and Family Proceedings Act 1984; or
    (c) as both a divorce and civil partnership proceedings court by such orders.
The Principal Registry of the Family Division of the High Court is to be treated as a designated adoption centre and as an intercountry adoption centre (Children (Allocation of Proceedings) (Amendment No. 2) Order 2005, article 16).

The following rules apply in relation to where the application must be issued:
    (a) An application issued in the county court must be issued in a county court which is also a designated adoption centre under Schedule 3 to the Children (Allocation of Proceedings) (Amendment No. 2) Order 2005, article 13(d). If the application is issued in a designated court which is not an adoption centre, the proceedings will be transferred to a convenient adoption centre.
    (b) Proceedings under the 2002 Act (save for proceedings under section 23 of the 2002 Act – varying placement orders) to vary or revoke an order must be made in the court in which the order was made (Children (Allocation of Proceedings) Order 1991, article 4(1A) as inserted by the 2005 Order, article 8(b)). An application under section 23 of the Act for the variation of a placement order must be made in the magistrates' court.
    (c) Any application under the Act to extend, vary or discharge an order, or the determination of which may have the effect of varying or discharging an order, should be made to the court in which the order was made. This is subject to the following exceptions:
        (i) an application for an order under section 8, 14A or 14D (special guardianship order or the variation or discharge of such a order) of the Children Act 1989 as amended, which would have the effect of varying or discharging an order made by a county court in accordance with section 10(1)(b) or section 14A(6)(b) or 14D(2), must be made in a designated county court (Children (Allocation of Proceedings) Order 1991, article 4(2) as amended by the 2005 Order, article 8);

(ii) an application to vary, extend or discharge an order made by a county court under section 38 of the Children Act 1989 (interim care order), or an order which would have the effect of extending or varying or discharging such an order, must be made to a care centre (Children (Allocation of Proceedings) Order 1991, article 4(3)). This provision would apply, for instance, where care proceedings are pending and an application is made for a special guardianship order which, if granted, would have the effect of discharging any interim care order made.

Magistrates' courts

An application under section 23 of the 2002 Act (to vary a placement order) must be made in the magistrates' court (family proceedings court) (Children (Allocation of Proceedings) 1991, article 3(1)(r) as amended by the 2005 Order, article 6).

Applications in pending proceedings

(a) Where an application has been made for an adoption order and has not been disposed of, the following related applications must be made in the court in which the adoption proceedings are pending:

  (i) an application for leave to apply for a residence order by a parent or guardian of the child under section 29(4)(b) of the 2002 Act (see page 76);

  (ii) an application for leave to apply for a special guardianship order, by any person under section 29(5)(b) of the 2002 Act, where a placement order is in force (see page 76);

  (iii) an application for a residence order under section 8 of the Children Act 1989, where section 28(1)(a) applies – that is, where a parent or guardian of the child applies for a residence order, where a child has been placed for adoption under section 19 of the 2002 Act, or an adoption agency is authorised to place a child for adoption, and where leave has been given to make the application under section 28(1)(a);

  (iv) an application for a residence order under section 8 of the Children Act 1989, where section 29(4)(b) of the 2002 Act applies; that is, where, in a pending adoption application, an application is made by a parent or guardian for a residence order, leave to do so having been granted;

  (v) an application under section 14A of the Children Act 1989 as amended, for a special guardianship order where section 28(1)(b) applies; that is, an application by a guardian of the child, who has been given permission to make such application under section 28(1)(b); or

(vi) an application under section 14A of the Children Act 1989 as amended, for a special guardianship order where section 29(5)(b) of the 2002 Act applies, that is, an application for a special guardianship order by any person, where a placement order is in force in respect of the child and the court has given permission to make such an application; or

(vii) an application under section 37(a) of the 2002 Act for leave to remove a child to whom section 36(1)(a) applies. Section 36(1) applies when the child who is the subject of the application has his home with any person ("the people concerned") with whom the child has not been placed by an adoption agency, and the people concerned have: (a) applied for an adoption order or a Convention adoption order in respect of the child and the application is pending; (b) have given notice of intention to adopt; or (c) have applied for leave to apply for an adoption order under section 42(6); and the application is pending;

(viii) an application by a parent or guardian of a child, under section 47(3) or (5) of the 2002 Act, for leave to oppose the making of an adoption order.

(Children (Allocation of Proceedings) Order, 1991 article 3B inserted by the 2005 Order, article 7).

(b) Where an application for a placement order is pending, an application for leave to remove the child from the accommodation provided by the local authority, under section 30(2)(b) of the 2002 Act, should be commenced in the court in which the proceedings for the placement order is pending.

(c) Where an application has been made for leave under section 42(6) of the 2002 Act to allow an application for an adoption order to be made where the child has not had his home with the applicants for the "relevant period", any application for leave to remove the child under 38(3)(a) or 40(2)(a) of the Act should be made in the court in which the proceedings for permission to make the application under section 42(6) are pending.

(Children (Allocation of Proceedings Order 1991, article 3B, inserted by the 2005 Order, article 7).

Where an order is in force

(a) Where a special guardianship order is in force in respect of a child, an application under section 14C(3), for leave to change the child's name or to remove him from the United Kingdom, must be commenced in the court in which the special guardianship order was made.

(b) Where a placement order is in force in respect of a child, the following applications must be commenced in the court in which the

placement order was made:
- (i) leave to apply to revoke the placement order under section 24(2)(a) of the 2002 Act;
- (ii) leave to place the child for adoption under section 24(5) of 2002 Act;
- (iii) leave to apply for contact under section 26(3)(f) of the 2002 Act;
- (iv) leave to apply to change the child's name or remove him from the United Kingdom under section 28(2)(b) of the 2002 Act;
- (v) a contact order under section 26 of the 2002 Act.

See the Children (Allocation of Proceedings Order, 1991 article 3C, inserted by the 2005 Order, article 7.

5. The Transfer of Proceedings

Sections 38 and 39 of the Matrimonial and Family Proceedings Act 1984 do not apply to proceedings under the 2002 Act (Children (Allocation of Proceedings) (Amendment No. 2) Order 2005, article 5).

Transfer of proceedings from one magistrates' court to another
Proceedings under the 2002 Act commenced in one magistrates' court ("the transferring court") may be transferred to another magistrates' court ("the receiving court") if two conditions are fulfilled, namely:
- (a) where, having regard to the principle set out in section 1(2), Children Act 1989 or section 1(3) of the 2002 Act, as the case may be, that delay is prejudicial to the child, the transferring court considers that the transfer is in the interests of the child because:
  - (i) it is likely significantly to accelerate the determination of the proceedings;
  - (ii) it would be appropriate for those proceedings to be heard together with any other family proceedings which are pending in the receiving court; or
- (b) for some other reason,

and the receiving court, by its justices' clerk (as defined in rule 1(2) of the Family Proceedings Courts (Children Act 1989) Rules 1991) consents to the transfer

(Children (Allocation of Proceedings) Order 1991, article 6 as amended).

Transfer of proceedings from the magistrates' court to the county court
A magistrates' court may transfer proceedings to a designated county court, which is an adoption centre, of its own initiative, or on the application of a party. It may do so where it considers transfer to be in the interests of the child, having regard, first, to the principle set out in section 1(2) of the Children Act 1989 and section 1(3) of the 2002 Act, that delay is prejudicial

to the child (Children (Allocation of Proceedings) Order 1991, articles 8 and 17(1) as amended); and secondly, to the following other matters:

(a) whether the proceedings are exceptionally grave, important or complex because of:

    (i) complicated or conflicting evidence about the risk involved to the child's physical or moral well-being or about other matters relating to the welfare of the child,

    (ii) the number of parties,

    (iii) conflict with the law of another jurisdiction,

    (iv) some novel or difficult point of law, or

    (v) some question of general public interest;

(b) whether it would be appropriate for those proceedings to be heard together with other family proceedings which are pending in that court;

(c) whether transfer is likely to avoid delay where no other method of doing so, including a transfer to another magistrates' court, is appropriate and delay would seriously prejudice the interests of the child who is the subject of the proceedings.

The magistrates' court may also transfer to a county court proceedings under the Adoption Act 1976 or the 2002 Act where the above provisions do not apply, if, having regard to the principles set out in section 1(2) of the Children Act 1989 or section 1(3) of the 2002 Act, it considers that in the interests of the child the proceedings could be dealt with more appropriately in the county court (Children (Allocation of Proceedings) Order 1991, article 8 as amended by the 2005 Order).

A county court to which a case has been transferred by the magistrates' court may transfer the case back, if the county court, having regard to the principle that delay is prejudicial to the child, and the interests of the child, considers that the criterion applied by the magistrates' court for the transfer does not apply, or no longer applies (Children (Allocation of Proceedings) Order 1991, article 11 as amended).

Appeal against refusal by a magistrates' court to transfer an application
Where a magistrates' court refuses an application for a transfer to the county court, a party to the proceedings may apply to the appropriate county court adoption centre for such a transfer. The county court hearing the application may transfer the proceedings to itself if it considers that it is in the interest of the child to do so, having regard to the principle that delay is prejudicial to the child, and to the matters set out above.

On such an application the court may, instead of retaining the case, transfer the proceedings to the High Court if, having regard to the "delay" principle, it considers that the proceedings are appropriate for determination in the High Court and that such determination is in the interests of the child. (Children (Allocation of Proceedings) Order 1991, article 9(3) as amended.)

Transfer from one county court to another
A county court may transfer proceedings under the Act to another appropriate designated county court (adoption centre) where the court, having regard to the principle that delay is prejudicial to the child, considers the transfer to be in the interests of the child. The transfer must be to an adoption centre, or to a receiving court which is presided over by a judge or district judge authorised to deal with adoption cases. (Children (Allocation of Proceedings) Order 1991, article 10 as amended.)

Transfer from the county court to the High Court
The county court may transfer proceedings to the High Court if, again having regard to the principle that delay is prejudicial to the child, it considers that the proceedings are appropriate for determination in the High Court and that such determination would be in the interests of the child (Children (Allocation of Proceedings) Order 1991, article 12, as amended).

Transfer from the High Court to the county court
The High Court may transfer proceedings under the 2002 Act to a designated county court which is an adoption centre where, having regard to the principle that delay is prejudicial to the child, it considers that such determination would be in the interests of the child (Children (Allocation of Proceedings) Order 1991, article 13 as amended). If the application is for a Convention order, or an adoption order where section 83 of the 2002 Act applies (bringing a foreign child into the UK for adoption), the transfer must be to an intercountry adoption centre (article 15).

Transfer from the county court to the magistrates' court
A county court may transfer back to a magistrates' court, before trial, proceedings under the Adoption Act 1976 or the 2002 Act which were transferred to it under article 17(1) (see above). It may do so if, having regard to the principle that delay is prejudicial to the child, the county court considers that the criterion cited by the magistrates' court as the reason for the transfer does not apply, or no longer applies because proceedings with which the transferred proceedings were to be heard have been determined; or because the transfer would not accelerate the determination of the proceedings (Children (Allocation of Proceedings) Order 1991, article 11 as amended).

6. Starting Proceedings

There are some six different types of procedure provided for in the Family Procedure (Adoption) Rules 2005. These are:
   (a) Part 5 procedure;
   (b) Part 9 procedure;

    (c) Part 10 procedure;

    (d) withdrawal of application procedure;

    (e) procedure for application for a recovery order;

    (f) procedure for an interim injunction.

These are discussed in turn below. It should be borne in mind that at the time of writing, practice directions pursuant to the rules had not been issued.

Confidentiality

If the identity of the applicant(s) is not to be disclosed in proceedings for an adoption order, an application should be made, to the court officer, before proceedings are issued, for a serial number to be assigned to the applicant(s). The court duly assigns a number (rule 20). The effect is that the court officer ensures that any application or notice sent out does not disclose the identity or likely identity of the applicant(s) or any other party to the application. The proceedings are conducted in a manner so as to ensure that the identity of the applicant is not disclosed to anyone who is not already aware of it, unless the applicant consents to such a disclosure (rule 20(4)).

    Unless the court directs otherwise, a party is not required to reveal:

    (a) his private address or telephone number;

    (b) the address of the child;

    (c) the name of the person with whom the child is living, if that person is not the applicant; or

    (d) in relation to an application under section 28(2) (for permission to change the child's surname), the proposed new surname of the child).

These particulars must be disclosed to the court (on Form A65), but will not be revealed to any person unless the court directs otherwise. Where a person changes his home address during the course of the proceedings, he must give notice of the change to the court (rule 21).

7. Part 5 Procedure

Part 5 procedure applies to applications for:

    (a) an adoption order;

    (b) a placement order;

    (c) a contact order under section 26 of the 2002 Act (related to placement proceedings; see page 74);

    (d) the variation or revocation of a contact order under section 27;

    (e) an order giving permission to change a child's surname or remove the child from the United Kingdom under section 28(2) or (3);

    (f) a section 84 order (parental responsibility order prior to removal of a child abroad);

    (g) a section 88 order (direction by the High Court that section 67(3) (status conferred by adoption) does not apply or does not apply to

any extent specified in the order);
(h) a section 89 order, which means:
  (i) an order annulling a Convention adoption or Convention order;
  (ii) an order providing for an overseas adoption or determination under section 91 to cease to be valid; or
  (iii) an order determining the extent, if any, to which a determination under section 91 has been affected by a subsequent determination under that section;
(i) any other order that may be referred to in a practice direction (rule 22).

Subject to the form of consent by a parent or guardian to an adoption, the prescribed forms set out in the relevant practice direction or otherwise identified, or forms to the like effect, must be used. At the time of going to press prescribed forms have been identified in respect of applications under:

- section 22, for a placement order: Form A50;
- section 24, for the revocation of a placement order: Form A52;
- section 26, for a contact order: Form A53;
- section 27(1)(b), for the variation or revocation of a contact order: Form A54;
- section 28, to change a child's surname: Form A55;
- section 28, for permission to remove a child from the United Kingdom: Form A56;
- section 41, for a recovery order: Form A57;
- section 46, for an adoption order: Form A58.

Application for an adoption order
In the case of an application for an adoption order, the following documents should accompany the application in Form A58 (original plus three copies), but readers are advised, when preparing an application, to ascertain whether any further rules, regulations or practice directions, made since this book was prepared in November 2005, confirm or amend the list below, and to read the notes which accompany the form:

(a) in the case of a joint application by a married couple, a certified copy of their marriage certificate;
(b) if the application is by a same-sex couple, a certified copy of the civil partnership registration;
(c) if the applicant's husband or wife or civil partner has died, a certified copy of the death certificate;
(d) if the applicant is divorced or the civil partnership has been dissolved, a copy of the decree absolute or decree of nullity, or a copy of the dissolution order or nullity order of the civil partnership;
(e) in any other joint application, documentary evidence of the relationship of the applicants to each other;
(f) reports by a registered medical practitioner made not more than

three months before the application is issued, on the health of the child and each of the applicants (such reports are also required in an application for a section 84 order), except where:

(i) the child was placed for adoption with the applicants by an adoption agency,

(ii) the child is the child of one of the applicants, or

(iii) the applicant is a partner of a parent of the child.

Health reports must contain the matters set out in the relevant practice direction (rule 30);

(g) proof of the identity of the child:

(i) the application must identify the child by reference to a full certified copy of an entry in the register of live-births. Where the child has previously been adopted, a copy of the entry in the Adopted Children Register should be attached;

(ii) it is also necessary for a form of consent to identify the child by reference to a full certified copy of an entry in the register of live-births attached to the form; and

(iii) the copy of the entry in the registers of live-births referred to must be the same, or relate to the same, entry in the registers of live-births as the copy of the entry in the registers of live-births attached to the form of consent.

Where the child's precise date of birth is not proved to the satisfaction of the court, the court determines the probable date of birth. A placement order identifying the probable date and place of birth of the child is sufficient proof of the date and place of birth in adoption proceedings and in proceedings for a section 84 order (rule 33).

Where the child's place of birth cannot be proved to the satisfaction of the court, the child may be treated as having been born in the registration district of the court where it is probable that the child may have been born in the United Kingdom, the Channel Islands or the Isle of Man; in any other case, the particulars of the country of birth may be omitted from the placement order, the adoption order or section 84 order;

(h) if the child has been placed for adoption or freed for adoption, a sealed and certified copy of the placement order or freeing order as the case may be;

(i) the consent of the parent or guardian in the appropriate form if applicable; if consent is not forthcoming, a statement setting out the grounds on which consent is sought to be dispensed with;

(j) the appropriate fee for issuing the application;

(k) where the applicant is seeking an order that the consent of the parent or guardian be dispensed with, the statement setting out briefly the facts relied on to support the request, with sufficient copies for the respondents who are to be served with the notice.

Application for a placement order

An application for a placement order is in Form A50. The court requires the completed form and three copies of it. If the child's address is not to be disclosed, the address should be omitted from Form A50 and given instead on Form A65 (Confidential information), which should then be filed. The grounds for the application should be briefly given. For the circumstances in which a placement order should be sought and the conditions which must be satisfied before an order may be made, see Chapter 5.

The documents which should accompany the application include:

(a) a certified copy of an entry in the register of live-births. Where the child has been previously adopted, a certified copy of the entry in the Adopted Children Register;

(b) where a maintenance order has been made in the child's favour, or some person is liable to pay maintenance for the child under an agreement or under the Child Support Act 1991, a certified copy of the order, or a copy of the agreement or the maintenance award;

(c) if a final care order has been made, a sealed copy of the order;

(d) where a contact order or any other order under the Children Act 1989 or otherwise in respect of the child is in existence, a sealed copy of the order;

(e) if there is in existence a parental responsibility agreement or order in favour of the child's father who was not at the time of the child's birth married to the mother of the child, a certified copy of the agreement or order;

(f) if the parent or guardian has given consent, a copy of the form of consent appropriately signed and witnessed;

(g) where a parent, having given consent, has subsequently withdrawn the consent, a copy of the notice withdrawing the consent;

(h) where the the court is being asked to dispense with the consent of the parent or guardian of the child, a statement of facts setting out briefly the history of the case and the facts relied on to establish the grounds on which dispensation is sought (see Chapter 8). Sufficient copies of the statement of facts should be filed for service on the respondents to the application;

(i) the court fee.

See also the notes on completing the form.

Application of the revocation of a placement order

An application for the revocation of a placement order must be in Form A52. Again, the completed form should be filed with three copies, and the following documents:

(a) a certified copy of the child's birth certificate;

(b) a sealed copy of the placement order;

(c) a copy of any previous orders made by any court in respect of the child;

(d) if the child has been previously adopted, a sealed copy of the adoption order and the details of the adoptive parents;

(e) if the child's parents were not married at the time of his birth, a copy of any parental responsibility agreement or order made in favour of the natural father of the child; and

(f) the appropriate court fee.

See also the notes on completing the form. A brief statement of the grounds on which the order is sought should be set out; see page 69 *et seq* for the circumstances in which an application to revoke a placement order may be applied for, and the conditions that must be satisfied for such an order to be made. It should be noted, however, that anyone other than the local authority which is authorised to place the child for adoption, and the child who is the subject of the placement order, must first seek the court's permission to make the application. An application for such permission must be made under Part 9 of the Family Proceedings (Adoption) Rules using Form FP2 (application notice; see further page 415). Where the child has been placed and it is intended to keep confidential the details of the person with whom the child is placed, it is essential to apply for a serial number. The details which are to remain confidential should not be inserted in the application form but on Form A65, which must be filed with the court along with the application. Where a serial number has been given, it must be entered in Part 2, paragraph (e), of the form.

Application for a contact order under section 26

An application for a contact order may be made by:

(a) the child;

(b) the adoption agency;

(c) any parent or guardian of the child;

(d) any person in whose favour there was a contact order under the Children Act 1989 which will cease to have effect on the making of a placement order;

(e) any person in whose favour a residence order has been made immediately before the adoption agency was authorised to place the child for adoption or placed the child for adoption at the time when the child was less than six weeks old;

(f) any person who has had the care of the child pursuant to an order made by the High Court under its inherent jurisdiction, e.g., wardship;

(g) any person who has applied for and been granted the permission of the court to make the application (see page 415).

In the case of any person, for example the prospective adopter(s), whose identity and details are not to be disclosed, the appropriate information should be inserted not on the application form, but on Form A65. In appropriate cases a serial number should be applied for.

The application form (Form A53) should be accompanied by three copies of it, and the following documents:

(a) any contact order made under section 8 of the Children Act 1989;

(b) any residence order;

(c) any orders made under the inherent jurisdiction of the court;

(d) any adoption order made in respect of the child if the child was previously adopted, and details of the adoptive parents;

(e) the appropriate court fee.

See also the notes which accompany the form.

Application for the variation or revocation of a contact order

The variation or revocation of a contact order may be applied for only by:

(a) the child in respect of whom the contact order has been made;

(b) the adoption agency that is authorised to place the child or has placed the child for adoption; and

(c) any person named in the contact order.

Form A54 should be used to make the application. The court requires the original plus three copies. A sealed copy of the contact order in force should be filed with the application. Any other order made in respect of the child should also be attached to the application. See above for the procedure where it is intended that details of the prospective adopters should not be disclosed. The appropriate fee must be paid at the time of issuing the application.

Application for permission to change the child's surname

This application is made under section 28, in Form A55. The completed application form, with three copies, should be filed together with the court fee and any relevant documents. Again, where it is intended that certain details should not be disclosed to the parent or guardian of the child, or it is intended to keep the identity of the prospective adopters confidential, the procedure outlined above should be followed. Where there have been earlier care proceedings, details must be provided and, where appropriate, sealed copies of the orders made should be attached to the application form. Any parental responsibility order or agreement in favour of the natural father of the child must also be attached. See also the notes to Form A55.

Application for permission to remove the child from the United Kingdom

The application, in Form A56, is generally made by the adoption agency or the person(s) with whom the child has been placed for adoption. If the prospective adopters wish their identity kept confidential, they must indicate this and apply for a serial number. Where the child's address is not to be disclosed, Form A65 should be completed and filed. The following documents should be attached to the application:

(a) a sealed copy of any placement order which is in force in respect of the child;

(b) any other orders made in respect of the child (see above). Details of these orders will need to be provided in the application form;

(c) any orders relating to any sibling of the child whether of full or half blood. Details of these orders must be provided in the application form.

The applicant must set out briefly the grounds upon which the application is made and refer to any supporting evidence.

Dispensing with consent

In an application for a child to be placed for adoption, or for an adoption order except a Convention order, or for a section 84 order, where the applicant is asking the court to dispense with the consent of the parent or guardian of the child, the applicant must give notice of the request on the application form or at any later stage. He must then file a statement of facts setting out a summary of the history and the facts relied on for seeking dispensation of consent (for the grounds for seeking to dispense with consent, see Chapter 8). Where a serial number has been assigned, the applicant must ensure that the statement of facts does not disclose his identity. See rule 27(1) and (2).

Parties

The persons who should be applicants and respondents are set out in Tables 1 and 2 of rule 23 of the Family Procedure (Adoption) Rules. these are reproduced in Appendix B at pages 520 to 521.

In addition, a child may be made a party to the proceedings at the direction of the court where the child wishes to make an application, give evidence or make a legal submission which has not been given or made by any other party, or there are special circumstances.

Any other person or body may be made a respondent to the proceedings or removed from the proceedings as a party.

In either of the above cases the court will give directions relating to the disclosure of evidence, documents to be filed and the management of the case (rule 23).

Where the application concerns the adoption of a foreign child by a British citizen, notice of the application should be served on the Home Office.

Issue of the application

An application is issued when the court officer seals, or otherwise authenticates with the stamp of the court, the application form. Other documents which must be stamped are the order, if any, and any other document required to be sealed or stamped by virtue of any rule or practice direction. The court officer may place the seal or stamp on the document by hand or by printing a facsimile of the seal on the document, whether electronically or otherwise. The document purporting to bear the court's seal or stamp is admissible in evidence without further proof. Practice directions are expected to make further provisions relating to court documents (rule 9).

Definitions

Rule 24 (see below) refers to the steps that the court and court officer are required to take as soon as practicable after the application is issued. A "court officer" means, in the High Court and a county court, a member of staff; and in the magistrates' court, the designated officer (rule 6(1)).

Where the rules or a practice direction require "the court" to perform any act, then, except where any rule, practice direction, other enactment or the Family Proceedings (Allocation of Judiciary) Directions [1999] 2 FLR 799 provides otherwise, that act may be performed:

(a) in relation to proceedings in the High Court or in a district registry, by any judge or district judge of that court, including a district judge of the Principal Registry of the Family Division. The Family Proceedings (Allocation of Judiciary) Directions provide that circuit judges, deputy circuit judges, recorders (subject to certain exceptions), district judges and deputy district judges must be nominated as judges to whom adoption proceedings may be allocated by the President of the Family Division;

(b) in relation to proceedings in the county court, by any judge or district judge, including a district judge of the Principal Registry of the Family Division when the Principal Registry is treated as if it were a county court; and

(c) in relation to proceedings in a magistrates' court:

(i) by any family proceedings court constituted in accordance with sections 66 and 67 of the Magistrates' Courts Act 1980;

(ii) by a single justice of the peace who is a member of the family panel, where an application without notice is made under section 41(2) for a recovery order and in accordance with the relevant practice direction.

The Justices' Clerks Rules 2005 (SI 2005 No. 545) as amended by the Justices' Clerks (Amendment) Rules 2005 (SI 2005 No. 2796) make provision for a justices' clerk or assistant clerk to carry out certain functions of a single justice of the peace.

A deputy High Court judge and a district judge, including a district judge of the Principal Registry of the Family Division, may not try a claim for a declaration of incompatibility pursuant to section 4 of the Human Rights Act 1998.

Steps to be taken by the court

As soon as practicable after the application is issued, the court is required to consider the following:

(a) if the application is for an adoption order, whether section 48(1) of the 2002 Act applies to the application, and whether it would be proper to hear the application. Section 48(1) prohibits the court from hearing an application for an adoption order in relation to a child where a previous application for an adoption order, a Scottish or Northern Irish adoption order, or an adoption order in the Isle of Man or any of the Channel Islands was made in respect of the child by the same person and was refused by any court, unless for any other reason it is proper to hear the case;

(b) whether to give directions as provided by rule 26, instead of setting a date for a first directions hearing;

(c) whether to set a date for the first directions hearing;

(d) whether to appoint a guardian in accordance with rule 59. If the application is opposed, the court appoints a children's guardian, unless it is satisfied that it is not necessary to do so to safeguard the interest of the child;

(e) whether to appoint a reporting officer in accordance with rule 69;

(f) whether a report relating to the welfare of the child is required, and if so, request a report in accordance with rule 73;

(g) where a request has been made that the consent of a parent should be dispensed with on the ground that the parent is incapable of giving consent, then unless a litigation friend has already been appointed, whether to appoint a litigation friend (see page 411) under rule 55(1), or give directions for the making of an application to appoint a litigation friend (rule 27(4)). This may be relevant where, for example, there have been care proceedings and the parent was represented by a litigation friend because of incapacity and the court then had a medical, psychiatric and or psychological report on the parent to support the case;

(h) whether to set a date for the hearing of the application;

(i) whether to do anything else that may be set out in a practice direction.

In addition, the court (or a court officer; see below) must, as soon as practicable after an application for an adoption order or a section 84 order has been issued:

(j) in a non-agency case, ask a CAFCASS officer or the Assembly to file any relevant form of consent to an adoption order or a section 84 order, and ask the local authority to prepare a report on the suitability of the prospective adopters if one has not already been prepared;

(k) where the child is placed for adoption by an adoption agency, ask the adoption agency to file the relevant form of consent to:

  (i) the child's being placed for adoption,

  (ii) the adoption order,

  (iii) the future adoption order under section 20,

  (iv) the section 84 order;

(l) ask the adoption agency to confirm whether a statement under section 20(4)(a) has been made and, if so, to file that statement. It must also ask that if such a statement, having been made, is subsequently withdrawn under section 20(4)(b), that withdrawal must be filed as soon as it is received by the adoption agency. The court must ask the adoption agency to file a report on the suitability of the prospective adopters if one has not already been prepared.

In addition to the above, where the application is for a placement order, as soon as practicable after the application is issued, the court must also:

  (i) consider whether a report giving the local authority's reasons for placing the child for adoption is required, and if so must direct the local authority to prepare such a report; and

  (ii) direct the CAFCASS officer or the Assembly to file any form of consent to the child's being placed for adoption.

See rule 24.

The court officer must:

(a) subject to any directions given by the court, give notice of any directions hearing set by the court to the parties and to any children's guardian, reporting officer or children and family reporter;

(b) serve a copy of the application form (but, subject to (c) and (d) below, not the documents attached to it) on the persons referred to in the relevant practice direction;

(c) send a certified copy of the child's full birth certificate, or a copy of a certified copy of an entry in the Adopted Children Register, and any health report attached to an application for an adoption order, to: any children's guardian, reporting officer or children and family reporter, and the local authority to whom notice under section 44 of intention to adopt or apply for a section 84 order has been given;

(d) if the applicant is asking for the consent of a parent or guardian to be dispensed with under section 27, inform the parent(s) or guardian of the request, and send a copy of the statement of facts to the parent(s) or guardian; the children's guardian, reporting officer or children and family reporter; any local authority to whom a notice under section 44 of intention to adopt or apply for a section 84 order has been given; and any adoption agency which has placed the child for adoption;

(e) do anything else that may be set out in a practice direction (rule 24).

In addition, if the court has not done so (see (j) to (l) above) the court officer must:

(f) if the application is a non-agency case, ask a CAFCASS or Assembly officer to file any relevant form of consent to an adoption or section 84 order, and ask the local authority to file and prepare a report on the suitability of the prospective adopters if one has not already been prepared;

(g) in an agency case, ask the adoption agency to file any relevant form of consent to the child's being placed for adoption, to an adoption order, to a future adoption order or to a section 84 order, as the case may be. The agency is also asked to confirm whether any statement has been made under section 20(4)(a) of the Act, and if it has, to file it. The agency will also be asked to file any withdrawal of the statement under section 20(4)(b) as soon as it is received by the adoption agency, and to prepare a report on the suitability of the prospective adopters;

(h) where the application is for a placement order, ask the CAFCASS or Assembly officer to file any form of consent to the child's being placed for adoption.

Service of any document which has been issued or prepared by a court officer is served by the court officer, except where a practice direction provides otherwise or the court directs otherwise. Where the court officer is required to serve a document, it is for the court to decide which of the methods of service specified in rule 35(1) should be used (see rule 36, rule 24 above and further page 414).

The court officer:

(a) gives notice of the first directions hearing to the parties and to any reporting officer, guardian or children and family reporter;

(b) sends a copy of the application form, the child's birth certificate, health report and any other document attached to the application form, to the child's guardian, the reporting officer, the family reporter, the appropriate local authority on whom notice of intention to adopt or apply for a section 84 order has been served, and any other person referred to in the relevant practice direction;

(c) if the applicant seeks to dispense with the consent of the parent or guardian of the child, and a statement of facts has been served, setting out the grounds for seeking to dispense with consent, sends a copy of the statement of facts to the persons in (a) and (b) above and to any adoption agency which has placed the child for adoption (rule 24);

(d) informs the parent or guardian of the child of the request for consent to be dispensed with, and, provided the statement of fact is framed so that it does not disclose the identity of the applicants, sends a copy of the statement of facts to the parent or guardian of the child.

First directions hearing

The first directions hearing must take place within four weeks of the date on which the application was issued, unless the court otherwise directs (rule 25). The court may direct otherwise, for example, where it has given directions without a hearing and set the initial timetable for filing the necessary reports. The parties and their legal representatives must attend the first directions hearing unless the court otherwise directs.

At the directions hearing, the court gives directions relating to any of the matters set out above and in rule 26(1) to (3). Thus the court should, as appropriate:

(a) set a timetable for filing any report relating to the suitability of the applicants to adopt; any report from the local authority, children's guardian, reporting officer or children and family reporter; if a statement of facts has been filed, any amended statement of facts; and any other evidence;

(b) give directions relating to the reports and other evidence;

(c) consider whether an alternative dispute resolution procedure is appropriate, and if so, give directions relating to the use of such procedure;

(d) consider whether the child or any other person should be made a party to the proceedings and, if so, give directions in accordance with rule 23(2) or (3) joining that child or person as a party;

(e) give directions relating to the appointment of a litigation friend for any patient or a child who is not the subject of the proceedings unless a litigation has already been appointed (see below, page 411);

(f) consider whether the case needs to be transferred to another court, and if so, give directions for transfer (see above, page 386);

(g) give directions about tracing parents or any other person the court considers to be relevant to the proceedings;

(h) give directions on service of witness statements. The court may give directions as to the order in which witness statements are to be served, and whether or not the witness statements are filed (rule 126);

(i) consider the service of any witness statement;

(j) control the evidence by giving directions as to the issues on which it requires evidence, the nature of the evidence it requires to decide those issues, and the way in which the evidence is to be placed before the court. It may exclude evidence and limit cross-examination where appropriate (rule 123). It may direct the way in which the evidence is to be led. In appropriate cases, directions are made for evidence to be given by video link or by other means (rule 125), for instance, to avoid delay, or to protect the witness or to his identity. (See further rules 122 to 139);

(k) consider whether a witness summons needs to be issued requiring the attendance of a witness to attend court to give evidence or produce documents (rule 141);

(l) consider whether evidence should be given by deposition (rule 146);

(m) give directions on service of documents where appropriate;

(n) give directions on disclosure of information and evidence to the parties. The court must consider whether to disclose a confidential report to each party to the proceedings, and if so, whether the document should be edited to delete any information, particularly information relating to the identity of a person who has been assigned a serial number under rule 20(2) or any other personal matter referred to in rule 21 (see above);

(o) give directions relating to disclosure against a person who is not a party to the proceedings (see below);

(p) consider whether any document or information should be withheld from a party (see below);

(q) consider whether directions need to be given for an expert to be instructed, and if so, give appropriate directions;

(r) set another directions or case management hearing;

(s) if appropriate, fix the date for the final hearing. If the date for the final hearing is not given at the first directions hearing, it may be dealt with at any further directions hearing or case management hearing. Notice of the date and place of the final hearing, and of the fact that unless the person wishes or the court directs the person need not attend, is given to the parties, any children's guardian, reporting officer or children and family reporter, by the court officer (rule 31). The court has the power to direct any person to attend a final hearing (rule 32(4)). (See rules 140 to 145).

At any stage of the proceedings the court may, of its own initiative or on the application of any party, children's guardian, reporting officer, or children and family reporter, set a date, of which notice will be given, for further directions to be given (rule 26(5) and (6)).

Joining or discharging a party

The rules do not provide any criteria to be applied when deciding whether or not to join a person as a party. Case law may offer some assistance. The court is likely to consider the merit of an application and whether the person has a good and arguable case to put forward: *Re M (Minors in Care) (Contact: Grandmother's Application for Leave)* [1995] 2 FLR 86. Whether the person has an alternative view or an option to put forward is an important factor. If he does not have such a view, it may be considered that it would be open to him to give evidence in support of a person who is a party to the proceedings: *North Yorkshire County Council v G* [1993] 2 FLR 732. Where the natural parent does not have parental responsibility for the child there is a presumption that he should be joined, unless there is a good reason for refusing his application; but if the parent applies late in the proceedings, despite having had an opportunity to do so earlier, the application is likely to be refused on the ground that he has denied himself the right to a fair trial and therefore could not rely on a breach of his article 6 right. Any right he may have under article 8 to respect for private and family life must be balanced against that of the child and the child's need for a conclusion of the proceedings and certainty in his life: *Re P (Care Proceedings: Father's Application to be Joined as a Party)* [2001] 1 FLR 781.

Disclosure of documents and information
Rules 77 to 85 of the Family Procedure (Adoption) Rules deal with documents and the disclosure of documents and information. Proceedings under the 2002 Act are held in private. All evidence filed in the proceedings, including the reports of the reporting officer, the children's guardian, the children and family reporter, the local authority and of any expert instructed, is therefore confidential and must not be disclosed to any third party. The only exceptions are where the court gives permission; the court directs otherwise; a relevant practice direction so requires; or disclosure is to a person who is a party to the proceedings, a legal representative of that party, or a professional legal adviser. A "professional legal adviser" means a barrister, solicitor, solicitor's employee or other authorised litigator as defined in section 119 of the Courts and Legal Services Act 1990, who is providing advice to a party but is not instructed to represent that party in the proceedings. The evidence is also disclosed to other professional people involved in the proceedings, any expert instructed on the authorisation of the court, the Legal Services Commission and any professional person acting in furtherance of the protection of children. The latter includes:

(a) an officer of a local authority exercising child protection functions;
(b) a police officer who is exercising powers under section 46 of the Children Act 1989 (the removal and accommodation of children by police in a case of emergency where the police have reasonable cause to believe that a child is likely to suffer significant harm) or who is serving in a child protection unit or a paedophile unit of a police force;
(c) any professional persons attending a child protection conference or review in relation to the child who is the subject of the proceedings;
(d) an officer of the NSPCC
(rule 78).

Where a report is confidential, the court considers whether to permit disclosure of the entire document or only part of it to each party to the proceedings. Where a party has been assigned a serial number, information relating to that person, and in particular information relating to that person's identity, is not disclosed. Generally, a party is permitted disclosure, but only in so far it as relates to the individual concerned. Although the starting point, in considering any application for disclosure, is for all information relevant to the court's decision to be disclosed, this is qualified. Confidential evidence is generally not disclosed unless disclosure is required in the interest of fairness and justice, and provided that disclosure would not result in harm to a child. Any violation of rights under the European Convention is also relevant.

Where disclosure of material to a party may be damaging to the child concerned, the court may direct that the information should be withheld, but such a direction is given only in exceptional circumstances. The question of disclosure has been considered in a number of cases relating to children, for example, *Re B (A Minor) (Confidential Evidence: Disclosure)* [1993] Fam 42, [1993] 2 WLR 20, [1993] 1 All ER 931, [1993] 1 FLR 191 (CA); *Re G (Minors) (Welfare Report: Disclosure)* [1993] 2 FLR 293 (CA); *Re M (Minors) (Disclosure of Evidence)* [1994] 1 FLR 790. In determining an application for disclosure, the court applies the principles set out in the House of Lords' decision in *Re D (Minors) (Adoption Reports: Confidentiality)* [1996] AC 593, [1995] 3 WLR 483, [1995] 4 All ER 385, [1995] 2 FLR 687. Those principles were referred to in *Re B (Disclosure to Other Parties)* [2001] 1017 and *Re X (Children) (Adoption: Confidential Procedure)* [2002] EWCA Civ 828 [2002] 2 FLR 476. The principles in *Re D* were stated in the judgment of Lord Mustill as follows:

"It is a fundamental principle of fairness that a party is entitled to the disclosure of all materials which may be taken into account by the court when reaching a decision adverse to that party. This principle applies with particular force to proceedings designed to lead to an order for adoption, since the consequences of such an order are so lasting and far reaching.

When deciding whether to direct that notwithstanding rule 53(2) of the Adoption Rules 1984 a party referred to in a confidential report supplied by an adoption agency, a local authority, a reporting officer or a guardian *ad litem* shall not be entitled to inspect that part of the report which refers to him or her, the court should first consider whether disclosure of the material would involve a real possibility of significant harm to the child.

If it would, the court should next consider whether the overall interests of the child would benefit from non-disclosure, weighing on the one hand the interests of the child in having the material properly tested, and on the other both the magnitude of the risk that harm will occur and the gravity of the harm if it does occur.

If the court is satisfied that the interests of the child point towards non-disclosure, the next and final step is for the court to weigh that consideration and its strength in the circumstances of the case, against the interest of the parent or other party in having an opportunity to see and respond to the material. In the latter regard the court should take into account the importance of the material to the issues in the case.

Non-disclosure should be the exception and not the rule. The court should be rigorous in its examination of the risk and the gravity of the feared harm to the child, and should order non-disclosure only when the case for doing so is compelling."

In *Re B*, the court considered the impact of the European Convention on Human Rights on the issue of non-disclosure, and held that the parties' rights to a fair trial are absolute, but that the decision-making process, although it must be fair to a party, must also be such as to afford due respect to the interests of the children and other parties and the witnesses safeguarded by article 8. Therefore, a party's right to disclosure could be qualified and may be acceptable if it is reasonably directed towards a clear and proper objective and directed to the pursuit of the legitimate aim of respecting some other person's rights under article 8. A balance would need to be struck in a way which was fair and which achieved a reasonable relationship of proportionality between the means employed and the aim sought to be achieved, having regard to the seriousness of the interests at stake and the gravity of the interference with the various rights involved. Non-disclosure could be justified only when the case for doing so was compelling or where it was strictly necessary, the court being rigorous in its examination of the risk and the gravity of the feared harm to the child or other person whose article 8 rights were said to be engaged. Any difficulties caused by limiting a person's rights to see all the documents must be sufficiently counterbalanced by procedures to ensure that everyone involved in the proceedings received a fair trial.

Re X concerned non-disclosure of information about the prospective adopters to the natural parents of the child. The court held that when determining non-disclosure the issue was one of:

"striking a fair balance between the various interests involved; the interests of the parties; but particularly the birth parents and the children themselves, in a fair trial of the issues, in which the evidence on each side can be properly tested and relevant arguments properly advanced before the court, the interests of the children, their birth family and their prospective adoptive family, in protecting their family and private lives from unjustified interference; and the interests of the children in being protected from harm and damage to their welfare, whether in the short, medium or longer term. Hence, the tripartite test in *Re D* is still the appropriate way of approaching this balance, provided that the relevant interests of the adults are also taken into account" (Hale LJ, as she then was).

The welfare of the child is not the paramount consideration (*Re M* above). The court will need to strike a balance between welfare and other considerations and the need to ensure a fair trial. In *Re B, R and C (Children)*

(Care: Duty of Disclosure: Appeals) [2002] EWCA Civ 1825, [2003] Fam Law 305, the Court of Appeal emphasised that the court should withhold evidence from another party if such disclosure would be so detrimental to the child as to outweigh the normal requirement of a fair trial. It is, however, important to ensure that notice of the application to withhold information is given to the party who would be affected by such an order, and he should be given the opportunity to make representations to the court. Consideration should be given to whether the material could be disclosed initially to counsel to consider whether a further application is necessary (see *Official Solicitor v K* [1965] AC 201, [1963] 3 WLR 408, [1963] 3 All ER 191, (1963) 1 FL Rep 520).

Documents held by the court
Except as provided in the Family Procedure (Adoption) Rules, any practice direction or any direction given by the court, no document or order held by the court in proceedings under the 2002 Act is open to inspection by any person. No copy of any such document or order, or of an extract from any such document or order, may be taken or given to any person. The duty of confidentiality extends to any document in the custody or possession of the adoption agency which does not form part of the proceedings, as the agency is required by the Adoption Agencies Regulations to maintain the confidentiality, safekeeping and security of any adoption information (see pages 169 and 374).

Disclosure by a person not a party to the proceedings
The court may direct disclosure by a person who is not a party to the proceedings, provided evidence is adduced to justify such disclosure. Disclosure may be directed where the documents in question are likely to support the case of the applicant or adversely affect the case of one of the other parties to the proceedings, and disclosure is necessary in order to dispose fairly of the application or to save costs. See rule 79. An example of the circumstances in which such a direction may be made would be where relevant evidence is held by the police. Save in the magistrates' court, this rule does not limit any other power the court may have to order disclosure before proceedings are started and against a person who is not a party to the proceedings.

Cases decided under the Children Act 1989, where the court has determined the issue of obtaining evidence from non-parties, may also be of assistance.

Where an order under rule 79 is made, it should:
(a) specify the documents or class(es) of document which the person to whom the order is directed is required to disclose;
(b) direct him to specify those documents which are no longer in his control, or in respect of which he claims a right or duty to withhold

inspection;
(c) require the person to indicate what has happened to any documents which are no longer in his control; and
(d) specify the time and place for disclosure and inspection (rule 79(4)).

Public interest immunity
A person may apply to withhold inspection or disclosure of a document on the ground that disclosure would damage the public interest. The limits of public interest immunity are not clear and the categories of document to which the immunity may extend may vary according to the circumstances. This type of application may be dealt with without notice to any other person, and is confidential. The person seeking to make such a claim must state in writing that he has such a right or duty, and the grounds upon which he claims that right or duty. On such an application, the court may direct the person seeking the order for non-disclosure to produce the document to the court and invite any person, whether or not a party, to make representations. See rule 81. Any order made on such an application must not, unless the court otherwise directs, be served on any other person and is not open to inspection by any other person.

Experts
No party may call an expert to give evidence or put in an expert's report without the permission of the court (rule 157). Any application to adduce such evidence must identify the expert, where practicable, the field in which the expert's evidence is required and the likely fees and expenses of the expert. In most cases the court directs that a single joint expert be instructed under rule 160. The procedure for instructing the single joint expert is set out in rules 159, 161 to 167. The expert, whether instructed jointly or not, has a duty to help the court on the matters within his expertise, and this duty overrides any obligation to the person who has instructed him or by whom he is paid (rule 156). The guidance issued on the Protocol for Judicial Case Management in Public Law Cases should be followed where appropriate.

In evaluating the evidence of a medical expert, particularly relating to injury, guidelines given following the case of *R v Cannings* [2004] EWCA Crim 1, [2004] 1 WLR 2607, [2004] 1 All ER 725 should be applied.

Reports by the adoption agency or local authority
The adoption agency or local authority must file the report on the suitability of the applicant to adopt a child. If it has not already been filed, the court will give a direction setting out the time within which the report should be filed. The report must cover the matters specified in the relevant practice direction and any other matter as the court may direct. This report is confidential, but will be disclosed to the children's guardian, the reporting officer and the

children and family reporter (rule 29).

The guardian
In applications for a placement order, an adoption order or a section 84 order, the court appoints a children's guardian where the child is a party to the proceedings, unless it is satisfied that it is not necessary to do so (for example where the parent consents to the application). A guardian should be appointed as soon as practicable after the application is made (rule 24). At any stage of the proceedings the court may appoint a children's guardian of its own initiative or on the application of any party to the proceedings (rule 59). A court should grant such an application unless it considers that the appointment is not necessary to safeguard the interest of the child. Where an appointment is made, the person appointed in the first instance should be the guardian who acted as the children's guardian in any previous proceedings, for example, in care proceedings; or, in the case of an application for an adoption order, the guardian appointed in the placement proceedings (rule 59 (3) and (4)). If the court refuses to appoint a children's guardian, it must give its reasons for so doing, the reasons must be recorded and CAFCASS or the Assembly must be notified of the decision (rule 60(1)).

The guardian's duty is to safeguard the interests of the child and to provide the court with such assistance as it may require. In this respect the guardian:

(a) must make such investigations as are necessary for him to safeguard the interests of the child, but in particular he must seek to contact or interview such persons as he thinks appropriate or as the court directs, and obtain such professional assistance as is available to him or which the court directs him to obtain;

(b) must appoint a solicitor for the child, unless a solicitor has already been appointed, and instruct him on all matters relevant to the interests of the child, including the possibilities for appeal arising in the course of the proceedings;

(c) give advice to the child as is appropriate having regard to his understanding;

(d) advise the court on the following matters:
  (i) whether the child is of sufficient understanding for any purpose, including refusal to submit to a medical or psychiatric examination or assessment that the court has the power to require, direct or order;
  (ii) the wishes of the child in respect of any matter relevant to the proceedings, including his attendance at court;
  (iii) the appropriate forum for the proceedings;
  (iv) the appropriate timing of the proceedings or any part of them;
  (v) the options available to it in respect of the child and the suitability of each such option, including what order should be

made in determining the application;

  (vi) any other matter on which the court seeks advice or of which he considers that the court should be informed.

  (vii) where it appears to the guardian that the child is instructing his own solicitor or intends to conduct and is capable of conducting the proceedings on his own behalf, he must inform the court of that fact. In this event the role of the guardian will be confined to the matters referred to in rule 64(2), or as the court may direct;

(e) must file a report advising on the interest of the child unless the court directs otherwise;

(f) consider who should be joined as a party to the proceedings to safeguard the interests of the child, and inform the court of the same;

(g) must serve and accept documents on behalf of the child as required by the rules;

(h) must advise the child, if he is of sufficient understanding, of the contents of the documents served;

(i) must bring all records and documents which have been disclosed during his investigations and which he considers would be of assistance in the proper determination of the proceedings to the attention of the court, and unless the court otherwise directs, to the attention of the other parties to the proceedings

(j) must, having regard to the age and understanding of the child, notify the child of the court's decision, and explain to him that decision in an age-appropriate manner

(rules 63 to 67).

The appointment of a children's guardian continues for such time as is specified in the appointment or until terminated by the court. If the court terminates the appointment it must give reasons for so doing so; a note of the reasons given must be recorded by the court or a court officer (rule 61).

The solicitor for the child

A solicitor appointed for the child must represent him in accordance with the instructions received from the children's guardian, unless, having taken into account the views of the guardian and any direction given by the court, the solicitor considers that the child wishes to give instructions which conflict with those of the guardian and that the child is able, having regard to his understanding, to give such instructions on his own behalf. In such a case the solicitor must conduct proceedings in accordance with the instructions of the child (rule 68(1)(a)).

Where the child has sufficient understanding to instruct a solicitor and wishes to do so, the solicitor must receive instructions from the child. Where a guardian has not been appointed and the child fails to give instructions, the solicitor must conduct the case in furtherance of the child's best interests (rule 68(1)(b) and (c)).

A child who is of sufficient understanding may apply to the court for the appointment of a solicitor, or an order terminating the appointment of his solicitor. In such an event, the solicitor and the children's guardian must be given an opportunity to make representations. The children's guardian also has similar rights. The rule does not make any provision on how the representation should be made. It is therefore open to the court to determine whether any such representation should be given orally or in writing, and when it should be made. The court must give its reasons for making or refusing the order sought (rule 68(3) and (4)). This rule mirrors rule 4.12(5) of the Family Proceedings Rules 1991.

The child's understanding

The rules refer, in a number of instances, to the understanding of the child. The following cases may be of assistance when the question whether the child is of sufficient understanding arises: *Re H (A Minor) (Role of Official Solicitor)* [1994] Fam 11, [1993] 3 WLR 1109, [1994] 4 All ER 762, [1993] 2 FLR 552; *Re S (A Minor) (Independent Representation)* [1993] Fam 263, [1993] 2 WLR 801, [1993] 3 All ER 36, [1993] 2 FLR 437.

The question of a child's understanding to instruct a solicitor has frequently arisen in cases under the Children Act 1989 and the Family Proceedings Rules 1991, particularly in cares cases. In *Re H (A Minor) (Care Proceedings: Child's Wishes)* [1993] 1 FLR 440, Thorpe LJ gave some guidance on the test to be applied. He stated that a child aged fifteen would not necessarily have sufficient understanding to instruct a solicitor, but that the test was lower than that required under section 38(6) (of the Children Act 1989) which allows a child to refuse to submit to medical or psychiatric examination or assessment. The child had to have sufficient rationality within the understanding to instruct a solicitor, and it might be that the level of emotional disturbance would be such as to remove the necessary degree of rationality that leads to coherent and consistent instruction being given. In cases where the child was intelligent and able but emotionally disturbed, the guardian should be retained so that he could make representations, but it was also important that the child's wishes and feelings were presented.

In *Re S (A Minor) (Independent Representation)* (above), when considering the test under rule 9.2A of the Family Proceedings Rules 1991, the Court of Appeal held that:

"what has become known as the 'Gillick competence' is the appropriate test in relation to the sufficiency of a child's understanding under the Children Act 1989 and the rules. Different children have different levels of understanding at the same age and understanding has to be assessed relatively to the issues in the proceedings. Where any sound judgment on these issues call for insight and imagination which only maturity and experience can bring, both the court and the solicitor will be slow to conclude that the child's understanding is sufficient."

The court also stated that it would not generally allow a child to participate in proceedings as a party without legal representation. The issue therefore turns on the question whether the child has sufficient understanding to give coherent instructions.

In *Re H (Minor) (Role of the Official Solicitor)* (above), it was held that participating as a party goes beyond instructing a solicitor and includes the ability to give evidence and to be cross-examined. Each case is to be considered in the light of all the circumstances. In such cases it was not for the court, in applying the test, to take account of what the court may or not consider to be in the best interest of the child. In *Re N (A Child) (Contact: Leave to Defend and Remove Guardian)* [2003] 1 FLR 652 it was held that the question was not whether the child was capable of giving instructions to the solicitor, but whether the child was of sufficient understanding to be able to cope with the ramifications of the proceedings and to give considered instructions of sufficient objectivity. The nature of the proceedings and the length of the proceedings are also relevant factors. See also *Re A (Care: Discharge Application by Child)* [1995] 1 FLR 599 and *Re C (Residence: Child's Application for Leave)* [1995] 1 FLR 927.

The reporting officer

A reporting officer may be appointed by the court in an application for a placement order, an adoption order or a section 84 order where it appears that a parent or guardian of the child is willing to consent to the application and the parent or guardian is in England or Wales. The same person may be appointed as the reporting officer for two or more parents or guardians. The appointment must be made as soon as practicable after the application has been made (rule 24).

The reporting officer must:

(a) witness the signature by a parent or guardian on the document in which consent is given;

(b) ensure, so far as is reasonably practicable, that the parent or guardian is giving his consent unconditionally and with full understanding of what is involved;

(c) investigate all the circumstances relevant to a parent's or guardian's consent to the placing of the child for adoption, or the making of an adoption order or a section 84 order;

(d) on completing his investigation, make a written report within the time specified by the court in any direction or order;

(e) draw the attention of the court to any matters which, in his opinion, may be of assistance to the court in considering the application;

(f) file an interim report if a parent is unwilling to consent to the application;

(g) file an interim report at any time before the final hearing if he considers it necessary and ask the court for further directions;

(h) attend all directions hearing unless the court directs otherwise.

The reporting officer's report is a confidential document. See rules 69 to 72.

The children and family reporter

In any application for a placement order, adoption order or section 84 order, the court may ask a children and family reporter to prepare a report on matters relating to the welfare of the child. The appointment should be made as soon as practicable after the application is made. See rules 73 and 24.

The children and family reporter must:

(a) comply with any request made to him for a report;

(b) provide the court with such other assistance as it may require;

(c) make such investigations as may be necessary for him to perform his duties;

(d) contact or seek to interview such persons as he thinks appropriate or as the court directs;

(e) obtain such professional assistance as is available to him which he thinks appropriate or which the court directs him to obtain;

(f) notify the child of such of the contents of his report as he considers appropriate to the age and understanding of the child, including any reference to the child's own views on the application and his recommendation;

(g) if he does notify the child of any of the contents of the report, give an explanation to the child in an age-appropriate manner;

(h) attend all directions hearings unless the court directs otherwise;

(i) advise the court on the wishes and feeling of the child;

(j) advise the court whether joining any other person as a party to the proceedings would be likely to safeguard the interests of the child;

(k) consider whether it is in the interests of the child to be made a party to the proceedings and, if so, notify the court and give his reasons for that opinion

(rule 74).

Litigation friend

The information given below is subject to such further requirements as may be set out in a practice direction.

Appointment of the court's initiative: The court will consider appointing a litigation friend for a child who is the subject of proceedings but does not have a children's guardian; a "non-subject" child; and a patient. A "child" is any person who is under the age of eighteen years and who is a subject of the proceedings. A "non-subject child" means a child under the age of eighteen years who is a party to the proceedings but is not a subject of the proceedings. In adoption proceedings, it includes a child who has attained the age of eighteen before the proceedings are concluded (rule 6(1)). A "patient" means a party to proceedings who, by reason of mental disorder within the meaning of the Mental Health Act 1983, is incapable of managing and administering his property or affairs. See rules 6(1) and 49.

The court may, on its own initiative, or on the application of a person who wishes to be a litigation friend or a party to the proceedings, make an order appointing as litigation friend:

(a) the Official Solicitor;

(b) in the case of a non-subject child, a CAFCASS officer or a Welsh family proceedings officer (if he consents); or

(c) some other person (if he consents).

Furthermore, at any stage of the proceedings the court may direct that a party make an application for an order appointing a litigation friend (rule 55(1) to (3)). An application for the appointment of a litigation friend must be supported by evidence (rule 55(4)).

Appointment on application: If the court has not appointed a litigation friend, a person authorised under Part VII of the Mental Health Act 1983 to conduct legal proceedings in the name of the patient or on his behalf is entitled to be the litigation friend of the patient in the proceedings to which his authority extends. If the court has not appointed a litigation friend, or in the case of a patient there is no authorised person under the Mental Health Act 1983 to act as litigation friend, a person may act as litigation friend if:

(a) he can fairly and competently conduct proceedings on behalf of the non-subject child or patient;

(b) he has no interest adverse to that of the non-subject child or patient; and

(c) he undertakes to pay any costs which the non-subject child or the patient may be ordered to pay in relation to the proceedings, subject to any right he may have to be repaid from the assets of the non-subject or the patient. This provision does not apply to the Official Solicitor, a CAFCASS officer or a Welsh family proceedings officer (rule 53).

Except where the application is made by the Official Solicitor, a CAFCASS officer or a Welsh family proceedings officer, any other applicant to be appointed as a litigation friend must file a copy of the order or other document which constitutes his authorisation to act, or a certificate of suitability stating that he satisfies the conditions in (a) to (c) above (rule 54).

Termination of appointment: The court may direct that a person who has been appointed as a litigation friend should no longer act, or direct that the appointment is terminated, or appoint a new litigation friend in substitution for the existing one. An application for any of these orders must be supported by evidence (rule 56). A litigation friend's appointment in any event comes to an end when a non-subject reaches the age of eighteen. In the case of the litigation friend of a patient, who subsequently ceases to be a patient, the appointment continues until the court makes an order, on the application of the former patient, the litigation friend, or a party (rule 59).

The litigation friend of a non-subject child: A non-subject child must have a litigation friend to conduct proceedings on his behalf unless:

    (a) he has obtained the court's permission to conduct the proceedings without a litigation friend; or

    (b) a solicitor considers that the child is able, having regard to his understanding, to give instructions in relation to the proceedings and he has accepted instructions from the child to act for him in the proceedings, and, if the proceedings have begun, he is already acting for the child

(rule 51(1)).

If, during the course of the proceedings, the solicitor acting for a non-subject child without a litigation friend considers that the non-subject child does not have sufficient understanding to participate as a party in the proceedings without a litigation friend, he must inform the court immediately (rule 51(7)).

The non-subject child who has a litigation friend may, at any stage of the proceedings, apply to the court for permission to conduct the proceedings without the litigation friend. Notice of the application must be given to the litigation friend (rule 51(3)). The court may grant permission, if it considers that the non-subject child concerned has sufficient understanding to conduct the proceedings without the litigation friend (rule 51(4)). But if, having given permission, the court considers that the non-subject child does not after all have that understanding, the court may revoke the permission (rule 51(4) and (6)). In exercising its powers the court may require the litigation friend to take such part in the proceedings as the court directs (rule 51(5)). Where permission is revoked the court may, if it considers it necessary to protect the interests of the non-subject child concerned, appoint a litigation friend for the non-subject child (rule 51(8)).

Consent

On consent and the withdrawal of consent generally, see pages 61 to 63. For the role of the reporting officer in consent, see page 410 above. The consent of any parent or guardian of a child to a placement order, or advance consent to the adoption of a child, must be given in the form required by the relevant practice direction, or a form to the like effect (rule 28(1)). Consent to the making of an adoption order or a section 84 order must likewise be given in the form required by the relevant practice direction or a form to the like effect (rule 28(2)). Any consent to a Convention adoption order must be in a form which complies with the internal law relating to adoption of the Convention country in which the child is habitually resident (rule 28(3)). A consent form executed in Scotland must be witnessed by a justice of the peace or a sheriff; in Northern Ireland it must be witnessed by a justice of the peace (rule 28(4) and (5)). Any form of consent executed outside the United Kingdom must be witnessed by any person for the time being authorised by law in the place where the document is executed to administer an oath or any judicial or other legal process; a British Consular officer; a notary public; or, if the person executing the document is serving in any of the regular armed forces of the Crown, an officer holding a commission in any of those forces (rule 28(6)).

Service

A copy of the application and any documents attached to it are served by a court officer on any children's guardian, reporting officer, children and family reporter and the local authority. If the application includes an application for an order dispensing with the consent of the parent or guardian of the child, the parent or guardian must be informed, and a statement of facts (which does not identify the applicant(s)) is filed with the application and sent to the parent or guardian. A copy of an unedited version of the statement of facts must also be sent to the children's guardian, reporting officer, children and family reporter and the local authority (rules 24 and 36). Any other document filed in the proceedings is served by the court officer, except where a practice direction which provides otherwise, or the court so directs (rule 36(1)).

If a party to the proceedings is unrepresented, the document may be served on him either by delivering it to him personally or by delivering it or sending it by first class post to his residence or last known residence. If a document is served personally after 5 pm on a business day, or at any time on a day which is not a business day, it is treated as served on the next business day. If it is served by first class post it is deemed served on the second day after it was served. See rule 38.

If a party to the proceedings is legally represented, service is effected by delivering the document to the solicitor or sending it by first class post or by document exchange to the solicitor's address for service. Where service is effected by first class post, it is deemed to have been effected on the second day after it was posted. Where service is effected by document exchange, it is deemed served on the second day after it was left at the document exchange (rule 38(1)).

For service outside the jurisdiction, see rules 42 to 48.

A notice of hearing must be served on all parties irrespective of whether or not they are legally represented (rule 35(2)).

An alternative method of service may be directed by the court, in which case the direction must specify the method of service and the date the document(s) in question are to be deemed to be served (rule 35(3) and (4)). The court may also direct that service of any document be dispensed with (rule 39).

8. Part 9 Procedure

The information given below is subject to such further requirements as may be set out in a practice direction.

The procedure under Part 9 applies to any application which is made:

(a) in the course of existing proceedings;

(b) to commence proceedings other than those to which Part 5 applies; or

(c) in connection with proceedings which have been concluded

(rule 86(2)).

Applications under the following sections of the Act or the rules are *excluded* from the Part 9 procedure:

(a) section 60(3) (order to prevent disclosure of information to an adopted person);

(b) section 79(4) (order for Registrar General to give information referred to in section 79(3));

(c) rule 27 (request to dispense with consent);

(d) rule 59(2) (appointment of a children's guardian);

(e) rule 84 (disclosure of information to an adopted child);

(f) rule 106 (withdrawal of application);

(g) rule 107 (recovery orders)

(rule 86(3)).

A practice direction may also provide that this procedure may not be used in relation to particular applications.

Much of what is said above in respect of Part 5 procedure applies also to Part 9: see disclosure (see page 402); experts (page 406); the guardian (page 407); the solicitor for the child (page 408); the reporting officer (page 410); the children and family reporter (page 411); litigation friends (page 411) and service (page 414).

Application

Application should be made by filing an application notice in Form FP2, unless a rule or practice direction provides for the application to be made without notice, or the court dispenses with the requirement for an application notice (rule 87). The application must state what order the applicant is seeking and, briefly, the grounds. If the application notice is verified by a statement of truth, it may be relied on as evidence (rule 90). The applicant must file any written evidence in support of the application at the time the application is made, together with a draft of the order sought. Sufficient copies must be lodged for service on each respondent to the application.

Respondents

Where there are existing proceedings, or the proceedings have concluded, the respondents are the parties to the original application. Where there are no existing proceedings, the respondent(s) is as follows:

(a) if notice of intention to adopt or apply for a section 84 order has been made, the local authority to whom notice has been given;

(ii) in the case of an application for permission to apply for contact under section 26(3)(f) of the Act or permission to apply for an adoption order under section 42(6), any person who, in accordance with rule 23, would be a party to the proceedings if permission is granted; and

(c) any other person as the court may direct
(rule 86(4)).

Procedure

A copy of the application notice must be served on each respondent unless a rule or practice direction provides that this is not necessary, or the court grants permission to make the application without notice (rule 88). The application must be served on the respondent at least seven days before it is listed for hearing. The court may, however, abridge time and hear the application if the court considers that sufficient notice has been given (rule 91(4)).

An application may be dealt with without a hearing where the parties agree the terms of the order sought; or the parties agree that the matter may be disposed of without a hearing; or the court does not consider that a hearing would be appropriate (rule 92). In any event, where an order or direction is given without a hearing, the order must include a statement that any party or person affected by the order may apply to the court, under rule 94, to set aside or vary the order, within seven days of the receipt of the order on the person.

Where an application is listed for hearing and the court is satisfied that the respondent has been served, but has failed to attend the hearing, the court may proceed to hear the application in his absence. Having made an order in the respondent's absence, the court may, on application or of its own initiative, re-list the application (rule 95).

Where the court dismisses the application and refuses leave to appeal on the ground that the application is totally without merit, the order must record the fact, and the court must at the same time consider whether it is appropriate to make a civil restraint order (rule 96).

For service outside the jurisdiction, see rules 42 to 48.

9. Part 10 Procedure

Part 10 procedure applies:

(a) where Part 9 procedure does not apply and there is no form prescribed by rule or practice direction in which to make the application; and the applicant is seeking the court's decision on a question which is unlikely to involve substantial dispute of fact;

(b) where a rule or practice direction in relation to any specified type of proceedings requires or permits the use of Part 10 procedure and disapplies or modifies any of the Part 10 rules to those proceedings;

(c) to an application made under section 60(3) (order to prevent disclosure of information to an adopted person) (rule 105);

(d) to an application under section 79(4) (order for Registrar General to give information referred to in section 79(3)); and

(e) to an application under rule 108 for a direction of the High Court regarding fathers without parental responsibility.

Part 10 procedure does not apply to any of the applications listed under Part 9 (see page 415) or where a practice direction provides that the Part 10 procedure may not be used in relation to the type of application in question.

The procedure set out in rules 98 to 104 applies to applications made under Part 10 (see Appendix B, pages 542 to 544). Again, much of what is said above in respect of Part 5 procedure applies also to Part 10: see disclosure (see page 402); experts (page 406); the guardian (page 407); the solicitor for the child (page 408); the reporting officer (page 410); the children and family reporter (page 411); litigation friends (page 411) and service (page 414). Practice directions under Part 10 may provide alternative procedures and should be consulted.

10. Withdrawal of Application

An application may be withdrawn with the permission of the court, but the applicant must file a written request for permission, setting out his reasons for the request. The rules do not identify how this written request should be made. It is likely that a form will be prescribed, as in the case of Children Act 1989 applications, where Form C2 is used. This form requires that the name and date of birth of the child concerned, the identity of the person making the request and the relationship of that person to the child should be set out. The reasons for the request are relevant and should be given. An oral request for withdrawal may be made where all the relevant parties and the children's guardian, reporting officer or the children and family reporter are present. See re *F (A Minor) (Care Order: Withdrawal of Application)* [1993] 2 FLR 9, where it was held that an oral application should not be dealt with in the absence of the children's guardian. If it is not possible to deal with an oral application immediately, the application should be adjourned for a written application to be made and for the court to hear representations. If a written request is made, all the relevant parties are informed of the request and, where appropriate, the court may deal with the request without a hearing, provided the parties, the children's guardian, and the reporting officer or the children and family reporter have had an opportunity to make written representations to the court about the request. See rule 106. This procedure is similar to the procedure in rule 4.5 of the Family Proceedings Rules 1991.

Cases decided under those rules may be relevant to the approach which the court is likely to adopt.

Since the application for withdrawal does not involve the court in considering directly whether a court order should be varied or discharged, the welfare checklist in the Children Act 1989 does not apply: *London Borough of Southwark v B* [1993] 2 FLR 559. The checklist may, however, be used to assist the court in making a decision. The paramountcy test may be a relevant consideration where, for example, the court is considering whether the withdrawal of the proceedings would promote or conflict with the child's welfare. Much will depend on the facts of the individual case and all the circumstances. In *Re F (A Minor) (Care Order: Withdrawal of Application)* [1993] 2 FLR 9 it was held that an application to withdraw an application is a matter which must be considered carefully, and that the court should hear the representations of a children's guardian.

Where an application is made to withdraw the application on the ground that to continue with it would amount to an infringement of the parents' article 8 rights, the question whether such interference is necessary to protect one of the interests set out in article 8(2) of the Convention should be considered (see *Re N (A Child) (Leave to Withdraw Care Proceedings)* [2000] 1 FLR 134).

For the parties to the application, see rule 23, above, page 395.

11. Application for a Recovery Order

An application for any of the recovery orders referred to in section 41(2) may be made in the High Court or the county court without notice, provided that, where the application is made by telephone, the applicant files the application on the next business day, or, in any other case, at the time the application is made.

If the application is made in the magistrates' court, the permission of the court is required to make the application without notice. If permission is granted, the application must be filed at the time the application is made, or as directed by the court.

Where the court refuses to make the order on an application without notice, it may direct that the application be filed, and the matter then follows the procedure set out in Part 5. See rule 107.

The respondents to an application for a recovery order are:

(a) in pending proceedings for a placement order, an adoption order or a section 84 order, all the parties in the proceedings;

(b) an adoption agency authorised to place the child for adoption or which has placed the child for adoption;

(c) any local authority to which notice of intention to adopt or apply for a section 84 order has been given;

(d) any person having parental responsibility for the child;

(e) any person in whose favour there is provision for contact;

(f) any person who was caring for the child immediately before the application is made;

(g) any person whom the applicant alleges to have effected, or to have been or be responsible for, taking or keeping the child

(rule 107(3)).

The application is made in form A57; see the form for the documents which must accompany it, and the notes on completing the form.

12. Application for an Injunction

The High Court and the county court (but not a magistrates' court) may grant an interim injunction, whether or not there has been an application, before proceedings are commenced or after judgment has been given, unless a rule, practice direction or other enactment provides otherwise. A practice direction on interim injunctions is likely to be issued and should be followed.

An interim injunction may be granted before an application has been made if the matter is urgent or it is otherwise desirable to do so in the interests of justice, but in such a case the court may require that an application is made.

If an application for an interim injunction is made without notice, it must be supported by evidence setting out the grounds for the application and the reason notice has not been given. The court may entertain the application if it appears that there are good reasons for not giving notice. In exercising its discretion, the court must apply the overriding objective and the adoption welfare principle.

If the court has granted an interim injunction and the application has been stayed other than by agreement between the parties, the interim injunction must be set aside unless the court orders that it should continue to have effect.

See rules 117 to 121.

13. Application for the Amendment or Revocation of an Order

An application under section 55 of the 2002 Act for the revocation of an adoption order on legitimation, or under paragraph 4 of schedule 1 to amend an adoption order or to revoke a direction in an adoption order (see pages 147 to 148) may be made by an application notice (rule 113). The rule does not indicate the form the notice should take but it is likely that a form will be prescribed.

The court may direct that the application may be made without serving notice on any person, or that it should be served on such persons as it directs (rule 113(1) and (2)).

Where the court makes an order granting the application, the court officer must send to the Registrar General a notice specifying the amendments, or informing him of the revocation of the order and giving sufficient particulars of the order to enable the Registrar General to identify the case.

The court also has the power to correct an accidental slip or omission, on the application of a party, without notice to the other parties (rule 113(4) and (5)).

14. Disputing the Court's Jurisdiction

An application by a respondent to any application who wishes to dispute the jurisdiction of the court to hear the case, or argue that the court should not exercise its jurisdiction, must apply to the court for an order declaring that it has no such jurisdiction, or should not exercise any jurisdiction it may have (rule 115(1)).

The application must be made within fourteen days of the date on which the notice of the directions hearing is sent to the parties. It is likely that a form of application will be prescribed.

Rule 115(2) provides that the application must be supported by evidence which must be filed with the application notice (rule 115(5)), but does not give any further details of the form this evidence should take. The applicant is not required to file any further evidence before the hearing of the application. The rule is silent on the part the parties to the application may wish to take. Where such an application is made, the other parties to the proceedings will need to be given time to make representations and to file evidence. Directions will therefore be needed. It is likely that further provisions will be made in a practice direction.

If the respondent does not make an application within fourteen days, he loses the right to make it later, rule 115(3) providing that in these circumstances he is to be treated as having accepted that the court has jurisdiction to hear the application. There is no provision in the rule for an application for extension of time. A practice direction may, however, make such provision.

An order containing a declaration that the court has no jurisdiction or will not exercise its jurisdiction may make further provisions. Such further provisions may include setting aside the application; discharging any order made before the application was made, or, where applicable, before the application form was served; and staying the proceedings (rule 115(4)).

15. Human Rights

Rule 116 deals with the situation where a person seeks to rely on any provision of or right arising under the Human Rights Act 1998, or seeks a remedy under that Act. Such a person must inform the court in his application, or otherwise in writing. He must specify the Convention right which it is alleged has been infringed and give details of the alleged infringement; and state the relief sought and whether it includes a declaration of incompatibility.

Where a declaration of incompatibility is sought, notice of twenty-one days, or such other period as the court directs, must be given to the Crown. If notice to be joined as party has been given, the Crown or a Minister should be joined as a party on giving notice to the court.

If a claim is made under section 7(1) of the Human Rights Act 1998, that a public authority has acted unlawfully in respect of a judicial act, the claim must be set out in the application form or the appeal notice. Notice must again be given to the Crown.

If the Crown or Minister has not applied to be joined as a party within twenty-one days or such other period specified by the court, the court has a discretion to join the appropriate person as a party in any event (rule 116(5)). A practice direction or rule may provide for, or the court may give directions for, the filing of written statements, affidavits, verification of documents by a statement of truth, or the discharge of any other procedural obligations by an appropriate officer acting on behalf of the Crown (rule 116(7)).

Matters in which issues under the Human Rights Act 1998 are raised must be dealt with in the High Court.

Further requirements are expected to be issued by way of practice direction and should be followed.

16. Witness Statements and Evidence

The provisions on witness statements and evidence in the Family Procedure (Adoption) Rules mirror those in the Civil Procedure Rules 1998, and it is likely that practice directions in relation to the Family Procedure (Adoption) Rules will set out further details. Any practice direction under Part 15 should also be consulted.

A witness statement is a written statement signed by a person which contains the evidence which that person is allowed to give orally. It must comply with the requirements in the relevant practice direction (rule 130). As under the Civil Procedure Rules, the witness statement must contain a statement of truth. Proceedings for contempt of court may be brought against a person if he makes, or causes to be made, a false statement in a document which is verified by a statement of truth, without an honest belief in its truth (rule 133). This rule does not apply to the magistrates' court. Proceedings for contempt may, however, be brought only by the Attorney General or with the court's permission. In determining whether to grant permission to bring contempt proceedings, the court will have regard to the overriding objective, and, in particular, the concept of proportionality.

Where parties are legally represented it is the duty of solicitors to ensure that they follow the Law Society's *Guide to the Professional Conduct of Solicitors,* and of barristers, the rules and guidance in the *Code of Conduct for the Bar in England and Wales.*

The general rule is that any fact that needs to be proved by the evidence of a witness may be proved at the final hearing by oral evidence, and at any other hearing by evidence in writing, but this is subject to any directions which the court may give. Although a witness may give evidence orally, there are requirements that the witness statement must be served before the final hearing of any application. The court will give directions on the issues which it requires to be covered in a witness statement, and the way in which that evidence may be placed before the court. Unless the court otherwise directs, a witness statement is treated as the oral evidence in chief of the witness (rule 127(2)). The court may give such a direction where, for instance, the witness's evidence is contentious and his credibility is contested. The court may give permission for the evidence to be amplified, and for the witness to give evidence on new matters which have arisen since the statement was made, provided there is good reason to do so (rule 127(3) and (4)).

If a party has filed a witness statement which has been served on all the other parties in the proceedings, and wishes to rely on the evidence of that witness at the final hearing, the party must call the witness to give oral evidence and to be cross-examined, unless the court directs otherwise. A witness called to give evidence may be cross-examined on his witness statement whether or not the statement, or any part of it, is referred to during the witness's evidence in chief (rule 132).

In any issue arising about a witness statement and the giving of oral evidence and cross-examination, the court, when making its decision and exercising its discretion, must apply the overriding objective and the court's power to control evidence.

Evidence in proceedings other than the final hearing
In all hearings other than final hearings, evidence is by way of witness statement, unless the court directs otherwise. If all the evidence that a party requires is set out in the person's application form or his application notice and is verified by a statement of truth, there is no need to file any further statement; the person can rely on matters set out in the application form or the application notice (rule 128). A party who wishes to cross-examine the witness may apply to the court for permission to do so. Such an application should be made before the hearing, in order to give notice to the party who is to be cross-examined and to ensure that sufficient court time is allowed.

Witness summaries
A witness summary is a summary of the evidence, if known, which would otherwise be included in a witness statement; or, if the evidence is not

known, the matters about which the party filing the witness summary proposes to question the witness. Unless the court directs otherwise, it must contain the name and address of the intended witness.

Where a party is required to file a witness statement for the final hearing but is unable to obtain it, he may apply without notice for permission to file a witness summary instead. The application for permission should explain why permission is required. If permission is granted, the witness summary must be filed and served within the period in which the witness statement would have had to be filed, unless the court directs otherwise.

See rule 131.

Affidavit evidence

Evidence may be given by affidavit, instead of or in addition to by witness statement, if this is required by the court, or if a provision in any other rule, practice direction or other enactment so requires (rule 134). The affidavit must comply with the requirements in the relevant practice direction. Under the Civil Procedure Rules, extensive provisions on affidavit evidence are made by way of practice direction (see PD 32), and it is likely that the same or similar provisions will be made under the Family Procedure (Adoption) Rules 2005. A person may make an affidavit outside the jurisdiction, but it must comply with the rules and the practice direction, or the law of the place where the person makes the affidavit (rule 136).

Notice to admit facts

A party may admit the truth of the whole or any part of another's party's case by giving notice in writing. A party may serve notice on another, requiring him to admit the fact(s) or part of the case specified in the notice. The rules do not provide any further detail on how this is to be done, but it is likely that a practice direction will make provisions on the form of the notice, time limits and service. The court may allow a party to amend or withdraw an admission made. See rule 122.

Plans, photographs and models

Unless the court directs otherwise, evidence such as plans, photographs or models, which is not contained in a witness statement, affidavit or report, may not be received in evidence at the final hearing unless the party intending to rely on such evidence has given notice to the court, and the court has given permission for the evidence to be introduced.

Application for permission to rely on such evidence must be made not later than the latest date for filing witness statements. If there are to be no witness statements, or it is intended to rely on the evidence solely in order to disprove an allegation made in a witness statement, the notice must be given at least twenty-one days before the hearing at which the evidence is proposed to be put in. If the evidence forms part of expert evidence, notice must be given when the expert's report is filed.

Where the evidence is being produced to the court for any reason other than as part of factual or expert evidence, notice must be given at least twenty-one days before the hearing at which it is proposed to produce the evidence.

When notice of the application is given, the court may direct that every other party be given an opportunity to inspect the evidence and to agree to its admission without further proof. See rule 138.

The rules do not make any provision as to the form of notice, or whether the notice is to be given orally or in writing. It is likely that a practice direction will deal with these points. If not, it would be prudent to make an application for permission to introduce such evidence in writing, accompanied by a notice to admit, and serve it on the other parties to give them an opportunity to agree the evidence, or the introduction of it, without a hearing.

Evidence of finding on question of foreign law

Rule 139 mirrors rule 33.7 of the Civil Procedure Rules. It sets out the procedure to be followed when it is intended to put in evidence a finding on a question of law by virtue of the Civil Evidence Act 1972. A party who wishes to rely on such evidence must give notice of his intention to do so. If there are witness statements, he must do so not later than the latest date for filing those statements, otherwise not less than twenty-one days before the hearing at which it is proposed to put the finding in evidence. Again, there is no provision on the form of notice to be used, but it is suggested that the procedure set out above under *Plans, photographs and models* would be appropriate. The notice must specify the question on which the finding was made, and enclose a copy of a document in which it is reported or recorded. See rule 139.

Witnesses summons, depositions and evidence for foreign courts

The procedure on witnesses, depositions and evidence for foreign courts is set out in rules 140 to 153; see Appendix B, pages 551 to 553.

17. Orders

An order takes effect on the date it is made, or on such other date as the court may direct.

Rule 112 provides that a final order must be served by the court officer within seven days of the date on which the order was made, or such shorter period as the court may direct, as follows:

An adoption order

    (a) on the applicant (rule 112(1)(a);

    (b) on every respondent (rule 112(1)(f);

(c) on the Registrar General; the order served must be sealed and authenticated with the stamp of the court or certified as a true copy (rule 112(1)(b));

(d) on any other person with the permission of the court (rule 112(1)(f));

(e) on the relevant Central Authority in the case of a Convention adoption order (rule 112(c)).

A section 89 order

(a) on the Registrar General; the order served must be sealed and authenticated with the stamp of the court or certified as a true copy (rule 112(1)(b));

(b) in the case of a Convention adoption order or a Convention adoption, on the Central Authority; the adopters; the adoption agency; the local authority (rule 112(1) and (2)(d)); and any other person with the permission of the court (rule 112(3));

An order quashing or revoking, or allowing an appeal against, an adoption order

(a) on the Registrar General; the copy served must be sealed and authenticated with the stamp of the court or certified as a true copy (rule 112(1)(b));

(b) on every respondent (rule 112(1)(f));

(c) on any other person with the permission of the court (rule 112(1)(f)).

Contact or variation of contact order

Unless the court directs otherwise a copy of a contact order or variation or revocation of a contact order must be sent to:

(a) the applicant;

(b) the person with whom the child is living;

(c) the adoption agency;

(d) the local authority; and

(e) any other person with the permission of the court.

Notice of orders

A court officer must send notice of the making of an adoption order or section 84 order to:

(a) any court in Great Britain which appears to him to have made any order relating to parental responsibility for, and maintenance of, the child; and

(b) the Principal Registry of the Family Division, if it appears that a parental responsibility agreement has been recorded there

(rule 112(2)).

Any other order

A copy of any order made during the course of the proceedings must be sent to all the parties to those proceedings, unless the court directs otherwise (rule 112(4)).

Costs

The court may at any time make such orders as to costs as it thinks just, including an order relating to the payment of expenses incurred by any CAFCASS officer or Welsh family proceedings officer. The provisions of the Civil Procedure Rules as outlined on page 379 apply to costs in proceedings (rule 110).

19. Appeals

An appeal against a decision relating to the assessment of costs may be brought only with permission. In all cases, permission to appeal may be required by a relevant practice direction (rule 173(1)(b)). Appeals from a magistrates' court are to the High Court and are governed by section 94 of the Children Act 1989.

An application for permission to appeal must be made to the lower court, if that is a county court or a High Court, at the hearing at which the decision to be appealed against was made, or to the appeal court in an appeal notice. For the procedure and time limits, see rules 174, 175 and 176, and any practice directions made under the rules.

If permission to appeal is refused by the lower court, a further application for permission to appeal may be made to the appeal court (rule 173(3)). The application will be dealt with without a hearing. If the appeal court refuses permission to appeal, the proposed appellant may request that the decision be reconsidered at a hearing. If such a request is made, it must be filed within seven days beginning with the date on which the notice that permission has been refused was served (rule 173(5)).

Permission to appeal will be given only where the court considers that the appeal would have a real prospect of success, or there is some other compelling reason why the appeal should be heard. If permission is granted, it may limit the issues to he heard and may impose conditions (rule 173(6)) and (7)).

On the powers of the appeal court, and the hearing, see rules 179 to 183 and any practice directions made under the rules.

On the destination of an appeal, see the Access to Justice Act 1999 (Destination of Appeals) (Family Proceedings) Order 2005, SI 2005 No. 3276.

Appendix A

Adoption and Children Act 2002

CONTENTS

PART 1: ADOPTION

CHAPTER 1: INTRODUCTORY

CHAPTER 5: THE REGISTERS
Adopted Children Register etc.

Adoption Contact Register

General

CHAPTER 6: ADOPTIONS WITH A FOREIGN ELEMENT
Bringing children into and out of the United Kingdom

Overseas adoptions

Miscellaneous

CHAPTER 7: MISCELLANEOUS
Restrictions

Information

Proceedings

The Children and Family Court Advisory and Support Service

Evidence

Scotland, Northern Ireland and the Islands

General

PART 2: AMENDMENTS OF THE CHILDREN ACT 1989

PART 3: MISCELLANEOUS AND FINAL PROVISIONS
CHAPTER 1: MISCELLANEOUS

Advertisements in the United Kingdom

Adoption and Children Act Register

Other miscellaneous provisions

Amendments etc.

CHAPTER 2: FINAL PROVISIONS

An Act to restate and amend the law relating to adoption; to make further amendments of the law relating to children; to amend section 93 of the Local Government Act 2000; and for connected purposes.   [7th November 2002]

BE IT ENACTED by the Queen's most Excellent Majesty, by and with the advice and consent of the Lords Spiritual and Temporal, and Commons, in this present Parliament assembled, and by the authority of the same, as follows:–

PART 1: ADOPTION
CHAPTER 1: INTRODUCTORY

1   Considerations applying to the exercise of powers

(1) This section applies whenever a court or adoption agency is coming to a decision relating to the adoption of a child.

(2) The paramount consideration of the court or adoption agency must be the child's welfare, throughout his life.

(3) The court or adoption agency must at all times bear in mind that, in general, any delay in coming to the decision is likely to prejudice the child's welfare.

(4) The court or adoption agency must have regard to the following matters (among others)–

(a) the child's ascertainable wishes and feelings regarding the decision (considered in the light of the child's age and understanding),

(b) the child's particular needs,

(c) the likely effect on the child (throughout his life) of having ceased to be a member of the original family and become an adopted person,

(d) the child's age, sex, background and any of the child's characteristics which the court or agency considers relevant,

(e) any harm (within the meaning of the Children Act 1989 (c. 41)) which the child has suffered or is at risk of suffering,

(f) the relationship which the child has with relatives, and with any other person in relation to whom the court or agency considers the relationship to be relevant, including–

(i) the likelihood of any such relationship continuing and the value to the child of its doing so,

(ii) the ability and willingness of any of the child's relatives, or of any such person, to provide the child with a secure environment in which the child can develop, and otherwise to meet the child's needs,

(iii) the wishes and feelings of any of the child's relatives, or of any such person, regarding the child.

(5) In placing the child for adoption, the adoption agency must give due consideration to the child's religious persuasion, racial origin and cultural and linguistic background.

(6) The court or adoption agency must always consider the whole range of powers available to it in the child's case (whether under this Act or the Children Act 1989); and the court must not make any order under this Act unless it considers that making the order would be better for the child than not doing so.

(7) In this section, "coming to a decision relating to the adoption of a child", in relation to a court, includes–

(a) coming to a decision in any proceedings where the orders that might be made by the court include an adoption order (or the revocation of such an order), a placement order (or the revocation of such an order) or an order under section 26 (or the revocation or variation of such an order),

(b) coming to a decision about granting leave in respect of any action (other than the initiation of proceedings in any court) which may be taken by an adoption agency or individual under this Act,

but does not include coming to a decision about granting leave in any other circumstances.

(8) For the purposes of this section–

(a) references to relationships are not confined to legal relationships,

(b) references to a relative, in relation to a child, include the child's mother and father.

CHAPTER 2: THE ADOPTION SERVICE

The Adoption Service

2   Basic definitions

(1) The services maintained by local authorities under section 3(1) may be collectively

referred to as "the Adoption Service", and a local authority or registered adoption society may be referred to as an adoption agency.

(2) In this Act, "registered adoption society" means a voluntary organisation which is an adoption society registered under Part 2 of the Care Standards Act 2000 (c. 14); but in relation to the provision of any facility of the Adoption Service, references to a registered adoption society or to an adoption agency do not include an adoption society which is not registered in respect of that facility.

(3) A registered adoption society is to be treated as registered in respect of any facility of the Adoption Service unless it is a condition of its registration that it does not provide that facility.

(4) No application for registration under Part 2 of the Care Standards Act 2000 may be made in respect of an adoption society which is an unincorporated body.

(5) In this Act–

"the 1989 Act" means the Children Act 1989 (c. 41),

"adoption society" means a body whose functions consist of or include making arrangements for the adoption of children,

"voluntary organisation" means a body other than a public or local authority the activities of which are not carried on for profit.

(6) In this Act, "adoption support services" means–

(a) counselling, advice and information, and

(b) any other services prescribed by regulations,

in relation to adoption.

(7) The power to make regulations under subsection (6)(b) is to be exercised so as to secure that local authorities provide financial support.

(8) In this Chapter, references to adoption are to the adoption of persons, wherever they may be habitually resident, effected under the law of any country or territory, whether within or outside the British Islands.

3   **Maintenance of Adoption Service**

(1) Each local authority must continue to maintain within their area a service designed to meet the needs, in relation to adoption, of:

(a) children who may be adopted, their parents and guardians,

(b) persons wishing to adopt a child, and

(c) adopted persons, their parents, natural parents and former guardians;

and for that purpose must provide the requisite facilities.

(2) Those facilities must include making, and participating in, arrangements–

(a) for the adoption of children, and

(b) for the provision of adoption support services.

(3) As part of the service, the arrangements made for the purposes of subsection (2)(b)–

(a) must extend to the provision of adoption support services to persons who are within a description prescribed by regulations,

(b) may extend to the provision of those services to other persons.

(4) A local authority may provide any of the requisite facilities by securing their provision by–

(a) registered adoption societies, or

(b) other persons who are within a description prescribed by regulations of persons who may provide the facilities in question.

(5) The facilities of the service must be provided in conjunction with the local authority's other social services and with registered adoption societies in their area, so that help may be given in a co-ordinated manner without duplication, omission or avoidable delay.

(6) The social services referred to in subsection (5) are the functions of a local authority which are social services functions within the meaning of the Local Authority Social Services Act 1970 (c. 42) (which include, in particular, those functions in so far as they relate to children).

4   **Assessments etc. for adoption support services**

(1) A local authority must at the request of–

(a) any of the persons mentioned in paragraphs (a) to (c) of section 3(1), or

(b) any other person who falls within a description prescribed by regulations

(subject to subsection (7)(a)),
carry out an assessment of that person's needs for adoption support services.

(2) A local authority may, at the request of any person, carry out an assessment of that person's needs for adoption support services.

(3) A local authority may request the help of the persons mentioned in paragraph (a) or (b) of section 3(4) in carrying out an assessment.

(4) Where, as a result of an assessment, a local authority decide that a person has needs for adoption support services, they must then decide whether to provide any such services to that person.

(5) If–
   (a) a local authority decide to provide any adoption support services to a person, and
   (b) the circumstances fall within a description prescribed by regulations,
the local authority must prepare a plan in accordance with which adoption support services are to be provided to the person and keep the plan under review.

(6) Regulations may make provision about assessments, preparing and reviewing plans, the provision of adoption support services in accordance with plans and reviewing the provision of adoption support services.

(7) The regulations may in particular make provision–
   (a) as to the circumstances in which a person mentioned in paragraph (b) of subsection (1) is to have a right to request an assessment of his needs in accordance with that subsection,
   (b) about the type of assessment which, or the way in which an assessment, is to be carried out,
   (c) about the way in which a plan is to be prepared,
   (d) about the way in which, and time at which, a plan or the provision of adoption support services is to be reviewed,
   (e) about the considerations to which a local authority are to have regard in carrying out an assessment or review or preparing a plan,
   (f) as to the circumstances in which a local authority may provide adoption support services subject to conditions,
   (g) as to the consequences of conditions imposed by virtue of paragraph (f) not being met (including the recovery of any financial support provided by a local authority),
   (h) as to the circumstances in which this section may apply to a local authority in respect of persons who are outside that local authority's area,
   (i) as to the circumstances in which a local authority may recover from another local authority the expenses of providing adoption support services to any person.

(8) A local authority may carry out an assessment of the needs of any person under this section at the same time as an assessment of his needs is made under any other enactment.

(9) If at any time during the assessment of the needs of any person under this section, it appears to a local authority that–
   (a) there may be a need for the provision of services to that person by a Primary Care Trust (in Wales, a Health Authority or Local Health Board), or
   (b) there may be a need for the provision to him of any services which fall within the functions of a local education authority (within the meaning of the Education Act 1996 (c. 56)),
the local authority must notify that Primary Care Trust, Health Authority, Local Health Board or local education authority.

(10) Where it appears to a local authority that another local authority could, by taking any specified action, help in the exercise of any of their functions under this section, they may request the help of that other local authority, specifying the action in question.

(11) A local authority whose help is so requested must comply with the request if it is consistent with the exercise of their functions.

5   **Local authority plans for adoption services**
   (1) Each local authority must prepare a plan for the provision of the services maintained under section 3(1) and secure that it is published.

   (2) The plan must contain information of a description prescribed by regulations (subject to subsection (4)(b)).

(3) The regulations may make provision requiring local authorities–

    (a) to review any plan,

    (b) in the circumstances prescribed by the regulations, to modify that plan and secure its publication or to prepare a plan in substitution for that plan and secure its publication.

(4) The appropriate Minister may direct–

    (a) that a plan is to be included in another document specified in the direction,

    (b) that the requirements specified in the direction as to the description of information to be contained in a plan are to have effect in place of the provision made by regulations under subsection (2).

(5) Directions may be given by the appropriate Minister for the purpose of making provision in connection with any duty imposed by virtue of this section including, in particular, provision as to–

    (a) the form and manner in which, and the time at which, any plan is to be published,

    (b) the description of persons who are to be consulted in the preparation of any plan,

    (c) the time at which any plan is to be reviewed.

(6) Subsections (2) to (5) apply in relation to a modified or substituted plan (or further modified or substituted plan) as they apply in relation to a plan prepared under subsection (1).

(7) Directions given under this section may relate–

    (a) to a particular local authority,

    (b) to any class or description of local authorities, or

    (c) except in the case of a direction given under subsection (4)(b), to local authorities generally,

and accordingly different provision may be made in relation to different local authorities or classes or descriptions of local authorities.

6   **Arrangements on cancellation of registration**

Where, by virtue of the cancellation of its registration under Part 2 of the Care Standards Act 2000 (c. 14), a body has ceased to be a registered adoption society, the appropriate Minister may direct the body to make such arrangements as to the transfer of its functions relating to children and other transitional matters as seem to him expedient.

7   **Inactive or defunct adoption societies etc.**

(1) This section applies where it appears to the appropriate Minister that–

    (a) a body which is or has been a registered adoption society is inactive or defunct, or

    (b) a body which has ceased to be a registered adoption society by virtue of the cancellation of its registration under Part 2 of the Care Standards Act 2000 has not made such arrangements for the transfer of its functions relating to children as are specified in a direction given by him.

(2) The appropriate Minister may, in relation to such functions of the society as relate to children, direct what appears to him to be the appropriate local authority to take any such action as might have been taken by the society or by the society jointly with the authority.

(3) A local authority are entitled to take any action which–

    (a) apart from this subsection the authority would not be entitled to take, or would not be entitled to take without joining the society in the action, but

    (b) they are directed to take under subsection (2).

(4) The appropriate Minister may charge the society for expenses necessarily incurred by him or on his behalf in securing the transfer of its functions relating to children.

(5) Before giving a direction under subsection (2) the appropriate Minister must, if practicable, consult both the society and the authority.

8   **Adoption support agencies**

(1) In this Act, "adoption support agency" means an undertaking the purpose of which, or one of the purposes of which, is the provision of adoption support services; but an undertaking is not an adoption support agency–

    (a) merely because it provides information in connection with adoption other than for the purpose mentioned in section 98(1), or

(b) if it is excepted by virtue of subsection (2).

"Undertaking" has the same meaning as in the Care Standards Act 2000 (c. 14).

(2) The following are excepted–

(a) a registered adoption society, whether or not the society is registered in respect of the provision of adoption support services,

(b) a local authority,

(c) a local education authority (within the meaning of the Education Act 1996 (c. 56)),

(d) a Special Health Authority, Primary Care Trust (in Wales, a Health Authority or Local Health Board), NHS trust or NHS foundation trust,[1]

(e) the Registrar General,

(f) any person, or description of persons, excepted by regulations.

(3) In section 4 of the Care Standards Act 2000 (basic definitions)–

(a) after subsection (7) there is inserted-

"(7A) "Adoption support agency" has the meaning given by section 8 of the Adoption and Children Act 2002.",

(b) in subsection (9)(a) (construction of references to descriptions of agencies), for "or a voluntary adoption agency" there is substituted "a voluntary adoption agency or an adoption support agency".

Regulations

9   General power to regulate adoption etc. agencies

(1) Regulations may make provision for any purpose relating to–

(a) the exercise by local authorities or voluntary adoption agencies of their functions in relation to adoption, or

(b) the exercise by adoption support agencies of their functions in relation to adoption.

(2) The extent of the power to make regulations under this section is not limited by sections 10 to 12, 45, 54, 56 to 65 and 98 or by any other powers exercisable in respect of local authorities, voluntary adoption agencies or adoption support agencies.

(3) Regulations may provide that a person who contravenes or fails to comply with any provision of regulations under this section is to be guilty of an offence and liable on summary conviction to a fine not exceeding level 5 on the standard scale.

(4) In this section and section 10, "voluntary adoption agency" means a voluntary organisation which is an adoption society.

10   Management etc. of agencies

(1) In relation to local authorities, voluntary adoption agencies and adoption support agencies, regulations under section 9 may make provision as to–

(a) the persons who are fit to work for them for the purposes of the functions mentioned in section 9(1),

(b) the fitness of premises,

(c) the management and control of their operations,

(d) the number of persons, or persons of any particular type, working for the purposes of those functions,

(e) the management and training of persons working for the purposes of those functions,

(f) the keeping of information.

(2) Regulations made by virtue of subsection (1)(a) may, in particular, make provision for prohibiting persons from working in prescribed positions unless they are registered in, or in a particular part of, one of the registers maintained under section 56(1) of the Care Standards Act 2000 (c. 14) (registration of social care workers).

(3) In relation to voluntary adoption agencies and adoption support agencies, regulations under section 9 may–

(a) make provision as to the persons who are fit to manage an agency, including provision prohibiting persons from doing so unless they are registered in, or in a particular part of, one of the registers referred to in subsection (2),

(b) impose requirements as to the financial position of an agency,

---

[1] Section 8(2)(d) is printed as amended by the Health and Social Care (Community Health and Standards) Act 2003, schedule 4, paragraph 125.

(c) make provision requiring the appointment of a manager,

(d) in the case of a voluntary adoption agency, make provision for securing the welfare of children placed by the agency, including provision as to the promotion and protection of their health,

(e) in the case of an adoption support agency, make provision as to the persons who are fit to carry on the agency.

(4) Regulations under section 9 may make provision as to the conduct of voluntary adoption agencies and adoption support agencies, and may in particular make provision–

(a) as to the facilities and services to be provided by an agency,

(b) as to the keeping of accounts,

(c) as to the notification to the registration authority of events occurring in premises used for the purposes of an agency,

(d) as to the giving of notice to the registration authority of periods during which the manager of an agency proposes to be absent, and specifying the information to be given in such a notice,

(e) as to the making of adequate arrangements for the running of an agency during a period when its manager is absent,

(f) as to the giving of notice to the registration authority of any intended change in the identity of the manager,

(g) as to the giving of notice to the registration authority of changes in the ownership of an agency or the identity of its officers,

(h) requiring the payment of a prescribed fee to the registration authority in respect of any notification required to be made by virtue of paragraph (g),

(i) requiring arrangements to be made for dealing with complaints made by or on behalf of those seeking, or receiving, any of the services provided by an agency and requiring the agency or manager to take steps for publicising the arrangements.

11   Fees

(1) Regulations under section 9 may prescribe–

(a) the fees which may be charged by adoption agencies in respect of the provision of services to persons providing facilities as part of the Adoption Service (including the Adoption Services in Scotland and Northern Ireland),

(b) the fees which may be paid by adoption agencies to persons providing or assisting in providing such facilities.

(2) Regulations under section 9 may prescribe the fees which may be charged by local authorities in respect of the provision of prescribed facilities of the Adoption Service where the following conditions are met.

(3) The conditions are that the facilities are provided in connection with–

(a) the adoption of a child brought into the United Kingdom for the purpose of adoption, or

(b) a Convention adoption, an overseas adoption or an adoption effected under the law of a country or territory outside the British Islands.

(4) Regulations under section 9 may prescribe the fees which may be charged by adoption agencies in respect of the provision of counselling, where the counselling is provided in connection with the disclosure of information in relation to a person's adoption.

12   Independent review of determinations

(1) Regulations under section 9 may establish a procedure under which any person in respect of whom a qualifying determination has been made by an adoption agency may apply to a panel constituted by the appropriate Minister for a review of that determination.

(2) The regulations must make provision as to the description of determinations which are qualifying determinations for the purposes of subsection (1).

(3) The regulations may include provision as to–

(a) the duties and powers of a panel (including the power to recover the costs of a review from the adoption agency by which the determination reviewed was made),

(b) the administration and procedures of a panel,

(c) the appointment of members of a panel (including the number, or any limit on the number, of members who may be appointed and any conditions for appointment),

(d) the payment of fees to members of a panel,[2]

(e) the duties of adoption agencies in connection with reviews conducted under the regulations,

(f) the monitoring of any such reviews.

(4) The appropriate Minister may make an arrangement with an organisation under which functions in relation to the panel are performed by the organisation on his behalf.

(5) If the appropriate Minister makes such an arrangement with an organisation, the organisation is to perform its functions under the arrangement in accordance with any general or special directions given by the appropriate Minister.

(6) The arrangement may include provision for payments to be made to the organisation by the appropriate Minister.

(7) Where the appropriate Minister is the Assembly, subsections (4) and (6) also apply as if references to an organisation included references to the Secretary of State.

(8) In this section, "organisation" includes a public body and a private or voluntary organisation.

Supplemental

13   Information concerning adoption

(1) Each adoption agency must give to the appropriate Minister any statistical or other general information he requires about–

(a) its performance of all or any of its functions relating to adoption,

(b) the children and other persons in relation to whom it has exercised those functions.

(2) The following persons–

(a) the designated officer for each magistrates' court,[3]

(b) the relevant officer of each county court,

(c) the relevant officer of the High Court,

must give to the appropriate Minister any statistical or other general information he requires about the proceedings under this Act of the court in question.

(3) In subsection (2), "relevant officer", in relation to a county court or the High Court, means the officer of that court who is designated to act for the purposes of that subsection by a direction given by the Lord Chancellor.

(4) The information required to be given to the appropriate Minister under this section must be given at the times, and in the form, directed by him.

(5) The appropriate Minister may publish from time to time abstracts of the information given to him under this section.

14   Default power of appropriate Minister

(1) If the appropriate Minister is satisfied that any local authority have failed, without reasonable excuse, to comply with any of the duties imposed on them by virtue of this Act or of section 1 or 2(4) of the Adoption (Intercountry Aspects) Act 1999 (c. 18), he may make an order declaring that authority to be in default in respect of that duty.

(2) An order under subsection (1) must give the appropriate Minister's reasons for making it.

(3) An order under subsection (1) may contain such directions as appear to the appropriate Minister to be necessary for the purpose of ensuring that, within the period specified in the order, the duty is complied with.

(4) Any such directions are enforceable, on the appropriate Minister's application, by a mandatory order.

15   Inspection of premises etc.

(1) The appropriate Minister may arrange for any premises in which–

(a) a child is living with a person with whom the child has been placed by an adoption agency, or

(b) a child in respect of whom a notice of intention to adopt has been given under section 44 is, or will be, living,

to be inspected from time to time.

(2) The appropriate Minister may require an adoption agency–

(a) to give him any information, or

---

[2] Section 12(3)(d) is printed as amended by the Children Act 2004, section 57.

[3] Section 13(2)(a) is printed as amended by the Courts Act 2003, schedule 8, paragraph 411.

(b) to allow him to inspect any records (in whatever form they are held),

relating to the discharge of any of its functions in relation to adoption which the appropriate Minister specifies.

(3) An inspection under this section must be conducted by a person authorised by the appropriate Minister.

(4) An officer of a local authority may only be so authorised with the consent of the authority.

(5) A person inspecting any premises under subsection (1) may–

(a) visit the child there,

(b) make any examination into the state of the premises and the treatment of the child there which he thinks fit.

(6) A person authorised to inspect any records under this section may at any reasonable time have access to, and inspect and check the operation of, any computer (and associated apparatus) which is being or has been used in connection with the records in question.

(7) A person authorised to inspect any premises or records under this section may–

(a) enter the premises for that purpose at any reasonable time,

(b) require any person to give him any reasonable assistance he may require.

(8) A person exercising a power under this section must, if required to do so, produce a duly authenticated document showing his authority.

(9) Any person who intentionally obstructs another in the exercise of a power under this section is guilty of an offence and liable on summary conviction to a fine not exceeding level 3 on the standard scale.

16   Distribution of functions in relation to registered adoption societies

After section 36 of the Care Standards Act 2000 (c. 14) there is inserted–

"36A Voluntary adoption agencies: distribution of functions

(1) This section applies to functions relating to voluntary adoption agencies conferred on the registration authority by or under this Part or under Chapter 2 of Part 1 of the Adoption and Children Act 2002.

(2) Subject to the following provisions, functions to which this section applies are exercisable–

(a) where the principal office of an agency is in England, by the Commission,

(b) where the principal office of an agency is in Wales, by the Assembly.

(3) So far as those functions relate to the imposition, variation or removal of conditions of registration, they may only be exercised after consultation with the Assembly or (as the case may be) the Commission.

(4) But–

(a) where such a function as is mentioned in subsection (3) is exercisable by the Commission in relation to an agency which has a branch in Wales, it is exercisable only with the agreement of the Assembly,

(b) where such a function as is mentioned in subsection (3) is exercisable by the Assembly in relation to an agency which has a branch in England, it is exercisable only with the agreement of the Commission.

(5) The functions conferred on the registration authority by sections 31 and 32 of this Act in respect of any premises of a voluntary adoption agency are exercisable–

(a) where the premises are in England, by the Commission

(b) where the premises are in Wales, by the Assembly.

(6) In spite of subsections (2) to (5), regulations may provide for any function to which this section applies to be exercisable by the Commission instead of the Assembly, or by the Assembly instead of the Commission, or by one concurrently with the other, or by both jointly or by either with the agreement of or after consultation with the other.

(7) In this section, "regulations" means regulations relating to England and Wales."

17   Inquiries

(1) The appropriate Minister may cause an inquiry to be held into any matter connected with the functions of an adoption agency.

(2) Before an inquiry is begun, the appropriate Minister may direct that it is to be held in private.

(3) Where no direction has been given, the person holding the inquiry may if he thinks fit hold it, or any part of it, in private.

(4) Subsections (2) to (5) of section 250 of the Local Government Act 1972 (c. 70) (powers in relation to local inquiries) apply in relation to an inquiry under this section as they apply in relation to a local inquiry under that section.

CHAPTER 3: PLACEMENT FOR ADOPTION AND ADOPTION ORDERS

Placement of children by adoption agency for adoption

18 Placement for adoption by agencies

(1) An adoption agency may–

(a) place a child for adoption with prospective adopters, or

(b) where it has placed a child with any persons (whether under this Part or not), leave the child with them as prospective adopters,

but, except in the case of a child who is less than six weeks old, may only do so under section 19 or a placement order.

(2) An adoption agency may only place a child for adoption with prospective adopters if the agency is satisfied that the child ought to be placed for adoption.

(3) A child who is placed or authorised to be placed for adoption with prospective adopters by a local authority is looked after by the authority.

(4) If an application for an adoption order has been made by any persons in respect of a child and has not been disposed of–

(a) an adoption agency which placed the child with those persons may leave the child with them until the application is disposed of, but

(b) apart from that, the child may not be placed for adoption with any prospective adopters.

"Adoption order" includes a Scottish or Northern Irish adoption order.

(5) References in this Act (apart from this section) to an adoption agency placing a child for adoption–

(a) are to its placing a child for adoption with prospective adopters, and

(b) include, where it has placed a child with any persons (whether under this Act or not), leaving the child with them as prospective adopters;

and references in this Act (apart from this section) to a child who is placed for adoption by an adoption agency are to be interpreted accordingly.

(6) References in this Chapter to an adoption agency being, or not being, authorised to place a child for adoption are to the agency being or (as the case may be) not being authorised to do so under section 19 or a placement order.

(7) This section is subject to sections 30 to 35 (removal of children placed by adoption agencies).

19 Placing children with parental consent

(1) Where an adoption agency is satisfied that each parent or guardian of a child has consented to the child–

(a) being placed for adoption with prospective adopters identified in the consent, or

(b) being placed for adoption with any prospective adopters who may be chosen by the agency,

and has not withdrawn the consent, the agency is authorised to place the child for adoption accordingly.

(2) Consent to a child being placed for adoption with prospective adopters identified in the consent may be combined with consent to the child subsequently being placed for adoption with any prospective adopters who may be chosen by the agency in circumstances where the child is removed from or returned by the identified prospective adopters.

(3) Subsection (1) does not apply where–

(a) an application has been made on which a care order might be made and the application has not been disposed of, or

(b) a care order or placement order has been made after the consent was given.

(4) References in this Act to a child placed for adoption under this section include a child who was placed under this section with prospective adopters and continues to be placed with them, whether or not consent to the placement has been withdrawn.

(5) This section is subject to section 52 (parental etc. consent).

20 Advance consent to adoption

(1) A parent or guardian of a child who consents to the child being placed for adoption

by an adoption agency under section 19 may, at the same or any subsequent time, consent to the making of a future adoption order.

(2) Consent under this section–

(a) where the parent or guardian has consented to the child being placed for adoption with prospective adopters identified in the consent, may be consent to adoption by them, or

(b) may be consent to adoption by any prospective adopters who may be chosen by the agency.

(3) A person may withdraw any consent given under this section.

(4) A person who gives consent under this section may, at the same or any subsequent time, by notice given to the adoption agency–

(a) state that he does not wish to be informed of any application for an adoption order, or

(b) withdraw such a statement.

(5) A notice under subsection (4) has effect from the time when it is received by the adoption agency but has no effect if the person concerned has withdrawn his consent.

(6) This section is subject to section 52 (parental etc. consent).

21   Placement orders

(1) A placement order is an order made by the court authorising a local authority to place a child for adoption with any prospective adopters who may be chosen by the authority.

(2) The court may not make a placement order in respect of a child unless–

(a) the child is subject to a care order,

(b) the court is satisfied that the conditions in section 31(2) of the 1989 Act (conditions for making a care order) are met, or

(c) the child has no parent or guardian.

(3) The court may only make a placement order if, in the case of each parent or guardian of the child, the court is satisfied–

(a) that the parent or guardian has consented to the child being placed for adoption with any prospective adopters who may be chosen by the local authority and has not withdrawn the consent, or

(b) that the parent's or guardian's consent should be dispensed with.

This subsection is subject to section 52 (parental etc. consent).

(4) A placement order continues in force until–

(a) it is revoked under section 24,

(b) an adoption order is made in respect of the child, or

(c) the child marries or forms a civil partnership or attains the age of 18 years.[4]

"Adoption order" includes a Scottish or Northern Irish adoption order.

22   Applications for placement orders

(1) A local authority must apply to the court for a placement order in respect of a child if–

(a) the child is placed for adoption by them or is being provided with accommodation by them,

(b) no adoption agency is authorised to place the child for adoption,

(c) the child has no parent or guardian or the authority consider that the conditions in section 31(2) of the 1989 Act are met, and

(d) the authority are satisfied that the child ought to be placed for adoption.

(2) If–

(a) an application has been made (and has not been disposed of) on which a care order might be made in respect of a child, or

(b) a child is subject to a care order and the appropriate local authority are not authorised to place the child for adoption,

the appropriate local authority must apply to the court for a placement order if they are satisfied that the child ought to be placed for adoption.

(3) If–

(a) a child is subject to a care order, and

(b) the appropriate local authority are authorised to place the child for adoption

---

[4] Section 21(4)(c) is printed as amended by the Civil Partnership Act 2004, section 79(1).

under section 19,
the authority may apply to the court for a placement order.

(4) If a local authority–

(a) are under a duty to apply to the court for a placement order in respect of a child, or

(b) have applied for a placement order in respect of a child and the application has not been disposed of,

the child is looked after by the authority.

(5) Subsections (1) to (3) do not apply in respect of a child–

(a) if any persons have given notice of intention to adopt, unless the period of four months beginning with the giving of the notice has expired without them applying for an adoption order or their application for such an order has been withdrawn or refused, or

(b) if an application for an adoption order has been made and has not been disposed of.

"Adoption order" includes a Scottish or Northern Irish adoption order.

(6) Where–

(a) an application for a placement order in respect of a child has been made and has not been disposed of, and

(b) no interim care order is in force,

the court may give any directions it considers appropriate for the medical or psychiatric examination or other assessment of the child; but a child who is of sufficient understanding to make an informed decision may refuse to submit to the examination or other assessment.

(7) The appropriate local authority–

(a) in relation to a care order, is the local authority in whose care the child is placed by the order, and

(b) in relation to an application on which a care order might be made, is the local authority which makes the application.

23 Varying placement orders

(1) The court may vary a placement order so as to substitute another local authority for the local authority authorised by the order to place the child for adoption.

(2) The variation may only be made on the joint application of both authorities.

24 Revoking placement orders

(1) The court may revoke a placement order on the application of any person.

(2) But an application may not be made by a person other than the child or the local authority authorised by the order to place the child for adoption unless–

(a) the court has given leave to apply, and

(b) the child is not placed for adoption by the authority.

(3) The court cannot give leave under subsection (2)(a) unless satisfied that there has been a change in circumstances since the order was made.

(4) If the court determines, on an application for an adoption order, not to make the order, it may revoke any placement order in respect of the child.

(5) Where–

(a) an application for the revocation of a placement order has been made and has not been disposed of, and

(b) the child is not placed for adoption by the authority,

the child may not without the court's leave be placed for adoption under the order.

25 Parental responsibility

(1) This section applies while–

(a) a child is placed for adoption under section 19 or an adoption agency is authorised to place a child for adoption under that section, or

(b) a placement order is in force in respect of a child.

(2) Parental responsibility for the child is given to the agency concerned.

(3) While the child is placed with prospective adopters, parental responsibility is given to them.

(4) The agency may determine that the parental responsibility of any parent or guardian, or of prospective adopters, is to be restricted to the extent specified in the

determination.

26   Contact

(1) On an adoption agency being authorised to place a child for adoption, or placing a child for adoption who is less than six weeks old, any provision for contact under the 1989 Act ceases to have effect.

(2) While an adoption agency is so authorised or a child is placed for adoption–

(a) no application may be made for any provision for contact under that Act, but

(b) the court may make an order under this section requiring the person with whom the child lives, or is to live, to allow the child to visit or stay with the person named in the order, or for the person named in the order and the child otherwise to have contact with each other.

(3) An application for an order under this section may be made by–

(a) the child or the agency,

(b) any parent, guardian or relative,

(c) any person in whose favour there was provision for contact under the 1989 Act which ceased to have effect by virtue of subsection (1),

(d) if a residence order was in force immediately before the adoption agency was authorised to place the child for adoption or (as the case may be) placed the child for adoption at a time when he was less than six weeks old, the person in whose favour the order was made,

(e) if a person had care of the child immediately before that time by virtue of an order made in the exercise of the High Court's inherent jurisdiction with respect to children, that person,

(f) any person who has obtained the court's leave to make the application.

(4) When making a placement order, the court may on its own initiative make an order under this section.

(5) This section does not prevent an application for a contact order under section 8 of the 1989 Act being made where the application is to be heard together with an application for an adoption order in respect of the child.

(6) In this section, "provision for contact under the 1989 Act" means a contact order under section 8 of that Act or an order under section 34 of that Act (parental contact with children in care).

27   Contact: supplementary

(1) An order under section 26–

(a) has effect while the adoption agency is authorised to place the child for adoption or the child is placed for adoption, but

(b) may be varied or revoked by the court on an application by the child, the agency or a person named in the order.

(2) The agency may refuse to allow the contact that would otherwise be required by virtue of an order under that section if–

(a) it is satisfied that it is necessary to do so in order to safeguard or promote the child's welfare, and

(b) the refusal is decided upon as a matter of urgency and does not last for more than seven days.

(3) Regulations may make provision as to–

(a) the steps to be taken by an agency which has exercised its power under subsection (2),

(b) the circumstances in which, and conditions subject to which, the terms of any order under section 26 may be departed from by agreement between the agency and any person for whose contact with the child the order provides,

(c) notification by an agency of any variation or suspension of arrangements made (otherwise than under an order under that section) with a view to allowing any person contact with the child.

(4) Before making a placement order the court must–

(a) consider the arrangements which the adoption agency has made, or proposes to make, for allowing any person contact with the child, and

(b) invite the parties to the proceedings to comment on those arrangements.

(5) An order under section 26 may provide for contact on any conditions the court

considers appropriate.

28   Further consequences of placement
    (1) Where a child is placed for adoption under section 19 or an adoption agency is authorised to place a child for adoption under that section–
        (a) a parent or guardian of the child may not apply for a residence order unless an application for an adoption order has been made and the parent or guardian has obtained the court's leave under subsection (3) or (5) of section 47,
        (b) if an application has been made for an adoption order, a guardian of the child may not apply for a special guardianship order unless he has obtained the court's leave under subsection (3) or (5) of that section.
    (2) Where–
        (a) a child is placed for adoption under section 19 or an adoption agency is authorised to place a child for adoption under that section, or
        (b) a placement order is in force in respect of a child,
then (whether or not the child is in England and Wales) a person may not do either of the following things, unless the court gives leave or each parent or guardian of the child gives written consent.
    (3) Those things are–
        (a) causing the child to be known by a new surname, or
        (b) removing the child from the United Kingdom.
    (4) Subsection (3) does not prevent the removal of a child from the United Kingdom for a period of less than one month by a person who provides the child's home.

29   Further consequences of placement orders
    (1) Where a placement order is made in respect of a child and either–
        (a) the child is subject to a care order, or
        (b) the court at the same time makes a care order in respect of the child,
the care order does not have effect at any time when the placement order is in force.
    (2) On the making of a placement order in respect of a child, any order mentioned in section 8(1) of the 1989 Act, and any supervision order in respect of the child, ceases to have effect.
    (3) Where a placement order is in force–
        (a) no prohibited steps order, residence order or specific issue order, and
        (b) no supervision order or child assessment order,
may be made in respect of the child.
    (4) Subsection (3)(a) does not apply in respect of a residence order if–
        (a) an application for an adoption order has been made in respect of the child, and
        (b) the residence order is applied for by a parent or guardian who has obtained the court's leave under subsection (3) or (5) of section 47 or by any other person who has obtained the court's leave under this subsection.
    (5) Where a placement order is in force, no special guardianship order may be made in respect of the child unless–
        (a) an application has been made for an adoption order, and
        (b) the person applying for the special guardianship order has obtained the court's leave under this subsection or, if he is a guardian of the child, has obtained the court's leave under section 47(5).
    (6) Section 14A(7) of the 1989 Act applies in respect of an application for a special guardianship order for which leave has been given as mentioned in subsection (5)(b) with the omission of the words "the beginning of the period of three months ending with".
    (7) Where a placement order is in force–
        (a) section 14C(1)(b) of the 1989 Act (special guardianship: parental responsibility) has effect subject to any determination under section 25(4) of this Act,
        (b) section 14C(3) and (4) of the 1989 Act (special guardianship: removal of child from UK etc.) does not apply.

Removal of children who are or may be placed by adoption agencies
30   General prohibitions on removal
    (1) Where–
        (a) a child is placed for adoption by an adoption agency under section 19, or

(b) a child is placed for adoption by an adoption agency and either the child is less than six weeks old or the agency has at no time been authorised to place the child for adoption,

a person (other than the agency) must not remove the child from the prospective adopters.

(2) Where–

(a) a child who is not for the time being placed for adoption is being provided with accommodation by a local authority, and

(b) the authority have applied to the court for a placement order and the application has not been disposed of,

only a person who has the court's leave (or the authority) may remove the child from the accommodation.

(3) Where subsection (2) does not apply, but–

(a) a child who is not for the time being placed for adoption is being provided with accommodation by an adoption agency, and

(b) the agency is authorised to place the child for adoption under section 19 or would be so authorised if any consent to placement under that section had not been withdrawn,

a person (other than the agency) must not remove the child from the accommodation.

(4) This section is subject to sections 31 to 33 but those sections do not apply if the child is subject to a care order.

(5) This group of sections (that is, this section and those sections) apply whether or not the child in question is in England and Wales.

(6) This group of sections does not affect the exercise by any local authority or other person of any power conferred by any enactment, other than section 20(8) of the 1989 Act (removal of children from local authority accommodation).

(7) This group of sections does not prevent the removal of a child who is arrested.

(8) A person who removes a child in contravention of this section is guilty of an offence and liable on summary conviction to imprisonment for a term not exceeding three months, or a fine not exceeding level 5 on the standard scale, or both.

31   Recovery by parent etc. where child not placed or is a baby

(1) Subsection (2) applies where–

(a) a child who is not for the time being placed for adoption is being provided with accommodation by an adoption agency, and

(b) the agency would be authorised to place the child for adoption under section 19 if consent to placement under that section had not been withdrawn.

(2) If any parent or guardian of the child informs the agency that he wishes the child to be returned to him, the agency must return the child to him within the period of seven days beginning with the request unless an application is, or has been, made for a placement order and the application has not been disposed of.

(3) Subsection (4) applies where–

(a) a child is placed for adoption by an adoption agency and either the child is less than six weeks old or the agency has at no time been authorised to place the child for adoption, and

(b) any parent or guardian of the child informs the agency that he wishes the child to be returned to him,

unless an application is, or has been, made for a placement order and the application has not been disposed of.

(4) The agency must give notice of the parent's or guardian's wish to the prospective adopters who must return the child to the agency within the period of seven days beginning with the day on which the notice is given.

(5) A prospective adopter who fails to comply with subsection (4) is guilty of an offence and liable on summary conviction to imprisonment for a term not exceeding three months, or a fine not exceeding level 5 on the standard scale, or both.

(6) As soon as a child is returned to an adoption agency under subsection (4), the agency must return the child to the parent or guardian in question.

32   Recovery by parent etc. where child placed and consent withdrawn

(1) This section applies where–

(a) a child is placed for adoption by an adoption agency under section 19, and

(b) consent to placement under that section has been withdrawn,

unless an application is, or has been, made for a placement order and the application has not been disposed of.

(2) If a parent or guardian of the child informs the agency that he wishes the child to be returned to him–

(a) the agency must give notice of the parent's or guardian's wish to the prospective adopters, and

(b) the prospective adopters must return the child to the agency within the period of 14 days beginning with the day on which the notice is given.

(3) A prospective adopter who fails to comply with subsection (2)(b) is guilty of an offence and liable on summary conviction to imprisonment for a term not exceeding three months, or a fine not exceeding level 5 on the standard scale, or both.

(4) As soon as a child is returned to an adoption agency under this section, the agency must return the child to the parent or guardian in question.

(5) Where a notice under subsection (2) is given, but–

(a) before the notice was given, an application for an adoption order (including a Scottish or Northern Irish adoption order), special guardianship order or residence order, or for leave to apply for a special guardianship order or residence order, was made in respect of the child, and

(b) the application (and, in a case where leave is given on an application to apply for a special guardianship order or residence order, the application for the order) has not been disposed of,

the prospective adopters are not required by virtue of the notice to return the child to the agency unless the court so orders.

33   Recovery by parent etc. where child placed and placement order refused

(1) This section applies where–

(a) a child is placed for adoption by a local authority under section 19,

(b) the authority have applied for a placement order and the application has been refused, and

(c) any parent or guardian of the child informs the authority that he wishes the child to be returned to him.

(2) The prospective adopters must return the child to the authority on a date determined by the court.

(3) A prospective adopter who fails to comply with subsection (2) is guilty of an offence and liable on summary conviction to imprisonment for a term not exceeding three months, or a fine not exceeding level 5 on the standard scale, or both.

(4) As soon as a child is returned to the authority, they must return the child to the parent or guardian in question.

34   Placement orders: prohibition on removal

(1) Where a placement order in respect of a child–

(a) is in force, or

(b) has been revoked, but the child has not been returned by the prospective adopters or remains in any accommodation provided by the local authority,

a person (other than the local authority) may not remove the child from the prospective adopters or from accommodation provided by the authority.

(2) A person who removes a child in contravention of subsection (1) is guilty of an offence.

(3) Where a court revoking a placement order in respect of a child determines that the child is not to remain with any former prospective adopters with whom the child is placed, they must return the child to the local authority within the period determined by the court for the purpose; and a person who fails to do so is guilty of an offence.

(4) Where a court revoking a placement order in respect of a child determines that the child is to be returned to a parent or guardian, the local authority must return the child to the parent or guardian as soon as the child is returned to the authority or, where the child is in accommodation provided by the authority, at once.

(5) A person guilty of an offence under this section is liable on summary conviction to imprisonment for a term not exceeding three months, or a fine not exceeding level 5 on the standard scale, or both.

(6) This section does not affect the exercise by any local authority or other person of a power conferred by any enactment, other than section 20(8) of the 1989 Act.

(7) This section does not prevent the removal of a child who is arrested.

(8) This section applies whether or not the child in question is in England and Wales.

35   Return of child in other cases

(1) Where a child is placed for adoption by an adoption agency and the prospective adopters give notice to the agency of their wish to return the child, the agency must–

(a) receive the child from the prospective adopters before the end of the period of seven days beginning with the giving of the notice, and

(b) give notice to any parent or guardian of the child of the prospective adopters' wish to return the child.

(2) Where a child is placed for adoption by an adoption agency, and the agency–

(a) is of the opinion that the child should not remain with the prospective adopters, and

(b) gives notice to them of its opinion,

the prospective adopters must, not later than the end of the period of seven days beginning with the giving of the notice, return the child to the agency.

(3) If the agency gives notice under subsection (2)(b), it must give notice to any parent or guardian of the child of the obligation to return the child to the agency.

(4) A prospective adopter who fails to comply with subsection (2) is guilty of an offence and liable on summary conviction to imprisonment for a term not exceeding three months, or a fine not exceeding level 5 on the standard scale, or both.

(5) Where–

(a) an adoption agency gives notice under subsection (2) in respect of a child,

(b) before the notice was given, an application for an adoption order (including a Scottish or Northern Irish adoption order), special guardianship order or residence order, or for leave to apply for a special guardianship order or residence order, was made in respect of the child, and

(c) the application (and, in a case where leave is given on an application to apply for a special guardianship order or residence order, the application for the order) has not been disposed of,

prospective adopters are not required by virtue of the notice to return the child to the agency unless the court so orders.

(6) This section applies whether or not the child in question is in England and Wales.

Removal of children in non-agency cases

36   Restrictions on removal

(1) At any time when a child's home is with any persons ("the people concerned") with whom the child is not placed by an adoption agency, but the people concerned–

(a) have applied for an adoption order in respect of the child and the application has not been disposed of,

(b) have given notice of intention to adopt, or

(c) have applied for leave to apply for an adoption order under section 42(6) and the application has not been disposed of,

a person may remove the child only in accordance with the provisions of this group of sections (that is, this section and sections 37 to 40).

The reference to a child placed by an adoption agency includes a child placed by a Scottish or Northern Irish adoption agency.

(2) For the purposes of this group of sections, a notice of intention to adopt is to be disregarded if–

(a) the period of four months beginning with the giving of the notice has expired without the people concerned applying for an adoption order, or

(b) the notice is a second or subsequent notice of intention to adopt and was given during the period of five months beginning with the giving of the preceding notice.

(3) For the purposes of this group of sections, if the people concerned apply for leave to apply for an adoption order under section 42(6) and the leave is granted, the application for leave is not to be treated as disposed of until the period of three days beginning with the granting of the leave has expired.

(4) This section does not prevent the removal of a child who is arrested.

(5) Where a parent or guardian may remove a child from the people concerned in accordance with the provisions of this group of sections, the people concerned must at the request of the parent or guardian return the child to the parent or guardian at once.

(6) A person who–

(a) fails to comply with subsection (5), or

(b) removes a child in contravention of this section,

is guilty of an offence and liable on summary conviction to imprisonment for a term not exceeding three months, or a fine not exceeding level 5 on the standard scale, or both.

(7) This group of sections applies whether or not the child in question is in England and Wales.

37   Applicants for adoption

If section 36(1)(a) applies, the following persons may remove the child–

(a) a person who has the court's leave,

(b) a local authority or other person in the exercise of a power conferred by any enactment, other than section 20(8) of the 1989 Act.

38   Local authority foster parents

(1) This section applies if the child's home is with local authority foster parents.

(2) If–

(a) the child has had his home with the foster parents at all times during the period of five years ending with the removal and the foster parents have given notice of intention to adopt, or

(b) an application has been made for leave under section 42(6) and has not been disposed of,

the following persons may remove the child.

(3) They are–

(a) a person who has the court's leave,

(b) a local authority or other person in the exercise of a power conferred by any enactment, other than section 20(8) of the 1989 Act.

(4) If subsection (2) does not apply but–

(a) the child has had his home with the foster parents at all times during the period of one year ending with the removal, and

(b) the foster parents have given notice of intention to adopt,

the following persons may remove the child.

(5) They are–

(a) a person with parental responsibility for the child who is exercising the power in section 20(8) of the 1989 Act,

(b) a person who has the court's leave,

(c) a local authority or other person in the exercise of a power conferred by any enactment, other than section 20(8) of the 1989 Act.

39   Partners of parents

(1) This section applies if a child's home is with a partner of a parent and the partner has given notice of intention to adopt.

(2) If the child's home has been with the partner for not less than three years (whether continuous or not) during the period of five years ending with the removal, the following persons may remove the child–

(a) a person who has the court's leave,

(b) a local authority or other person in the exercise of a power conferred by any enactment, other than section 20(8) of the 1989 Act.

(3) If subsection (2) does not apply, the following persons may remove the child–

(a) a parent or guardian,

(b) a person who has the court's leave,

(c) a local authority or other person in the exercise of a power conferred by any enactment, other than section 20(8) of the 1989 Act.

40   Other non-agency cases

(1) In any case where sections 37 to 39 do not apply but–

(a) the people concerned have given notice of intention to adopt, or

(b) the people concerned have applied for leave under section 42(6) and the

application has not been disposed of,
the following persons may remove the child.
   (2) They are–
      (a) a person who has the court's leave,
      (b) a local authority or other person in the exercise of a power conferred by any
      enactment, other than section 20(8) of the 1989 Act.

Breach of restrictions on removal

41   Recovery orders
   (1) This section applies where it appears to the court–
      (a) that a child has been removed in contravention of any of the preceding
      provisions of this Chapter or that there are reasonable grounds for believing that a
      person intends to remove a child in contravention of those provisions, or
      (b) that a person has failed to comply with section 31(4), 32(2), 33(2), 34(3) or
      35(2).
   (2) The court may, on the application of any person, by an order–
      (a) direct any person who is in a position to do so to produce the child on request to
      any person mentioned in subsection (4),
      (b) authorise the removal of the child by any person mentioned in that subsection,
      (c) require any person who has information as to the child's whereabouts to
      disclose that information on request to any constable or officer of the court,
      (d) authorise a constable to enter any premises specified in the order and search for
      the child, using reasonable force if necessary.
   (3) Premises may only be specified under subsection (2)(d) if it appears to the court
that there are reasonable grounds for believing the child to be on them.
   (4) The persons referred to in subsection (2) are–
      (a) any person named by the court,
      (b) any constable,
      (c) any person who, after the order is made under that subsection, is authorised to
      exercise any power under the order by an adoption agency which is authorised to
      place the child for adoption.
   (5) A person who intentionally obstructs a person exercising a power of removal
conferred by the order is guilty of an offence and liable on summary conviction to a fine
not exceeding level 3 on the standard scale.
   (6) A person must comply with a request to disclose information as required by the
order even if the information sought might constitute evidence that he had committed an
offence.
   (7) But in criminal proceedings in which the person is charged with an offence (other
than one mentioned in subsection (8))–
      (a) no evidence relating to the information provided may be adduced, and
      (b) no question relating to the information may be asked,
by or on behalf of the prosecution, unless evidence relating to it is adduced, or a question
relating to it is asked, in the proceedings by or on behalf of the person.
   (8) The offences excluded from subsection (7) are–
      (a) an offence under section 2 or 5 of the Perjury Act 1911 (c. 6) (false statements
      made on oath otherwise than in judicial proceedings or made otherwise than on
      oath),
      (b) an offence under section 44(1) or (2) of the Criminal Law (Consolidation)
      (Scotland) Act 1995 (c. 39) (false statements made on oath or otherwise than on
      oath).
   (9) An order under this section has effect in relation to Scotland as if it were an order
made by the Court of Session which that court had jurisdiction to make.

Preliminaries to adoption

42   Child to live with adopters before application
   (1) An application for an adoption order may not be made unless–
      (a) if subsection (2) applies, the condition in that subsection is met,
      (b) if that subsection does not apply, the condition in whichever is applicable of
      subsections (3) to (5) applies.
   (2) If –

(a) the child was placed for adoption with the applicant or applicants by an adoption agency or in pursuance of an order of the High Court, or

(b) the applicant is a parent of the child,

the condition is that the child must have had his home with the applicant or, in the case of an application by a couple, with one or both of them at all times during the period of ten weeks preceding the application.

(3) If the applicant or one of the applicants is the partner of a parent of the child, the condition is that the child must have had his home with the applicant or, as the case may be, applicants at all times during the period of six months preceding the application.

(4) If the applicants are local authority foster parents, the condition is that the child must have had his home with the applicants at all times during the period of one year preceding the application.

(5) In any other case, the condition is that the child must have had his home with the applicant or, in the case of an application by a couple, with one or both of them for not less than three years (whether continuous or not) during the period of five years preceding the application.

(6) But subsections (4) and (5) do not prevent an application being made if the court gives leave to make it.

(7) An adoption order may not be made unless the court is satisfied that sufficient opportunities to see the child with the applicant or, in the case of an application by a couple, both of them together in the home environment have been given–

(a) where the child was placed for adoption with the applicant or applicants by an adoption agency, to that agency,

(b) in any other case, to the local authority within whose area the home is.

(8) In this section and sections 43 and 44(1)–

(a) references to an adoption agency include a Scottish or Northern Irish adoption agency,

(b) references to a child placed for adoption by an adoption agency are to be read accordingly.

43   Reports where child placed by agency

Where an application for an adoption order relates to a child placed for adoption by an adoption agency, the agency must–

(a) submit to the court a report on the suitability of the applicants and on any other matters relevant to the operation of section 1, and

(b) assist the court in any manner the court directs.

44   Notice of intention to adopt

(1) This section applies where persons (referred to in this section as "proposed adopters") wish to adopt a child who is not placed for adoption with them by an adoption agency.

(2) An adoption order may not be made in respect of the child unless the proposed adopters have given notice to the appropriate local authority of their intention to apply for the adoption order (referred to in this Act as a "notice of intention to adopt").

(3) The notice must be given not more than two years, or less than three months, before the date on which the application for the adoption order is made.

(4) Where–

(a) if a person were seeking to apply for an adoption order, subsection (4) or (5) of section 42 would apply, but

(b) the condition in the subsection in question is not met,

the person may not give notice of intention to adopt unless he has the court's leave to apply for an adoption order.

(5) On receipt of a notice of intention to adopt, the local authority must arrange for the investigation of the matter and submit to the court a report of the investigation.

(6) In particular, the investigation must, so far as practicable, include the suitability of the proposed adopters and any other matters relevant to the operation of section 1 in relation to the application.

(7) If a local authority receive a notice of intention to adopt in respect of a child whom they know was (immediately before the notice was given) looked after by another local authority, they must, not more than seven days after the receipt of the notice, inform the

other local authority in writing that they have received the notice.

(8) Where–

(a) a local authority have placed a child with any persons otherwise than as prospective adopters, and

(b) the persons give notice of intention to adopt,

the authority are not to be treated as leaving the child with them as prospective adopters for the purposes of section 18(1)(b).

(9) In this section, references to the appropriate local authority, in relation to any proposed adopters, are–

(a) in prescribed cases, references to the prescribed local authority,

(b) in any other case, references to the local authority for the area in which, at the time of giving the notice of intention to adopt, they have their home,

and "prescribed" means prescribed by regulations.

45   Suitability of adopters

(1) Regulations under section 9 may make provision as to the matters to be taken into account by an adoption agency in determining, or making any report in respect of, the suitability of any persons to adopt a child.

(2) In particular, the regulations may make provision for the purpose of securing that, in determining the suitability of a couple to adopt a child, proper regard is had to the need for stability and permanence in their relationship.

The making of adoption orders

46   Adoption orders

(1) An adoption order is an order made by the court on an application under section 50 or 51 giving parental responsibility for a child to the adopters or adopter.

(2) The making of an adoption order operates to extinguish–

(a) the parental responsibility which any person other than the adopters or adopter has for the adopted child immediately before the making of the order,

(b) any order under the 1989 Act or the Children (Northern Ireland) Order 1995 (S.I. 1995/755 (N.I. 2)),

(c) any order under the Children (Scotland) Act 1995 (c. 36) other than an excepted order, and

(d) any duty arising by virtue of an agreement or an order of a court to make payments, so far as the payments are in respect of the adopted child's maintenance or upbringing for any period after the making of the adoption order.

"Excepted order" means an order under section 9, 11(1)(d) or 13 of the Children (Scotland) Act 1995 or an exclusion order within the meaning of section 76(1) of that Act.

(3) An adoption order–

(a) does not affect parental responsibility so far as it relates to any period before the making of the order, and

(b) in the case of an order made on an application under section 51(2) by the partner of a parent of the adopted child, does not affect the parental responsibility of that parent or any duties of that parent within subsection (2)(d).

(4) Subsection (2)(d) does not apply to a duty arising by virtue of an agreement–

(a) which constitutes a trust, or

(b) which expressly provides that the duty is not to be extinguished by the making of an adoption order.

(5) An adoption order may be made even if the child to be adopted is already an adopted child.

(6) Before making an adoption order, the court must consider whether there should be arrangements for allowing any person contact with the child; and for that purpose the court must consider any existing or proposed arrangements and obtain any views of the parties to the proceedings.

47   Conditions for making adoption orders

(1) An adoption order may not be made if the child has a parent or guardian unless one of the following three conditions is met; but this section is subject to section 52 (parental etc. consent).

(2) The first condition is that, in the case of each parent or guardian of the child, the court is satisfied–

(a) that the parent or guardian consents to the making of the adoption order,

(b) that the parent or guardian has consented under section 20 (and has not withdrawn the consent) and does not oppose the making of the adoption order, or

(c) that the parent's or guardian's consent should be dispensed with.

(3) A parent or guardian may not oppose the making of an adoption order under subsection (2)(b) without the court's leave.

(4) The second condition is that–

(a) the child has been placed for adoption by an adoption agency with the prospective adopters in whose favour the order is proposed to be made,

(b) either-

(i) the child was placed for adoption with the consent of each parent or guardian and the consent of the mother was given when the child was at least six weeks old, or

(ii) the child was placed for adoption under a placement order, and

(c) no parent or guardian opposes the making of the adoption order.

(5) A parent or guardian may not oppose the making of an adoption order under the second condition without the court's leave.

(6) The third condition is that the child is free for adoption by virtue of an order made–

(a) in Scotland, under section 18 of the Adoption (Scotland) Act 1978 (c. 28), or

(b) in Northern Ireland, under Article 17(1) or 18(1) of the Adoption (Northern Ireland) Order 1987 (S.I. 1987/2203 (N.I. 22)).

(7) The court cannot give leave under subsection (3) or (5) unless satisfied that there has been a change in circumstances since the consent of the parent or guardian was given or, as the case may be, the placement order was made.

(8) An adoption order may not be made in relation to a person who is or has been married.

(8A) An adoption order may not be made in relation to a person who is or has been a civil partner.[5]

(9) An adoption order may not be made in relation to a person who has attained the age of 19 years.

48   Restrictions on making adoption orders

(1) The court may not hear an application for an adoption order in relation to a child, where a previous application to which subsection (2) applies made in relation to the child by the same persons was refused by any court, unless it appears to the court that, because of a change in circumstances or for any other reason, it is proper to hear the application.

(2) This subsection applies to any application–

(a) for an adoption order or a Scottish or Northern Irish adoption order, or

(b) for an order for adoption made in the Isle of Man or any of the Channel Islands.

49   Applications for adoption

(1) An application for an adoption order may be made by–

(a) a couple, or

(b) one person,

but only if it is made under section 50 or 51 and one of the following conditions is met.

(2) The first condition is that at least one of the couple (in the case of an application under section 50) or the applicant (in the case of an application under section 51) is domiciled in a part of the British Islands.

(3) The second condition is that both of the couple (in the case of an application under section 50) or the applicant (in the case of an application under section 51) have been habitually resident in a part of the British Islands for a period of not less than one year ending with the date of the application.

(4) An application for an adoption order may only be made if the person to be adopted has not attained the age of 18 years on the date of the application.

(5) References in this Act to a child, in connection with any proceedings (whether or not concluded) for adoption, (such as "child to be adopted" or "adopted child") include a person who has attained the age of 18 years before the proceedings are concluded.

50   Adoption by couple

(1) An adoption order may be made on the application of a couple where both of them

---

[5] Section 47(8A) was inserted by the Civil Partnership Act 2004, section 79(3).

have attained the age of 21 years.

(2) An adoption order may be made on the application of a couple where–

(a) one of the couple is the mother or the father of the person to be adopted and has attained the age of 18 years, and

(b) the other has attained the age of 21 years.

51   Adoption by one person

(1) An adoption order may be made on the application of one person who has attained the age of 21 years and is not married or a civil partner.[6]

(2) An adoption order may be made on the application of one person who has attained the age of 21 years if the court is satisfied that the person is the partner of a parent of the person to be adopted.

(3) An adoption order may be made on the application of one person who has attained the age of 21 years and is married if the court is satisfied that–

(a) the person's spouse cannot be found,

(b) the spouses have separated and are living apart, and the separation is likely to be permanent, or

(c) the person's spouse is by reason of ill-health, whether physical or mental, incapable of making an application for an adoption order.

(3A) An adoption order may be made on the application of one person who has attained the age of 21 years and is a civil partner if the court is satisfied that–

(a) the person's civil partner cannot be found,

(b) the civil partners have separated and are living apart, and the separation is likely to be permanent, or

(c) the person's civil partner is by reason of ill-health, whether physical or mental, incapable of making an application for an adoption order.[7]

(4) An adoption order may not be made on an application under this section by the mother or the father of the person to be adopted unless the court is satisfied that–

(a) the other natural parent is dead or cannot be found,

(b) by virtue of section 28 of the Human Fertilisation and Embryology Act 1990 (c. 37), there is no other parent, or

(c) there is some other reason justifying the child's being adopted by the applicant alone,

and, where the court makes an adoption order on such an application, the court must record that it is satisfied as to the fact mentioned in paragraph (a) or (b) or, in the case of paragraph (c), record the reason.

Placement and adoption: general

52   Parental etc. consent

(1) The court cannot dispense with the consent of any parent or guardian of a child to the child being placed for adoption or to the making of an adoption order in respect of the child unless the court is satisfied that–

(a) the parent or guardian cannot be found or lacks capacity (within the meaning of the Mental Capacity Act 2005) to give consent, or[8]

(b) the welfare of the child requires the consent to be dispensed with.

(2) The following provisions apply to references in this Chapter to any parent or guardian of a child giving or withdrawing–

(a) consent to the placement of a child for adoption, or

(b) consent to the making of an adoption order (including a future adoption order).

(3) Any consent given by the mother to the making of an adoption order is ineffective if it is given less than six weeks after the child's birth.

(4) The withdrawal of any consent to the placement of a child for adoption, or of any consent given under section 20, is ineffective if it is given after an application for an adoption order is made.

(5) "Consent" means consent given unconditionally and with full understanding of what is involved; but a person may consent to adoption without knowing the identity of the persons in whose favour the order will be made.

---

[6] Section 51(1) is printed as amended by the Civil Partnership Act 2004, section 79(4).

[7] Section 51(3A) was inserted by the Civil Partnership Act 2004, section 79(5).

[8] Section 52(1)(a) is printed as it is to be amended by the Mental Capacity Act 2005, schedule 6, paragraph 45.

(6) "Parent" (except in subsections (9) and (10) below) means a parent having parental responsibility.

(7) Consent under section 19 or 20 must be given in the form prescribed by rules, and the rules may prescribe forms in which a person giving consent under any other provision of this Part may do so (if he wishes).

(8) Consent given under section 19 or 20 must be withdrawn–

(a) in the form prescribed by rules, or

(b) by notice given to the agency.

(9) Subsection (10) applies if–

(a) an agency has placed a child for adoption under section 19 in pursuance of consent given by a parent of the child, and

(b) at a later time, the other parent of the child acquires parental responsibility for the child.

(10) The other parent is to be treated as having at that time given consent in accordance with this section in the same terms as those in which the first parent gave consent.

53 **Modification of 1989 Act in relation to adoption**

(1) Where–

(a) a local authority are authorised to place a child for adoption, or

(b) a child who has been placed for adoption by a local authority is less than six weeks old,

regulations may provide for the following provisions of the 1989 Act to apply with modifications, or not to apply, in relation to the child.

(2) The provisions are–

(a) section 22(4)(b), (c) and (d) and (5)(b) (duty to ascertain wishes and feelings of certain persons),

(b) paragraphs 15 and 21 of Schedule 2 (promoting contact with parents and parents' obligation to contribute towards maintenance).

(3) Where a registered adoption society is authorised to place a child for adoption or a child who has been placed for adoption by a registered adoption society is less than six weeks old, regulations may provide–

(a) for section 61 of that Act to have effect in relation to the child whether or not he is accommodated by or on behalf of the society,

(b) for subsections (2)(b) to (d) and (3)(b) of that section (duty to ascertain wishes and feelings of certain persons) to apply with modifications, or not to apply, in relation to the child.

(4) Where a child's home is with persons who have given notice of intention to adopt, no contribution is payable (whether under a contribution order or otherwise) under Part 3 of Schedule 2 to that Act (contributions towards maintenance of children looked after by local authorities) in respect of the period referred to in subsection (5).

(5) That period begins when the notice of intention to adopt is given and ends if–

(a) the period of four months beginning with the giving of the notice expires without the prospective adopters applying for an adoption order, or

(b) an application for such an order is withdrawn or refused.

(6) In this section, "notice of intention to adopt" includes notice of intention to apply for a Scottish or Northern Irish adoption order.

54 **Disclosing information during adoption process**

Regulations under section 9 may require adoption agencies in prescribed circumstances to disclose in accordance with the regulations prescribed information to prospective adopters.

55 **Revocation of adoptions on legitimation**

(1) Where any child adopted by one natural parent as sole adoptive parent subsequently becomes a legitimated person on the marriage of the natural parents, the court by which the adoption order was made may, on the application of any of the parties concerned, revoke the order.

(2) In relation to an adoption order made by a magistrates' court, the reference in subsection (1) to the court by which the order was made includes a court acting for the same petty sessions area.

Disclosure of information in relation to a person's adoption

56   Information to be kept about a person's adoption

(1) In relation to an adopted person, regulations may prescribe–

(a) the information which an adoption agency must keep in relation to his adoption,

(b) the form and manner in which it must keep that information.

(2) Below in this group of sections (that is, this section and sections 57 to 65), any information kept by an adoption agency by virtue of subsection (1)(a) is referred to as section 56 information.

(3) Regulations may provide for the transfer in prescribed circumstances of information held, or previously held, by an adoption agency to another adoption agency.

57   Restrictions on disclosure of protected etc. information

(1) Any section 56 information kept by an adoption agency which–

(a) is about an adopted person or any other person, and

(b) is or includes identifying information about the person in question,

may only be disclosed by the agency to a person (other than the person the information is about) in pursuance of this group of sections.

(2) Any information kept by an adoption agency–

(a) which the agency has obtained from the Registrar General on an application under section 79(5) and any other information which would enable the adopted person to obtain a certified copy of the record of his birth, or

(b) which is information about an entry relating to the adopted person in the Adoption Contact Register,

may only be disclosed to a person by the agency in pursuance of this group of sections.

(3) In this group of sections, information the disclosure of which to a person is restricted by virtue of subsection (1) or (2) is referred to (in relation to him) as protected information.

(4) Identifying information about a person means information which, whether taken on its own or together with other information disclosed by an adoption agency, identifies the person or enables the person to be identified.

(5) This section does not prevent the disclosure of protected information in pursuance of a prescribed agreement to which the adoption agency is a party.

(6) Regulations may authorise or require an adoption agency to disclose protected information to a person who is not an adopted person.

58   Disclosure of other information

(1) This section applies to any section 56 information other than protected information.

(2) An adoption agency may for the purposes of its functions disclose to any person in accordance with prescribed arrangements any information to which this section applies.

(3) An adoption agency must, in prescribed circumstances, disclose prescribed information to a prescribed person.

59   Offence

Regulations may provide that a registered adoption society which discloses any information in contravention of section 57 is to be guilty of an offence and liable on summary conviction to a fine not exceeding level 5 on the standard scale.

60   Disclosing information to adopted adult

(1) This section applies to an adopted person who has attained the age of 18 years.

(2) The adopted person has the right, at his request, to receive from the appropriate adoption agency–

(a) any information which would enable him to obtain a certified copy of the record of his birth, unless the High Court orders otherwise,

(b) any prescribed information disclosed to the adopters by the agency by virtue of section 54.

(3) The High Court may make an order under subsection (2)(a), on an application by the appropriate adoption agency, if satisfied that the circumstances are exceptional.

(4) The adopted person also has the right, at his request, to receive from the court which made the adoption order a copy of any prescribed document or prescribed order relating to the adoption.

(5) Subsection (4) does not apply to a document or order so far as it contains

information which is protected information.

61   Disclosing protected information about adults

(1) This section applies where–

(a) a person applies to the appropriate adoption agency for protected information to be disclosed to him, and

(b) none of the information is about a person who is a child at the time of the application.

(2) The agency is not required to proceed with the application unless it considers it appropriate to do so.

(3) If the agency does proceed with the application it must take all reasonable steps to obtain the views of any person the information is about as to the disclosure of the information about him.

(4) The agency may then disclose the information if it considers it appropriate to do so.

(5) In deciding whether it is appropriate to proceed with the application or disclose the information, the agency must consider–

(a) the welfare of the adopted person,

(b) any views obtained under subsection (3),

(c) any prescribed matters,

and all the other circumstances of the case.

(6) This section does not apply to a request for information under section 60(2) or to a request for information which the agency is authorised or required to disclose in pursuance of regulations made by virtue of section 57(6).

62   Disclosing protected information about children

(1) This section applies where–

(a) a person applies to the appropriate adoption agency for protected information to be disclosed to him, and

(b) any of the information is about a person who is a child at the time of the application.

(2) The agency is not required to proceed with the application unless it considers it appropriate to do so.

(3) If the agency does proceed with the application, then, so far as the information is about a person who is at the time a child, the agency must take all reasonable steps to obtain–

(a) the views of any parent or guardian of the child, and

(b) the views of the child, if the agency considers it appropriate to do so having regard to his age and understanding and to all the other circumstances of the case,

as to the disclosure of the information.

(4) And, so far as the information is about a person who has at the time attained the age of 18 years, the agency must take all reasonable steps to obtain his views as to the disclosure of the information.

(5) The agency may then disclose the information if it considers it appropriate to do so.

(6) In deciding whether it is appropriate to proceed with the application, or disclose the information, where any of the information is about a person who is at the time a child–

(a) if the child is an adopted child, the child's welfare must be the paramount consideration,

(b) in the case of any other child, the agency must have particular regard to the child's welfare.

(7) And, in deciding whether it is appropriate to proceed with the application or disclose the information, the agency must consider–

(a) the welfare of the adopted person (where subsection (6)(a) does not apply),

(b) any views obtained under subsection (3) or (4),

(c) any prescribed matters,

and all the other circumstances of the case.

(8) This section does not apply to a request for information under section 60(2) or to a request for information which the agency is authorised or required to disclose in pursuance of regulations made by virtue of section 57(6).

63   Counselling

(1) Regulations may require adoption agencies to give information about the

availability of counselling to persons–

(a) seeking information from them in pursuance of this group of sections,

(b) considering objecting or consenting to the disclosure of information by the agency in pursuance of this group of sections, or

(c) considering entering with the agency into an agreement prescribed for the purposes of section 57(5).

(2) Regulations may require adoption agencies to make arrangements to secure the provision of counselling for persons seeking information from them in prescribed circumstances in pursuance of this group of sections.

(3) The regulations may authorise adoption agencies–

(a) to disclose information which is required for the purposes of such counselling to the persons providing the counselling,

(b) where the person providing the counselling is outside the United Kingdom, to require a prescribed fee to be paid.

(4) The regulations may require any of the following persons to provide counselling for the purposes of arrangements under subsection (2)–

(a) a local authority, a council constituted under section 2 of the Local Government etc. (Scotland) Act 1994 (c. 39) or a Health and Social Services Board established under Article 16 of the Health and Personal Social Services (Northern Ireland) Order 1972 (S.I. 1972/1265 (N.I. 14)),

(b) a registered adoption society, an organisation within section 144(3)(b) or an adoption society which is registered under Article 4 of the Adoption (Northern Ireland) Order 1987 (S.I. 1987/2203 (N.I. 22)),

(c) an adoption support agency in respect of which a person is registered under Part 2 of the Care Standards Act 2000 (c. 14).

(5) For the purposes of subsection (4), where the functions of a Health and Social Services Board are exercisable by a Health and Social Services Trust, the reference in sub-paragraph (a) to a Board is to be read as a reference to the Health and Social Services Trust.

64   Other provision to be made by regulations

(1) Regulations may make provision for the purposes of this group of sections, including provision as to–

(a) the performance by adoption agencies of their functions,

(b) the manner in which information may be received, and

(c) the matters mentioned below in this section.

(2) Regulations may prescribe–

(a) the manner in which agreements made by virtue of section 57(5) are to be recorded,

(b) the information to be provided by any person on an application for the disclosure of information under this group of sections.

(3) Regulations may require adoption agencies–

(a) to give to prescribed persons prescribed information about the rights or opportunities to obtain information, or to give their views as to its disclosure, given by this group of sections,

(b) to seek prescribed information from, or give prescribed information to, the Registrar General in prescribed circumstances.

(4) Regulations may require the Registrar General–

(a) to disclose to any person (including an adopted person) at his request any information which the person requires to assist him to make contact with the adoption agency which is the appropriate adoption agency in the case of an adopted person specified in the request (or, as the case may be, in the applicant's case),

(b) to disclose to the appropriate adoption agency any information which the agency requires about any entry relating to the adopted person on the Adoption Contact Register.

(5) Regulations may provide for the payment of a prescribed fee in respect of the disclosure in prescribed circumstances of any information in pursuance of section 60, 61 or 62; but an adopted person may not be required to pay any fee in respect of any information disclosed to him in relation to any person who (but for his adoption) would be

related to him by blood (including half blood), marriage or civil partnership.[9]

(6) Regulations may provide for the payment of a prescribed fee by an adoption agency obtaining information under subsection (4)(b).

65   Sections 56 to 65: interpretation

(1) In this group of sections–

"appropriate adoption agency", in relation to an adopted person or to information relating to his adoption, means–

(a) if the person was placed for adoption by an adoption agency, that agency or (if different) the agency which keeps the information in relation to his adoption,

(b) in any other case, the local authority to which notice of intention to adopt was given,

"prescribed" means prescribed by subordinate legislation,

"regulations" means regulations under section 9,

"subordinate legislation" means regulations or, in relation to information to be given by a court, rules.

(2) But–

(a) regulations under section 63(2) imposing any requirement on a council constituted under section 2 of the Local Government etc. (Scotland) Act 1994 (c. 39), or an organisation within section 144(3)(b), are to be made by the Scottish Ministers,

(b) regulations under section 63(2) imposing any requirement on a Health and Social Services Board established under Article 16 of the Health and Personal Social Services (Northern Ireland) Order 1972 (S.I. 1972/ 1265 (N.I. 14)), or an adoption society which is registered under Article 4 of the Adoption (Northern Ireland) Order 1987 (S.I. 1987/2203 (N.I. 22)), are to be made by the Department of Health, Social Services and Public Safety.

(3) The power of the Scottish Ministers or of the Department of Health, Social Services and Public Safety to make regulations under section 63(2) includes power to make–

(a) any supplementary, incidental or consequential provision,

(b) any transitory, transitional or saving provision,

which the person making the regulations considers necessary or expedient.

(4) Regulations prescribing any fee by virtue of section 64(6) require the approval of the Chancellor of the Exchequer.

(5) Regulations making any provision as to the manner in which any application is to be made for the disclosure of information by the Registrar General require his approval.

CHAPTER 4: STATUS OF ADOPTED CHILDREN

66   Meaning of adoption in Chapter 4

(1) In this Chapter "adoption" means–

(a) adoption by an adoption order or a Scottish or Northern Irish adoption order,

(b) adoption by an order made in the Isle of Man or any of the Channel Islands,

(c) an adoption effected under the law of a Convention country outside the British Islands, and certified in pursuance of Article 23(1) of the Convention (referred to in this Act as a "Convention adoption"),

(d) an overseas adoption, or

(e) an adoption recognised by the law of England and Wales and effected under the law of any other country;

and related expressions are to be interpreted accordingly.

(2) But references in this Chapter to adoption do not include an adoption effected before the day on which this Chapter comes into force (referred to in this Chapter as "the appointed day").

(3) Any reference in an enactment to an adopted person within the meaning of this Chapter includes a reference to an adopted child within the meaning of Part 4 of the Adoption Act 1976 (c. 36).

67   Status conferred by adoption

(1) An adopted person is to be treated in law as if born as the child of the adopters or

---

[9] Section 64(5) is printed as amended by the Civil Partnership Act 2004, section 79(6).

adopter.

(2) An adopted person is the legitimate child of the adopters or adopter and, if adopted by–

  (a) a couple, or

  (b) one of a couple under section 51(2),

is to be treated as the child of the relationship of the couple in question.

(3) An adopted person–

  (a) if adopted by one of a couple under section 51(2), is to be treated in law as not being the child of any person other than the adopter and the other one of the couple, and

  (b) in any other case, is to be treated in law, subject to subsection (4), as not being the child of any person other than the adopters or adopter;

but this subsection does not affect any reference in this Act to a person's natural parent or to any other natural relationship.

(4) In the case of a person adopted by one of the person's natural parents as sole adoptive parent, subsection (3)(b) has no effect as respects entitlement to property depending on relationship to that parent, or as respects anything else depending on that relationship.

(5) This section has effect from the date of the adoption.

(6) Subject to the provisions of this Chapter and Schedule 4, this section–

  (a) applies for the interpretation of enactments or instruments passed or made before as well as after the adoption, and so applies subject to any contrary indication, and

  (b) has effect as respects things done, or events occurring, on or after the adoption.

68   Adoptive relatives

(1) A relationship existing by virtue of section 67 may be referred to as an adoptive relationship, and–

  (a) an adopter may be referred to as an adoptive parent or (as the case may be) as an adoptive father or adoptive mother,

  (b) any other relative of any degree under an adoptive relationship may be referred to as an adoptive relative of that degree.

(2) Subsection (1) does not affect the interpretation of any reference, not qualified by the word "adoptive", to a relationship.

(3) A reference (however expressed) to the adoptive mother and father of a child adopted by–

  (a) a couple of the same sex, or

  (b) a partner of the child's parent, where the couple are of the same sex,

is to be read as a reference to the child's adoptive parents.

69   Rules of interpretation for instruments concerning property

(1) The rules of interpretation contained in this section apply (subject to any contrary indication and to Schedule 4) to any instrument so far as it contains a disposition of property.

(2) In applying section 67(1) and (2) to a disposition which depends on the date of birth of a child or children of the adoptive parent or parents, the disposition is to be interpreted as if–

  (a) the adopted person had been born on the date of adoption,

  (b) two or more people adopted on the same date had been born on that date in the order of their actual births;

but this does not affect any reference to a person's age.

(3) Examples of phrases in wills on which subsection (2) can operate are-

  1. Children of A "living at my death or born afterwards".

  2. Children of A "living at my death or born afterwards before any one of such children for the time being in existence attains a vested interest and who attain the age of 21 years".

  3. As in example 1 or 2, but referring to grandchildren of A instead of children of A.

  4. A for life "until he has a child", and then to his child or children.

Note. Subsection (2) will not affect the reference to the age of 21 years in example 2.

(4) Section 67(3) does not prejudice–

(a) any qualifying interest, or

(b) any interest expectant (whether immediately or not) upon a qualifying interest.

"Qualifying interest" means an interest vested in possession in the adopted person before the adoption.

(5) Where it is necessary to determine for the purposes of a disposition of property effected by an instrument whether a woman can have a child–

(a) it must be presumed that once a woman has attained the age of 55 years she will not adopt a person after execution of the instrument, and

(b) if she does so, then (in spite of section 67) that person is not to be treated as her child or (if she does so as one of a couple) as the child of the other one of the couple for the purposes of the instrument.

(6) In this section, "instrument" includes a private Act settling property, but not any other enactment.

70   Dispositions depending on date of birth

(1) Where a disposition depends on the date of birth of a person who was born illegitimate and who is adopted by one of the natural parents as sole adoptive parent, section 69(2) does not affect entitlement by virtue of Part 3 of the Family Law Reform Act 1987 (c. 42) (dispositions of property).

(2) Subsection (1) applies for example where–

(a) a testator dies in 2001 bequeathing a legacy to his eldest grandchild living at a specified time,

(b) his unmarried daughter has a child in 2002 who is the first grandchild,

(c) his married son has a child in 2003,

(d) subsequently his unmarried daughter adopts her child as sole adoptive parent.

In that example the status of the daughter's child as the eldest grandchild of the testator is not affected by the events described in paragraphs (c) and (d).

71   Property devolving with peerages etc.

(1) An adoption does not affect the descent of any peerage or dignity or title of honour.

(2) An adoption does not affect the devolution of any property limited (expressly or not) to devolve (as nearly as the law permits) along with any peerage or dignity or title of honour.

(3) Subsection (2) applies only if and so far as a contrary intention is not expressed in the instrument, and has effect subject to the terms of the instrument.

72   Protection of trustees and personal representatives

(1) A trustee or personal representative is not under a duty, by virtue of the law relating to trusts or the administration of estates, to enquire, before conveying or distributing any property, whether any adoption has been effected or revoked if that fact could affect entitlement to the property.

(2) A trustee or personal representative is not liable to any person by reason of a conveyance or distribution of the property made without regard to any such fact if he has not received notice of the fact before the conveyance or distribution.

(3) This section does not prejudice the right of a person to follow the property, or any property representing it, into the hands of another person, other than a purchaser, who has received it.

73   Meaning of disposition

(1) This section applies for the purposes of this Chapter.

(2) A disposition includes the conferring of a power of appointment and any other disposition of an interest in or right over property; and in this subsection a power of appointment includes any discretionary power to transfer a beneficial interest in property without the furnishing of valuable consideration.

(3) This Chapter applies to an oral disposition as if contained in an instrument made when the disposition was made.

(4) The date of death of a testator is the date at which a will or codicil is to be regarded as made.

(5) The provisions of the law of intestate succession applicable to the estate of a deceased person are to be treated as if contained in an instrument executed by him (while

of full capacity) immediately before his death.

74   Miscellaneous enactments

(1) Section 67 does not apply for the purposes of–

(a) section 1 of and Schedule 1 to the Marriage Act 1949 or Schedule 1 to the Civil Partnership Act 2004 (prohibited degrees of kindred and affinity), or

(b) sections 64 and 65 of the Sexual Offences Act 2003 (sex with adult relative).[10]

(2) Section 67 does not apply for the purposes of any provision of–

(a) the British Nationality Act 1981 (c. 61),

(b) the Immigration Act 1971 (c. 77),

(c) any instrument having effect under an enactment within paragraph (a) or (b), or

(d) any other provision of the law for the time being in force which determines British citizenship, British overseas territories citizenship, the status of a British National (Overseas) or British Overseas citizenship.

75   Pensions

Section 67(3) does not affect entitlement to a pension which is payable to or for the benefit of a person and is in payment at the time of the person's adoption.

76   Insurance

(1) Where a child is adopted whose natural parent has effected an insurance with a friendly society or a collecting society or an industrial insurance company for the payment on the death of the child of money for funeral expenses, then–

(a) the rights and liabilities under the policy are by virtue of the adoption transferred to the adoptive parents, and

(b) for the purposes of the enactments relating to such societies and companies, the adoptive parents are to be treated as the person who took out the policy.

(2) Where the adoption is effected by an order made by virtue of section 51(2), the references in subsection (1) to the adoptive parents are to be read as references to the adopter and the other one of the couple.

CHAPTER 5: THE REGISTERS

Adopted Children Register etc.

77   Adopted Children Register

(1) The Registrar General must continue to maintain in the General Register Office a register, to be called the Adopted Children Register.

(2) The Adopted Children Register is not to be open to public inspection or search.

(3) No entries may be made in the Adopted Children Register other than entries–

(a) directed to be made in it by adoption orders, or

(b) required to be made under Schedule 1.

(4) A certified copy of an entry in the Adopted Children Register, if purporting to be sealed or stamped with the seal of the General Register Office, is to be received as evidence of the adoption to which it relates without further or other proof.

(5) Where an entry in the Adopted Children Register contains a record–

(a) of the date of birth of the adopted person, or

(b) of the country, or the district and sub-district, of the birth of the adopted person,

a certified copy of the entry is also to be received, without further or other proof, as evidence of that date, or country or district and sub-district, (as the case may be) in all respects as if the copy were a certified copy of an entry in the registers of live-births.

(6) Schedule 1 (registration of adoptions and the amendment of adoption orders) is to have effect.

78   Searches and copies

(1) The Registrar General must continue to maintain at the General Register Office an index of the Adopted Children Register.

(2) Any person may–

(a) search the index,

(b) have a certified copy of any entry in the Adopted Children Register.

(3) But a person is not entitled to have a certified copy of an entry in the Adopted Children Register relating to an adopted person who has not attained the age of 18 years

[10] Section 74(1) is printed as amended by the Civil Partnership Act 2004, section 79(7) and the Sexual Offences Act 2003, Schedule 6, paragraph 47.

unless the applicant has provided the Registrar General with the prescribed particulars.

"Prescribed" means prescribed by regulations made by the Registrar General with the approval of the Chancellor of the Exchequer.

(4) The terms, conditions and regulations as to payment of fees, and otherwise, applicable under the Births and Deaths Registration Act 1953 (c. 20), and the Registration Service Act 1953 (c. 37), in respect of–

(a) searches in the index kept in the General Register Office of certified copies of entries in the registers of live-births,

(b) the supply from that office of certified copies of entries in those certified copies,

also apply in respect of searches, and supplies of certified copies, under subsection (2).

79   Connections between the register and birth records

(1) The Registrar General must make traceable the connection between any entry in the registers of live-births or other records which has been marked "Adopted" and any corresponding entry in the Adopted Children Register.

(2) Information kept by the Registrar General for the purposes of subsection (1) is not to be open to public inspection or search.

(3) Any such information, and any other information which would enable an adopted person to obtain a certified copy of the record of his birth, may only be disclosed by the Registrar General in accordance with this section.

(4) In relation to a person adopted before the appointed day the court may, in exceptional circumstances, order the Registrar General to give any information mentioned in subsection (3) to a person.

(5) On an application made in the prescribed manner by the appropriate adoption agency in respect of an adopted person a record of whose birth is kept by the Registrar General, the Registrar General must give the agency any information relating to the adopted person which is mentioned in subsection (3).

"Appropriate adoption agency" has the same meaning as in section 65.

(6) In relation to a person adopted before the appointed day, Schedule 2 applies instead of subsection (5).

(7) On an application made in the prescribed manner by an adopted person a record of whose birth is kept by the Registrar General and who–

(a) is under the age of 18 years, and

(b) intends to be married or form a civil partnership,

the Registrar General must inform the applicant whether or not it appears from information contained in the registers of live-births or other records that the applicant and the intended spouse or civil partner may be within the prohibited degrees of relationship for the purposes of the Marriage Act 1949 (c. 76).[11]

(8) Before the Registrar General gives any information by virtue of this section, any prescribed fee which he has demanded must be paid.

(9) In this section–

"appointed day" means the day appointed for the commencement of sections 56 to 65,

"prescribed" means prescribed by regulations made by the Registrar General with the approval of the Chancellor of the Exchequer.

Adoption Contact Register

80   Adoption Contact Register

(1) The Registrar General must continue to maintain at the General Register Office in accordance with regulations a register in two Parts to be called the Adoption Contact Register.

(2) Part 1 of the register is to contain the prescribed information about adopted persons who have given the prescribed notice expressing their wishes as to making contact with their relatives.

(3) The Registrar General may only make an entry in Part 1 of the register for an adopted person–

(a) a record of whose birth is kept by the Registrar General,

(b) who has attained the age of 18 years, and

(c) who the Registrar General is satisfied has such information as is necessary to enable him to obtain a certified copy of the record of his birth.

---

[11] Section 79(7) is printed as amended by the Civil Partnership Act 2004, section 79(8)(b).

(4) Part 2 of the register is to contain the prescribed information about persons who have given the prescribed notice expressing their wishes, as relatives of adopted persons, as to making contact with those persons.

(5) The Registrar General may only make an entry in Part 2 of the register for a person–

(a) who has attained the age of 18 years, and

(b) who the Registrar General is satisfied is a relative of an adopted person and has such information as is necessary to enable him to obtain a certified copy of the record of the adopted person's birth.

(6) Regulations may provide for–

(a) the disclosure of information contained in one Part of the register to persons for whom there is an entry in the other Part,

(b) the payment of prescribed fees in respect of the making or alteration of entries in the register and the disclosure of information contained in the register.

81   **Adoption Contact Register: supplementary**

(1) The Adoption Contact Register is not to be open to public inspection or search.

(2) In section 80, "relative", in relation to an adopted person, means any person who (but for his adoption) would be related to him by blood (including half blood), marriage or civil partnership.[12]

(3) The Registrar General must not give any information entered in the register to any person except in accordance with subsection (6)(a) of that section or regulations made by virtue of section 64(4)(b).

(4) In section 80, "regulations" means regulations made by the Registrar General with the approval of the Chancellor of the Exchequer, and "prescribed" means prescribed by such regulations.

General

82   **Interpretation**

(1) In this Chapter–

"records" includes certified copies kept by the Registrar General of entries in any register of births,

"registers of live-births" means the registers of live-births made under the Births and Deaths Registration Act 1953 (c. 20).

(2) Any register, record or index maintained under this Chapter may be maintained in any form the Registrar General considers appropriate; and references (however expressed) to entries in such a register, or to their amendment, marking or cancellation, are to be read accordingly.

CHAPTER 6: ADOPTIONS WITH A FOREIGN ELEMENT

Bringing children into and out of the United Kingdom

83   **Restriction on bringing children in**

(1) This section applies where a person who is habitually resident in the British Islands (the "British resident")–

(a) brings, or causes another to bring, a child who is habitually resident outside the British Islands into the United Kingdom for the purpose of adoption by the British resident, or

(b) at any time brings, or causes another to bring, into the United Kingdom a child adopted by the British resident under an external adoption effected within the period of six months ending with that time.

The references to adoption, or to a child adopted, by the British resident include a reference to adoption, or to a child adopted, by the British resident and another person.

(2) But this section does not apply if the child is intended to be adopted under a Convention adoption order.

(3) An external adoption means an adoption, other than a Convention adoption, of a child effected under the law of any country or territory outside the British Islands, whether or not the adoption is–

(a) an adoption within the meaning of Chapter 4, or

(b) a full adoption (within the meaning of section 88(3)).

---

[12] Section 81(2) is printed as amended by the Civil Partnership Act 2004, section 79(9).

(4) Regulations may require a person intending to bring, or to cause another to bring, a child into the United Kingdom in circumstances where this section applies–

(a) to apply to an adoption agency (including a Scottish or Northern Irish adoption agency) in the prescribed manner for an assessment of his suitability to adopt the child, and

(b) to give the agency any information it may require for the purpose of the assessment.

(5) Regulations may require prescribed conditions to be met in respect of a child brought into the United Kingdom in circumstances where this section applies.

(6) In relation to a child brought into the United Kingdom for adoption in circumstances where this section applies, regulations may–

(a) provide for any provision of Chapter 3 to apply with modifications or not to apply,

(b) if notice of intention to adopt has been given, impose functions in respect of the child on the local authority to which the notice was given.

(7) If a person brings, or causes another to bring, a child into the United Kingdom at any time in circumstances where this section applies, he is guilty of an offence if–

(a) he has not complied with any requirement imposed by virtue of subsection (4), or

(b) any condition required to be met by virtue of subsection (5) is not met,

before that time, or before any later time which may be prescribed.

(8) A person guilty of an offence under this section is liable–

(a) on summary conviction to imprisonment for a term not exceeding six months, or a fine not exceeding the statutory maximum, or both,

(b) on conviction on indictment, to imprisonment for a term not exceeding twelve months, or a fine, or both.

(9) In this section, "prescribed" means prescribed by regulations and "regulations" means regulations made by the Secretary of State, after consultation with the Assembly.

84   Giving parental responsibility prior to adoption abroad

(1) The High Court may, on an application by persons who the court is satisfied intend to adopt a child under the law of a country or territory outside the British Islands, make an order giving parental responsibility for the child to them.

(2) An order under this section may not give parental responsibility to persons who the court is satisfied meet those requirements as to domicile, or habitual residence, in England and Wales which have to be met if an adoption order is to be made in favour of those persons.

(3) An order under this section may not be made unless any requirements prescribed by regulations are satisfied.

(4) An application for an order under this section may not be made unless at all times during the preceding ten weeks the child's home was with the applicant or, in the case of an application by two people, both of them.

(5) Section 46(2) to (4) has effect in relation to an order under this section as it has effect in relation to adoption orders.

(6) Regulations may provide for any provision of this Act which refers to adoption orders to apply, with or without modifications, to orders under this section.

(7) In this section, "regulations" means regulations made by the Secretary of State, after consultation with the Assembly.

85   Restriction on taking children out

(1) A child who–

(a) is a Commonwealth citizen, or

(b) is habitually resident in the United Kingdom,

must not be removed from the United Kingdom to a place outside the British Islands for the purpose of adoption unless the condition in subsection (2) is met.

(2) The condition is that–

(a) the prospective adopters have parental responsibility for the child by virtue of an order under section 84, or

(b) the child is removed under the authority of an order under section 49 of the Adoption (Scotland) Act 1978 (c. 28) or Article 57 of the Adoption (Northern

Ireland) Order 1987 (S.I. 1987/2203 (N.I. 22)).

(3) Removing a child from the United Kingdom includes arranging to do so; and the circumstances in which a person arranges to remove a child from the United Kingdom include those where he–

(a) enters into an arrangement for the purpose of facilitating such a removal of the child,

(b) initiates or takes part in any negotiations of which the purpose is the conclusion of an arrangement within paragraph (a), or

(c) causes another person to take any step mentioned in paragraph (a) or (b).

An arrangement includes an agreement (whether or not enforceable).

(4) A person who removes a child from the United Kingdom in contravention of subsection (1) is guilty of an offence.

(5) A person is not guilty of an offence under subsection (4) of causing a person to take any step mentioned in paragraph (a) or (b) of subsection (3) unless it is proved that he knew or had reason to suspect that the step taken would contravene subsection (1).

But this subsection only applies if sufficient evidence is adduced to raise an issue as to whether the person had the knowledge or reason mentioned.

(6) A person guilty of an offence under this section is liable–

(a) on summary conviction to imprisonment for a term not exceeding six months, or a fine not exceeding the statutory maximum, or both,

(b) on conviction on indictment, to imprisonment for a term not exceeding twelve months, or a fine, or both.

(7) In any proceedings under this section–

(a) a report by a British consular officer or a deposition made before a British consular officer and authenticated under the signature of that officer is admissible, upon proof that the officer or the deponent cannot be found in the United Kingdom, as evidence of the matters stated in it, and

(b) it is not necessary to prove the signature or official character of the person who appears to have signed any such report or deposition.

86   Power to modify sections 83 and 85

(1) Regulations may provide for section 83 not to apply if–

(a) the adopters or (as the case may be) prospective adopters are natural parents, natural relatives or guardians of the child in question (or one of them is), or

(b) the British resident in question is a partner of a parent of the child,

and any prescribed conditions are met.

(2) Regulations may provide for section 85(1) to apply with modifications, or not to apply, if–

(a) the prospective adopters are parents, relatives or guardians of the child in question (or one of them is), or

(b) the prospective adopter is a partner of a parent of the child,

and any prescribed conditions are met.

(3) On the occasion of the first exercise of the power to make regulations under this section–

(a) the statutory instrument containing the regulations is not to be made unless a draft of the instrument has been laid before, and approved by a resolution of, each House of Parliament, and

(b) accordingly section 140(2) does not apply to the instrument.

(4) In this section, "prescribed" means prescribed by regulations and "regulations" means regulations made by the Secretary of State after consultation with the Assembly.

Overseas adoptions

87   Overseas adoptions

(1) In this Act, "overseas adoption"–

(a) means an adoption of a description specified in an order made by the Secretary of State, being a description of adoptions effected under the law of any country or territory outside the British Islands, but

(b) does not include a Convention adoption.

(2) Regulations may prescribe the requirements that ought to be met by an adoption of any description effected after the commencement of the regulations for it to be an

overseas adoption for the purposes of this Act.

(3) At any time when such regulations have effect, the Secretary of State must exercise his powers under this section so as to secure that subsequently effected adoptions of any description are not overseas adoptions for the purposes of this Act if he considers that they are not likely within a reasonable time to meet the prescribed requirements.

(4) In this section references to this Act include the Adoption Act 1976 (c. 36).

(5) An order under this section may contain provision as to the manner in which evidence of any overseas adoption may be given.

(6) In this section–

"adoption" means an adoption of a child or of a person who was a child at the time the adoption was applied for,

"regulations" means regulations made by the Secretary of State after consultation with the Assembly.

Miscellaneous

88   Modification of section 67 for Hague Convention adoptions

(1) If the High Court is satisfied, on an application under this section, that each of the following conditions is met in the case of a Convention adoption, it may direct that section 67(3) does not apply, or does not apply to any extent specified in the direction.

(2) The conditions are–

(a) that under the law of the country in which the adoption was effected, the adoption is not a full adoption,

(b) that the consents referred to in Article 4(c) and (d) of the Convention have not been given for a full adoption or that the United Kingdom is not the receiving State (within the meaning of Article 2 of the Convention),

(c) that it would be more favourable to the adopted child for a direction to be given under subsection (1).

(3) A full adoption is an adoption by virtue of which the child is to be treated in law as not being the child of any person other than the adopters or adopter.

(4) In relation to a direction under this section and an application for it, sections 59 and 60 of the Family Law Act 1986 (c. 55) (declarations under Part 3 of that Act as to marital status) apply as they apply in relation to a direction under that Part and an application for such a direction.

89   Annulment etc. of overseas or Hague Convention adoptions

(1) The High Court may, on an application under this subsection, by order annul a Convention adoption or Convention adoption order on the ground that the adoption is contrary to public policy.

(2) The High Court may, on an application under this subsection–

(a) by order provide for an overseas adoption or a determination under section 91 to cease to be valid on the ground that the adoption or determination is contrary to public policy or that the authority which purported to authorise the adoption or make the determination was not competent to entertain the case, or

(b) decide the extent, if any, to which a determination under section 91 has been affected by a subsequent determination under that section.

(3) The High Court may, in any proceedings in that court, decide that an overseas adoption or a determination under section 91 is to be treated, for the purposes of those proceedings, as invalid on either of the grounds mentioned in subsection (2)(a).

(4) Subject to the preceding provisions, the validity of a Convention adoption, Convention adoption order or overseas adoption or a determination under section 91 cannot be called in question in proceedings in any court in England and Wales.

90   Section 89: supplementary

(1) Any application for an order under section 89 or a decision under subsection (2)(b) or (3) of that section must be made in the prescribed manner and within any prescribed period.

"Prescribed" means prescribed by rules.

(2) No application may be made under section 89(1) in respect of an adoption unless immediately before the application is made–

(a) the person adopted, or

(b) the adopters or adopter,

habitually reside in England and Wales.

(3) In deciding in pursuance of section 89 whether such an authority as is mentioned in section 91 was competent to entertain a particular case, a court is bound by any finding of fact made by the authority and stated by the authority to be so made for the purpose of determining whether the authority was competent to entertain the case.

91   Overseas determinations and orders

(1) Subsection (2) applies where any authority of a Convention country (other than the United Kingdom) or of the Channel Islands, the Isle of Man or any British overseas territory has power under the law of that country or territory–

(a) to authorise, or review the authorisation of, an adoption order made in that country or territory, or

(b) to give or review a decision revoking or annulling such an order or a Convention adoption.

(2) If the authority makes a determination in the exercise of that power, the determination is to have effect for the purpose of effecting, confirming or terminating the adoption in question or, as the case may be, confirming its termination.

(3) Subsection (2) is subject to section 89 and to any subsequent determination having effect under that subsection.

CHAPTER 7: MISCELLANEOUS

Restrictions

92   Restriction on arranging adoptions etc.

(1) A person who is neither an adoption agency nor acting in pursuance of an order of the High Court must not take any of the steps mentioned in subsection (2).

(2) The steps are–

(a) asking a person other than an adoption agency to provide a child for adoption,

(b) asking a person other than an adoption agency to provide prospective adopters for a child,

(c) offering to find a child for adoption,

(d) offering a child for adoption to a person other than an adoption agency,

(e) handing over a child to any person other than an adoption agency with a view to the child's adoption by that or another person,

(f) receiving a child handed over to him in contravention of paragraph (e),

(g) entering into an agreement with any person for the adoption of a child, or for the purpose of facilitating the adoption of a child, where no adoption agency is acting on behalf of the child in the adoption,

(h) initiating or taking part in negotiations of which the purpose is the conclusion of an agreement within paragraph (g),

(i) causing another person to take any of the steps mentioned in paragraphs (a) to (h).

(3) Subsection (1) does not apply to a person taking any of the steps mentioned in paragraphs (d), (e), (g), (h) and (i) of subsection (2) if the following condition is met.

(4) The condition is that–

(a) the prospective adopters are parents, relatives or guardians of the child (or one of them is), or

(b) the prospective adopter is the partner of a parent of the child.

(5) References to an adoption agency in subsection (2) include a prescribed person outside the United Kingdom exercising functions corresponding to those of an adoption agency, if the functions are being exercised in prescribed circumstances in respect of the child in question.

(6) The Secretary of State may, after consultation with the Assembly, by order make any amendments of subsections (1) to (4), and any consequential amendments of this Act, which he considers necessary or expedient.

(7) In this section–

(a) "agreement" includes an arrangement (whether or not enforceable),

(b) "prescribed" means prescribed by regulations made by the Secretary of State after consultation with the Assembly.

93   **Offence of breaching restrictions under section 92**

(1) If a person contravenes section 92(1), he is guilty of an offence; and, if that person is an adoption society, the person who manages the society is also guilty of the offence.

(2) A person is not guilty of an offence under subsection (1) of taking the step mentioned in paragraph (f) of section 92(2) unless it is proved that he knew or had reason to suspect that the child was handed over to him in contravention of paragraph (e) of that subsection.

(3) A person is not guilty of an offence under subsection (1) of causing a person to take any of the steps mentioned in paragraphs (a) to (h) of section 92(2) unless it is proved that he knew or had reason to suspect that the step taken would contravene the paragraph in question.

(4) But subsections (2) and (3) only apply if sufficient evidence is adduced to raise an issue as to whether the person had the knowledge or reason mentioned.

(5) A person guilty of an offence under this section is liable on summary conviction to imprisonment for a term not exceeding six months, or a fine not exceeding £10,000, or both.

94   **Restriction on reports**

(1) A person who is not within a prescribed description may not, in any prescribed circumstances, prepare a report for any person about the suitability of a child for adoption or of a person to adopt a child or about the adoption, or placement for adoption, of a child.

"Prescribed" means prescribed by regulations made by the Secretary of State after consultation with the Assembly.

(2) If a person–

(a) contravenes subsection (1), or

(b) causes a person to prepare a report, or submits to any person a report which has been prepared, in contravention of that subsection,

he is guilty of an offence.

(3) If a person who works for an adoption society–

(a) contravenes subsection (1), or

(b) causes a person to prepare a report, or submits to any person a report which has been prepared, in contravention of that subsection,

the person who manages the society is also guilty of the offence.

(4) A person is not guilty of an offence under subsection (2)(b) unless it is proved that he knew or had reason to suspect that the report would be, or had been, prepared in contravention of subsection (1).

But this subsection only applies if sufficient evidence is adduced to raise an issue as to whether the person had the knowledge or reason mentioned.

(5) A person guilty of an offence under this section is liable on summary conviction to imprisonment for a term not exceeding six months, or a fine not exceeding level 5 on the standard scale, or both.

95   **Prohibition of certain payments**

(1) This section applies to any payment (other than an excepted payment) which is made for or in consideration of–

(a) the adoption of a child,

(b) giving any consent required in connection with the adoption of a child,

(c) removing from the United Kingdom a child who is a Commonwealth citizen, or is habitually resident in the United Kingdom, to a place outside the British Islands for the purpose of adoption,

(d) a person (who is neither an adoption agency nor acting in pursuance of an order of the High Court) taking any step mentioned in section 92(2),

(e) preparing, causing to be prepared or submitting a report the preparation of which contravenes section 94(1).

(2) In this section and section 96, removing a child from the United Kingdom has the same meaning as in section 85.

(3) Any person who–

(a) makes any payment to which this section applies,

(b) agrees or offers to make any such payment, or

(c) receives or agrees to receive or attempts to obtain any such payment, is guilty of an offence.

(4) A person guilty of an offence under this section is liable on summary conviction to imprisonment for a term not exceeding six months, or a fine not exceeding £10,000, or both.

96   Excepted payments

(1) A payment is an excepted payment if it is made by virtue of, or in accordance with provision made by or under, this Act, the Adoption (Scotland) Act 1978 (c. 28) or the Adoption (Northern Ireland) Order 1987 (S.I. 1987/2203 (N.I. 22)).

(2) A payment is an excepted payment if it is made to a registered adoption society by–
(a) a parent or guardian of a child, or
(b) a person who adopts or proposes to adopt a child,
in respect of expenses reasonably incurred by the society in connection with the adoption or proposed adoption of the child.

(3) A payment is an excepted payment if it is made in respect of any legal or medical expenses incurred or to be incurred by any person in connection with an application to a court which he has made or proposes to make for an adoption order, a placement order, or an order under section 26 or 84.

(4) A payment made as mentioned in section 95(1)(c) is an excepted payment if–
(a) the condition in section 85(2) is met, and
(b) the payment is made in respect of the travel and accommodation expenses reasonably incurred in removing the child from the United Kingdom for the purpose of adoption.

97   Sections 92 to 96: interpretation

In sections 92 to 96–
(a) "adoption agency" includes a Scottish or Northern Irish adoption agency,
(b) "payment" includes reward,
(c) references to adoption are to the adoption of persons, wherever they may be habitually resident, effected under the law of any country or territory, whether within or outside the British Islands.

Information

98   Pre-commencement adoptions: information

(1) Regulations under section 9 may make provision for the purpose of–
(a) assisting persons adopted before the appointed day who have attained the age of 18 to obtain information in relation to their adoption, and
(b) facilitating contact between such persons and their relatives.

(2) For that purpose the regulations may confer functions on–
(a) registered adoption support agencies,
(b) the Registrar General,
(c) adoption agencies.

(3) For that purpose the regulations may–
(a) authorise or require any person mentioned in subsection (2) to disclose information,
(b) authorise or require the disclosure of information contained in records kept under section 8 of the Public Records Act 1958 (c. 51) (court records),
and may impose conditions on the disclosure of information, including conditions restricting its further disclosure.

(4) The regulations may authorise the charging of prescribed fees by any person mentioned in subsection (2) or in respect of the disclosure of information under subsection (3)(b).

(5) An authorisation or requirement to disclose information by virtue of subsection (3)(a) has effect in spite of any restriction on the disclosure of information in Chapter 5.

(6) The making of regulations by virtue of subsections (2) to (4) which relate to the Registrar General requires the approval of the Chancellor of the Exchequer.

(7) In this section–
"appointed day" means the day appointed for the commencement of sections 56 to 65,
"registered adoption support agency" means an adoption support agency in respect of which a person is registered under Part 2 of the Care Standards Act 2000 (c. 14),

"relative", in relation to an adopted person, means any person who (but for his adoption) would be related to him by blood (including half blood), marriage or civil partnership.[13]

Proceedings

99   Proceedings for offences

Proceedings for an offence by virtue of section 9 or 59 may not, without the written consent of the Attorney General, be taken by any person other than the Commission for Social Care Inspection or the Assembly.[14]

100   Appeals

In section 94 of the 1989 Act (appeals under that Act), in subsections (1)(a) and (2), after "this Act" there is inserted "or the Adoption and Children Act 2002".

101   Privacy

(1) Proceedings under this Act in the High Court or a County Court may be heard and determined in private.

(2) In section 12 of the Administration of Justice Act 1960 (c. 65) (publication of information relating to proceedings in private), in subsection (1)(a)(ii), after "1989" there is inserted "or the Adoption and Children Act 2002".

(3) In section 97 of the 1989 Act (privacy for children involved in certain proceedings), after "this Act" in subsections (1) and (2) there is inserted "or the Adoption and Children Act 2002".

The Children and Family Court Advisory and Support Service

102   Officers of the Service

(1) For the purposes of–

(a) any relevant application,

(b) the signification by any person of any consent to placement or adoption,

rules must provide for the appointment in prescribed cases of an officer of the Children and Family Court Advisory and Support Service ("the Service") or a Welsh family proceedings officer.[15]

(2) The rules may provide for the appointment of such an officer in other circumstances in which it appears to the Lord Chancellor to be necessary or expedient to do so.

(3) The rules may provide for the officer–

(a) to act on behalf of the child upon the hearing of any relevant application, with the duty of safeguarding the interests of the child in the prescribed manner,

(b) where the court so requests, to prepare a report on matters relating to the welfare of the child in question,

(c) to witness documents which signify consent to placement or adoption,

(d) to perform prescribed functions.

(4) A report prepared in pursuance of the rules on matters relating to the welfare of a child must–

(a) deal with prescribed matters (unless the court orders otherwise), and

(b) be made in the manner required by the court.

(5) A person who–

(a) in the case of an application for the making, varying or revocation of a placement order, is employed by the local authority which made the application,

(b) in the case of an application for an adoption order in respect of a child who was placed for adoption, is employed by the adoption agency which placed him, or

(c) is within a prescribed description,

is not to be appointed under subsection (1) or (2).

(6) In this section, "relevant application" means an application for–

(a) the making, varying or revocation of a placement order,

(b) the making of an order under section 26, or the varying or revocation of such an order,

(c) the making of an adoption order, or

---

[13] Section 98(7) is printed as amended by the Civil Partnership Act 2004, section 79(10).

[14] Section 99 is printed as amended by the Health and Social Care (Community Health and Standards) Act 2003, schedule 9, paragraph 32.

[15] Section 102(1) is printed as amended by the Children Act 2004, schedule 3, paragraph 16(2).

(d) the making of an order under section 84.

(7) Rules may make provision as to the assistance which the court may require an officer of the Service or Welsh family proceedings officer to give to it.[16]

(8) In this section and section 103, "Welsh family proceedings officer" has the meaning given by section 35 of the Children Act 2004.[17]

103　Right of officers of the Service to have access to adoption agency records

(1) Where an officer of the Service or Welsh family proceedings officer has been appointed to act under section 102(1), he has the right at all reasonable times to examine and take copies of any records of, or held by, an adoption agency which were compiled in connection with the making, or proposed making, by any person of any application under this Part in respect of the child concerned.

(2) Where an officer of the Service or Welsh family proceedings officer takes a copy of any record which he is entitled to examine under this section, that copy or any part of it is admissible as evidence of any matter referred to in any—

(a) report which he makes to the court in the proceedings in question, or

(b) evidence which he gives in those proceedings.[18]

(3) Subsection (2) has effect regardless of any enactment or rule of law which would otherwise prevent the record in question being admissible in evidence.

Evidence

104　Evidence of consent

(1) If a document signifying any consent which is required by this Part to be given is witnessed in accordance with rules, it is to be admissible in evidence without further proof of the signature of the person by whom it was executed.

(2) A document signifying any such consent which purports to be witnessed in accordance with rules is to be presumed to be so witnessed, and to have been executed and witnessed on the date and at the place specified in the document, unless the contrary is proved.

Scotland, Northern Ireland and the Islands

105　Effect of certain Scottish orders and provisions

(1) A Scottish adoption order or an order under section 25 of the Adoption (Scotland) Act 1978 (c. 28) (interim adoption orders) has effect in England and Wales as it has in Scotland, but as if references to the parental responsibilities and the parental rights in relation to a child were to parental responsibility for the child.

(2) An order made under section 18 of the Adoption (Scotland) Act 1978 (freeing orders), and the revocation or variation of such an order under section 20 or 21 of that Act, have effect in England and Wales as they have effect in Scotland, but as if references to the parental responsibilities and the parental rights in relation to a child were to parental responsibility for the child.

(3) Any person who—

(a) contravenes section 27(1) of that Act (removal where adoption agreed etc.), or

(b) contravenes section 28(1) or (2) of that Act (removal where applicant provided home),

is guilty of an offence and liable on summary conviction to imprisonment for a term not exceeding three months, or a fine not exceeding level 5 on the standard scale, or both.

(4) Orders made under section 29 of that Act (order to return or not to remove child) are to have effect in England and Wales as if they were orders of the High Court under section 41 of this Act.

106　Effect of certain Northern Irish orders and provisions

(1) A Northern Irish adoption order or an order under Article 26 of the Adoption (Northern Ireland) Order 1987 (S.I. 1987/2203 (N.I. 22)) (interim orders) has effect in England and Wales as it has in Northern Ireland.

(2) An order made under Article 17 or 18 of the Adoption (Northern Ireland) Order 1987 (freeing orders), or the variation or revocation of such an order under Article 20 or 21 of that Order, have effect in England and Wales as they have in Northern Ireland.

---

[16] Section 102(7) is printed as amended by the Children Act 2004, schedule 3, paragraph 16(3).

[17] Section 102(8) was inserted by the Children Act 2004, schedule 3, paragraph 16(4).

[18] Section 103(1) and (2) are printed as amended by the Children Act 2004, schedule 3, paragraph 17.

(3) Any person who–
(a) contravenes Article 28(1) or (2) of the Adoption (Northern Ireland) Order 1987 (removal where adoption agreed etc.), or
(b) contravenes Article 29(1) or (2) of that Order (removal where applicant provided home),
is guilty of an offence and liable on summary conviction to imprisonment for a term not exceeding three months, or a fine not exceeding level 5 on the standard scale, or both.

(4) Orders made under Article 30 of that Order (order to return or not to remove child) are to have effect in England and Wales as if they were orders of the High Court under section 41 of this Act.

107   Use of adoption records from other parts of the British Islands
Any document which is receivable as evidence of any matter–
(a) in Scotland under section 45(2) of the Adoption (Scotland) Act 1978 (c. 28),
(b) in Northern Ireland under Article 63(1) of the Adoption (Northern Ireland) Order 1987, or
(c) in the Isle of Man or any of the Channel Islands under an enactment corresponding to section 77(3) of this Act,
is also receivable as evidence of that matter in England and Wales.

108   Channel Islands and the Isle of Man
(1) Regulations may provide–
(a) for a reference in any provision of this Act to an order of a court to include an order of a court in the Isle of Man or any of the Channel Islands which appears to the Secretary of State to correspond in its effect to the order in question,
(b) for a reference in any provision of this Act to an adoption agency to include a person who appears to the Secretary of State to exercise functions under the law of the Isle of Man or any of the Channel Islands which correspond to those of an adoption agency and for any reference in any provision of this Act to a child placed for adoption by an adoption agency to be read accordingly,
(c) for a reference in any provision of this Act to an enactment (including an enactment contained in this Act) to include a provision of the law of the Isle of Man or any of the Channel Islands which appears to the Secretary of State to correspond in its effect to the enactment,
(d) for any reference in any provision of this Act to the United Kingdom to include the Isle of Man or any of the Channel Islands.

(2) Regulations may modify any provision of this Act, as it applies to any order made, or other thing done, under the law of the Isle of Man or any of the Channel Islands.

(3) In this section, "regulations" means regulations made by the Secretary of State after consultation with the Assembly.

General

109   Avoiding delay
(1) In proceedings in which a question may arise as to whether an adoption order or placement order should be made, or any other question with respect to such an order, the court must (in the light of any rules made by virtue of subsection (2))–
(a) draw up a timetable with a view to determining such a question without delay, and
(b) give such directions as it considers appropriate for the purpose of ensuring that the timetable is adhered to.

(2) Rules may–
(a) prescribe periods within which prescribed steps must be taken in relation to such proceedings, and
(b) make other provision with respect to such proceedings for the purpose of ensuring that such questions are determined without delay.

110   Service of notices etc.
Any notice or information required to be given by virtue of this Act may be given by post.

PART 2: AMENDMENTS OF THE CHILDREN ACT 1989

111   Parental responsibility of unmarried father
(1) Section 4 of the 1989 Act (acquisition of responsibility by the father of a child who

is not married to the child's mother) is amended as follows.

(2) In subsection (1) (cases where parental responsibility is acquired), for the words after "birth" there is substituted ", the father shall acquire parental responsibility for the child if–

    (a) he becomes registered as the child's father under any of the enactments specified in subsection (1A);

    (b) he and the child's mother make an agreement (a "parental responsibility agreement") providing for him to have parental responsibility for the child; or

    (c) the court, on his application, orders that he shall have parental responsibility for the child."

(3) After that subsection there is inserted–

    "(1A) The enactments referred to in subsection (1)(a) are–

        (a) paragraphs (a), (b) and (c) of section 10(1) and of section 10A(1) of the Births and Deaths Registration Act 1953;

        (b) paragraphs (a), (b)(i) and (c) of section 18(1), and sections 18(2)(b) and 20(1)(a) of the Registration of Births, Deaths and Marriages (Scotland) Act 1965; and

        (c) sub-paragraphs (a), (b) and (c) of Article 14(3) of the Births and Deaths Registration (Northern Ireland) Order 1976.

    (1B) The Lord Chancellor may by order amend subsection (1A) so as to add further enactments to the list in that subsection."

(4) For subsection (3) there is substituted–

    "(2A) A person who has acquired parental responsibility under subsection (1) shall cease to have that responsibility only if the court so orders.

(3) The court may make an order under subsection (2A) on the application–

        (a) of any person who has parental responsibility for the child; or

        (b) with the leave of the court, of the child himself,

    subject, in the case of parental responsibility acquired under subsection (1)(c), to section 12(4)."

(5) Accordingly, in section 2(2) of the 1989 Act (a father of a child who is not married to the child's mother shall not have parental responsibility for the child unless he acquires it in accordance with the provisions of the Act), for the words from "shall not" to "acquires it" there is substituted "shall have parental responsibility for the child if he has acquired it (and has not ceased to have it)".

(6) In section 104 of the 1989 Act (regulations and orders)–

        (a) in subsection (2), after "section" there is inserted "4(1B),", and

        (b) in subsection (3), after "section" there is inserted "4(1B) or".

(7) Paragraph (a) of section 4(1) of the 1989 Act, as substituted by subsection (2) of this section, does not confer parental responsibility on a man who was registered under an enactment referred to in paragraph (a), (b) or (c) of section 4(1A) of that Act, as inserted by subsection (3) of this section, before the commencement of subsection (3) in relation to that paragraph.

112   Acquisition of parental responsibility by step-parent

After section 4 of the 1989 Act there is inserted–

"4A Acquisition of parental responsibility by step-parent

(1) Where a child's parent ("parent A") who has parental responsibility for the child is married to a person who is not the child's parent ("the step-parent")–

    (a) parent A or, if the other parent of the child also has parental responsibility for the child, both parents may by agreement with the step-parent provide for the step-parent to have parental responsibility for the child; or

    (b) the court may, on the application of the step-parent, order that the step-parent shall have parental responsibility for the child.

(2) An agreement under subsection (1)(a) is also a "parental responsibility agreement", and section 4(2) applies in relation to such agreements as it applies in relation to parental responsibility agreements under section 4.

(3) A parental responsibility agreement under subsection (1)(a), or an order under subsection (1)(b), may only be brought to an end by an order of the court made on the application–

    (a) of any person who has parental responsibility for the child; or

(b) with the leave of the court, of the child himself.

(4) The court may only grant leave under subsection (3)(b) if it is satisfied that the child has sufficient understanding to make the proposed application."

113 Section 8 orders: local authority foster parents

In section 9 of the 1989 Act (restrictions on making section 8 orders)–

(a) in subsection (3)(c), for "three years" there is substituted "one year", and

(b) subsection (4) is omitted.

114 Residence orders: extension to age of 18

(1) In section 12 of the 1989 Act (residence orders and parental responsibility), after subsection (4) there is inserted–

"(5) The power of a court to make a residence order in favour of any person who is not the parent or guardian of the child concerned includes power to direct, at the request of that person, that the order continue in force until the child reaches the age of eighteen (unless the order is brought to an end earlier); and any power to vary a residence order is exercisable accordingly.

(6) Where a residence order includes such a direction, an application to vary or discharge the order may only be made, if apart from this subsection the leave of the court is not required, with such leave".

(2) In section 9 of that Act (restrictions on making section 8 orders), at the beginning of subsection (6) there is inserted "Subject to section 12(5)".

(3) In section 91 of that Act (effect and duration of orders), in subsection (10), after "9(6)" there is inserted "or 12(5)".

115 Special guardianship

(1) After section 14 of the 1989 Act there is inserted–

"Special guardianship

14A Special guardianship orders

(1) A "special guardianship order" is an order appointing one or more individuals to be a child's "special guardian" (or special guardians).

(2) A special guardian–

(a) must be aged eighteen or over; and

(b) must not be a parent of the child in question,

and subsections (3) to (6) are to be read in that light.

(3) The court may make a special guardianship order with respect to any child on the application of an individual who–

(a) is entitled to make such an application with respect to the child; or

(b) has obtained the leave of the court to make the application,

or on the joint application of more than one such individual.

(4) Section 9(3) applies in relation to an application for leave to apply for a special guardianship order as it applies in relation to an application for leave to apply for a section 8 order.

(5) The individuals who are entitled to apply for a special guardianship order with respect to a child are–

(a) any guardian of the child;

(b) any individual in whose favour a residence order is in force with respect to the child;

(c) any individual listed in subsection (5)(b) or (c) of section 10 (as read with subsection (10) of that section);

(d) a local authority foster parent with whom the child has lived for a period of at least one year immediately preceding the application.

(6) The court may also make a special guardianship order with respect to a child in any family proceedings in which a question arises with respect to the welfare of the child if–

(a) an application for the order has been made by an individual who falls within subsection (3)(a) or (b) (or more than one such individual jointly); or

(b) the court considers that a special guardianship order should be made even though no such application has been made.

(7) No individual may make an application under subsection (3) or (6)(a) unless, before the beginning of the period of three months ending with the date of the

application, he has given written notice of his intention to make the application–

(a) if the child in question is being looked after by a local authority, to that local authority, or

(b) otherwise, to the local authority in whose area the individual is ordinarily resident.

(8) On receipt of such a notice, the local authority must investigate the matter and prepare a report for the court dealing with–

(a) the suitability of the applicant to be a special guardian;

(b) such matters (if any) as may be prescribed by the Secretary of State; and

(c) any other matter which the local authority consider to be relevant.

(9) The court may itself ask a local authority to conduct such an investigation and prepare such a report, and the local authority must do so.

(10) The local authority may make such arrangements as they see fit for any person to act on their behalf in connection with conducting an investigation or preparing a report referred to in subsection (8) or (9).

(11) The court may not make a special guardianship order unless it has received a report dealing with the matters referred to in subsection (8).

(12) Subsections (8) and (9) of section 10 apply in relation to special guardianship orders as they apply in relation to section 8 orders.

(13) This section is subject to section 29(5) and (6) of the Adoption and Children Act 2002.

14B Special guardianship orders: making

(1) Before making a special guardianship order, the court must consider whether, if the order were made–

(a) a contact order should also be made with respect to the child, and

(b) any section 8 order in force with respect to the child should be varied or discharged.

(2) On making a special guardianship order, the court may also–

(a) give leave for the child to be known by a new surname;

(b) grant the leave required by section 14C(3)(b), either generally or for specified purposes.

14C Special guardianship orders: effect

(1) The effect of a special guardianship order is that while the order remains in force–

(a) a special guardian appointed by the order has parental responsibility for the child in respect of whom it is made; and

(b) subject to any other order in force with respect to the child under this Act, a special guardian is entitled to exercise parental responsibility to the exclusion of any other person with parental responsibility for the child (apart from another special guardian).

(2) Subsection (1) does not affect–

(a) the operation of any enactment or rule of law which requires the consent of more than one person with parental responsibility in a matter affecting the child; or

(b) any rights which a parent of the child has in relation to the child's adoption or placement for adoption.

(3) While a special guardianship order is in force with respect to a child, no person may–

(a) cause the child to be known by a new surname; or

(b) remove him from the United Kingdom,

without either the written consent of every person who has parental responsibility for the child or the leave of the court.

(4) Subsection (3)(b) does not prevent the removal of a child, for a period of less than three months, by a special guardian of his.

(5) If the child with respect to whom a special guardianship order is in force dies, his special guardian must take reasonable steps to give notice of that fact to–

(a) each parent of the child with parental responsibility; and

(b) each guardian of the child,

but if the child has more than one special guardian, and one of them has taken such steps in relation to a particular parent or guardian, any other special guardian need not do so as respects that parent or guardian.

(6) This section is subject to section 29(7) of the Adoption and Children Act 2002.

14D Special guardianship orders: variation and discharge

(1) The court may vary or discharge a special guardianship order on the application of–

    (a) the special guardian (or any of them, if there are more than one);

    (b) any parent or guardian of the child concerned;

    (c) any individual in whose favour a residence order is in force with respect to the child;

    (d) any individual not falling within any of paragraphs (a) to (c) who has, or immediately before the making of the special guardianship order had, parental responsibility for the child;

    (e) the child himself; or

    (f) a local authority designated in a care order with respect to the child.

(2) In any family proceedings in which a question arises with respect to the welfare of a child with respect to whom a special guardianship order is in force, the court may also vary or discharge the special guardianship order if it considers that the order should be varied or discharged, even though no application has been made under subsection (1).

(3) The following must obtain the leave of the court before making an application under subsection (1)–

    (a) the child;

    (b) any parent or guardian of his;

    (c) any step-parent of his who has acquired, and has not lost, parental responsibility for him by virtue of section 4A;

    (d) any individual falling within subsection (1)(d) who immediately before the making of the special guardianship order had, but no longer has, parental responsibility for him.

(4) Where the person applying for leave to make an application under subsection (1) is the child, the court may only grant leave if it is satisfied that he has sufficient understanding to make the proposed application under subsection (1).

(5) The court may not grant leave to a person falling within subsection (3)(b)(c) or (d) unless it is satisfied that there has been a significant change in circumstances since the making of the special guardianship order.

14E Special guardianship orders: supplementary

(1) In proceedings in which any question of making, varying or discharging a special guardianship order arises, the court shall (in the light of any rules made by virtue of subsection (3))–

    (a) draw up a timetable with a view to determining the question without delay; and

    (b) give such directions as it considers appropriate for the purpose of ensuring, so far as is reasonably practicable, that the timetable is adhered to.

(2) Subsection (1) applies also in relation to proceedings in which any other question with respect to a special guardianship order arises.

(3) The power to make rules in subsection (2) of section 11 applies for the purposes of this section as it applies for the purposes of that.

(4) A special guardianship order, or an order varying one, may contain provisions which are to have effect for a specified period.

(5) Section 11(7) (apart from paragraph (c)) applies in relation to special guardianship orders and orders varying them as it applies in relation to section 8 orders.

14F Special guardianship support services

(1) Each local authority must make arrangements for the provision within their area of special guardianship support services, which means–

    (a) counselling, advice and information; and

(b) such other services as are prescribed,

in relation to special guardianship.

(2) The power to make regulations under subsection (1)(b) is to be exercised so as to secure that local authorities provide financial support.

(3) At the request of any of the following persons–

(a) a child with respect to whom a special guardianship order is in force;

(b) a special guardian;

(c) a parent;

(d) any other person who falls within a prescribed description,

a local authority may carry out an assessment of that person's needs for special guardianship support services (but, if the Secretary of State so provides in regulations, they must do so if he is a person of a prescribed description, or if his case falls within a prescribed description, or if both he and his case fall within prescribed descriptions).

(4) A local authority may, at the request of any other person, carry out an assessment of that person's needs for special guardianship support services.

(5) Where, as a result of an assessment, a local authority decide that a person has needs for special guardianship support services, they must then decide whether to provide any such services to that person.

(6) If–

(a) a local authority decide to provide any special guardianship support services to a person, and

(b) the circumstances fall within a prescribed description,

the local authority must prepare a plan in accordance with which special guardianship support services are to be provided to him, and keep the plan under review.

(7) The Secretary of State may by regulations make provision about assessments, preparing and reviewing plans, the provision of special guardianship support services in accordance with plans and reviewing the provision of special guardianship support services.

(8) The regulations may in particular make provision–

(a) about the type of assessment which is to be carried out, or the way in which an assessment is to be carried out;

(b) about the way in which a plan is to be prepared;

(c) about the way in which, and the time at which, a plan or the provision of special guardianship support services is to be reviewed;

(d) about the considerations to which a local authority are to have regard in carrying out an assessment or review or preparing a plan;

(e) as to the circumstances in which a local authority may provide special guardianship support services subject to conditions (including conditions as to payment for the support or the repayment of financial support);

(f) as to the consequences of conditions imposed by virtue of paragraph (e) not being met (including the recovery of any financial support provided);

(g) as to the circumstances in which this section may apply to a local authority in respect of persons who are outside that local authority's area;

(h) as to the circumstances in which a local authority may recover from another local authority the expenses of providing special guardianship support services to any person.

(9) A local authority may provide special guardianship support services (or any part of them) by securing their provision by–

(a) another local authority; or

(b) a person within a description prescribed in regulations of persons who may provide special guardianship support services,

and may also arrange with any such authority or person for that other authority or that person to carry out the local authority's functions in relation to assessments under this section.

(10) A local authority may carry out an assessment of the needs of any person for the purposes of this section at the same time as an assessment of his needs is made under any other provision of this Act or under any other enactment.

(11) Section 27 (co-operation between authorities) applies in relation to the exercise of functions of a local authority under this section as it applies in relation to the exercise of functions of a local authority under Part 3.

14G Special guardianship support services: representations
(1) Every local authority shall establish a procedure for considering representations (including complaints) made to them by any person to whom they may provide special guardianship support services about the discharge of their functions under section 14F in relation to him.
(2) Regulations may be made by the Secretary of State imposing time limits on the making of representations under subsection (1).
(3) In considering representations under subsection (1), a local authority shall comply with regulations (if any) made by the Secretary of State for the purposes of this subsection."
   (2) The 1989 Act is amended as follows.
   (3) In section 1 (welfare of the child), in subsection (4)(b), after "discharge" there is inserted "a special guardianship order or".
   (4) In section 5 (appointment of guardians)–
      (a) in subsection (1)-
         (i) in paragraph (b), for "or guardian" there is substituted ", guardian or special guardian", and
         (ii) at the end of paragraph (b) there is inserted "; or (c) paragraph (b) does not apply, and the child's only or last surviving special guardian dies.",
      (b) in subsection (4), at the end there is inserted "; and a special guardian of a child may appoint another individual to be the child's guardian in the event of his death", and
      (c) in subsection (7), at the end of paragraph (b) there is inserted "or he was the child's only (or last surviving) special guardian".

116   Accommodation of children in need etc.
   (1) In section 17 of the 1989 Act (provision of services for children in need, their families and others), in subsection (6) (services that may be provided in exercise of the functions under that section) after "include" there is inserted "providing accommodation and".
   (2) In section 22 of that Act (general duty of local authority in relation to children looked after by them), in subsection (1) (looked after children include those provided with accommodation, with exceptions) before "23B" there is inserted "17".
   (3) In section 24A of that Act (advice and assistance for certain children and young persons aged 16 or over), in subsection (5), for "or, in exceptional circumstances, cash" there is substituted "and, in exceptional circumstances, assistance may be given–
      (a) by providing accommodation, if in the circumstances assistance may not be given in respect of the accommodation under section 24B, or
      (b) in cash".

117   Inquiries by local authorities into representations
   (1) In section 24D of the 1989 Act (representations: sections 23A to 24B), after subsection (1) there is inserted–
      "(1A) Regulations may be made by the Secretary of State imposing time limits on the making of representations under subsection (1)."
   (2) Section 26 of that Act (procedure for considering other representations) is amended as follows.
   (3) In subsection (3) (which makes provision as to the persons by whom, and the matters in respect of which, representations may be made), for "functions under this Part" there is substituted "qualifying functions".
   (4) After that subsection there is inserted–
      "(3A) The following are qualifying functions for the purposes of subsection (3)–
         (a) functions under this Part,
         (b) such functions under Part 4 or 5 as are specified by the Secretary of State in regulations.
      (3B) The duty under subsection (3) extends to representations (including complaints) made to the authority by–

(a) any person mentioned in section 3(1) of the Adoption and Children Act 2002 (persons for whose needs provision is made by the Adoption Service) and any other person to whom arrangements for the provision of adoption support services (within the meaning of that Act) extend,

(b) such other person as the authority consider has sufficient interest in a child who is or may be adopted to warrant his representations being considered by them,

about the discharge by the authority of such functions under the Adoption and Children Act 2002 as are specified by the Secretary of State in regulations."

(5) In subsection (4) (procedure to require involvement of independent person), after paragraph (b) there is inserted–

"but this subsection is subject to subsection (5A)."

(6) After that subsection there is inserted–

"(4A) Regulations may be made by the Secretary of State imposing time limits on the making of representations under this section."

(7) After subsection (5) there is inserted–

"(5A) Regulations under subsection (5) may provide that subsection (4) does not apply in relation to any consideration or discussion which takes place as part of a procedure for which provision is made by the regulations for the purpose of resolving informally the matters raised in the representations."

118   Review of cases of looked after children

(1) In section 26 of the 1989 Act (review of cases of looked after children, etc.), in subsection (2) (regulations as to reviews)–

(a) in paragraph (e), "to consider" is omitted and after "their care" there is inserted–

"(i) to keep the section 31A plan for the child under review and, if they are of the opinion that some change is required, to revise the plan, or make a new plan, accordingly,

(ii) to consider",

(b) in paragraph (f), "to consider" is omitted and after the second mention of "the authority" there is inserted–

"(i) if there is no plan for the future care of the child, to prepare one,

(ii) if there is such a plan for the child, to keep it under review and, if they are of the opinion that some change is required, to revise the plan or make a new plan, accordingly,

(iii) to consider",

(c) after paragraph (j) there is inserted-

"(k) for the authority to appoint a person in respect of each case to carry out in the prescribed manner the functions mentioned in subsection (2A) and any prescribed function".

(2) After that subsection there is inserted–

"(2A) The functions referred to in subsection (2)(k) are–

(a) participating in the review of the case in question,

(b) monitoring the performance of the authority's functions in respect of the review,

(c) referring the case to an officer of the Children and Family Court Advisory and Support Service, if the person appointed under subsection (2)(k) considers it appropriate to do so.

(2B) A person appointed under subsection (2)(k) must be a person of a prescribed description.

(2C) In relation to children whose cases are referred to officers under subsection (2A)(c), the Lord Chancellor may by regulations–

(a) extend any functions of the officers in respect of family proceedings (within the meaning of section 12 of the Criminal Justice and Court Services Act 2000) to other proceedings,

(b) require any functions of the officers to be performed in the manner prescribed by the regulations."

119   Advocacy services
> After section 26 of the 1989 Act there is inserted–
>> **"26A Advocacy services**
>> (1) Every local authority shall make arrangements for the provision of assistance to–
>>> (a) persons who make or intend to make representations under section 24D; and
>>> (b) children who make or intend to make representations under section 26.
>> (2) The assistance provided under the arrangements shall include assistance by way of representation.
>> (3) The arrangements–
>>> (a) shall secure that a person may not provide assistance if he is a person who is prevented from doing so by regulations made by the Secretary of State; and
>>> (b) shall comply with any other provision made by the regulations in relation to the arrangements.
>> (4) The Secretary of State may make regulations requiring local authorities to monitor the steps that they have taken with a view to ensuring that they comply with regulations made for the purposes of subsection (3).
>> (5) Every local authority shall give such publicity to their arrangements for the provision of assistance under this section as they consider appropriate."

120   Meaning of "harm" in the 1989 Act
In section 31 of the 1989 Act (care and supervision orders), at the end of the definition of "harm" in subsection (9) there is inserted "including, for example, impairment suffered from seeing or hearing the ill-treatment of another".

121   Care plans
> (1) In section 31 of the 1989 Act (care and supervision orders), after subsection (3) there is inserted–
>> "(3A) No care order may be made with respect to a child until the court has considered a section 31A plan."
> (2) After that section there is inserted–
>> **"31A Care orders: care plans**
>> (1) Where an application is made on which a care order might be made with respect to a child, the appropriate local authority must, within such time as the court may direct, prepare a plan ("a care plan") for the future care of the child.
>> (2) While the application is pending, the authority must keep any care plan prepared by them under review and, if they are of the opinion some change is required, revise the plan, or make a new plan, accordingly.
>> (3) A care plan must give any prescribed information and do so in the prescribed manner.
>> (4) For the purposes of this section, the appropriate local authority, in relation to a child in respect of whom a care order might be made, is the local authority proposed to be designated in the order.
>> (5) In section 31(3A) and this section, references to a care order do not include an interim care order.
>> (6) A plan prepared, or treated as prepared, under this section is referred to in this Act as a "section 31A plan"."
> (3) If–
>> (a) before subsection (2) comes into force, a care order has been made in respect of a child and a plan for the future care of the child has been prepared in connection with the making of the order by the local authority designated in the order, and
>> (b) on the day on which that subsection comes into force the order is in force, or would be in force but for section 29(1) of this Act,
> the plan is to have effect as if made under section 31A of the 1989 Act.

122   Interests of children in proceedings
> (1) In section 41 of the 1989 Act (specified proceedings)–
>> (a) in subsection (6), after paragraph (h) there is inserted-
>>> "(hh) on an application for the making or revocation of a placement order (within the meaning of section 21 of the Adoption and Children Act 2002);",

(b) after that subsection there is inserted–

"(6A) The proceedings which may be specified under subsection (6)(i) include (for example) proceedings for the making, varying or discharging of a section 8 order."

(2) In section 93 of the 1989 Act (rules of court), in subsection (2), after paragraph (b) there is inserted–

"(bb) for children to be separately represented in relevant proceedings,".

PART 3: MISCELLANEOUS AND FINAL PROVISIONS

CHAPTER 1: MISCELLANEOUS

Advertisements in the United Kingdom

123   Restriction on advertisements etc.

(1) A person must not–

(a) publish or distribute an advertisement or information to which this section applies, or

(b) cause such an advertisement or information to be published or distributed.

(2) This section applies to an advertisement indicating that–

(a) the parent or guardian of a child wants the child to be adopted,

(b) a person wants to adopt a child,

(c) a person other than an adoption agency is willing to take any step mentioned in paragraphs (a) to (e), (g) and (h) and (so far as relating to those paragraphs) (i) of section 92(2),

(d) a person other than an adoption agency is willing to receive a child handed over to him with a view to the child's adoption by him or another, or

(e) a person is willing to remove a child from the United Kingdom for the purposes of adoption.

(3) This section applies to–

(a) information about how to do anything which, if done, would constitute an offence under section 85 or 93, section 11 or 50 of the Adoption (Scotland) Act 1978 (c. 28) or Article 11 or 58 of the Adoption (Northern Ireland) Order 1987 (S.I. 1987/2203 (N.I. 22)) (whether or not the information includes a warning that doing the thing in question may constitute an offence),

(b) information about a particular child as a child available for adoption.

(4) For the purposes of this section and section 124–

(a) publishing or distributing an advertisement or information means publishing it or distributing it to the public and includes doing so by electronic means (for example, by means of the internet),

(b) the public includes selected members of the public as well as the public generally or any section of the public.

(5) Subsection (1) does not apply to publication or distribution by or on behalf of an adoption agency.

(6) The Secretary of State may by order make any amendments of this section which he considers necessary or expedient in consequence of any developments in technology relating to publishing or distributing advertisements or other information by electronic or electro-magnetic means.

(7) References to an adoption agency in this section include a prescribed person outside the United Kingdom exercising functions corresponding to those of an adoption agency, if the functions are being exercised in prescribed circumstances.

"Prescribed" means prescribed by regulations made by the Secretary of State.

(8) Before exercising the power conferred by subsection (6) or (7), the Secretary of State must consult the Scottish Ministers, the Department of Health, Social Services and Public Safety and the Assembly.

(9) In this section–

(a) "adoption agency" includes a Scottish or Northern Irish adoption agency,

(b) references to adoption are to the adoption of persons, wherever they may be habitually resident, effected under the law of any country or territory, whether within or outside the British Islands.

124   Offence of breaching restriction under section 123

(1) A person who contravenes section 123(1) is guilty of an offence.

(2) A person is not guilty of an offence under this section unless it is proved that he knew or had reason to suspect that section 123 applied to the advertisement or information.

But this subsection only applies if sufficient evidence is adduced to raise an issue as to whether the person had the knowledge or reason mentioned.

(3) A person guilty of an offence under this section is liable on summary conviction to imprisonment for a term not exceeding three months, or a fine not exceeding level 5 on the standard scale, or both.

Adoption and Children Act Register

125 Adoption and Children Act Register

(1) Her Majesty may by Order in Council make provision for the Secretary of State to establish and maintain a register, to be called the Adoption and Children Act Register, containing–

(a) prescribed information about children who are suitable for adoption and prospective adopters who are suitable to adopt a child,

(b) prescribed information about persons included in the register in pursuance of paragraph (a) in respect of things occurring after their inclusion.

(2) For the purpose of giving assistance in finding persons with whom children may be placed for purposes other than adoption, an Order under this section may–

(a) provide for the register to contain information about such persons and the children who may be placed with them, and

(b) apply any of the other provisions of this group of sections (that is, this section and sections 126 to 131), with or without modifications.

(3) The register is not to be open to public inspection or search.

(4) An Order under this section may make provision about the retention of information in the register.

(5) Information is to be kept in the register in any form the Secretary of State considers appropriate.

126 Use of an organisation to establish the register

(1) The Secretary of State may make an arrangement with an organisation under which any function of his under an Order under section 125 of establishing and maintaining the register, and disclosing information entered in, or compiled from information entered in, the register to any person is performed wholly or partly by the organisation on his behalf.

(2) The arrangement may include provision for payments to be made to the organisation by the Secretary of State.

(3) If the Secretary of State makes an arrangement under this section with an organisation, the organisation is to perform the functions exercisable by virtue of this section in accordance with any directions given by the Secretary of State and the directions may be of general application (or general application in any part of Great Britain) or be special directions.

(4) An exercise of the Secretary of State's powers under subsection (1) or (3) requires the agreement of the Scottish Ministers (if the register applies to Scotland) and of the Assembly (if the register applies to Wales).

(5) References in this group of sections to the registration organisation are to any organisation for the time being performing functions in respect of the register by virtue of arrangements under this section.

127 Use of an organisation as agency for payments

(1) An Order under section 125 may authorise an organisation with which an arrangement is made under section 126 to act as agent for the payment or receipt of sums payable by adoption agencies to other adoption agencies and may require adoption agencies to pay or receive such sums through the organisation.

(2) The organisation is to perform the functions exercisable by virtue of this section in accordance with any directions given by the Secretary of State; and the directions may be of general application (or general application in any part of Great Britain) or be special directions.

(3) An exercise of the Secretary of State's power to give directions under subsection (2) requires the agreement of the Scottish Ministers (if any payment agency provision applies to Scotland) and of the Assembly (if any payment agency provision applies to

Wales).

128   Supply of information for the register

(1) An Order under section 125 may require adoption agencies to give prescribed information to the Secretary of State or the registration organisation for entry in the register.

(2) Information is to be given to the Secretary of State or the registration organisation when required by the Order and in the prescribed form and manner.

(3) An Order under section 125 may require an agency giving information which is entered on the register to pay a prescribed fee to the Secretary of State or the registration organisation.

(4) But an adoption agency is not to disclose any information to the Secretary of State or the registration organisation–

(a) about prospective adopters who are suitable to adopt a child, or persons who were included in the register as such prospective adopters, without their consent,

(b) about children suitable for adoption, or persons who were included in the register as such children, without the consent of the prescribed person.

(5) Consent under subsection (4) is to be given in the prescribed form.

129   Disclosure of information

(1) Information entered in the register, or compiled from information entered in the register, may only be disclosed under subsection (2) or (3).

(2) Prescribed information entered in the register may be disclosed by the Secretary of State or the registration organisation–

(a) where an adoption agency is acting on behalf of a child who is suitable for adoption, to the agency to assist in finding prospective adopters with whom it would be appropriate for the child to be placed,

(b) where an adoption agency is acting on behalf of prospective adopters who are suitable to adopt a child, to the agency to assist in finding a child appropriate for adoption by them.

(3) Prescribed information entered in the register, or compiled from information entered in the register, may be disclosed by the Secretary of State or the registration organisation to any prescribed person for use for statistical or research purposes, or for other prescribed purposes.

(4) An Order under section 125 may prescribe the steps to be taken by adoption agencies in respect of information received by them by virtue of subsection (2).

(5) Subsection (1) does not apply –

(a) to a disclosure of information with the authority of the Secretary of State, or

(b) to a disclosure by the registration organisation of prescribed information to the Scottish Ministers (if the register applies to Scotland) or the Assembly (if the register applies to Wales).

(6) Information disclosed to any person under subsection (2) or (3) may be given on any prescribed terms or conditions.

(7) An Order under section 125 may, in prescribed circumstances, require a prescribed fee to be paid to the Secretary of State or the registration organisation–

(a) by a prescribed adoption agency in respect of information disclosed under subsection (2), or

(b) by a person to whom information is disclosed under subsection (3).

(8) If any information entered in the register is disclosed to a person in contravention of subsection (1), the person disclosing it is guilty of an offence.

(9) A person guilty of an offence under subsection (8) is liable on summary conviction to imprisonment for a term not exceeding three months, or a fine not exceeding level 5 on the standard scale, or both.

130   Territorial application

(1) In this group of sections, "adoption agency" means–

(a) a local authority in England,

(b) a registered adoption society whose principal office is in England.

(2) An Order under section 125 may provide for any requirements imposed on adoption agencies in respect of the register to apply–

(a) to Scottish local authorities and to voluntary organisations providing a registered adoption service,

(b) to local authorities in Wales and to registered adoption societies whose principal offices are in Wales,

and, in relation to the register, references to adoption agencies in this group of sections include any authorities or societies mentioned in paragraphs (a) and (b) to which an Order under that section applies those requirements.

(3) For the purposes of this group of sections, references to the register applying to Scotland or Wales are to those requirements applying as mentioned in paragraph (a) or, as the case may be, (b) of subsection (2).

(4) An Order under section 125 may apply any provision made by virtue of section 127–

(a) to Scottish local authorities and to voluntary organisations providing a registered adoption service,

(b) to local authorities in Wales and to registered adoption societies whose principal offices are in Wales.

(5) For the purposes of this group of sections, references to any payment agency provision applying to Scotland or Wales are to provision made by virtue of section 127 applying as mentioned in paragraph (a) or, as the case may be, (b) of subsection (4).

131 Supplementary

(1) In this group of sections–

(a) "organisation" includes a public body and a private or voluntary organisation,

(b) "prescribed" means prescribed by an Order under section 125,

(c) "the register" means the Adoption and Children Act Register,

(d) "Scottish local authority" means a local authority within the meaning of the Regulation of Care (Scotland) Act 2001 (asp 4),

(e) "voluntary organisation providing a registered adoption service" has the same meaning as in section 144(3).

(2) For the purposes of this group of sections–

(a) a child is suitable for adoption if an adoption agency is satisfied that the child ought to be placed for adoption,

(b) prospective adopters are suitable to adopt a child if an adoption agency is satisfied that they are suitable to have a child placed with them for adoption.

(3) Nothing authorised or required to be done by virtue of this group of sections constitutes an offence under section 93, 94 or 95.

(4) No recommendation to make an Order under section 125 is to be made to Her Majesty in Council unless a draft has been laid before and approved by resolution of each House of Parliament.

(5) If any provision made by an Order under section 125 would, if it were included in an Act of the Scottish Parliament, be within the legislative competence of that Parliament, no recommendation to make the Order is to be made to Her Majesty in Council unless a draft has been laid before, and approved by resolution of, the Parliament.

(6) No recommendation to make an Order under section 125 containing any provision in respect of the register is to be made to Her Majesty in Council if the register applies to Wales or the Order would provide for the register to apply to Wales, unless a draft has been laid before, and approved by resolution of, the Assembly.

(7) No recommendation to make an Order under section 125 containing any provision by virtue of section 127 is to be made to Her Majesty in Council if any payment agency provision applies to Wales or the Order would provide for any payment agency provision to apply to Wales, unless a draft has been laid before, and approved by resolution of, the Assembly.

Other miscellaneous provisions

132 Amendment of Adoption (Scotland) Act 1978: contravention of sections 30 to 36 of this Act [not reproduced here]

133 Scottish restriction on bringing children into or out of United Kingdom [not reproduced here]

134 Amendment of Adoption (Scotland) Act 1978: overseas adoptions [not reproduced here]

135   Adoption and fostering: criminal records

(1) Part 5 of the Police Act 1997 (c. 50) (certificates of criminal records) is amended as follows.

(2) In section 113 (criminal record certificates), in subsection (3A), for "his suitability" there is substituted "the suitability of the applicant, or of a person living in the same household as the applicant, to be a foster parent or".

(3) In section 115 (enhanced criminal record certificates), in subsection (6A), for "his suitability" there is substituted "the suitability of the applicant, or of a person living in the same household as the applicant, to be a foster parent or".

136   Payment of grants in connection with welfare services

(1) Section 93 of the Local Government Act 2000 (c. 22) (payment of grants for welfare services) is amended as follows.

(2) In subsection (1) (payment of grants by the Secretary of State), for the words from "in providing" to the end there is substituted–

"(a) in providing, or contributing to the provision of, such welfare services as may be determined by the Secretary of State, or

(b) in connection with any such welfare services."

(3) In subsection (2) (payment of grants by the Assembly), for the words from "in providing" to the end there is substituted–

"(a) in providing, or contributing to the provision of, such welfare services as may be determined by the Assembly, or

(b) in connection with any such welfare services."

(4) After subsection (6) there is inserted–

"(6A) Before making any determination under subsection (3) or (5) the Secretary of State must obtain the consent of the Treasury."

137   Extension of the Hague Convention to British overseas territories

(1) Her Majesty may by Order in Council provide for giving effect to the Convention in any British overseas territory.

(2) An Order in Council under subsection (1) in respect of any British overseas territory may, in particular, make any provision corresponding to provision which in relation to any part of Great Britain is made by the Adoption (Intercountry Aspects) Act 1999 (c. 18) or may be made by regulations under section 1 of that Act.

(3) The British Nationality Act 1981 (c. 61) is amended as follows.

(4) In section 1 (acquisition of British citizenship by birth or adoption)–

(a) in subsection (5), at the end of paragraph (b) there is inserted "effected under the law of a country or territory outside the United Kingdom",

(b) at the end of subsection (5A)(b) there is inserted "or in a designated territory",

(c) in subsection (8), the words following "section 50" are omitted.

(5) In section 15 (acquisition of British overseas territories citizenship)–

(a) after subsection (5) there is inserted–

"(5A) Where–

(a) a minor who is not a British overseas territories citizen is adopted under a Convention adoption,

(b) on the date on which the adoption is effected–

(i) the adopter or, in the case of a joint adoption, one of the adopters is a British overseas territories citizen, and

(ii) the adopter or, in the case of a joint adoption, both of the adopters are habitually resident in a designated territory, and

(c) the Convention adoption is effected under the law of a country or territory outside the designated territory,

the minor shall be a British overseas territories citizen as from that date.",

(b) in subsection (6), after "order" there is inserted "or a Convention adoption".

(6) In section 50 (interpretation), in subsection (1)–

(a) after the definition of "company" there is inserted–

""Convention adoption" means an adoption effected under the law of a country or territory in which the Convention is in force, and certified in pursuance of Article 23(1) of the Convention",

(b) after the definition of "Crown service under the government of the United Kingdom" there is inserted–

""designated territory" means a qualifying territory, or the Sovereign Base Areas of Akrotiri and Dhekelia, which is designated by Her Majesty by Order in Council under subsection (14)".

(7) After subsection (13) of that section there is inserted–

"(14) For the purposes of the definition of "designated territory" in subsection (1), an Order in Council may–

(a) designate any qualifying territory, or the Sovereign Base Areas of Akrotiri and Dhekelia, if the Convention is in force there, and

(b) make different designations for the purposes of section 1 and section 15;

and, for the purposes of this subsection and the definition of "Convention adoption" in subsection (1), "the Convention" means the Convention on the Protection of Children and Co-operation in respect of Intercountry Adoption, concluded at the Hague on 29th May 1993.

An Order in Council under this subsection shall be subject to annulment in pursuance of a resolution of either House of Parliament."

138   Proceedings in Great Britain

Proceedings for an offence by virtue of section 9, 59, 93, 94, 95 or 129–

(a) may not be brought more than six years after the commission of the offence but, subject to that,

(b) may be brought within a period of six months from the date on which evidence sufficient in the opinion of the prosecutor to warrant the proceedings came to his knowledge.

In relation to Scotland, "the prosecutor" is to be read as "the procurator fiscal".

Amendments etc.

139   Amendments, transitional and transitory provisions, savings and repeals

(1) Schedule 3 (minor and consequential amendments) is to have effect.

(2) Schedule 4 (transitional and transitory provisions and savings) is to have effect.

(3) The enactments set out in Schedule 5 are repealed to the extent specified.

CHAPTER 2: FINAL PROVISIONS

140   Orders, rules and regulations

(1) Any power to make subordinate legislation conferred by this Act on the Lord Chancellor, the Secretary of State, the Scottish Ministers, the Assembly or the Registrar General is exercisable by statutory instrument.

(2) A statutory instrument containing subordinate legislation made under any provision of this Act (other than section 14 or 148 or an instrument to which subsection (3) applies) is to be subject to annulment in pursuance of a resolution of either House of Parliament.

(3) A statutory instrument containing subordinate legislation–

(a) under section 9 which includes provision made by virtue of section 45(2),

(b) under section 92(6), 94 or 123(6), or

(c) which adds to, replaces or omits any part of the text of an Act,

is not to be made unless a draft of the instrument has been laid before, and approved by resolution of, each House of Parliament.

(4) Subsections (2) and (3) do not apply to an Order in Council or to subordinate legislation made–

(a) by the Scottish Ministers, or

(b) by the Assembly, unless made jointly by the Secretary of State and the Assembly.

(5) A statutory instrument containing regulations under section 63(2) made by the Scottish Ministers is to be subject to annulment in pursuance of a resolution of the Scottish Parliament.

(6) The power of the Department of Health, Social Services and Public Safety to make regulations under section 63(2) is to be exercisable by statutory rule for the purposes of the Statutory Rules (Northern Ireland) Order 1979 (S.I. 1979/ 1573 (N.I. 12)); and any such regulations are to be subject to negative resolution within the meaning of section 41(6) of the Interpretation Act (Northern Ireland) 1954 (c. 33 (N.I.)) as if they were statutory instruments within the meaning of that Act.

(7) Subordinate legislation made under this Act may make different provision for different purposes.

(8) A power to make subordinate legislation under this Act (as well as being exercisable in relation to all cases to which it extends) may be exercised in relation to–

(a) those cases subject to specified exceptions, or

(b) a particular case or class of case.

(9) In this section, "subordinate legislation" does not include a direction.

141 Rules of procedure

(1) Rules may be made in accordance with Part 1 of Schedule 1 to the Constitutional Reform Act 2005 in respect of any matter to be prescribed by rules made by virtue of this Act and dealing generally with all matters of procedure.[19]

(2) Subsection (1) does not apply in relation to proceedings before magistrates' courts, but the power to make rules conferred by section 144 of the Magistrates' Courts Act 1980 (c. 43) includes power to make provision in respect of any of the matters mentioned in that subsection.

(3) In the case of an application for a placement order, for the variation or revocation of such an order, or for an adoption order, the rules must require any person mentioned in subsection (4) to be notified–

(a) of the date and place where the application will be heard, and

(b) of the fact that, unless the person wishes or the court requires, the person need not attend.

(4) The persons referred to in subsection (3) are–

(a) in the case of a placement order, every person who can be found whose consent to the making of the order is required under subsection (3)(a) of section 21 (or would be required but for subsection (3)(b) of that section) or, if no such person can be found, any relative prescribed by rules who can be found,

(b) in the case of a variation or revocation of a placement order, every person who can be found whose consent to the making of the placement order was required under subsection (3)(a) of section 21 (or would have been required but for subsection (3)(b) of that section),

(c) in the case of an adoption order-

(i) every person who can be found whose consent to the making of the order is required under subsection (2)(a) of section 47 (or would be required but for subsection (2)(c) of that section) or, if no such person can be found, any relative prescribed by rules who can be found,

(ii) every person who has consented to the making of the order under section 20 (and has not withdrawn the consent) unless he has given a notice under subsection (4)(a) of that section which has effect,

(iii) every person who, if leave were given under section 47(5), would be entitled to oppose the making of the order.

(5) Rules made in respect of magistrates' courts may provide–

(a) for enabling any fact tending to establish the identity of a child with a child to whom a document relates to be proved by affidavit, and

(b) for excluding or restricting in relation to any facts that may be so proved the power of a justice of the peace to compel the attendance of witnesses.

(6) Rules may, for the purposes of the law relating to contempt of court, authorise the publication in such circumstances as may be specified of information relating to proceedings held in private involving children.[20]

142 Supplementary and consequential provision

(1) The appropriate Minister may by order make–

(a) any supplementary, incidental or consequential provision,

(b) any transitory, transitional or saving provision,

which he considers necessary or expedient for the purposes of, in consequence of or for giving full effect to any provision of this Act.

(2) For the purposes of subsection (1), where any provision of an order extends to England and Wales, and Scotland or Northern Ireland, the appropriate Minister in relation to the order is the Secretary of State.

---

[19] Section 141(1) is printed as it is to be amended by the Constitutional Reform Act 2005, schedule 1, part 2, paragraph 27.

[20] Section 141(6) was inserted by the Children Act 2004, section 62(6).

(3) Before making an order under subsection (1) containing provision which would, if included in an Act of the Scottish Parliament, be within the legislative competence of that Parliament, the appropriate Minister must consult the Scottish Ministers.

(4) Subsection (5) applies to any power of the Lord Chancellor, the Secretary of State or the Assembly to make regulations, rules or an order by virtue of any other provision of this Act, any power to make rules under section 141 or any power of Her Majesty to make an Order in Council by virtue of section 125.[21]

(5) The power may be exercised so as to make–

    (a) any supplementary, incidental or consequential provision,

    (b) any transitory, transitional or saving provision,

which the person exercising the power considers necessary or expedient.

(6) The provision which may be made under subsection (1) or (5) includes provision modifying Schedule 4 or amending or repealing any enactment or instrument.

In relation to an Order in Council, "enactment" in this subsection includes an enactment comprised in, or in an instrument made under, an Act of the Scottish Parliament.

(7) The power of the Registrar General to make regulations under Chapter 5 of Part 1 may, with the approval of the Chancellor of the Exchequer, be exercised so as to make–

    (a) any supplementary, incidental or consequential provision,

    (b) any transitory, transitional or saving provision,

which the Registrar General considers necessary or expedient.

143   Offences by bodies corporate and unincorporated bodies

(1) Where an offence under this Act committed by a body corporate is proved to have been committed with the consent or connivance of, or to be attributable to any neglect on the part of, any director, manager, secretary or other similar officer of the body, or a person purporting to act in any such capacity, that person as well as the body is guilty of the offence and liable to be proceeded against and punished accordingly.

(2) Where the affairs of a body corporate are managed by its members, subsection (1) applies in relation to the acts and defaults of a member in connection with his functions of management as it applies to a director of a body corporate.

(3) Proceedings for an offence alleged to have been committed under this Act by an unincorporated body are to be brought in the name of that body (and not in that of any of its members) and, for the purposes of any such proceedings in England and Wales or Northern Ireland, any rules of court relating to the service of documents have effect as if that body were a corporation.

(4) A fine imposed on an unincorporated body on its conviction of an offence under this Act is to be paid out of the funds of that body.

(5) If an unincorporated body is charged with an offence under this Act–

    (a) in England and Wales, section 33 of the Criminal Justice Act 1925 (c. 86) and Schedule 3 to the Magistrates' Courts Act 1980 (c. 43) (procedure on charge of an offence against a corporation),

    (b) in Northern Ireland, section 18 of the Criminal Justice Act (Northern Ireland) 1945 (c. 15 (N.I.)) and Schedule 4 to the Magistrates' Courts (Northern Ireland) Order 1981 (S.I. 1981/1675 (N.I. 26)) (procedure on charge of an offence against a corporation),

have effect in like manner as in the case of a corporation so charged.

(6) Where an offence under this Act committed by an unincorporated body (other than a partnership) is proved to have been committed with the consent or connivance of, or to be attributable to any neglect on the part of, any officer of the body or any member of its governing body, he as well as the body is guilty of the offence and liable to be proceeded against and punished accordingly.

(7) Where an offence under this Act committed by a partnership is proved to have been committed with the consent or connivance of, or to be attributable to any neglect on the part of, a partner, he as well as the partnership is guilty of the offence and liable to be proceeded against and punished accordingly.

---

[21] Section 142(4) is printed as it is to be amended by the Constitutional Reform Act 2005, schedule 1, part 2, paragraph 28.

144 **General interpretation etc.**
(1) In this Act–
"appropriate Minister" means-
(a) in relation to England, Scotland or Northern Ireland, the Secretary of State,
(b) in relation to Wales, the Assembly,
and in relation to England and Wales means the Secretary of State and the Assembly acting jointly,
"the Assembly" means the National Assembly for Wales,
"body" includes an unincorporated body,
"by virtue of" includes "by" and "under",
"child", except where used to express a relationship, means a person who has not attained the age of 18 years,
"the Convention" means the Convention on Protection of Children and Co-operation in respect of Intercountry Adoption, concluded at the Hague on 29th May 1993,
"Convention adoption order" means an adoption order which, by virtue of regulations under section 1 of the Adoption (Intercountry Aspects) Act 1999 (c. 18) (regulations giving effect to the Convention), is made as a Convention adoption order,
"Convention country" means a country or territory in which the Convention is in force,
"court" means, subject to any provision made by virtue of Part 1 of Schedule 11 to the 1989 Act, the High Court, a county court or a magistrates' court,
"enactment" includes an enactment comprised in subordinate legislation,
"fee" includes expenses,
"guardian" has the same meaning as in the 1989 Act and includes a special guardian within the meaning of that Act,
"information" means information recorded in any form,
"local authority" means any unitary authority, or any county council so far as they are not a unitary authority,
"Northern Irish adoption agency" means an adoption agency within the meaning of Article 3 of the Adoption (Northern Ireland) Order 1987 (S.I. 1987/2203 (N.I. 22)),
"Northern Irish adoption order" means an order made, or having effect as if made, under Article 12 of the Adoption (Northern Ireland) Order 1987,
"notice" means a notice in writing,
"registration authority" (in Part 1) has the same meaning as in the Care Standards Act 2000 (c. 14),
"regulations" means regulations made by the appropriate Minister, unless they are required to be made by the Lord Chancellor, the Secretary of State or the Registrar General,
"relative", in relation to a child, means a grandparent, brother, sister, uncle or aunt, whether of the full blood or half blood or by marriage or civil partnership,
"rules" means rules made under section 141(1) or made by virtue of section 141(2) under section 144 of the Magistrates' Courts Act 1980 (c. 43),
"Scottish adoption order" means an order made, or having effect as if made, under section 12 of the Adoption (Scotland) Act 1978 (c. 28),
"subordinate legislation" has the same meaning as in the Interpretation Act 1978 (c. 30),
"unitary authority" means–
(a) the council of any county so far as they are the council for an area for which there are no district councils,
(b) the council of any district comprised in an area for which there is no county council,
(c) the council of a county borough,
(d) the council of a London borough,
(e) the Common Council of the City of London.
(2) Any power conferred by this Act to prescribe a fee by Order in Council or regulations includes power to prescribe–
(a) a fee not exceeding a prescribed amount,
(b) a fee calculated in accordance with the Order or, as the case may be, regulations,
(c) a fee determined by the person to whom it is payable, being a fee of a

reasonable amount.

(3) In this Act, "Scottish adoption agency" means–

(a) a local authority, or

(b) a voluntary organisation providing a registered adoption service;

but in relation to the provision of any particular service, references to a Scottish adoption agency do not include a voluntary organisation unless it is registered in respect of that service or a service which, in Scotland, corresponds to that service.

Expressions used in this subsection have the same meaning as in the Regulation of Care (Scotland) Act 2001 (asp 4) and "registered" means registered under Part 1 of that Act.

(4) In this Act, a couple means–

(a) a married couple, or

(aa) two people who are civil partners of each other, or

(b) two people (whether of different sexes or the same sex) living as partners in an enduring family relationship.

(5) Subsection (4)(b) does not include two people one of whom is the other's parent, grandparent, sister, brother, aunt or uncle.

(6) References to relationships in subsection (5)–

(a) are to relationships of the full blood or half blood or, in the case of an adopted person, such of those relationships as would exist but for adoption, and

(b) include the relationship of a child with his adoptive, or former adoptive, parents,

but do not include any other adoptive relationships.

(7) For the purposes of this Act, a person is the partner of a child's parent if the person and the parent are a couple but the person is not the child's parent.[22]

145   Devolution: Wales

(1) The references to the Adoption Act 1976 (c. 36) and to the 1989 Act in Schedule 1 to the National Assembly for Wales (Transfer of Functions) Order 1999 (S.I. 1999/672) are to be treated as referring to those Acts as amended by virtue of this Act.

(2) This section does not affect the power to make further Orders varying or omitting those references.

(3) In Schedule 1 to that Order, in the entry for the Adoption Act 1976, "9" is omitted.

(4) The functions exercisable by the Assembly under sections 9 and 9A of the Adoption Act 1976 (by virtue of paragraphs 4 and 5 of Schedule 4 to this Act) are to be treated for the purposes of section 44 of the Government of Wales Act 1998 (c. 38) (parliamentary procedures for subordinate legislation) as if made exercisable by the Assembly by an Order in Council under section 22 of that Act.

146   Expenses

There shall be paid out of money provided by Parliament–

(a) any expenditure incurred by a Minister of the Crown by virtue of this Act,

(b) any increase attributable to this Act in the sums payable out of money so provided under any other enactment.

147   Glossary

Schedule 6 (glossary) is to have effect.

148   Commencement

(1) This Act (except sections 116 and 136, this Chapter and the provisions mentioned in subsections (5) and (6)) is to come into force on such day as the Secretary of State may by order appoint.

(2) Before making an order under subsection (1) (other than an order bringing paragraph 53 of Schedule 3 into force) the Secretary of State must consult the Assembly.

(3) Before making an order under subsection (1) bringing sections 123 and 124 into force, the Secretary of State must also consult the Scottish Ministers and the Department of Health, Social Services and Public Safety.

(4) Before making an order under subsection (1) bringing sections 125 to 131 into force, the Secretary of State must also consult the Scottish Ministers.

(5) The following are to come into force on such day as the Scottish Ministers may by

---

[22] Section 144 is printed as amended by the Civil Partnership Act 2004, sections 79(11) and 144(4).

order appoint–

    (a) section 41(5) to (9), so far as relating to Scotland,

    (b) sections 132 to 134,

    (c) paragraphs 21 to 35 and 82 to 84 of Schedule 3,

    (d) paragraphs 15 and 23 of Schedule 4,

    (e) the entries in Schedule 5, so far as relating to the provisions mentioned in paragraphs (c) and (d),

    (f) section 139, so far as relating to the provisions mentioned in the preceding paragraphs.

    (6) Sections 2(6), 3(3) and (4), 4 to 17, 27(3), 53(1) to (3), 54, 56 to 65 and 98, paragraphs 13, 65, 66 and 111 to 113 of Schedule 3 and paragraphs 3 and 5 of Schedule 4 are to come into force on such day as the appropriate Minister may by order appoint.

149   Extent

    (1) The amendment or repeal of an enactment has the same extent as the enactment to which it relates.

    (2) Subject to that and to the following provisions, this Act except section 137 extends to England and Wales only.

    (3) The following extend also to Scotland and Northern Ireland–

    (a) sections 63(2) to (5), 65(2)(a) and (b) and (3), 123 and 124,

    (b) this Chapter, except sections 141 and 145.

    (4) The following extend also to Scotland–

    (a) section 41(5) to (9),

    (b) sections 125 to 131,

    (c) section 138,

    (d) section 139, so far as relating to provisions extending to Scotland.

    (5) In Schedule 4, paragraph 23 extends only to Scotland.

150   Short title

    This Act may be cited as the Adoption and Children Act 2002.

SCHEDULES

SCHEDULE 1: REGISTRATION OF ADOPTIONS

Registration of adoption orders

1   (1) Every adoption order must contain a direction to the Registrar General to make in the Adopted Children Register an entry in the form prescribed by regulations made by the Registrar General with the approval of the Chancellor of the Exchequer.

    (2) Where, on an application to a court for an adoption order in respect of a child, the identity of the child with a child to whom an entry in the registers of live-births or other records relates is proved to the satisfaction of the court, any adoption order made in pursuance of the application must contain a direction to the Registrar General to secure that the entry in the register or, as the case may be, record in question is marked with the word "Adopted".

    (3) Where an adoption order is made in respect of a child who has previously been the subject of an adoption order made by a court in England or Wales under Part 1 of this Act or any other enactment–

    (a) sub-paragraph (2) does not apply, and

    (b) the order must contain a direction to the Registrar General to mark the previous entry in the Adopted Children Register with the word "Re-adopted".

    (4) Where an adoption order is made, the prescribed officer of the court which made the order must communicate the order to the Registrar General in the prescribed manner; and the Registrar General must then comply with the directions contained in the order.

    "Prescribed" means prescribed by rules.

Registration of adoptions in Scotland, Northern Ireland, the Isle of Man and the Channel Islands

2   (1) Sub-paragraphs (2) and (3) apply where the Registrar General is notified by the authority maintaining a register of adoptions in a part of the British Islands outside England and Wales that an order has been made in that part authorising the adoption of a child.

    (2) If an entry in the registers of live-births or other records (and no entry in the

Adopted Children Register) relates to the child, the Registrar General must secure that the entry is marked with–

    (a) the word "Adopted", followed by

    (b) the name, in brackets, of the part in which the order was made.

(3) If an entry in the Adopted Children Register relates to the child, the Registrar General must mark the entry with–

    (a) the word "Re-adopted", followed by

    (b) the name, in brackets, of the part in which the order was made.

(4) Where, after an entry in either of the registers or other records mentioned in sub-paragraphs (2) and (3) has been so marked, the Registrar General is notified by the authority concerned that–

    (a) the order has been quashed,

    (b) an appeal against the order has been allowed, or

    (c) the order has been revoked,

the Registrar General must secure that the marking is cancelled.

(5) A copy or extract of an entry in any register or other record, being an entry the marking of which is cancelled under sub-paragraph (4), is not to be treated as an accurate copy unless both the marking and the cancellation are omitted from it.

Registration of other adoptions

3   (1) If the Registrar General is satisfied, on an application under this paragraph, that he has sufficient particulars relating to a child adopted under a registrable foreign adoption to enable an entry to be made in the Adopted Children Register for the child he must make the entry accordingly.

(2) If he is also satisfied that an entry in the registers of live-births or other records relates to the child, he must–

    (a) secure that the entry is marked "Adopted", followed by the name, in brackets, of the country in which the adoption was effected, or

    (b) where appropriate, secure that the overseas registers of births are so marked.

(3) An application under this paragraph must be made, in the prescribed manner, by a prescribed person and the applicant must provide the prescribed documents and other information.

(4) An entry made in the Adopted Children Register by virtue of this paragraph must be made in the prescribed form.

(5) In this Schedule "registrable foreign adoption" means an adoption which satisfies prescribed requirements and is either–

    (a) adoption under a Convention adoption, or

    (b) adoption under an overseas adoption.

(6) In this paragraph–

    (a) "prescribed" means prescribed by regulations made by the Registrar General with the approval of the Chancellor of the Exchequer,

    (b) "overseas register of births" includes–

        (i) a register made under regulations made by the Secretary of State under section 41(1)(g), (h) or (i) of the British Nationality Act 1981 (c. 61),

        (ii) a record kept under an Order in Council made under section 1 of the Registration of Births, Deaths and Marriages (Special Provisions) Act 1957 (c. 58) (other than a certified copy kept by the Registrar General).

Amendment of orders and rectification of Registers and other records

4   (1) The court by which an adoption order has been made may, on the application of the adopter or the adopted person, amend the order by the correction of any error in the particulars contained in it.

(2) The court by which an adoption order has been made may, if satisfied on the application of the adopter or the adopted person that within the period of one year beginning with the date of the order any new name–

    (a) has been given to the adopted person (whether in baptism or otherwise), or

    (b) has been taken by the adopted person,

either in place of or in addition to a name specified in the particulars required to be entered in the Adopted Children Register in pursuance of the order, amend the order by substituting or, as the case may be, adding that name in those particulars.

(3) The court by which an adoption order has been made may, if satisfied on the application of any person concerned that a direction for the marking of an entry in the registers of live-births, the Adopted Children Register or other records included in the order in pursuance of paragraph 1(2) or (3) was wrongly so included, revoke that direction.

(4) Where an adoption order is amended or a direction revoked under sub-paragraphs (1) to (3), the prescribed officer of the court must communicate the amendment in the prescribed manner to the Registrar General.

"Prescribed" means prescribed by rules.

(5) The Registrar General must then–

(a) amend the entry in the Adopted Children Register accordingly, or

(b) secure that the marking of the entry in the registers of live-births, the Adopted Children Register or other records is cancelled,

as the case may be.

(6) Where an adoption order is quashed or an appeal against an adoption order allowed by any court, the court must give directions to the Registrar General to secure that–

(a) any entry in the Adopted Children Register, and

(b) any marking of an entry in that Register, the registers of live-births or other records as the case may be, which was effected in pursuance of the order,

is cancelled.

(7) Where an adoption order has been amended, any certified copy of the relevant entry in the Adopted Children Register which may be issued pursuant to section 78(2)(b) must be a copy of the entry as amended, without the reproduction of–

(a) any note or marking relating to the amendment, or

(b) any matter cancelled in pursuance of it.

(8) A copy or extract of an entry in any register or other record, being an entry the marking of which has been cancelled, is not to be treated as an accurate copy unless both the marking and the cancellation are omitted from it.

(9) If the Registrar General is satisfied–

(a) that a registrable foreign adoption has ceased to have effect, whether on annulment or otherwise, or

(b) that any entry or mark was erroneously made in pursuance of paragraph 3 in the Adopted Children Register, the registers of live-births, the overseas registers of births or other records,

he may secure that such alterations are made in those registers or other records as he considers are required in consequence of the adoption ceasing to have effect or to correct the error.

"Overseas register of births" has the same meaning as in paragraph 3.

(10) Where an entry in such a register is amended in pursuance of sub-paragraph (9), any copy or extract of the entry is not to be treated as accurate unless it shows the entry as amended but without indicating that it has been amended.

Marking of entries on re-registration of birth on legitimation

5 (1) Without prejudice to paragraphs 2(4) and 4(5), where, after an entry in the registers of live-births or other records has been marked in accordance with paragraph 1 or 2, the birth is re-registered under section 14 of the Births and Deaths Registration Act 1953 (c. 20) (re-registration of births of legitimated persons), the entry made on the re-registration must be marked in the like manner.

(2) Without prejudice to paragraph 4(9), where an entry in the registers of live-births or other records is marked in pursuance of paragraph 3 and the birth in question is subsequently re-registered under section 14 of that Act, the entry made on re-registration must be marked in the like manner.

Cancellations in registers on legitimation

6 (1) This paragraph applies where an adoption order is revoked under section 55(1).

(2) The prescribed officer of the court must communicate the revocation in the prescribed manner to the Registrar General who must then cancel or secure the cancellation of–

(a) the entry in the Adopted Children Register relating to the adopted person, and

(b) the marking with the word "Adopted" of any entry relating to the adopted person in the registers of live-births or other records.

"Prescribed" means prescribed by rules.

(3) A copy or extract of an entry in any register or other record, being an entry the marking of which is cancelled under this paragraph, is not to be treated as an accurate copy unless both the marking and the cancellation are omitted from it.

SCHEDULE 2: DISCLOSURE OF BIRTH RECORDS BY REGISTRAR GENERAL

1   On an application made in the prescribed manner by an adopted person–

(a) a record of whose birth is kept by the Registrar General, and

(b) who has attained the age of 18 years,

the Registrar General must give the applicant any information necessary to enable the applicant to obtain a certified copy of the record of his birth.

"Prescribed" means prescribed by regulations made by the Registrar General with the approval of the Chancellor of the Exchequer.

2   (1) Before giving any information to an applicant under paragraph 1, the Registrar General must inform the applicant that counselling services are available to the applicant–

(a) from a registered adoption society, an organisation within section 144(3)(b) or an adoption society which is registered under Article 4 of the Adoption (Northern Ireland) Order 1987 (S.I. 1987/2203 (N.I. 22)),

(b) if the applicant is in England and Wales, at the General Register Office or from any local authority or registered adoption support agency,

(c) if the applicant is in Scotland, from any council constituted under section 2 of the Local Government etc. (Scotland) Act 1994 (c. 39),

(d) if the applicant is in Northern Ireland, from any Board.

(2) In sub-paragraph (1)(b), "registered adoption support agency" means an adoption support agency in respect of which a person is registered under Part 2 of the Care Standards Act 2000 (c. 14).

(3) In sub-paragraph (1)(d), "Board" means a Health and Social Services Board established under Article 16 of the Health and Personal Social Services (Northern Ireland) Order 1972 (S.I. 1972/1265 (N.I. 14)); but where the functions of a Board are exercisable by a Health and Social Services Trust, references in that sub-paragraph to a Board are to be read as references to the Health and Social Services Trust.

(4) If the applicant chooses to receive counselling from a person or body within sub-paragraph (1), the Registrar General must send to the person or body the information to which the applicant is entitled under paragraph 1.

3   (1) Where an adopted person who is in England and Wales–

(a) applies for information under paragraph 1 or Article 54 of the Adoption (Northern Ireland) Order 1987, or

(b) is supplied with information under section 45 of the Adoption (Scotland) Act 1978 (c. 28),

the persons and bodies mentioned in sub-paragraph (2) must, if asked by the applicant to do so, provide counselling for the applicant.

(2) Those persons and bodies are–

(a) the Registrar General,

(b) any local authority,

(c) a registered adoption society, an organisation within section 144(3)(b) or an adoption society which is registered under Article 4 of the Adoption (Northern Ireland) Order 1987.

4   (1) Where a person–

(a) was adopted before 12th November 1975, and

(b) applies for information under paragraph 1,

the Registrar General must not give the information to the applicant unless the applicant has attended an interview with a counsellor arranged by a person or body from whom counselling services are available as mentioned in paragraph 2.

(2) Where the Registrar General is prevented by sub-paragraph (1) from giving information to a person who is not living in the United Kingdom, the Registrar General may give the information to any body which–

(a) the Registrar General is satisfied is suitable to provide counselling to that person, and

(b) has notified the Registrar General that it is prepared to provide such counselling.

SCHEDULE 3: MINOR AND CONSEQUENTIAL AMENDMENTS

The Marriage Act 1949 (c. 76)

1   Section 3 of the Marriage Act 1949 (marriage of person aged under eighteen) is amended as follows.

2   In subsection (1), for "person or persons specified in subsection (1A) of this section" there is substituted "appropriate persons".

3   For subsection (1A) there is substituted–

"(1A) The appropriate persons are–

(a) if none of paragraphs (b) to (h) apply, each of the following-

(i) any parent of the child who has parental responsibility for him; and

(ii) any guardian of the child;

(b) where a special guardianship order is in force with respect to a child, each of the child's special guardians, unless any of paragraphs (c) to (g) applies;

(c) where a care order has effect with respect to the child, the local authority designated in the order, and each parent, guardian or special guardian (in so far as their parental responsibility has not been restricted under section 33(3) of the Children Act 1989), unless paragraph (e) applies;

(d) where a residence order has effect with respect to the child, the persons with whom the child lives, or is to live, as a result of the order, unless paragraph (e) applies;

(e) where an adoption agency is authorised to place the child for adoption under section 19 of the Adoption and Children Act 2002, that agency or, where a care order has effect with respect to the child, the local authority designated in the order;

(f) where a placement order is in force with respect to the child, the appropriate local authority;

(g) where a child has been placed for adoption with prospective adopters, the prospective adopters (in so far as their parental responsibility has not been restricted under section 25(4) of the Adoption and Children Act 2002), in addition to those persons specified in paragraph (e) or (f);

(h) where none of paragraphs (b) to (g) apply but a residence order was in force with respect to the child immediately before he reached the age of sixteen, the persons with whom he lived, or was to live, as a result of the order."

4   For subsection (1B) there is substituted–

"(1B) In this section–

"guardian of a child", "parental responsibility", "residence order", "special guardian", "special guardianship order" and "care order" have the same meaning as in the Children Act 1989;

"adoption agency", "placed for adoption", "placement order" and "local authority" have the same meaning as in the Adoption and Children Act 2002;

"appropriate local authority" means the local authority authorised by the placement order to place the child for adoption."

5   In subsection (2), for "The last foregoing subsection" there is substituted "Subsection (1)".

The Births and Deaths Registration Act 1953 (c. 20)

6   In section 10 of the Births and Deaths Registration Act 1953 (registration of father where parents not married)–

(a) in subsection (1)(d)(i), for "a parental responsibility agreement made between them in relation to the child" there is substituted "any agreement made between them under section 4(1)(b) of the Children Act 1989 in relation to the child",

(b) in subsection (1)(d)(ii), for "the Children Act 1989" there is substituted "that Act",

(c) in subsection (3), the words following "the Family Law Reform Act 1987" are omitted.

7   In section 10A of the Births and Deaths Registration Act 1953 (re-registration of father where parents not married)–

(a) in subsection (1)(d)(i), for "a parental responsibility agreement made between them in relation to the child" there is substituted "any agreement made between them under section 4(1)(b) of the Children Act 1989 in relation to the child",

(b) in subsection (1)(d)(ii), for "the Children Act 1989" there is substituted "that Act".

The Sexual Offences Act 1956 (c. 69)

8   In section 28 of the Sexual Offences Act 1956 (causing or encouraging prostitution of, intercourse with, or indecent assault on, girl under sixteen), in subsection (4), the "or" at the end of paragraph (a) is omitted, and after that paragraph there is inserted–
       "(aa) a special guardianship order under that Act is in force with respect to her and he is not her special guardian; or".

The Health Services and Public Health Act 1968 (c. 46)

9   The Health Services and Public Health Act 1968 is amended as follows.

10   In section 64 (financial assistance by the Secretary of State to certain voluntary organisations), in subsection (3)(a)(xviii), for "the Adoption Act 1976" there is substituted "the Adoption and Children Act 2002".

11   In section 65 (financial and other assistance by local authorities to certain voluntary organisations), in subsection (3)(b), for "the Adoption Act 1976" there is substituted "the Adoption and Children Act 2002".

The Local Authority Social Services Act 1970 (c. 42)

12   The Local Authority Social Services Act 1970 is amended as follows.

13   In section 7D (default powers of Secretary of State as respects social services functions of local authorities), in subsection (1), after "the Children Act 1989" there is inserted "section 1 or 2(4) of the Adoption (Intercountry Aspects) Act 1999 or the Adoption and Children Act 2002".

14   In Schedule 1 (enactments conferring functions assigned to social services committee)–
       (a) the entry relating to the Adoption Act 1976 is omitted,
       (b) in the entry relating to the Children Act 1989, after "Consent to application for residence order in respect of child in care" there is inserted "Functions relating to special guardianship orders",
       (c) in the entry relating to the Adoption (Intercountry Aspects) Act 1999–
              (i) in the first column, for "Section" there is substituted "Sections 1 and",
              (ii) in the second column, for "Article 9(a) to (c) of" there is substituted "regulations made under section 1 giving effect to" and at the end there is inserted "and functions under Article 9(a) to (c) of the Convention",
       and at the end of the Schedule there is inserted–
       "Adoption and Children Act 2002   Maintenance of Adoption Service;
                                            functions of local authority as adoption
                                            agency."

The Immigration Act 1971 (c. 77)

15   In section 33(1) of the Immigration Act 1971 (interpretation)–
       (a) in the definition of "Convention adoption", after "1978" there is inserted "or in the Adoption and Children Act 2002",
       (b) in the definition of "legally adopted", for "section 72(2) of the Adoption Act 1976" there is substituted "section 87 of the Adoption and Children Act 2002".

The Legitimacy Act 1976 (c. 31)

16   The Legitimacy Act 1976 is amended as follows.

17   In section 4 (legitimation of adopted child)–
       (a) in subsection (1), after "1976" there is inserted "or section 67 of the Adoption and Children Act 2002",
       (b) in subsection (2)–
              (i) in paragraph (a), after "39" there is inserted "or subsection (3)(b) of the said section 67",
              (ii) in paragraph (b), after "1976" there is inserted "or section 67, 68 or 69 of the Adoption and Children Act 2002".

18   In section 6 (dispositions depending on date of birth), at the end of subsection (2) there is inserted "or section 69(2) of the Adoption and Children Act 2002".

The Adoption Act 1976 (c. 36)

19   In section 38 of the Adoption Act 1976 (meaning of "adoption" in Part 4), in subsection (2), after "1975" there is inserted "but does not include an adoption of a kind mentioned in paragraphs (c) to (e) of subsection (1) effected on or after the day which is the appointed day for the purposes of Chapter 4 of Part 1 of the Adoption and Children Act 2002".

ADOPTION LAW MANUAL

The National Health Service Act 1977 (c. 49)

20 In section 124A(3) of the National Health Service Act 1977 (information provided by the Registrar General to the Secretary of State), the "or" at the end of paragraph (a) is omitted and after that paragraph there is inserted–
"(aa) entered in the Adopted Children Register maintained by the Registrar General under the Adoption and Children Act 2002; or".

The Adoption (Scotland) Act 1978 (c. 28)
[Paragraphs 21 to 35 relate to Scotland only and are not reproduced here.]

The Magistrates' Courts Act 1980 (c. 43)

36 The Magistrates' Courts Act 1980 is amended as follows.
37 In section 65 (meaning of family proceedings), in subsection (1), for paragraph (h) there is substituted–
"(h) the Adoption and Children Act 2002;".
38 In section 69 (sitting of magistrates' courts for family proceedings), in subsections (2) and (3), for "the Adoption Act 1976" there is substituted "the Adoption and Children Act 2002".
39 In section 71 (newspaper reports of family proceedings)–
(a) in subsection (1), "(other than proceedings under the Adoption Act 1976)" is omitted,
(b) in subsection (2)–
(i) for "the Adoption Act 1976" there is substituted "the Adoption and Children Act 2002",
(ii) the words following "(a) and (b)" are omitted.
40 In Part 1 of Schedule 6 (fees to be taken by justices' chief executives), in the entry relating to family proceedings–
(a) for "the Adoption Act 1976, except under section 21 of that Act", there is substituted "the Adoption and Children Act 2002, except under section 23 of that Act",
(b) in paragraph (c), for "section 21 of the Adoption Act 1976" there is substituted "section 23 of the Adoption and Children Act 2002".

The Mental Health Act 1983 (c. 20)

41 In section 28 of the Mental Health Act 1983 (nearest relative of minor under guardianship, etc.), in subsection (3), after ""guardian"" there is inserted "includes a special guardian (within the meaning of the Children Act 1989), but".

The Child Abduction Act 1984 (c. 37)

42 (1) Section 1 of the Child Abduction Act 1984 (offence of abduction of child by parent, etc.) is amended as follows.
(2) In subsection (2), after paragraph (c) there is inserted–
(ca) he is a special guardian of the child; or".
(3) In subsection (3)(a), after sub-paragraph (iii) there is inserted–
"(iiia) any special guardian of the child;".
(4) In subsection (4), for paragraphs (a) and (b) there is substituted–
"(a) he is a person in whose favour there is a residence order in force with respect to the child, and he takes or sends the child out of the United Kingdom for a period of less than one month; or
(b) he is a special guardian of the child and he takes or sends the child out of the United Kingdom for a period of less than three months."
(5) In subsection (5A), the "or" at the end of sub-paragraph (i) of paragraph (a) is omitted, and after that sub-paragraph there is inserted–
"(ia) who is a special guardian of the child; or".
(6) In subsection (7)(a), after " "guardian of a child," " there is inserted ""special guardian," ".
43 (1) The Schedule to that Act (modifications of section 1 for children in certain cases) is amended as follows.
(2) In paragraph 3 (adoption and custodianship), for sub-paragraphs (1) and (2) there is substituted–
"(1) This paragraph applies where–
(a) a child is placed for adoption by an adoption agency under section 19 of

496

the Adoption and Children Act 2002, or an adoption agency is authorised to place the child for adoption under that section; or

(b) a placement order is in force in respect of the child; or

(c) an application for such an order has been made in respect of the child and has not been disposed of; or

(d) an application for an adoption order has been made in respect of the child and has not been disposed of; or

(e) an order under section 84 of the Adoption and Children Act 2002 (giving parental responsibility prior to adoption abroad) has been made in respect of the child, or an application for such an order in respect of him has been made and has not been disposed of.

(2) Where this paragraph applies, section 1 of this Act shall have effect as if–

(a) the reference in subsection (1) to the appropriate consent were–

(i) in a case within sub-paragraph (1)(a) above, a reference to the consent of each person who has parental responsibility for the child or to the leave of the High Court;

(ii) in a case within sub-paragraph (1)(b) above, a reference to the leave of the court which made the placement order;

(iii) in a case within sub-paragraph (1)(c) or (d) above, a reference to the leave of the court to which the application was made;

(iv) in a case within sub-paragraph (1)(e) above, a reference to the leave of the court which made the order or, as the case may be, to which the application was made;

(b) subsection (3) were omitted;

(c) in subsection (4), in paragraph (a), for the words from "in whose favour" to the first mention of "child" there were substituted "who provides the child's home in a case falling within sub-paragraph (1)(a) or (b) of paragraph 3 of the Schedule to this Act"; and

(d) subsections (4A), (5), (5A) and (6) were omitted."

(3) In paragraph 5 (interpretation), in sub-paragraph (a), for the words from "and "adoption order"" to the end there is substituted ", "adoption order", "placed for adoption by an adoption agency" and "placement order" have the same meaning as in the Adoption and Children Act 2002; and".

The Matrimonial and Family Proceedings Act 1984 (c. 42)

44   In section 40 of the Matrimonial and Family Proceedings Act 1984 (family proceedings rules), in subsection (2), in paragraph (a), after "the Adoption Act 1968" the "or" is omitted and after "the Adoption Act 1976" there is inserted "or section 141(1) of the Adoption and Children Act 2002".

The Child Abduction and Custody Act 1985 (c. 60)

45   In Schedule 3 to the Child Abduction and Custody Act 1985 (custody orders), in paragraph 1, the "and" at the end of paragraph (b) is omitted and after that paragraph there is inserted–

"(bb) a special guardianship order (within the meaning of the Act of 1989); and",
and paragraph (c)(v) is omitted.

The Family Law Act 1986 (c. 55)

46   The Family Law Act 1986 is amended as follows.

47   In section 1 (orders to which Part 1 applies), in subsection (1), after paragraph (a) there is inserted–

"(aa) a special guardianship order made by a court in England and Wales under the Children Act 1989;

(ab) an order made under section 26 of the Adoption and Children Act 2002 (contact), other than an order varying or revoking such an order".

48   In section 2 (jurisdiction: general), after subsection (2) there is inserted–

"(2A) A court in England and Wales shall not have jurisdiction to make a special guardianship order under the Children Act 1989 unless the condition in section 3 of this Act is satisfied.

(2B) A court in England and Wales shall not have jurisdiction to make an order under section 26 of the Adoption and Children Act 2002 unless the condition in section 3 of this

Act is satisfied."

49   In section 57 (declarations as to adoptions effected overseas)–

(a) for subsection (1)(a) there is substituted–

"(a) a Convention adoption, or an overseas adoption, within the meaning of the Adoption and Children Act 2002, or",

(b) in subsection (2)(a), after "1976" there is inserted "or section 67 of the Adoption and Children Act 2002".

The Family Law Reform Act 1987 (c. 42)

50   The Family Law Reform Act 1987 is amended as follows.

51   In section 1 (general principle), for paragraph (c) of subsection (3) there is substituted–

"(c) is an adopted person within the meaning of Chapter 4 of Part 1 of the Adoption and Children Act 2002".

52   In section 19 (dispositions of property), in subsection (5), after "1976" there is inserted "or section 69 of the Adoption and Children Act 2002".

The Adoption (Northern Ireland) Order 1987 (S.I. 1987/2203 (N.I. 22))

53   In Article 2(2) (interpretation), in the definition of "prescribed", for "Articles 54" there is substituted "Articles 53(3B) and (3D), 54".

The Children Act 1989 (c. 41)

54   The Children Act 1989 is amended as follows.

55   In section 8 (residence, contact and other orders with respect to children), in subsection (4), for paragraph (d) there is substituted–

"(d) the Adoption and Children Act 2002;".

56   In section 10 (power of court to make section 8 orders)–

(a) in subsection (4)(a), for "or guardian" there is substituted ", guardian or special guardian",

(b) after subsection (4)(a) there is inserted–

"(aa) any person who by virtue of section 4A has parental responsibility for the child;",

(c) after subsection (5) there is inserted–

"(5A) A local authority foster parent is entitled to apply for a residence order with respect to a child if the child has lived with him for a period of at least one year immediately preceding the application.",

(d) after subsection (7) there is inserted–

"(7A) If a special guardianship order is in force with respect to a child, an application for a residence order may only be made with respect to him, if apart from this subsection the leave of the court is not required, with such leave."

57   In section 12 (residence orders and parental responsibility), in subsection (3)–

(a) paragraph (a) is omitted,

(b) in paragraph (b), for "section 55 of the Act of 1976" there is substituted "section 84 of the Adoption and Children Act 2002".

58   In section 16 (family assistance orders), in subsection (2)(a), for "or guardian" there is substituted ", guardian or special guardian".

59   In section 20 (provision of accommodation for children: general), in subsection (9), the "or" at the end of paragraph (a) is omitted and after that paragraph there is inserted–

"(aa) who is a special guardian of the child; or".

60   In section 24 (persons qualifying for advice and assistance)–

(a) for subsection (1) there is substituted–

"(1) In this Part "a person qualifying for advice and assistance" means a person to whom subsection (1A) or (1B) applies.

(1A) This subsection applies to a person–

(a) who has reached the age of sixteen but not the age of twenty-one;

(b) with respect to whom a special guardianship order is in force (or, if he has reached the age of eighteen, was in force when he reached that age); and

(c) who was, immediately before the making of that order, looked after by a local authority.

(1B) This subsection applies to a person to whom subsection (1A) does not apply, and who–

(a) is under twenty-one; and

(b) at any time after reaching the age of sixteen but while still a child was, but is no longer, looked after, accommodated or fostered.",

(b) in subsection (2), for "subsection (1)(b)" there is substituted "subsection (1B)(b)",

(c) in subsection (5), before paragraph (a) there is inserted–

"(za) in the case of a person to whom subsection (1A) applies, a local authority determined in accordance with regulations made by the Secretary of State;".

61   In section 24A (advice and assistance for qualifying persons)–

(a) in subsection (2)(b), after "a person" there is inserted "to whom section 24(1A) applies, or to whom section 24(1B) applies and",

(b) in subsection (3)(a), after "if" there is inserted "he is a person to whom section 24(1A) applies, or he is a person to whom section 24(1B) applies and".

62   In section 24B (assistance with employment, education and training), in each of subsections (1) and (3)(b), after "of" there is inserted "section 24(1A) or".

63   In section 33 (effect of care order)–

(a) in subsection (3)(b), for "a parent or guardian of the child" there is substituted"–

(i) a parent, guardian or special guardian of the child; or

(ii) a person who by virtue of section 4A has parental responsibility for the child,",

(b) in subsection (5), for "a parent or guardian of the child who has care of him" there is substituted "a person mentioned in that provision who has care of the child",

(c) in subsection (6)(b)–

(i) sub-paragraph (i) is omitted,

(ii) in sub-paragraph (ii), for "section 55 of the Act of 1976" there is substituted "section 84 of the Adoption and Children Act 2002",

(d) in subsection (9), for "a parent or guardian of the child" there is substituted "a person mentioned in that provision".

64   In section 34 (parental contact etc. with children in care)–

(a) in subsection (1)(b), after "guardian" there is inserted "or special guardian", and

(b) after subsection (1)(b) there is inserted–

"(ba) any person who by virtue of section 4A has parental responsibility for him;".

65   In section 80 (inspection of children's homes by persons authorised by Secretary of State), in subsection (1), paragraphs (e) and (f) are omitted.

66   In section 81 (inquiries), in subsection (1), paragraph (b) is omitted.

67   In section 88 (amendments of adoption legislation), subsection (1) is omitted.

68   In section 91 (effect and duration of orders, etc.)–

(a) after subsection (5) there is inserted–

"(5A) The making of a special guardianship order with respect to a child who is the subject of–

(a) a care order; or

(b) an order under section 34,

discharges that order.",

(b) in subsection (7), after "4(1)" there is inserted "4A(1)",

(c) in subsection (8)(a), after "4" there is inserted "or 4A".

69   In section 102 (power of constable to assist in exercise of certain powers to search for children or inspect premises), in subsection (6), paragraph (c) is omitted.

70   In section 105 (interpretation), in subsection (1)–

(a) in the definition of "adoption agency", for "section 1 of the Adoption Act 1976" there is substituted "section 2 of the Adoption and Children Act 2002",

(b) at the appropriate place there is inserted–

""section 31A plan" has the meaning given by section 31A(6);",

(c) in the definition of "parental responsibility agreement", for "section 4(1)" there is substituted "sections 4(1) and 4A(2)",

(d) the definition of "protected child" is omitted,

(e) after the definition of "special educational needs" there is inserted–

""special guardian" and "special guardianship order" have the meaning given by section 14A;".

71   In Schedule 1 (financial provision for children)–

(a) in paragraph 1 (orders for financial relief against parents)–

(i) in sub-paragraph (1), for "or guardian" there is substituted ", guardian or special guardian"" and

(ii) in sub-paragraph (6), after "order" there is inserted "or a special guardianship order",

(b) in paragraph 6 (variation etc of orders for periodical payments), in sub-paragraph (8), after "guardian" there is inserted "or special guardian",

(c) in paragraph 8 (financial relief under other enactments), in sub-paragraph (1) and in sub-paragraph (2)(b), after "residence order" there is inserted "or a special guardianship order",

(d) in paragraph 14 (financial provision for child resident in country outside England and Wales), in sub-paragraph (1)(b), after "guardian" there is inserted "or special guardian".

72   In Schedule 2, in paragraph 19 (arrangements by local authorities to assist children to live abroad)–

(a) in sub-paragraph (4) (arrangements to assist children to live abroad), after "guardian," there is inserted "special guardian,",

(b) in sub-paragraph (6), for the words from the beginning to "British subject)" there is substituted "Section 85 of the Adoption and Children Act 2002 (which imposes restrictions on taking children out of the United Kingdom)",

(c) after sub-paragraph (8) there is inserted–

"(9) This paragraph does not apply to a local authority placing a child for adoption with prospective adopters."

73   In Schedule 8 (privately fostered children), in paragraph 5, for sub-paragraphs (a) and (b) there is substituted "he is placed in the care of a person who proposes to adopt him under arrangements made by an adoption agency within the meaning of–

(a) section 2 of the Adoption and Children Act 2002;

(b) section 1 of the Adoption (Scotland) Act 1978; or

(c) Article 3 of the Adoption (Northern Ireland) Order 1987".

74   Part 1 of Schedule 10 is omitted.

75   In Schedule 11 (jurisdiction), in paragraphs 1 and 2, for the words "the Adoption Act 1976", wherever they occur, there is substituted "the Adoption and Children Act 2002".

The Human Fertilisation and Embryology Act 1990 (c. 37)

76   The Human Fertilisation and Embryology Act 1990 is amended as follows.

77   In section 27 (meaning of mother), in subsection (2), for "child of any person other than the adopter or adopters" there is substituted "woman's child".

78   In section 28 (meaning of father), in subsection (5)(c), for "child of any person other than the adopter or adopters" there is substituted "man's child".

79   In section 30 (parental orders in favour of gamete donors), in subsection (10) for "Adoption Act 1976" there is substituted "Adoption and Children Act 2002".

The Courts and Legal Services Act 1990 (c. 41)

80   In section 58A of the Courts and Legal Services Act 1990 (conditional fee agreements: supplementary), in subsection (2), for paragraph (b) there is substituted–

"(b) the Adoption and Children Act 2002;".

The Child Support Act 1991 (c. 48)

81   In section 26 of the Child Support Act 1991 (disputes about parentage), in subsection (3), after "1976" there is inserted "or Chapter 4 of Part 1 of the Adoption and Children Act 2002".

The Children (Scotland) Act 1995 (c. 36)

84   [not reproduced here]

The Family Law Act 1996 (c. 27)

85   The Family Law Act 1996 is amended as follows.

86   In section 62 (meaning of "relevant child" etc.)–

(a) in subsection (2), in paragraph (b), after "the Adoption Act 1976" there is inserted ", the Adoption and Children Act 2002",

(b) in subsection (5), for the words from "has been freed" to "1976"" there is substituted "falls within subsection (7)".

87   At the end of that section there is inserted–

"(7) A child falls within this subsection if–

(a) an adoption agency, within the meaning of section 2 of the Adoption and Children Act 2002, has power to place him for adoption under section 19 of that Act (placing children with parental consent) or he has become the subject of an order under section 21 of that Act (placement orders), or

(b) he is freed for adoption by virtue of an order made–

(i) in England and Wales, under section 18 of the Adoption Act 1976,

(ii) in Scotland, under section 18 of the Adoption (Scotland) Act 1978, or

(iii) in Northern Ireland, under Article 17(1) or 18(1) of the Adoption (Northern Ireland) Order 1987."

88 In section 63 (interpretation of Part 4)–

(a) in subsection (1), for the definition of "adoption order", there is substituted–

""adoption order" means an adoption order within the meaning of section 72(1) of the Adoption Act 1976 or section 46(1) of the Adoption and Children Act 2002;",

(b) in subsection (2), after paragraph (h) there is inserted–

"(i) the Adoption and Children Act 2002."

The Housing Act 1996 (c. 52)

89 Section 178 of the Housing Act 1996 (meaning of associated person) is amended as follows.

90 In subsection (2), for the words from "has been freed" to "1976" there is substituted "falls within subsection (2A)".

91 After that subsection there is inserted–

"(2A) A child falls within this subsection if–

(a) an adoption agency, within the meaning of section 2 of the Adoption and Children Act 2002, is authorised to place him for adoption under section 19 of that Act (placing children with parental consent) or he has become the subject of an order under section 21 of that Act (placement orders), or

(b) he is freed for adoption by virtue of an order made–

(i) in England and Wales, under section 18 of the Adoption Act 1976,

(ii) in Scotland, under section 18 of the Adoption (Scotland) Act 1978, or

(iii) in Northern Ireland, under Article 17(1) or 18(1) of the Adoption (Northern Ireland) Order 1987."

92 In subsection (3), for the definition of "adoption order", there is substituted–

""adoption order" means an adoption order within the meaning of section 72(1) of the Adoption Act 1976 or section 46(1) of the Adoption and Children Act 2002;".

The Police Act 1997 (c. 50)

93 In section 115 of the Police Act 1997 (enhanced criminal records), in subsection (5)(h), for "section 11 of the Adoption Act 1976" there is substituted "section 2 of the Adoption and Children Act 2002".[23]

The Protection of Children Act 1999 (c. 14)

94 In section 2B of the Protection of Children Act 1999 (individuals named in the findings of certain inquiries), in subsection (7), after paragraph (a) there is inserted–

"(vi) section 17 of the Adoption and Children Act 2002;".

The Adoption (Intercountry Aspects) Act 1999 (c. 18)

95 The following provisions of the Adoption (Intercountry Aspects) Act 1999 cease to have effect in relation to England and Wales: sections 3, 6, 8, 9 and 11 to 13.

96 Section 2 of that Act (accredited bodies) is amended as follows.

97 In subsection (2A)–

(a) for the words from the beginning to "2000" there is substituted "A registered adoption society",

(b) for "agency" there is substituted "society".

98 For subsection (5) there is substituted–

"(5) In this section, "registered adoption society" has the same meaning as in section 2 of the Adoption and Children Act 2002 (basic definitions); and expressions used in this section in its application to England and Wales which are also used in that Act have the same meanings as in that Act."

99 In subsection (6)–

(a) the words "in its application to Scotland" are omitted,

(b) after "expressions" there is inserted "used in this section in its application to Scotland".

100 Section 14 (restriction on bringing children into the United Kingdom for adoption) is

[23] Paragraph 93 is to be repealed by the Serious Organised Crime and Police Act 2005, schedule 17, part 2.

omitted.
101   In section 16(1) (devolution: Wales), the words ", or section 17 or 56A of the 1976 Act," are omitted.

The Access to Justice Act 1999 (c. 22)
102   In Schedule 2 to the Access to Justice Act 1999 (Community Legal Service: excluded services), in paragraph 2(3)(c)–
        (a) for "section 27 or 28 of the Adoption Act 1976" there is substituted "section 36 of the Adoption and Children Act 2002",
        (b) for "an order under Part II or section 29 or 55" there is substituted "a placement order or adoption order (within the meaning of the Adoption and Children Act 2002) or an order under section 41 or 84".

The Care Standards Act 2000 (c. 14)
103   The Care Standards Act 2000 is amended as follows.
104   In section 4 (basic definitions), in subsection (7), for "the Adoption Act 1976" there is substituted "the Adoption and Children Act 2002".
105   At the end of section 5 (registration authorities) there is inserted–
        "(2) This section is subject to section 36A."
106   In section 11 (requirement to register), in subsection (3), for "reference in subsection (1) to an agency does" there is substituted "references in subsections (1) and (2) to an agency do".
107   In section 14 (2) (offences conviction of which may result in cancellation of registration), for paragraph (d) there is substituted–
        "(d) an offence under regulations under section 1(3) of the Adoption (Intercountry Aspects) Act 1999,
        (e) an offence under the Adoption and Children Act 2002 or regulations made under it".
108   In section 16(2) (power to make regulations providing that no application for registration may be made in respect of certain agencies which are unincorporated bodies), "or a voluntary adoption agency" is omitted.
109   In section 22(10) (disapplication of power to make regulations in the case of voluntary adoption agencies), at the end there is inserted "or adoption support agencies".
110   In section 23 (standards), at the end of subsection (4)(d) there is inserted "or proceedings against a voluntary adoption agency for an offence under section 9(4) of the Adoption Act 1976 or section 9 of the Adoption and Children Act 2002".
111   In section 31 (inspections by authorised persons), in subsection (3)(b), for "section 9(2) of the Adoption Act 1976" there is substituted "section 9 of the Adoption and Children Act 2002".
112   In section 43 (introductory), in subsection (3)(a)–
        (a) for "the Adoption Act 1976" there is substituted "the Adoption and Children Act 2002",
        (b) after "children" there is inserted "or the provision of adoption support services (as defined in section 2(6) of the Adoption and Children Act 2002)".
113   In section 46 (inspections: supplementary), in subsection (7)(c), for "section 9(3) of the Adoption Act 1976" there is substituted "section 9 of the Adoption and Children Act 2002".
114   In section 48 (regulation of fostering functions), at the end of subsection (1) there is inserted–
        "(f) as to the fees or expenses which may be paid to persons assisting local authorities in making decisions in the exercise of such functions""
115   In section 55(2)(b) (definition of "social care worker"), for "or a voluntary adoption agency" there is substituted ", a voluntary adoption agency or an adoption support agency".
116   In section 121 (general interpretation)–
        (a) in subsection (1), in the definition of "voluntary organisation", for "the Adoption Act 1976" there is substituted "the Adoption and Children Act 2002",
        (b) in subsection (13), in the appropriate place in the table there is inserted-
        "Adoption support agency   Section 4"
117   In Schedule 4 (minor and consequential amendments), paragraph 27(b) is omitted.

The Criminal Justice and Court Services Act 2000 (c. 43)

118   In section 12(5) of the Criminal Justice and Court Services Act 2000 (meaning of "family proceedings" in relation to CAFCASS), paragraph (b) (supervision orders under the 1989 Act) and the preceding "and" are omitted.

SCHEDULE 4: TRANSITIONAL AND TRANSITORY PROVISIONS AND SAVINGS

General rules for continuity

1   (1) Any reference (express or implied) in Part 1 or any other enactment, instrument or document to–

(a) any provision of Part 1, or

(b) things done or falling to be done under or for the purposes of any provision of Part 1,

must, so far as the nature of the reference permits, be construed as including, in relation to the times, circumstances or purposes in relation to which the corresponding provision repealed by this Act had effect, a reference to that corresponding provision or (as the case may be) to things done or falling to be done under or for the purposes of that corresponding provision.

(2) Any reference (express or implied) in any enactment, instrument or document to–

(a) a provision repealed by this Act, or

(b) things done or falling to be done under or for the purposes of such a provision,

must, so far as the nature of the reference permits, be construed as including, in relation to the times, circumstances or purposes in relation to which the corresponding provision of Part 1 has effect, a reference to that corresponding provision or (as the case may be) to things done or falling to be done under or for the purposes of that corresponding provision.

General rule for old savings

2   (1) The repeal by this Act of an enactment previously repealed subject to savings does not affect the continued operation of those savings.

(2) The repeal by this Act of a saving made on the previous repeal of an enactment does not affect the operation of the saving in so far as it is not specifically reproduced in this Act but remains capable of having effect.

Adoption support services

3   (1) The facilities to be provided by local authorities as part of the service maintained under section 1(1) of the Adoption Act 1976 (c. 36) include such arrangements as the authorities may be required by regulations to make for the provision of adoption support services to prescribed persons.

(2) Regulations under sub-paragraph (1) may require a local authority–

(a) at the request of a prescribed person, to carry out an assessment of his needs for adoption support services,

(b) if, as a result of the assessment, the authority decide that he has such needs, to decide whether to provide any such services to him,

(c) if the authority decide to provide any such services to a person, and the circumstances fall within a description prescribed by the regulations, to prepare a plan in accordance with which the services are to be provided to him and keep the plan under review.

(3) Subsections (6) and (7) (except paragraph (a)) of section 4 of this Act apply to regulations under sub-paragraph (1) as they apply to regulations made by virtue of that section.

(4) Section 57(1) of the Adoption Act 1976 (prohibited payments) does not apply to any payment made in accordance with regulations under sub-paragraph (1).

Regulation of adoption agencies

4   (1) In section 9 of the Adoption Act 1976–

(a) for "Secretary of State" in subsections (2) and (3) there is substituted "appropriate Minister", and

(b) at the end of that section there is inserted–

"(5) In this section and section 9A, "the appropriate Minister" means–

(a) in relation to England, the Secretary of State,

(b) in relation to Wales, the National Assembly for Wales,

and in relation to England and Wales, means the Secretary of State and the Assembly acting jointly."

(2) Until the commencement of the repeal by this Act of section 9(2) of the Adoption Act 1976, section 36A of the Care Standards Act 2000 (c. 14) (inserted by section 16 of this Act) is to have effect as if, after "2002", there were inserted "or under section 9(2) of the Adoption Act 1976".

Independent review mechanism

5   After section 9 of the Adoption Act 1976 (c. 36) there is inserted–

"9A Independent review of determinations

(1) Regulations under section 9 may establish a procedure under which any person in respect of whom a qualifying determination has been made by an adoption agency may apply to a panel constituted by the appropriate Minister for a review of that determination.

(2) The regulations must make provision as to the description of determinations which are qualifying determinations for the purposes of subsection (1).

(3) The regulations may include provision as to–

(a) the duties and powers of a panel (including the power to recover the costs of a review from the adoption agency by which the determination reviewed was made),

(b) the administration and procedures of a panel,

(c) the appointment of members of a panel (including the number, or any limit on the number, of members who may be appointed and any conditions for appointment),

(d) the payment of expenses of members of a panel,

(e) the duties of adoption agencies in connection with reviews conducted under the regulations,

(f) the monitoring of any such reviews.

(4) The appropriate Minister may make an arrangement with an organisation under which functions in relation to the panel are performed by the organisation on his behalf.

(5) If the appropriate Minister makes such an arrangement with an organisation, the organisation is to perform its functions under the arrangement in accordance with any general or special directions given by the appropriate Minister.

(6) The arrangement may include provision for payments to be made to the organisation by the appropriate Minister.

(7) Where the appropriate Minister is the National Assembly for Wales, subsections (4) and (6) also apply as if references to an organisation included references to the Secretary of State.

(8) In this section, "organisation" includes a public body and a private or voluntary organisation."

Pending applications for freeing orders

6   Nothing in this Act affects any application for an order under section 18 of the Adoption Act 1976 (freeing for adoption) where–

(a) the application has been made and has not been disposed of immediately before the repeal of that section, and

(b) the child in relation to whom the application is made has his home immediately before that repeal with a person with whom he has been placed for adoption by an adoption agency.

Freeing orders

7   (1) Nothing in this Act affects any order made under section 18 of the Adoption Act 1976 (c. 36) and–

(a) sections 19 to 21 of that Act are to continue to have effect in relation to such an order, and

(b) Part 1 of Schedule 6 to the Magistrates' Courts Act 1980 (c. 43) is to continue to have effect for the purposes of an application under section 21 of the Adoption Act 1976 in relation to such an order.

(2) Section 20 of that Act, as it has effect by virtue of this paragraph, is to apply as if, in subsection (3)(c) after "1989" there were inserted–

"(iia) any care order, within the meaning of that Act".

(3) Where a child is free for adoption by virtue of an order made under section 18 of that Act, the third condition in section 47(6) is to be treated as satisfied.

Pending applications for adoption orders

8 Nothing in this Act affects any application for an adoption order under section 12 of the Adoption Act 1976 where–

(a) the application has been made and has not been disposed of immediately before the repeal of that section, and

(b) the child in relation to whom the application is made has his home immediately before that repeal with a person with whom he has been placed for adoption by an adoption agency.

Notification of adoption applications

9 Where a notice given in respect of a child by the prospective adopters under section 22(1) of the Adoption Act 1976 is treated by virtue of paragraph 1(1) as having been given for the purposes of section 44(2) in respect of an application to adopt the child, section 42(3) has effect in relation to their application for an adoption order as if for "six months" there were substituted "twelve months".

Adoptions with a foreign element

10 In section 13 of the Adoption Act 1976 (child to live with adopters before order is made)–

(a) in subsection (1)(a), at the beginning there is inserted "(subject to subsection (1A))",

(b) after subsection (1) there is inserted–

"(1A) Where an adoption is proposed to be effected by a Convention adoption order, the order shall not be made unless at all times during the preceding six months the child had his home with the applicants or one of them.",

(c) in subsection (2), after "subsection (1)" there is inserted "or (1A)",

(d) subsection (4) is omitted.

11 In section 56 of the Adoption Act 1976 (restriction on removal of children for adoption outside Great Britain)–

(a) in subsection (1), "not being a parent or guardian or relative of the child" is omitted,

(b) at the end of that section there is inserted-

"(4) Regulations may provide for subsection (1) to apply with modifications, or not to apply, if–

(a) the prospective adopters are parents, relatives or guardians of the child in question (or one of them is), or

(b) the prospective adopter is a step-parent of the child,

and any prescribed conditions are met.

(5) On the occasion of the first exercise of the power to make regulations under subsection (4)–

(a) the regulations shall not be made unless a draft of the regulations has been approved by a resolution of each House of Parliament, and

(b) accordingly section 67(2) does not apply to the statutory instrument containing the regulations.

(6) In this section, "prescribed" means prescribed by regulations and "regulations" means regulations made by the Secretary of State, after consultation with the National Assembly for Wales."

12 For section 56A of the Adoption Act 1976 (c. 36) there is substituted–

"56A Restriction on bringing children into the United Kingdom

(1) This section applies where a person who is habitually resident in the British Islands (the "British resident")–

(a) brings, or causes another to bring, a child who is habitually resident outside the British Islands into the United Kingdom for the purpose of adoption by the British resident, or

(b) at any time brings, or causes another to bring, into the United Kingdom a child adopted by the British resident under an external adoption effected within the period of six months ending with that time.

The references to adoption, or to a child adopted, by the British resident include a reference to adoption, or to a child adopted, by the British resident and another person.

(2) But this section does not apply if the child is intended to be adopted under a Convention adoption order.

(3) An external adoption means an adoption, other than a Convention adoption, of a child effected under the law of any country or territory outside the British Islands, whether

or not the adoption is–

    (a) an adoption within the meaning of Part IV of this Act, or

    (b) a full adoption (within the meaning of section 39(3A)).

(4) Regulations may require a person intending to bring, or to cause another to bring, a child into the United Kingdom in circumstances where this section applies–

    (a) to apply to an adoption agency (including an adoption agency within the meaning of section 1 of the Adoption (Scotland) Act 1978 or Article 3 of the Adoption (Northern Ireland) Order 1987) in the prescribed manner for an assessment of his suitability to adopt the child, and

    (b) to give the agency any information it may require for the purpose of the assessment.

(5) Regulations may require prescribed conditions to be met in respect of a child brought into the United Kingdom in circumstances where this section applies.

(6) In relation to a child brought into the United Kingdom for adoption in circumstances where this section applies, regulations may provide for any provision of Part II to apply with modifications or not to apply.

(7) If a person brings, or causes another to bring, a child into the United Kingdom at any time in circumstances where this section applies, he is guilty of an offence if–

    (a) he has not complied with any requirement imposed by virtue of subsection (4), or

    (b) any condition required to be met by virtue of subsection (5) is not met,

before that time, or before any later time which may be prescribed.

(8) A person guilty of an offence under this section is liable–

    (a) on summary conviction to imprisonment for a term not exceeding six months, or a fine not exceeding the statutory maximum, or both,

    (b) on conviction on indictment, to imprisonment for a term not exceeding twelve months, or a fine, or both.

(9) Regulations may provide for the preceding provisions of this section not to apply if–

    (a) the adopters or (as the case may be) prospective adopters are natural parents, natural relatives or guardians of the child in question (or one of them is), or

    (b) the British resident in question is a step-parent of the child,

and any prescribed conditions are met.

(10) On the occasion of the first exercise of the power to make regulations under subsection (9)–

    (a) the regulations shall not be made unless a draft of the regulations has been approved by a resolution of each House of Parliament, and

    (b) accordingly section 67(2) does not apply to the statutory instrument containing the regulations.

(11) In this section, "prescribed" means prescribed by regulations and "regulations" means regulations made by the Secretary of State, after consultation with the National Assembly for Wales."

13   In section 72 of the Adoption Act 1976 (c. 36) (interpretation), subsection (3B) is omitted.

Advertising

14   In section 58 of the Adoption Act 1976 (c. 36) (restrictions on advertisements)–

    (a) after subsection (1) there is inserted–

        "(1A) Publishing an advertisement includes doing so by electronic means (for example, by means of the internet).",

    (b) in subsection (2), for the words following "conviction" there is substituted "to imprisonment for a term not exceeding three months, or a fine not exceeding level 5 on the standard scale, or both".

15   In section 52 of the Adoption (Scotland) Act 1978 (c. 28) (restriction on advertisements)–

    (a) after subsection (1) there is inserted–

        "(1A) Publishing an advertisement includes doing so by electronic means (for example, by means of the internet).",

    (b) in subsection (2), for the words following "conviction" there is substituted "to imprisonment for a term not exceeding three months, or a fine not exceeding level 5 on the standard scale, or both""

16   (1) The Secretary of State may make regulations providing for the references to an

adoption agency in–
    (a) section 58(1)(c) of the Adoption Act 1976, and
    (b) section 52(1)(c) of the Adoption (Scotland) Act 1978,
to include a prescribed person outside the United Kingdom exercising functions corresponding to those of an adoption agency, if the functions are being exercised in prescribed circumstances.
"Prescribed" means prescribed by the regulations.
    (2) Before exercising the power conferred by sub-paragraph (1) in relation to the Adoption (Scotland) Act 1978, the Secretary of State must consult the Scottish Ministers.

Status
17   (1) Section 67–
    (a) does not apply to a pre-1976 instrument or enactment in so far as it contains a disposition of property, and
    (b) does not apply to any public general Act in its application to any disposition of property in a pre-1976 instrument or enactment.
    (2) Section 73 applies in relation to this paragraph as if this paragraph were contained in Chapter 4 of Part 1; and an instrument or enactment is a pre-1976 instrument or enactment for the purposes of this Schedule if it was passed or made at any time before 1st January 1976.

18   Section 69 does not apply to a pre-1976 instrument.
19   In section 70(1), the reference to Part 3 of the Family Law Reform Act 1987 (c. 42) includes Part 2 of the Family Law Reform Act 1969 (c. 46).

Registration of adoptions
20   (1) The power of the court under paragraph 4(1) of Schedule 1 to amend an order on the application of the adopter or adopted person includes, in relation to an order made before 1st April 1959, power to make any amendment of the particulars contained in the order which appears to be required to bring the order into the form in which it would have been made if paragraph 1 of that schedule had applied to the order.
    (2) In relation to an adoption order made before the commencement of the Adoption Act 1976 (c. 36), the reference in paragraph 4(3) of that Schedule to paragraph 1(2) or (3) is to be read–
    (a) in the case of an order under the Adoption of Children Act 1926 (c. 29), as a reference to section 12(3) and (4) of the Adoption of Children Act 1949 (c. 98),
    (b) in the case of an order under the Adoption Act 1950 (c. 26), as a reference to section 18(3) and (4) of that Act,
    (c) in the case of an order under the Adoption Act 1958 (c. 5), as a reference to section 21(4) and (5) of that Act.

The Child Abduction Act 1984 (c. 37)
21   Paragraph 43 of Schedule 3 does not affect the Schedule to the Child Abduction Act 1984 in its application to a child who is the subject of–
    (a) an order under section 18 of the Adoption Act 1976 freeing the child for adoption,
    (b) a pending application for such an order, or
    (c) a pending application for an order under section 12 of that Act.

The Courts and Legal Services Act 1990 (c. 41)
22   Paragraph 80 of Schedule 3 does not affect section 58A(2)(b) of the Courts and Legal Services Act 1990 in its application to proceedings under the Adoption Act 1976 (c. 36).

The Children (Scotland) Act 1995 (c. 36)
23   [not reproduced here]

SCHEDULE 5: REPEALS
Short title and chapter; Extent of repeal

Births and Deaths Registration Act 1953 (c. 20). In section 10(3), the words following "the Family Law Reform Act 1987".
Sexual Offences Act 1956 (c. 69). In section 28(4), the "or" at the end of paragraph (a).
Local Authority Social Services Act 1970 (c. 42). In Schedule 1, the entry relating to the Adoption Act 1976.
Adoption Act 1976 (c. 36). The whole Act, except Part 4 and paragraph 6 of Schedule 2.
Criminal Law Act 1977 (c. 45). In Schedule 12, the entries relating to the Adoption Act 1976.

National Health Service Act 1977 (c. 49). In section 124A(3), the "or" at the end of paragraph (a).

Domestic Proceedings and Magistrates' Courts Act 1978 (c. 22). Sections 73(2), 74(2) and 74(4).

Adoption (Scotland) Act 1978 (c. 28). [Not reproduced here.]

Magistrates' Courts Act 1980 (c. 43). In section 71(1) the words "(other than proceedings under the Adoption Act 1976)". In section 71(2) the words following "(a) and (b)". In Schedule 7, paragraphs 141 and 142.

British Nationality Act 1981 (c. 61). In section 1(8), the words following "section 50".

Mental Health Act 1983 (c. 20). In Schedule 4, paragraph 45.

Health and Social Services and Social Security Adjudications Act 1983 (c. 41). In Schedule 2, paragraphs 29 to 33, 35 and 36. In Schedule 9, paragraph 19.

County Courts Act 1984 (c. 28). In Schedule 2, paragraph 58.

Child Abduction Act 1984 (c. 37). In section 1(5A)(a), the "or" at the end of sub-paragraph (i).

Matrimonial and Family Proceedings Act 1984 (c. 42). In section 40(2)(a), after "the Adoption Act 1968", the word "or". In Schedule 1, paragraph 20.

Child Abduction and Custody Act 1985 (c. 60). In Schedule 3, in paragraph 1, the "and" at the end of paragraph (b). In Schedule 3, in paragraph 1(c), paragraph (v).

Family Law Reform Act 1987 (c. 42). In Schedule 3, paragraphs 2 to 5.

Children Act 1989 (c. 41). Section 9(4). Section 12(3)(a). In section 20(9), the "or" at the end of paragraph (a). In section 26(2)(e) and (f), the words "to consider". Section 33(6)(b)(i). Section 80(1)(e) and (f). Section 81(1)(b). Section 88(1). Section 102(6)(c). In section 105(1), the definition of "protected child". In Schedule 10, Part 1.

National Health Service and Community Care Act 1990 (c. 19). In Schedule 9, paragraph 17.

Human Fertilisation and Embryology Act 1990 (c. 37). In Schedule 4, paragraph 4.

Courts and Legal Services Act 1990 (c. 41). In Schedule 16, paragraph 7.

Local Government (Wales) Act 1994 (c. 19). In Schedule 10, paragraph 9.

Health Authorities Act 1995 (c. 17). In Schedule 1, paragraph 101.

Adoption (Intercountry Aspects) Act 1999 (c. 18). In section 2(6), the words "in its application to Scotland". Section 7(3). Section 14. In section 16(1), the words ", or section 17 or 56A of the 1976 Act,". In Schedule 2, paragraph 3.

Access to Justice Act 1999 (c. 22). In Schedule 13, paragraph 88.

Care Standards Act 2000 (c. 14). In section 16(2), the words "or a voluntary adoption agency". In Schedule 4, paragraphs 5 and 27(b).

Local Government Act 2000 (c. 22). In Schedule 5, paragraph 16.

Criminal Justice and Court Services Act 2000 (c. 43). Section 12(5)(b) and the preceding "and". In Schedule 7, paragraphs 51 to 53.

This Act. In Schedule 4, paragraphs 3 to 5 and 10 to 16.

SCHEDULE 6: GLOSSARY

In this Act, the expressions listed in the left-hand column below have the meaning given by, or are to be interpreted in accordance with, the provisions of this Act or (where stated) of the 1989 Act listed in the right-hand column.

Expression	Provision
the 1989 Act	section 2(5)
Adopted Children Register	section 77
Adoption and Children Act Register	section 125
adoption (in relation to Chapter 4 of Part 1)	section 66
adoption agency	section 2(1)
adoption agency placing a child for adoption	section 18(5)
Adoption Contact Register	section 80
adoption order	section 46(1)
Adoption Service	section 2(1)
adoption society	section 2(5)
adoption support agency	section 8
adoption support services	section 2(6)
appointed day (in relation to Chapter 4 of Part 1)	section 66(2)
appropriate Minister	section 144
Assembly	section 144
body	section 144

by virtue of...section 144
care order...section 105(1) of the 1989 Act
child...sections 49(5) and 144
child assessment order...section 43(2) of the 1989 Act
child in the care of a local authority..section 105(1) of the 1989 Act
child looked after by a local authority.....................................section 22 of the 1989 Act
child placed for adoption by an adoption agency.................... section 18(5)
child to be adopted, adopted child.............................. section 49(5)
consent (in relation to making adoption orders or
    placing for adoption).. section 52
the Convention...section 144
Convention adoption...section 66(1)(c)
Convention adoption order... section 144
Convention country..section 144
couple..section 144(4)
court.. section 144
disposition (in relation to Chapter 4 of Part 1)........................ section 73
enactment.. section 144
fee ....section 144
guardian...section 144
information...section 144
interim care order..section 38 of the 1989 Act
local authority... section 144
local authority foster parent..................................... section 23(3) of the 1989 Act
Northern Irish adoption agency.. section 144
Northern Irish adoption order.. section 144
notice...section 144
notice of intention to adopt..................................... section 44(2)
overseas adoption..section 87
parental responsibility...section 3 of the 1989 Act
partner, in relation to a parent of a child.................................section 144(7)
placement order..section 21
placing, or placed, for adoption.. sections 18(5) and 19(4)
prohibited steps order..section 8(1) of the 1989 Act
records (in relation to Chapter 5 of Part 1)............................. section 82
registered adoption society...................................... section 2(2)
registers of live-births (in relation to Chapter 5 of Part 1)........section 82
registration authority (in Part 1)..section 144
regulations..section 144
relative...section 144, read with section 1(8)
residence order..section 8(1) of the 1989 Act
rules...section 144
Scottish adoption agency.. section 144(3)
Scottish adoption order... section 144
specific issue order...section 8(1) of the 1989 Act
subordinate legislation... section 144
supervision order..section 31(11) of the 1989 Act
unitary authority..section 144
voluntary organisation... section 2(5)

Appendix B

The Family Procedure (Adoption) Rules 2005
SI 2005 No 2795

Made: 10th October 2005.
Laid before Parliament: 12th October 2005.
Coming into force: 30th December 2005.

PART 19: APPEALS

The Family Procedure Rule Committee makes the following Rules in exercise of the powers conferred by sections 75 and 76 of the Courts Act 2003, sections 52(7) and (8), 60(4), 90(1), 102, 109(2) and 141(1) and (3) of, and paragraphs 1(4), 4(4) and 6(2) of Schedule 1 to, the Adoption and Children Act 2002[24] and section 54(1) of the Access to Justice Act 1999.

In accordance with section 79 of the Courts Act 2003 the Committee has consulted with persons it considered appropriate.

These Rules may be cited as the Family Procedure (Adoption) Rules 2005.

PART 1: OVERRIDING OBJECTIVE

The overriding objective

1.—(1) These Rules are a new procedural code with the overriding objective of enabling the court to deal with cases justly, having regard to the welfare issues involved.

(2) Dealing with a case justly includes, so far as is practicable—

(a) ensuring that it is dealt with expeditiously and fairly;

(b) dealing with the case in ways which are proportionate to the nature, importance and complexity of the issues;

(c) ensuring that the parties are on an equal footing;

(d) saving expense; and

(e) allotting to it an appropriate share of the court's resources, while taking into account the need to allot resources to other cases.

Application by the court of the overriding objective

2. The court must seek to give effect to the overriding objective when it—

(a) exercises any power given to it by these Rules; or

(b) interprets any rule.

Duty of the parties

3. The parties are required to help the court to further the overriding objective.

Court's duty to manage cases

4.—(1) The court must further the overriding objective by actively managing cases.

(2) Active case management includes—

(a) encouraging the parties to co-operate with each other in the conduct of the proceedings;

(b) identifying at an early stage—

(i) the issues; and

(ii) who should be a party to the proceedings;

---

[24] Section 102 was amended by section 40 of, and paragraphs 15 and 16 of Schedule 3 to, the Children Act 2004. Section 141(1) was amended, and section 141(2) was revoked, by section 109 of, paragraph 413 of Schedule 8, and Schedule 10, to the Courts Act 2003. Section 141(6) was inserted by section 62(6) of the Children Act 2004.

(c) deciding promptly—
    (i)   which issues need full investigation and hearing and which do not; and
    (ii) the procedure to be followed in the case;
(d) deciding the order in which issues are to be resolved;
(e) encouraging the parties to use an alternative dispute resolution procedure if the court considers that appropriate and facilitating the use of such procedure;
(f) helping the parties to settle the whole or part of the case;
(g) fixing timetables or otherwise controlling the progress of the case;
(h) considering whether the likely benefits of taking a particular step justify the cost of taking it;
(i) dealing with as many aspects of the case as it can on the same occasion;
(j) dealing with the case without the parties needing to attend at court;
(k) making use of technology; and
(l) giving directions to ensure that the case proceeds quickly and efficiently.

PART 2: INTERPRETATION AND APPLICATION OF OTHER RULES

Extent and application of other rules

5.—(1) Unless the context otherwise requires, these Rules apply to proceedings in—
    (a) the High Court;
    (b) a county court; and
    (c) a magistrates' court.

(2) Rule 35.15 of the CPR shall apply in detailed assessment proceedings in the High Court and a county court.

(3) Subject to paragraph (4), Parts 43, 44 (except rules 44.3(2) and (3) and 44.9 to 44.12A), 47 and 48 and rule 45.6 of the CPR apply to costs in proceedings, with the following modifications—
    (a) in rule 43.2(1)(c)(ii), "district judge" includes a district judge of the principal registry of the Family Division;
    (b) after rule 43.2(1)(d)(iv), insert—
        "or (v) a magistrates' court."; and
    (c) in rule 48.7(1) after "section 51(6) of the Supreme Court Act 1981" insert "or section 145A of the Magistrates' Courts Act 1980[25]".

(4) Part 47 of the CPR does not apply to proceedings in a magistrates' court.

(5) Parts 50 and 70 to 74 of, and Schedules 1 and 2 to, the CPR apply, as far as they are relevant, to the enforcement of orders made in proceedings in the High Court and county courts with necessary modifications.

Interpretation

6.—(1) In these Rules—
"the Act" means Part 1 of the Adoption and Children Act 2002;
"the 1989 Act" means the Children Act 1989;
"adoption proceedings" means proceedings for the making of an adoption order under the Act;
"application notice" means a document in which the applicant states his intention to seek a court order in accordance with the procedure in Part 9;
"business day" means any day other than—
    (a) a Saturday, Sunday, Christmas Day or Good Friday; or
    (b) a bank holiday under the Banking and Financial Dealings Act 1971, in England and Wales;
"Central Authority" means, in relation to England, the Secretary of State for Education and Skills, and in relation to Wales, the National Assembly for Wales;
"child"—
    (a) means, subject to paragraph (b), a person under the age of 18 years who is the subject of the proceedings; and
    (b) in adoption proceedings, also includes a person who has attained the age of 18 years before the proceedings are concluded;
"children and family reporter" means an officer of the Service or a Welsh family proceedings officer who prepares a report on matters relating to the welfare of the child;
"children's guardian" means an officer of the Service or a Welsh family proceedings

---

[25] Section 145A was inserted by section 112 of the Courts and Legal Services Act 1990.

officer appointed to act on behalf of a child who is a party to the proceedings with the duty of safeguarding the interests of the child;

"civil restraint order" means an order restraining a party—

(a) from making any further applications in current proceedings (a limited civil restraint order);

(b) from making certain applications in specified courts (an extended civil restraint order); or

(c) from making any application in specified courts (a general civil restraint order);

"court officer" means, in the High Court and a county court, a member of court staff, and in a magistrates' court, the designated officer;

"CPR" means the Civil Procedure Rules 1998 [SI 1998 No. 3132];

"detailed assessment proceedings" means the procedure by which the amount of costs is decided in accordance with Part 47 of the CPR;

"filing", in relation to a document, means delivering it, by post or otherwise, to the court office;

"jurisdiction" means, unless the context requires otherwise, England and Wales and any part of the territorial waters of the United Kingdom adjoining England and Wales;

"legal representative" means a barrister or a solicitor, solicitor's employee or other authorised litigator (as defined in section 119 of the Courts and Legal Services Act 1990) who has been instructed to act for a party in relation to an application;

"litigation friend" has the meaning given by section 1 of Part 7;

"non-subject child" means a person under the age of 18 years who is a party to the proceedings but is not the subject of the proceedings;

"officer of the Service" has the meaning given by section 11(3) of the Criminal Justice and Court Services Act 2000;

"patient" means a party to proceedings who, by reason of mental disorder within the meaning of the Mental Health Act 1983, is incapable of managing and administering his property and affairs;

"placement proceedings" means proceedings for the making, varying or revoking of a placement order under the Act;

"proceedings" means, unless the context otherwise requires, proceedings brought under the Act (whether at first instance or appeal) or proceedings for the purpose of enforcing an order made in any proceedings under that Act, as the case may be;

"provision for contact" means a contact order under section 8 or 34 of the 1989 Act or a contact order under section 26;

"reporting officer" means an officer of the Service or a Welsh family proceedings officer appointed to witness the documents which signify a parent or guardian's consent to the placing of the child for adoption or to the making of an adoption order or a section 84 order;

"section 84 order" means an order made by the High Court under section 84 giving parental responsibility prior to adoption abroad;

"section 88 direction" means a direction given by the High Court under section 88 that section 67(3) (status conferred by adoption) does not apply or does not apply to any extent specified in the direction;

"section 89 order" means an order made by the High Court under section 89—

(a) annulling a Convention adoption or Convention adoption order;

(b) providing for an overseas adoption or determination under section 91 to cease to be valid; or

(c) deciding the extent, if any, to which a determination under section 91 has been affected by a subsequent determination under that section;

"the Service Regulation" means Council Regulation (EC) No 1348/2000 of 29 May 2000 on the service in the Member States of judicial and extrajudicial documents in civil or commercial matters;

"Welsh family proceedings officer" has the meaning given by section 35(4) of the Children Act 2004.

(2) A section or Schedule referred to by number alone means the section or Schedule so numbered in the Adoption and Children Act 2002.

(3) Any provision in these Rules—

(a) requiring or permitting directions to be given by the court is to be taken as including provision for such directions to be varied or revoked; and

(b) requiring or permitting a date to be set is to be taken as including provision for that date to be set aside.

Power to perform functions of the court

7.—(1) Where these Rules or a practice direction provide for the court to perform any act then, except where any rule or practice direction, any other enactment, or the Family Proceedings (Allocation to Judiciary)[26] Directions, provides otherwise, that act may be performed—

(a) in relation to proceedings in the High Court or in a district registry, by any judge or district judge of that Court including a district judge of the principal registry of the Family Division;

(b) in relation to proceedings in a county court, by any judge or district judge including a district judge of the principal registry of the Family Division when the principal registry of the Family Division is treated as if it were a county court[27]; and

(c) in relation to proceedings in a magistrates' court—

    (i) by any family proceedings court constituted in accordance with sections 66 and 67 of the Magistrates' Courts Act 1980[28]; or

    (ii) by a single justice of the peace who is a member of the family panel—

        (aa) where an application without notice is made under section 41(2) (recovery orders); and

        (bb) in accordance with the relevant practice direction.

(The Justices' Clerks Rules 2005 make provision for a justices' clerk or assistant clerk to carry out certain functions of a single justice of the peace.)

(2) A deputy High Court judge and a district judge, including a district judge of the principal registry of the Family Division, may not try a claim for a declaration of incompatibility in accordance with section 4 of the Human Rights Act 1998.

Court's discretion as to where it deals with cases

8. The court may deal with a case at any place that it considers appropriate.

Court documents

9.—(1) A court officer must seal[29], or otherwise authenticate with the stamp of the court, the following documents on issue—

(a) the application form;

(b) the order; and

(c) any other document which a rule or practice direction requires it to seal or stamp.

(2) The court officer may place the seal or the stamp on the document—

(a) by hand; or

(b) by printing a facsimile of the seal on the document whether electronically or otherwise.

(3) A document purporting to bear the court's seal or stamp will be admissible in evidence without further proof.

(4) The relevant practice direction contains provisions about court documents.

Computation of time

10.—(1) This rule shows how to calculate any period of time for doing any act which is specified—

(a) by these Rules;

(b) by a practice direction; or

(c) by a direction or order of the court.

(2) A period of time expressed as a number of days must be computed as clear days.

(3) In this rule "clear days" means that in computing the numbers of days—

---

[26] The Family Proceedings (Allocation to Judiciary) Directions [1999] 2 FLR 799 provides that circuit judges, deputy circuit judges, recorders (subject to certain exceptions), district judges and deputy district judges must be nominated as a judge to whom adoption proceedings may be allocated by the President of the Family Division.

[27] By virtue of article 19 of the Children (Allocation of Proceedings) Order 1991 (S.I. 1991/1677) the principal registry of the Family Division is treated as a county court.

[28] Section 67 was substituted by section 49 of the Courts Act 2003.

[29] A seal is a mark which the court puts on a document to indicate that the document has been issued by the court.

(a) the day on which the period begins; and

(b) if the end of the period is defined by reference to an event, the day on which that event occurs

are not included.

(4) Where the specified period is 7 days or less and would include a day which is not a business day, that day does not count.

(5) When the period specified—

(a) by these Rules or a practice direction; or

(b) by any direction or order of the court,

for doing any act at the court office ends on a day on which the office is closed, that act will be in time if done on the next day on which the court office is open.

Dates for compliance to be calendar dates and to include time of day

11.—(1) Where the court makes an order or gives a direction which imposes a time limit for doing any act, the last date for compliance must, wherever practicable—

(a) be expressed as a calendar date; and

(b) include the time of day by which the act must be done.

(2) Where the date by which an act must be done is inserted in any document, the date must, wherever practicable, be expressed as a calendar date.

(3) Where "month" occurs in any order, direction or other document, it means a calendar month.

PART 3: GENERAL CASE MANAGEMENT POWERS

The court's general powers of management

12.—(1) The list of powers in this rule is in addition to any powers given to the court by any other rule or practice direction or by any other enactment or any powers it may otherwise have.

(2) Except where these Rules provide otherwise, the court may—

(a) extend or shorten the time for compliance with any rule, practice direction or court direction (even if an application for extension is made after the time for compliance has expired);

(b) adjourn or bring forward a hearing;

(c) require a party or a party's legal representative to attend the court;

(d) hold a hearing and receive evidence by telephone or by using any other method of direct oral communication;

(e) direct that part of any proceedings be dealt with as separate proceedings;

(f) stay the whole or part of any proceedings or judgment either generally or until a specified date or event;

(g) consolidate proceedings;

(h) hear two or more applications on the same occasion;

(i) direct a separate hearing of any issue;

(j) decide the order in which issues are to be heard;

(k) exclude an issue from consideration;

(l) dismiss or give judgment on an application after a decision on a preliminary issue;

(m) direct any party to file and serve an estimate of costs; and

(n) take any other step or give any other direction for the purpose of managing the case and furthering the overriding objective.

(3) The court may not extend the period within which a section 89 order must be made.

(4) Paragraph (2)(f) does not apply to proceedings in a magistrates' court.

Exercise of powers of court's own initiative

13.—(1) Except where an enactment provides otherwise, the court may exercise the powers in rule 12 on an application or of its own initiative.

(Part 9 sets out the procedure for making an application.)

(2) Where the court proposes to exercise its powers of its own initiative—

(a) it may give any person likely to be affected an opportunity to make representations; and

(b) where it does so it must specify the time by and the manner in which the representations must be made.

(3) Where the court proposes to hold a hearing to decide whether to exercise its powers of its own initiative it must give each party likely to be affected at least 3 days' notice of the hearing.

(4) The court may exercise its powers of its own initiative, without hearing the parties or

giving them an opportunity to make representations.

(5) Where the court has exercised its powers under paragraph (4)—

(a) a party affected by the direction may apply to have it set aside or varied; and

(b) the direction must contain a statement of the right to make such an application.

(6) An application under paragraph (5)(a) must be made—

(a) within such period as may be specified by the court; or

(b) if the court does not specify a period, within 7 days beginning with the date on which the order was served on the party making the application.

(7) If the High Court or a county court of its own initiative dismisses an application (including an application for permission to appeal) and it considers that the application is totally without merit—

(a) the court's order must record that fact; and

(b) the court must at the same time consider whether it is appropriate to make a civil restraint order.

Court officer's power to refer to the court

14. Where these Rules require a step to be taken by a court officer—

(a) the court officer may consult the court before taking that step;

(b) the step may be taken by the court instead of the court officer.

General power of the court to rectify matters where there has been an error of procedure

15. Where there has been an error of procedure such as a failure to comply with a rule or practice direction—

(a) the error does not invalidate any step taken in the proceedings unless the court so orders; and

(b) the court may make an order to remedy the error.

Power of the court to make civil restraint orders

16. The relevant practice direction sets out—

(a) the circumstances in which the High Court or a county court has the power to make a civil restraint order against a party to proceedings;

(b) the procedure where a party applies for a civil restraint order against another party; and

(c) the consequences of the court making a civil restraint order.

PART 4: HOW TO START PROCEEDINGS

Forms

17. Subject to rule 28(2) and (3), the forms set out in the relevant practice direction or forms to the like effect must be used in the cases to which they apply.

Documents to be attached to the application form

18. The application form must have attached to it any documents referred to in the application form.

How to start proceedings

19.—(1) Proceedings are started when a court officer issues an application at the request of the applicant.

(2) An application is issued on the date entered in the application form by the court officer. (Restrictions on where proceedings may be started are set out in the Children (Allocation of Proceedings) Order 1991[SI 1991/1677 as amended by SI 2005/2797 and others].)

Application for a serial number

20.—(1) This rule applies to any application in proceedings by a person who intends to adopt the child.

(2) If the applicant wishes his identity to be kept confidential in the proceedings, he may, before those proceedings have started, request a court officer to assign a serial number to him to identify him in connection with the proceedings, and a number will be assigned to him.

(3) The court may at any time direct that a serial number identifying the applicant in the proceedings referred to in paragraph (2) must be removed.

(4) If a serial number has been assigned to a person under paragraph (2)—

(a) the court officer will ensure that any application form or application notice sent in accordance with these Rules does not contain information which discloses, or is likely to disclose, the identity of that person to any other party to that application who is not already aware of that person's identity; and

(b) the proceedings on the application will be conducted with a view to securing that the applicant is not seen by or made known to any party who is not already aware of his identity except with his consent.

Personal details

21.—(1) Unless the court directs otherwise, a party is not required to reveal—

(a) the address or telephone number of their private residence;

(b) the address of the child;

(c) the name of a person with whom the child is living, if that person is not the applicant; or

(d) in relation to an application under section 28(2) (application for permission to change the child's surname), the proposed new surname of the child.

(2) Where a party does not wish to reveal any of the particulars in paragraph (1), he must give notice of those particulars to the court and the particulars will not be revealed to any person unless the court directs otherwise.

(3) Where a party changes his home address during the course of proceedings, he must give notice of the change to the court.

PART 5: PROCEDURE FOR APPLICATIONS IN ADOPTION, PLACEMENT AND RELATED PROCEEDINGS

Application of this Part

22. The rules in this Part apply to the following proceedings—

(a) adoption proceedings;

(b) placement proceedings; or

(c) proceedings for—

(i) the making of a contact order under section 26;

(ii) the variation or revocation of a contact order under section 27;

(iii) an order giving permission to change a child's surname or remove a child from the United Kingdom under section 28(2) and (3);

(iv) a section 84 order;

(v) a section 88 direction;

(vi) a section 89 order; or

(vii) any other order that may be referred to in a practice direction.

(Parts 9 and 10 set out the procedure for making an application in proceedings not dealt with in this Part.)

Who the parties are

23.—(1) In relation to the proceedings set out in column 1 of each of the following tables, column 2 of Table 1 sets out who the application may be made by and column 2 of Table 2 sets out who the respondents to those proceedings will be.

Table 1

Proceedings for	*Applicants*
An adoption order (section 46)	The prospective adopters (section 50 and 51).
A section 84 order	The prospective adopters asking for parental responsibility prior to adoption abroad.
A placement order (section 21)	A local authority (section 22).
An order varying a placement order (section 23)	The joint application of the local authority authorised by the placement order to place the child for adoption and the local authority which is to be substituted for that authority (section 23).
An order revoking a placement order (section 24)	The child; the local authority authorised to place the child for adoption; or where the child is not placed for adoption by the authority, any other person who has the permission of the court to apply (section 24).
A contact order (section 26)	The child; the adoption agency; any parent, guardian or relative; any person in whose favour there was provision for

contact under the 1989 Act which ceased to have effect on an adoption agency being authorised to place a child for adoption, or placing a child for adoption who is less than six weeks old (section 26(1)); a person in whose favour there was a residence order in force immediately before the adoption agency was authorised to place the child for adoption or placed the child for adoption at a time when he was less than six weeks old; a person who by virtue of an order made in the exercise of the High Court's inherent jurisdiction with respect to children had care of the child immediately before that time; or any person who has the permission of the court to make the application (section 26).

An order varying or revoking a contact order (section 27)	The child; the adoption agency; or any person named in the contact order (section 27(1)).
An order permitting the child's name to be changed or the removal of the child from the United Kingdom (section 28(2) and (3))	Any person including the adoption agency or the local authority authorised to place, or which has placed, the child for adoption (section 28(2)).
A section 88 direction	The adopted child; the adopters; any parent; or any other person.
A section 89 order	The adopters; the adopted person; any parent; the relevant Central Authority; the adoption agency; the local authority to whom notice under section 44 (notice of intention to adopt or apply for a section 84 order) has been given; the Secretary of State for the Home Department; or any other person.

Table 2

Proceedings for	*Respondents*
An adoption order (section 46) or a section 84 order	Each parent who has parental responsibility for the child or guardian of the child unless he has given notice under section 20(4)(a) (statement of wish not to be informed of any application for an adoption order) which has effect; any person in whose favour there is provision for contact; any adoption agency having parental responsibility for the child under section 25; any adoption agency which has taken part at any stage in the arrangements for adoption of the child; any local authority to whom notice under section 44 (notice of intention to adopt or apply for a section 84 order) has been given; any local authority or voluntary organisation which has parental responsibility for, is looking after, or is caring for, the child; and the child where: • permission has been granted to a parent or guardian to oppose the making of the adoption order (section 47(3) or 47(5)); • he opposes the making of an adoption order; • a children and family reporter recommends that it is in the best interests of the child to be a party to the proceedings and that recommendation is accepted by the court; • he is already an adopted child; • any party to the proceedings or the child is opposed to the arrangements for allowing any person contact with the child, or a person not being allowed contact with the child after the making of the adoption order; • the application is for a Convention adoption order or a section 84 order; • he has been brought into the United Kingdom in the circumstances where section 83(1) applies (restriction on bringing children in); • the application is for an adoption order other than a Convention adoption order and the

prospective adopters intend the child to live in a country or territory outside the British Islands after the making of the adoption order; or • the prospective adopters are relatives of the child.

A placement order (section 21)	Each parent who has parental responsibility for the child or guardian of the child; any person in whose favour an order under the 1989 Act is in force in relation to the child; any adoption agency or voluntary organisation which has parental responsibility for, is looking after, or is caring for, the child; the child; and the parties or any persons who are or have been parties to proceedings for a care order in respect of the child where those proceedings have led to the application for the placement order.
An order varying a placement order (section 23)	The parties to the proceedings leading to the placement order which it is sought to have varied except the child who was the subject of those proceedings; and any person in whose favour there is provision for contact.
An order revoking a placement order (section 24)	The parties to the proceedings leading to the placement order which it is sought to have revoked; and any person in whose favour there is provision for contact.
A contact order (section 26)	The adoption agency authorised to place the child for adoption or which has placed the child for adoption; the person with whom the child lives or is to live; each parent with parental responsibility for the child or guardian of the child; and the child where: • the adoption agency authorised to place the child for adoption or which has placed the child for adoption or a parent with parental responsibility for the child opposes the making of the contact order under section 26; • he opposes the making of the contact order under section 26; • existing provision for contact is to be revoked; • relatives of the child do not agree to the arrangements for allowing any person contact with the child, or a person not being allowed contact with the child; or • he is suffering or is at risk of suffering harm within the meaning of the 1989 Act.
An order varying or revoking a contact order (section 27)	The parties to the proceedings leading to the contact order which it is sought to have varied or revoked; and any person named in the contact order.
An order permitting the child's name to be changed or the removal of the child from the United Kingdom (section 28(2) and (3))	The parties to proceedings leading to any placement order; the adoption agency authorised to place the child for adoption or which has placed the child for adoption; any prospective adopters with whom the child is living; and each parent with parental responsibility for the child or guardian of the child.
A section 88 direction	The adopters; the parents; the adoption agency; the local authority to whom notice under section 44 (notice of intention to apply for a section 84 order) has been given; and the Attorney-General.
A section 89 order:	The adopters; the parents; the adoption agency; and the local authority to whom notice under section 44 (notice to adopt or apply for a section 84 order) has been given.

(2) The court may at any time direct that a child, who is not already a respondent to proceedings, be made a respondent to proceedings where—

    (a) the child—

        (i)   wishes to make an application; or

    (ii)   has evidence to give to the court or a legal submission to make which has not been given or made by any other party; or

  (b) there are other special circumstances.

(3) The court may at any time direct that—

  (a) any other person or body be made a respondent to proceedings; or

  (b) a respondent be removed.

(4) If the court makes a direction for the addition or removal of a party, it may give consequential directions about—

  (a) serving a copy of the application form on any new respondent;

  (b) serving relevant documents on the new party; and

  (c) the management of the proceedings.

What the court or a court officer will do when the application has been issued

24.—(1) As soon as practicable after the application has been issued in proceedings—

  (a) the court will—

    (i)   if section 48(1) (restrictions on making adoption orders) applies, consider whether it is proper to hear the application;

    (ii) subject to paragraph (4), set a date for the first directions hearing;

    (iii) appoint a children's guardian in accordance with rule 59;

    (iv) appoint a reporting officer in accordance with rule 69;

    (v)   consider whether a report relating to the welfare of the child is required, and if so, request such a report in accordance with rule 73;

    (vi) set a date for the hearing of the application; and

    (vii) do anything else that may be set out in a practice direction; and

  (b) a court officer will—

    (i)   subject to receiving confirmation in accordance with paragraph (2)(b)(ii), give notice of any directions hearing set by the court to the parties and to any children's guardian, reporting officer or children and family reporter;

    (ii) serve a copy of the application form (but, subject to sub-paragraphs (iii) and (iv), not the documents attached to it) on the persons referred to in the relevant practice direction;

    (iii) send a copy of the certified copy of the entry in the register of live-births or Adopted Children Register and any health report attached to an application for an adoption order to—

      (aa) any children's guardian, reporting officer or children and family reporter; and

      (bb) the local authority to whom notice under section 44 (notice of intention to adopt or apply for a section 84 order) has been given;

    (iv) if notice under rule 27 has been given (request to dispense with consent of parent or guardian), in accordance with that rule inform the parent or guardian of the request and send a copy of the statement of facts to—

      (aa) the parent or guardian;

      (bb) any children's guardian, reporting officer or children and family reporter;

      (cc) any local authority to whom notice under section 44 (notice of intention to adopt or apply for a section 84 order) has been given; and

      (dd) any adoption agency which has placed the child for adoption; and

    (v)   do anything else that may be set out in a practice direction.

(2) In addition to the matters referred to in paragraph (1), as soon as practicable after an application for an adoption order or a section 84 order has been issued the court or the court officer will—

  (a) where the child is not placed for adoption by an adoption agency—

    (i)   ask either the Service or the Assembly to file any relevant form of consent to an adoption order or a section 84 order; and

    (ii) ask the local authority to prepare a report on the suitability of the prospective adopters if one has not already been prepared; and

  (b) where the child is placed for adoption by an adoption agency, ask the adoption agency to—

    (i)   file any relevant form of consent to—

      (aa) the child being placed for adoption;

      (bb) an adoption order;

(cc)   a future adoption order under section 20; or

(dd)   a section 84 order;

(ii)   confirm whether a statement has been made under section 20(4)(a) (statement of wish not to be informed of any application for an adoption order) and if so, to file that statement;

(iii)   file any statement made under section 20(4)(b) (withdrawal of wish not to be informed of any application for an adoption order) as soon as it is received by the adoption agency; and

(iv)   prepare a report on the suitability of the prospective adopters if one has not already been prepared.

(3) In addition to the matters referred to in paragraph (1), as soon as practicable after an application for a placement order has been issued—

(a)   the court will consider whether a report giving the local authority's reasons for placing the child for adoption is required, and if so, will direct the local authority to prepare such a report; and

(b)   the court or the court officer will ask either the Service or the Assembly to file any form of consent to the child being placed for adoption.

(4) Where it considers it appropriate the court may, instead of setting a date for a first directions hearing, give the directions provided for by rule 26.

Date for first directions hearing

25. Unless the court directs otherwise, the first directions hearing must be within 4 weeks beginning with the date on which the application is issued.

The first directions hearing

26.—(1) At the first directions hearing in the proceedings the court will—

(a)   fix a timetable for the filing of—

(i)   any report relating to the suitability of the applicants to adopt a child;

(ii)   any report from the local authority;

(iii)   any report from a children's guardian, reporting officer or children and family reporter;

(iv)   if a statement of facts has been filed, any amended statement of facts;

(v)   any other evidence, and

give directions relating to the reports and other evidence;

(b)   consider whether an alternative dispute resolution procedure is appropriate and, if so, give directions relating to the use of such procedure;

(c)   consider whether the child or any other person should be a party to the proceedings and, if so, give directions in accordance with rule 23(2) or (3) joining that child or person as a party;

(d)   give directions relating to the appointment of a litigation friend for any patient or non-subject child unless a litigation friend has already been appointed;

(e)   consider whether the case needs to be transferred to another court and, if so, give directions to transfer the proceedings to another court in accordance with any order made by the Lord Chancellor under Part I of Schedule 11 to the 1989 Act;

(f)   give directions about—

(i)   tracing parents or any other person the court considers to be relevant to the proceedings;

(ii)   service of documents;

(iii)   subject to paragraph (2), disclosure as soon as possible of information and evidence to the parties; and

(iv)   the final hearing; and

(2) Rule 77(2) applies to any direction given under paragraph (1)(f)(iii) as it applies to a direction given under rule 77(1).

(3) In addition to the matters referred to in paragraph (1), the court will give any of the directions listed in the relevant practice direction in proceedings for—

(a)   a Convention adoption order;

(b)   a section 84 order;

(c)   a section 88 direction;

(d)   a section 89 order; or

(e)   an adoption order where section 83(1) applies (restriction on bringing children in).

(4) The parties or their legal representatives must attend the first directions hearing unless the court directs otherwise.

(5) Directions may also be given at any stage in the proceedings—

    (a) of the court's own initiative; or

    (b) on the application of a party or any children's guardian or, where the direction concerns a report by a reporting officer or children and family reporter, the reporting officer or children and family reporter.

(6) For the purposes of giving directions or for such purposes as the court directs—

    (a) the court may set a date for a further directions hearing or other hearing; and

    (b) the court officer will give notice of any date so fixed to the parties and to any children's guardian, reporting officer or children and family reporter.

(7) After the first directions hearing the court will monitor compliance with the court's timetable and directions by the parties.

Requesting the court to dispense with the consent of any parent or guardian

27.—(1) The following paragraphs apply where the applicant wants to ask the court to dispense with the consent of any parent or guardian of a child to—

    (a) the child being placed for adoption;

    (b) the making of an adoption order except a Convention adoption order; or

    (c) the making of a section 84 order.

(2) The applicant requesting the court to dispense with the consent must—

    (a) give notice of the request in the application form or at any later stage by filing a written request setting out the reasons for the request; and

    (b) file a statement of facts setting out a summary of the history of the case and any other facts to satisfy the court that—

        (i) the parent or guardian cannot be found or is incapable of giving consent; or

        (ii) the welfare of the child requires the consent to be dispensed with.

(3) If a serial number has been assigned to the applicant under rule 20, the statement of facts supplied under paragraph (2)(b) must be framed so that it does not disclose the identity of the applicant.

(4) On receipt of the notice of the request—

    (a) a court officer will—

        (i) inform the parent or guardian of the request; and

        (ii) send a copy of the statement of facts filed in accordance with paragraph (2)(b) to—

            (aa) the parent or guardian;

            (bb) any children's guardian, reporting officer or children and family reporter;

            (cc) any local authority to whom notice under section 44 (notice of intention to adopt or apply for a section 84 order) has been given; and

            (dd) any adoption agency which has placed the child for adoption; and

    (b) if the applicant considers that the parent or guardian is incapable of giving consent, the court will consider whether to—

        (i) appoint a litigation friend for the parent or guardian under rule 55(1); or

        (ii) give directions for an application to be made under rule 55(3),

    unless a litigation friend is already appointed for that parent or guardian.

Consent

28.—(1) Consent of any parent or guardian of a child—

    (a) under section 19, to the child being placed for adoption; and

    (b) under section 20, to the making of a future adoption order

must be given in the form required by the relevant practice direction or a form to the like effect.

(2) Subject to paragraph (3), consent—

    (a) to the making of an adoption order; or

    (b) to the making of a section 84 order,

may be given in the form required by the relevant practice direction or a form to the like effect.

(3) Any consent to a Convention adoption order must be in a form which complies with the internal law relating to adoption of the Convention country of which the child is habitually resident.

(4) Any form of consent executed in Scotland must be witnessed by a Justice of the Peace or a Sheriff.

(5) Any form of consent executed in Northern Ireland must be witnessed by a Justice of the Peace.

(6) Any form of consent executed outside the United Kingdom must be witnessed by—

    (a) any person for the time being authorised by law in the place where the document is executed to administer an oath for any judicial or other legal purpose;

    (b) a British Consular officer;

    (c) a notary public; or

    (d) if the person executing the document is serving in any of the regular armed forces of the Crown, an officer holding a commission in any of those forces.

Reports by the adoption agency or local authority

29.—(1) The adoption agency or local authority must file the report on the suitability of the applicant to adopt a child within the timetable fixed by the court.

(2) A local authority that is directed to prepare a report on the placement of the child for adoption must file that report within the timetable fixed by the court.

(3) The reports must cover the matters specified in the relevant practice direction.

(4) The court may at any stage request a further report or ask the adoption agency or local authority to assist the court in any other manner.

(5) A court officer will send a copy of any report referred to in this rule to any children's guardian, reporting officer or children and family reporter.

(6) Any report to the court under this rule will be confidential.

Health reports

30.—(1) Reports by a registered medical practitioner ("health reports") made not more than three months earlier on the health of the child and of each applicant must be attached to an application for an adoption order or a section 84 order except where—

    (a) the child was placed for adoption with the applicant by an adoption agency;

    (b) the applicant or one of the applicants is a parent of the child; or

    (c) the applicant is the partner of a parent of the child.

(2) Health reports must contain the matters set out in the relevant practice direction.

(3) Any health report will be confidential.

Notice of final hearing

31. A court officer will give notice to the parties, any children's guardian, reporting officer or children and family reporter and to any other person that may be referred to in a practice direction—

    (a) of the date and place where the application will be heard; and

    (b) of the fact that, unless the person wishes or the court requires, the person need not attend.

The final hearing

32.—(1) Any person who has been given notice in accordance with rule 31 may attend the final hearing and, subject to paragraph (2), be heard on the question of whether an order should be made.

(2) A person whose application for the permission of the court to oppose the making of an adoption order under section 47(3) or (5) has been refused is not entitled to be heard on the question of whether an order should be made.

(3) Any member or employee of a party which is a local authority, adoption agency or other body may address the court at the final hearing if he is authorised to do so.

(4) The court may direct that any person must attend a final hearing.

(5) Paragraphs (6) and (7) apply to—

    (a) an adoption order;

    (b) a section 84 order; or

    (c) a section 89 order.

(6) Subject to paragraphs (7) and (8), the court cannot make an order unless the applicant and the child personally attend the final hearing.

(7) The court may direct that the applicant or the child need not attend the final hearing.

(8) In a case of adoption by a couple[30] under section 50 the court may make an adoption order

---

[30] A couple is defined in section 144(4) of the Adoption and Children Act 2002.

after personal attendance of one only of the applicants if there are special circumstances.

(9) The court cannot make a placement order unless a legal representative of the applicant attends the final hearing.

Proof of identity of the child

33.—(1) Unless the contrary is shown, the child referred to in the application will be deemed to be the child referred to in the form of consent—

    (a) to the child being placed for adoption;

    (b) to the making of an adoption order; or

    (c) to the making of a section 84 order

where the conditions in paragraph (2) apply.

(2) The conditions are—

    (a) the application identifies the child by reference to a full certified copy of an entry in the registers of live-births;

    (b) the form of consent identifies the child by reference to a full certified copy of an entry in the registers of live-births attached to the form; and

    (c) the copy of the entry in the registers of live-births referred to in sub-paragraph (a) is the same or relates to the same entry in the registers of live-births as the copy of the entry in the registers of live-births attached to the form of consent.

(3) Where the child is already an adopted child paragraph (2) will have effect as if for the references to the registers of live-births there were substituted references to the Adopted Children Register.

(4) Subject to paragraph (7), where the precise date of the child's birth is not proved to the satisfaction of the court, the court will determine the probable date of birth.

(5) The probable date of the child's birth may be specified in the placement order, adoption order or section 84 order as the date of his birth.

(6) Subject to paragraph (7), where the child's place of birth cannot be proved to the satisfaction of the court—

    (a) he may be treated as having been born in the registration district of the court where it is probable that the child may have been born in—

        (i)   the United Kingdom;

        (ii) the Channel Islands; or

        (iii) the Isle of Man; or

    (b) in any other case, the particulars of the country of birth may be omitted from the placement order, adoption order or section 84 order.

(7) A placement order identifying the probable date and place of birth of the child will be sufficient proof of the date and place of birth of the child in adoption proceedings and proceedings for a section 84 order.

PART 6: SERVICE

SECTION 1: GENERAL RULES ABOUT SERVICE

Scope of this Part

34. The rules in this Part apply to the service of documents, including a document that is required to be given or sent by these Rules or any practice direction, except where—

    (a) any other enactment, a rule in another Part or a practice direction makes a different provision; or

    (b) the court directs otherwise.

Methods of service

35.—(1) Subject to paragraph (2), a document may be served—

    (a) where it is not known whether a solicitor is acting on behalf of a party—

        (i)   by delivering it to the party personally; or

        (ii) by delivering it at, or by sending it by first class post to, the party's residence or last known residence; or

    (b) where a solicitor is known to be acting on behalf of a party—

        (i)   by delivering the document at, or sending it by first class post to, the solicitor's address for service; or

        (ii) through a document exchange in accordance with the relevant practice direction.

(2) A notice of hearing must be served in accordance with paragraph (1)(a)(i) or (ii) irrespective of whether a solicitor is acting on behalf of a party.

(3) Where it appears to the court that there is a good reason to authorise service by a method not permitted by paragraph (1), the court may direct that service is effected by an alternative method.

(4) A direction that service is effected by an alternative method must specify—

    (a) the method of service; and

    (b) the date when the document will be deemed to be served.

Who is to serve

36.—(1) A document which has been issued or prepared by a court officer will be served by the court officer except where—

    (a) a practice direction provides otherwise; or

    (b) the court directs otherwise.

(2) Where a court officer is to serve a document, it is for the court to decide which of the methods of service specified in rule 35(1) is to be used.

Service of documents on children and patients

37.—(1) The following table shows the person on whom a document must be served if it is a document which would otherwise be served on a child, non-subject child or patient—

Nature of party	Type of document	Person to be served
Child who is not also a patient	Any document	The solicitor acting for the child; where there is no such solicitor, the children's guardian or the children and family reporter.
Non-subject child who is not also a patient	Application form	One of the non-subject child's parents or guardians; if there is no parent or guardian, the person with whom the non-subject child resides or in whose care the non-subject child is.
Patient	Application form	The person authorised under Part VII of the Mental Health Act 1983 to conduct the proceedings in the name of the patient or on his behalf; if there is no person so authorised, the person with whom the patient resides or in whose care the patient is.
Non-subject child or patient	Application for an order appointing a litigation friend, where the non-subject child or patient has no litigation friend	See rule 57
	Any other document	The litigation friend who is conducting proceedings on behalf of the non-subject child or patient.

(2) Where a child is directed by the court to serve a document, service is to be effected by—

    (a) the solicitor acting for the child;

    (b) where there is no such solicitor, the children's guardian;

    (c) where there is neither a solicitor or children's guardian, the litigation friend; or

    (d) where there is neither a solicitor, children's guardian, or litigation friend, a court officer.

(3) Where a non-subject child or patient is directed by the court to serve a document, service is to be effected by—

    (a) the solicitor acting for the non-subject child or patient; or

    (b) where there is no such solicitor, the litigation friend.

(4) The court may give directions permitting a document to be served on the child, non-subject child or patient, or on some other person other than the person specified in the table in this rule.

(5) The court may direct that, although a document has been served on someone other than the person specified in the table, the document is to be treated as if it had been properly served.

(6) This rule does not apply where a non-subject child is conducting proceedings without a litigation friend in accordance with rule 51.

Deemed service

38.—(1) Unless the contrary is proved, a document which is served in accordance with these Rules or any relevant practice direction will be deemed to be served on the day shown in the following table—

Method of service	*Deemed day of service*
First class post	The second day after it was posted.
Document exchange	The second day after it was left at the document exchange.
Delivering the document to address	The day after the document was delivered to that address.

(2) If a document is served personally—
    (a) after 5 p.m. on a business day; or
    (b) at any time on a day which is not a business day
it will be treated as being served on the next business day.

Power of court to dispense with service

39. Where a rule or practice direction requires a document to be served, the court may direct that the requirement is dispensed with.

Certificate of service

40.—(1) Where a rule, practice direction or court order requires a certificate of service, the certificate must state the details set out in the following table—

Method of service	*Details to be certified*
Post	Date of posting.
Personal	Date of personal service.
Document exchange	Date of delivery to the document exchange.
Delivery of document to address	Date when the document was delivered to the address.
Alternative method permitted by the Court	As required by the court.

(2) Where an application form is to be served by the applicant he must file a certificate of service within 7 days beginning with the date on which the application form was served.

Notice of non-service

41. Where a person fails to serve any document under these Rules or as directed by the court he must file a certificate of non-service stating the reason why service has not been effected.

SECTION 2: SERVICE OUT OF THE JURISDICTION

Scope and definitions

42.—(1) This Section contains rules about—
    (a) service out of the jurisdiction; and
    (b) the procedure for serving out of the jurisdiction.
(Rule 6 defines "jurisdiction".)

(2) In this Section—
    "application form" includes application notice; and
"the Hague Convention" means the Convention on the service abroad of judicial and extra-judicial documents in civil or commercial matters signed at the Hague on November 15, 1965 [Cmnd 3986].

Service of documents

43.—(1) Any document to be served for the purposes of these Rules may be served out of the jurisdiction without the permission of the court.

(2) Subject to paragraph (4) or (5), any document served out of the jurisdiction in a country in which English is not the official language must be accompanied by a translation of the document—
    (a) in the official language of the country in which the document is to be served; or
    (b) if there is more than one official language of the country, in any one of those languages which is appropriate to the place in that country in which the document is to be served.

(3) Every translation filed under this rule must be signed by the translator to certify that the translation is accurate.

(4) Any document served out of the jurisdiction in a country in which English is not the official language need not be accompanied by a translation of the document where—

    (a) the person on whom the document is to be served is able to read and understand English; and

    (b) service of the document is to be effected directly on that person.

(5) Paragraphs (2) and (3) do not apply where service is to be effected in accordance with the Service Regulation.

Method of service – general provisions

44.—(1) Where an application form is to be served out of the jurisdiction, it may be served by any method—

    (a) permitted by the law of the country in which it is to be served; or

    (b) provided for by—

        (i) rule 45 (service through foreign governments, judicial authorities and British Consular authorities); or

        (ii) rule 47 (service in accordance with the Service Regulation).

(2) Nothing in this rule or in any court order will authorise or require any person to do anything in the country where the application form is to be served which is against the law of that country.

Service through foreign governments, judicial authorities and British Consular authorities

45.—(1) Where an application form is to be served on a respondent in any country which is a party to the Hague Convention, the application form may be served—

    (a) through the authority designated under the Hague Convention in respect of that country; or

    (b) if the law of that country permits—

        (i) through the judicial authorities of that country; or

        (ii) through a British Consular authority in that country.

(2) Where an application form is to be served on a respondent in any country which is not a party to the Hague Convention, the application form may be served, if the law of that country so permits—

    (a) through the government of that country, where that government is willing to serve it; or

    (b) through a British Consular authority in that country.

(3) Paragraph (2) does not apply where the application form is to be served in—

    (a) Scotland, Northern Ireland, the Isle of Man or the Channel Islands;

    (b) any Commonwealth State; or

    (c) any United Kingdom Overseas Territory listed in the relevant practice direction.

(4) This rule does not apply where service is to be effected in accordance with the Service Regulation.

Procedure where service is to be through foreign governments, judicial authorities and British Consular authorities

46.—(1) This rule applies where the applicant wishes to serve the application form through—

    (a) the judicial authorities of the country where the application form is to be served;

    (b) a British Consular authority in that country;

    (c) the authority designated under the Hague Convention in respect of that country; or

    (d) the government of that country.

(2) Where this rule applies, the applicant must file—

    (a) a request for service of the application form by the method in paragraph (1) that he has chosen;

    (b) a copy of the application form;

    (c) any translation required under rule 43; and

    (d) any other documents, copies of documents or translations required by the relevant practice direction.

(3) When the applicant files the documents specified in paragraph (2), a court officer will—

    (a) seal, or otherwise authenticate with the stamp of the court, the copy of the application form; and

    (b) forward the documents to the Senior Master of the Queen's Bench Division.

(4) The Senior Master will send documents forwarded under this rule—

    (a) where the application form is being served through the authority designated under the Hague Convention, to that authority; or

    (b) in any other case, to the Foreign and Commonwealth Office with a request that it arranges for the application to be served by the method indicated in the request for service filed under paragraph (2) or, where that request indicates alternative methods, by the most convenient method.

(5) An official certificate will be evidence of the facts stated in the certificate if it—

    (a) states that the application form has been served in accordance with this rule either personally, or in accordance with the law of the country in which service was effected;

    (b) specifies the date on which the application form was served; and

    (c) is made by—

        (i) a British Consular authority in the country where the application form was served;

        (ii) the government or judicial authorities in that country; or

        (iii) any other authority designated in respect of that country under the Hague Convention.

(6) A document purporting to be an official certificate under paragraph (5) will be treated as such a certificate, unless it is proved not to be.

(7) This rule does not apply where service is to be effected in accordance with the Service Regulation.

Service in accordance with the Service Regulation

47.—(1) This rule applies where an application form is to be served in accordance with the Service Regulation.

(2) The applicant must file the application form and any translations or other documents required by the Service Regulation.

(3) When the applicant files the documents referred to in paragraph (2), a court officer will—

    (a) seal, or otherwise authenticate with the stamp of the court, the copy of the application form; and

    (b) forward the documents to the Senior Master of the Queen's Bench Division.

(The Service Regulation is annexed to the relevant practice direction.)

Undertaking to be responsible for expenses of the Foreign and Commonwealth Office

48. Every request for service filed under rule 46 (service through foreign governments, judicial authorities etc.) must contain an undertaking by the person making the request—

    (a) to be responsible for all expenses incurred by the Foreign and Commonwealth Office or foreign judicial authority; and

    (b) to pay those expenses to the Foreign and Commonwealth Office or foreign judicial authority on being informed of the amount.

PART 7: LITIGATION FRIEND, CHILDREN'S GUARDIAN, REPORTING OFFICER AND CHILDREN AND FAMILY REPORTER
SECTION 1: LITIGATION FRIEND

Application of this Section

49.—(1) This Section—

    (a) contains special provisions which apply in proceedings involving non-subject children and patients; and

    (b) sets out how a person becomes a litigation friend.

(2) The provisions of this Section also apply to a child who does not have a children's guardian, in which case, any reference to a "non-subject child" in these Rules is to be taken as including a child.

Requirement for litigation friend in proceedings

50.—(1) Subject to rule 51, a non-subject child must have a litigation friend to conduct proceedings on his behalf.

(2) A patient must have a litigation friend to conduct proceedings on his behalf.

Circumstances in which the non-subject child does not need a litigation friend

51.—(1) A non-subject child may conduct proceedings without a litigation friend—

    (a) where he has obtained the court's permission to do so; or

(b) where a solicitor—
- (i) considers that the non-subject child is able, having regard to his understanding, to give instructions in relation to the proceedings; and
- (ii) has accepted instructions from that child to act for him in the proceedings and, if the proceedings have begun, he is already acting.

(2) An application for permission under paragraph (1)(a) may be made by the non-subject child without notice.

(3) Where a non-subject child has a litigation friend in proceedings and he wishes to conduct the remaining stages of the proceedings without a litigation friend, the non-subject child may apply to the court, on notice to the litigation friend, for permission for that purpose and for the removal of the litigation friend.

(4) Where the court is considering whether to—
- (a) grant permission under paragraph (1)(a); or
- (b) grant permission under paragraph (3) and remove a litigation friend

it will grant the permission sought and, as the case may be, remove the litigation friend if it considers that the non-subject child concerned has sufficient understanding to conduct the proceedings concerned or proposed without a litigation friend.

(5) In exercising its powers under paragraph (4) the court may require the litigation friend to take such part in the proceedings as the court directs.

(6) The court may revoke any permission granted under paragraph (1)(a) where it considers that the non-subject child does not have sufficient understanding to participate as a party in the proceedings concerned without a litigation friend.

(7) Where a solicitor is acting for a non-subject child in proceedings without a litigation friend by virtue of paragraph (1)(b) and either of the conditions specified in paragraph (1)(b)(i) or (ii) cease to be fulfilled, he must inform the court immediately.

(8) Where—
- (a) the court revokes any permission under paragraph (6); or
- (b) either of the conditions specified in paragraph (1)(b)(i) or (ii) is no longer fulfilled

the court may, if it considers it necessary in order to protect the interests of the non-subject child concerned, appoint a person to be that child's litigation friend.

Stage of proceedings at which a litigation friend becomes necessary

52.—(1) This rule does not apply where a non-subject child is conducting proceedings without a litigation friend in accordance with rule 51.

(2) A person may not without the permission of the court take any step in proceedings except—
- (a) filing an application form; or
- (b) applying for the appointment of a litigation friend under rule 55

until the non-subject child or patient has a litigation friend.

(3) If a party becomes a patient during proceedings, no party may take any step in proceedings without the permission of the court until the patient has a litigation friend.

Who may be a litigation friend for a patient without a court order

53.—(1) This rule does not apply if the court has appointed a person to be a litigation friend.

(2) A person authorised under Part VII of the Mental Health Act 1983 to conduct legal proceedings in the name of a patient or on his behalf is entitled to be the litigation friend of the patient in any proceedings to which his authority extends.

(3) If nobody has been appointed by the court or, in the case of a patient, authorised under Part VII of the Mental Health Act 1983, a person may act as a litigation friend if he—
- (a) can fairly and competently conduct proceedings on behalf of the non-subject child or patient;
- (b) has no interest adverse to that of the non-subject child or patient; and
- (c) subject to paragraph (4), undertakes to pay any costs which the non-subject child or patient may be ordered to pay in relation to the proceedings, subject to any right he may have to be repaid from the assets of the non-subject child or patient.

(4) Paragraph (3)(c) does not apply to the Official Solicitor, an officer of the Service or a Welsh family proceedings officer.

How a person becomes a litigation friend without a court order

54.—(1) If the court has not appointed a litigation friend, a person who wishes to act as a litigation friend must follow the procedure set out in this rule.

(2) A person authorised under Part VII of the Mental Health Act 1983 must file an official copy[31] of the order or other document which constitutes his authorisation to act.

(3) Any other person must file a certificate of suitability stating that he satisfies the conditions specified in rule 53(3).

(4) A person who is to act as a litigation friend must file —

    (a) the authorisation; or

    (b) the certificate of suitability

at the time when he first takes a step in the proceedings on behalf of the non-subject child or patient.

(5) A court officer will send the certificate of suitability to every person on whom, in accordance with rule 37(1) (service on parent, guardian etc.), the application form should be served.

(6) This rule does not apply to the Official Solicitor, an officer of the Service or a Welsh family proceedings officer.

How a person becomes a litigation friend by court order

55. — (1) The court may make an order appointing —

    (a) the Official Solicitor;

    (b) in the case of a non-subject child, an officer of the Service or a Welsh family proceedings officer (if he consents); or

    (c) some other person (if he consents)

as a litigation friend.

(2) An order appointing a litigation friend may be made by the court of its own initiative or on the application of —

    (a) a person who wishes to be a litigation friend; or

    (b) a party to the proceedings.

(3) The court may at any time direct that a party make an application for an order under paragraph (2).

(4) An application for an order appointing a litigation friend must be supported by evidence.

(5) Unless the court directs otherwise, a person appointed under this rule to be a litigation friend for a non-subject child or patient will be treated as a party for the purpose of any provision in these Rules requiring a document to be served on, or sent to, or notice to be given to, a party to the proceedings.

(6) Subject to rule 53(4), the court may not appoint a litigation friend under this rule unless it is satisfied that the person to be appointed complies with the conditions specified in rule 53(3).

Court's power to change litigation friend and to prevent person acting as litigation friend

56. — (1) The court may —

    (a) direct that a person may not act as a litigation friend;

    (b) terminate a litigation friend's appointment; or

    (c) appoint a new litigation friend in substitution for an existing one.

(2) An application for an order under paragraph (1) must be supported by evidence.

(3) Subject to rule 53(4), the court may not appoint a litigation friend under this rule unless it is satisfied that the person to be appointed complies with the conditions specified in rule 53(3).

Appointment of litigation friend by court order – supplementary

57. — (1) A copy of the application for an order under rule 55 or 56 must be sent by a court officer to every person on whom, in accordance with rule 37(1) (service on parent, guardian etc.), the application form should be served.

(2) Where an application for an order under rule 55 is in respect of a patient, the court officer must also send a copy of the application to the patient unless the court directs otherwise.

(3) A copy of an application for an order under rule 56 must also be sent to —

    (a) the person who is the litigation friend, or who is purporting to act as the litigation friend, when the application is made; and

    (b) the person who it is proposed should be the litigation friend, if he is not the applicant.

Procedure where appointment of litigation friend comes to an end

58. — (1) When a non-subject child who is not a patient reaches the age of 18, a litigation friend's appointment comes to an end.

---

[31] An official copy is a copy of an official document supplied and marked as such by the office that issued the original.

(2) When a party ceases to be a patient, the litigation friend's appointment continues until it is brought to an end by a court order.

(3) An application for an order under paragraph (2) may be made by—
 (a) the former patient;
 (b) the litigation friend; or
 (c) a party.

(4) A court officer will send a notice to the other parties stating that the appointment of the non-subject child or patient's litigation friend to act has ended.

SECTION 2: CHILDREN'S GUARDIAN

Appointment of children's guardian

59.—(1) In proceedings to which Part 5 applies, the court will appoint a children's guardian where the child is a party to the proceedings unless it is satisfied that it is not necessary to do so to safeguard the interests of the child.

(2) At any stage in proceedings where the child is a party to the proceedings—
 (a) a party may apply, without notice to the other parties unless the court directs otherwise, for the appointment of a children's guardian; or
 (b) the court may of its own initiative appoint a children's guardian.

(3) The court will grant an application under paragraph (2)(a) unless it considers that such an appointment is not necessary to safeguard the interests of the child.

(4) When appointing a children's guardian the court will consider the appointment of anyone who has previously acted as a children's guardian of the same child.

What the court or a court officer will do once the court has made a decision about appointing a children's guardian

60.—(1) Where the court refuses an application under rule 59(2)(a) it will give reasons for the refusal and the court or a court officer will—
 (a) record the refusal and the reasons for it; and
 (b) as soon as practicable, notify the parties and either the Service or the Assembly of a decision not to appoint a children's guardian.

(2) Where the court appoints a children's guardian under rule 59 a court officer will record the appointment and, as soon as practicable, will—
 (a) inform the parties and either the Service or the Assembly; and
 (b) unless it has already been sent, send the children's guardian a copy of the application and copies of any document filed with the court in the proceedings.

(3) A court officer also has a continuing duty to send the children's guardian a copy of any other document filed with the court during the course of the proceedings.

Termination of the appointment of the children's guardian

61.—(1) The appointment of a children's guardian under rule 59 continues for such time as is specified in the appointment or until terminated by the court.

(2) When terminating an appointment in accordance with paragraph (1), the court will give reasons for doing so, a note of which will be taken by the court or a court officer.

Powers and duties of the children's guardian

62.—(1) The children's guardian is to act on behalf of the child upon the hearing of any application in proceedings to which Part 5 applies with the duty of safeguarding the interests of the child.

(2) The children's guardian must also provide the court with such other assistance as it may require.

How the children's guardian exercises his duties – investigations and appointment of solicitor

63.—(1) The children's guardian must make such investigations as are necessary for him to carry out his duties and must, in particular—
 (a) contact or seek to interview such persons as he thinks appropriate or as the court directs; and
 (b) obtain such professional assistance as is available to him which he thinks appropriate or which the court directs him to obtain.

(2) The children's guardian must—
 (a) appoint a solicitor for the child unless a solicitor has already been appointed;
 (b) give such advice to the child as is appropriate having regard to his understanding; and

(c) where appropriate instruct the solicitor representing the child on all matters relevant to the interests of the child, including possibilities for appeal, arising in the course of proceedings.

(3) Where the children's guardian is authorised in the terms mentioned by and in accordance with section 15(1) of the Criminal Justice and Court Services Act 2000 or section 37(1) of the Children Act 2004 (right of officer of the Service or Welsh family proceedings officer to conduct litigation or exercise a right of audience), paragraph (2)(a) will not apply if he intends to have conduct of the proceedings on behalf of the child unless—

(a) the child wishes to instruct a solicitor direct; and
(b) the children's guardian or the court considers that he is of sufficient understanding to do so.

Where the child instructs a solicitor or conducts proceedings on his own behalf

64.—(1) Where it appears to the children's guardian that the child—
(a) is instructing his solicitor direct; or
(b) intends to conduct and is capable of conducting the proceedings on his own behalf
he must inform the court of that fact.

(2) Where paragraph (1) applies, the children's guardian—
(a) must perform the duties set out in rules 62, 63, 65 to 67 and this rule, other than those duties in rule 63(2)(a) and (c), and such other duties as the court may direct;
(b) must take such part in the proceedings as the court may direct; and
(c) may, with the permission of the court, have legal representation in the conduct of those duties.

How the children's guardian exercises his duties – attendance at court, advice to the court and reports

65.—(1) The children's guardian or the solicitor appointed under section 41(3) of the 1989 Act or in accordance with rule 63(2)(a) must attend all directions hearings unless the court directs otherwise.

(2) The children's guardian must advise the court on the following matters—
(a) whether the child is of sufficient understanding for any purpose including the child's refusal to submit to a medical or psychiatric examination or other assessment that the court has the power to require, direct or order;
(b) the wishes of the child in respect of any matter relevant to the proceedings including his attendance at court;
(c) the appropriate forum for the proceedings;
(d) the appropriate timing of the proceedings or any part of them;
(e) the options available to it in respect of the child and the suitability of each such option including what order should be made in determining the application; and
(f) any other matter on which the court seeks his advice or on which he considers that the court should be informed.

(3) The advice given under paragraph (2) may, subject to any direction of the court, be given orally or in writing.

(4) The children's guardian must—
(a) unless the court directs otherwise, file a written report advising on the interests of the child in accordance with the timetable set by the court; and
(b) where practicable, notify any person the joining of whom as a party to those proceedings would be likely, in his opinion, to safeguard the interests of the child, of the court's power to join that person as a party under rule 23 and must inform the court—
(i) of any notification;
(ii) of anyone whom he attempted to notify under this paragraph but was unable to contact; and
(iii) of anyone whom he believes may wish to be joined to the proceedings.

(5) Any report to the court under this rule will be confidential.

(Part 9 sets out the procedure for making an application to be joined as a party in proceedings.)

How the children's guardian exercises his duties – service of documents and inspection of records

66.—(1) The children's guardian must—
(a) serve documents on behalf of the child in accordance with rule 37(2)(b); and

(b) accept service of documents on behalf of the child in accordance with the table in rule 37(1),

and, where the child has not himself been served and has sufficient understanding, advise the child of the contents of any document so served.

(2) Where the children's guardian inspects records of the kinds referred to in—

    (a) section 42 of the 1989 Act (right to have access to local authority records); or

    (b) section 103 (right to have access to adoption agency records)

he must bring all records and documents which may, in his opinion, assist in the proper determination of the proceedings to the attention of—

    (i)   the court; and

    (ii)   unless the court directs otherwise, the other parties to the proceedings.

How the children's guardian exercises his duties – communication of a court's decision to the child

67. The children's guardian must ensure that, in relation to a decision made by the court in the proceedings—

    (a) if he considers it appropriate to the age and understanding of the child, the child is notified of that decision; and

    (b) if the child is notified of the decision, it is explained to the child in a manner appropriate to his age and understanding.

Solicitor for child

68.—(1) A solicitor appointed under section 41(3) of the 1989 Act or in accordance with rule 63(2)(a) must represent the child—

    (a) in accordance with instructions received from the children's guardian unless the solicitor considers, having taken into account the views of the children's guardian and any direction of the court under rule 64(2)—

        (i)   that the child wishes to give instructions which conflict with those of the children's guardian; and

        (ii)   that he is able, having regard to his understanding, to give such instructions on his own behalf,

    in which case the solicitor must conduct the proceedings in accordance with instructions received from the child;

    (b) where no children's guardian has been appointed and the condition in section 41(4)(b) of the 1989 Act is satisfied, in accordance with instructions received from the child; or

    (c) in default of instructions under sub-paragraph (a) or (b), in furtherance of the best interests of the child.

(2) A solicitor appointed under section 41(3) of the 1989 Act or in accordance with rule 63(2)(a) must—

    (a) serve documents on behalf of the child in accordance with rule 37(2)(a); and

    (b) accept service of documents on behalf of the child in accordance with the table in rule 37(1),

and, where the child has not himself been served and has sufficient understanding, advise the child of the contents of any document so served.

(3) Where the child wishes an appointment of a solicitor under section 41(3) of the 1989 Act or in accordance with rule 63(2)(a) to be terminated—

    (a) he may apply to the court for an order terminating the appointment; and

    (b) the solicitor and the children's guardian will be given an opportunity to make representations.

(4) Where the children's guardian wishes an appointment of a solicitor under section 41(3) of the 1989 Act or in accordance with rule 63(2)(a) to be terminated—

    (a) he may apply to the court for an order terminating the appointment; and

    (b) the solicitor and, if he is of sufficient understanding, the child, will be given an opportunity to make representations.

(5) When terminating an appointment in accordance with paragraph (3) or (4), the court will give its reasons for so doing, a note of which will be taken by the court or a court officer.

(6) The court or a court officer will record the appointment under section 41(3) of the 1989 Act or in accordance with rule 63(2)(a) or the refusal to make the appointment.

SECTION 3: REPORTING OFFICER

When the court appoints a reporting officer

69. In proceedings to which Part 5 applies, the court will appoint a reporting officer where—

(a) it appears that a parent or guardian of the child is willing to consent to the placing of the child for adoption, to the making of an adoption order or to a section 84 order; and

(b) that parent or guardian is in England or Wales.

Appointment of the same reporting officer in respect of two or more parents or guardians

70. The same person may be appointed as the reporting officer for two or more parents or guardians of the child.

The duties of the reporting officer

71. The reporting officer must witness the signature by a parent or guardian on the document in which consent is given to—

(a) the placing of the child for adoption;

(b) the making of an adoption order; or

(c) the making of a section 84 order.

How the reporting officer exercises his duties

72.—(1) The reporting officer must—

(a) ensure so far as reasonably practicable that the parent or guardian is—

(i) giving consent unconditionally; and

(ii) with full understanding of what is involved;

(b) investigate all the circumstances relevant to a parent's or guardian's consent to the placing of the child for adoption or to the making of an adoption order or a section 84 order; and

(c) on completing his investigations the reporting officer must—

(i) make a report in writing to the court in accordance with the timetable set by the court, drawing attention to any matters which, in his opinion, may be of assistance to the court in considering the application; or

(ii) make an interim report to the court if a parent or guardian of the child is unwilling to consent to the placing of the child for adoption or to the making of an adoption order or section 84 order.

(2) On receipt of an interim report under paragraph (1)(c)(ii) a court officer must inform the applicant that a parent or guardian of the child is unwilling to consent to the placing of the child for adoption or to the making of an adoption order or section 84 order.

(3) The reporting officer may at any time before the final hearing make an interim report to the court if he considers necessary and ask the court for directions.

(4) The reporting officer must attend all directions hearings unless the court directs otherwise.

(5) Any report to the court under this rule will be confidential.

SECTION 4: CHILDREN AND FAMILY REPORTER

Request by court for a welfare report in respect of the child

73.—(1) In proceedings to which Part 5 applies, where the court is considering an application for an order in proceedings the court may ask a children and family reporter to prepare a report on matters relating to the welfare of the child.

(2) It is the duty of a children and family reporter to—

(a) comply with any request for a report under this rule; and

(b) provide the court with such other assistance as it may require.

(3) Any report to the court under this rule will be confidential.

How the children and family reporter exercises his powers and duties

74.—(1) The children and family reporter must make such investigations as may be necessary for him to perform his powers and duties and must, in particular—

(a) contact or seek to interview such persons as he thinks appropriate or as the court directs; and

(b) obtain such professional assistance as is available to him which he thinks appropriate or which the court directs him to obtain.

(2) The children and family reporter must—

(a) notify the child of such contents of his report (if any) as he considers appropriate to the age and understanding of the child, including any reference to the child's own

      views on the application and his recommendation; and
- (b) if he does notify the child of any contents of his report, explain them to the child in a manner appropriate to his age and understanding.

(3) The children and family reporter must—
- (a) attend all directions hearings unless the court directs otherwise;
- (b) advise the court of the child's wishes and feelings;
- (c) advise the court if he considers that the joining of a person as a party to the proceedings would be likely to safeguard the interests of the child;
- (d) consider whether it is in the best interests of the child for the child to be made a party to the proceedings, and if so, notify the court of his opinion together with the reasons for that opinion; and
- (e) where the court has directed that a written report be made, file the report in accordance with the timetable set by the court.

SECTION 5: WHO CAN ACT AS CHILDREN'S GUARDIAN, REPORTING OFFICER AND CHILDREN AND FAMILY REPORTER

Persons who may not be appointed as children's guardian, reporting officer or children and family reporter

75.—(1) In adoption proceedings or proceedings for a section 84 order or a section 89 order, a person may not be appointed as a children's guardian, reporting officer or children and family reporter if he—
- (a) is a member, officer or servant of a local authority which is a party to the proceedings;
- (b) is, or has been, a member, officer or servant of a local authority or voluntary organisation who has been directly concerned in that capacity in arrangements relating to the care, accommodation or welfare of the child during the five years prior to the commencement of the proceedings; or
- (c) is a serving probation officer who has, in that capacity, been previously concerned with the child or his family.

(2) In placement proceedings, a person described in paragraph (1)(b) or (c) may not be appointed as a children's guardian, reporting officer or children and family reporter.

Appointment of the same person as children's guardian, reporting officer and children and family reporter

76. The same person may be appointed to act as one or more of the following—
- (a) the children's guardian;
- (b) the reporting officer; and
- (c) the children and family reporter.

PART 8: DOCUMENTS AND DISCLOSURE OF DOCUMENTS AND INFORMATION

Confidential reports to the court and disclosure to the parties

77.—(1) The court will consider whether to give a direction that a confidential report be disclosed to each party to the proceedings.

(2) Before giving such a direction the court will consider whether any information should be deleted including information which—
- (a) discloses, or is likely to disclose, the identity of a person who has been assigned a serial number under rule 20(2); or
- (b) discloses the particulars referred to in rule 21(1) where a party has given notice under rule 21(2) (disclosure of personal details).

(3) The court may direct that the report will not be disclosed to a party.

Communication of information relating to proceedings

78.—(1) For the purposes of the law relating to contempt of court, information (whether or not it is recorded in any form) relating to proceedings held in private may be communicated—
- (a) where the court gives permission;
- (b) unless the court directs otherwise, in accordance with the relevant practice direction; or
- (c) where the communication is to—
  - (i) a party;
  - (ii) the legal representative of a party;
  - (iii) a professional legal adviser;

    (iv) an officer of the Service or a Welsh family proceedings officer;
    (v) a welfare officer;
    (vi) the Legal Services Commission;
    (vii) an expert whose instruction by a party has been authorised by the court; or
    (viii) a professional acting in furtherance of the protection of children.

(2) In this rule—

"professional acting in furtherance of the protection of children" includes—

    (a) an officer of a local authority exercising child protection functions;
    (b) a police officer who is—
        (i) exercising powers under section 46 of the 1989 Act; or
        (ii) serving in a child protection unit or a paedophile unit of a police force;
    (c) any professional person attending a child protection conference or review in relation to a child who is the subject of the proceedings to which the information relates; or
    (d) an officer of the National Society for the Prevention of Cruelty to Children;

"professional legal adviser" means a barrister or a solicitor, solicitor's employee or other authorised litigator (as defined in section 119 of the Courts and Legal Services Act 1990) who is providing advice to a party but is not instructed to represent that party in the proceedings;

"welfare officer" means a person who has been asked to prepare a report under section 7(1)(b) of the 1989 Act.

Orders for disclosure against a person not a party

79.—(1) This rule applies where an application is made to the court under any Act for disclosure by a person who is not a party to the proceedings[32].

(2) The application must be supported by evidence.

(3) The court may make an order under this rule only where—

    (a) the documents of which disclosure is sought are likely to support the case of the applicant or adversely affect the case of one of the other parties to the proceedings; and
    (b) disclosure is necessary in order to dispose fairly of the application or to save costs.

(4) An order under this rule must—

    (a) specify the documents or the classes of documents which the respondent must disclose; and
    (b) require the respondent, when making disclosure, to specify any of those documents—
        (i) which are no longer in his control; or
        (ii) in respect of which he claims a right or duty to withhold inspection.

(5) Such an order may—

    (a) require the respondent to indicate what has happened to any documents which are no longer in his control; and
    (b) specify the time and place for disclosure and inspection.

(6) This rule does not apply to proceedings in a magistrates' court.

Rules not to limit other powers of the court to order disclosure

80.—(1) Rule 79 does not limit any other power which the court may have to order—

    (a) disclosure before proceedings have started; and
    (b) disclosure against a person who is not a party to proceedings.

(2) This rule does not apply to proceedings in a magistrates' court.

Claim to withhold inspection or disclosure of a document

81.—(1) A person may apply, without notice, for an order permitting him to withhold disclosure of a document on the ground that disclosure would damage the public interest.

(2) Unless the court orders otherwise, an order of the court under paragraph (1)—

    (a) must not be served on any other person; and
    (b) must not be open to inspection by any person.

(3) A person who wishes to claim that he has a right or a duty to withhold inspection of a document, or part of a document, must state in writing—

    (a) that he has such a right or duty; and
    (b) the grounds on which he claims that right or,duty.

(4) The statement referred to in paragraph (3) must be made to the person wishing to inspect the document.

---

[32] An application for disclosure against a person who is not a party to proceedings is permitted under section 34 of the Supreme Court Act 1981 or section 53 of the County Courts Act 1984.

(5) A party may apply to the court to decide whether a claim made under paragraph (3) should be upheld.

(6) For the purpose of deciding an application under paragraph (1) (application to withhold disclosure) or paragraph (3) (claim to withhold inspection) the court may—

    (a) require the person seeking to withhold disclosure or inspection of a document to produce that document to the court; and

    (b) invite any person, whether or not a party, to make representations.

(7) An application under paragraph (1) or (5) must be supported by evidence.

(8) This rule does not affect any rule of law which permits or requires a document to be withheld from disclosure or inspection on the ground that its disclosure or inspection would damage the public interest.

(9) This rule does not apply to proceedings in a magistrates' court.

Custody of documents

82. All documents relating to proceedings under the Act must, while they are in the custody of the court, be kept in a place of special security.

Inspection and copies of documents

83. Subject to the provisions of these Rules, any practice direction or any direction given by the court—

    (a) no document or order held by the court in proceedings under the Act will be open to inspection by any person; and

    (b) no copy of any such document or order, or of an extract from any such document or order, will be taken by or given to any person.

Disclosing information to an adopted adult

84.—(1) The adopted person has the right, at his request, to receive from the court which made the adoption order a copy of the following—

    (a) the application form for an adoption order (but not the documents attached to that form);

    (b) the adoption order and any other orders relating to the adoption proceedings;

    (c) orders allowing any person contact with the child after the adoption order was made; and

    (d) any other document or order referred to in the relevant practice direction.

(2) The court will remove any protected information from any copy of a document or order referred to in paragraph (1) before the copies are given to the adopted person.

(3) This rule does not apply to an adopted person under the age of 18 years.

(4) In this rule "protected information" means information which would be protected information under section 57(3) if the adoption agency gave the information and not the court.

Translation of documents

85.—(1) Where a translation of any document is required for the purposes of proceedings for a Convention adoption order the translation must—

    (a) unless the court directs otherwise, be provided by the applicant; and

    (b) be signed by the translator to certify that the translation is accurate.

(2) This rule does not apply where the document is to be served in accordance with the Service Regulation.

PART 9: PROCEDURE FOR OTHER APPLICATIONS IN PROCEEDINGS

Types of application for which Part 9 procedure may be followed

86.—(1) The Part 9 procedure is the procedure set out in this Part.

(2) An applicant may use the Part 9 procedure if the application is made—

    (a) in the course of existing proceedings;

    (b) to commence proceedings other than those to which Part 5 applies; or

    (c) in connection with proceedings which have been concluded.

(Rule 22 lists the proceedings to which Part 5 applies.)

(3) Paragraph (2) does not apply—

    (a) to applications made in accordance with—

        (i) section 60(3) (order to prevent disclosure of information to an adopted person);

        (ii) section 79(4) (order for Registrar General to give any information referred to in section 79(3));

        (iii) rule 27 (request to dispense with consent);

       (iv)   rule 59(2) (appointment of children's guardian);

       (v)   rule 84 (disclosure of information to adopted adult);

       (vi)   rule 106 (withdrawal of application); or

       (vii) rule 107 (recovery orders); or

   (b) if a practice direction provides that the Part 9 procedure may not be used in relation to the type of application in question.

(4) The following persons are to be respondents to an application under this Part—

   (a) where there are existing proceedings or the proceedings have concluded, the parties to those proceedings;

   (b) where there are no existing proceedings—

       (i)   if notice has been given under section 44 (notice of intention to adopt or apply for a section 84 order), the local authority to whom notice has been given; and

       (ii)   if an application is made in accordance with—

           (aa) section 26(3)(f) (permission to apply for contact order); or

           (bb) section 42(6) (permission to apply for adoption order),

      any person who, in accordance with rule 23, will be a party to the proceedings brought if permission is granted; and

   (c) any other person as the court may direct.

Application notice to be filed

87.—(1) Subject to paragraph (2), the applicant must file an application notice.

(2) An applicant may make an application without filing an application notice if—

   (a) this is permitted by a rule or practice direction; or

   (b) the court dispenses with the requirement for an application notice.

Notice of an application

88.—(1) Subject to paragraph (2), a copy of the application notice will be served on each respondent.

(2) An application may be made without serving a copy of the application notice if this is permitted by—

   (a) a rule;

   (b) a practice direction; or

   (c) the court.

(Rule 91 deals with service of a copy of the application notice.)

Time when an application is made

89. Where an application must be made within a specified time, it is so made if the court receives the application notice within that time.

What an application notice must include

90.—(1) An application notice must state—

   (a) what order the applicant is seeking; and

   (b) briefly, why the applicant is seeking the order.

(2) The applicant may rely on the matters set out in his application notice as evidence if the application is verified by a statement of truth.

Service of a copy of an application notice

91.—(1) A court officer will serve a copy of the application notice—

   (a) as soon as practicable after it is filed; and

   (b) in any event at least 7 days before the court is to deal with the application.

(2) The applicant must, when he files the application notice, file a copy of any written evidence in support.

(3) When a copy of an application notice is served by a court officer it will be accompanied by—

   (a) a notice of the date and place where the application will be heard;

   (b) a copy of any witness statement in support; and

   (c) a copy of any draft order which the applicant has attached to his application.

(4) If—

   (a) an application notice is served; but

   (b) the period of notice is shorter than the period required by these Rules or a practice direction,

the court may direct that, in the circumstances of the case, sufficient notice has been given and hear the application.

(5) This rule does not require written evidence—

    (a) to be filed if it has already been filed; or

    (b) to be served on a party on whom it has already been served.

Applications which may be dealt with without a hearing

92. The court may deal with an application without a hearing if—

    (a) the parties agree as to the terms of the order sought;

    (b) the parties agree that the court should dispose of the application without a hearing; or

    (c) the court does not consider that a hearing would be appropriate.

Service of application where application made without notice

93.—(1) This rule applies where the court has disposed of an application which it permitted to be made without service of a copy of the application notice.

(2) Where the court makes an order, whether granting or dismissing the application, a copy of the application notice and any evidence in support will, unless the court directs otherwise, be served with the order on all the parties in the proceedings.

(3) The order must contain a statement of the right to make an application to set aside or vary the order under rule 94.

Application to set aside or vary order made without notice

94.—(1) A person who was not served with a copy of the application notice before an order was made under rule 93 may apply to have the order set aside or varied.

(2) An application under this rule must be made within 7 days beginning with the date on which the order was served on the person making the application.

Power of the court to proceed in the absence of a party

95.—(1) Where the applicant or any respondent fails to attend the hearing of an application, the court may proceed in his absence.

(2) Where—

    (a) the applicant or any respondent fails to attend the hearing of an application; and

    (b) the court makes an order at the hearing,

the court may, on application or of its own initiative, re-list the application.

Dismissal of totally without merit applications

96. If the High Court or a county court dismisses an application (including an application for permission to appeal) and it considers that the application is totally without merit—

    (a) the courts order must record that fact; and

    (b) the court must at the same time consider whether it is appropriate to make a civil restraint order.

PART 10: ALTERNATIVE PROCEDURE FOR APPLICATIONS

Types of application for which Part 10 procedure may be followed

97.—(1) The Part 10 procedure is the procedure set out in this Part.

(2) An applicant may use the Part 10 procedure where the procedure set out in Part 9 does not apply and—

    (a) there is no form prescribed by a rule or practice direction in which to make the application;

    (b) he seeks the court's decision on a question which is unlikely to involve a substantial dispute of fact; or

    (c) paragraph (5) applies.

(3) The court may at any stage direct that the application is to continue as if the applicant had not used the Part 10 procedure and, if it does so, the court may give any directions it considers appropriate.

(4) Paragraph (2) does not apply—

    (a) to applications made in accordance with—

        (i)   rule 27 (request to dispense with consent);

        (ii)   rule 59(2) (appointment of children's guardian);

        (iii) rule 84 (disclosure of information to adopted adult);

        (iv) rule 106 (withdrawal of application); or

        (v)   rule 107 (recovery orders); or

    (b) if a practice direction provides that the Part 10 procedure may not be used in relation to the type of application in question.

(5) A rule or practice direction may, in relation to a specified type of proceedings—

    (a) require or permit the use of the Part 10 procedure; and

    (b) disapply or modify any of the rules set out in this Part as they apply to those proceedings.

Contents of the application

98.—(1) In this Part "application" means an application made under this Part.

(2) Where the applicant uses the Part 10 procedure the application must state—

    (a) that this Part applies;

    (b) (i) the question which the applicant wants the court to decide; or

        (ii) the order which the applicant is seeking and the legal basis of the application for that order;

    (c) if the application is being made under an enactment, what that enactment is;

    (d) if the applicant is applying in a representative capacity, what that capacity is; and

    (e) if the respondent appears or is to appear in a representative capacity, what that capacity is.

(3) A court officer will serve a copy of the application on the respondent.

Issue of application without naming respondents

99.—(1) A practice direction may set out circumstances in which an application may be issued under this Part without naming a respondent.

(2) The practice direction may set out those cases in which an application for permission must be made before the application is issued.

(3) The application for permission—

    (a) need not be served on any other person; and

    (b) must be accompanied by a copy of the application that the applicant proposes to issue.

(4) Where the court gives permission it will give directions about the future management of the application.

Acknowledgement of service

100.—(1) Subject to paragraph (2), each respondent must file an acknowledgement of service within 14 days beginning with the date on which the application is served.

(2) If the application is to be served out of the jurisdiction the respondent must file an acknowledgement of service within the period set out in the practice direction supplementing Part 6, section 2.

(3) A court officer will serve the acknowledgement of service on the applicant and any other party.

(4) The acknowledgement of service must—

    (a) state whether the respondent contests the application;

    (b) state, if the respondent seeks a different order from that set out in the application, what that order is; and

    (c) be signed by the respondent or his legal representative.

Consequence of not filing an acknowledgement of service

101.—(1) This rule applies where—

    (a) the respondent has failed to file an acknowledgement of service; and

    (b) the time period for doing so has expired.

(2) The respondent must attend the hearing of the application but may not take part in the hearing unless the court gives permission.

Filing and serving written evidence

102.—(1) The applicant must file written evidence on which he intends to rely when he files his application.

(2) A court officer will serve the applicant's evidence on the respondent with the application.

(3) A respondent who wishes to rely on written evidence must file it when he files his acknowledgement of service.

(4) A court officer will serve the respondent's evidence, if any, on the other parties with the acknowledgement of service.

(5) The applicant may, within 14 days beginning with the date on which a respondent's evidence was served on him, file further written evidence in reply.

(6) If he does so, a court officer will serve a copy of that evidence on the other parties.

(7) The applicant may rely on the matters set out in his application as evidence under this rule if the application is verified by a statement of truth.

Evidence – general

103.—(1) No written evidence may be relied on at the hearing of the application unless—

    (a) it has been served in accordance with rule 102; or

    (b) the court gives permission.

(2) The court may require or permit a party to give oral evidence at the hearing.

(3) The court may give directions requiring the attendance for cross-examination of a witness who has given written evidence.

Procedure where respondent objects to use of the Part 10 procedure

104.—(1) Where a respondent contends that the Part 10 procedure should not be used because—

    (a) there is a substantial dispute of fact; and

    (b) the use of the Part 10 procedure is not required or permitted by a rule or practice direction,

he must state his reasons when he files his acknowledgement of service.

(2) When the court receives the acknowledgement of service and any written evidence it will give directions as to the future management of the case.

Applications under section 60(3) and 79(4) or rule 108

105.—(1) The Part 10 procedure must be used in an application made in accordance with—

    (a) section 60(3) (order to prevent disclosure of information to an adopted person);

    (b) section 79(4) (order for Registrar General to give any information referred to in section 79(3)); and

    (c) rule 108 (directions of High Court regarding fathers without parental responsibility).

(2) The respondent to an application made in accordance with paragraph (1)(b) is the Registrar General.

PART 11: MISCELLANEOUS

Withdrawal of application

106.—(1) An application may be withdrawn with the permission of the court.

(2) Subject to paragraph (3), a person seeking permission to withdraw an application must file a written request for permission setting out the reasons for the request.

(3) The request under paragraph (2) may be made orally to the court if the parties and any children's guardian, reporting officer or children and family reporter are present.

(4) A court officer will notify the other parties and any children's guardian, reporting officer or children and family reporter of a written request.

(5) The court may deal with a written request under paragraph (2) without a hearing if the other parties and any children's guardian, reporting officer or children and family reporter have had an opportunity to make written representations to the court about the request.

Application for recovery orders

107.—(1) An application for any of the orders referred to in section 41(2) (recovery orders) may—

    (a) in the High Court or a county court, be made without notice in which case the applicant must file the application—

        (i) where the application is made by telephone, the next business day after the making of the application; or

        (ii) in any other case, at the time when the application is made; and

    (b) in a magistrates' court, be made, with the permission of the court, without notice in which case the applicant must file the application at the time when the application is made or as directed by the court.

(2) Where the court refuses to make an order on an application without notice it may direct that the application is made on notice in which case the application will proceed in accordance with Part 5.

(3) The respondents to an application under this rule are—

    (a) in a case where—

        (i) placement proceedings;

        (ii) adoption proceedings; or

      (iii)   proceedings for a section 84 order

are pending, all parties to those proceedings;

    (b) any adoption agency authorised to place the child for adoption or which has placed the child for adoption;

    (c) any local authority to whom notice under section 44 (notice of intention to adopt or apply for a section 84 order) has been given;

    (d) any person having parental responsibility for the child;

    (e) any person in whose favour there is provision for contact;

    (f) any person who was caring for the child immediately prior to the making of the application; and

    (g) any person whom the applicant alleges to have effected or to have been or to be responsible for taking or keeping the child.

Inherent jurisdiction and fathers without parental responsibility

108. Where no proceedings have started an adoption agency or local authority may ask the High Court for directions on the need to give a father without parental responsibility notice of the intention to place a child for adoption.

Timing of applications for section 89 order

109. An application for a section 89 order must be made within 2 years beginning with the date on which—

    (a) the Convention adoption or Convention adoption order; or

    (b) the overseas adoption or determination under section 91

to which it relates was made.

Costs

110. The court may at any time make such order as to costs as it thinks just including an order relating to the payment of expenses incurred by any officer of the Service or a Welsh family proceedings officer.

(Rule 5(3) provides that Parts 43, 44 (except rules 44.3(2) and (3) and 44.9 to 44.12A), 47 and 48 and rule 45.6 of the CPR apply to costs in proceedings.)

Orders

111.—(1) An order takes effect from the date when it is made, or such later date as the court may specify.

(2) In proceedings in Wales a party may request that an order be drawn up in Welsh as well as English.

Copies of orders

112.—(1) Within 7 days beginning with the date on which the final order was made in proceedings or such shorter time as the court may direct a court officer will send—

    (a) a copy of the order to the applicant;

    (b) a copy, which is sealed, authenticated with the stamp of the court or certified as a true copy, of—

        (i)   an adoption order;

        (ii) a section 89 order; or

        (iii) an order quashing or revoking an adoption order or allowing an appeal against an adoption order

to the Registrar General;

    (c) a copy of a Convention adoption order to the relevant Central Authority;

    (d) a copy of a section 89 order relating to a Convention adoption order or a Convention adoption to the—

        (i)   relevant Central Authority;

        (ii) adopters;

        (iii) adoption agency; and

    (iv) local authority;

    (e) unless the court directs otherwise, a copy of a contact order or a variation or revocation of a contact order to the—

        (i)   person with whom the child is living;

        (ii) adoption agency; and

        (iii) local authority; and

    (f) a notice of the making or refusal of—

    (i)   the final order; or

    (ii)   an order quashing or revoking an adoption order or allowing an appeal against an order in proceedings

to every respondent and, with the permission of the court, any other person.

(2) The court officer will also send notice of the making of an adoption order or a section 84 order to—

    (a) any court in Great Britain which appears to him to have made any such order as is referred to in section 46(2) (order relating to parental responsibility for, and maintenance of, the child); and

    (b) the principal registry of the Family Division, if it appears to him that a parental responsibility agreement has been recorded at the principal registry.

(3) A copy of any final order may be sent to any other person with the permission of the court.

(4) The court officer will send a copy of any order made during the course of the proceedings to all the parties to those proceedings unless the court directs otherwise.

(5) If an order has been drawn up in Welsh as well as English in accordance with rule 111(2) any reference in this rule to sending an order is to be taken as a reference to sending both the Welsh and English orders.

Amendment and revocation of orders

113.—(1) Subject to paragraph (2), an application under—

    (a) section 55 (revocation of adoptions on legitimation); or

    (b) paragraph 4 of Schedule 1 (amendment of adoption order and revocation of direction)

may be made without serving a copy of the application notice.

(2) The court may direct that an application notice be served on such persons as it thinks fit.

(3) Where the court makes an order granting the application, a court officer will send the Registrar General a notice—

    (a) specifying the amendments; or

    (b) informing him of the revocation,

giving sufficient particulars of the order to enable the Registrar General to identify the case.

(4) The court may at any time correct an accidental slip or omission in an order.

(5) A party may apply for a correction under paragraph (4) without notice to the other parties.

Keeping of registers

114.—(1) A magistrates' court officer will keep a register in which there will be entered a minute or memorandum of every adjudication of the court in proceedings to which these Rules apply.

(2) The register may be stored in electronic form on the court computer system and entries in the register will include, where relevant, the following particulars—

    (a) the name and address of the applicant;

    (b) the name of the child including, in adoption proceedings, the name of the child prior to, and after, adoption;

    (c) the age and sex of the child;

    (d) the nature of the application; and

    (e) the minute of adjudication.

(3) The part of the register relating to adoption proceedings will be kept separately to any other part of the register and will—

    (a) not contain particulars of any other proceedings; and

    (b) be kept by the court in a place of special security.

PART 12: DISPUTING THE COURT'S JURISDICTION

Procedure for disputing the court's jurisdiction

115.—(1) A respondent who wishes to—

    (a) dispute the court's jurisdiction to hear the application; or

    (b) argue that the court should not exercise its jurisdiction

may apply to the court for an order declaring that it has no such jurisdiction or should not exercise any jurisdiction which it may have.

(2) An application under this rule must—

    (a) be made within 14 days beginning with the date on which the notice of the directions hearing is sent to the parties; and

    (b) be supported by evidence.

(3) If the respondent does not make an application within the period specified in paragraph (2)

he is to be treated as having accepted that the court has jurisdiction to hear the application.

(4) An order containing a declaration that the court has no jurisdiction or will not exercise its jurisdiction may also make further provision including—

    (a) setting aside the application form;

    (b) discharging any order made before the application was commenced or, where applicable, before the application form was served; and

    (c) staying the proceedings.

(5) If a respondent makes an application under this rule, he must file his written evidence in support with the application notice, but he need not before the hearing of the application file any other written evidence.

(6) Paragraph (4) does not apply to proceedings in a magistrates' court.

PART 13: HUMAN RIGHTS

Human Rights Act 1998

116.—(1) A party who seeks to rely on any provision of or right arising under the Human Rights Act 1998 or seeks a remedy available under that Act must inform the court in his application or otherwise in writing specifying—

    (a) the Convention right which it is alleged has been infringed and details of the alleged infringement; and

    (b) the relief sought and whether this includes a declaration of incompatibility.

(2) The High Court may not make a declaration of incompatibility unless 21 days' notice, or such other period of notice as the court directs, has been given to the Crown.

(3) Where notice has been given to the Crown, a Minister, or other person permitted by that Act, will be joined as a party on giving notice to the court.

(4) Where a claim is made under section 7(1) of the Human Rights Act 1998 (claim that public authority acted unlawfully) in respect of a judicial act—

    (a) that claim must be set out in the application form or the appeal notice; and

    (b) notice must be given to the Crown.

(5) Where paragraph (4) applies and the appropriate person (as defined in section 9(5) of the Human Rights Act 1998) has not applied within 21 days, or such other period as the court directs, beginning with the date on which the notice to be joined as a party was served, the court may join the appropriate person as a party.

(6) On any application concerning a committal order, if the court ordering the release of the person concludes that his Convention rights have been infringed by the making of the order to which the application or appeal relates, the judgment or order should so state, but if the court does not do so, that failure will not prevent another court from deciding the matter.

(7) Where by reason of a rule, practice direction or court order the Crown is permitted or required—

    (a) to make a witness statement;

    (b) to swear an affidavit;

    (c) to verify a document by a statement of truth; or

    (d) to discharge any other procedural obligation,

that function will be performed by an appropriate officer acting on behalf of the Crown, and the court may if necessary nominate an appropriate officer.

(8) In this rule—

"Convention right" has the same meaning as in the Human Rights Act 1998; and

"declaration of incompatibility" means a declaration of incompatibility under section 4 of the Human Rights Act 1998.

(A practice direction makes provision for the notices mentioned in this rule.)

PART 14: INTERIM INJUNCTIONS

Scope of this Part

117. The rules in this Part do not apply to proceedings in a magistrates' court.

Order for interim injunction

118.—(1) The court may grant an interim injunction.

(2) Paragraph (1) does not limit any other power which the court may have to grant an injunction.

(3) The court may grant an interim injunction whether or not there has been an application.

Time when an order for an interim injunction may be made

119.—(1) An order for an interim injunction may be made at any time, including—

    (a) before proceedings are started; and

    (b) after judgment has been given.

(Rule 19 provides that proceedings are started when the court issues an application form.)

    (2) However—

    (a) paragraph (1) is subject to any rule, practice direction or other enactment which provides otherwise; and

    (b) the court may grant an interim injunction before an application has been made only if—

        (i) the matter is urgent; or

        (ii) it is otherwise desirable to do so in the interests of justice.

(3) Where the court grants an interim injunction before an application has been commenced, it may give directions requiring an application to be commenced.

How to apply for an interim injunction

120.—(1) The court may grant an interim injunction on an application made without notice if it appears to the court that there are good reasons for not giving notice.

(2) An application for an interim injunction must be supported by evidence, unless the court orders otherwise.

(3) If the applicant makes an application without giving notice, the evidence in support of the application must state the reasons why notice has not been given.

(Rule 12 lists general case-management powers of the court.)

(Part 9 contains general rules about making an application.)

Interim injunction to cease if application is stayed

121. If—

    (a) the court has granted an interim injunction; and

    (b) the application is stayed other than by agreement between the parties,

the interim injunction shall be set aside unless the court orders that it should continue to have effect even though the application is stayed.

PART 15: ADMISSIONS AND EVIDENCE

Making an admission

122.—(1) A party may admit the truth of the whole or any part of another party's case by giving notice in writing.

(2) The court may allow a party to amend or withdraw an admission.

Power of court to control evidence

123.—(1) The court may control the evidence by giving directions as to—

    (a) the issues on which it requires evidence;

    (b) the nature of the evidence which it requires to decide those issues; and

    (c) the way in which the evidence is to be placed before the court.

(2) The court may use its power under this rule to exclude evidence that would otherwise be admissible.

(3) The court may limit cross-examination.

Evidence of witnesses – general rule

124.—(1) The general rule is that any fact which needs to be proved by the evidence of witnesses is to be proved—

    (a) at final hearing, by their oral evidence; and

    (b) at any other hearing, by their evidence in writing.

(2) This is subject—

    (a) to any provision to the contrary contained in these Rules or elsewhere; or

    (b) to any order of the court.

Evidence by video link or other means

125. The court may allow a witness to give evidence through a video link or by other means.

Service of witness statements for use at final hearing

126.—(1) A witness statement is a written statement signed by a person which contains the evidence which that person would be allowed to give orally.

(2) The court will give directions about the service of any witness statement of the oral evidence which a party intends to rely on in relation to any issues of fact to be decided at the final hearing on the other parties.

(3) The court may give directions as to—

    (a) the order in which witness statements are to be served; and

    (b) whether or not the witness statements are to be filed.

Use at final hearing of witness statements which have been served

127.—(1) If—

    (a) a party has filed a witness statement which has been served on the other parties; and

    (b) he wishes to rely at the final hearing on the evidence of the witness who made the statement,

he must call the witness to give oral evidence unless the court directs otherwise or he puts the statement in as hearsay evidence.

(2) Where a witness is called to give oral evidence under paragraph (1), his witness statement shall stand as his evidence in chief unless the court directs otherwise.

(3) A witness giving oral evidence at final hearing may with the permission of the court—

    (a) amplify his witness statement; and

    (b) give evidence in relation to new matters which have arisen since the witness statement was served on the other parties.

(4) The court will give permission under paragraph (3) only if it considers that there is good reason not to confine the evidence of the witness to the contents of his witness statement.

(5) If a party who has filed a witness statement which has been served on the other parties does not—

    (a) call the witness to give evidence at final hearing; or

    (b) put the witness statement in as hearsay evidence, any other party may put the witness statement in as hearsay evidence.

Evidence in proceedings other than at final hearing

128.—(1) Subject to paragraph (2), the general rule is that evidence at hearings other than the final hearing is to be by witness statement unless the court, a practice direction or any other enactment requires otherwise.

(2) At hearings other than the final hearing, a party may, rely on the matters set out in—

    (a) his application form; or

    (b) his application notice, if it is verified by a statement of truth.

Order for cross-examination

129.—(1) Where, at a hearing other than the final hearing, evidence is given in writing, any party may apply to the court for permission to cross-examine the person giving the evidence.

(2) If the court gives permission under paragraph (1) but the person in question does not attend as required by the order, his evidence may not be used unless the court gives permission.

Form of witness statement

130. A witness statement must comply with the requirements set out in the relevant practice direction.

Witness summaries

131.—(1) A party who—

    (a) is required to file a witness statement for use at final hearing; but

    (b) is unable to obtain one, may apply, without notice, for permission to file a witness summary instead.

(2) A witness summary is a summary of—

    (a) the evidence, if known, which would otherwise be included in a witness statement; or

    (b) if the evidence is not known, the matters about which the party filing the witness summary proposes to question the witness.

(3) Unless the court directs otherwise, a witness summary must include the name and address of the intended witness.

(4) Unless the court directs otherwise, a witness summary must be filed within the period in which a witness statement would have had to be filed.

(5) Where a party files a witness summary, so far as practicable, rules 126 (service of witness statements for use at final hearing), 127(3) (amplifying witness statements), and 130 (form of witness statement) shall apply to the summary.

Cross-examination on a witness statement

132. Where a witness is called to give evidence at final hearing, he may be cross-examined on his witness statement whether or not the statement or any part of it was referred to during the witness's evidence in chief.

False statements

133.—(1) Proceedings for contempt of court may be brought against a person if he makes, or causes to be made, a false statement in a document verified by a statement of truth without an honest belief in its truth.

(2) Proceedings under this rule may be brought only—
    (a) by the Attorney General; or
    (b) with the permission of the court.

(3) This rule does not apply to proceedings in a magistrates' court.

Affidavit evidence

134. Evidence must be given by affidavit instead of or in addition to a witness statement if this is required by the court, a provision contained in any other rule, a practice direction or any other enactment.

Form of affidavit

135. An affidavit must comply with the requirements set out in the relevant practice direction.

Affidavit made outside the jurisdiction

136. A person may make an affidavit outside the jurisdiction in accordance with—
    (a) this Part; or
    (b) the law of the place where he makes the affidavit.

Notarial acts and instruments

137. A notarial act or instrument may be received in evidence without further proof as duly authenticated in accordance with the requirements of law unless the contrary is proved.

Use of plans, photographs and models as evidence

138.—(1) This rule applies to evidence (such as a plan, photograph or model) which is not—
    (a) contained in a witness statement, affidavit or expert's report; and
    (b) to be given orally at the final hearing.

(2) This rule includes documents which may be received in evidence without further proof under section 9 of the Civil Evidence Act 1995[33].

(3) Unless the court orders otherwise the evidence shall not be receivable at the final hearing unless the party intending to put it in evidence has given notice to the court in accordance with this rule and the court will give directions about service of the notice on any other party.

(4) Where the party intends to use the evidence as evidence of any fact then, subject to paragraph (6), he must give notice not later than the latest date for filing witness statements.

(5) He must give notice at least 21 days before the hearing at which he proposes to put in the evidence, if—
    (a) there are not to be witness statements; or
    (b) he intends to put in the evidence solely in order to disprove an allegation made in a witness statement.

(6) Where the evidence forms part of expert evidence, he must give notice when the expert's report is filed.

(7) Where the evidence is being produced to the court for any reason other than as part of factual or expert evidence, he must give notice at least 21 days before the hearing at which he proposes to put in the evidence.

(8) Where a party has given notice that he intends to put in the evidence, the court may direct that every other party be given an opportunity to inspect it and to agree to its admission without further proof.

Evidence of finding on question of foreign law

139.—(1) This rule sets out the procedure which must be followed by a party who intends to put in evidence a finding on a question of foreign law by virtue of section 4(2) of the Civil Evidence Act 1972.

(2) He must give the court notice of his intention—

---

[33] Section 9 of the Civil Evidence Act 1995 provides that documents forming part of the records of a business or public authority, as defined in that section, may be received in evidence without further proof.

    (a) if there are to be witness statements, not later than the latest date for filing them; or

    (b) otherwise, not less than 21 days before the hearing at which he proposes to put the finding in evidence

and the court will give directions about service of the notice on any other party.

(3) The notice must—

    (a) specify the question on which the finding was made; and

    (b) enclose a copy of a document where it is reported or recorded.

PART 16: WITNESSES, DEPOSITIONS AND EVIDENCE FOR FOREIGN COURTS
SECTION 1: WITNESSES AND DEPOSITIONS

Scope of this Section

140.—(1) This Section of this Part provides—

    (a) for the circumstances in which a person may be required to attend court to give evidence or to produce a document; and

    (b) for a party to obtain evidence before a hearing to be used at the hearing.

(2) This Section, except for rule 149(2) to (4), does not apply to proceedings in a magistrates' court.

(Section 97 of the Magistrates' Courts Act 1980 sets out the procedure for obtaining a witness summons in proceedings in a magistrates' court.)

Witness summonses

141.—(1) A witness summons is a document issued by the court requiring a witness to—

    (a) attend court to give evidence; or

    (b) produce documents to the court.

(2) A witness summons must be in the relevant form.

(3) There must be a separate witness summons for each witness.

(4) A witness summons may require a witness to produce documents to the court either—

    (a) on the date fixed for a hearing; or

    (b) on such date as the court may direct.

(5) The only documents that a summons under this rule can require a person to produce before a hearing are documents which that person could be required to produce at the hearing.

Issue of a witness summons

142.—(1) A witness summons is issued on the date entered on the summons by the court.

(2) A party must obtain permission from the court where he wishes to—

    (a) have a summons issued less than 7 days before the date of the final hearing;

    (b) have a summons issued for a witness to attend court to give evidence or to produce documents on any date except the date fixed for the final hearing; or

    (c) have a summons issued for a witness to attend court to give evidence or to produce documents at any hearing except the final hearing.

(3) A witness summons must be issued by—

    (a) the court where the case is proceeding; or

    (b) the court where the hearing in question will be held.

(4) The court may set aside or vary a witness summons issued under this rule.

Time for serving a witness summons

143.—(1) The general rule is that a witness summons is binding if it is served at least 7 days before the date on which the witness is required to attend before the court or tribunal.

(2) The court may direct that a witness summons shall be binding although it will be served less than 7 days before the date on which the witness is required to attend before the court or tribunal.

(3) A witness summons which is—

    (a) served in accordance with this rule; and

    (b) requires the witness to attend court to give evidence,

is binding until the conclusion of the hearing at which the attendance of the witness is required.

Who is to serve a witness summons

144.—(1) Unless the court directs otherwise, a witness summons is to be served by the court.

(2) Where the court is to serve the witness summons, the party on whose behalf it is issued must deposit, in the court office, the money to be paid or offered to the witness under rule 145.

Right of witness to travelling expenses and compensation for loss of time

145. At the time of service of a witness summons the witness must be offered or paid—

    (a) a sum reasonably sufficient to cover his expenses in travelling to and from the court; and

    (b) such sum by way of compensation for loss of time as may be specified in the relevant practice direction.

Evidence by deposition

146.—(1) A party may apply for an order for a person to be examined before the hearing takes place.

(2) A person from whom evidence is to be obtained following an order under this rule is referred to as a "deponent" and the evidence is referred to as a "deposition".

(3) An order under this rule shall be for a deponent to be examined on oath before—

    (a) a judge or district judge, including a district judge of the principal registry of the Family Division;

    (b) an examiner of the court; or

    (c) such other person as the court appoints.

(4) The order may require the production of any document which the court considers is necessary for the purposes of the examination.

(5) The order must state the date, time and place of the examination.

(6) At the time of service of the order the deponent must be offered or paid—

    (a) a sum reasonably sufficient to cover his expenses in travelling to and from the place of examination; and

    (b) such sum by way of compensation for loss of time as may be specified in the relevant practice direction.

(7) Where the court makes an order for a deposition to be taken, it may also order the party who obtained the order to file a witness statement or witness summary in relation to the evidence to be given by the person to be examined.

(Part 15 contains the general rules about witness statements and witness summaries.)

Conduct of examination

147.—(1) Subject to any directions contained in the order for examination, the examination must be conducted in the same way as if the witness were giving evidence at a final hearing.

(2) If all the parties are present, the examiner may conduct the examination of a person not named in the order for examination if all the parties and the person to be examined consent.

(3) The examiner will conduct the examination in private unless he considers it is not appropriate to do so.

(4) The examiner must ensure that the evidence given by the witness is recorded in full.

(5) The examiner must send a copy of the deposition—

    (a) to the person who obtained the order for the examination of the witness; and

    (b) to the court where the case is proceeding.

(6) The court will make directions as to the service of a copy of the deposition on the other parties.

Enforcing attendance of witness

148.—(1) If a person served with an order to attend before an examiner—

    (a) fails to attend; or

    (b) refuses to be sworn for the purpose of the examination or to answer any lawful question or produce any document at the examination,

a certificate of his failure or refusal, signed by the examiner, must be filed by the party requiring the deposition.

(2) On the certificate being filed, the party requiring the deposition may apply to the court for an order requiring that person to attend or to be sworn or to answer any question or produce any document, as the case may be.

(3) An application for an order under this rule may be made without notice.

(4) The court may order the person against whom an order is made under this rule to pay any costs resulting from his failure or refusal.

Use of deposition at a hearing

149.—(1) A deposition ordered under rule 146 may be given in evidence at a hearing unless the court orders otherwise.

(2) A party intending to put in evidence a deposition at a hearing must file notice of his intention to do so on the court and the court will make directions about serving the notice on every other party.

(3) He must file the notice at least 21 days before the day fixed for the hearing.

(4) The court may require a deponent to attend the hearing and give evidence orally.

Where a person to be examined is out of the jurisdiction – letter of request

150. — (1) This rule applies where a party wishes to take a deposition from a person who is —

    (a)   out of the jurisdiction; and

    (b)   not in a Regulation State within the meaning of Section 2 of this Part.

(2) The High Court may order the issue of a letter of request to the judicial authorities of the country in which the proposed deponent is.

(3) A letter of request is a request to a judicial authority to take the evidence of that person, or arrange for it to be taken.

(4) The High Court may make an order under this rule in relation to county court proceedings.

(5) If the government of a country allows a person appointed by the High Court to examine a person in that country, the High Court may make an order appointing a special examiner for that purpose.

(6) A person may be examined under this rule on oath or affirmation or in accordance with any procedure permitted in the country in which the examination is to take place.

(7) If the High Court makes an order for the issue of a letter of request, the party who sought the order must file —

    (a)   the following documents and, subject to paragraph (8), a translation of them, —

        (i)   a draft letter of request;

        (ii)   a statement of the issues relevant to the proceedings; and

        (iii)   a list of questions or the subject matter of questions to be put to the person to be examined; and

    (b)   an undertaking to be responsible for the Secretary of State's expenses.

(8) There is no need to file a translation if —

    (a)   English is one of the official languages of the country where the examination is to take place; or

    (b)   a practice direction has specified that country as a country where no translation is necessary.

Fees and expenses of examiner of the court

151. — (1) An examiner of the court may charge a fee for the examination.

(2) He need not send the deposition to the court unless the fee is paid.

(3) The examiner's fees and expenses must be paid by the party who obtained the order for examination.

(4) If the fees and expenses due to an examiner are not paid within a reasonable time, he may report that fact to the court.

(5) The court may order the party who obtained the order for examination to deposit in the court office a specified sum in respect of the examiner's fees and, where it does so, the examiner will not be asked to act until the sum has been deposited.

(6) An order under this rule does not affect any decision as to the party who is ultimately to bear the costs of the examination.

SECTION 2: TAKING OF EVIDENCE – MEMBER STATES OF THE EUROPEAN UNION

Interpretation

152. In this Section—

"designated court" has the meaning given in the relevant practice direction;

"Regulation State" has the same meaning as "Member State" in the Taking of Evidence Regulation, that is all Member States except Denmark;

"the Taking of Evidence Regulation" means Council Regulation (EC) No. 1206/2001 of 28 May 2001 on co-operation between the courts of the Member States in the taking of evidence in civil and commercial matters.

Where a person to be examined is in another Regulation State

153. — (1) This rule applies where a party wishes to take a deposition from a person who is in another Regulation State —

    (a)   outside the jurisdiction; and

(b) in a Regulation State.

(2) The court may order the issue of a request to a designated court ("the requested court") in the Regulation State in which the proposed deponent is.

(3) If the court makes an order for the issue of a request, the party who sought the order must file—

(a) a draft Form A as set out in the annex to the Taking of Evidence Regulation (request for the taking of evidence);

(b) subject to paragraph (4), a translation of the form;

(c) an undertaking to be responsible for costs sought by the requested court in relation to—

(i)   fees paid to experts and interpreters; and

(ii)   where requested by that party, the use of special procedures or communications technology; and

(d) an undertaking to be responsible for the court's expenses.

(4) There is no need to file a translation if—

(a) English is one of the official languages of the Regulation State where the examination is to take place; or

(b) the Regulation State has indicated, in accordance with the Taking of Evidence Regulation, that English is a language which it will accept.

(5) Where article 17 of the Taking of Evidence Regulation (direct taking of evidence by the requested court) allows evidence to be taken directly in another Regulation State, the court may make an order for the submission of a request in accordance with that article.

(6) If the court makes an order for the submission of a request under paragraph (5), the party who sought the order must file—

(a) a draft Form I as set out in the annex to the Taking of Evidence Regulation (request for direct taking of evidence);

(b) subject to paragraph (4), a translation of the form; and

(c) an undertaking to be responsible for the court's expenses.

PART 17: EXPERTS

Duty to restrict expert evidence

154. Expert evidence shall be restricted to that which is reasonably required to resolve the proceedings.

Interpretation

155. A reference to an "expert" in this Part—

(a) is a reference to an expert who has been instructed to give or prepare evidence for the purpose of court proceedings; and

(b) does not include—

(i)   a person who is within a prescribed description for the purposes of section 94(1) of the Act (persons who may prepare a report for any person about the suitability of a child for adoption or of a person to adopt a child or about the adoption, or placement for adoption, of a child); or

(ii)   an officer of the Service or a Welsh family proceedings officer when acting in that capacity.

(Regulation 3 of the Restriction on the Preparation of Adoption Reports Regulations 2005 (S.I. 2005/1711) sets out which persons are within a prescribed description for the purposes of section 94(1) of the Act.)

Experts – overriding duty to the court

156.—(1) It is the duty of an expert to help the court on the matters within his expertise.

(2) This duty overrides any obligation to the person from whom he has received instructions or by whom he is paid.

Court's power to restrict expert evidence

157.—(1) No party may call an expert or put in evidence an expert's report without the court's permission.

(2) When a party applies for permission under this rule he must identify—

(a) the field in which he wishes to rely on expert evidence; and

(b) where practicable the expert in that field on whose evidence he wishes to rely.

(3) If permission is granted under this rule it shall be in relation only to the expert named or

the field identified under paragraph (2).

(4) The court may limit the amount of the expert's fees and expenses that the party who wishes to rely on the expert may recover from any other party.

General requirement for expert evidence to be given in a written report

158. Expert evidence is to be given in a written report unless the court directs otherwise.

Written questions to experts

159.—(1) A party may put to—

(a) an expert instructed by another party; or

(b) a single joint expert appointed under rule 160,

written questions about his report.

(2) Written questions under paragraph (1)—

(a) may be put once only;

(b) must be put within 5 days beginning with the date on which the expert's report was served; and

(c) must be for the purpose only of clarification of the report,

unless in any case—

(i)   the court gives permission;

(ii)   the other party agrees; or

(iii) any practice direction provides otherwise.

(3) An expert's answers to questions put in accordance with paragraph (1) shall be treated as part of the expert's report.

(4) Where—

(a) a party has put a written question to an expert instructed by another party in accordance with this rule; and

(b) the expert does not answer that question,

the court may make one or both of the following orders in relation to the party who instructed the expert—

(i)   that the party may not rely on the evidence of that expert; or

(ii)   that the party may not recover the fees and expenses of that expert from any other party.

Court's power to direct that evidence is to be given by a single joint expert

160.—(1) Where two or more parties wish to submit expert evidence on a particular issue, the court may direct that the evidence on that issue is to given by one expert only.

(2) The parties wishing to submit the expert evidence are called "the instructing parties".

(3) Where the instructing parties cannot agree who should be the expert, the court may—

(a) select the expert from a list prepared or identified by the instructing parties; or

(b) direct that the expert be selected in such other manner as the court may direct.

Instructions to a single joint expert

161.—(1) Where the court gives a direction under rule 160 for a single joint expert to be used, each instructing party may give instructions to the expert.

(2) When an instructing party gives instructions to the expert he must, at the same time, send a copy of the instructions to the other instructing parties.

(3) The court may give directions about—

(a) the payment of the expert's fees and expenses; and

(b) any inspection, examination or experiments which the expert wishes to carry out.

(4) The court may, before an expert is instructed, limit the amount that can be paid by way of fees and expenses to the expert.

(5) Unless the court otherwise directs, the instructing parties are jointly and severally liable for the payment of the expert's fees and expenses.

Power of court to direct a party to provide information

162.—(1) Where a party has access to information which is not reasonably available to the other party, the court may direct the party who has access to the information to prepare and file a document recording the information.

(2) A court officer will send a copy of that document to the other party.

Contents of report

163.—(1) An expert's report must comply with the requirements set out in the relevant practice direction.

(2) At the end of an expert's report there must be a statement that—

(a) the expert understands his duty to the court; and

(b) he has complied with that duty.

(3) The expert's report must state the substance of all material instructions, whether written or oral, on the basis of which the report was written.

(4) The instructions referred to in paragraph (3) shall not be privileged against disclosure.

Use by one party of expert's report disclosed by another

164. Where a party has disclosed an expert's report, any party may use that expert's report as evidence at the final hearing.

Discussions between experts

165.—(1) The court may, at any stage, direct a discussion between experts for the purpose of requiring the experts to—

(a) identify and discuss the expert issues in the proceedings; and

(b) where possible, reach an agreed opinion on those issues.

(2) The court may specify the issues which the experts must discuss.

(3) The court may direct that following a discussion between the experts they must prepare a statement for the court showing—

(a) those issues on which they agree; and

(b) those issues on which they disagree and a summary of their reasons for disagreeing.

Consequence of failure to disclose expert's report

166. A party who fails to disclose an expert's report may not use the report at the final hearing or call the expert to give evidence orally unless the court gives permission.

Expert's right to ask court for directions

167.—(1) An expert may file a written request for directions to assist him in carrying out his function as an expert.

(2) An expert must, unless the court directs otherwise, provide a copy of any proposed request for directions under paragraph (1)—

(a) to the party instructing him, at least 7 days before he files the request; and

(b) to all other parties, at least 4 days before he files it.

(3) The court, when it gives directions, may also direct that a party be served with a copy of the directions.

PART 18: CHANGE OF SOLICITOR

Change of solicitor – duty to give notice

168.—(1) This rule applies where—

(a) a party for whom a solicitor is acting wants to change his solicitor;

(b) a party, after having conducted the application in person, appoints a solicitor to act on his behalf (except where the solicitor is appointed only to act as an advocate for a hearing); or

(c) a party, after having conducted the application by a solicitor, intends to act in person.

(2) Where this rule applies, the party or his solicitor (where one is acting) must—

(a) file notice of the change; and

(b) where paragraph (1)(a) or (c) applies, serve notice of the change on the former solicitor.

(3) The court will give directions about serving notice of the change on every other party.

(4) The notice filed at court must state that notice has been served as required by paragraph (2)(b).

(5) Subject to paragraph (6), where a party has changed his solicitor or intends to act in person, the former solicitor will be considered to be the party's solicitor unless and until—

(a) notice is filed and served in accordance with paragraphs (2) and (3); or

(b) the court makes an order under rule 169 and the order is served as required by paragraph (3) of that rule.

(6) Where the certificate of a LSC funded client or an assisted person is revoked or discharged—

(a) the solicitor who acted for that person will cease to be the solicitor acting in the case as soon as his retainer is determined under regulation 4 of the Community Legal Service (Costs) Regulations 2000[S.I. 2000/441]; and

(b) if that person wishes to continue where he appoints a solicitor to act on his behalf, paragraph (2) will apply as if he had previously conducted the application in person;

(7) In this rule—

"assisted person" means an assisted person within the statutory provisions relating to legal aid;

"certificate" means a certificate issued under the Funding Code (approved under section 9 of the Access to Justice Act 1999);

"LSC funded client" means an individual who receives services funded by the Legal Services Commission as part of the Community Legal Service within the meaning of Part I of the Access to Justice Act 1999.

Order that a solicitor has ceased to act

169.—(1) A solicitor may apply for an order declaring that he has ceased to be the solicitor acting for a party.

(2) Where an application is made under this rule—

(a) notice of the application must be given to the party for whom the solicitor is acting, unless the court directs otherwise; and

(b) the application must be supported by evidence.

(3) Where the court makes an order that a solicitor has ceased to act—

(a) the court will give directions about serving the order on every party to the proceedings; and

(b) if it is served by a party or the solicitor, the party or the solicitor (as the case may be) must file a certificate of service.

Removal of solicitor who has ceased to act on application of another party

170.—(1) Where—

(a) a solicitor who has acted for a party—

(i) has died;

(ii) has become bankrupt;

(iii) has ceased to practice; or

(iv) cannot be found; and

(b) the party has not given notice of a change of solicitor or notice of intention to act in person as required by rule 168(2),

any other party may apply for an order declaring that the solicitor has ceased to be the solicitor acting for the other party in the case.

(2) Where an application is made under this rule, notice of the application must be given to the party to whose solicitor the application relates unless the court directs otherwise.

(3) Where the court makes an order made under this rule—

(a) the court will give directions about serving the order on every party to the proceedings; and

(b) where it is served by a party, that party must file a certificate of service.

PART 19: APPEALS

Scope and interpretation

171.—(1) The rules in this Part apply to appeals to—

(a) the High Court; and

(b) a county court.

(2) This Part does not apply to an appeal in detailed assessment proceedings against a decision of an authorised court officer.

(Rules 47.20 to 47.23 of the CPR deal with appeals against a decision of an authorised court officer in detailed assessment proceedings.)

(3) In this Part—

"appeal" includes an appeal by way of case stated;

"appeal court" means the court to which an appeal is made;

"appeal notice" means an appellant's or respondent's notice;

"appellant" means a person who brings or seeks to bring an appeal;

"lower court" means the court from whose decision an appeal is brought;

"respondent" means—

(a) a person other than the appellant who was a party to the proceedings in the lower court and who is affected by the appeal; and

(b) a person who is permitted by the appeal court to be a party to the appeal.

(4) This Part is subject to any rule, enactment or practice direction which sets out special provisions with regard to any particular category of appeal.

Parties to comply with the practice direction

172. All parties to an appeal must comply with the relevant practice direction.

Permission

173.—(1) An appellant or respondent requires permission to appeal—

    (a) against a decision in assessment proceedings relating to costs in proceedings where the decision appealed against was made by a district judge or a costs judge; or

    (b) as provided by the relevant practice direction.

(2) An application for permission to appeal may be made—

    (a) to the lower court, if that court is a county court or the High Court, at the hearing at which the decision to be appealed was made; or

    (b) to the appeal court in an appeal notice.

(Rule 174 sets out the time limits for filing an appellant's notice at the appeal court. Rule 175 sets out the time limits for filing a respondent's notice at the appeal court. Any application for permission to appeal to the appeal court must be made in the appeal notice (see rules 174(1) and 175(3).)

(3) Where the lower court refuses an application for permission to appeal, a further application for permission to appeal may be made to the appeal court.

(4) Where the appeal court, without a hearing, refuses permission to appeal, the person seeking permission may request the decision to be reconsidered at a hearing.

(5) A request under paragraph (4) must be filed within 7 days beginning with the date on which the notice that permission has been refused was served.

(6) Permission to appeal will only be given where—

    (a) the court considers that the appeal would have a real prospect of success; or

    (b) there is some other compelling reason why the appeal should be heard.

(7) An order giving permission may—

    (a) limit the issues to be heard; and

    (b) be made subject to conditions.

(8) In this rule "costs judge" means a taxing master of the Supreme Court.

Appellant's notice

174.—(1) Where the appellant seeks permission from the appeal court it must be requested in the appellant's notice.

(2) The appellant must file the appellant's notice at the appeal court within—

    (a) such period as may be directed by the lower court, if that court is a county court or the High Court; or

    (b) (i)   where the lower court makes no such direction; or

         (ii) the lower court is a magistrates' court,

14 days beginning with the date on which the decision of the lower court that the appellant wishes to appeal was made.

(3) Unless the appeal court directs otherwise, an appeal notice must be served on the persons referred to in paragraph (4)—

    (a) as soon as practicable; and

    (b) in any event not later than 7 days,

after it is filed.

(4) The persons referred to in paragraph (3) are—

    (a) each respondent;

    (b) any children's guardian, reporting officer or children and family reporter; and

    (c) where the appeal is from a magistrates' court, the court officer.

(5) Unless the appeal court directs otherwise, a court officer will serve the appeal notice.

Respondent's notice

175.—(1) A respondent may file a respondent's notice.

(2) A respondent who—

    (a) is seeking permission to appeal from the appeal court; or

    (b) wishes to ask the appeal court to uphold the order of the lower court for reasons different from or additional to those given by the lower court,

must file a respondent's notice.

(3) Where the respondent seeks permission from the appeal court it must be requested in the respondent's notice.

(4) A respondent's notice must be filed within—

    (a) such period as may be directed by the lower court, if that court is a county court or the High Court; or

    (b) (i)   where the lower court makes no such direction; or

          (ii)   the lower court is a magistrates' court,

14 days beginning with the date referred to in paragraph (5).

(5) The date referred to in paragraph (4) is—

    (a) the date on which the respondent is served with the appellant's notice where—

          (i)   permission to appeal was given by the lower court; or

          (ii)   permission to appeal is not required;

    (b) the date on which the respondent is served with notification that the appeal court has given the appellant permission to appeal; or

    (c) the date on which the respondent is served with notification that the application for permission to appeal and the appeal itself are to be heard together.

(6) Unless the appeal court directs otherwise, a respondent's notice must be served on the appellant and any other respondent—

    (a) as soon as practicable; and

    (b) in any event not later than 7 days,

after it is filed.

(7) Unless the appeal court directs otherwise, a court officer will serve a respondent's notice.

Variation of time

176.—(1) An application to vary the time limit for filing an appeal notice must be made to the appeal court.

(2) The parties may not agree to extend any date or time limit set by—

    (a) these Rules;

    (b) the relevant practice direction; or

    (c) an order of the appeal court or the lower court.

(Rule 12(2)(a) provides that the court may extend or shorten the time for compliance with any rule, practice direction or court order (even if an application for extension is made after the time for compliance has expired).)

(Rule 12(2)(b) provides that the court may adjourn or bring forward a hearing.)

Stay

177. Unless the appeal court or the lower court, other than a magistrates' court, orders otherwise an appeal shall not operate as a stay of any order or decision of the lower court.

Amendment of appeal notice

178. An appeal notice may not be amended without the permission of the appeal court.

Striking out appeal notices and setting aside or imposing conditions on permission to appeal

179.—(1) The appeal court may—

    (a) strike out the whole or part of an appeal notice;

    (b) set aside permission to appeal in whole or in part; or

    (c) impose or vary conditions upon which an appeal may be brought.

(2) The court will only exercise its powers under paragraph (1) where there is a compelling reason for doing so.

(3) Where a party was present at the hearing at which permission was given he may not subsequently apply for an order that the court exercise its powers under paragraphs (1)(b) or (c).

Appeal court's powers

180.—(1) In relation to an appeal the appeal court has all the powers of the lower court.

(Rule 171(4) provides that this Part is subject to any enactment that sets out special provisions with regard to any particular category of appeal.)

(2) The appeal court has power to—

    (a) affirm, set aside or vary any order or judgment made or given by the lower court;

    (b) refer any application or issue for determination by the lower court;

    (c) order a new hearing;

    (d) make orders for the payment of interest; and

    (e) make a costs order.

(3) The appeal court may exercise its powers in relation to the whole or part of an order of the lower court.

(Rule 12 contains general rules about the court's case management powers.)

    (4) If the appeal court—

        (a) refuses an application for permission to appeal;

        (b) strikes out an appellant's notice; or

        (c) dismisses an appeal,

and it considers that the application, the appellant's notice or the appeal is totally without merit, the provisions of paragraph (5) must be complied with.

    (5) Where paragraph (4) applies—

        (a) the court's order must record the fact that it considers the application, the appellant's notice or the appeal to be totally without merit; and

        (b) the court must at the same time consider whether it is appropriate to make a civil restraint order.

Hearing of appeals

181.—(1) Every appeal will be limited to a review of the decision of the lower court unless—

        (a) a practice direction makes different provision for a particular category of appeal; or

        (b) the court considers that in the circumstances of an individual appeal it would be in the interests of justice to hold a re-hearing.

    (2) Unless it orders otherwise, the appeal court will not receive—

        (a) oral evidence; or

        (b) evidence which was not before the lower court.

    (3) The appeal court will allow an appeal where the decision of the lower court was—

        (a) wrong; or

        (b) unjust because of a serious procedural or other irregularity in the proceedings in the lower court.

    (4) The appeal court may draw any inference of fact which it considers justified on the evidence.

    (5) At the hearing of the appeal a party may not rely on a matter not contained in his appeal notice unless the appeal court gives permission.

Assignment of appeals to the Court of Appeal

182.—(1) Where the court from or to which an appeal is made or from which permission to appeal is sought ("the relevant court") considers that—

        (a) an appeal which is to be heard by a county court or the High Court would raise an important point of principle or practice; or

        (b) there is some other compelling reason for the Court of Appeal to hear it,

the relevant court may order the appeal to be transferred to the Court of Appeal.

    (2) This rule does not apply to proceedings in a magistrates' court.

Reopening of final appeals

183.—(1) The High Court will not reopen a final determination of any appeal unless—

        (a) it is necessary to do so in order to avoid real injustice;

        (b) the circumstances are exceptional and make it appropriate to reopen the appeal; and

        (c) there is no alternative effective remedy.

    (2) In paragraphs (1), (3), (4) and (6), "appeal" includes an application for permission to appeal.

    (3) This rule does not apply to appeals to a county court.

    (4) Permission is needed to make an application under this rule to reopen a final determination of an appeal.

    (5) There is no right to an oral hearing of an application for permission unless, exceptionally, the judge so directs.

    (6) The judge will not grant permission without directing the application to be served on the other party to the original appeal and giving him an opportunity to make representations.

    (7) There is no right of appeal or review from the decision of the judge on the application for permission, which is final.

    (8) The procedure for making an application for permission is set out in the practice direction.

Index